Fodor's

New
TWELFTH EDITION

Pacific Northwest

The complete guide, thoroughly up-to-date

Packed with details that will make your trip

The must-see sights, off and on the beaten path

What to see, what to skip

Mix-and-match vacation itineraries

City strolls, countryside adventures

Smart lodging and dining options

Essential local do's and taboos

Transportation tips, distances and directions

Key contacts, savvy travel tips

When to go, what to pack

Clear, accurate, easy-to-use maps

Books to read, videos to watch, background essays

Portions of this book appear in *Fodor's Seattle & Vancouver*

Fodor's Travel Publications, Inc.
New York • Toronto • London • Sydney • Auckland
www.fodors.com/

Fodor's Pacific Northwest

EDITOR: Daniel Mangin

Editorial Contributors: Stephanie Adler, Alex Aron, Christopher Baty, Linda Cabasin, Langdon Faust, Julie Fay, Tom Gaunt, Wier Harman, Jeff Kuechle, Christina Knight, Deborah Margaritov, Donald S. Olson, Melissa Rivers, Michael Rozendal, Stephen Sadis, Glenn W. Sheehan, Heidi Sarna, M. T. Schwartzman (Gold Guide editor), Bill Sherwonit, Dinah A. Spritzer

Editorial Production: Janet Foley, Melissa Klurman

Maps: David Lindroth, *cartographer*; Steven K. Amsterdam, *map editor*

Design: Fabrizio La Rocca, *creative director*; Guido Caroti, *associate art director*; Jolie Novak, *photo editor*

Production/Manufacturing: Rebecca Zeiler

Cover Photograph: J.A. Kraulis/Masterfile

Copyright

Twelfth Edition

ISBN 0–679–03516–8

Special Sales

Fodor's Travel Publications are available at special discounts for bulk purchases for sales promotions or premiums. Special editions, including personalized covers, excerpts of existing guides, and corporate imprints, can be created in large quantities for special needs. For more information, contact your local bookseller or write to Special Markets, Fodor's Travel Publications, 201 East 50th Street, New York, NY 10022. Inquiries from Canada should be directed to your local Canadian bookseller or sent to Random House of Canada, Ltd., Marketing Department, 1265 Aerowood Drive, Mississauga, Ontario L4W 1B9. Inquiries from the United Kingdom should be sent to Fodor's Travel Publications, 20 Vauxhall Bridge Road, London SW1V 2SA, England.

PRINTED IN THE UNITED STATES OF AMERICA

10 9 8 7 6 5 4 3 2 1

CONTENTS

ON THE ROAD WITH FODOR'S

WE'RE ALWAYS THRILLED to get letters from readers, especially one like this:

It took us an hour to decide what book to buy and we now know we picked the best one. Your book was wonderful, easy to follow, very accurate, and good on pointing out eating places, informal as well as formal. When we saw other people using your book, we would look at each other and smile.

Our editors and writers are deeply committed to making every Fodor's guide "the best one"—not only accurate but always charming, brimming with sound recommendations and solid ideas, right on the mark in describing restaurants and hotels, and full of fascinating facts that make you view your destination in a rich new light.

About Our Writers

Our success in achieving our goals—and in helping to make your trip the best of all possible vacations—is a credit to the hard work of our writers.

Freelance writer **Alex Aron,** who revised and updated the Washington chapter, lived in the state for eight years and continues to spend half the year working in and around the Seattle area. The rest of her year is spent in Brooklyn teaching in the New York City public schools.

Tom Gaunt works as editor of the magazine section of the *Business Journal of Portland.* A native of the state, Tom has covered Northwest politics and culture for the past 12 years. His writing has appeared in *Pacific Northwest, Omni,* and the *Oregon Magazine of Nature, Exploration and Science.*

After seven invigorating years in Seattle— exploring its restaurants and parks, frequenting its theaters and cinemas, and actually *enjoying* its climate (well, at least in summer)—**Wier Harman** now endures a self-imposed exile in New Haven, Connecticut, at the Yale School of Drama. He does, however, hold a return-trip ticket.

Novelist and playwright **Donald S. Olson,** who wrote the Portland and Oregon chapters, put nearly 5,000 miles on his car updating *Fodor's Pacific Northwest.* His travel writing on Oregon has appeared in the *New York Times, Travel & Leisure, Passport Newsletter,* and *Diversion* magazine. Donald has also contributed to *National Geographic* and *Readers Digest: The Most Scenic Drives in America.*

Melissa Rivers, who updated the Vancouver and British Columbia chapters, travels throughout the Pacific Northwest on assignments for Fodor's.

Washington resident and freelance writer **Stephen Sadis** revised the Grand Coulee Dam and Spokane sections of the Washington chapter, adding new walking tours, restaurants, and lodgings.

New This Year

We've completely revised our guide to the Pacific Northwest, adding new coverage throughout the region. Wier Harman wrote new neighborhood walking tours for Seattle, Alex Aron added new sights in western and eastern Washington, Donald S. Olson wrote new walking tours in Portland and added four new tours of Oregon, and Melissa Rivers revamped the dining and lodging sections of the Vancouver chapter and wrote new exploring tours of British Columbia.

All the maps in this edition of *Fodor's Pacific Northwest* have been completely revised, and we've added new western Canada, Portland, Eugene, eastern Oregon, Seattle, San Juan Islands, Spokane, and Saltspring Island maps.

We're proud to announce that the American Society of Travel Agents has endorsed Fodor's as its guidebook series of choice. ASTA is the world's largest and most influential travel trade association, operating in more than 170 countries, with 27,000 members pledged to adhere to a strict code of ethics reflecting the Society's motto, "Integrity in Travel." ASTA shares Fodor's devotion to providing smart, honest travel information and advice to travelers, and we've long recommended that our readers consult ASTA member agents for their experience and professionalism.

On the Web, check out the Fodor's site (www.fodors.com/) for information on major destinations around the world and travel-savvy interactive features. The Web site also lists the 85-plus radio stations nationwide that carry the *Fodor's Travel Show,* a live call-in program that airs every weekend. Tune in to hear guests discuss their wonderful adventures—or call in for answers to your most pressing travel questions.

How to Use This Book

Organization

Up front is the **Gold Guide,** an easy-to-use section divided alphabetically by topic. Under each listing you'll find tips and information that will help you tour the Pacific Northwest. You'll also find addresses and telephone numbers of organizations and companies that offer destination-related services and detailed information and publications.

The first chapter in the guide, **Destination: Pacific Northwest,** helps get you in the mood for your trip. New and Noteworthy cues you in on trends and happenings, What's Where gets you oriented, Pleasures and Pastimes describes the activities and sights that make the Pacific Northwest unique, Fodor's Choice lists our top picks in several categories, and Festivals and Seasonal Events alerts you to special events you'll want to seek out.

Destination chapters in *Fodor's Pacific Northwest* are arranged by state or province, with full chapters for Portland, Seattle, and Vancouver. Each city chapter begins with an Exploring section subdivided by neighborhood; each subsection recommends a walking or driving tour and lists sights in alphabetical order. Each regional chapter is divided by geographical area; within each area, towns are covered in logical geographical order, and attractive stretches of road and minor points of interest between them are indicated by the designation En Route. Throughout, Off the Beaten Path sights appear after the places from which they are most easily accessible. And within town sections, all restaurants and lodgings are grouped together.

To help you decide what to visit in the time you have, all chapters begin with recommended itineraries; you can mix and match those from several chapters to create a complete vacation. The A to Z section that ends all chapters covers getting there and getting around. It also provides helpful contacts and resources.

At the end of the book you'll find **Portraits,** an essay about the Pacific Northwest, followed by suggestions for any pretrip research you want to do, from recommended reading to videotapes that have the Pacific Northwest as a backdrop.

Icons and Symbols

★	Our special recommendation
✕	Restaurant
🏠	Lodging establishment
✕🏠	Lodging establishment whose restaurant warrants a special trip
⚠	Campgrounds
☾	Good for kids (rubber duckie)
☞	Sends you to another section of the guide for more information
⊠	Address
☎	Telephone number
☉	Opening and closing times
💷	Admission prices (those we give apply to adults; substantially reduced fees are almost always available for children, students, and senior citizens)

Numbers in white and black circles (e.g., ② and ❷) that appear on the maps, in the margins, and within the tours correspond to one another.

Dining and Lodging

The restaurants and lodgings we list are the cream of the crop in each price range. In city chapters, price charts appear at the beginning of the dining and lodging sections. In the regional chapters, price charts appear in the Pleasures and Pastimes section that follows each chapter introduction. Prices in the Vancouver and British Columbia chapters are in Canadian dollars. Prices in the Portland, Seattle, Oregon, Washington, and Southeast Alaska chapters are in U.S. dollars.

Hotel Facilities

We always list the facilities that are available—but we don't specify whether they cost extra: When pricing accommodations, always ask what's included. Assume that all rooms have private baths unless otherwise noted.

Restaurant Reservations and Dress Codes

Reservations are always a good idea; we note only when they're essential or when they are not accepted. Book as far ahead as you can, and reconfirm when you get to town. Unless otherwise noted, the restaurants listed are open daily for lunch and dinner. Dining throughout the Pacific Northwest is generally casual. We mention dress only when men are required to wear a jacket or a jacket and tie.

Credit Cards

The following abbreviations are used: **AE**, American Express; **D**, Discover; **DC**, Diners Club; **MC**, MasterCard; and **V**, Visa.

Don't Forget to Write

You can use this book in the confidence that all prices and opening times are based on information supplied to us at press time; Fodor's cannot accept responsibility for any errors. Time inevitably brings changes, so always confirm information when it matters—especially if you're making a detour to visit a specific place. In addition, when making reservations be sure to mention if you have a disability or are traveling with children, if you prefer a private bath or a certain type of bed, or if you have specific dietary needs or other concerns.

Were the restaurants we recommended as described? Did our hotel picks exceed your expectations? Did you find a museum we recommended a waste of time? If you have complaints, we'll look into them and revise our entries when the facts warrant it. If you've discovered a special place that we haven't included, we'll pass the information along to our correspondents and have them check it out. So send us your feedback, positive and negative: e-mail us at editors@fodors.com (specifying the name of the book on the subject line) or write to the *Pacific Northwest* editor at Fodor's, 201 East 50th Street, New York, New York 10022. Have a wonderful trip!

Karen Cure
Editorial Director

The Pacific Northwest

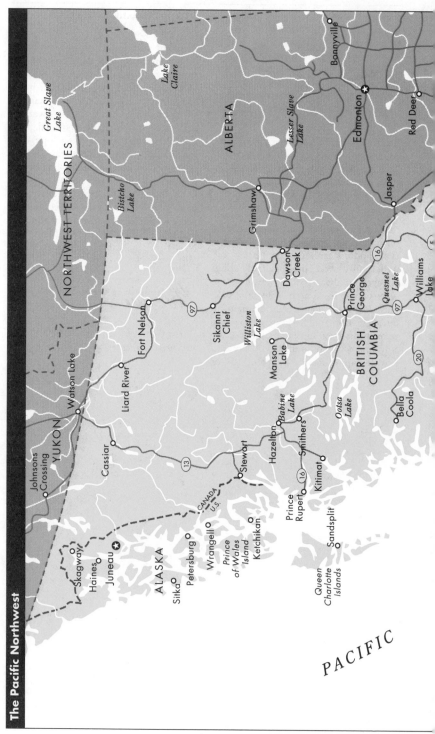

PACIFIC

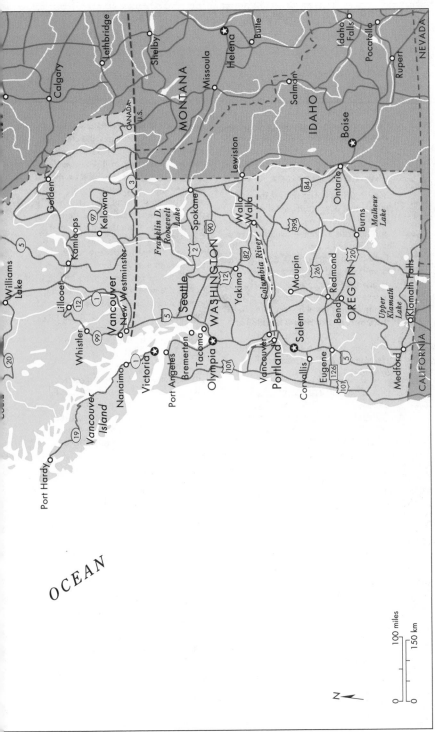

OCEAN

100 miles

150 km

N

SMART TRAVEL TIPS A TO Z

Basic Information on Traveling in the Pacific Northwest, Savvy Tips to Make Your Trip a Breeze, and Companies and Organizations to Contact

A

AIR TRAVEL

MAJOR AIRLINE OR LOW-COST CARRIER?

Major airlines offer the greatest number of departures; smaller airlines—including regional, low-cost, and no-frills airlines—usually have a more limited number of flights daily. Low-cost airlines offer a definite price advantage and fewer restrictions, such as advance-purchase requirements. Safety wise, low-cost carriers as a group have a good history, but **check the safety record before booking** any low-cost carrier; call the Federal Aviation Administration's Consumer Hotline (☞ Airline Complaints, *below*).

➤ MAJOR AIRLINES: **Air B.C.** (☎ 604/688–5515 or 250/360–9074; 800/776–3000 in the U.S.). **Air Canada** (☎ 800/776–3000). **Air North Ltd.** (☎ 800/764–0407). **Alaska** (☎ 800/426–0333). **American** (☎ 800/433–7300). **British Airways** (☎ 800/247–9297 in the U.S.; 0345/222–111 in the U.K.). **Continental** (☎ 800/525–0280). **Delta** (☎ 800/221–1212). **EVA Airways** (☎ 800/695–1188). **Hawaiian** (☎ 800/367–5320). **Japan** (☎ 800/525–3663). **Northwest** (☎ 800/225–2525). **Thai** (☎ 800/426–5204). **TWA** (☎ 800/221–2000). **United/United Express** (☎ 800/241–6522). **US Airways/US Airways Express** (☎ 800/428–4322).

➤ SMALLER AIRLINES: **America West** (☎ 800/235–9292). **Canadian** (☎ 800/426–7000). **Horizon Air** (☎ 800/547–9308). **Reno Air** (☎ 800/736–6247). **Skywest** (☎ 800/453–9417). **Southwest** (☎ 800/435–9792). **Westjet** (☎ 800/538–5696). **Western Pacific** ☎ 800/930–3030).

GET THE LOWEST FARE

The least-expensive airfares to the Pacific Northwest are priced for round-trip travel. Major airlines usually require that you **book in advance and buy the ticket within 24 hours,** and you may have to **stay over a Saturday night.** It's smart to **call a number of airlines, and when you are quoted a good price, book it on the spot**—the same fare may not be available on the same flight the next day. Airlines generally allow you to change your return date for a fee of $25–$50. If you don't use your ticket you can apply the cost toward the purchase of a new ticket, again for a small charge. However, most low-fare tickets are nonrefundable. To get the lowest airfare, **check different routings.** If your destination or home city has more than one gateway, compare prices to and from different airports. Also price off-peak flights, which may be significantly less expensive. If you're flying to Vancouver, remember that penalties for refunds or scheduling changes are stiffer for international tickets, usually about $150. International flights are also sensitive to the season: **plan to fly in the off season** for the cheapest fares.

To save money on flights from the United Kingdom and back, **look into an APEX or Super-PEX ticket.** APEX tickets must be booked in advance and have certain restrictions. Super-PEX tickets can be purchased at the airport on the day of departure—subject to availability.

DON'T STOP UNLESS YOU MUST

When you book, **look for nonstop flights** and remember that "direct" flights stop at least once. Try to **avoid connecting flights,** which require a change of plane. Two airlines may jointly operate a connecting flight, so ask if your airline operates every segment—you may find that your preferred carrier flies you only part of the way.

AVOID GETTING BUMPED

Airlines routinely overbook planes, knowing that not everyone with a ticket will show up, but sometimes everyone does. When that happens, airlines ask for volunteers to give up their seats. In return, these volunteers usually get a certificate for a free flight and are rebooked on the next flight out. If there are not enough volunteers, the airline must choose who will be denied boarding. The first to get bumped are passengers who checked in late and those flying on discounted tickets, **so get to the gate and check in as early as possible,** especially during peak periods.

Always **bring a photo ID to the airport.** You may be asked to show it before you are allowed to check in.

ENJOY THE FLIGHT

For more legroom, **request an emergency-aisle seat.** Don't sit in the row in front of the emergency aisle or in front of a bulkhead, where seats may not recline. If you don't like airline food, **ask for special meals when booking.** These can be vegetarian, low-cholesterol, or kosher, for example.

COMPLAIN IF NECESSARY

If your baggage goes astray or your flight goes awry, complain right away. Most carriers require that you file a claim immediately.

➤ AIRLINE COMPLAINTS: **Aviation Consumer Protection Division** (✉ U.S. Dept. of Transportation, C-75, Room 4107, Washington, DC 20590, ☎ 202/366–2220). **Federal Aviation Administration (FAA) Consumer Hotline** (☎ 800/322–7873).

WITHIN THE PACIFIC NORTHWEST

The leading regional carriers in the Pacific Northwest include **Horizon Air** and **United Express.** The two airlines provide frequent service between cities in Washington and Oregon. Horizon Air flies from Seattle to Vancouver and Victoria.

The major regional carrier in western Canada is **Air B.C.,** which has daily flights from Vancouver and Victoria into Seattle. **Air B.C.** also has several daily flights between Vancouver and Portland. **Helijet Airways** provides jet helicopter service from Vancouver and Seattle's Boeing Field to Victoria.

In addition to its regular airport service, Air B.C. has floatplane service

between Vancouver and Victoria harbors. **Kenmore Air** has scheduled flights from Seattle's Lake Union to Victoria and points in the San Juan Islands. Along with several other floatplane companies, Kenmore provides fly-in service to remote fishing resorts along the coast of British Columbia.

➤ REGIONAL AIRLINES: **Air B.C.** (☎ 604/688–5515 or 250/360–9074; 800/776–3000 in the U.S.). **Harbor Air** (☎ 800/359–3220). **Helijet Airways** (☎ 604/682–1468). **Horizon Air** (☎ 800/547–9308). **Kenmore Air** (☎ 206/486–8400 or 800/543–9595). **United Express** (☎ 800/241–6522).

AIRPORTS & TRANSFERS

The major gateways are **Portland International Airport, Sea-Tac (Seattle-Tacoma) International Airport,** and **Vancouver International Airport.** Nonstop flying time from New York to Seattle or Portland is approximately 5 hours; flights from Chicago are about 4–4½ hours; flights between Los Angeles and Seattle take 2½ hours. Flights from New York to Vancouver take about 8 hours with connections; from Chicago, about 4½ hours nonstop; and from Los Angeles, about 3 hours nonstop.

➤ AIRPORT INFORMATION: **Portland International Airport** (✉ N.E. Airport Way at I–205, ☎ 503/335–1234), **Sea-Tac International Airport** (☎ 206/431–4444).**Vancouver International Airport** (☎ 604/276–6101).

TRANSFERS

See the A to Z sections at the end of the Portland, Seattle, and Vancouver chapters for information about airport transfers to the center of each city.

B

BUS TRAVEL

WITHIN THE PACIFIC NORTHWEST

➤ BUS LINES AND SIGHTSEEING COMPANIES: **Gray Line** (☎ 503/285–9845 or 800/422–7042 in Portland; 206/624–5077 or 800/544–0739 in Seattle; 604/681–8687 or [from U.S. only] 800/663–0667 in Vancouver; 250/388–5248 or [from the U.S. only] 800/663–8390 in Victoria; 907/277–5581 or 800/544–2206 in Alaska).

Greyhound (☎ 800/231–2222).
Pacific Coach Lines (☎ 800/661–
1725), for travel from Vancouver to
Victoria.

DISCOUNT PASSES

The **AlaskaPass Travelpass** provides
transportation aboard any Alaska or
British Columbia ferry as well as
many connecting bus and train services. Greyhound's **Ameripass**, valid
on all U.S. routes, allows unlimited
bus travel within a 7-, 15-, 30-, or
60-day period. Greyhound Lines of
Canada offers the **CanPass**, valid for
7, 15, 30, or 60 days of unlimited bus
travel within Canada.

➤ PASSES: **AlaskaPass Travelpass** (☎
800/248–7598). **Ameripass** (☎ 800/
231–2222). **CanPass** (☎ 604/662–
3222).

BUSINESS HOURS

WASHINGTON & OREGON

Most retail stores in downtown
locations in Washington and Oregon
are open on weekdays and Saturday
from 9:30 to 6 and on Sunday between noon and 5; suburban shopping malls are usually open until 9
except on Sunday. Downtown stores
sometimes stay open late Thursday
and Friday nights. Normal banking
hours are between 9 and 6 on weekdays; some branches are also open on
Saturday morning.

BRITISH COLUMBIA

In British Columbia, most stores are
open from Saturday to Tuesday
between 9 and 6, and from Wednesday to Friday between 9 AM and 9 PM.
Normal banking hours in Canada are
from 9 to 4 on weekdays, and 9 to 3
on Saturday. Some branches may be
closed Monday.

SOUTHEAST ALASKA

In Southeast Alaska, most city retail
outlets are open daily except Sunday
from 10 to 6 or 7. Shopping malls
stay open until 8 or 9. Most banks
operate from 10 to 3.

C

CAMERAS, CAMCORDERS, &
COMPUTERS

Always **keep your film, tape, or
computer disks out of the sun.** Carry
an extra supply of batteries, and **be**

**prepared to turn on your camera,
camcorder, or laptop** to prove to
security personnel that the device is
real. Always **ask for hand inspection
of film,** which becomes clouded after
successive exposure to airport x-ray
machines, and **keep videotapes and
computer disks away from metal
detectors.**

➤ PHOTO HELP: Kodak Information
Center (☎ 800/242–2424). *Kodak
Guide to Shooting Great Travel Pic-
tures,* available in bookstores or from
Fodor's Travel Publications (☎ 800/
533–6478; $16.50 plus $4 shipping).

CAR RENTAL

Rates in Portland begin at $33 a day
and $145 a week. Rates in Seattle
begin at $50 a day and $155 a week.
Rates in Vancouver begin at $23 a
day and $133 a week. This does not
include tax on car rentals, which is
15% in Vancouver and 18.3% in
Seattle.

➤ MAJOR AGENCIES: **Alamo** (☎ 800/
327–9633; 0800/272–2000 in the
U.K.). **Avis** (☎ 800/331–1212; 800/
879–2847 in Canada). **Budget** (☎
800/527–0700; 0800/181181 in the
U.K.). **Dollar** (☎ 800/800–4000;
0990/565656 in the U.K., where it is
known as Eurodollar). **Hertz** (☎ 800/
654–3131; 800/263–0600 in Canada;
0345/555888 in the U.K.). **National
InterRent** (☎ 800/227–7368; 01345/
222525 in the U.K., where it is
known as Europcar InterRent).

CUT COSTS

When pricing cars, **ask about the
location of the rental lot.** Some off-
airport locations offer lower rates,
and their lots are only minutes from
the terminal via complimentary
shuttle. You also may want to **price
local car-rental companies,** whose
rates may be lower still, although
their service and maintenance may
not be as good as those of a name-
brand agency. Remember to ask
about required deposits, cancellation
penalties, and drop-off charges if
you're planning to pick up the car in
one city and leave it in another.

Also **ask your travel agent about a
company's customer-service record.**
How has it responded to late plane
arrivals and vehicle mishaps? Are
there often lines at the rental
counter, and, if you're traveling

during a holiday period, does a confirmed reservation guarantee you a car?

NEED INSURANCE?

When driving a rented car you are generally responsible for any damage to or loss of the vehicle. You also are liable for any property damage or personal injury that you may cause while driving. Before you rent, **see what coverage you already have** under the terms of your personal auto-insurance policy and credit cards.

For about $14 a day, rental companies sell protection, known as a collision- or loss-damage waiver (CDW or LDW), that eliminates your liability for damage to the car; it's always optional and should never be automatically added to your bill.

In most states you don't need a CDW if you have personal auto insurance or other liability insurance. However, **make sure you have enough coverage to pay for the car.** If you do not have auto insurance or an umbrella policy that covers damage to third parties, purchasing a CDW or LDW is highly recommended.

BEWARE SURCHARGES

Before you pick up a car in one city and leave it in another, **ask about drop-off charges or one-way service fees,** which can be substantial. Note, too, that some rental agencies charge extra if you return the car before the time specified on your contract. To avoid a hefty refueling fee, **fill the tank just before you turn in the car,** but be aware that gas stations near the rental outlet may overcharge.

MEET THE REQUIREMENTS

In the United States you must be 21 to rent a car, and rates may be higher if you're under 25. You'll pay extra for child seats (about $3 per day), which are compulsory for children under five, and for additional drivers (about $2 per day). Residents of the United Kingdom will need a reservation voucher, a passport, a U.K. driver's license, and a travel policy that covers each driver in order to pick up a car.

DRIVING

If you are renting a car, don't forget to **arrange for a car seat** when you reserve.

HOTELS

Most hotels in the Pacific Northwest allow children under a certain age to stay in their parents' room at no extra charge, but others charge them as extra adults; **ask about the cutoff age for children's discounts.**

FLYING

As a general rule, infants under two not occupying a seat fly free on U.S. flights, at greatly reduced fares and occasionally for free on international flights. If your children are two or older **ask about children's airfares.**

In general, the adult baggage allowance applies to children paying half or more of the adult fare. When booking flights to Canada, **ask about carry-on allowances for those traveling with infants.** In general, for babies charged 10% of the adult fare, you are allowed one carry-on bag and a collapsible stroller, which may have to be checked; you may be limited to less if the flight is full.

According to the FAA it's a good idea to use safety seats aloft for children weighing less than 40 pounds. Airlines, however, can set their own policies: U.S. carriers allow FAA-approved models but usually require that you buy a ticket, even if your child would otherwise ride free, since the seats must be strapped into regular seats. Airline rules vary regarding their use; **check your airline's policy about using safety seats during take-off and landing.** Safety seats cannot obstruct any of the other passengers in the row, so get an appropriate seat assignment as early as possible.

When making your reservation, **request children's meals or a free-standing bassinet** if you need them; the latter are available only to those seated at the bulkhead, where there's enough legroom. Remember, however, that bulkhead seats may not have their own overhead bins, and there's no storage space in front of you—a major inconvenience.

GROUP TRAVEL

➤ FAMILY-FRIENDLY TOUR OPERATORS: **Grandtravel** (✉ 6900 Wisconsin Ave., Suite 706, Chevy Chase, MD 20815, ☎ 301/986–0790 or 800/247–7651) for people traveling with grandchildren ages 7–17. **Families Welcome!** (✉ 92 N. Main St., Ashland, OR 97520, ☎ 541/482–6121 or 800/326–0724, FAX 541/482–0660).

CONSUMER PROTECTION

Whenever possible, **pay with a major credit card** so you can cancel payment if necessary. This is a good practice whether you're buying travel arrangements before your trip or shopping at your destination.

If you're doing business with a particular company for the first time, **contact your local Better Business Bureau and the attorney general's offices** in your state and the company's home state, as well. Have any complaints been filed?

Finally, if you're buying a package or tour, always **consider travel insurance** that includes default coverage (☞ Insurance, *below*).

➤ LOCAL BBBS: **Alaska Better Business Bureau** (✉ 2805 Bering St., Suite 2, Anchorage 99503-3819, ☎ 907/562–0704). **British Columbia Better Business Bureaus** (✉ 788 Beatty St., Suite 404, Vancouver V6B2M1, ☎ 604/682–2711 for mainland British Columbia; ✉ 1005 Langley St., Room 201, Victoria V8W 1V7, ☎ 250/386–6348 for Vancouver Island). **Oregon Better Business Bureau** (✉ 333 S.W. 5th Ave., Suite 300, Portland 97204, ☎ 503/226–3981). **Washington Better Business Bureau** (✉ Box 68926, Sea-Tac 98168-0926, ☎ 206/431–2222). **Council of Better Business Bureaus** (✉ 4200 Wilson Blvd., Suite 800, Arlington, VA 22203, ☎ 703/276–0100, FAX 703/525–8277).

CRUISING

More than 30 ships, of all sizes, offer cruises to Alaska. You can sail the Inside Passage on a small ship carrying a handful of passengers or cross the Gulf of Alaska in the company of more than 1,000 other people. For the latest information on which cruise lines and ships are sailing to Alaska, see *Fodor's Cruises and Ports of Call* or *Fodor's Alaska Ports of Call.*

Cruise ships travel the Inside Passage and Gulf of Alaska from mid-May to late September. The most popular ports of embarkation are Vancouver and Seward (port city for Anchorage), but cruises also leave from San Francisco and Seattle. To get the best deal on a cruise, **consult a cruise-only travel agency.**

➤ INFORMATION: **Cruise Lines International Association** (✉ 500 5th Ave., Suite 631, New York, NY 10004, ☎ 212/921–0066).

CUSTOMS & DUTIES

ENTERING THE U.S.

You may bring home $400 worth of foreign goods duty-free if you've been out of the country for at least 48 hours and haven't already used the $400 allowance or any part of it in the past 30 days.

Travelers 21 and older may bring back 1 liter of alcohol duty-free. In addition, regardless of your age, you are allowed 200 cigarettes and 100 non-Cuban cigars. (At press time, a federal rule restricting tobacco access to persons 18 years and older did not apply to importation.) Antiques, which the U.S. Customs Service defines as objects more than 100 years old, enter duty-free, as do original works of art done entirely by hand, including paintings, drawings, and sculptures.

You may also send packages home duty-free: up to $200 worth of goods for personal use, with a limit of one parcel per addressee per day (and no alcohol or tobacco products or perfume worth more than $5); label the package PERSONAL USE, and attach a list of its contents and their retail value. Do not label the package UNSOLICITED GIFT, or your duty-free exemption will drop to $100. Mailed items do not affect your duty-free allowance on your return.

➤ INFORMATION: **U.S. Customs Service** (Inquiries, ✉ Box 7407, Washington, DC 20044, ☎ 202/927–6724; complaints, ☞ Office of Regulations and Rulings, 1301 Constitution Ave. NW, Washington, DC 20229; registration of equipment, ✉ Resource Management, 1301 Constitution Ave.

NW, Washington, DC 20229, ☎ 202/927–0540).

ENTERING CANADA

If you've been out of Canada for at least seven days, you may bring in C$500 worth of goods duty-free. If you've been away for fewer than seven days but more than 48 hours, the duty-free allowance drops to C$200; if your trip lasts 24–48 hours, the allowance is C$50. You may not pool allowances with family members. Goods claimed under the C$500 exemption may follow you by mail; those claimed under the lesser exemptions must accompany you.

Alcohol and tobacco products may be included in the seven-day and 48-hour exemptions but not in the 24-hour exemption. If you meet the age requirements of the province or territory through which you reenter Canada, you may bring in, duty-free, 1.14 liters (40 imperial ounces) of wine or liquor *or* 24 12-ounce cans or bottles of beer or ale. If you are 16 or older, you may bring in, duty-free, 200 cigarettes and 50 cigars; these items must accompany you.

You may send an unlimited number of gifts worth up to C$60 each duty-free to Canada. Label the package UNSOLICITED GIFT—VALUE UNDER $60. Alcohol and tobacco are excluded.

➤ INFORMATION: **Revenue Canada** (⊠ 2265 St. Laurent Blvd. S, Ottawa, Ontario K1G 4K3, ☎ 613/993–0534, 800/461–9999 in Canada).

ENTERING THE U.K.

From countries outside the EU, including the United States and Canada, you may import, duty-free, 200 cigarettes or 50 cigars; 1 liter of spirits or 2 liters of fortified or sparkling wine or liqueurs; 2 liters of still table wine; 60 milliliters of perfume; 250 milliliters of toilet water; plus £136 worth of other goods, including gifts and souvenirs.

➤ INFORMATION: **HM Customs and Excise** (⊠ Dorset House, Stamford St., London SE1 9NG, ☎ 0171/202–4227).

D

DISABILITIES & ACCESSIBILITY

ACCESS IN THE PACIFIC NORTHWEST

The **Easter Seal Society** publishes *Access Seattle,* a free guide to the city's services for people with disabilities. **Tourism British Columbia's** accommodations guide describes the accessibility of lodging facilities throughout the province. If you drop by the **Vancouver Tourist Information Centre,** you can look in the center's General Information binder for the list of area attractions that are wheelchair accessible. **Access Alaska** provides information and referral to visitors with disabilities. **Challenge Alaska** provides recreational opportunities for people with disabilities. Activities include downhill and cross-country skiing, sea kayaking, canoeing, camping, fishing, swimming, dogsledding, and backpacking.

➤ LOCAL RESOURCES: **Access Alaska** (⊠ 3710 Woodland Dr., Suite 900, Anchorage, AK 99517, ☎ 907/248–4777). **Challenge Alaska** (⊠ Box 110065, Anchorage, AK 99511-0065, ☎ 907/563–2658). **Easter Seal Society** (⊠ 521 2nd Ave. W, Seattle, WA 98119, ☎ 206/281–5700). **Tourism British Columbia** (☞ Parliament Bldg., Victoria, BC V8V 1X4, ☎ 800/633–6000). **Vancouver Tourist Information Centre** (⊠ 200 Burrard St., Vancouver, BC Z6C 3L6, ☎ 604/683–2000).

TIPS & HINTS

When discussing accessibility with an operator or reservationist, **ask hard questions.** Are there any stairs, inside *or* out? Are there grab bars next to the toilet *and* in the shower/tub? How wide is the doorway to the room? To the bathroom? For the most extensive facilities meeting the latest legal specifications, **opt for newer accommodations,** which are more likely to have been designed with access in mind. Older buildings or ships may offer more limited facilities. Be sure to **discuss your needs before booking.**

➤ COMPLAINTS: **Disability Rights Section** (⊠ U.S. Dept. of Justice, Box 66738, Washington, DC 20035-6738, ☎ 202/514–0301 or 800/514–0301, FAX 202/307–1198, TTY 202/514–

THE GOLD GUIDE / SMART TRAVEL TIPS

0383 or 800/514–0383) for general complaints. **Aviation Consumer Protection Division** (☞ Air Travel, *above*) for airline-related problems. **Civil Rights Office** (✉ U.S. Dept. of Transportation, Departmental Office of Civil Rights, S-30, 400 7th St. SW, Room 10215, Washington, DC 20590, ☎ 202/366–4648) for problems with surface transportation.

TRAVEL AGENCIES & TOUR OPERATORS

The Americans with Disabilities Act requires that travel firms serve the needs of all travelers. That said, you should note that some agencies and operators specialize in making travel arrangements for individuals and groups with disabilities.

➤ TRAVELERS WITH MOBILITY PROBLEMS: **Access Adventures** (✉ 206 Chestnut Ridge Rd., Rochester, NY 14624, ☎ 716/889–9096), run by a former physical-rehabilitation counselor. **Hinsdale Travel Service** (✉ 201 E. Ogden Ave., Suite 100, Hinsdale, IL 60521, ☎ 630/325–1335), a travel agency that benefits from the advice of wheelchair traveler Janice Perkins. **Wheelchair Journeys** (✉ 16979 Redmond Way, Redmond, WA 98052, ☎ 425/885–2210 or 800/313–4751), for general travel arrangements.

➤ TRAVELERS WITH DEVELOPMENTAL DISABILITIES: **New Directions** (✉ 5276 Hollister Ave., Suite 207, Santa Barbara, CA 93111, ☎ 805/967–2841, FAX 805/964–7344). **Sprout** (✉ 893 Amsterdam Ave., New York, NY 10025, ☎ 212/222–9575 or 888/222–9575, FAX 212/222–9768).

DISCOUNTS & DEALS

Be a smart shopper and **compare all your options before making a choice.** A plane ticket bought with a promotional coupon may not be cheaper than the least expensive fare from a discount ticket agency. For high-price travel purchases, such as packages or tours, keep in mind that what you get is just as important as what you save. Just because something is cheap doesn't mean it's a bargain.

LOOK IN YOUR WALLET

When you use your credit card to make travel purchases, you may get free travel-accident insurance, colli-sion-damage insurance, and medical or legal assistance, depending on the card and the bank that issued it. American Express, MasterCard, and Visa provide one or more of these services, so **get a copy of your credit card's travel-benefits policy.** If you are a member of the American Automobile Association (AAA) or an oil-company-sponsored road-assistance plan, always **ask hotel or car-rental reservationists about auto-club discounts.** Some clubs offer additional discounts on tours, cruises, or admission to attractions. And don't forget that auto-club membership entitles you to free maps and trip-planning services.

DIAL FOR DOLLARS

To save money, **look into "1-800" discount reservations services,** which use their buying power to get a better price on hotels, airline tickets, even car rentals. When booking a room, always **call the hotel's local toll-free number** (if one is available) rather than the central reservations number—you'll often get a better price. Always ask about special packages or corporate rates.

➤ AIRLINE TICKETS: ☎ 800/FLY–4–LESS. 800/FLY–ASAP.

➤ HOTEL ROOMS: **Central Reservation Service (CRS)** (☎ 800/548–3311). **RMC Travel** (☎ 800/245–5738). **Steigenberger Reservation Service** (☎ 800/223–5652).

SAVE ON COMBOS

Packages and guided tours can both save you money, but don't confuse the two. When you buy a package, your travel remains independent, just as though you had planned and booked the trip yourself. Fly-drive packages, which combine airfare and car rental, are often a good deal.

JOIN A CLUB?

Many companies sell discounts in the form of travel clubs and coupon books, but these cost money. You must use participating advertisers to get a deal, and only after you recoup the initial membership cost or book price do you begin to save. If you plan to use the club or coupons frequently you may save considerably. Before signing up, find out what discounts you get for free.

➤ Discount Clubs: **Entertainment Travel Editions** (✉ 2125 Butterfield Rd., Troy, MI 48084, ☎ 800/445–4137; $23–$48, depending on destination). **Great American Traveler** (✉ Box 27965, Salt Lake City, UT 84127, ☎ 800/548–2812; $49.95 per year). **Moment's Notice Discount Travel Club** (✉ 7301 New Utrecht Ave., Brooklyn, NY 11204, ☎ 718/234–6295; $25 per year, single or family). **Privilege Card International** (✉ 237 E. Front St., Youngstown, OH 44503, ☎ 330/746–5211 or 800/236–9732; $74.95 per year). **Sears's Mature Outlook** (✉ Box 9390, Des Moines, IA 50306, ☎ 800/336–6330; $14.95 per year). **Travelers Advantage** (✉ CUC Travel Service, 3033 S. Parker Rd., Suite 1000, Aurora, CO 80014, ☎ 800/548–1116 or 800/648–4037; $49 per year, single or family). **Worldwide Discount Travel Club** (✉ 1674 Meridian Ave., Miami Beach, FL 33139, ☎ 305/534–2082; $50 per year family, $40 single).

DRIVING

FROM THE U.S.

The U.S. interstate highway network provides quick and easy access to the Pacific Northwest in spite of imposing mountain barriers. From the south, Interstate 5 (I–5) runs from the U.S.–Mexican border through California, into Oregon and Washington, and ends at the U.S.–Canadian border. From the east, I–90 stretches from Boston to Seattle. I–84 runs from the midwestern states to Portland.

The main entry point into Canada by car is on I–5 at Blaine, Washington, 30 miles south of Vancouver. Two major highways enter British Columbia from the east: the Trans–Canada Highway (the longest highway in the world, running more than 5,000 miles from St. John's, Newfoundland, to Victoria, British Columbia) and the Yellowhead Highway, which runs through northern British Columbia from the Rocky Mountains to Prince Rupert.

Border-crossing procedures are usually quick and simple (☞ Passports & Visas, *below*). The I–5 border crossing at Blaine, Washington, is open 24 hours. The peak traffic time northbound into Canada is 4 PM. Southbound, expect delays in the evening and on weekend mornings. There are smaller border stations at other points between Washington and British Columbia, but they may be closed at night.

WITHIN THE PACIFIC NORTHWEST

Except for a short distance north of Vancouver, there are no roads along the rugged mainland coast of British Columbia and Southeast Alaska.

Alaskan cities such as Juneau have no direct access by road; cars must be brought in by ferry. Skagway and Haines are the only towns in Southeast Alaska accessible directly by road. The trip—a grueling 1,650 mi from Seattle—passes through British Columbia and the Yukon Territory.

AUTO CLUBS

The American Automobile Association (AAA) and the Canadian Automobile Association (CAA) provide full services to members of any of the Commonwealth Motoring Conference (CMC) clubs, including the Automobile Association, the Royal Automobile Club, and the Royal Scottish Automobile Club. Services are also available to members of the Alliance Internationale de l'Automobile (AIT), the Fédération Internationale de l'Automobile (FIA), and the Federation of Interamerican Touring and Automobile Clubs (FITAC). Members receive travel information, itineraries, maps, tour books, information about road and weather conditions, emergency road services, and travel-agency services.

➤ Auto Clubs: In the United States, **American Automobile Association** (☎ 800/564–6222). In the United Kingdom, **Automobile Association** (AA, ☎ 0990/500–600), **Royal Automobile Club** (RAC, ☎ 0990/722–722 membership; 0345/121–345 insurance).

INSURANCE

Vehicle insurance is compulsory in the United States and Canada. Motorists are required to produce evidence of insurance if they become involved in an accident. Upon arrival, visitors from foreign countries should contact an insurance agent or broker to obtain the necessary insurance for North America.

SPEED LIMITS

The speed limit on U.S. interstate highways is generally 65 miles per hour in rural areas and 55 miles per hour in urban zones and on secondary highways. In Canada (where the metric system is used), the speed limit is usually 100 kph (62 mph) on expressways and 80 kph (50 mph) on secondary roads.

WINTER DRIVING

Winter driving in the Pacific Northwest can present challenges. In coastal areas, the mild, damp climate contributes to roadways that are frequently wet. Winter snowfalls are not common (generally only once or twice a year), but when snow does fall, traffic grinds to a halt and the roadways become treacherous and stay that way until the snow melts.

Tire chains, studs, or snow tires are essential equipment for winter travel in mountain areas. If you're planning to drive into high elevations, be sure to check the weather forecast beforehand. Even the main-highway mountain passes may close because of snow conditions.

E

EMERGENCIES

For **police, ambulance,** or **other emergencies** in Alaska, Oregon, and Washington, dial 911. For **police, fire** and **ambulance** in Vancouver and Victoria, B.C., dial 911; dial "0" elsewhere in the province.

F

FERRIES

Ferries are an important link in the transportation network of the Pacific Northwest. In some areas, ferries provide the only form of access into and out of communities. In other places, ferries transport thousands of commuters a day to and from work in the cities. For visitors, ferries are one of the best ways to get a feel for the region and its ties to the sea.

WASHINGTON

If you are planning to use the Washington State Ferries, try to **avoid peak commuter hours.** The heaviest traffic flows are eastbound in the mornings and on Sunday evening, and westbound on Saturday morning and

weekday afternoons. The best times for travel are from 9 to 3 and after 7 PM on weekdays. In July and August, you may have to wait up to three hours to take a car aboard one of the popular San Juan Islands ferries. Walk-on space is always available; if possible, **leave your car behind.**

The vessels of **Washington State Ferries** carry more than 23 million passengers a year between points on Puget Sound and the San Juan Islands. Reservations are not available on any domestic routes.

➤ FERRY COMPANY: **Washington State Ferries** (✉ Colman Dock, Pier 52, Seattle, WA 98104, ☎ 206/464–6400; 800/843–3779 in WA).

BRITISH COLUMBIA

B.C. Ferries operates ferries between the mainland and Vancouver Island and elsewhere, carrying passengers, cars, campers, RVs, trucks, and buses. Peak traffic times are Friday afternoon, Saturday morning, and Sunday afternoon, especially during summer months and on holiday weekends.

Black Ball Transport's MV *Coho* makes daily crossings year-round, from Port Angeles to Victoria. The *Coho* can carry 800 passengers and 100 cars across the Strait of Juan de Fuca in 1½ hours. Advance reservations are not accepted.

Clipper Navigation operates three passenger-only jet catamarans between Seattle and Victoria. One makes the trip in two hours, another makes it in three hours, and the third, which takes the scenic route, makes it in five hours. The company also operates the *Princess Marguerite III* car and passenger ferry between Seattle and Victoria, with one round-trip daily from mid-May to mid-September. The sailing time is 4½ hours each way.

➤ FERRY COMPANIES: **B.C. Ferries** (✉ 1112 Fort St., Victoria, BC V8V 4V2, ☎ 250/386–3431 in Victoria or 604/277–0277 in Vancouver; 888/223–3779 in British Columbia only). **Black Ball Transport** (✉ 430 Belleville St., Victoria, BC V8V 1W9, ☎ 604/386–2202 in Victoria or 360/457–4491 in Port Angeles). **Clipper Navigation** (✉ 2701 Alaskan Way, Pier 69, Seattle, WA 98121, ☎ 250/

480–5555 in Victoria; 206/448–5000 in Seattle; 800/888–2535 in the U.S. only).

➤ DISCOUNT PASSES: The **AlaskaPass Travelpass** (✉ Box 351, Vashon Island, WA 98070, ☎ 800/248–7598) provides transportation aboard any British Columbia ferry as well as many connecting bus and train services. Passes of varying lengths enable the independent traveler to exercise a high degree of flexibility in choosing an itinerary.

SOUTHEAST ALASKA

The ferries of the **Alaska Marine Highway** system travel within Alaska and between Bellingham, Washington, and the towns of the Inside Passage. The Marine Highway links up with British Columbia Ferries in Prince Rupert.

➤ FERRY LINES: **Alaska Marine Highway** (✉ Box 25535, Juneau 99802-5535, ☎ 907/465–3941 or 800/642–0066, FAX 907/277–4829). **British Columbia Ferries** (✉ 1112 Fort St., Victoria, BC V8V 4V2, ☎ 250/386–3431, FAX 250/381—5452).

G
GAY & LESBIAN TRAVEL

LOCAL INFORMATION

➤ COMMUNITY RESOURCES: Portland: **Hotline** (☎ 800/777–2437). Seattle: **Greater Seattle Business Assn.** (☎ 206/443–4722). Vancouver: **Prideline B.C.** (✉ 1170 Bute St., ☎ 604/684–6869); **Vancouver Lesbian Connection** (✉ 876 Commercial Dr., ☎ 604/254–8458).

➤ PUBLICATIONS: Portland: *Just Out* (☎ 503/236–1252). Seattle: *Seattle Gay News* (☎ 206/324–4297). Vancouver: *Angles* (☎ 604/688–0265).

➤ GAY- & LESBIAN-FRIENDLY TRAVEL AGENCIES: **Advance Damron** (✉ 1 Greenway Plaza, Suite 800, Houston, TX 77046, ☎ 713/850–1140 or 800/695–0880, FAX 713/888–1010). **Club Travel** (✉ 8739 Santa Monica Blvd., West Hollywood, CA 90069, ☎ 310/358–2200 or 800/429–8747, FAX 310/358–2222). **Islanders/Kennedy Travel** (✉ 183 W. 10th St., New York, NY 10014, ☎ 212/242–3222 or 800/988–1181, FAX 212/929–8530). **Now Voyager** (✉ 4406 18th St., San Francisco, CA 94114, ☎ 415/626–1169 or 800/255–6951, FAX 415/626–8626). **Yellowbrick Road** (✉ 1500 W. Balmoral Ave., Chicago, IL 60640, ☎ 773/561–1800 or 800/642–2488, FAX 773/561–4497). **Skylink Women's Travel** (✉ 3577 Moorland Ave., Santa Rosa, CA 95407, ☎ 707/585–8355 or 800/225–5759, FAX 707/584–5637).

I
INSURANCE

Travel insurance is the best way to **protect yourself against financial loss.** The most useful policies are trip-cancellation-and-interruption, default, medical, and comprehensive insurance.

Without insurance you will lose all or most of your money if you cancel your trip, regardless of the reason. It's essential that you **buy trip-cancellation-and-interruption insurance,** particularly if your airline ticket, cruise, or package tour is nonrefundable and cannot be changed. Look for a policy that will cover the cost of your trip plus the nondiscounted price of a one-way airline ticket, should you need to return home early. Also **consider default or bankruptcy insurance,** which protects you against a supplier's failure to deliver.

Medicare generally does not cover health-care costs outside the United States, nor do many privately issued policies. If your own policy does not cover you outside the United States, **consider buying supplemental medical coverage.** Remember that travel health insurance is different from a medical-assistance plan.

Citizens of the United Kingdom can buy an annual travel-insurance policy valid for most vacations during the year in which it's purchased. If you are pregnant or have a preexisting medical condition, make sure you're covered. According to the Association of British Insurers, it's wise to buy extra medical coverage when you visit the United States.

If you have purchased an expensive vacation, comprehensive insurance is a must. **Look for comprehensive policies that include trip-delay insurance,** which will protect you in the event that weather problems cause you to miss your flight, tour, or cruise. A few insurers sell waivers for preexisting medical conditions. Companies that offer both features include Access America, Carefree Travel Insurance, Travel Insured International, and Travel Guard International (☞ *below*).

Always **buy travel insurance directly from the insurance company**; if you buy it from a travel agency or tour operator that goes out of business you probably will not be covered for the agency or operator's default, a major risk. Before you make any purchase, **review your existing health and home-owner's policies** to find out whether they cover expenses incurred while traveling.

➤ TRAVEL INSURERS: In the United States, **Access America** (⊠ 6600 W. Broad St., Richmond, VA 23230, ☎ 804/285–3300 or 800/284–8300), **Carefree Travel Insurance** (⊠ Box 9366, 100 Garden City Plaza, Garden City, NY 11530, ☎ 516/294–0220 or 800/323–3149), **Near Travel Services** (⊠ Box 1339, Calumet City, IL 60409, ☎ 708/868–6700 or 800/654–6700), **Travel Guard International** (⊠ 1145 Clark St., Stevens Point, WI 54481, ☎ 715/345–0505 or 800/826–1300), **Travel Insured International** (⊠ Box 280568, East Hartford, CT 06128–0568, ☎ 860/528–7663 or 800/243–3174), **Travelex Insurance Services** (⊠ 11717 Burt St., Suite 202, Omaha, NE 68154-1500, ☎ 402/445–8637 or 800/228–9792, FAX 800/867–9531), **Wallach & Company** (⊠ 107 W. Federal St., Box 480, Middleburg, VA 20118, ☎ 540/687–3166 or 800/237–6615). In Canada, **Mutual of Omaha** (⊠ Travel Division, 500 University Ave., Toronto, Ontario M5G 1V8, ☎ 416/598–4083, 800/268–8825 in Canada). In the United Kingdom, **Association of British Insurers** (⊠ 51 Gresham St., London EC2V 7HQ, ☎ 0171/600–3333).

L

LODGING

Although the hotel and motel price categories are standard, the prices listed under each may vary from one area to another. This variation reflects local price standards. In all cases, price ranges for each category are clearly stated before each listing.

APARTMENT, HOME, & VILLA RENTALS

Home-exchange directories list rentals (often second homes owned by prospective house swappers), and some services search for a house or apartment for you (even a castle if that's your fancy) and handle the paperwork. Some send an illustrated catalog; others send photographs only of specific properties, sometimes at a charge. Up-front registration fees may apply.

➤ RENTAL AGENTS/EXCHANGE CLUB: **Europa-Let/Tropical Inn-Let** (⊠ 92 N. Main St., Ashland, OR 97520, ☎ 541/482–5806 or 800/462–4486, FAX 541/482–0660). **HomeLink International** (⊠ Box 650, Key West, FL 33041, ☎ 305/294–7766 or 800/638–3841, FAX 305/294–1148) charges $83 per year. **Rent-a-Home International** (⊠ 7200 34th Ave. NW, Seattle, WA 98117, ☎ 206/789–9377 or 800/488–7368, FAX 206/789–9379). **Hideaways International** (⊠ 767 Islington St., Portsmouth, NH 03801, ☎ 603/430–4433 or 800/843–4433, FAX 603/430–4444) is a travel club whose members arrange rentals among themselves; yearly membership is $99.

B&BS/INNS

➤ RESERVATION SERVICES: **A Northwest Bed & Breakfast Reservation Service** (⊠ 610 S.W. Broadway, Portland, OR 97205, ☎ 503/243–7616). **A Traveller's Reservation Service** (⊠ Box 492, Mercer Island, WA 98040, ☎ 206/232–2345). **Best Canadian Bed & Breakfast Network** (⊠ 1090 W. King Edward Ave., Vancouver, BC V6H 1Z4, ☎ 604/738–7207). Before leaving the United Kingdom, you can book a B&B through **American Bed & Breakfast, Inter-Bed Network** (⊠ 31 Ernest Rd., Colchester, Essex CO7 9LQ, ☎ 0206/223162).

CAMPING

Oregon, Washington, Alaska, and British Columbia have excellent government-run campgrounds. A few accept advance camping reservations, but most do not. Privately operated campgrounds sometimes have extra amenities such as laundry rooms and swimming pools. For more information, contact the state or provincial tourism department.

HOTELS

Many business-oriented properties offer special weekend rates, sometimes up to 50% off regular prices. However, these deals are usually not extended during peak summer months, when hotels are normally full.

➤ NATIONAL CHAINS: **Canadian Pacific** (☎ 800/828–7447). **Courtyard by Marriott** (☎ 800/321–2211). **Delta** (☎ 800/877–1133). **Doubletree** (☎ 800/528–0444). **Embassy Suites Hotels** (☎ 800/362–2779). **Four Seasons** (☎ 800/332–3442). **Hilton** (☎ 800/445–8667). **Holiday Inn** (☎ 800/465–4329). **Hyatt** (☎ 800/233–1234). **Marriott** (☎ 800/228–9290). **Ramada** (☎ 800/228–2828). **Red Lion Hotels and Inns** (☎ 800/547–8010). **Sheraton** (☎ 800/325–3535). **Stouffer** (☎ 800/468–3571). **West Coast Hotels/Coast Hotels** (☎ 800/426–0670). **Westin** (☎ 800/228–3000).

MOTELS/MOTOR INNS

➤ NATIONAL CHAINS: **Best Western** (☎ 800/528–1234). **Days Inn** (☎ 800/325–2525). **La Quinta Inns** (☎ 800/531–5900). **Motel 6** (☎ 800/440–6000). **Quality Inns** (☎ 800/228–5151). **Super 8 Motels** (☎ 800/848–8888). **Travelodge** (☎ 800/255–3050). **Nendel's** (☎ 800/547–0106), **Sandman Inns** (☎ 800/726–3626), and **Shilo Inns** (☎ 800/222–2244) are regional chains.

RESORTS

Resorts in the Pacific Northwest run the gamut from rural fishing lodges to luxury showpieces. Whistler, British Columbia, is a year-round destination with skiing, golf, tennis, swimming, mountain biking, and horseback riding. Two resorts in Washington with grand settings are the Inn at Semi-Ah-Moo in Blaine and the Rosario Resort in the San Juan Islands. On the Washington side of the Columbia River, just across the Oregon border, is Skamania Lodge. Timberline Lodge on Mount Hood in Oregon is a longtime favorite of visitors to the state. Most of the Oregon coast is resort country; Salishan Lodge at Gleneden Beach is perhaps the most famous in the area.

M

MAIL

Postage rates vary for different classes of mail and destinations. Check with the local post office for rates before mailing a letter or parcel. At press time, it cost 32¢ to mail a standard letter anywhere within the United States. Mail to Canada costs 40¢ per first ounce, and 23¢ for each additional ounce; mail to Great Britain and other foreign countries costs 50¢ per half ounce.

First-class rates in Canada are 45¢ for up to 30 grams of mail delivered within Canada, 52¢ for up to 30 grams delivered to the United States, 70¢ for 30 to 50 grams. International mail and postcards run 90¢ for up to 20 grams, $1.37 for 20–50 grams.

RECEIVING MAIL

Visitors can have letters or parcels sent to them while they are traveling by using the following address: Name of addressee, c/o General Delivery, Main Post Office, City and State/Province, U.S./Canada, Zip Code (U.S.) or Postal Code (Canada). Contact the nearest post office for further details. Any item mailed to "General Delivery" must be picked up by the addressee in person within 15 days or it will be returned to the sender.

MONEY

The United States and Canada both use the same currency denominations—dollars and cents—although each currency has a different value on the world market. In the United States, the most common paper currency comes in $1, $5, $10, and $20 bills. Common notes in Canada include the $2, $5, $10, and $20 bills. (Canada recently phased out its $1 bill, replacing it with a $1 gold-colored coin nicknamed the "loonie" by Canadians because it contains a picture of a loon on one side.) Coins in both countries come in denominations of 1¢ (penny), 5¢ (nickel), 10¢ (dime), 25¢ (quarter), and 50¢ (half-dollar).

ATMS

Before leaving home, **make sure that your credit cards have been programmed for ATM use.**

➤ ATM Locations: **Cirrus** (☎ 800/424–7787). **Plus** (☎ 800/843–7587).

COSTS

Prices for meals and accommodations in the Pacific Northwest are generally lower than in other major North American regions. Prices for first-class hotel rooms in major cities (Seattle, Portland, Vancouver, and Victoria) range from $100 to $200 a night, although you can still find some "value" hotel rooms for $65 to $90 a night.

As a rule, costs outside the major cities are lower, but prices for rooms and meals at some of the major deluxe resorts can rival or exceed those at the best big-city hotels. In Alaska, food costs are higher because the state has to import virtually all of its produce.

Prices in Canada are always quoted in Canadian dollars in this guide. When comparing prices with those in the United States, costs should be calculated via the current rate of exchange. At press time (late fall 1997) the rate was US$1 to C$1.29 and £1 to C$2.18, but this exchange rate can vary considerably. Check with a bank or other financial institution for the current rate. A good way to be sure you're getting the best exchange rate is by using your credit card. The issuing bank will convert your bill at the current rate.

TRAVELER'S CHECKS

Whether or not to buy traveler's checks depends on where you are headed. **Take cash if your trip includes rural areas** and small towns, traveler's checks to cities. If your checks are lost or stolen, they can usually be replaced within 24 hours. To ensure a speedy refund, buy your checks yourself (don't ask someone else to make the purchase). When making a claim for stolen or lost checks, the person who bought the checks should make the call.

P

PACKING FOR THE PACIFIC NORTHWEST

Summer days are warm but evenings can cool off substantially. Your best bet is to **dress in layers**—sweatshirts, sweaters, and jackets are removed or put on as the day progresses. If you plan to explore the region's cities on foot, or if you choose to hike along mountain trails or beaches, take comfortable walking shoes.

Dining out is usually an informal affair, although some restaurants require a jacket and tie for men and dresses for women. Residents tend to dress conservatively when going to the theater or symphony, but it's not uncommon to see some patrons wearing jeans. In other words, almost anything is acceptable for most occasions.

If you're heading for Alaska, **take a collapsible umbrella or a rain slicker.** Passengers aboard Alaska-bound cruise ships should check with their travel agents about the dress code on board. Some vessels expect formal attire for dinner, while others do not. In all cases, you will need a waterproof coat and warm clothes if you plan to spend time on deck.

If you plan on hiking or camping during the summer, insect repellent is a must. Bring an extra pair of eyeglasses or contact lenses in your carry-on luggage, and if you have a health problem, **pack enough medication** to last the entire trip. It's important that you **don't put prescription drugs or valuables in luggage to be checked**: It might go astray.

LUGGAGE

In general you are entitled to check two bags on flights within the United States and on international flights leaving the United States. A third piece may be brought on board, but it must fit easily under the seat in front of you or in the overhead compartment.

Airline liability for baggage is limited to $1,250 per person on flights within the United States. On international flights it amounts to $9.07 per pound or $20 per kilogram for checked baggage (roughly $640 per 70-pound bag) and $400 per passenger for unchecked baggage. Insurance for losses exceeding these amounts can be bought from the airline at check-in for about $10 per $1,000 of coverage; this coverage excludes a rather extensive list of items, which is shown on your airline ticket.

Before departure, **itemize your bags' contents** and their worth, and label the bags with your name, address, and phone number. (If you use your home address, cover it so that potential thieves can't see it readily.) Inside each bag, **pack a copy of your itinerary.** At check-in, **make sure that each bag is correctly tagged** with the destination airport's three-letter code. If your bags arrive damaged or fail to arrive at all, file a written report with the airline before leaving the airport.

PARKS

NATIONAL PARKS

You may be able to **save money on park entrance fees** by getting a discount pass. The Golden Eagle Pass ($25) gets you and your companions free admission to all parks for one year. (Camping and parking are extra.) Both the Golden Age Passport, for U.S. citizens or permanent residents age 62 and older, and the Golden Access Passport, for travelers with disabilities, entitle holders to free entry to all national parks, plus 50% off fees for many facilities and services. Both passports are free; you must show proof of age and U.S. citizenship or permanent residency (such as a U.S. passport, driver's license, or birth certificate) or proof of disability. All three passes are available at all national park entrances. Golden Eagle and Golden Access passes are also available by mail.

➤ PASSES BY MAIL: **National Park Service** (✉ Department of the Interior, Washington, DC 20240).

PASSPORTS & VISAS

If you're traveling to British Columbia or the Yukon, **get a passport even if you don't need one to enter Canada**—it's always the best form of I.D. It's also a good idea to **make photocopies of the data page;** leave one copy with someone at home and keep another with you, separated from your passport. If you lose your passport, promptly call the nearest embassy or consulate and the local police; having a copy of the data page can speed replacement.

U.S. & CANADIAN CITIZENS

Canadian and U.S. citizens do not need a passport to travel between the United States and Canada.

U.K. CITIZENS

British citizens need a valid passport to enter the United States. If you are staying for fewer than 90 days on vacation, with a return or onward ticket, you probably will not need a visa. However, you will need to fill out the Visa Waiver Form, 1-94W, supplied by the airline. Citizens of the United Kingdom need only a valid passport to enter Canada for stays of up to 90 days.

➤ INFORMATION: **London Passport Office** (☎ 0990/21010) for fees and documentation requirements and to request an emergency passport. **U.S. Embassy Visa Information Line** (☎ 01891/200–290) for U.S. visa information; calls cost 49p per minute or 39p per minute cheap rate. **U.S. Embassy Visa Branch** (✉ 5 Upper Grosvenor St., London W1A 2JB) for U.S. visa information; send a self-addressed, stamped envelope. Write the **U.S. Consulate General** (✉ Queen's House, Queen St., Belfast BTI 6EO) if you live in Northern Ireland.

S

SENIOR-CITIZEN TRAVEL

To qualify for age-related discounts, **mention your senior-citizen status up front** when booking hotel reservations (not when checking out) and before you're seated in restaurants (not when paying the bill). Discounts may be limited to certain menus, days, or hours. When renting a car, **ask about promotional car-rental discounts,** which can be cheaper than senior-citizen rates.

➤ EDUCATIONAL TRAVEL PROGRAMS: **Elderhostel** (✉ 75 Federal St., 3rd floor, Boston, MA 02110, ☎ 617/426–8056).

SPORTS

BICYCLING

➤ ASSOCIATIONS: **Portland Wheelmen Touring Club** (☎ 503/257–7982). **Cascade Bicycle Club** (Seattle; ☎ 206/522–2453), and **Bicycling Association of British Columbia** (☎ 604/737–3034.

CLIMBING/MOUNTAINEERING

➤ INFORMATION: **Mazama Club** (Portland; ☎ 503/227–2345). **The Mountaineers** (Seattle; ☎ 800/553–

4453). **Alpine Club of Canada** (⊠ Box 2040, Canmore, Alberta T0L 0M0, ☎ 403/678–3200).

FISHING

➤ INFORMATION/LICENSES: **Oregon Department of Fish and Wildlife** (⊠ Box 59, Portland, OR 97207, ☎ 503/229–5403). **Washington Department of Fish and Wildlife** (⊠ 600 Capitol Way, Olympia, WA 98501–0091, ☎ 360/902–2200). For saltwater fishing in British Columbia: **Department of Fisheries and Oceans** (⊠ 555 W. Hastings St., Suite 400, Vancouver, BC V6B 5G3, ☎ 604/666–0384). For freshwater fishing in British Columbia: **Ministry of Environment, Fish and Wildlife Information** (⊠ Parliament Bldgs., Victoria, BC V8V 1X5, ☎ 604/387–9740). **Alaska Department of Fish and Game** (⊠ Box 25526, Juneau, AK 99802, ☎ 907/465–4180).

HIKING

➤ INFORMATION: **U.S. Forest Service and National Parks Outdoor Recreation Information Center** (⊠ 222 Yale Ave. N, Seattle, WA 98109, ☎ 206/470–4064).

HUNTING

➤ FACILITIES/LICENSES: **Oregon Department of Fish and Wildlife** (⊠ Box 59, Portland, OR 97207, ☎ 503/229–5403). **Washington State Department of Fish and Wildlife** (⊠ 600 Capitol Way N, Olympia, WA 98501, ☎ 360/902–2200). **British Columbia Ministry of Environment, Wildlife Branch** (⊠ 810 Blanshard St., Victoria, BC V8W 2H1, ☎ 604/387–9740). **Alaska Department of Fish and Game** (⊠ Box 25526, Juneau, AK 99802, ☎ 907/465–4190).

SKIING

➤ PASSES & INFORMATION: **Oregon Department of Transportation** (☎ 503/986–3006 for information and Sno-Park permits). **Office of Winter Recreation, Parks and Recreation Commission** (⊠ 7150 Cleanwater La., Olympia, WA 98504, ☎ 360/902–8500) for information and Sno-Park permits). **Canada West Ski Areas Association** (⊠ 3313 32nd Ave., Suite 103, Vernon, V1T 2M8, ☎ 250/542–9020). **Alaska Parks and Recreation Department** (☎ 907/586–5226 for information).

STUDENTS

➤ STUDENT IDs & SERVICES: **Council on International Educational Exchange** (⊠ CIEE, 205 E. 42nd St., 14th floor, New York, NY 10017, ☎ 212/822–2600 or 888/268–6245, FAX 212/822–2699), for mail orders only, in the United States. **Travel Cuts** (⊠ 187 College St., Toronto, Ontario M5T 1P7, ☎ 416/979–2406 or 800/667–2887) in Canada.

➤ HOSTELING: **Hostelling International–American Youth Hostels** (⊠ 733 15th St. NW, Suite 840, Washington, DC 20005, ☎ 202/783–6161, FAX 202/783–6171). **Hostelling International–Canada** (⊠ 400-205 Catherine St., Ottawa, Ontario K2P 1C3, ☎ 613/237–7884, FAX 613/237–7868). **Youth Hostel Association of England and Wales** (⊠ Trevelyan House, 8 St. Stephen's Hill, St. Albans, Hertfordshire AL1 2DY, ☎ 01727/855215 or 01727/845047, FAX 01727/844126). Membership in the United States, $25; in Canada, C$26.75; in the United Kingdom, £9.30.

T
TAXES

Oregon and Alaska have no sales tax, although most cities levy a tax on hotel rooms. Portland, for example, has a 9% room tax. The sales tax in Washington is between 7% and 8.2%, depending on the municipality. Seattle adds 5% to the rate for hotel rooms. Canada's 7% Goods & Services Tax (GST) is added to hotel bills but will be rebated to foreign visitors. The provincial and municipal tax in British Columbia ranges from 8% to 10%

GST

Canada's Goods and Services Tax (GST) is 7%, applicable on virtually every purchase except basic groceries and a few other items. Visitors to Canada may claim a full rebate of the GST on any goods taken out of the country as well as on short-term accommodations. Rebates can be claimed either immediately on departure from Canada at participating duty-free shops or by mail. Rebate forms can be obtained at most stores and hotels in Canada or by writing to Revenue Canada (⊠ Visitor's Rebate Program, Ottawa, Ontario K1A 1J5, ☎ 902/432–5608; 800/668–4748 in

Canada). Claims must be for a minimum of $7 worth of tax and can be submitted up to a year from the date of purchase. Purchases made during multiple visits to Canada can be grouped together for rebate purposes.

TELEPHONES

In 1996 and 1997 several new telephone area codes were added in the Pacific Northwest. The area code for Portland and surrounding areas is 503; 541 is used in the rest of Oregon. The metropolitan Seattle area code is 206; 253, 425, and 360 are used in the rest of western Washington, and 509 is used in eastern Washington. Area codes for British Columbia are 604 in the Vancouver area and 250 elsewhere in the province. Alaska uses 907, except for the town of Hyder in Southeast Alaska, which uses the 604 area code.

Pay telephones cost 25¢ for local calls. Charge phones are also found in many locations. These phones can be used to charge a call to a telephone-company credit card, your home phone, or the party you are calling: You do not need to deposit 25¢. For directory assistance, dial 1, the area code, and 555–1212. For local directory assistance, dial 1 followed by 555–1212. You can dial most international calls directly. Dial 0 to reach an operator.

Many hotels place a surcharge on local calls made from your room and include a service charge on long-distance calls. It may be cheaper for you to make your calls from a pay phone in the hotel lobby rather than from your room.

CALLING HOME

AT&T, MCI, and Sprint long-distance services make calling home relatively convenient and let you avoid hotel surcharges.

➤ ACCESS CODES: AT&T (☎ 800/225–5288 in the U.S. and Canada). MCI (☎ 10222, U.S. and Canada); Sprint (☎ 800/877–8000 in the U.S. and Canada).

TIPPING

Tips and service charges are usually not automatically added to a bill in the United States or Canada. If service is satisfactory, customers generally give waiters, waitresses, taxi drivers, barbers, hairdressers, and so forth a tip of 15%–20% of the total bill. Bellhops, doormen, and porters at airports and railway stations are generally tipped $1 for each item of luggage.

TOUR OPERATORS

Operators that handle several hundred thousand travelers per year can use their purchasing power to give you a good price. Their high volume may also indicate financial stability. But some small companies provide more personalized service; because they tend to specialize, they may also be more knowledgeable about a given area.

A GOOD DEAL?

The more your package or tour includes, the better you can predict the ultimate cost of your vacation. Make sure you know exactly what is covered, and **beware of hidden costs.** Are taxes, tips, and service charges included? Transfers and baggage handling? Entertainment and excursions? These can add up.

If the package or tour you are considering is priced lower than in your wildest dreams, **be skeptical.** Also, **make sure your travel agent knows the accommodations** and other services. Ask about the hotel's location, room size, beds, and whether it has a pool, room service, or programs for children, if you care about these. Has your agent been there in person or sent others you can contact?

BUYER BEWARE

Each year consumers are stranded or lose their money when tour operators—even very large ones with excellent reputations—go out of business. So **check out the operator.** Find out how long the company has been in business, and ask several agents about its reputation. **Don't book unless the firm has a consumer-protection program.**

Members of the National Tour Association and United States Tour Operators Association are required to set aside funds to cover your payments and travel arrangements in case the company defaults. Nonmembers may carry insurance instead. Look for the details, and for the name of an underwriter with a solid reputation, in the operator's brochure. When it comes

THE GOLD GUIDE / SMART TRAVEL TIPS

SMART TRAVEL TIPS / THE GOLD GUIDE

to tour operators, **don't trust escrow accounts.** Although the Department of Transportation watches over charter-flight operators, no regulatory body prevents tour operators from raiding the till. You may want to protect yourself by buying travel insurance that includes a tour-operator default provision. For more information, *see* Consumer Protection, *above.*

It's also a good idea to choose a company that participates in the American Society of Travel Agents' Tour Operator Program (TOP). This gives you a forum if there are any disputes between you and your tour operator; ASTA will act as mediator.

➤ TOUR-OPERATOR RECOMMENDA-TIONS: **American Society of Travel Agents** (☞ Travel Agencies, *below*). **National Tour Association** (✉ NTA, 546 E. Main St., Lexington, KY 40508, ☎ 606/226–4444 or 800/755–8687). **United States Tour Operators Association** (✉ USTOA, 342 Madison Ave., Suite 1522, New York, NY 10173, ☎ 212/599–6599, FAX 212/599–6744).

USING AN AGENT

Travel agents are excellent resources. But it's a good idea to **collect brochures from several agencies,** because some agents' suggestions may be influenced by relationships with tour and package firms that reward them for volume sales. If you have a special interest, **find an agent with expertise in that area;** ASTA (☞ Travel Agencies, *below*) has a database of specialists worldwide. Do some homework on your own, too: Local tourism boards can provide information about lesser-known and small-niche operators, some of which may sell only direct.

SINGLE TRAVELERS

Prices for packages and tours are usually quoted per person, based on two sharing a room. If traveling solo, you may be required to pay the full double-occupancy rate. Some operators eliminate this surcharge if you agree to be matched with a roommate of the same sex, even if one is not found by departure time.

TRAIN TRAVEL

Amtrak, the U.S. passenger rail system, has daily service to the Pacific Northwest from the Midwest and California. The *Empire Builder* takes a northern route from Chicago to Seattle. The *Coast Starlight* begins in Los Angeles, makes stops throughout western Oregon and Washington, and terminates in Seattle.

Canada's passenger service, **VIA Rail Canada,** operates transcontinental routes on the *Canadian* three times weekly between eastern Canada and Vancouver. A second train, the *Skeena,* runs three times weekly between Jasper, Alberta, to the British Columbia port city of Prince Rupert.

WITHIN THE PACIFIC NORTHWEST

Amtrak's *Mt. Baker International* travels between Seattle and Vancouver. The **Great Canadian Railtour Co., Ltd.,** operates the *Rocky Mountaineer,* a two-day rail cruise between Vancouver and the Canadian Rockies that runs from May to October. There are two routes—one to Banff/Calgary and the other to Jasper—through landscapes considered to be the most spectacular in the world. An overnight hotel stop is made in Kamloops.

On Vancouver Island, **VIA Rail** runs the *E&N Railway* daily from Victoria north to Courtenay. **B.C. Rail** operates daily service from its North Vancouver terminal to the town of Prince George. At Prince George, it is possible to connect with VIA Rail's *Skeena* service east to Jasper and Alberta or west to Prince Rupert.

The Seattle-based **American Orient Express Railway Company** operates several trips in the Northwest aboard its luxury cars, including one that travels from Portland through Washington and into Idaho before terminating at Glacier Mountain·National Park.

➤ RAILWAY COMPANIES: **American Orient Express Railway Company** (☎ 206/441–2725). **Amtrak** (☎ 800/872–7245). **B.C. Rail** (☎ 604/631–3500 or 800/663–8238). **Great Canadian Railtour Co., Ltd.** (☎ 800/665–7245). **VIA Rail Canada** (☎ 604/383–4324 or 800/561–3949).

RAIL PASSES

VIA Rail Canada (☞ *above*) offers a Canrailpass that is good for 30 days.

System-wide passes cost $268 (good from mid-January to mid-May and mid-October to mid-December) and $420 (good from mid-May to mid-October). Youth passes (age 24 and under) are $377 in peak season and $258 during the off-season. Prices are quoted in U.S. dollars. Tickets can be purchased in the United States or the United Kingdom from a travel agent, from **Long Haul Leisurail** (✉ Box 113, Peterborough PE1 1LE, ☎ 0733/51780), or upon arrival in Canada. This offer does not apply to Canadian citizens.

TRAVEL AGENCIES

A good travel agent puts your needs first. Look for an agency that has been in business at least five years, emphasizes customer service, and has someone on staff who specializes in your destination. In addition, **make sure the agency belongs to the American Society of Travel Agents** (ASTA). If your travel agency is also acting as your tour operator, *see* Buyer Beware in Tour Operators, *above.*

➤ LOCAL AGENT REFERRALS: **American Society of Travel Agents (ASTA,** ☎ 800/965–2782 24-hr hot line, FAX 703/684–8319). **Alliance of Canadian Travel Associations** (✉ Suite 201, 1729 Bank St., Ottawa, Ontario K1V 7Z5, ☎ 613/521–0474, FAX 613/521–0805). **Association of British Travel Agents** (✉ 55–57 Newman St., London W1P 4AH, ☎ 0171/637–2444, FAX 0171/637–0713).

U

U.S. GOVERNMENT

The U.S. government can be an excellent source of inexpensive travel information. When planning your trip, **find out what government materials are available.**

➤ PAMPHLETS: **Consumer Information Center** (✉ Consumer Information Catalogue, Pueblo, CO 81009, ☎ 719/948–3334) for a free catalog that includes travel titles.

V

VISITOR INFORMATION

➤ OREGON: **Portland/Oregon Visitors Association** (✉ 2 World Trade Center, 26 S.W. Salmon St., 97204, ☎ 503/222–2223 or 800/345–3214).

➤ WASHINGTON: **Visitors Information Center** (✉ Washington State Convention Center, 800 Convention Pl., Seattle, WA 98104, ☎ 206/461–5840). **Washington State Tourism** (✉ 101 General Administration Bldg., Olympia 98504, ☎ 800/544–1800).

➤ BRITISH COLUMBIA: **Tourism British Columbia** (✉ Parliament Building, Victoria, BC V8V 1X4, ☎ 800/663–6000). **Vancouver Tourist Info Centre** (✉ 200 Broward St., Vancouver, BC Z6C 3L6, ☎ 604/683–2000).

➤ ALASKA: **Alaska Division of Tourism** (✉ Box 110801, Juneau 99811-0801, ☎ 907/465–2010 or 800/762–5275).

W

WHEN TO GO

The Pacific Northwest's mild climate is best from June through September. Hotels in the major tourist destinations are often filled in July and August, so it's important to book reservations in advance. Summer temperatures generally range in the 70s, and rainfall is usually minimal. Nights, however, can be cool.

Spring and fall are also excellent times to visit. The weather usually remains quite good, and the prices for accommodations, transportation, and tours can be lower (and the crowds much smaller) in the most popular destinations. In winter, the coastal rain turns to snow in the nearby mountains, making the region a skier's dream.

CLIMATE

Average daytime summer highs are in the 70s; winter temperatures are generally in the 40s. Snow is uncommon in the lowland areas. The Pacific Northwest's reputation for rain is somewhat misleading. The amount of rainfall in the region varies greatly. In the coastal mountains, for example, 160 inches of rain falls annually, creating temperate rain forests. In eastern Oregon, Washington, and British Columbia, near-desert conditions prevail, with rainfall as low as 6 inches per year.

Seattle has an average of only 36 inches of rainfall a year—less than New York, Chicago, or Miami. The wetness, however, is concentrated during the winter months, when cloudy skies and drizzly weather persist.

THE GOLD GUIDE / SMART TRAVEL TIPS

➤ FORECASTS: **Weather Channel Connection** (☎ 900/932–8437), 95¢ per minute from a Touch-Tone phone.

The following are average daily maximum and minimum temperatures for major cities in the Pacific Northwest region.

Climate in the Pacific Northwest

PORTLAND

Jan.	44F	7C	May	67F	19C	Sept.	74F	23C
	33	1		46	8		51	10
Feb.	50F	10C	June	72F	22C	Oct.	63F	17C
	36	2		52	11		45	7
Mar.	54F	12C	July	79F	26C	Nov.	52F	11C
	37	3		55	13		39	4
Apr.	60F	15C	Aug.	78F	25C	Dec.	46F	8C
	41	5		55	13		35	2

SEATTLE

Jan.	45F	7C	May	66F	19C	Sept.	69F	20C
	35	2		47	8		52	11
Feb.	50F	10C	June	70F	21C	Oct.	62F	16C
	37	3		52	11		47	8
Mar.	53F	12C	July	76F	24C	Nov.	51F	10C
	38	3		56	13		40	4
Apr.	59F	13C	Aug.	75F	24C	Dec.	47F	8C
	42	5		55	13		37	3

VANCOUVER

Jan.	41F	5C	May	63F	17C	Sept.	64F	18C
	32	0		46	8		50	10
Feb.	46F	8C	June	66F	19C	Oct.	57F	14C
	34	1		52	11		43	6
Mar.	48F	9C	July	72F	22C	Nov.	48F	9C
	36	2		55	13		37	3
Apr.	55F	13C	Aug.	72F	22C	Dec.	45F	7C
	41	5		55	13		34	1

JUNEAU

Jan.	29F	−2C	May	55F	13C	Sept.	56F	13C
	18	−8		38	3		42	6
Feb.	34F	1C	June	62F	16C	Oct.	47F	8C
	22	−6		44	7		36	2
Mar.	38F	3C	July	64F	18C	Nov.	37F	3C
	26	−4		48	9		28	−2
Apr.	47F	8C	Aug.	62F	17C	Dec.	32F	0C
	31	−1		46	8		23	−5

1 Destination: Pacific Northwest

THE LAY OF THE LAND

IT WAS GETTING DARK high in the Oregon Cascades as we rowed ashore at the small, isolated lake. The peaks, just wrapped in an autumn snow, were blurred by the dusk. With less than an hour of light left, we decided one of us should get back to camp quickly, unencumbered, while the other deflated the raft and carried it the 4 miles back to camp, with little chance of making it out before pitch blackness fell over the dense forest.

Maybe it was because my brother is older and has bad knees, or perhaps it was just because I was soaking wet and needed to change anyway. But I elected to be the one who walked in the dark.

Soon I was alone with the lake as a wispy fog slipped in from the upper basin; the tall firs creaked in the wind and to the east, barely visible now, three rugged peaks shrugged in the distance. I knew that my brother, rapidly moving away, was the only other human near me. Behind me were hundreds of tiny lakes like this one, all empty and quiet in their own seldom-explored basins.

I was very alone, feeling at once joyous and frightened, exalted and exhausted, both overwhelmed and completely free. I had not just *connected* with nature in some fleeting, superficial way; I had melded with it. Things of the world below the meadows, canyons, and forests simply did not exist. There were only those moments of scary wonder as I got into some dry clothes and prepared to walk through the woods in the dark.

The sensation of being alone with nature, of being in the very cup of her hands, is something that is familiar to those who live in the Pacific Northwest. There are certainly more remote areas, but here man seems to have found his niche in the ecosystem and, more or less, stays there as pleased with his failures to conquer nature as with his occasional, temporary successes.

To understand the people of the Pacific Northwest—and there are roughly 12.5 million of us in an area about the size of Western Europe—one has to understand the land and the climate and how the two combine to cast their spell. For even in the cities of the Pacific Northwest, nature is never far away. In Seattle, Mount Rainier and the Olympic Mountains enchant commuters stuck in traffic; in Vancouver, British Columbia, the Coast Range juts out over downtown, keeping the metropolis in line; and in Portland, 5,000 acres of forestland in the hills north of the city center harbor deer, elk, and the odd bear and cougar. It's not a zoo, it's just there, a piece of almost primeval forest. No matter how many planes Seattle's Boeing Company churns out, or how many chips come out of Oregon's high-tech Silicon Forest, or how many shares of stock change hands in the volatile Vancouver Stock Exchange, the relationship with nature and the wilds is not altered. There is always this mixture of respect and love, fear and admiration, topped off with simple awe.

These feelings come naturally when you survey the landscape, but still there are the simultaneous sensations of solitude and inclusion. To understand, look at the far corners of this land: southern Alaska and southeastern Oregon.

SWATHED IN SITKA SPRUCE, the islands scattered below the Alaskan mountains are like small individual worlds. Roads and people are few. The intrepid can kayak through the inlets and fjords for days on end, catching salmon or watching the glaciers peel majestically off into the sea, sheet by sheet. Roughly in the middle of this region is Juneau, the only state capital that is inaccessible by road. Here it is common for legislative aides to live in makeshift camps in the hills above town and ski to the state's modest capitol building. Behind the coast ranges are deep, remote river canyons and lakes that stretch all the way east to where the mighty Rockies dribble off into a few bumps on the tundra. Moving south along Coastal British Columbia, the terrain is no less steep, but the glaciers shrink back into the hanging valleys, leaving only a few waterfalls. Other than fishing vessels and the occasional cruise ship, this is lonely country, beautiful, but often pelted with wild rain storms and blizzards that blast straight across the north Pacific.

Likewise, southeastern Oregon is solitary country. It is a land of extremes, a high desert where it is not at all uncommon, especially in the spring or fall, to find the highest and lowest temperature reading in the lower 48 states in the same county. A 100-mile drive across the desert and scrubland is not likely to turn up another soul. What people there are here—many of them descendants of Basque settlers a century ago—tend to their stock on the arid plains. The land is dominated by Steens Mountain, a 60-mile-long slab of desert floor that over the millennia gradually tilted upward. From the west, the gain in elevation is barely noticeable at first, just a steppe rolling into the distance. But after 30 miles of bad road, the mountain simply breaks off into space, the Alvord Desert a gasping 5,000 feet below. And beyond, the gray horizon fades into Nevada and Idaho.

WHETHER IT IS the cathedral-like island forests of southern Alaska or the sagebrush-covered frontier of southeastern Oregon, the awe is there—subtle yet omnipresent. In many ways, the land here shapes us, mellowing and hypnotizing us until other ways of life seem improbably complicated. I don't know how many people I've known come back from visiting New York or San Francisco or some other famously bustling place and say something like along the lines of, "It was very exciting, but I don't know why anyone would go to the trouble of living there."

Go to the trouble . . . A key phrase. In the Pacific Northwest, going to the trouble is more likely to be the consequence of some recreational choice. You go to the trouble of rafting a river just for the hell of it; you go to the trouble of hiking to the top of a butte you've never climbed before; or you go to the trouble of taking a road in the baking deserts of eastern Oregon and

Washington just to see the mirages disappear as you approach them.

Okay, so Pacific Northwesterners may seem a bit flaky—carefree, perhaps—but some say this contagious attitude simply comes with the land. The Native Americans of the Pacific Northwest had it pretty easy compared with their brethren on the Great Plains. Whereas a family of Sioux may have needed to scour 100 square miles of land to get enough food to live on, West Coast Indians only needed to dip into the river for fish or take a few steps out of the village for game. Sure, the weather was damp, but wood for shelter and warmth was plentiful and the time saved gathering food went toward monumental projects of art such as the totems of Coastal British Columbia.

In the Pacific Northwest, rich is defined as living a clean life; nature deals the bonuses. What people here compromise in salaries, they are compensated for by having the opportunity to hike, fish, hunt, or just wake up every morning with a view of a forest. Some might call this simple living; others just call it wacky. Some examples: Portland twice elected as mayor a local tavern owner who bikes around the city in lederhosen and calls out "Whoop, whoop" at the drop of a photo opportunity. And a few years ago, there was a strong effort (serious does not seem to be the right word) to make the rock-and-roll classic "Louie, Louie" the state song of Washington.

Is there some sort of pattern here? Perhaps all the rain twists great and creative minds? When the explorers Lewis and Clark arrived almost 200 years ago, the rain almost drove them crazy, and that was after only one winter! Imagine a lifetime of gray winters; you look out of your window in October at a line of dark clouds rolling in from the west and know there will be only a handful of clear days (probably below freezing) until mid-March. Northwest author Ken Kesey has blamed everything from impotence to union problems on this drizzly season. True, residents of the Pacific Northwest drink more and are more likely to commit suicide than others in the country, but it may be that the weather helps us keep a sense of the absurd and the macabre; for example, in Portland's Oregon Convention Center the men's rooms have etchings of Oregon waterfalls perched above the urinals.

So we're a little eccentric. But remember, when an impulse sends you ripping down an untracked ski run or landing a thrashing steelhead in a river at flood stage, the humdrum details of daily life become pretty ridiculous, like some sort of cosmic joke, and you fade back to a private place, to *your* lake beneath the peaks. Just before dark.

– By Tom Gaunt

NEW AND NOTEWORTHY

"Urban density" is the current buzz phrase in fast-growing Portland. To prevent suburban sprawl and protect outlying farmland and green spaces, the city is encouraging new housing and development in urban areas. The result is a major building boom. Traffic, previously not a problem in Portland, has increased significantly. A western extension of the city's light-rail system, scheduled to open in fall 1998, will reach as far as Hillsboro and include a stop at the Metro Washington Park Zoo, whose transit station, 260 feet below ground, will be the deepest in the nation.

Environmental issues are part of the everyday life of the residents of Oregon, and the state is currently grappling with a big one: how to keep wild salmon from becoming extinct. Clear-cutting by timber companies, pollution from grazing cattle, and the damming of major waterways have all led to deterioration of habitats. The situation is so serious, particularly along the Columbia and Snake rivers, that previously unmentionable plans—such as dismantling some of the dams to create free-flowing areas—are being considered.

Nearly every top-of-the-line arts organization and sports franchise in Seattle has undergone or is planning a major remodeling or change of venue. The Paramount Theatre recently completed a stunning renovation, the Seattle Repertory Theatre and A Contemporary Theatre celebrated the opening of new spaces, and the Seattle Symphony is due for a 1998 move into a new $99 million downtown facility. The recently rebuilt Key Arena (formerly the Coliseum) at last provides a worthy home for perennial National Basketball Association contenders the Seattle Supersonics, and the Seattle Mariners baseball team and the Seattle Seahawks football team will both have new facilities within the next few years.

An increase in direct flights—a result of the Open Skies agreement signed by the United States and Canada—has further enhanced the status of Vancouver as a Pacific Rim player, as did Amtrak's restoration of daily train service between the city and Seattle. A ride on the *Mt. Baker International* train, which follows the coast most of the way, is a truly glorious way to take in the region's scenery.

Alaska is celebrating the centennial of the great rush to the Klondike that lasted from 1897 to 1898. Across the state, festivals, races, and other events will have special gold-rush themes this year. Native groups are becoming increasingly active in hosting visitors, and nowhere is this trend more obvious than in Juneau and Ketchikan. Juneau's Mount Roberts Tram complex expanded in 1997—it now includes an observatory, a theater, a cultural center, shops, and a restaurant.

WHAT'S WHERE

Oregon

Although the climate and landscape of Oregon vary dramatically from place to place, much of the state enjoys a constant level of natural splendor. The Pacific coast is a wild and rocky 300-mi stretch dotted with small towns. In the northeast are the Columbia River Gorge and Mount Hood, dramatic examples of the power of earth and water. On the gentler side, the Willamette Valley is a lush wine-producing region and home to Eugene and other important cities. Oregon's largest city, Portland, in the northwest part of the state, is among the nation's most livable—not surprising given its unspoiled setting and host of urban amenities.

Washington

From the islands that dot Puget Sound to the peak of Mount Rainier to the Yakima Valley's vineyards, Washington presents hundreds of opportunities to appreciate the great outdoors. Watch whales from coastal lighthouses, dine on fresh seafood in waterside towns, tramp through dripping rain forests, hike high mountains— or head straight to Seattle, the Pacific Northwest's hippest city, where the green hills and bay views are best appreciated from a coffee bar, and the music and art scenes change as frequently as the tides.

British Columbia

Canada's westernmost province contains Pacific beaches, forested islands, year-round skiing, world-class fishing—a wealth of outdoor action and beauty. Its towns and cities, from Anglophile Victoria to the placid Gulf Islands, reflect the diversity of its inhabitants. Cosmopolitan Vancouver enjoys a spectacular setting. Tall fir trees stand practically downtown, rock spires tower close by, the ocean is at your doorstep, and residents who have come from every corner of the earth create a young and vibrant atmosphere.

Southeast Alaska

The glacier-filled fjords of the Inside Passage are Southeast Alaska's most famous attraction; what a century ago was the route to the Klondike goldfields is today the centerpiece of many Alaskan cruises. Juneau, the state's capital, is also in the Southeast, as are a number of interesting small towns. Petersburg and Ketchikan (which is also known for its totem-pole carving) are traditional fishing villages; an onion-dome cathedral accents Sitka, the capital of Russian America; and each fall up to 4,000 eagles gather outside Haines.

PLEASURES AND PASTIMES

Beaches

The coasts of Oregon, Washington, and British Columbia have long, sandy beaches that run for miles at a stretch. But the waters are generally too cold or treacherous for swimming. Even in summertime, beachgoers must be prepared to dress warmly. The most accessible ocean beaches in the Pacific Northwest are in Oregon. Those in Washington and western Vancouver Island are more remote; even in summer, the beaches are never crowded. The gravel

shores of Washington's Puget Sound and British Columbia's Inside Passage attract few swimmers or sunbathers but are popular for beachcombing and viewing marine life.

Canoeing and Rafting

The area's swift rivers provide challenges to canoeists and kayakers. Many of these rivers should be attempted only by experienced boaters. June through September are prime months for white-water rafting.

Charters

Cruising and deep-sea-fishing charters are available from many ports throughout the Pacific Northwest. Campbell River on British Columbia's Vancouver Island, Neah Bay and Port Angeles on Washington's Olympic Peninsula, Westport on the Long Beach Peninsula in southern Washington, and Depoe Bay in Oregon are leading ports.

Climbing and Mountaineering

The mountains of the Pacific Northwest have given many an adventurer quite a challenge. It is no coincidence that many members of the U.S. expedition teams to Mount Everest come from this region.

Dining

Many restaurants in the Northwest serve local specialties—salmon, crab, oysters, and other seafood delicacies—in dishes that, reflecting the region's ties to Asia and the Pacific Islands, often incorporate the ingredients and techniques of Japanese, Korean, Thai, and other cuisines. Unless otherwise noted, casual but neat dress is appropriate at all of the restaurants reviewed.

Fishing

The coastal regions and inland lakes and rivers of the Pacific Northwest are known for excellent fishing. Lodges, many of which are accessible only by seaplane, cater to anglers in search of the ultimate fishing experience. Visiting sportsmen must possess a nonresident license for the state or province in which they plan to fish. Licenses are easily obtainable at sporting-goods stores, bait shops, and other outlets in fishing areas.

Golf

The Northwest has many excellent golf courses, but not all of them are open to the public. Consequently, visitors may find it difficult to arrange a tee time at a popular course. If you are a member of a golf club at home, check to see if your club has a reciprocal playing arrangement with private clubs in the areas that you will be visiting.

Sailboarding

The Columbia River, particularly at Hood River, Oregon, is one of the world's premier locations for windsurfing. Puget Sound and some of the inland lakes in Washington are other venues for the sport. Sailboard rentals and lessons are available from local specialty shops. In British Columbia, the town of Squamish is quickly becoming another major windsurfing destination.

Skiing

Moist air off the Pacific Ocean dumps snow on the coastal mountains, providing excellent skiing from November through the end of March and sometimes into April. Resort and lift-ticket prices tend to be less expensive here than at the internationally known ski destinations, but the slopes, especially on weekends, can be crowded. Winter driving in these high elevations usually requires a four-wheel-drive vehicle or tire chains.

Wildlife Viewing

Sea lions, seals, dolphins, and whales are a few of the marine mammals that can be observed in bays, near headlands, and along the coast. In the spring and summer, thousands of gray whales pass by the British Columbia, Washington, and Oregon coasts on their seasonal migration from Alaska to Baja. One of the easiest and most exciting ways to see them is by taking a whale-watching boat excursion. In the forests and along coastal rivers and estuaries deer, bald eagles, herons, and egrets are commonly seen. The dedicated birders who annually trek to the Northwest find that their efforts are amply rewarded.

FODOR'S CHOICE

Portland

Sights and Attractions

★ **International Rose Test Garden.** Three breathtaking terraced gardens on 4 acres high above the city are planted with 10,000 rose bushes in more than 400 varieties.

★ **Japanese Garden.** This serene oasis is considered the most authentic Japanese garden outside Japan.

★ **Nob Hill/Northwest 23rd Avenue.** The fine old Victorian homes of the Nob Hill neighborhood surround Portland's trendiest shopping street, chockablock with boutiques, restaurants, and coffee bars.

★ **Oregon Museum of Science and Industry.** A great place for children, the museum houses the Northwest's largest astronomy center (with an Omnimax theater and a 200-seat planetarium), a hands-on computer facility, a space wing with a mission-control center, and even its own submarine, the USS *Blueback.*

★ **Pioneer Courthouse Square.** Downtown Portland's heart and soul, a broad brick plaza with a purple tile fountain and whimsical weather vane, is surrounded by department stores and handsome office towers.

★ **Pittock Mansion.** The opulent French Renaissance–style mansion, completed in 1914, is perched above the city on landscaped grounds with vistas of the city and the Cascade Range.

★ **Portland Saturday Market.** Vendors at North America's largest open-air handicraft market sell crystals, beaded hats, stained glass, jewelry, flags, rubber stamps, decorative boots, and other handmade items. Street entertainers and food booths enhance the festive atmosphere.

Restaurants

★ **Couvron.** Portland's finest restaurant for contemporary French cuisine has a casual but elegant interior and a menu high on charm and creativity. *$$$–$$$$*

★ **Zefiro.** The chef at this attractive restaurant combines Southeast Asian and Mediterranean ingredients and cooking techniques. *$$$–$$$$*

★ **The Heathman.** The French-trained chef of this sophisticated hotel dining room changes his menu with the season to make use of fresh Northwest fish, game, wild mushrooms, and produce. *$$$*

★ **Assaggio.** Authentic Italian cuisine is cooked to perfection at this small Sellwood trattoria painted in burnt-sienna colors and decorated in classical motifs. *$–$$*

★ **Misohapi.** Tongue-in-chic decor and delicious Vietnamese and Thai dishes—at amazingly low prices—make this small restaurant one of the brightest spots on Northwest 23rd Avenue. $

Hotels and Inns

⭐ **Governor Hotel.** Small and quiet, the Governor is the most atmospherically "Northwestern" of Portland's many renovated luxury accommodations, more like an Arts and Crafts–style club than a bustling downtown hotel. $$$$

⭐ **Heathman Hotel.** Superior service, an award-winning restaurant, and elegant public areas have earned this centrally located hotel a reputation for quality. $$$$

⭐ **Doubletree Hotel/Lloyd Center.** This well-appointed business-oriented hotel is within walking distance of the Lloyd Center shopping mall, the MAX light-rail system, and the Oregon Convention Center. $$$

⭐ **MacMaster House.** Less than 10 minutes by foot from fashionable Northwest 23rd Avenue, this 17-room Colonial Revival mansion built in 1886 is a comfortable, funky, and fascinating bed-and-breakfast inn. $$

⭐ **Ramada Inn Airport.** Business travelers speak highly of this facility with well-equipped suites and a business center with computers, fax machines, and individual workstations. $$

Oregon

Sights and Attractions

⭐ **Cape Perpetua.** The highest lookout point on the Oregon coast is part of a 2,700-acre scenic area with a visitor center and several hiking trails, including one that winds through a rain forest to an enormous 500-year-old Sitka spruce.

⭐ **Columbia River Gorge.** From Crown Point, a 730-foot-high bluff, there's an unparalleled 30-mile view down the gorge created by America's second-largest river.

⭐ **Columbia River Maritime Museum, Astoria.** The observation tower of a World War II submarine and the personal belongings of the passengers of area shipwrecks are among the exhibits here.

⭐ **Crater Lake National Park.** Rain and snowmelt have filled the caldera left by the eruption of Mount Mazama, creating a sapphire-blue lake—at a depth of 1,900 feet, the nation's deepest—so clear that sunlight penetrates 400 feet.

⭐ **Fort Clatsop National Memorial, Astoria.** Lewis and Clark's humble winter fort, a log stockade built in 1805 at the conclusion of their trailblazing journey across North America, has been faithfully reconstructed on what is believed to be its original site.

⭐ **John Day Fossil Beds National Monument.** Three high-desert sites in central Oregon's scenic John Day Valley contain the richest collection of prehistoric plant and animal fossils in the world.

⭐ **Mount Hood.** The majestic Cascade Range peak is less than an hour's drive from Portland.

⭐ **Oregon Coast Aquarium, Newport.** The home of Keiko, the orca who starred in *Free Willy,* is part of a 4½-acre complex with re-creations of Pacific marine habitats.

⭐ **Oregon Shakespeare Festival, Ashland.** More than 100,000 theater lovers come to the Rogue Valley every year to see some of the finest Shakespearean productions this side of Stratford-upon-Avon—plus works by Ibsen, Williams, and other playwrights.

⭐ **Sea Lion Caves, Florence.** An elevator at Oregon's best-known coastal attraction takes visitors down an impressive sea cave, a year-round home for wild Stellar sea lions.

Restaurants

⭐ **Chateaulin, Ashland.** An ivy-covered storefront houses this romantic restaurant that dispenses French food, local wines, and gracious service with equal facility. $$$

⭐ **Chez Jeannette, Gleneden Beach.** Fresh seafood and local produce receive a sophisticated Parisian spin at this whitewashed cottage-restaurant near Lincoln City. $$$

⭐ **Nick's Italian Café, McMinnville.** Ask any wine maker in the valley to name his or her favorite wine-country restaurant, and chances are that Nick's will head the list. $$$

⭐ **The Bistro, Cannon Beach.** A profusion of flowers and candlelight makes this 12-table restaurant a most romantic dining establishment. $$

⭐ **Blue Heron Bistro, Coos Bay.** Subtle preparations of local seafood and homemade pasta with an international flair are the highlights of the far-ranging menu at this busy bistro. *$$*

⭐ **La Serre, Yachats.** The chef at what many consider to be the best restaurant on the Oregon coast has a deft touch with seafood, which is always impeccably fresh and never deep fried. *$$*

Hotels and Inns

⭐ **Tu Tu Tun Lodge, near Gold Beach.** Famous for its food, fishing, and hospitality, this rustically elegant fishing resort sits on the fabled Rogue River. *$$$$*

⭐ **Timberline Lodge, Mount Hood.** A National Historic Landmark that has withstood howling winter storms for more than six decades, the lodge warms its guests with hospitality, hearty food, and rustic rooms. *$$$*

⭐ **Under the Greenwood Tree, Medford-Ashland.** Luxurious rooms, stunning 10-acre gardens, and breakfasts cooked by the owner, a Cordon Bleu–trained chef, make a visit here memorable. *$$$*

⭐ **Excelsior Inn, Eugene.** The rooms in this sophisticated European-style hotel—a former frat house—are furnished in a refreshingly understated manner. *$$–$$$*

⭐ **Flying M Ranch, Yamhill.** "Daniel Boone–eclectic" might be the best description of the decor at this great log lodge, the centerpiece of a 625-acre complex of cabins and riverside hotel units. *$$–$$$*

⭐ **Mt. Ashland Inn, Ashland.** Cedar logged on the property was used to build this lodge. The views of Mount Shasta are as magnificent as the forested setting. *$$–$$$*

⭐ **The Steamboat Inn, Steamboat.** A veritable Who's Who of the world's top fly fishermen have visited Oregon's most famous fishing lodge; others come simply to relax in the reading nooks or on the broad decks of the riverside cabins. *$$–$$$*

⭐ **Chetco River Inn, near Brookings.** Acres of forest surround this splendidly remote inn where guests hike, hunt wild mushrooms, or relax in front of the fireplace. *$$*

⭐ **Mattey House Bed & Breakfast, Lafayette.** Antiques and hand-screened wallpapers decorate this 100-year-old Victorian home that's now a favorite wine-country B&B. *$$*

⭐ **Stang Manor Bed & Breakfast, La Grande.** A timber baron built this stylish Georgian Revival mansion in eastern Oregon. *$$*

⭐ **The Sylvia Beach Hotel, Newport.** This 1912 beachfront hotel has a literary theme—each of the antiques-filled rooms is named for a famous writer, and no two are decorated alike. *$$*

Seattle

Sights and Attractions

⭐ **Ballard Locks.** Follow the fascinating progress of fishing boats and pleasure craft through the locks, part of the Lake Washington Ship Canal, then watch as salmon and trout make the same journey via a ladder that allows migrating fish to swim upstream on a gradual incline.

⭐ **Floatplane flight from Lake Union to Friday Harbor.** Hop on the plane that lands on the sea for unforgettable views of Puget Sound and the San Juan Islands.

⭐ **Museum of Flight.** Exhibits on the history of human flight fill the Red Barn, Boeing's original airplane factory, and the Great Gallery contains more than 20 classic airplanes, dating from the Wright brothers to the jet era.

⭐ **Pike Place Market.** It's fun here anytime, but there's no place in the world quite like Pike Place Market in full swing on a Saturday afternoon. "If we get separated, I'll meet you by the pig in an hour." But watch for low-flying fish!

⭐ **Space Needle.** There's nothing like the view of the city at night from the observation deck of this Seattle landmark.

⭐ **Washington Park Arboretum.** The Arboretum is a true Seattle gem, a 200-acre mixed-use park that's perfect for a picnic, a stroll through the Greenhouse, or a quiet afternoon in the immaculate Japanese Garden.

⭐ **Woodland Park Zoo.** Many of the more than 300 species of animals in this award-winning 92-acre botanical garden roam free in climate-specific habitats.

Restaurants

⭐ **Fullers.** Consistently ranked at or near the top of Seattle's restaurants in local and national publications, Fullers delivers a rare commodity: a dining experience of exceptional poise and restraint, born out of unconventional, even visionary, risk-taking. *$$$$*

★ **Lampreia.** The subtle beige-and-gold interior of this Belltown restaurant is the perfect backdrop for chef-owner Scott Carsberg's clean, sophisticated cuisine. *$$$$*

★ **Rover's.** An intimate escape from the energy of downtown, Rover's offers exceptional French cooking with a menu (changing daily) founded on fresh, locally available ingredients, selected and prepared by chef-owner Thierry Rautureau. *$$$$*

★ **Dahlia Lounge.** The easygoing ambience of the Dahlia Lounge perfectly suits chef Tom Douglas's penchant for simple, if uncommon, preparations. His signature Dungeness crab cakes lead an ever-evolving menu focused on regional ingredients. *$$$*

★ **Metropolitan Grill.** This clubby downtown spot serves custom-aged mesquite-broiled steaks—the best in Seattle—in a classic steak-house atmosphere. *$$$*

★ **Palace Kitchen.** Northwest ingredients are again the centerpiece of Tom Douglas's latest venture, which has a gorgeous curved bar and an open kitchen. *$$$*

★ **Ray's Boathouse.** The view of Puget Sound may be the drawing card, but the seafood is fresh, well prepared, and complemented by one of the area's finest wine lists. *$$$*

★ **Saigon Gourmet.** This small café in the International District is about as plain as they get, but the Vietnamese food is superb and the prices are incredibly low. *$*

★ **Four Seasons Olympic Hotel.** Seattle's most elegant hotel has a 1920s Renaissance Revival–style grandeur; public rooms are appointed with marble, wood paneling, potted plants, and thick rugs, and furnished with plush armchairs. *$$$$*

★ **Sorrento.** Sitting high on First Hill, this deluxe European-style hotel, designed to look like an Italian villa, has wonderful views overlooking downtown and the waterfront. *$$$$*

★ **Inn at the Market.** This sophisticated but unpretentious hotel, right up the street from the Pike Place Market, combines the best aspects of a small French country inn with the informality of the Pacific Northwest. *$$$–$$$$*

★ **Gaslight Inn.** Rooms at this Capitol Hill bed-and-breakfast inn range from a cozy crow's nest to large rooms and suites with gas fireplaces, carved antique beds, and ceiling fans. *$$–$$$*

★ **Marriott Sea-Tac.** The luxurious Marriott near the airport has a five-story tropical atrium that's complete with a waterfall, a dining area, an indoor pool, and a lounge. *$$–$$$*

Washington

Sights and Attractions

★ **A ferry ride through the San Juan Islands.** Nothing beats the view of the islands from the waters of Puget Sound.

★ **Mount Rainier National Park.** Magnificent Mount Rainier is the centerpiece of a park with hiking and cross-country ski trails, lakes and rivers, and ample camping facilities.

★ **Point Defiance Zoo and Aquarium, Tacoma.** The zoo's re-creations of natural habitats provide close-up views of whales, walruses, sharks, polar bears, octopuses, apes, reptiles, and birds.

★ **Snoqualmie Falls.** Spring and summer snowmelt turns the Snoqualmie River into a thundering torrent as it cascades through a 268-foot rock gorge to a deep pool below.

★ **Whale-watching on Long Beach Peninsula.** Climb the North Head Lighthouse and watch for a whale blow—the vapor that spouts into the air when a whale exhales—as gray whales pass by on their way back and forth from breeding grounds in warmer waters.

Restaurants

★ **C'est Si Bon.** French expatriates Norbert and Michele Juhasz run this locally famous French restaurant—the classiest eatery on the decidedly informal Olympic Peninsula. *$$$–$$$$*

★ **The Ark, Nahcotta.** The oysters at the Ark couldn't be fresher—they're raised in beds behind the restaurant. *$$$*

★ **Christina's.** The modern decor at the premier Orcas restaurant includes original artwork and copper-top tables. The seasonal menu changes daily but generally emphasizes fresh local fish and seafood. *$$$*

★ **The Herbfarm, Snoqualmie.** To devotees of Northwest cuisine, the intimate Herbfarm ranks as a temple. *$$$*

★ **Birchfield Manor, Yakima.** All entrées at the Yakima wine country's best restaurant come with an exotic homemade bread of the day. *$$–$$$*

★ **Springtree Café.** Chef James Boyle devises his inventive daily menu around fresh seafood and Waldron Island organic produce and herbs, creating savory dishes that you won't soon forget. *$$–$$$*

★ **Alice's Restaurant, Tenino.** Homey and intimate, this restaurant in a rural farmhouse serves six-course, prix-fixe dinners of innovative yet classic American cuisine. *$$*

Hotels and Inns

★ **Domaine Madeleine, Port Angeles.** The rooms at this small and romantic inn have views of the water, fireplaces, Jacuzzis, TVs with VCRs, and CD/tape players. Breakfast is a feast. *$$$$*

★ **Majestic Hotel, Anacortes.** An old mercantile building in the San Juan Islands has been turned into one of the finest small hotels in the Northwest. *$$$–$$$$*

★ **Spring Bay Inn, Orcas Island.** Former park rangers run this B&B on acres of woodland. All the rooms have bay views, wood-burning fireplaces, feather beds, and private sitting areas. *$$$–$$$$*

★ **Guest House Cottages, Whidbey Island.** The five very private log cabins here, surrounded by 25 forested acres, have feather beds, VCRs, whirlpool tubs, country antiques, and fireplaces. *$$$*

★ **Inn at Langley, Whidbey Island.** This concrete-and-wood Frank Lloyd Wright–inspired structure rests on the edge of a bluff that descends to a beach. *$$$*

★ **Salish Lodge, Snoqualmie.** The rooms at this favorite getaway of Seattleites have views of Snoqualmie Falls or the Snoqualmie River. Elaborate Saturday and Sunday brunches include eggs, bacon, fish, fresh fruit, pancakes, and a locally renowned oatmeal. *$$$*

★ **James House, Port Townsend.** This splendid Victorian-era B&B that overlooks downtown has a serene atmosphere. *$$–$$$*

★ **Shelburne Inn, Seaview.** Impeccably maintained, this antiques-filled inn retains an air of refinement. The gourmet breakfast is unforgettable. *$$–$$$*

Vancouver

Sights and Attractions

★ **Dr. Sun Yat-Sen Gardens.** No power tools, screws, or nails were used in the construction of these gardens, built in the 1980s.

★ **Granville Island.** This small sandbar's refurbished industrial buildings and tin sheds, painted in upbeat primary colors, house restaurants, a public market, marine activities, and artisans' studios.

★ **Museum of Anthropology.** Vancouver's most spectacular museum displays aboriginal art from the Pacific Northwest and around the world.

★ **Stanley Park.** An afternoon in this 1,000-acre wilderness park, blocks from downtown, can include beaches, the ocean, the harbor, Douglas fir and cedar forests, and a good look at the North Shore mountains.

Restaurants

★ **Chartwell.** Named after Sir Winston Churchill's country home, the flagship dining room at the Four Seasons Hotel serves robust, inventive Continental food in a British-club atmosphere. *$$$–$$$$*

★ **Star Anise.** Pacific Rim cuisine with French flair shines in this intimate restaurant on the west side of town. *$$$*

★ **Tojo's.** Hidekazu Tojo is a sushi-making legend here, with more than 2,000 special preparations stored in his creative mind. *$$$*

★ **Villa del Lupo.** The top chefs in town come here for Italian food. The decor sets a romantic tone, but come prepared to roll up your sleeves and mop up the sauce with a chunk of crusty bread. *$$$*

★ **Imperial Chinese Seafood.** This Cantonese restaurant has two-story floor-to-ceiling windows with stupendous views of Stanley Park and the North Shore mountains across Coal Harbour. *$$–$$$*

★ **Rubina Tandoori.** For the best East Indian food in the city, try Rubina Tandoori, 20 minutes from downtown. The large menu spans most of the subcontinent's cuisines. $$

★ **Phnom Penh Restaurant.** You'll taste unusually robust Vietnamese and Cambodian fare at this restaurant on the fringes of Chinatown. $

Hotels and Inns

★ **Sutton Place.** The rooms at the Sutton Place are furnished with rich, dark woods reminiscent of 19th-century France. Despite its size, the hotel feels intimate. $$$$

★ **Waterfront Centre Hotel.** The lobby and many rooms at this 23-story glass hotel have views of Burrard Inlet. The hotel is across from Canada Place, which can be reached from the hotel by an underground walkway. $$$$

★ **Hotel Vancouver.** The copper roof of this grand château-style hotel dominates Vancouver's skyline. The two-floor suites are plush, and even the standard guest rooms have an air of prestige. $$$

★ **Rosedale on Robson.** If you plan to be in town for a while and want to keep expenses down by doing some of your own cooking, consider this all-suites property downtown. $$–$$$

★ **English Bay Inn.** The rooms at this renovated 1930s Tudor house have wonderful sleigh beds with matching armoires. A small, sunny English country garden brightens the back of the inn. $$

★ **West End Guest House.** This lovely Victorian house is a true "painted lady," from its gracious front parlor, cozy fireplace, and early 1900s furniture to its green-trimmed pink exterior. $$

★ **Hostelling International Vancouver Downtown.** Vancouver's newest hostel, conveniently located in the West End downtown, is tidy and secure. $

British Columbia

Sights and Attractions

★ **Butchart Gardens, Victoria.** This world-class horticultural collection grows more than 700 varieties of flowers and has Italian, Japanese, and English rose gardens.

★ **Craigdarroch Castle.** The lavish mansion of British Columbia's first millionaire is now a museum that surveys life at the end of the 19th century.

★ **Minter Gardens, Rosedale.** This compound contains beautifully presented theme gardens—Chinese, rose, English, fern, fragrance, and more—along with aviaries and ponds.

★ **O'Keefe Historic Ranch, Vernon.** For a window on cattle-ranch life at the turn of the century, visit the O'Keefe house, a late-19th-century Victorian mansion opulently furnished with original antiques.

★ **Pacific Rim National Park, Vancouver Island.** The first national marine park in Canada comprises a hard-packed white-sand beach, a group of islands, and a demanding coastal hiking trail.

Restaurants

★ **The Marina Restaurant, Victoria.** Locals love this round restaurant overlooking the Oak Bay Marina; imaginative seafood dishes are the highlights of the diverse menu. $$–$$$

★ **Mahle House, Nanaimo.** The intimate setting and innovative Northwest cuisine make a visit here one of the finest dining experiences in the region. $$

★ **The Old House Restaurant, Courtenay.** This bi-level restaurant offers casual dining in a restored 1938 house with large cedar beams and a stone fireplace. $$

★ **Royal Coachman Inn, Campbell River, Vancouver Island.** Informal, blackboard-menu restaurants like this one dot the landscape of the island, but here the menu, which changes daily, is surprisingly daring. $–$$

Hotels and Inns

★ **Hastings House, Saltspring Island.** You'll feel more than pampered at one of the finest country inns in North America. $$$$

★ **April Point Lodge and Fishing Resort, Campbell River, Vancouver Island.** Spread across a point of Quadra Island and stretching into Discovery Passage, the 1944 cedar lodge is surrounded by refurbished fishermen's cabins and guest houses. $$$–$$$$

★ **Ocean Pointe Resort, Victoria.** Public rooms and half the guest rooms have views of downtown Victoria and the parliament buildings. $$$

Southeast Alaska

Sights and Attractions

★ **Abraham Lincoln Totem Pole, Ketchikan.** The top-hatted image of Abe Lincoln crowns one of Alaska's most curious totem poles.

★ **Alaska State Museum, Juneau.** On view at one of Alaska's top museums are stuffed brown bears, a replica of a two-story-high eagle nesting tree, a 40-foot walrus-skin *umiak* (whaling boat), a re-created interior of a Tlingit tribal house, mining exhibits, and contemporary art.

★ **Klondike Gold Rush National Historical Park, Skagway.** A former White Pass & Yukon Route rail depot contains exhibits, photos, and artifacts from the White Pass and Chilkoot trails.

Restaurants

★ **Channel Club, Sitka.** If you've never dined on halibut cheeks, you don't know what you're missing. The decor is nautical, with fishnet floats, whale baleen, and whalebone carvings hanging on the walls. $$–$$$

★ **Salmon Falls Resort, Ketchikan.** The dining area of the resort overlooks the waters of Clover Passage, where sunsets are often a vivid red. Seafood fresh from adjacent waters is especially good; try the halibut and the prawns stuffed with crabmeat. $$

★ **The Fiddlehead, Juneau.** This is probably Juneau's favorite restaurant, a delightful place where healthful dishes come in generous portions. $–$$

★ **Beachcomber Inn, Petersburg.** Seafood with a distinctly Norwegian flair is the specialty in this restored cannery building on the shores of Wrangell Narrows. $

Hotels and Inns

★ **Westmark Shee Atika, Sitka.** Stay here for a night or two and you'll come away with an increased appreciation for Southeast Alaskan native art and culture. Many rooms overlook Crescent Harbor and the islands in the waters beyond; others have mountain and forest views. $$$$

★ **The Prospector, Juneau.** Business travelers and legislators favor this small, modern hotel. Very large rooms have contemporary furnishings, bright watercolors of Alaskan nature, and views of the channel, mountains, or city. $$$–$$$$

★ **Ingersoll Hotel, Ketchikan.** Old-fashioned patterned wallpaper, wood wainscoting, and etched-glass windows on the oak registration desk set an old-fashioned mood for this three-story downtown hotel, built in the 1920s. The rooms are standard, but the views are sublime. $$$

★ **Golden North Hotel.** Pioneer Skagway families contributed gold-rush furnishings to each of this historic hotel's lovingly restored rooms. $$

FESTIVALS AND SEASONAL EVENTS

Listed below are some of the major events that take place in the Pacific Northwest. For more information about them, *see* the listing for the city or region in which they occur, or phone the appropriate state or provincial visitors bureau. *See* Visitor Information *in* the Gold Guide for bureau phone numbers.

OREGON

➤ MID-FEB.–EARLY NOV.: The **Oregon Shakespeare Festival** in Ashland presents classic and contemporary plays in repertory.

➤ APR.: The **Hood River Valley Blossom Festival** is a springtime floral spectacle.

➤ MAY: The **Cinco de Mayo Festival** in Portland is one of the largest such celebrations this side of Guadalajara. In late May, the **Brookings Azalea Festival** shows off the azaleas of Oregon's southern coast.

➤ LATE MAY–LATE JUNE: The **Portland Rose Festival** packs diverse events—an air show, three parades, auto racing, and a riverside carnival among them—into 25 days.

➤ JUNE: **Sandcastle Day** transforms Cannon Beach into a sculptured fantasyland.

➤ MID-JUNE–EARLY SEPT.: The **Britt Festivals** present concerts, musical theater and dance at an outdoor amphitheater in historic Jacksonville.

➤ LATE JUNE–MID-JULY: The **Oregon Bach Festival** in Eugene celebrates the works of the great composer.

➤ JULY: The **Oregon Coast Music Festival** in Coos Bay, North Bend, and Charleston presents classical bluegrass, jazz, and other concerts. The **Oregon Brewer's Festival**, a beer-lover's delight, is held in Portland. The **Waterfront Blues Festival** in Portland features Oregon's finest blues artists along with national recording stars.

➤ MID-JULY: The **Salem Art Fair and Festival,** Oregon's biggest art fair, includes exhibits, food, entertainment, and tours of historic mansions.

➤ AUG.: The **Mount Hood Festival of Jazz** brings nationally acclaimed jazz musicians to Gresham for performances in an outdoor setting.

➤ LATE AUG.–EARLY SEPT.: The **Oregon State Fair** takes place in Salem the 11 days before Labor Day.

➤ MID-SEPT.: **Oktoberfest** draws half a million people to Mount Angel for an extravaganza of Bavarian food, beer, wine, and cabaret.

WASHINGTON

➤ LATE MAR.–MID-APR.: The **Skagit Valley Tulip Festival** is a showcase of millions of colorful tulips and daffodils.

➤ MAY: The **Viking Fest** celebrates the Norwegian community of Poulsbo's proud heritage.

➤ MEMORIAL DAY WEEKEND: The **Northwest Folklife Festival** in Seattle is one of the nation's largest folk-music festivals.

➤ LATE JUNE–EARLY JULY: **Fort Vancouver Days** in Vancouver include a chili cook-off, musical events, and fireworks.

➤ JULY: **Bite of Seattle,** an event at the Seattle Center, showcases the fare at the city's finest restaurants. The **Pacific Northwest Arts Fair,** a juried show in Bellevue, presents the works of several hundred artists.

➤ MID-JULY–EARLY AUG.: **Seafair** in Seattle begins with a torchlight parade and ends with a Blue Angels air show and hydroplane races.

➤ LATE AUG.: The **Washington State International Kite Festival** sends kites of all shapes and sizes flying above Long Beach.

➤ LATE AUG.–EARLY SEPT.: **Bumbershoot** is a beloved Seattle showcase for music, dance, theater, comedy, and the visual and literary arts.

➤ EARLY–MID-SEPT.: The **Western Washington Fair** brings top entertainment, animals, food, exhibits, and rides to the town of Puyallup.

➤ EARLY SEPT.: The **Wooden Boat Festival** of Port Townsend includes historic boat displays, demonstrations, and a street fair.

BRITISH COLUMBIA

➤ JAN.: The **Polar Bear Swim** on New Year's Day in Vancouver is said to bring good luck all year. **Skiing competitions** take place at most alpine ski resorts (through February).

➤ MAR.: The **Pacific Rim Whale Festival** on Vancouver Island's west coast celebrates the spring migration of gray whales with guided tours by whale experts and accompanying music and dancing. Northwest vintages take center stage at the **Vancouver International Wine Festival.**

➤ APR.: The **TerrifVic Jazz Party** in Victoria presents top international Dixieland bands.

➤ MAY: **Cloverdale Rodeo** in Surrey is rated sixth in the world by the Pro Rodeo Association. **Vancouver Children's Festival** provides free open-air stage performances.

➤ JUNE: **Canadian International Dragon Boat Festival** in Vancouver includes entertainment, exotic foods, and the ancient "awakening the dragons" ritual of long, slender boats decorated with huge dragon heads.

➤ JUNE–SEPT.: **Whistler Summer Festivals** present daily street entertainment and music festivals at the international ski and summer resort.

➤ JULY 1: **Canada Day** inspires celebrations around the country in honor of Canada's birthday. In Vancouver, **Canada Place** hosts an entire day of free outdoor concerts followed by a fireworks display in the inner harbor. Victoria stages the daylong **Great**

Canadian Family Picnic in Beacon Hill Park. The event usually includes children's games, bands, food booths, and fireworks.

➤ JULY: The **Harrison Festival of the Arts** focuses on ethnic music, dance, and theater, such as African, Caribbean, or Central American. The **Vancouver Sea Festival** celebrates the city's nautical heritage with the World Championship Bathtub Race, sailing regattas, and windsurfing races.

➤ AUG.: The **Abbotsford International Airshow** is three days of flight performances and a large-aircraft display. The **Pacific National Exhibition** in Vancouver has parades, exhibits, sports, entertainment, and logging contests. The **Squamish Days Loggers Sports Festival** draws loggers from around the world to compete in a series of incredible feats.

➤ SEPT.: Cars speed through downtown Vancouver in the **Molson Indy Formula 1 race.**

➤ OCT.: The **Okanagan Wine Festivals** take place in the Okanagan-Similkameen area. The **Vancouver International Film Festival** brings top directors and films to the city.

➤ DEC.: The **Carol Ships,** sailboats full of carolers and decorated with colored lights, ply the waters of the Vancouver harbor.

ALASKA

➤ EARLY FEB.: The **Tent City Winter Festival** in Wrangell captures the flavor of Alaska's early days.

➤ LATE MAR.: **Seward's Day,** which commemorates the signing of the 1867 treaty purchasing Alaska from Russia, is celebrated around the state on the last Monday in March.

➤ EARLY APR.: The **Alaska Folk Festival** in Juneau is a mix of music, handmade crafts, and foods.

➤ MAY: The **Little Norway Festival** in picturesque Petersburg celebrates the town's Scandinavian heritage. The **Juneau Jazz and Classics Festival** presents nationally known musicians. The **Southeast Alaska State Fair** takes place in Haines and includes contests, a timber show, and agriculture, home-arts, fine-arts, and crafts exhibits.

➤ JUNE: The **Sitka Summer Music Festival** is a monthlong series of chamber-music performances.

➤ MID-OCT.: The **Alaska Day Celebration** brings out the whole town of Sitka to celebrate the day—October 18—the United States acquired Alaska from Russia. The weeklong festival includes a period costume ball and a parade.

2 Portland

Oregon's largest city is among America's most livable—not surprising, given its verdant natural setting and host of urban amenities. To find out the secret to Portland's allure, stroll through the city's parks and gardens, explore its intriguing neighborhoods and lively downtown, peruse the galleries and museums, or just sit back and enjoy the buzz at any of the dozens of coffeehouses, cafés, and microbreweries.

By Donald S.
Olson

PORTLAND IS LOADED WITH ENERGY. For decades this
inland port on the Willamette River was the undiscovered gem of the West Coast, often overlooked
by visitors seeking more sophisticated milieus. But in the last decade,
people have begun flocking here in unprecedented numbers.

The city's proximity to mountains, ocean, and desert adds an element
of natural grandeur to its urban character. Majestic Mount Hood, about
70 mi to the east, acts as a kind of mascot, and on a clear day several
peaks of the Cascade Range are visible, including Mount St. Helen's,
which dusted the city with ash when it erupted in 1980. The west side
of town is built on a series of forested hills that descend to the downtown area, the Willamette River, and the flatter east side. Filled with
stately late-19th-century and modern architecture, linked by an effec-
tive and intelligent transit system, and home to a vital arts scene, Portland is a place where there's much to do day or night, rain or shine.

The quality of life remains a high and constant priority here. As far
back as 1852, with the establishment of the Boulevard, Portland began
setting aside city land as parks. This legacy has added immeasurably
to the city's attractiveness and environmental mystique. Included
among Portland's 250 parks, public gardens, and greenways are the
nation's largest urban wilderness, the world's smallest park, and the
only extinct volcano in the lower 48 states within a city's limits.

A temperate climate and plenty of precipitation keep Portland green
year-round and make it a paradise for gardeners. The City of Roses,
as it's known, celebrates its favorite flower with a monthlong Rose Festival—a June extravaganza with auto and boat races, visiting navy ships,
and a grand parade second in size only to Pasadena's Rose Parade. But
the floral spectacle really starts three months earlier, when streets and
gardens bloom with the colors of flowering trees, camellias, rhododendrons, and azaleas.

The arts here flourish in unexpected places: You'll find artworks in police stations, office towers, banks, playgrounds, and on the sides of buildings. The brick-paved transit mall downtown is a veritable outdoor
gallery of fountains and sculptures. As for the performing arts, Portland is home to several professional theater companies, the Oregon Symphony, the Portland Opera, and Chamber Music Northwest, to name
just a few. Those into nightlife will also find some of the best live-band
and club action in the country.

Portland, which began as an Indian clearing of about 1 square mile,
has become a metropolis of 485,000 people; within its now 132-
square-mi borders are 90 diverse and distinct neighborhoods. A center for sports and sportswear makers, the Portland metropolitan area
contains the headquarters and factories of Jantzen, Nike, Columbia
Sportswear, and Pendleton. High-tech shipbuilding, furniture, fabricated-
metals, and other manufacturers have broadened the region's economic base even further. And its prime location at the confluence of
the Columbia and Willamette rivers has helped Portland become the
third-largest port on the West Coast. Five main terminals export automobiles, steel, livestock, grain, and timber products. Shipyards repair tankers, tugboats, cruise ships, and navy vessels.

For all its emphasis on the future, though, Portland has not forgotten
its past. Architectural preservation is a major preoccupation, particularly when it comes to the 1860s brick buildings with cast-iron columns

and the 1890s ornate terra-cotta designs that grace areas like the Skidmore Old Town, Yamhill, and Glazed Terra-Cotta national historic districts. In the Pearl District, older industrial buildings are being given new life as residential lofts, restaurants, office space, galleries, and boutiques.

The future will undoubtedly bring more people to Portland. To curb urban sprawl, the city has instituted an "urban growth boundary" and is actively promoting "urban density" schemes within the inner city. In the process it has revitalized several older neighborhoods and created some entirely new ones. Not all Portlanders are happy with the results, which have brought increased traffic congestion and constant construction. For many, however, the city is better than ever, bursting with fresh energy and a new level of sophistication.

EXPLORING PORTLAND

The Willamette River is Portland's east–west dividing line. Burnside Street separates north from south. The city's 200-ft-long blocks make them easy to walk, but you can also explore the downtown core by either MAX light rail or Tri-Met bus (☞ Getting Around *in* Portland A to Z, *below*).

Downtown Portland, stretching from the Willamette River to roughly Northwest and Southwest 12th avenues, dominates the city's near west side. Two Northwest neighborhoods are within walking distance of downtown. The newest, a former industrial area now called the **Pearl District,** extends north from West Burnside Street to Northwest Marshall Street between Northwest 8th and 15th avenues. One of Portland's oldest neighborhoods, **Nob Hill,** lies west of the Pearl District. Grand old houses line the streets of this dense, mixed-use area anchored by fashion-conscious Northwest 23rd Avenue. Across the Willamette River on Portland's east side, the **Hawthorne District,** along Southeast Hawthorne Boulevard from Southeast 17th Avenue to Southeast 43rd Avenue, has attracted bohemian and artsy types with its coffeehouses, music clubs, funky shops, and galleries. **Sellwood,** in the city's southeast corner between Southeast Tacoma Street and Southeast 13th Avenue, is a modest neighborhood known for its antiques stores. The section of **Northeast Portland** closest to the Willamette River has been redefined by the new Rose Quarter stadium and Convention Center. Northeast Broadway is the major commercial artery, Lloyd Center the main shopping hub.

Great Itineraries

IF YOU HAVE 1 DAY

Spend the morning exploring the parks, museums, and historic districts in downtown Portland. To get the flavor of a Portland neighborhood, stroll along Northwest 23rd Avenue and through Nob Hill in the early afternoon. From there, drive up into the northwest hills to the Pittock Mansion. Just minutes away, in the southwest hills, are the famous rose gardens and Japanese Garden in Washington Park.

IF YOU HAVE 3 DAYS

On your first day, explore downtown Portland, Northwest 23rd Avenue and Nob Hill, the Pittock Mansion, and the gardens in Washington Park. On the second morning, visit the Oregon Museum of Science and Industry (OMSI), have lunch in Sellwood, and then head to Hoyt Arboretum, Forest Park, or both. Head back to east Portland on your third day to check out the Hawthorne District. Then, to gain a historical perspective, drive to Oregon City or Fort Vancouver.

Downtown

Portland has one of the most successful and attractive downtown urban cores in America. Clean, compact, and filled with parks, plazas, and fountains, it holds a mix of new and historic buildings. Hotels, shopping, museums, restaurants, and entertainment can all be found here, and the entire downtown area is part of the Tri-Met transit system's Fareless Square, meaning that you can ride any bus for free.

Numbers in the text correspond to numbers in the margin and on the Downtown Portland map.

A Good Walk

Begin at Southwest Morrison Street and Southwest 6th Avenue at **Pioneer Courthouse Square** ①. From the square, walk south on 6th Avenue for two blocks. At the corner of 6th Avenue and Salmon Street is **NikeTown** ②. Continue one block south to Main Street and one block west to Broadway and the **Portland Center for the Performing Arts** ③. Behind the center are the tree-lined **South Park Blocks** along Park Avenue. On the east side of Park at Jefferson Street, a mural of Lewis and Clark and the Oregon Trail rises above the entrance to the **Oregon History Center** ④. West on Jefferson across the Park Blocks is the **Portland Art Museum** ⑤. Walk west on Jefferson and south on 11th Avenue to reach the **Old Church** ⑥. Loop back east to the Park Blocks along Columbia Street and head south on Park Avenue to Market Street, where the campus of **Portland State University** ⑦ begins.

Continue east on Market to 3rd Avenue and you'll reach the **Civic Auditorium** ⑧, which has a massive waterfall fountain. **KOIN Center** ⑨, the most distinctive high-rise in downtown Portland, occupies the next block to the north. Continue north for one block more on 3rd Avenue to **Terry Schrunk Plaza** ⑩. On the west side of the plaza is Portland's newly restored **City Hall** ⑪. The adjacent **Chapman and Lownsdale squares** ⑫ are flanked by the blue, postmodern **Portland Building** ⑬ to the west and the **Justice Center** ⑭ to the east. Rising beside the Justice Center, between Main and Salmon streets, is the **Mark O. Hatfield U.S. Courthouse** ⑮. The **State of Oregon Sports Hall of Fame** ⑯ is just north of Chapman Square on 4th Avenue, between Salmon and Taylor streets. Head east on Salmon to the **World Trade Center** on 2nd Avenue; the **Portland/Oregon Visitors Association** ⑰ occupies the building on Naito Parkway, a street most locals still call Front Avenue, the name it had before it was changed to honor a local real-estate mogul.

Cross Naito Parkway and enter **Governor Tom McCall Waterfront Park** and **Salmon Street Plaza.** The park extends north for about a mile to Burnside Street. Follow the park one block north to Taylor Street, where **Mill Ends Park** ⑱ sits in the middle of a traffic island on Naito Parkway. You are now in the **Yamhill National Historic District** of cast-iron and other buildings. If you are interested in art and architecture, zigzag back and forth between Southwest 5th and Southwest 6th avenues and the intersecting streets of Oak and Yamhill. This is the heart of the **Glazed Terra-Cotta National Historic District.**

TIMING

The entire downtown walk can be accomplished in about 90 minutes. If you're planning to stop at the Oregon History Center or Portland Art Museum (both closed on Monday), add at least one hour for each. Allot 15 or 30 minutes for the Sports Hall of Fame, which is closed on Sunday.

Sights to See

12 **Chapman and Lownsdale squares.** During the 1920s, these parks were segregated by sex: Chapman, between Madison and Main streets, was reserved for women, and Lownsdale, between Main and Salmon streets, was for men. The elk statue on Main Street, which separates the parks, was given to the city by former mayor David Thompson. It supposedly honors an elk that grazed here in the 1850s.

OFF THE
BEATEN PATH

CHILDREN'S MUSEUM – Hands-on play is the order of the day at this museum with exhibits, a clay shop, and a child-size grocery store. ⊠ *3037 S.W. 2nd Ave., between S.W. Barbour Blvd. and S.W. Woods St. near the Ross Island Bridge,* ☎ *503/823–2227.* ☜ *$3.50.* ☉ *Daily 9–5.*

11 **City Hall.** Portland's four-story, granite-faced City Hall, which was completed in 1895, is an example of the Renaissance Revival style popular in the late 19th century. Italian influences can be seen in the porch, the pink scagliola columns, the cornice embellishments, and other details. The building has been undergoing a major renovation, but it should reopen to the public in late spring 1998. ⊠ *1220 S.W. 5th Ave.,* ☎ *503/823–4000.* ☉ *Weekdays 8–5.*

8 **Civic Auditorium.** Home base for the Portland Opera and Oregon Ballet Theater, the Civic Auditorium also hosts traveling musicals and other theatrical extravaganzas. The building itself, part of the Portland Center for the Performing Arts (☞ *below*), is not particularly distinctive, but the **Ira Keller Fountain**, a series of 18-ft-high stone waterfalls across from the front entrance, is worth a look. ⊠ *S.W. 3rd Ave. and Clay St.,* ☎ *503/274–6560.*

Glazed Terra-Cotta National Historic District. A century ago, terra-cotta was often used in construction because of its availability and low cost; it could also be easily molded into the decorative details that were popular at the time. Elaborate lions' heads, griffins, floral displays, and other classical motifs adorn the rooflines of the district's many buildings that date from the late 1890s to the mid-1910s. Public art lines 5th and 6th avenues. On 5th you'll find a sculpture that reflects light and changing colors, a nude woman made of bronze, a copper and redwood creation inspired by the Norse god Thor, and a large limestone cat in repose. Sixth Avenue has a steel-and-concrete matrix, a granite-and-brick fountain, and an abstract modern depiction of an ancient Greek defending Crete. ⊠ *S.W. 5th and S.W. 6th Aves. between S.W. Oak and S.W. Yamhill Sts.*

Governor Tom McCall Waterfront Park. The park named for a former governor of Oregon revered for his statewide land-use planning initiatives stretches north along the Willamette River for about a mile to Burnside Street. Broad and grassy, it yields what may be the finest ground-level view of downtown Portland's bridges and skyline. The park, on the site of a former expressway, hosts many events, among them the Rose Festival, classical and blues concerts, and the Oregon Brewers' Festival. Bikers, joggers, and roller and in-line skaters enjoy the area year-round. The arching jets of water at the **Salmon Street Fountain** change configuration every few hours and are a favorite cooling-off spot during the dog days of summer. ⊠ *S.W. Naito Pkwy. (Front Ave.) from just south of the Hawthorne Bridge to the Burnside Bridge.*

14 **Justice Center.** This modern building houses the county court and support offices and, on the 16th floor, the **Police Museum**, which has uniforms, guns, and badges worn by the Portland Police Department. Thanks to a city ordinance requiring that 1% of the development

Downtown Portland

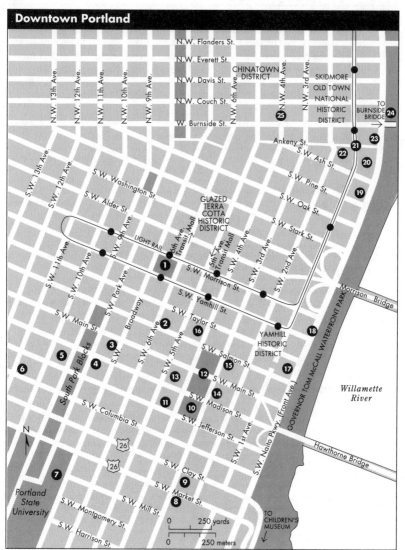

American Advertising Museum, **22**

Chapman and Lownsdale Squares, **12**

Chinatown Gate, **25**

City Hall, **11**

Civic Auditorium, **8**

Japanese-American Historical Plaza, **24**

Jeff Morris Memorial Fire Museum, **20**

Justice Center, **14**

KOIN Center, **9**

Mark O. Hatfield U.S. Courthouse, **15**

Mill Ends Park, **18**

NikeTown, **2**

Old Church, **6**

Oregon History Center, **4**

Oregon Maritime Center and Museum, **19**

Pioneer Courthouse Square, **1**

Portland Art Museum, **5**

Portland Building, **13**

Portland Center for the Performing Arts, **3**

Portland/Oregon Visitors Association, **17**

Portland Saturday Market, **23**

Portland State University, **7**

Skidmore Fountain, **21**

State of Oregon Sports Hall of Fame, **16**

Terry Schrunk Plaza, **10**

costs of new buildings be allotted to the arts, the center's hallways are lined with travertine sculptures, ceiling mosaics, stained-glass windows, and photographic murals. Visitors are welcome to peruse the works of art. ⊠ *1111 S.W. 2nd Ave.,* ☎ *503/823–0019.* ⌦ *Free.* ☾ *Mon.–Thurs. 10–3.*

❾ KOIN Center. An instant landmark after its completion in 1984, this handsome tower with a tapering form and a pyramidal top takes its design cues from early art deco skyscrapers. Made of brick with limestone trim and a blue metal roof, the tower houses offices (including those of KOIN, a local television and radio station), a multiplex cinema, and, on its top floors, some of the most expensive condominiums in Portland. ⊠ *S.W. Columbia St. and S.W. 3rd Ave.*

⓯ Mark O. Hatfield U.S. Courthouse. The New York architectural firm Kohn Pedersen Fox designed Portland's newest skyscraper, which was completed in 1997. The sophisticated exterior is clad in Indiana limestone, and the courtroom lobbies have expansive glass walls. Public rooftop terraces yield grand city views. ⊠ *S.W. 2nd Ave. between Main and Salmon Sts.*

⓲ Mill Ends Park. Sitting in the middle of a traffic island on Naito Parkway, this patch of urban tranquillity, at 24 inches in diameter, has been recognized by the *Guinness Book of Records* as the world's smallest official city park. ⊠ *S.W. Naito Pkwy. at Taylor St.*

❷ NikeTown. This futuristic F.A.O. Schwarz for the athletically inclined is a showplace for Nike, the international sportswear giant headquartered in Beaverton, just outside Portland. A life-size plaster cast of Michael Jordan captured in mid-jump dangles from the ceiling near the basketball shoes. Autographed sports memorabilia, video monitors, and statuary compete for your attention with the many products for sale. But don't expect any bargains: Prices are full retail and the word "sale" is almost as taboo around here as the name Reebok. ⊠ *930 S.W. 6th Ave.,* ☎ *503/221–6453.* ☾ *Mon.–Thurs. and Sat. 10–7, Fri. 10–8, Sun. 11:30–6:30.*

❻ Old Church. This building erected in 1882 is a prime example of Carpenter Gothic architecture. Tall spires and original stained-glass windows enhance its exterior of rough-cut lumber. The acoustically resonant church hosts free classical concerts at noon each Wednesday. If you're lucky, you'll get to hear one of the few operating Hook and Hastings tracker pipe organs. ⊠ *1422 S.W. 11th Ave.,* ☎ *503/222–2031.* ⌦ *Free.* ☾ *Weekdays 11–3, Sat. by appointment.*

❹ Oregon History Center. Impressive eight-story-high trompe l'oeil murals of Lewis and Clark and the Oregon Trail (the route the two pioneers took from the Midwest to the Oregon Territory) cover two sides of this downtown museum, which follows the state's story from prehistoric times to the present. The multisensory, hands-on "Portland!" exhibit presents a vivid slice of city life. Archaeological and anthropological artifacts, ship models, and memorabilia from the Oregon Trail are also on display in a series of dramatic galleries. The center's research library is open to the public; its bookstore is a good source for maps and publications on Northwest history. ⊠ *1200 S.W. Park Ave.,* ☎ *503/306–5200.* ⌦ *$6.* ☾ *Tues.–Sat. 10–5, Sun. noon–5.*

★ ❶ Pioneer Courthouse Square. Downtown Portland's public heart and commercial soul is centered in this amphitheatrical brick piazza whose design echoes the classic central plazas of European cities. Special events often take place in this premier people-watching venue, where the neatly dressed office crowd mingles with some of the city's stranger elements. The best time to be here is at noon, when a goofy weather machine blasts a fanfare, and a shining sun, stormy dragon, or blue heron rises out of a misty cloud to confirm the day's weather. Directly across the street is one of downtown Portland's most familiar landmarks, the classically sedate **Pioneer Courthouse.** Built in 1869, it's the oldest public building in the Northwest. ⊠ *701 S.W. 6th Ave., ☎ 503/ 223–1613.*

❺ Portland Art Museum. The treasures at the Northwest's oldest visual- and media-arts facility span 35 centuries of Asian, European, and American art, with collections of Native American, regional, and contemporary art. The film center presents the annual Portland International Film Festival in February and March and the Northwest Film Festival in early November. ⊠ *1219 S.W. Park Ave., ☎ 503/226–2811; 503/221–1156 for film schedule. ☜ $6. ☉ Tues.–Sun. 10–5.*

⓭ Portland Building. *Portlandia,* the second-largest hammered-copper statue in the world, surpassed only by the Statue of Liberty, kneels on the second-story balcony of one of the first postmodern buildings in the United States. The building itself generates strong feelings; chances are you'll either love it or hate it. The controversial structure, architect Michael Graves's first major design commission, is buff colored with brown and blue trim and exterior decorative touches. The interior spaces are dark and clumsily executed, but the **Metropolitan Center for Public Art,** on the second floor, is worth a brief visit. A permanent exhibit of public art includes a huge fiberglass mold of Portlandia's face and original works by local artists. ⊠ *1120 S.W. 5th Ave., ☎ 503/823– 5111. ☜ Free. ☉ Weekdays 8–6.*

❸ Portland Center for the Performing Arts. The "old building" and the hub of activity here is the **Arlene Schnitzer Concert Hall,** host to the Oregon Symphony, musical events of many genres, and lectures. Across Main Street, but still part of the center, is the 292-seat **Delores Winningstad Theater,** used for plays and special performances. Its stage design and dimensions are based on those of an Elizabethan-era stage. The 916-seat **Intermediate Theater,** which houses Portland Center Stage, a highly regarded resident theater company, is also part of the complex. The section of the street connecting the old and new buildings is sometimes blocked off for food fairs, art shows, and other events. ⊠ *S.W. Broadway and S.W. Main St., ☎ 503/796–9293.*

⓱ Portland/Oregon Visitors Association. You can pick up maps and literature about the city and the state at this agency inside World Trade Center Two. The three sleek, handsome World Trade Center buildings, designed by the Portland architectural firm Zimmer Gunsel Frasca, are connected by sky bridges. Retail stores, a restaurant, coffee shops, banks, and travel agencies occupy the ground floors. ⊠ *26 S.W. Salmon St., ☎ 503/222–2223 or 800/345–3214. ☉ Weekdays 9–5, Sat. 9–4.*

❼ Portland State University. The state's only urban university takes advantage of downtown's South Park Blocks to provide trees and greenery for its 15,000 students. The compact campus, located between Market Street and I–405, spreads west from the Park Blocks to 12th Avenue and east to 5th Avenue. Seven schools offer undergraduate, master's, and doctoral degrees.

⓰ State of Oregon Sports Hall of Fame. This museum houses sports memorabilia associated with prominent Oregonian athletes and organizations such as Heisman Trophy winner Terry Baker, the Portland Trail Blazers professional basketball team, and baseball player Mickey Lolich, who pitched for the Detroit Tigers in three World Series. ⊠ *321 S.W. Salmon St., ☎ 503/227–7466. ☜ $3. ☉ Mon.–Sat. 10–3.*

❿ Terry Schrunk Plaza. A terraced amphitheater of green lawn and brick, shaded by flowering cherry trees, the plaza is a popular lunch spot for the office crowd. ✉ *Between S.W. 3rd and 4th Aves. and S.W. Madison and Jefferson Sts.*

★ **Yamhill National Historic District.** Many examples of 19th-century cast-iron architecture have been preserved within this district's six square blocks. Because the cast-iron facade helped support the main structure, these buildings traditionally did not need big, heavy walls to bear the weight; the interior spaces could therefore be larger and more open. North and west of this area, along 2nd Avenue, galleries exhibit fine art, ceramics, photography, and posters. On the first Thursday of each month, new shows are unveiled and most galleries stay open until 9 PM. Call the Portland Art Museum at 503/226–2811 for details. ✉ *Between S.W. Naito Pkwy. and S.W. 3rd Ave. and S.W. Morrison and S.W. Taylor Sts.*

NEED A BREAK?	The **Rock Bottom Brewing Co.** (✉ 210 S.W. Morrison St., at S.W. 2nd Ave., ☎ 503/796–2739) is one of the ritzier examples of that authentically Portland experience, the brew pub. Have a pint of ale—brewed on the premises, of course—and sample the fine pub foods and snacks.

The Skidmore District and Chinatown

The Skidmore Old Town National Historic District, commonly called the Skidmore District or Old Town, is where Portland was born. The 20-square-block section, bounded by Oak Street to the south and Everett Street to the north, includes buildings of varying ages and architectural designs. Before it was renovated, this was skid row, and vestiges of that condition remain. The area is easily accessible from downtown via the MAX light-rail system.

Numbers in the text correspond to numbers in the margin and on the Downtown Portland map.

A Good Walk

Begin on Southwest Naito Parkway at the **Oregon Maritime Center and Museum** ⑲. Across Southwest Ash Street at the far northern corner of the Central Fire Station is the **Jeff Morris Memorial Fire Museum** ⑳. **Skidmore Fountain** ㉑, the centerpiece of Ankeny Square, is adjacent to the museum. West of the fountain at 2nd Avenue is the New Market Theater, which houses the **American Advertising Museum** ㉒. On Saturdays and Sundays this area is home to the **Portland Saturday Market** ㉓. Walk north one block on Naito Parkway past the Burnside Bridge to the **Japanese-American Historical Plaza** ㉔. Walk west on Burnside Street to Northwest 4th Avenue and the **Chinatown Gate** ㉕, the official entrance to the **Chinatown District.**

TIMING

Sights in the Skidmore District and Chinatown can be easily seen in an hour or less. Add a half hour if you're interested in the American Advertising Museum. It's best to do this walk during daylight hours because the street scene here can be intimidating.

Sights to See

㉒ American Advertising Museum. The New Market Theatre, a grand brick-and-cast-iron building that was Portland's first opera house when it was completed in 1872, houses this museum devoted exclusively to advertising. Exhibits celebrate memorable campaigns, print advertisements, radio and TV commercials, and novelty and specialty products. ✉ *50*

S.W. 2nd Ave., ☎ *503/226–0000.* 🖻 *$3.* ☉ *Wed.–Sat. 11–5, Sun. noon–5.*

㉕ Chinatown Gate. Recognizable by its five roofs, 64 dragons, and two huge lions, the Chinatown Gate is the official entrance to the **Chinatown District.** During the 1890s, Portland had the second-largest Chinese community in the United States. Today's Chinatown is compressed into several blocks with restaurants (though many locals prefer Chinese eateries outside the district), shops, and grocery stores. ⊠ *N.W. 4th Ave. and Burnside St.*

㉔ Japanese-American Historical Plaza. Take a moment to study the evocative figures cast into the bronze columns at the plaza's entrance; they show Japanese-Americans before, during, and after World War II—living daily life, fighting in battle for the United States, marching off to internment camps. More than 110,000 Japanese-Americans were interned by the American government during the war. This park, an oasis of meticulous landscaping and flowering cherry trees, was created to commemorate their experience and contributions. Simple blocks of granite carved with haiku poems describing the war experience powerfully evoke this dark episode in American history. ⊠ *East of Naito Pkwy. between W. Burnside and N.W. Couch Sts.*

㉒ Jeff Morris Memorial Fire Museum. This is not a museum you enter: The antique horse-drawn pumps and other fire-fighting equipment on display are visible through large plate-glass windows on the north side of the Central Fire Station building. Cast-iron medallions, capitals, and grillwork taken from other buildings decorate the wall; cast-iron columns mark the border of Ankeny Square, beside the museum. ⊠ *111 S.W. Naito Pkwy.*

㉑ Oregon Maritime Center and Museum. Local model makers created most of this museum's models of ships that plied the Columbia River. Prime street-level examples of cast-iron architecture grace the building's exterior. The admission fee includes entrance aboard the last operating stern-wheel steam tug in the United States, which is docked across the street. ⊠ *113 S.W. Naito Pkwy.,* ☎ *503/224–7724.* 🖻 *$4.* ☉ *Memorial Day–Labor Day, Fri.–Sun. 11–4; Labor Day–Memorial Day, Thurs.–Sun. 11–4.*

★ ㉓ Portland Saturday Market. On Saturday and Sunday from March to Christmas, the west side of the Burnside Bridge and the Skidmore Fountain environs is home to North America's largest open-air handicraft market. This is not upscale shopping by any means, but if you're looking for crystals, yard goods, beaded hats, stained glass, birdhouses, jewelry, flags, wood and rubber stamps, or custom footwear and decorative boots, you stand a good chance of finding them. Entertainers and food and produce booths add to the festive atmosphere. ⊠ *Under west end of the Burnside Bridge, from S.W. Naito Pkwy. to Ankeny Sq.,* ☎ *503/222–6072.* ☉ *Mar.–Dec., Sat. 10–5, Sun. 11–4:30.*

㉑ Skidmore Fountain. This unusually graceful fountain built in 1888 is the centerpiece of **Ankeny Square,** a plaza around which many community activities take place. Two nymphs uphold the brimming basin on top; citizens once quenched their thirst from the spouting lions' heads below, and horses drank from the granite troughs at the base of the fountain. ⊠ *S.W. Ankeny St. at S.W. Naito Pkwy.*

NEED A   For a break from sightseeing and shopping, settle into cool, dark **Kell's**
BREAK?   **Irish Restaurant & Pub** (⊠ 112 S.W. 2nd Ave., between S.W. Ash and

S.W. Pine Sts., ☎ 503/227–4057) for a pint of Guinness and authentic Irish pub fare—and be sure to ask the bartender how all those folded-up dollar bills got stuck to the ceiling.

Nob Hill and Vicinity

The showiest example of Portland's newly acquired urban chic is Northwest 23rd Avenue, a 20-block thoroughfare that cuts north–south through the neighborhood known as Nob Hill. Fashionable since the 1880s and still filled with Victorian residential architecture, the neighborhood is a mixed-use cornucopia of old Portland charm and new Portland trendiness. With its cafés, restaurants, galleries, and boutiques, it's a delightful place to stroll, shop, and people-watch.

Numbers in the text correspond to numbers in the margin and on the Nob Hill/Northwest 23rd Avenue map.

Two Good Walks

Northwest 23rd Avenue between West Burnside Street and Northwest Lovejoy Street—the east–west-running streets are in alphabetical order—is the heart of Nob Hill. There's such a profusion of coffee bars and cafés along the avenue that some locals call it Latte-land Central. The **Pettygrove House** ㉖, a Victorian gingerbread on the corner of 23rd Avenue and Pettygrove Street, was built by the man who gave Portland its name. Continue on 23rd Avenue past Pettygrove to Quimby Street to reach the **Clear Creek Distillery** ㉗.

There's much more to Nob Hill than Northwest 23rd Avenue, something you'll discover if you walk among the neighborhood's **Victorian residences** ㉘.

TIMING
Strolling along 23rd Avenue from Burnside Street to Pettygrove Street can take a half hour or half a day, depending on how many eateries or shops lure you in along the way. The tour of neighborhood Victorian residences can be done in about an hour.

Sights to See

㉗ **Clear Creek Distillery.** The distillery keeps such a low profile that it's practically invisible. But ring the bell and someone will unlock the wrought-iron gate and let you into a dim, quiet tasting room where you can sample Clear Creek's world-famous Oregon apple and pear brandies and grappas. ⊠ *1430 N.W. 23rd Ave.,* ☎ *503/248–9470.* ☉ *Weekdays 8–4:30 or by appointment.*

Northwest 23rd Avenue. You don't need a map of the avenue, just cash or credit cards. Some of the shops and restaurants are in newly designed quarters, and others are tucked into restored Victorian and other century-old homes and buildings. As it continues north past Lovejoy Street, the avenue begins to quiet down. Between Overton and Pettygrove streets, a block of open-porch frame houses converted into shops typifies the alternative, New Age side of Portland. **Clear Creek Distillery** (☞ *above*) is just before Quimby Street.

NEED A
BREAK?
You won't have any trouble finding a place to sit and caffeinate on Northwest 23rd. Two of Portland's largest coffee competitors, Coffee People and Starbucks, face each other on opposite sides of Hoyt Street. The best of the smaller cafés is **Torrefazione Italia** (⊠ 838 N.W. 23rd Ave., ☎ 503/228–1255), which exudes a bright Italian charm and serves delicious coffee (none of it flavored) in Deruta ceramic cups.

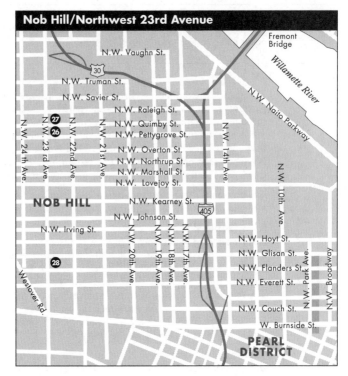

Nob Hill/Northwest 23rd Avenue

26 Pettygrove House. Back in 1845, after he'd bought much of what is now downtown Portland for $50, Francis Pettygrove and his partner, Asa Lovejoy, flipped a coin to decide who would name the still unbuilt city. Pettygrove won and chose Portland, after a town in his native Maine. His beautifully restored Victorian gingerbread house was built in 1892. ⊠ *2287 N.W. Pettygrove St.*

★ **28 Victorian residences.** Nob Hill's architectural heritage is amply evident in its Victorian-era homes. Most of the structures in the following tour are private residences and do not have identifying plaques.

Begin at 23rd Avenue and Flanders Street. The 1891 **Trevett-Nunn House** (⊠ 2347 N.W. Flanders St.), an excellent example of the Colonial Revival style, is the oldest extant residence designed by Whidden and Lewis, Portland's most distinguished architectural firm in the late 19th century. Continue east to the 1907 **Day Building** (⊠ 2068 N.W. Flanders St.), another example of the Colonial Revival style. The front facade of this apartment building has large, fluted columns rising more than 30 ft to ornate Corinthian capitals. Farther east is **Temple Beth Israel** (⊠ 1931 N.W. Flanders St.), which serves a congregation first organized in 1858. The imposing sandstone, brick, and stone structure with a massive domed roof and Byzantine styling was completed in 1928.

At Flanders and 17th Avenue head north (to the left) to Irving Street. The **Campbell Townhouses** (⊠ 1705–1719 N.W. Irving St.) are the only known example of brick row-house construction in Oregon. These six attached buildings with Queen Anne–style detailing, reminiscent of row houses in San Francisco and along the East Coast, have undergone virtually no structural modification since they were built in 1893. Continue west on Irving and north (to the right) on 18th Avenue to the **Ayer-Shea House** (⊠ 1809 N.W. Johnson St.), an elegant Colonial Revival house that was built in 1892 by Whidden and Lewis, who also designed Portland's City Hall.

Heading west on Johnson Street you'll pass the Italianate-style **Sprague-Marshall-Bowie House** (⊠ 2234 N.W. Johnson St.), built in 1882. A few doors away is the 1893 **Albert Tanner House** (⊠ 2248 N.W. Johnson St.), a rare Stick-style residence with a wraparound porch and richly decorated front gables. The 2½-story **Mary Smith House** (⊠ 2256 N.W. Johnson St.), which dates from 1906, is an unusual variation on the otherwise ubiquitous Colonial Revival style. It has a central second-story bow window and a full-length veranda with a central bowed portico supported by Ionic columns.

At 22nd Avenue, turn south (left) to reach the **Nathan Loeb House** (⊠ 726 N.W. 22nd Ave.), a fine late-19th-century Queen Anne–style structure. One of the most ornate Victorians in Portland, the Loeb House has turned-wood posts, wood arches with central pendants and sunburst spandrel patterns, and a projecting ground-floor section with an ornamental three-bay round arch window.

Continue south on 22nd Avenue and turn east (left) on Hoyt Street to reach the **Joseph Bergman House** (⊠ 2134 N.W. Hoyt St.), a High Victorian Italianate–style home built in 1885. Head two blocks east to 20th Avenue and two blocks south (to the right) to reach the **George Huesner House** (⊠ 333 N.W. 20th Ave.), an example of the rare Shingle style that came into vogue in the 1890s. It was designed by Edgar Lazarus, architect of landmarks such as Vista House in the Columbia River Gorge.

Washington Park and Forest Park

Numbers in the text correspond to numbers in the margin and on the West of the Willamette River map.

A Good Tour

Head west of downtown on West Burnside Street and south (turn left) on Southwest Tichner Drive to reach 322-acre **Washington Park,** home to the **Hoyt Arboretum** ㉙, the **International Rose Test Garden** ㉚, and the **Japanese Garden** ㉛. By car, the **Metro Washington Park Zoo** ㉜ and the **World Forestry Center** ㉝ can best be reached by heading west on U.S. 26. North of the park is the opulent **Pittock Mansion** ㉞. Also north of Washington Park is **Forest Park** ㉟.

TIMING

You could easily spend a day at either Washington Park or Forest Park; plan on at least two hours at the zoo, an hour or more at the arboretum, rose garden, and Japanese Garden, and an hour to tour the Pittock Mansion and its grounds.

Sights to See

㉟ **Forest Park.** One of the nation's largest (5,000 acres) urban wildernesses, this city-owned oasis, home to more than 100 species of birds and 50 species of mammals, contains more than 50 mi of trails. The **Portland Audubon Society** (⊠ 5151 N.W. Cornell Rd., ☎ 503/292–6855) supplies free maps and sponsors a bevy of bird-related activities in the heart of the only old-growth forest in a major U.S. city. Programs include guided bird-watching events, a hospital for injured and orphaned birds, and a gift shop stocked with books, feeders, and bird-lovers' paraphernalia. ⊠ *Take N.W. Lovejoy St. west to where it becomes Cornell Rd. and follow to the park,* ☎ *503/823–4492.* *Free.* ☉ *Dawn–dusk.*

㉙ **Hoyt Arboretum.** Ten miles of trails wind through the arboretum, which has more than 800 species of plants and one of the nation's largest

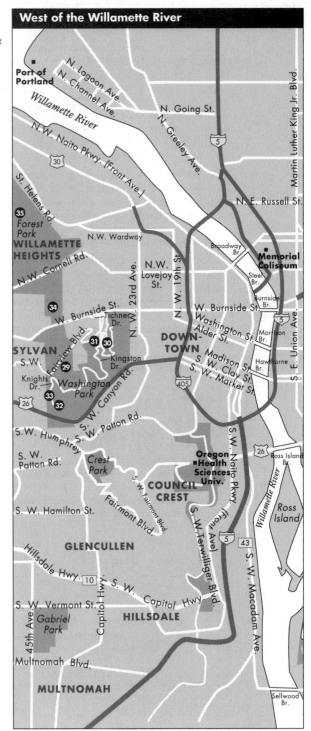

West of the Willamette River

collections of coniferous trees; pick up trail maps at the visitor center. Also here are the Winter Garden and a memorial to veterans of the Vietnam War. ⊠ *4000 S.W. Fairview Blvd.,* ☎ *503/228–8733.* 💷 *Free.* ⊙ *Arboretum daily dawn–dusk, visitor center most days 9–4.*

★ ㉚ **International Rose Test Garden.** Despite the name, these grounds are not an experimental greenhouse laboratory but three breathtaking terraced gardens, set on 4 acres, where 10,000 bushes and 400 varieties of roses grow. The flowers, many of them new varieties, are at their peak in June and July and September and October. From the gardens, there are highly photogenic views of the downtown skyline and, on fine days, the Fuji-shaped slopes of Mount Hood, 50 mi to the east. Summer concerts take place in the garden's amphitheater. ⊠ *400 S.W. Kingston Ave.,* ☎ *503/823–3636.* 💷 *Free.* ⊙ *Dawn–dusk.*

★ ㉛ **Japanese Garden.** The most authentic Japanese garden outside Japan is nestled among 5½ acres of Washington Park above the International Rose Test Garden. This serene oasis, designed by a Japanese landscape master and opened to the public in 1967, represents five separate garden styles: Strolling Pond Garden, Tea Garden, Natural Garden, Sand and Stone Garden, and Flat Garden. The Tea House was built in Japan and reconstructed here. The west side of the Pavilion has a majestic view of Portland and Mount Hood. ⊠ *611 S.W. Kingston Ave.,* ☎ *503/ 223–4070.* 💷 *$5.* ⊙ *Apr.–May and Sept., daily 10–6; June–Aug., daily 9–8; Oct.–Mar., daily 10–4.*

⊙ ㉜ **Metro Washington Park Zoo.** The zoo, which was established in 1887, has been a prolific breeding ground for Asian elephants. Major exhibits include an African section with rhinos, hippos, zebras, and pythons, plus an aviary with 15 species of birds. Other popular attractions include an Alaska Tundra exhibit, a penguinarium, and habitats for beavers, otters, and reptiles native to the west side of the Cascade Range. During the summer a 4-mi round-trip narrow-gauge train ($2.50) operates from the zoo to the International Rose Test Garden and the Japanese Garden. ⊠ *4001 S.W. Canyon Rd.,* ☎ *503/226–7627.* 💷 *$5.50; free 2nd Tues. of month after 3 PM.* ⊙ *Labor Day–Memorial Day, daily 9:30–6; Memorial Day–Labor Day, daily 9:30–4.*

★ ㉞ **Pittock Mansion.** Henry Pittock, the founder and publisher of the *Oregonian* newspaper, built this mansion, which combines French Renaissance and Victorian styles. The opulent manor, erected in 1914, is filled with art and antiques of the 1880s. The grounds, north of Washington Park and 1,000 ft above the city, have superb views of the skyline, rivers, and Cascade Range. ⊠ *3229 N.W. Pittock Dr.; from W. Burnside St. heading west, turn right on N.W. Barnes Rd. and follow signs,* ☎ *503/823–3624.* 💷 *$4.25.* ⊙ *Daily noon–4.*

⊙ ㉝ **World Forestry Center.** The center, across from the Metro Washington Park Zoo, takes its arboreal interests seriously—its spokesperson is a 70-ft-tall talking tree! Outside, a 1909 locomotive and antique logging equipment are displayed, and inside are two floors of exhibits, a multi-image "Forests of the World," a collection of 100-year-old wood, and a gift shop. ⊠ *4033 S.W. Canyon Rd.,* ☎ *503/228–1367.* 💷 *$3.* ⊙ *Memorial Day–Labor Day, daily 9–5; Labor Day–Memorial Day, daily 10–5.*

East of the Willamette River

Portland is known as the City of Roses, but the 10 distinctive bridges spanning the Willamette River have also earned it the name Bridgetown. The older drawbridges, near downtown, open several times a day to allow passage of large cargo ships and freighters.

Numbers in the text correspond to numbers in the margin and on the East of the Willamette River map.

A Good Tour

Most people visit Portland's east-side destinations separately, and by car rather than public transportation. **Laurelhurst Park** ㊱ is a stately enclave. The busy **Southeast Hawthorne Boulevard** corridor and the **Sellwood** neighborhood have interesting shopping areas. There are fewer tourist attractions per se, but **Mount Tabor Park** ㊲ and the **Crystal Springs Rhododendron Garden** ㊳ are worth exploring. Children usually enjoy the **Oregon Museum of Science and Industry** ㊴ and **Oaks Amusement Park** ㊵.

TIMING

You could spend a pleasant hour or so strolling each of the parks, gardens, and neighborhoods here. Plan to spend one to two hours at the Museum of Science and Industry or the amusement park.

Sights to See

㊳ **Crystal Springs Rhododendron Garden.** For much of the year this 7-acre retreat near Reed College is used by bird-watchers and those who want a restful stroll. But starting in April, thousands of rhododendron bushes and azaleas burst into flower. The peak blooming season for these woody shrubs is May; by late June the show is over. ⊠ *S.E. 28th Ave. (west side, 1 block north of Woodstock Blvd.),* ☎ *503/777–1734.* ☞ *$2 Mar.–Labor Day, Thurs.–Mon.; otherwise free.* ☉ *Daily dawn–dusk.*

㊱ **Laurelhurst Park.** Manicured lawns, stately trees, and a wildfowl pond make this 25-acre, southeast Portland park a favorite urban hangout. **Laurelhurst,** one of the city's most beautiful neighborhoods, surrounds the park. ⊠ *S.E. 39th Ave. between S.E. Ankeny and Oak Sts.* ☉ *Daily dawn–dusk.*

㊲ **Mount Tabor Park.** Dirt trails and an asphalt road wind through forested hillsides and past good picnic areas to the top of Mount Tabor, which looks out toward Portland's West Hills. Mount Tabor is an extinct volcano; the buttes and conical hills east of the park are evidence of the gigantic eruptions that formed the Cascade Range millions of years ago. ⊠ *S.E. 60th Ave. and Salmon St.*

☾ ㊵ **Oaks Amusement Park.** It may not be Disneyland, but there's a small-town charm to this park with thrill rides and miniature golf in summer and roller-skating year-round. Also in the park is the **Ladybug Theater** (☎ 503/232–2346), which presents shows for children. ⊠ *S.E. Spokane St. east of the Willamette River (from east side of Sellwood Bridge, take Grand Ave. north and Spokane west),* ☎ *503/233–5777.* ☞ *Park free, rides extra.* ☉ *Memorial Day–Labor Day, Tues.–Sun. noon–5; Labor Day–Oct., weekends noon–5.*

★ ☾ ㊴ **Oregon Museum of Science and Industry** (OMSI). An Omnimax theater and planetarium are among the main attractions at the Northwest's largest astronomy educational facility, which also has a hands-on computer center, a space wing with a mission-control center, and many permanent and touring scientific exhibits. Moored in the Willamette as part of the museum is a 240-ft submarine, the USS *Bluebook.* ⊠ *1945 S.E. Water Ave., south of the Morrison Bridge,* ☎ *503/797–4000.* ☞ *Museum and planetarium $6; Omnimax $5.50; USS Bluebook $3.50.* ☉ *Memorial Day–Labor Day, daily 9:30–7 (Thurs. until 8); Labor Day–Memorial Day, daily 9:30–5:30 (Thurs. until 8).*

Sellwood. The browsable neighborhood that begins just east of the Sellwood Bridge was once a separate town. Annexed by Portland in the

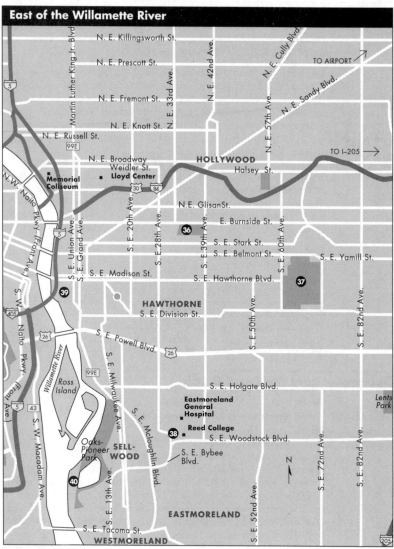

East of the Willamette River

Crystal Springs
Rhododendron
Garden, **38**

Laurelhurst Park, **36**

Mount Tabor
Park, **37**

Oaks Amusement
Park, **40**

Oregon Museum
of Science
and Industry, **39**

1890s, it retains a modest charm. On weekends the antiques stores along 13th Avenue do a brisk business. Each store is identified by a plaque that tells the date of construction and what the building was originally used for. ⊠ *S.E. 13th Ave. between Malden and Clatsop Sts.*

Southeast Hawthorne Boulevard. Though it's quickly becoming more upscale, this neighborhood with bookstores, coffeehouses, taverns, restaurants, antiques stores, and boutiques still has a countercultural feel. ⊠ *S.E. Hawthorne Blvd. between 30th and 42nd Aves.*

DINING

First-time visitors to Portland are often surprised by the diversity of restaurants and the low prices. Lovers of ethnic foods can choose from restaurants serving French, Indian, Italian, Japanese, Middle Eastern, Tex-Mex, Thai, and Vietnamese specialties. There's also Pacific Northwest cuisine, an emerging style that incorporates regional fish and game plus locally grown wild mushrooms and other produce.

Restaurants are arranged first by neighborhood and then by type of cuisine served.

CATEGORY	COST*
$$$$	over $35
$$$	$25–$35
$$	$15–$25
$	under $15

per person for a three-course meal, excluding drinks and service

Downtown and the Pearl District

American

$$–$$$ ✕ **Red Star Tavern & Roast House.** Cooked in a wood-burning oven, smoker, rotisserie, or grill, the cuisine at Red Star can best be described as American comfort food inspired by the bounty of the Northwest. Spit-roasted leg of lamb, maple-fired baby back ribs with a brown-ale glaze, and charred salmon with fennel sausage and Manila clams are some of the better entrées. The wine list includes regional and international vintages, and 12 local microbrews are on tap. The spacious restaurant, part of the Fifth Avenue Suites Hotel, has a lodge-style ambience, with tufted leather booths, murals, and copper accents. ⊠ *503 S.W. Alder St.,* ☎ *503/222–0005. AE, D, DC, MC, V.*

$ ✕ **Bridgeport Brew Pub.** The only food on the menu here is thick, hand-thrown pizza on sourdough beer-wort crust, served inside a cool, ivy-covered, century-old industrial building. The boisterous crowds wash down the pizza with frothing pints of Bridgeport's English-style ale, brewed on the premises. During the summer, the flower-festooned loading dock is transformed into a beer garden. ⊠ *1313 N.W. Marshall St.,* ☎ *503/241–7179. MC, V.*

$ ✕ **Pizzicato.** This local chain serves up gourmet pizzas topped by inventive combinations such as red potato and prosciutto. The restaurant interiors are clean, bright, and modern. Beer and wine are available. ⊠ *705 S.W. Alder St.,* ☎ *503/226–1007;* ⊠ *505 N.W. 23rd Ave.,* ☎ *503/242–0023. AE, MC. V.*

Eclectic

$$–$$$ ✕ **Bima Restaurant and Bar.** A restored warehouse in the artsy Pearl District contains one of the city's most popular restaurants and bars. The cuisine takes its cue from the gulf coast of Mexico, the southern United States, and the Caribbean. Pecan-crusted catfish, assorted fish and meat skewers, fish tacos, and luscious ribs are some of the spe-

cialties. There's a bar menu as well. ⊠ *1338 N.W. Hoyt St.,* ☎ *503/ 241–3465. AE, MC, V. Closed Sun.*

Greek

$–$$ ✕ **Alexis.** The Mediterranean decor here consists only of white walls and basic furnishings, but the authentic Greek flavor keeps the crowds coming for *kalamarakia* (deep-fried squid served with *tzatziki,* a yogurt dip), *horiatiki* (a Greek salad combination with feta cheese and Kalamata olives), and other traditional dishes. If you have trouble making up your mind, the gigantic Alexis platter includes a little of everything. ⊠ *215 W. Burnside St.,* ☎ *503/224–8577. AE, D, DC, MC, V. No lunch on weekends.*

Italian

$$–$$$ ✕ **Pazzo.** The aromas of roasted garlic and wood smoke greet patrons of the bustling, street-level dining room of the Hotel Vintage Plaza. Pazzo's frequently changing menu relies on deceptively simple new Italian cuisine—pastas, risottos, and grilled meats, fish, and poultry. Try the lamb chops with fennel and the artichoke risotto if they're being prepared. The decor is a mix of dark wood, terra-cotta, checkered tablecloths, and dangling Parma hams. ⊠ *422 S.W. Broadway,* ☎ *503/228– 1515. Reservations essential. AE, D, DC, MC, V.*

Japanese

$$$–$$$$ ✕ **Murata.** It's tiny and the prices are steep, but Murata has the finest sushi in town. *Uni* (sea urchin), *hamachi* (yellowtail tuna), *saba* (mackerel), *aji* (Spanish mackerel), and *kasu* (cod) are all outstanding. Reserve a day ahead for *kaiseki,* several courses assembled by the chef. ⊠ *200 S.W. Market St.,* ☎ *503/227–0080. AE, MC, V. Closed Sun. No lunch Sat.*

Lebanese

$ ✕ **Abou Karim.** More than half the menu is vegetarian, but the leg of lamb served on a bed of rice with lentil soup or a full salad is a favorite here. Health-conscious diners will find a special menu of meals low in saturated fats, and there is an outside area for dining in summer. A few plants and a Lebanese sword or two hanging on the wall are the only nods to atmosphere. ⊠ *221 S.W. Pine St.,* ☎ *503/223–5058. AE, D, MC, V. Closed Sun.*

Pacific Northwest

$$$$ ✕ **Atwater's.** Perched on the 30th floor of the U.S. Bancorp Tower, Atwater's has an outstanding view of the Willamette River, the Cascade Range, and the city's skyline. The cuisine is American but relies almost exclusively on ingredients indigenous to the Northwest—depending on the season everything from fresh seafood (ahi, Pacific salmon, Dungeness crab, sturgeon) to chicken and game. An 18,000-bottle enclosed "wine cellar" with labels from every wine-producing region in the world is a prominent feature of the dining room. Dansk linens, silver cutlery, crystal glasses, and an orchid on every table lend a touch of elegance. Musicians perform in the adjoining bar from Wednesday to Saturday. ⊠ *111 S.W. 5th Ave.,* ☎ *503/275–3600. Reservations essential. AE, D, DC, MC, V. No lunch.*

$$$ ✕ **Esplanade at RiverPlace.** Tall windows frame a view of the sailboat-filled marina and the Willamette River, providing a dramatic backdrop to this restaurant in the RiverPlace Hotel. The cuisine is gourmet Northwest—Dungeness crab cakes; plump scallops seared with fennel, red onion, and oyster mushrooms; duck with blackberry sauce—and the wine list includes many hard-to-find Northwest vintages. ⊠ *1510 S.W. Harbor Way,* ☎ *503/228–3233. Reservations essential. AE, D, DC, MC, V. No lunch Sat.*

34

Portland Dining

N.E. Graham St.

N.E. Graham St.

N.E. Knott St.

N.E. Russell St.

N.E. Thompson St

N.E. Thompson St.

N.E. 15th Ave.

I-5

N.E. Vancouver Ave.

N.E. 9th Ave.

E. River St.

N.E. Union Ave.

N.E. Hancock St

N.E. Hancock St.

N.E. Wheeler Ave.

N.E. Schuyler St.

24

N.E. Broadway

Parkway

Broadway
Bridge

**Memorial
Coliseum**

N.E. 2nd Ave.

N.E. Weidler St.

LLOYD DISTRICT

N.E. Halsey St.

N.E. Halsey St.

N.E. Wasco St.

Lloyd Center

N.E. Multnomah St.

**OLD
TOWN**

Steel
Bridge

N.E. 1st Ave.

N.E. Holladay St.

**Oregon
Convention
Center**

N.E. Lloyd Blvd.

I-84

N.E. Glisan St.

N.W. Park Ave.

N.W. Broadway

N.W. 6th Ave.

N.W. 5th Ave.

N.W. 4th Ave.

N.W. 3rd Ave.

N.E. Everett St.

26

27

N.W. Davis St.

Chinatown Gate

Burnside
Bridge

E. Burnside St.

N.E. Sandy Blvd.

W. Burnside St.

19

18 S.W. Ankeny St.

S.W. Ankeny St.

28

S.W. Pine St.

S.W.
Ash St.

20

S.E. Ash St.

S.W. Oak St.

21

S.W. Stark St.

S.E. 11th Ave.

S.E. 12th Ave.

S.E. 14th Ave.

S.E. 15th Ave.

13

S.W. Washington St.

S.W. 1st Ave.

Tom McCall
Waterfront
Park

99E 99E

S.E. Stark St.

14

S.W. Alder St.

Morrison
Bridge

S.E. Washington St.

W. Yamhill St.

S.W. 3rd Ave.

S.W. 2nd Ave.

S.E. 7th Ave.

S.E. 8th Ave.

Main St.

25

S.E. Union Ave.

S.E. Grand Ave.

S.E. Belmont St.

Madison St.

S.W. Naito Parkway (Front Ave.)

Willamette River

S.E. Water Ave.

S.E. 1st Ave.

S.E. 2nd Ave.

S.E. 3rd Ave.

29

efferson St.

lumbia St.

S.E. Main St.

30

y St.

S.E. Madison St.

TO
**HAWTHORNE
DISTRICT**

ket St.

17

22

Hawthorne
Bridge

S.E. Hawthorne Blvd.

S.E. Clay St.

S.W. 1st Ave.

S.W. Harbor Way

I-5

St.

23

S.E. Market St.

31

$$$ ✕ **The Heathman.** Chef Philippe Boulot, the French-trained former head
★   chef at New York's Mark Hotel, revels in the fresh fish, game, wild
mushrooms, and other ingredients of the Northwest. His menu changes
with the season and may include seared ahi tuna wrapped in locally
cured prosciutto and served with Oregon-truffle risotto; Normandy-
style braised rabbit in apple cider and mustard sauce, served with sage
white-wine gnocchi; or roasted pesto salmon with red onion–caper rel-
ish. The dining room, scented with wood smoke and adorned with Andy
Warhol prints, is a favorite for special occasions. ⊠ *Heathman Hotel,
1001 S.W. Broadway,* ☎ *503/241–4100. AE, D, DC, MC, V.*

Seafood

$$ ✕ **Jake's Famous Crawfish.** Diners have been enjoying fresh Northwest seafood in Jake's warren of wood-paneled dining rooms for more
than a century—the back bar came around Cape Horn during the 1880s,
and the chandeliers hanging from the high ceilings date from 1881. But
it wasn't until 1920, when crawfish was added to the menu, that the
restaurant began to get a national reputation. White-coated waiters can
take your order from a lengthy sheet of daily seafood specials year-
round, but try to come during crawfish season, from May to September, when you can sample the tasty crustacean in pie, cooked Creole
style, or in a Cajun-style stew over rice. ⊠ *401 S.W. 12th Ave.,* ☎ *503/
226–1419. AE, D, DC, MC, V. No lunch on weekends.*

$$ ✕ **Newport Bay at RiverPlace.** When it comes to river, bridge, and city-
skyline views, there's not a bad seat in this circular glass dining room
that literally floats on the Willamette River. Newport Bay seeks out
whatever is in season worldwide, which might include Oregon spring
salmon, Maine lobster, Australian lobster tail, Alaskan halibut, stur-
geon, or New Zealand roughy, as well as swordfish, marlin, and shark.
⊠ *RiverPlace, 0425 S.W. Montgomery St.,* ☎ *503/227–3474. AE, D,
DC, MC, V.*

$ ✕ **Dan & Louis's Oyster Bar.** Oysters here come fried, stewed, or on
the half shell. Crab stew—virtually impossible to find elsewhere in
town—is also a specialty. Founder Louis Wachsmuth, who started his
restaurant in 1907, was an avid collector of steins, plates, and marine
art. The collection has grown over the years to fill beams, nooks, cran-
nies, and nearly every inch of wall. ⊠ *208 S.W. Ankeny St.,* ☎ *503/
227–5906. AE, D, DC, MC, V.*

Nob Hill and Vicinity

American

$$–$$$ ✕ **The Ringside.** If you're in the mood for a juicy steak, head for this
Portland institution without further ado. There are other things on the
menu, but the Ringside has been famous for beef for more than 50 years.
The onion rings, made with Walla Walla sweets, are equally renowned.
⊠ *2165 N.W. Burnside St.,* ☎ *503/223–1513. Reservations essential.
AE, D, DC, MC, V. No lunch.*

$ ✕ **Kornblatt's.** Come to Kornblatt's for the best bagel in Portland. The
decor at this kosher deli is reminiscent of a 1950s diner; the fresh-cooked
pastrami, corned beef, and tongue are lean and tender, and the home-
smoked salmon and sablefish are simply the best. For breakfast, try
the poached eggs with spicy corned-beef hash. ⊠ *628 N.W. 23rd Ave.,*
☎ *503/242–0055. Reservations not accepted. MC, V.*

Eclectic

$$$–$$$$ ✕ **Zefiro.** Blond floors, pale green walls, lots of windows, and archi-
★   tectural lighting fixtures set the mood at Zefiro, where clarity and at-
tractive detail are the thematic touchstones of the dining room and
kitchen. The ever-changing menu combines Southeast Asian and

Mediterranean elements with gratifying results. Try the oysters with Thai sauce or any of the grilled fish dishes; the Caesar salad is justly popular. This is a place to see and be seen. ⊠ *500 N.W. 21st Ave.,* ☎ *503/226–3394. Reservations essential. AE, DC, MC, V. Closed Sun. No lunch Sat.*

$$ ✕ **Papa Haydn.** Many patrons come here just for the luscious desserts, but this corner restaurant also makes a convenient lunch or dinner stop. Top sandwiches include Gruyère cheese and Black Forest ham grilled on rustic Italian bread and the mesquite-grilled chicken breast on a roll with bacon, avocado, basil, and tomato. Favorite dinner entrées are the Bresola filet mignon and the pan-seared pork medallions with a pear-tarragon demi-glace. More versions of meat, fish, and poultry, grilled or cooked on a rotisserie, are available next door at the trendy Jo Bar. ⊠ *701 N.W. 23rd Ave.,* ☎ *503/228–7317. Reservations essential for Sun. brunch. AE, MC, V.*

French

$$$–$$$$ ✕ **Couvron.** Casual yet elegant Couvron is Portland's finest restaurant
★ for contemporary French cuisine. Chef Anthony Demes's signature dishes include a honey-glazed Oregon duck breast with curry and anise, a pan-roasted foie gras with summer truffles and diced organic root vegetables in a red wine sauce, a thyme-roasted Alaskan halibut, and sautéed salmon mignon on a chiffonade potato cake with stewed leeks. The Grand Marnier soufflé is otherworldly. ⊠ *1126 S.W. 18th Ave.,* ☎ *503/ 225–1844. Reservations essential. AE, MC, V. Closed Sun.–Mon. No lunch.*

Indian

$$ ✕ **Plainfield's Mayur.** Portland's finest Indian cuisine is served in a Victorian house amid quietly elegant surroundings. The tomato-curry soup and vegetarian dishes such as *dahi wadi* (crispy fried lentil croquettes) and basmati rice *biryani* (with silverleaf) are popular. Other specialties include lobster in brown onion sauce and lamb shanks in sandalwood sauce. For bread, try the garlic nan. This is one of the few Indian restaurants in North America to win an award from *Wine Spectator.* ⊠ *852 S.W. 21st Ave.,* ☎ *503/223–2995. AE, D, DC, MC, V. No lunch.*

Italian

$$ ✕ **Bastas.** Whoever thought a former Tastee-Freeze could be converted into an Italian restaurant with such stylish results? The walls at Bastas are painted with Italian earth shades and there's a small side garden for alfresco dining in good weather. The menu, drawn from all over Italy, includes pasta, fish, and meat dishes. ⊠ *410 N.W. 21st Ave.,* ☎ *503/274–1572. AE, MC, V.*

Vietnamese/Thai

$ ✕ **Misohapi.** For the price you can't beat Misohapi. The interior is hip
★ tongue-in-chic '90s modern with pastel walls, white fabric clouds supported by stainless-steel rods, and unusual lighting fixtures. The food is a mixture of Thai and Vietnamese with a sushi bar thrown in for good measure. Try the hot-and-sour seafood soup, the lemongrass seafood dish, or the peanutty pad thai noodles with shrimp. ⊠ *1123 N.W. 23rd Ave.,* ☎ *503/796–2012. MC, V. Closed Sun.*

East of the Willamette

Cajun

$ ✕ **Montage.** Spicy Cajun is the jumping-off point for the chef at this sassy bistro under the Morrison Bridge on Portland's east side. Jambalayas, blackened pork and catfish, hoppin' John, rabbit sausage, and old-fashioned macaroni dishes are served up from around noon till the wee hours in an atmosphere that's loud, crowded, and casually hip. ⊠ *301 S.E. Morrison St., ☎ 503/234–1324. Reservations not accepted. No credit cards. No lunch on weekends.*

Eclectic

$$ ✕ **Indigene.** Chef-owner Millie Howe wows regulars with her unique cuisine, which draws on the flavors of India, Latin America, Indonesia, and Europe. Depending on the season, diners may encounter rabbit with mustard, fresh rosemary, cream, and green peppercorns; fresh razor clams seared in butter and garlic; or a four-course Indian feast with fresh homemade chutneys. This intimate restaurant, accented with flowers and natural wood, has a pleasingly spare look. The small garden deck out back is a great place for a romantic dinner on a summer evening. ⊠ *3723 S.E. Division St., ☎ 503/238–1470. Reservations essential. MC, V. Closed Mon. No lunch (except Sun. brunch).*

Italian

$–$$ ✕ **Assaggio.** In an age of canned music it's pleasant to enter a restau-
★ rant and hear Maria Callas singing opera arias. But, then, everything about this Sellwood trattoria (food, decor, price) is extraordinarily pleasant. The Italian cooking is perhaps the most authentic in Portland, and many dishes are available as family-style samplers. Farfalle, fusilli, penne, and spaghetti dishes are properly cooked al dente and not overly sauced. For starters try the salad sampler or any of the *bruschette* (grilled garlic bread with various toppings). An excellent wine cellar favors Italian vintages. The interior, painted in a burnt-sienna shade and accented with classical architectural motifs, lovingly evokes Italy. ⊠ *7742 S.E. 13th Ave., ☎ 503/232–6151. MC, V. Closed Sun.–Mon. No lunch.*

Japanese

$$ ✕ **Hokkaido Japanese Cuisine and Sushi Bar.** The soothing sound of water flowing through a rock fountain greets diners at this restaurant with very reasonable prices. The sushi and sashimi are impeccably fresh and show occasional flashes of inspiration. Try the spider roll, a whole soft-shell crab surrounded by seaweed, rice, and wasabi. ⊠ *6744 N.E. Sandy Blvd., ☎ 503/288–3731. MC, V. Closed Mon. No lunch Sun.*

Southwestern

$$ ✕ **Esparza's Tex-Mex Cafe.** Be prepared for south-of-the-border craziness at this beloved local eatery. Wild West kitsch festoons the walls, but it isn't any wilder than some of the entrées that emerge from chef-owner Joe Esparza's kitchen. Look for offerings like lean smoked-sirloin tacos—Esparza's is renowned for its smoked meats—and, for the truly adventurous diner, ostrich enchiladas. ⊠ *2725 S.E. Ankeny St., at S.E. 28th Ave., ☎ 503/234–7909. AE, MC, V. Closed Sun.–Mon.*

Thai

$ ✕ **Bangkok Kitchen.** Chef-owner Srichan Miller juggles the lime, cilantro, coconut milk, lemongrass, curry, and hot peppers of classic Thai cuisine with virtuosity. Pay no attention to the '60s diner decor, and be sure to try one of the noodle dishes—the tender rice-stick noodles with shrimp, egg, fresh mint, chilies, and coconut are memorable. Order your dishes mild or medium-hot unless you have an asbestos tongue, and don't forget the cold Singha beer. ⊠ *2534 S.E. Belmont St., ☎ 503/236–7349. No credit cards. Closed Sun.–Mon. No lunch Sat.*

Vietnamese

$ ✕ **Yen Ha.** The vibrant flavors of Vietnam find full expression at crowded Yen Ha. Superb rice-paper rolls—translucent cylinders filled with pungent bean threads, fresh mint, and shrimp, then dipped in peanut sauce—and wonderful noodle dishes are among the star attractions. ⊠ *6820 N.E. Sandy Blvd.,* ☎ *503/287–3698. MC, V.*

Vietnamese/Thai

$ ✕ **Saigon Kitchen.** Consistently good Vietnamese and Thai food and friendly service have made Saigon Kitchen a neighborhood favorite. Fried salted calamari and fiery chili noodles with prawns or chicken are delectable standouts on the wide-ranging menu. The decor is nononsense diner, but don't let that deter you. ⊠ *835 N.E. Broadway,* ☎ *503/281–3669. AE, D, MC, V.*

LODGING

Many of the elegant hotels near the city center and waterfront appeal because of their proximity to the city's attractions. The all-suites hotels in the southwest suburbs provide space without requiring you to give up the extras. Budget travelers will need to sacrifice convenience to the airport or downtown. Some establishments offer senior-citizen discounts and family plans.

CATEGORY	COST*
$$$$	over $170
$$$	$110–$170
$$	$60–$110
$	under $60

All prices are for a standard double room, excluding 9% room tax.

Downtown

$$$$ ⊞ **Benson Hotel.** Portland's grandest hotel was built in 1912. The hand-carved Russian Circassian walnut paneling and the Italian white-marble staircase are among the noteworthy design touches in the public areas. In the guest rooms expect to find small crystal chandeliers, inlaid mahogany doors, and the original ceilings. ⊠ *309 S.W. Broadway, 97205,* ☎ *503/228–2000 or 800/426–0670,* ℻ *503/226–4603. 287 rooms. 2 restaurants, bar, coffee shop, in-room modem lines, minibars, room service, exercise room, laundry service, concierge, airport shuttle, parking (fee). AE, D, DC, MC, V.*

$$$$ ⊞ **Governor Hotel.** With its mahogany walls and mural of Northwest
★ Indians fishing in Celilo Falls, the clubby lobby of the distinctive Governor sets the overall tone for the hotel's 1920s Arts and Crafts style. Painted in soothing earth tones, the guest rooms have large windows and whirlpool tubs; some have fireplaces and balconies. ⊠ *611 S.W. 10th Ave., 97205,* ☎ *503/224–3400 or 800/554–3456,* ℻ *503/241–2122. 100 rooms. 2 restaurants, bar, sports bar, in-room modem lines, minibars, no-smoking rooms, room service, indoor lap pool, sauna, steam room, aerobics, exercise room, health club, indoor track, video games, laundry service and dry cleaning, concierge, business services, meeting rooms, parking (fee). AE, D, DC, MC, V.*

$$$$ ⊞ **Heathman Hotel.** Superior service, an award-winning restaurant, a
★ central downtown location (adjoining the Performing Arts Center), and swank public areas have earned the Heathman its reputation for quality. From the teak-panel lobby hung with Warhol prints to the rosewood elevators and marble fireplaces, this hotel exudes refinement. The guest rooms are luxuriously comfortable, if not overly spacious, and the bathrooms have plenty of marble and mirrors. Afternoon tea is served in the high-ceiling Tea Court, which becomes a popular gathering spot in the evenings. ⊠ *1009 S.W. Broadway, 97205,* ☎ *503/241–4100 or 800/551–0011,* ℻ *503/790–7110. 151 rooms. Restaurant, 2 bars, in-room modem lines, minibars, no-smoking floor, room service, exer-*

40

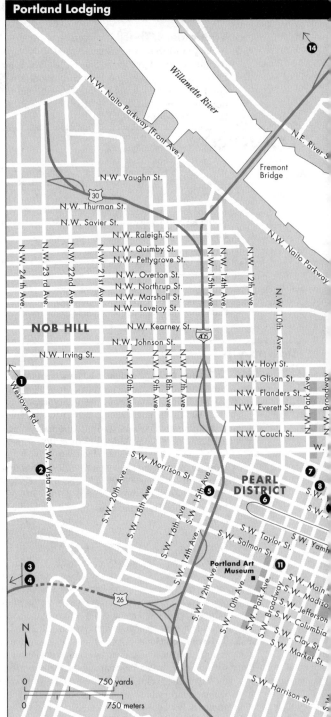

Portland Lodging

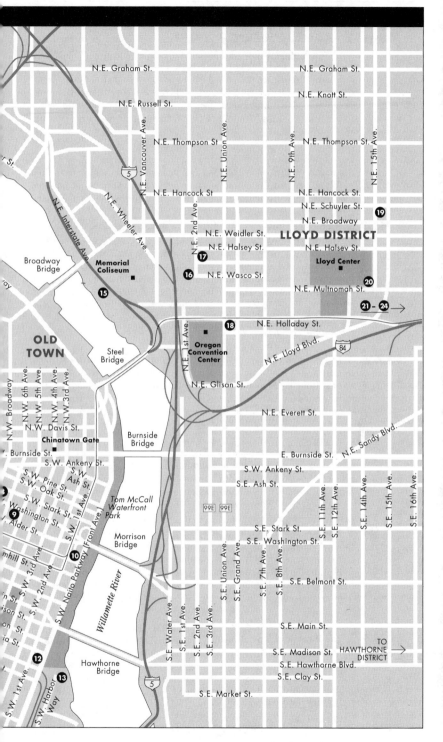

cise room, library, laundry service and dry cleaning, concierge, parking (fee). AE, D, DC, MC, V.

$$$$ ⚄ **Hotel Vintage Plaza.** This historic landmark takes its theme from the area's vineyards. Guests can fall asleep counting stars in top-floor rooms, where skylights and wall-to-wall conservatory-style windows rate highly among the special details. Hospitality suites have extra-large rooms with a full living area, and the deluxe rooms have a bar. All rooms are appointed in hunter green, deep plum, cerise, taupe, and gold; some rooms have hot tubs. Complimentary coffee and newspapers are available in the morning; wine is served in the evening, and an extensive collection of Oregon vintages is displayed in the tasting room. Two-story town-house suites are named after local wineries. ⊠ *422 S.W. Broadway, 97205,* ☎ *503/228–1212 or 800/243–0555,* ⅢX *503/228–3598. 107 rooms, 21 suites. Restaurant, piano bar, in-room modem lines, minibars, room service, exercise room, concierge, business services, meeting rooms, parking (fee). AE, D, DC, MC, V.*

$$$$ ⚄ **RiverPlace Hotel.** With its bright rooms, wing chairs, teak tables, and feather pillows, this hotel has the feeling of a private home. It has one of the best views in Portland, overlooking the river, the marina, and the city skyline. Amenities include a complimentary Continental breakfast, the morning newspaper, and valet parking in a locked garage. ⊠ *1510 S.W. Harbor Way, 97201,* ☎ *503/228–3233 or 800/227–1333,* ⅢX *503/295–6161. 39 rooms, 44 suites. 2 restaurants, bar, in-room modem lines, minibars, no-smoking rooms, room service, hot tub, sauna, concierge, business services, meeting rooms, parking (fee). AE, D, DC, MC, V.*

$$$–$$$$ ⚄ **Fifth Avenue Suites Hotel.** The 1912 Lipman Wolfe Department Store reopened as a boutique hotel in 1997. A tall vestibule with a marble mosaic floor leads to the art-filled lobby, where guests gather by the fireplace for an early-evening glass of wine or a complimentary Continental breakfast. Curtained sliding doors divide the 10-story property's 550-square-ft suites. Upholstered chairs, fringed ottomans, and other appointments in the sitting areas will make you feel right at home (or wish you had one like this). The large bathrooms are stocked with every amenity. ⊠ *506 S.W. Washington St., 97205,* ☎ *503/222–0001 or 800/711–2971,* ⅢX *503/222–0004. 221 suites. Restaurant, bar, in-room modem lines, minibars, no-smoking floor, room service, in-room VCRs, massage, health club, laundry service and dry cleaning, business services, meeting rooms, parking (fee). AE, D, DC, MC, V.*

$$$ ⚄ **Marriott Hotel.** The large rooms here are decorated in off-whites; the best ones look east to the Willamette and the Cascades. Champions Lounge, filled with sports memorabilia, is a singles' hot spot on weekends. ⊠ *1401 S.W. Naito Pkwy., 97201,* ☎ *503/226–7600,* ⅢX *503/221–1789. 503 rooms. Restaurant, 2 bars, no-smoking rooms, refrigerators, room service, indoor pool, barbershop, beauty salon, health club, coin laundry, laundry service and dry cleaning, concierge, business services, meeting rooms, parking (fee). AE, D, DC, MC, V.*

$$–$$$ ⚄ **The Riverside.** If you're concerned about location and value, consider this scrupulously maintained five-story hotel on the MAX light-rail line. East-facing rooms have a good view of the Willamette River and the Governor Tom McCall Waterfront Park; rooms on the west side, a trifle quieter, face downtown. Amenities here include coffeemakers and irons with boards, and guests have privileges at a nearby health club. ⊠ *50 S.W. Morrison St., 97204,* ☎ *503/221–0711 or 800/899–0247,* ⅢX *503/274–0312. 140 rooms. Restaurant, bar, no-smoking rooms, room service, dry cleaning, business services, meeting rooms, parking (fee). AE, D, DC, MC, V.*

$–$$ ⊞ **Mallory Hotel.** The years have been kind to this 1920s-vintage hotel eight blocks from the downtown core. Its gilt-ceiling lobby has fresh white paint and floral carpeting; crystal chandeliers and a leaded-glass skylight hark back to a more genteel era. The rooms are old-fashioned but clean and cheerful; corner suites and rooms on the east side of the building have impressive skyline views. The hotel is a favorite with visiting singers, writers, and artists of every stripe. The staff is friendly and knowledgeable. ⊠ *729 S.W. 15th Ave., 97205,* ☎ *503/223–6311 or 800/228–8657,* ℻ *503/223–0522. 144 rooms. Restaurant, bar. AE, D, DC, MC, V.*

East of the Willamette

$$$ ⊞ **Doubletree Hotel Lloyd Center.** This busy and well-appointed busi-
★ ness-oriented hotel maintains a huge traffic in meetings and special events. The public areas are a tasteful mix of marble, rose-and-green carpet, and antique-style furnishings. The large rooms, many with balconies, have views of the mountains or the city center. The Lloyd Center and the MAX light-rail line are across the street; the Oregon Convention Center is a five-minute walk away. ⊠ *1000 N.E. Multnomah St., 97232,* ☎ *503/281–6111 or 800/547–8010,* ℻ *503/284–8553. 476 rooms. 3 restaurants, 2 bars, in-room modem lines, room service, pool, exercise room, laundry service and dry cleaning, business services, meeting rooms, airport shuttle, parking (fee). AE, D, DC, MC, V.*

$$ ⊞ **Best Western Inn at the Convention Center.** Rooms here are done in pleasing creams and rusts; those with king-size beds usually come with wet bars. The inn is four blocks west of Lloyd Center, directly across the street from the Portland Convention Center, and on the MAX line. ⊠ *420 N.E. Holladay St., 97232,* ☎ *503/233–6331,* ℻ *503/233–2677. 97 rooms. Coffee shop, no-smoking floor, coin laundry, dry cleaning, meeting room, free parking. AE, D, DC, MC, V.*

$$ ⊞ **Portland Guest House.** Inside a Northeast Portland working-class Victorian home with a dusty heather exterior paint job, this cozy B&B near the Lloyd Center contains rooms with antique walnut furniture, original Northwest artworks, and phones. The rates include a gourmet breakfast. No smoking is permitted at this inn. ⊠ *1720 N.E. 15th St., 97212,* ☎ *503/282–1402. 7 rooms, 5 with bath. Free parking. AE, DC, MC, V.*

$$ ⊞ **Ramada Plaza Hotel.** Rooms here come with king- or queen-size beds and sofas, plus full-length mirrors and cable TVs. The Rose Garden arena, Memorial Coliseum, and Oregon Convention Center are within walking distance. ⊠ *1441 N.E. 2nd Ave., 97232,* ☎ *503/233–2401,* ℻ *503/238–7016. 238 rooms. Restaurant, bar, no-smoking floor, room service, pool, exercise room, dry cleaning, airport shuttle, free parking. AE, D, DC, MC, V.*

$$ ⊞ **Red Lion Inn Coliseum.** The restaurant and many of the rooms at the Red Lion overlook the Willamette River. A railroad line lies between the river and the hotel, making courtside rooms the better choice if you want peace and quiet. The rooms are standard but pleasing enough; decorated in pinks, whites, mauve, and sea-foam green, they have queen-size beds and modern oak furnishings. ⊠ *1225 N. Thunderbird Way, 97227,* ☎ *503/235–8311,* ℻ *503/232–2670. 211 rooms. Restaurant, bar, no-smoking rooms, room service, pool, laundry service and dry cleaning, airport shuttle, free parking. AE, D, DC, MC, V.*

$$ ⊞ **Rodeway Inn Convention Center.** Location is what this hotel is all about: The Rose Garden arena, Memorial Coliseum, and Oregon Convention Center are only three blocks away. The room rates include a Continental breakfast, and several dining establishments are within easy walking distance. ⊠ *1506 N.E. 2nd Ave., 97232,* ☎ *503/231–7665,*

FAX *503/236–6040. 44 rooms. No-smoking rooms, sauna, coin laundry, airport shuttle, free parking. AE, D, DC, MC, V.*

West of Downtown

$$$ 🖭 **Heron Haus.** This lovely B&B is inside a stately, 90-year-old Tudor-style mansion near Forest Park. Special features include a tulip-shape bathtub in one room and a tiled, seven-headed antique shower in another. All rooms have phones and work desks. Breakfast, included in the room rate, is a gourmet Continental affair. No smoking is allowed at Heron Haus. ⌧ *2545 N.W. Westover Rd., 97210,* ☎ *503/274–1846,* FAX *503/248–4055. 6 rooms. Breakfast room, in-room modem lines, no-smoking rooms, pool, business services, free parking. MC, V.*

$$–$$$ 🖭 **Greenwood Inn.** Rooms at this hotel in suburban Portland, a 10-minute drive west of downtown, are decorated with custom wood furnishings, original works of art, and southwestern shades of sand, ocher, pale green, and red; ask for one with a courtyard view and avoid the noisier rooms on the hotel's west side. You can dance to live bands three nights a week. The Pavilion restaurant, set among Japanese-style gardens beneath an atrium, serves Northwest cuisine and has an extensive wine cellar. ⌧ *10700 S.W. Allen Blvd., Beaverton 97005,* ☎ *503/643–7444 or 800/289–1300,* FAX *503/626–4553. 250 rooms. Restaurant, 2 bars, kitchenettes, no-smoking rooms, 2 pools, outdoor hot tub, exercise room, free parking. AE, D, DC, MC, V.*

$$ 🖭 **MacMaster House.** On King's Hill, less than 10 minutes by foot from
★ fashionable Northwest 23rd Avenue, this 17-room Colonial Revival mansion built in 1886 is comfortable, funky, and fascinating. A hybrid assortment of Victorian furniture and antiques fills the parlors, and the guest rooms on the second and third floors are charming without being too cute. The two suites with large, private, old-fashioned baths are the ones to choose, especially the spacious Artist's Studio, tucked garretlike under the dormers, with a high brass bed and fireplace. Patrick Long, who was Perry Ellis's private chef, prepares a justly renowned gourmet breakfast. ⌧ *1041 S.W. Vista Ave., 97205,* ☎ *503/223–7362 or 800/774–9523,* FAX *503/224–8808. 5 rooms share 2½ baths, 2 suites. Free parking. AE, D, DC, MC, V.*

$ 🖭 **Lamplighter Inn.** Although it's close to the freeway, noise coming into the hotel is muffled by highway embankments. The Lamplighter's color scheme runs to blues and mauves. The small shopping mall across the street has a supermarket, lounge, and sporting-goods and equipment stores; a Mongolian restaurant is nearby. ⌧ *10207 S.W. Parkway Ave., Beaverton 97225,* ☎ *503/297–2211,* FAX *503/297–0915. 56 rooms. Kitchenettes, free parking. AE, D, DC, MC, V.*

Portland International Airport Area

$$$–$$$$ 🖭 **Doubletree Hotel Jantzen Beach.** The four-story Doubletree has larger than average guest rooms, many with balconies and good views of the Columbia River and Vancouver, Washington. Standard amenities include coffeemakers and irons. Public areas glitter with brass and bright lights that accentuate the greenery and the burgundy, green, and rose color scheme. The seasonal menu at Maxi's Seafood Restaurant highlights ingredients fresh from Northwest fields, farms, and waters. ⌧ *909 N. Hayden Island Dr. (east of I–5's Jantzen Beach exit), 97217,* ☎ *503/283–4466,* FAX *503/735–4847. 320 rooms. Restaurant, bar, coffee shop, in-room modem lines, no-smoking rooms, room service, pool, outdoor hot tub, tennis court, exercise room, dry cleaning, concierge, business services, meeting rooms, airport shuttle, free parking. AE, D, DC, MC, V.*

$$$–$$$$ 🖭 **Shilo Inn Suites Hotel.** Each room at this all-suites hotel has three TV sets, a VCR, a microwave, four telephones, a wet bar, and two over-size beds; the rates include a Continental breakfast as well. The contemporary decor runs to soothing pale blues, light pinks, and light grays in both the public and private areas. ⊠ *11707 N.E. Airport Way, 97220,* ☎ *503/252–7500 or 800/222–2244,* 🅵🅰🆇 *503/254–0794. 200 rooms. Restaurant, bar, in-room modem lines, no-smoking floor, refrigerators, room service, in-room VCRs, indoor pool, hot tub, steam room, exercise room, coin laundry, laundry service and dry cleaning, concierge, business services, meeting rooms, airport shuttle, parking (fee). AE, D, DC, MC, V.*

$$–$$$ 🖭 **Ramada Inn Airport.** The business center at this facility has com-
★   puters, fax machines, and individual workstations. The 108 executive suites have microwaves, wet bars, refrigerators, and sitting areas. Spacious one- and two-bedroom suites have whirlpool tubs; standard rooms, with king-size beds, are decorated in quiet grays, browns, and pinks. ⊠ *6221 N.E. 82nd Ave., 97220,* ☎ *503/255–6511 or 800/272–6232,* 🅵🅰🆇 *503/255–8417. 202 rooms. Restaurant, bar, no-smoking rooms, room service, pool, outdoor hot tub, sauna, exercise room, coin laundry, laundry service and dry cleaning, business services, airport shuttle, parking (fee). AE, D, DC, MC, V.*

$$ 🖭 **Best Western Fortniter Motel.** Rooms here have a lived-in, put-your-feet-up feel. There is no room service, but the rates include a Continental breakfast and the motel provides a shuttle to a nearby restaurant. There's a fee to park during the busy summer months but none the rest of the year. ⊠ *4911 N.E. 82nd Ave., 97220,* ☎ *503/255–9771,* 🅵🅰🆇 *503/255–9774. 52 rooms. Kitchenettes, refrigerators, pool, coin laundry, laundry service and dry cleaning, airport shuttle, parking. AE, D, DC, MC, V.*

$$ 🖭 **Courtyard by Marriott.** This modern hotel is conveniently located ¾ mi from I–205. The average-size rooms are brightly decorated in teals and maroons. ⊠ *11550 N.E. Airport Way, 97220,* ☎ *503/252–3200 or 800/321–2211,* 🅵🅰🆇 *503/252–8921. 150 rooms. Restaurant, bar, in-room modem lines, no-smoking floors, room service, outdoor pool, outdoor hot tub, exercise room, coin laundry, laundry service and dry cleaning, business services, airport shuttle, free parking. AE, D, DC, MC, V.*

NIGHTLIFE AND THE ARTS

"A&E, The Arts and Entertainment Guide," published each Friday in the *Oregonian,* contains listings of performers, productions, events, and club entertainment. *Willamette Week,* published free each Wednesday and widely available throughout the metropolitan area, contains similar, but hipper, listings. *Just Out,* the city's gay and lesbian newspaper, is published bimonthly.

Nightlife

Portland's flourishing music scene encompasses everything from classical concerts to the latest permutations of rock and roll and hip-hop. The city has become something of a mecca for young rock bands, which perform in dance clubs scattered throughout the metropolitan area. Good jazz groups perform nightly in clubs and bars. Top-name musicians and performers in every genre regularly appear at the city's larger venues.

Bars and Lounges
DOWNTOWN

Many of the best bars and lounges in Portland are found in its restaurants. **Atwater's** (⊠ 111 S.W. 5th Ave., ☎ 503/275–3600) is the place to go to enjoy a panoramic city view and live music with your cocktail. The Pearl District's **Bima** (⌧ 1338 N.W. Hoyt St., ☎ 503/241–3465) has a large lounge with a good bar menu. **Brasserie Montmarte** (⌧ 626 S.W. Park Ave., ☎ 503/224–7181) is a popular late-night spot with free jazz and nightclublike decor. At the **Heathman Hotel** (⌧ 1001 S.W. Broadway, ☎ 503/241–4100) you can sit in the marble bar or the wood-panel Tea Court. **Huber's** (⌧ 411 S.W. 3rd Ave., ☎ 503/228–5686), the city's oldest restaurant, is noted for its Spanish coffee and old-fashioned ambience. The young and eclectic crowd at the **Lotus Cardroom and Cafe** (⌧ 932 S.W. 3rd Ave., ☎ 503/227–6185) comes to drink, dance, and play pool.

NOB HILL

Boisterous **Gypsy** (⌧ 625 N.W. 21st Ave., ☎ 503/796–1859) has a 1950s-like atmosphere. In the winter, you can sit by the fireplace in the softly lit bar at **L'Auberge** (⌧ 2601 N.W. Vaughn St., ☎ 503/223–3302); in the summer, tables are set out on the back deck. **Wildwood** (⌧ 1221 N.W. 21st Ave., ☎ 503/248–9663) is casually chic. At **Zefiro** (⌧ 500 N.W. 21st Ave., ☎ 503/226–3394) the atmosphere is likewise informally upscale.

Brew Pubs, Brew Theaters, and Microbreweries

In less than a decade Portland has become the unofficial microbrewery capital of America. Dozens of small breweries operating in the metropolitan area produce pale ales, bitters, bocks, barley wines, and stouts. Some have attached pub operations, where you can sample a foaming pint of house ale. An especially interesting facet of the microbrewery phenomenon is the "brew theaters"—former neighborhood movie houses, lovingly restored, whose patrons enjoy food, suds, and recent theatrical releases.

The **Bagdad Theatre and Pub** (⌧ 3702 S.E. Hawthorne Blvd., ☎ 503/230–0895) screens recent Hollywood films and serves microbrews. **Bridgeport Brew Pub** (⌧ 1318 N.W. Marshall St., ☎ 503/241–7179), Portland's oldest microbrewery, prepares hand-tossed pizza (☞ Dining, *above*) to accompany its ales. Portland Brewing's **Brewhouse Tap Room and Grill** (⌧ 2730 N.W. 31st Ave., ☎ 503/228–5269), part of a 27,000-square-ft brewery complex, has a large restaurant. The **Mission Theater** (⌧ 1624 N.W. Glisan St., ☎ 503/223–4031) was the first brew theater to show recent Hollywood offerings and serve locally brewed McMenamins ales.

The McMenamins chain of microbreweries includes some pubs in restored historic buildings. **Ringlers** (⌧ 1332 W. Burnside St., ☎ 503/225–0543) occupies the first floor of the building that houses the famous Crystal Ballroom (☞ Dancing, *below*). **Ringlers Annex** (⌧ 1223 S.W. Stark St., ☎ 503/525–0520), one block away from Ringlers, is a pie-shaped corner pub where you can puff a cigar while drinking beer, port, or a single-malt Scotch. **Widmer Brewing and Gasthaus** (⌧ 955 N. Russell St., ☎ 503/281–3333) brews German-style beers and has a full menu; you can tour the adjacent brewery during the daytime except on Sunday.

Coffeehouses and Teahouses

DOWNTOWN

Traditional English teas, complete with scones and Devonshire cream, are served with authentic English accents at the **British Tea Garden** (⌧ 725 S.W. 10th Ave., ☎ 503/221–7817). **Giant Steps** (1208 N.W. Glisan St., ☎ 503/226–2547), with its stark, angular, modern decor, is the artsy Pearl District's coffeehouse of choice. **Starbucks** (⌧ 720 S.W. Broadway, ☎ 503/223–2488) has cloned itself in just about every section of

Portland; its main downtown store at Pioneer Courthouse Square is a good place to sip a latte and people-watch. Local musicians play from Wednesday to Friday at **Ultra Penumbra** (⌧ 316 S.W. 9th Ave., ☎ 503/223–4497), a smaller, more personable café.

NOB HILL AND VICINITY

Coffee People (⌧ 533 N.W. 23rd Ave., ☎ 503/221–0235) and **Starbucks** (⌧ 605 N.W. 23rd Ave., ☎ 503/223–1747) are the largest coffee emporiums in Nob Hill, drawing crowds from early in the morning until late in the evening. **Torrefazione Italia** (⌧ 838 N.W. 23rd Ave., ☎ 503/228–1255), a smaller coffeehouse with the individualized charm the larger chains lack, serves the best cappuccino in town.

EAST PORTLAND

Sippers lounge on sofas and overstuffed chairs at **Pied Cow** (⌧ 3244 S.E. Belmont St., ☎ 503/230–4866), a laid-back alternative to more yuppified establishments. **Rimsky Korsakoffee House** (⌧ 707 S.E. 12th Ave., ☎ 503/232–2640), one of the city's first coffeehouses, is still one of the best, especially when it comes to desserts. **Torrefazione Italia** (⌧ 1403 N.E. Weidler St., ☎ 503/288–1608) has an east-side location in a busy area near Lloyd Center.

Comedy

Harvey's Comedy Club (⌧ 436 N.W. 6th Ave., ☎ 503/241–0338) presents stand-up comics nightly except Monday.

Dancing

McMenamins Crystal Ballroom (⌧ 1332 W. Burnside St., ☎ 503/225–0047), a famous Portland dance hall that dates from 1914, sat empty for three decades until being completely refurbished in 1997. Rudolph Valentino danced the tango here in 1923, and you may feel like doing the same once you step out onto the 7,500-square-ft "elastic" floor (it's built on ball bearings) and feel it bouncing beneath your feet. Bands perform everything from swing to hillbilly rock nightly except Monday.

Gay and Lesbian Clubs

Boxx's/The Brig/Panorama (⌧ Stark St. between 10th and 11th Aves., ☎ 503/221–7262) is a popular three-club bar-disco complex that's usually packed on weekends. Boxx's is a video bar. The Brig has a sunken dance floor. Panorama, a cavernous space, has a larger dance floor.

Brew Sisters Pub (⌧ 53 N.W. 1st Ave., ☎ 503/274–9901), a comfortable women's bar in Old Town, has exposed brick walls, wood floors, a pleasant back patio, and live music on weekends.

C. C. Slaughters (⌧ 1014 S.W. Stark St., ☎ 503/248–9135) is a casual western-motif bar with a dance floor.

Egyptian Room (⌧ 3701 S.E. Division St., ☎ 503/236–8689), Portland's most popular lesbian bar-disco, has pool tables and video poker games up front and a medium-size dance floor with a DJ spinning cool music in the back.

Scandals (⌧ 1038 S.W. Stark St., ☎ 503/227–5887), a danceless alternative for people who want to talk without screaming, has a low-key atmosphere and plate-glass windows that look out onto the street.

Music

BLUES, FOLK, AND ROCK

Candlelight Cafe and Bar (⌧ 2032 S.W. 5th Ave., ☎ 503/222–3378) presents blues nightly.

Dublin Pub (⌧ 6821 S.W. Beaverton–Hillsdale Hwy., ☎ 503/297–2889) pours more than 100 beers on tap and hosts Irish bands and rock groups.

Kell's (⌧ 112 S.W. 2nd Ave., ☎ 503/227–4057) serves up terrific Irish food and Celtic music nightly.

Key Largo Restaurant and Nightclub (⊠ 31 N.W. 1st Ave., ☎ 503/223–9919) is in a historic building with brick walls, an outdoor courtyard, and a dance floor. The club serves Cajun food and books top-drawer rock, blues, and folk acts.

La Luna (⊠ 215 S.E. 9th Ave., ☎ 503/241–5862) hosts hot rock acts—and occasional world beat, blues, and ethnic-music performers—in a nightclub setting.

Moody's (⊠ 424 S.W. 4th Ave., ☎ 503/223–4241) is the place to go for hard rock.

Satyricon (⊠ 125 N.W. 6th Ave., ☎ 503/243–2380) is Portland's leading outlet for grunge, punk, and other alternative rock music.

COUNTRY AND WESTERN

The Drum (⊠ 14601 S.E. Division St., ☎ 503/760–1400), Portland's top country club, books traditional country and contemporary country-rock performers.

Jubitz Truck Stop (⊠ 33 N.E. Middlefield Rd., ☎ 503/283–1111) presents live country music nightly.

JAZZ

Brasserie Montmartre (⊠ 626 S.W. Park Ave., ☎ 503/224–5552) presents duos on weeknights and quartets and larger groups on weekends.

Jazz de Opus (⊠ 33 N.W. 2nd Ave., ☎ 503/222–6077) books local musicians with national reputations seven nights a week.

Parchman Farm (⊠ 1204 S.E. Clay St., ☎ 503/235–7831) showcases prominent local jazz performers nightly.

The Arts

When it comes to arts funding, Oregon ranks very low. Yet Portland is home to a symphony orchestra, opera and dance companies, and a number of theater companies. Most Portland-based performing arts groups have their own box-office numbers; see individual listings. For other events, the main ticket outlets are **Ticketmaster** (☎ 503/224–8499) and **Fastixx** (☎ 503/224–8499).

Dance

Oregon Ballet Theatre (☎ 503/227–6867 or 888/922–5538) produces five classical and contemporary works a year, including a much-loved holiday *Nutcracker*. Most performances are at the Portland Civic Auditorium.

Film

Cinema 21 (⊠ 616 N.W. 21st Ave., ☎ 503/223–4515), in the Nob Hill area, is the city's most eclectic art-movie house; it also hosts the annual gay and lesbian film festival. For Hollywood blockbusters, new foreign films, and interesting low-budget sleepers, check out **KOIN Center Cinemas** (⊠ S.W. 3rd Ave. and Clay St., ☎ 503/225–5555, ext. 4608) downtown. The **Movie House** (⊠ 1220 S.W. Taylor St., ☎ 503/225–5555, ext. 4609), a restored theater in the former Portland Women's Club, shows critically acclaimed first-run British and American films. The **Northwest Film and Video Center** (⊠ 1219 S.W. Park Ave., ☎ 503/221–1156), a branch of the Portland Art Museum, screens all manner of art films, documentaries, and independent features and presents the three-week Portland International Film Festival in February and March.

Music

CHAMBER MUSIC

Chamber Music Northwest (☎ 503/223–3202) presents some of the most sought-after soloists, chamber musicians, and recording artists from the Portland area and abroad for a five-week summer concert series; performances take place at Reed College and Catlin Gabel School.

ORCHESTRAS

The **Oregon Symphony** (☎ 503/228–1353 or 800/228–7343) presents more than 40 classical, pop, children's, and family concerts each year at the Arlene Schnitzer Concert Hall. The **Portland Baroque Orchestra** (☎ 503/222–6000) performs works on period instruments in a season that runs from October to April. Performances are held in the city at Trinity Episcopal Church (✉ 147 N.W. 19th Ave.) and at St. Anne's Chapel, Marylhurst College (✉ Hwy. 43, 1 mi east of Lake Oswego), a half-hour drive from downtown.

Opera

Portland Opera (☎ 503/241–1802) and its orchestra and chorus stage five productions annually at the Portland Civic Auditorium (☞ *below*).

Performance Venues

Arlene Schnitzer Concert Hall (✉ Portland Center for the Performing Arts, S.W. Broadway and Main St., ☎ 503/796–9293) hosts rock stars, choral groups, lectures, and concerts by the Oregon Symphony and others.

Memorial Coliseum (✉ 1 Center Ct., Rose Quarter, ☎ 503/321–3211), a 12,000-seat venue in northeast Portland, books rock groups, touring shows, the Ringling Brothers circus, ice-skating extravaganzas, and sporting events.

Portland Center for the Performing Arts (✉ 1111 S.W. Broadway, ☎ 503/796–9293) schedules rock shows, symphony performances, lectures, and Broadway musicals (☞ Downtown *in* Exploring Portland, *above*).

Portland Civic Auditorium (✉ 222 S.W. Clay St., ☎ 503/796–9293), with 3,000 seats and outstanding acoustics, presents opera, ballet, country and rock concerts, and touring shows.

Roseland Theater (✉ 10 N.W. 6th Ave., ☎ 503/224–2038), which holds 1,400 people, specializes in rock and blues.

Theater

Artists Repertory Theatre (✉ 1516 S.W. Alder St., ☎ 503/241–1278) stages five productions a year—regional premieres, occasional commissioned works, and selected classics.

Cygnet Productions (☎ 503/230–8827) presents a consistently intriguing season of plays and staged readings in nontraditional spaces.

Oregon Puppet Theater (☎ 503/236–4034) stages five children's productions a year at different locations in town.

Portland Center Stage (✉ 1111 S.W. Broadway, ☎ 503/274–6588) produces six contemporary and classical works between October and April in the 800-seat Intermediate Theater.

Portland Repertory Theater (✉ 2 World Trade Center, 26 S.W. Salmon St., 3rd floor, ☎ 503/224–4491), the region's oldest professional theatrical company, presents five productions each year.

Tygres Heart Shakespeare Co. (✉ 1111 S.W. Broadway, ☎ 503/222–9220) mounts a fall, winter, and spring Shakespearean production in the intimate, court-style Winningstad Theatre.

OUTDOOR ACTIVITIES AND SPORTS

Portlanders are definitely oriented to the outdoors. Hikers, joggers, and mountain bikers take to the city's hundreds of miles of parks, paths, and trails. The Willamette and Columbia rivers are used for boating and water sports; unfortunately, it's not easy to rent any kind of boat for casual use. Big-sports fervor is reserved for Trail Blazer games, held at the Rose Quarter arena on the east side. The **Portland/Oregon Visitors Association** (☎ 503/222–2223 or 800/345–3214) provides information on sports events and outdoor activities in the city.

Participant Sports

Bicycling

Cyclists are common on Portland's streets, and numerous bike paths meander through parks and along the shoreline of the Willamette River. Designated routes include a 30-mi path northwest of downtown Portland along U.S. 30 and a path through northwest and southwest Portland on Terwilliger Boulevard to Lake Oswego. Other options are the 5½ mi of promenade along the Willamette River between the Broadway and Sellwood bridges and an east-side riverfront path between the Hawthorne and Burnside bridges. There is extensive off-road riding in Forest Park. Bikes can be rented downtown at **Bike Central** (⊠ 835 S.W. 2nd Ave., ☎ 503/227–4439).

Fishing

The Columbia and Willamette rivers are major sportfishing streams with opportunities for angling virtually year-round. Unfortunately, though salmon can still be caught here, runs have been greatly reduced in both rivers in recent years. The Willamette River offers prime fishing for bass, channel catfish, sturgeon, crappies, perch, panfish, and crayfish. It is also a good winter steelhead stream. June is the top shad month, with some of the best fishing occurring below Willamette Falls at Oregon City. The Columbia River is known for its salmon, sturgeon, walleye, and smelt.

OUTFITTERS

Outfitters throughout Portland operate guide services, including **G.I. Joe's** (⊠ 1140 N. Hayden Meadows Dr., ☎ 503/283–0312) and **Stewart Fly Shop** (⊠ 23830 N.E. Halsey St., ☎ 503/666–2471). Few outfitters rent equipment, so bring your own or be prepared to buy.

REGULATIONS

Local sport shops are the best sources of information on current fishing hot spots, which change from year to year. Detailed fishing regulations are available at local tackle shops or from the **Oregon Department of Fish and Wildlife** (⊠ 2501 S.W. 1st Ave., Portland 97201, ☎ 503/229–5403).

Golf

Broadmoor Golf Course (⊠ 3509 N.E. Columbia Blvd., ☎ 503/281–1337) is an 18-hole, par-72 course where the greens fee ranges from $20 to $22 and an optional cart costs $22. At the 18-hole, par-70 **Colwood National Golf Club** (⊠ 7313 N.E. Columbia Blvd., ☎ 503/254–5515), the greens fee runs from $18 to $31, plus $22 for an optional cart. On mornings and weekends, the $31 greens fee includes a cart. **Heron Lakes Golf Course** (⊠ 3500 N. Victory Blvd., ☎ 503/289–1818) consists of two 18-hole, par-72 courses: the less challenging Greenback, and the Great Blue, generally acknowledged to be the most difficult links in the greater Portland area. The greens fee at the Green, as it is locally known, ranges from $18 to $20, while the fee at the Blue is $29 at all times. An optional cart at either course costs $24.

Skiing

For information about permits for cross-country and downhill skiing, *see* Oregon A to Z *in* Chapter 3. Two places in Portland that rent skis and equipment are the **Mountain Shop** (⊠ 628 N.E. Broadway, ☎ 503/288–6768) and **REI** (⊠ 1798 Jantzen Beach Center, ☎ 503/283–1300).

Tennis
Glendoveer Golf Course (⊠ 14015 N.E. Glisan St., ☎ 503/253–7507) and the **Lake Oswego Indoor Tennis Center** (⊠ 2900 S.W. Diane Dr., ☎ 503/635–5550) have indoor tennis courts. The **Portland Tennis Center** (⊠ 324 N.E. 12th Ave., ☎ 503/823–3189) operates four indoor courts and eight lighted outdoor courts. The **St. John's Racquet Center** (⊠ 7519 N. Burlington Ave., ☎ 503/823–3629) has three indoor courts.

Portland Parks and Recreation (☎ 503/823–3189) operates 117 outdoor tennis courts (many with night lighting) at Washington Park, Grant Park, and many other locations. The courts are open on a first-come, first-served basis year-round, but you can reserve one, starting in March, for play from May to September.

Spectator Sports

Auto Racing
Portland International Raceway (⊠ West Delta Park, 1940 N. Victory Blvd., ☎ 503/285–6635) presents bicycle and drag racing and motocross on weeknights, and sports-car, motorcycle, and go-cart racing on weekends from April to September.

Portland Speedway (⊠ 9727 N. Martin Luther King Jr. Blvd., ☎ 503/285–2883) hosts demolition derbies and NASCAR and stock-car races from April to September. In June, it hosts the Budweiser Indy Car World Series, a 200-mi race that lures the top names on the Indy Car circuit.

Basketball
The **Rose Garden** (⊠ 1 Center Ct., ☎ 503/797–9617) is the 21,700-seat home court of the Portland Trail Blazers of the National Basketball Association.

Greyhound Racing
The season at **Multnomah Greyhound Park** (⊠ 223rd and N.E. Glisan Sts., ☎ 503/667–7700) starts in May and continues until mid-October.

Hockey
The **Portland Winter Hawks** (☎ 503/238–6366) of the Western Hockey League play home games at Memorial Coliseum (⊠ 1 Center Ct.) and at the Rose Garden (⊠ 1 Center Ct.).

Horse Racing
Thoroughbred and quarter horses race, rain or shine, at **Portland Meadows** (⊠ 1001 N. Schmeer Rd., ☎ 503/285–9144) from October to April.

SHOPPING

Portland's main shopping area is **downtown,** between Southwest 2nd and 10th avenues and between Southwest Stark and Morrison streets. **Nob Hill,** north of downtown along Northwest 21st and 23rd avenues, is home to eclectic clothing, gift, book, and food shops. Most of the city's fine-art galleries are concentrated in the **Pearl District,** north from Burnside Street to Marshall Street between Northwest 8th and 15th avenues. The storefronts and warehouses in this former industrial area have been converted into furniture, design, and other stores. **Sellwood,** 5 mi from the city center, south on Naito Parkway and east across the Sellwood Bridge, has more than 50 antiques and collectibles shops along Southeast 13th Avenue, plus specialty shops and outlet stores for sporting goods. **Southeast Hawthorne Boulevard** between 30th and 42nd avenues has an eclectic and often countercultural array of bookstores, coffeehouses, antiques stores, and boutiques.

The **Portland Saturday Market** (⊠ Burnside Bridge, underneath west end, ☎ 503/222–6072), open on Saturdays and Sundays, is a good place to find handcrafted items.

Portland merchants are generally open from Monday to Saturday between 9 or 10 AM and 6 PM and on Sundays between 11 AM or noon and 4 PM. Most shops in downtown's Pioneer Place, the east side's Lloyd Center, and the outlying malls are open until 9 PM every night.

Malls and Department Stores
Downtown/City Center
Meier and Frank (⊠ 621 S.W. 5th Ave., ☎ 503/223–0512), a department store that dates from 1857, has 10 floors of general merchandise at its main location downtown.
Nordstrom (⊠ 701 S.W. Broadway, ☎ 503/224–6666) sells fine-quality apparel and accessories and has a large footwear department. Bargain lovers should head for the Nordstrom Rack (⊠ 401 S.W. Morrison St., ☎ 503/299–1815) outlet across from Pioneer Place Mall.
Pioneer Place (⊠ 700 S.W. 5th Ave., ☎ 503/228–5800) holds 70 upscale specialty shops (including Williams-Sonoma, Coach, J. Crew, Godiva, and Caswell-Massey) in a three-story glass-roof atrium setting. You'll find good, inexpensive ethnic foods from 18 vendors in the Cascades Food Court in the basement.
Saks Fifth Avenue (⊠ 850 S.W. 5th Ave., ☎ 503/226–3200) has two floors of men's and women's clothing, jewelry, and other merchandise.

Beyond Downtown
NORTHEAST PORTLAND

The **Lloyd Center** (⊠ N.E. Multnomah St. at N.E. 9th Ave., ☎ 503/282–2511), which is on the MAX light-rail line, contains more than 170 shops, including four department stores, a large food court, a multiscreen cinema, and an ice-skating pavilion.

SOUTHEAST PORTLAND

Clackamas Town Center (⊠ Sunnyside Rd. at I–205's Exit 14, ☎ 503/653–6913) has five major department stores and more than 180 shops.

SOUTHWEST PORTLAND

Washington Square (⊠ 9585 S.W. Washington Sq. Rd., at S.W. Hall Blvd. and Hwy. 217, Tigard, ☎ 503/639–8860) contains five major department stores and 120 specialty shops.
The Water Tower (⊠ 5331 S.W. MacAdam Ave., ☎ 503/228–9431), in the John's Landing neighborhood, is a pleasant smaller mall with 35 specialty shops and six restaurants.

Specialty Stores
Antiques
You'll find many antiques shops in **Sellwood** (☞ *above*). Options elsewhere include the following:

Portland Antique Company (⊠ 1211 N.W. Glisan St., ☎ 503/223–0999) spreads over 35,000 square ft in the Pearl District. It houses the Northwest's largest selection of European and English antiques.
Shogun's Gallery (⊠ 206 N.W. 23rd Ave., ☎ 503/224–0328) specializes in Japanese and Chinese furniture, especially the lightweight wooden Japanese cabinets known as *tansu*. Also here are chairs, tea tables, altar tables, armoires, ikebana baskets, and Chinese wooden picnic boxes, all of them at least 100 years old and at extremely reasonable prices.

Star's Antique Mall (✉ 305 N.W. 21st Ave., ☎ 503/220–8180) rents out its 10,000-square-ft space in Nob Hill to a variety of antiques dealers; you might find anything from low-end 1950s kitsch to high-end treasures.

Art Dealers and Galleries

Butters Gallery, Ltd. (✉ 223 N.W. 9th Ave., ☎ 503/248–9378) has monthly exhibits of the works of nationally known and local artists in its Pearl District space.

In Her Image Gallery (✉ 3208 S.E. Hawthorne Blvd., ☎ 503/231–3726) specializes in statues, totems, and works of art dedicated to the great Earth goddesses.

Photographic Image Gallery (✉ 240 S.W. 1st Ave., ☎ 503/224–3543) carries prints by nationally known nature photographers Christopher Burkett and Joseph Holmes, among others, and has a large supply of photography posters.

Pulliam Deffenbaugh Gallery (✉ 522 N.W. 12th Ave., ☎ 503/228–6665) generally shows contemporary figurative and expressionistic works by Northwest artists.

Quintana Galleries of Native American Art (✉ 501 S.W. Broadway, ☎ 503/223–1729 or 800/321–1729) focuses on Northwest coast, Navajo, and Hopi art and jewelry, along with photogravures by Edward Curtis.

Twist (✉ 30 N.W. 23rd Pl., ☎ 503/224–0334; ✉ Pioneer Place, ☎ 503/222–3137) has a huge space in Nob Hill and a smaller shop downtown. In Nob Hill you'll find contemporary American ceramics, glass, furniture, sculpture, and handcrafted jewelry; downtown carries an assortment of objects, often with a pop, whimsical touch.

Books

Powell's City of Books (✉ 1005 W. Burnside St., ☎ 503/228–4651), the largest bookstore in the United States, carries new and used books, as well as rare and hard-to-find editions.

New Renaissance Bookshop (✉ 1338 N.W. 23rd Ave., ☎ 503/224–4929), between Overton and Pettygrove, is dedicated to New Age and metaphysical books and tapes.

Clothing

Elizabeth Street and Zelda's Shoe Bar (✉ 635 N.W. 23rd Ave., ☎ 503/226–8977), two connected boutiques in Nob Hill, carry a sophisticated, highly eclectic line of women's clothes, accessories, and shoes.

Fashion Passion (✉ 616 N.W. 23rd Ave., ☎ 503/223–4373) is a good place to go for men's and women's retro and vintage clothing and accessories.

Jane's Obsession (✉ 728 N.W. 23rd Ave., ☎ 503/221–1490), a porch-level shop in one of Northwest 23rd Avenue's "house boutiques," sells luxurious French and Italian lingerie.

Mario's (✉ 921 S.W. Morrison St., ☎ 503/227–3477), Portland's best store for fine men's clothing, carries designer lines by Canali, Armani, Vestimenta, Donna Karan, and Calvin Klein, among others.

Mario's for Women (✉ 811 S.W. Morrison St., ☎ 503/241–8111) stocks Armani, Calvin Klein, and Vesti.

Nob Hill Shoes (✉ 921 N.W. 23rd Ave., ☎ 503/224–8682), a tiny spot, sells men and women's Naot sandals from Israel and Swedish Bastad clogs. (These are big in Portland, which has entered its post-Birkenstock phase.)

Norm Thompson Outfitters (✉ 1805 N.W. Thurman St., ☎ 503/221–0764) carries classic fashions for men and women, innovative footwear, and one-of-a-kind gifts.

Portland Outdoor Store (⊠ 304 S.W. 3rd Ave., ☎ 503/222–1051) stubbornly resists all that is trendy, both in clothes and decor, but if you want authentic western gear—saddles, Stetsons, boots, or cowboy shirts—head here.

Gifts

Christmas at the Zoo (⊠ 118 N.W. 23rd Ave., ☎ 503/223–4048 or 800/223–5886) is crammed year-round with decorated trees and has Portland's best selection of European handblown glass ornaments and plush animals.

Made in Oregon (☎ 800/828–9673), which sells books, smoked salmon, local wines, Pendleton woolen goods, carvings made of myrtle wood, and other products made in the state, has shops at Portland International Airport, the Lloyd Center, the Galleria, Old Town, Washington Square, and Clackamas Town Center.

Jewelry

Carl Greve (⊠ 731 S.W. Morrison St., ☎ 503/223–7121), in operation since 1922, carries exclusive designer lines of fine jewelry, such as Mikimoto pearls, and has the state's only Tiffany boutique. The second floor is reserved for china, stemware, and housewares.

Music

Django Records (⊠ 1111 S.W. Stark St., ☎ 503/227–4381) is a must for collectors of tapes, compact discs, 45s, and vintage albums. **Music Millennium Northwest** (⊠ 801 N.W. 23rd Ave., ☎ 503/248–0163) stocks a huge selection of CDs and tapes in every possible musical category, from local punk to classical. **Classical Millenium** (⊠ 3144 E. Burnside St., ☎ 503/231–8909), the company's east-side location, has the best selection of classical CDs and tapes in Oregon.

Perfume

Aveda Lifestyle Store and Spa (⊠ 500 S.W. 5th Ave., ☎ 503/248–0615) sells the flower-based Aveda line of scents and skin-care products. **Perfume House** (⊠ 3328 S.E. Hawthorne Blvd., ☎ 503/234–5375) carries hundreds of brand-name fragrances for women and men.

Toys

Finnegan's Toys and Gifts (⊠ 922 S.W. Yamhill St., ☎ 503/221–0306), downtown Portland's largest toy store, stocks artistic, creative, educational, and other types of toys.

SIDE TRIPS

Oregon City

22 mi from downtown Portland, east on I–84 and south on I–205; 13 mi south of Portland on Hwy. 99E.

Oregon City (population 19,000) was the western terminus of the Oregon Trail. The city was founded in 1829, when Dr. John McLoughlin claimed the land for his employer, the Hudson Bay Company. In 1843 Oregon country's first provisional legislature convened here, and the town served as territorial capital from 1849 to 1852.

At the **End of the Oregon Trail Interpretive Center,** living-history interpreters, a multimedia show, and exhibits relate the compelling story of the 2,000-mi Oregon Trail journey. There are demonstrations by traditional craftspeople and a pioneer heritage garden. The 8½-acre site includes an amphitheater where the **Oregon Trail Pageant,** an outdoor music drama, is performed during July and August. ⊠ *1726 Washington St. (from I–205's Exit 10, take Hwy. 213 south and follow signs),* ☎

503/657–9336. ☎ $4.50. ⊙ Memorial Day–Sept., Mon.–Sat. 9–6, Sun. 10–5; Oct.–Memorial Day, Mon.–Sat. 9–5, Sun. 11–5.

The **John McLoughlin House National Historic Site** contains McLoughlin's 1846 home, many of his possessions, and 19th-century artifacts. The **McLoughlin Historic District,** which surrounds the home, is a neighborhood of picturesque houses and churches in architectural styles dating from the 1840s to the 1930s. ⊠ *713 Center St., between 7th and 8th Sts.,* ☎ *503/656–5146. ☎ $3. ⊙ Feb.–Dec., Tues.–Sat. 10–4, Sun. 1–4.*

Fort Vancouver

12 mi north of Portland on I–5, across the Columbia River into Washington State; take Exit 1-C and follow the signs to Officers' Row.

National Park Service staff and volunteers conduct tours through the **Fort Vancouver National Historic Site,** a reconstruction of the 1825 fur-trading headquarters of the Hudson Bay Company. Some furnishings are from the original fort. The visitor center has a museum, an audiovisual program, and a gift shop. Outside the front entrance of Fort Vancouver is the Officers' Row Historic District, 21 Victorian-style homes built between 1850 and 1906. Although they are not part of the fort, officers stationed there often occupied the houses. Among the more notable residents were Ulysses S. Grant and George C. Marshall. Some of the houses are still private residences; others have been converted into restaurants and commercial businesses. ⊠ *612 E. Reserve St., Vancouver, WA,* ☎ *360/696–7655. ☎ $2 Memorial Day–Labor Day; free rest of yr. ⊙ Memorial Day–Labor Day, daily 9–5; Labor Day–Memorial Day, daily 9–4.*

PORTLAND A TO Z

Arriving and Departing

By Bus

Greyhound (⊠ 550 N.W. 6th Ave., ☎ 503/243–2317 or 800/231–2222) services Portland from Seattle, Vancouver, San Francisco, and elsewhere.

By Car

Interstate 5 enters Portland from the north and south. **Interstate 84** is the major east-side corridor. **U.S. 26 and U.S. 30** are primary east–west thoroughfares. Bypass routes are **I–205,** which loops through east Portland, and **I–405,** which arcs around western downtown.

By Plane

Portland International Airport (⊠ N.E. Airport Way at I–205, ☎ 503/335–1234), about 12 mi from downtown in northeast Portland, is served by Air Canada, Alaska, American, America West, Continental, Delta, Hawaiian, Horizon, Northwest, Reno, Southwest Airlines, TWA, United, and Western Pacific. *See* Air Travel *in* the Gold Guide for airline phone numbers.

BETWEEN THE AIRPORT AND CITY CENTER

By Bus: Raz Tranz (☎ 503/246–3301) operates buses to some downtown Portland hotels, the Best Western Inn at the Convention Center, and the Amtrak and Greyhound depots. Departures are approximately every 30 minutes between 5 AM and midnight. The fare is $8.50 one-way and $15.50 round-trip. **Tri-Met** (☎ 503/238–7433) Bus 12 runs about every 15 minutes to and from the airport. The fare is $1.05.

By Car: From the airport, take the East Portland Freeway (I–205) south and the Banfield Freeway (I–84) west to the City Center exit. Going to the airport, take I–84 east to I–205 north; follow I–205 to the airport exit.

By Taxi: The trip between downtown Portland and the airport takes about 30 minutes by taxi. The fare is about $25.

By Train
Amtrak (☎ 800/872–7245) trains stop at Union Station (⌂ 800 N.W. 6th Ave.).

Getting Around

By Bus
Tri-Met (☎ 503/238–7433) operates bus service throughout the greater Portland area. The fares are the same for Tri-Met and the light-rail system (☞ *below*), and tickets can be used on either system. Buses are free throughout the entire downtown "Fareless Square," whose borders are Northwest Irving Street to the north, I–405 to the west and south, and the Willamette River to the east. The Tri-Met information office at Pioneer Courthouse Square (⌂ 6th Ave. and Morrison St.) is open on weekdays from 9 to 5.

By Car
Most city-center streets are one-way only, and Southwest 5th and 6th avenues between Burnside and Southwest Madison streets are limited to bus traffic. It is legal to turn right on a red light at most intersections (check the signs). Left turns from a one-way street onto another one-way street on a red light are also legal. Most parking meters are patrolled from 8 AM to 6 PM; many streets have posted rush-hour regulations. Sunday parking is free.

By Light Rail
Metropolitan Area Express (☎ 503/228–7246), or MAX, links the eastern and western Portland suburbs to downtown, the Lloyd Center district, the Convention Center, and the Rose Quarter. From downtown, transportation operates daily from 5:30 AM to 1 AM, with a fare of $1.05 for travel through one or two zones, $1.35 for three zones, and $3.25 for day tickets. A western extension, scheduled to open in fall 1998, will include a stop at the Metro Washington Park Zoo.

By Taxi
Taxi fare is $2.50 at flag drop plus $1.50 per mile. The first person pays by the meter, and each additional passenger pays $1. Cabs cruise the city streets, but it's better to phone for one. The major companies are **Broadway Cab** (☎ 503/227–1234), **New Rose City Cab** (☎ 503/282–7707), **Portland Taxi Company** (☎ 503/256–5400), and **Radio Cab** (☎ 503/227–1212).

Contacts and Resources

Emergencies
Ambulance (☎ 911). **Fire** (☎ 911). **Police** (☎ 911).

Eastmoreland Hospital (⌂ 2900 S.E. Steele St., ☎ 503/234–0411). **Emanuel Hospital and Health Center** (⌂ 2801 N.W. Gantenbien Ave., ☎ 503/280–3200). **Good Samaritan Hospital & Medical Center** (⌂ 1015 N.W. 22nd Ave., ☎ 503/229–7711). **Providence Portland Medical Center** (⌂ 4805 N.E. Glisan St., ☎ 503/230–6000). **Providence St. Vincent Hospital** (⌂ 9205 S.W. Barnes Rd., ☎ 503/297–4411).

Willamette Dental Group PC (⊠ 1933 S.W. Jefferson St., ☏ 503/644–3200) has offices throughout the metropolitan area and is open Saturdays.

Guided Tours

ORIENTATION

Gray Line Sightseeing (☏ 503/285–9845) operates city tours year-round; call for departure times.

SPECIAL-INTEREST

Sternwheeler Riverboat Tours (☏ 503/223–3928) departs year-round from RiverPlace Marina on two-hour excursions; there are also Friday-night dinner cruises. **Yachts-O-Fun Riverboat Cruises** (☏ 503/234–6665) operates dinner and Sunday-brunch cruises, Portland harbor excursions, and historical tours.

WALKING

The **Portland/Oregon Visitors Association** (☞ Visitor Information, *below*), which is open on weekdays from 9 to 5 and Saturday from 9 to 4, has brochures, maps, and guides to art galleries and select neighborhoods.

Late-Night Pharmacies

Fred Meyer has branches close to downtown (⊠ 100 N.W. 20th Pl., ☏ 503/226–7179) and near Lloyd Center (⊠ 3030 N.E. Weidler St., ☏ 503/280–1333); both in-store pharmacies are open until 10 PM.

Visitor Information

Portland/Oregon Visitors Association (⊠ 2 World Trade Center, 26 S.W. Salmon St., 97204, ☏ 503/222–2223 or 800/345–3214).

3 Oregon

Welcome to Oregon, where natural splendor is the rule, not the exception. The bounty includes the rocky Pacific coast, the wild Rogue and McKenzie rivers, and scenic knockouts like the Columbia River Gorge, Mount Hood, and Crater Lake. Old West memories linger on amid the vast grandeur of eastern Oregon's high desert, forests, and mountains. On the gentler side, the Willamette Valley is a lush wine-producing region where attractions commemorating the state's pioneer history mix with world-renowned cultural events.

AT ITS EASTERN END, Oregon begins in a high, sage-scented desert plateau that covers nearly two-thirds of the state's 96,000 square mi. Moving west, the landscape rises to 10,000-ft-high alpine peaks, meadows, and lakes; plunges to fertile farmland and forest; and ends at the cold, tumultuous Pacific. Within a 90-minute drive from Portland or Eugene you can lose yourself in the recreational landscape of your choice: a thriving wine country, uncrowded ocean beaches, snow-silvered mountain wilderness, or a monolith-studded desert that has been used as the backdrop for many a Hollywood western.

By Donald S. Olson

Oregonians, who have been called the hardest-working and the hardest-playing Americans, take full advantage of the outdoors. There is a story, never confirmed, that early pioneers arriving at a crossroads of the Oregon Trail found a pile of gold quartz or pyrite pointing the way south to California. The way north, on the other hand, was marked by a hand-lettered sign: TO OREGON. Oregonians like to think that the more literate of the pioneers found their way here, while the fortune hunters continued south.

Evidence of Oregon's earliest Native American inhabitants is tantalizingly rare, but what does exist suggests that tribes of nomadic hunter-gatherers had established themselves throughout the region many centuries before the first white explorers and settlers arrived. In eastern Oregon, a pair of 9,000-year-old sagebrush sandals (now in the Oregon Museum of Natural History in Eugene) and nets woven from reeds have been discovered; on the coast, ancient shell middens indicate that even the earliest Oregonians feasted on seafood. In the Columbia River Gorge, a recently unearthed male skeleton has archaeologists revising their time lines.

In 1792 Robert Gray, an American trading captain, followed a trail of debris and muddy water inland and discovered the Columbia River. Shortly thereafter, British Army Lieutenant William Broughton was dispatched to investigate Gray's find, and he sailed as far upriver as the rapids-choked mouth of the Columbia River Gorge.

Within a few years, a thriving seaborne fur trade had sprung up, with American and British entrepreneurs exchanging baubles, cloth, tools, weapons, and liquor with the native peoples for high-quality beaver and sea-otter pelts. By 1805, American explorers Meriwether Lewis and William Clark had arrived at the site of present-day Astoria after their epic overland journey, spurring an influx of white pioneers—mostly fur trappers and traders sent by John Jacob Astor's Pacific Fur Company in 1811 to do business and claim the land for the United States.

The English disputed American claims to the territory, on the basis of Broughton's exploration, and soon after the War of 1812 began, they negotiated the purchase of Astoria from Astor's company. It wasn't until 1846 that they formally renounced their claims in the region with the signing of the Oregon Treaty.

"Oregon Country" grew tremendously between 1841 and 1860, as more than 50,000 settlers from the eastern United States made the journey over the plains in their covered wagons. The majority settled in the Willamette Valley, where most of Oregon's 3.2 million residents still live. As settlers capitalized on gold-rush San Francisco's need for provisions and other supplies, Oregon reaped its own riches, and the lawless frontier gradually acquired a semblance of civilization. The

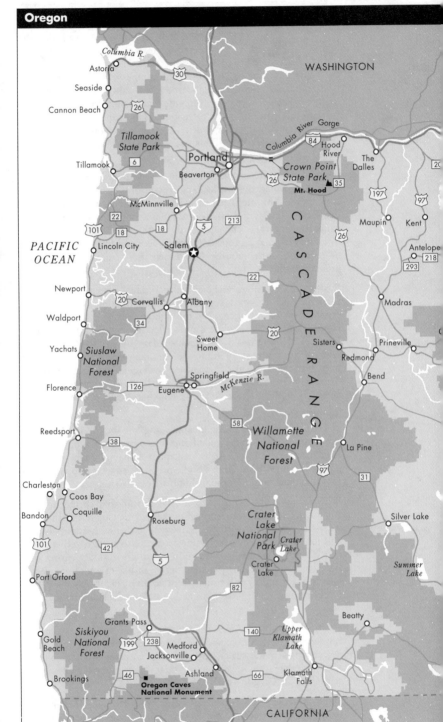

WASHINGTON

Columbia R.

Astoria

Seaside

Cannon Beach

30

26

Tillamook
State Park

6

Tillamook

Columbia River Gorge

84

Hood
River

The
Dalles

20

Portland

Beaverton

Crown Point
State Park

26

35

197

Mt. Hood

McMinnville

22

18

101

18

5

213

Salem

Maupin

Kent

97

Antelope

218

293

PACIFIC
OCEAN

Lincoln City

Newport

20

Corvallis

Albany

22

Madras

Waldport

34

Sweet
Home

20

Sisters

Prineville

Yachats

Siuslaw
National
Forest

Redmond

Bend

Florence

126

Springfield

Eugene

McKenzie R.

Reedsport

38

58

Willamette
National
Forest

La Pine

97

31

Charleston

Coos Bay

Coquille

Roseburg

Crater
Lake
National
Park

Crater
Lake

Silver Lake

Bandon

101

42

Summer
Lake

Port Orford

5

Crater
Lake

82

Beatty

Grants Pass

Siskiyou
National
Forest

199

238

140

Upper
Klamath
Lake

Gold
Beach

Medford

Jacksonville

Brookings

46

Ashland

66

Klamath
Falls

Oregon Caves
National Monument

CALIFORNIA

C A S C A D E   R A N G E

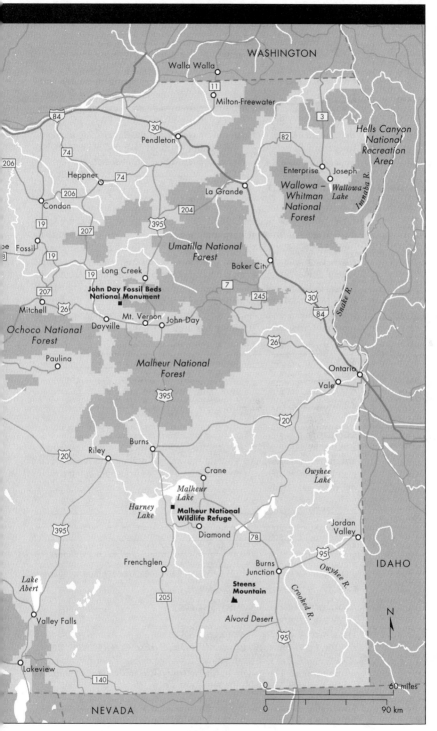

territory's residents voted down the idea of statehood three times, but in 1859, Oregon became the 33rd U.S. state.

Oregon's economy is still heavily dominated by timber (the state is America's largest producer of softwood), agriculture (hazelnuts, fruit, berries, wine, seed crops, livestock, and dairy products), and fishing. A major high-tech center known as the Silicon Forest, producing high-speed computer hardware and sophisticated instruments, has taken root west of Portland in the Tualatin Valley, side by side with the wine industry. Tourism grows in importance every year—Oregonians have discovered that the scenic and recreational treasures that thrill them also thrill visitors from all over the world. A sophisticated hospitality network has appeared, making Oregon more accessible than ever before.

Pleasures and Pastimes

Dining

Fresh foods grown, caught, and harvested in the Northwest are standard fare in gourmet restaurants throughout Oregon. Outside urban areas and resorts, most restaurants tend to be low-key and unpretentious, both in ambience and cuisine. On the coast, look for regional specialties—clam chowder, fresh fish (particularly salmon), sweet Dungeness crab, mussels, shrimp, and oysters. Elsewhere in the state fresh river fish, local lamb and beef, and seasonal game dishes appear on many menus. Desserts made with local fruits such as huckleberries and marionberries are always worth trying.

CATEGORY	COST*
$$$$	over $35
$$$	$25–$35
$$	$15–$25
$	under $15

per person for a three-course meal, excluding drinks and service

Lodging

Luxury hotels, sophisticated resorts, historic lodges, Old West hotels, and rustic inns are among Oregon's diverse accommodations. Cozy bed-and-breakfasts, many of them in Victorian-era houses in small towns, are often real finds.

CATEGORY	COST*
$$$$	over $170
$$$	$110–$170
$$	$60–$110
$	under $60

All prices are for a standard double room, excluding room tax, which varies from 6% to 9½% depending on location.

Outdoor Activities and Sports

BIKING AND HIKING

For the past 20 years, Oregon has set aside 1% of its highway funds for the development and maintenance of bikeways throughout the state, resulting in one of the most extensive networks of bicycle trails in the country. The system of hiking trails through state-park and national-forest lands is equally comprehensive.

BOATING, FISHING, AND RAFTING

Oregon's many waterways afford limitless opportunities for adventure. Many companies operate boating and white-water rafting tours, or you can rent equipment and head out on your own. Fishing requires a license. *See* Fishing *in* Oregon A to Z at the end of this chapter for advice on how to obtain one.

ROCKHOUNDING

Rockhounding—searching for semiprecious or unusual rocks—is very popular in the Ochocos in central Oregon and Harney County and the Stinkingwater Mountains in eastern Oregon. Agate, obsidian, jasper, and thundereggs are among the sought-after stones.

SKIING

Most Oregon downhillers congregate around Mount Hood and Mount Bachelor, but there is also skiing to the south, at Willamette Pass and Mount Ashland. The temperate Willamette Valley generally receives only a few inches of snow a year, but the Coast Range, the Cascade Range, and the Siskiyou Mountains are all Nordic skiers' paradises, crisscrossed by hundreds of miles of trails. Every major downhill ski resort in the state also has Nordic skiing, but don't rule out the many Forest Service trails and logging roads.

Wine Tasting

The Willamette Valley is Oregon's main region for viticulture—many area wineries are open for tours, tasting, or both. South of the Willamette Valley are the Umpqua Valley and Rogue River wine-growing regions. *See* Guided Tours *in* Oregon A to Z at the end of this chapter for a list of companies that conduct winery tours.

Exploring Oregon

Oregon's coastline stretches south from Astoria to the California border. Inland a bit, the fertile Willamette River valley also runs north–south. The mighty Columbia River travels west from the Cascade Range past the Mount Hood Wilderness Area to Astoria. The resort towns of Bend and Sisters are in Central Oregon, and the sparsely populated desert region is east of the Cascades.

Numbers in the text correspond to numbers in the margin and on the Oregon Coast and Willamette Valley/Wine Country; Salem; Eugene; Columbia River Gorge, the Cascades, and Central Oregon; and Eastern Oregon maps.

Great Itineraries

IF YOU HAVE 3 OR 4 DAYS

On your first day take U.S. 101 to the coastal resort town of **Cannon Beach,** and then continue south to ⚟ **Newport,** where Keiko, the orca whale in the *Free Willy* movies, is the star attraction at the **Oregon Coast Aquarium** ③. On day two drive east on U.S. 20, stopping briefly in **Corvallis** before continuing east on U.S. 20 and north on Interstate 5 (I–5) to **Salem** ⑥–⑩, the state capital. After touring Salem, visit one or more of the **Willamette Valley vineyards** before stopping in ⚟ **McMinnville** for the night. On day three take Highway 99W north toward Portland and connect with I–5 heading north to I–84. The interstate winds eastward to the **Columbia Gorge.** At Troutdale, get on the **Historic Columbia River Highway,** which passes **Multnomah Falls** ⑳ before rejoining I–84. Continue east to the **Bonneville Dam** ㉒ and **The Dalles** ㉓. If you'll be staying in the area four days, spend night three in ⚟ **Hood River** and swing down to **Mount Hood** ㉔ the next morning.

IF YOU HAVE 7 OR 8 DAYS

Begin in Oregon's northwest, in **Astoria,** where the Columbia River meets the Pacific Ocean. From there, continue south on U.S. 101 to ⚟ **Cannon Beach.** On day two head south from Cannon Beach to **Tillamook** and the oceanfront parks on the **Three Capes Loop** ②. Continue south to **Newport,** where the **Oregon Coast Aquarium** ③ is a must-see attraction. Spend the night south of Newport in the ⚟ **Florence** area. Drive south on day three to **Coos Bay** and **Bandon,** then east on Highway 42 over the Coast Range to pick up I–5 heading south to ⚑ **Ash-land** ⑱. On day four backtrack north on I–5 to **Medford,** where you can pick up Highway 62 heading north and then east to ⚑ **Crater Lake National Park** ⑯. Spend the night at the park, or backtrack west on Highway 62 and pick up Highway 230 north to Highway 138 west to I–5, which leads north to **Eugene** ⑫–⑮. (If you're not going to stay at Crater Lake, you'll need to get an early start from Medford.) If you've stayed at Crater Lake, on day five take Highway 138 east from the north end of the park to U.S. 97, which travels north past the **Newberry Volcanic National Monument** to ⚑ **Bend** ㉕. If you've spent the night in Eugene, travel east along the McKenzie River on Highway 126 to Highway 242 (closed in winter, in which case stay on 126) to U.S. 20. This route travels past the western-theme town of **Sisters** ㉖ to ⚑ **Bend** ㉕. On day six head north on U.S. 97 and east on Highway 126 and U.S. 26 past the **Ochoco National Forest** and the **John Day Fossil Beds National Monument** ㉝. You have three options for lodgings, depending on how much time you spend at the fossil beds: ⚑ **Mitchell** and ⚑ **John Day** ㉜ are both on U.S. 26; farther east on Highway 7 is ⚑ **Baker City** ㉛. On day seven, take scenic U.S. 30 north from Baker City to North Powder, and then continue north on I–84 to **La Grande** ㉘ and ⚑ **Pendleton** ㉗. If you have the time, spend the night in Pendleton, and on day eight drive west on I–84 to the **Columbia Gorge,** stopping at the **Bonneville Dam** ㉒ and **Multnomah Falls** ⑳.

When to Tour Oregon

Spring weather is changeable on both sides of the Cascades; this is the time when the landscape comes alive with wildflowers, flowering fruit trees (in the Hood River valley), and gardens bursting with rhododendrons and azaleas. February through May are the best months for whale-watching along the coast and bird-watching at the Malheur National Wildlife Refuge in southeastern Oregon. Jacksonville, Eugene, and Portland all host world-class summer music festivals; the theater season in Ashland lasts from February to October. Summer weather along the coast is chancy year-round, but clear days are more frequent in late summer and early fall. July and August are the prime months for visiting Crater Lake National Park, which is often snowed in for the rest of the year. Summer and fall are the best times to visit the many wineries in the Willamette Valley. Winters in western Oregon are usually mild, but they can be relentlessly rainy. To the east of the Cascade Range, winters are clearer, drier, and colder.

THE OREGON COAST

Oregon has 300 mi of white-sand beaches, not a grain of which is privately owned. U.S. 101, called Highway 101 by most Oregonians (it sometimes appears this way in addresses as well), parallels the coast the length of the state, past sea-tortured rocks, brooding headlands, hidden beaches, historic lighthouses, tiny ports, and the Pacific Ocean, a gleaming gunmetal gray stretching to the horizon. With its seaside hamlets and small hotels and resorts, the coast seems to have been created with pleasure in mind. South of Newport, the pace slows. The scenery and fishing and outdoor activities are just as rich as those in the towns to the north, but the area is less crowded and the commercialism less obvious.

Astoria and Vicinity

96 mi northwest of Portland on U.S. 30.

The mighty Columbia River meets the Pacific at Astoria, which was founded in 1811. The city was named for John Jacob Astor, then

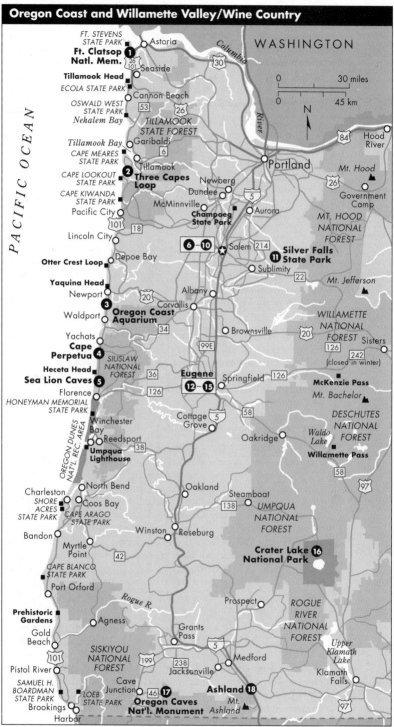

Oregon Coast and Willamette Valley/Wine Country

WASHINGTON

PACIFIC OCEAN

FT. STEVENS STATE PARK
Ft. Clatsop Natl. Mem. ➊
Astoria
Seaside
Tillamook Head
ECOLA STATE PARK
Cannon Beach
OSWALD WEST STATE PARK
Nehalem Bay
TILLAMOOK STATE FOREST

Columbia River

Tillamook Bay
Garibaldi
CAPE MEARES STATE PARK
Tillamook
CAPE LOOKOUT STATE PARK ➋ **Three Capes Loop**
CAPE KIWANDA STATE PARK
Pacific City
Lincoln City
Depoe Bay
Otter Crest Loop
Yaquina Head
Newport
Waldport ➌ **Oregon Coast Aquarium**
Yachats
Cape Perpetua ➍
SIUSLAW NATIONAL FOREST
Heceta Head
Sea Lion Caves ➎
Florence
HONEYMAN MEMORIAL STATE PARK
Winchester Bay
Reedsport
Umpqua Lighthouse
OREGON DUNES NAT'L REC. AREA
North Bend
Charleston
SHORE ACRES STATE PARK
Coos Bay
CAPE ARAGO STATE PARK
Bandon
Myrtle Point
CAPE BLANCO STATE PARK
Port Orford
Prehistoric Gardens
Gold Beach
Pistol River
SAMUEL H. BOARDMAN STATE PARK
LOEB STATE PARK
Brookings
Harbor

Portland
Newberg
Dundee
McMinnville
Champoeg State Park
Aurora
➏–➓ ✪ Salem 214
Silver Falls State Park ⓫
Sublimity
Albany
Corvallis
Brownsville
99E
Eugene ⓬–⓯
Springfield 126
Cottage Grove
Oakland
Steamboat
UMPQUA NATIONAL FOREST
Winston
Roseburg
Crater Lake National Park ⓰
Prospect
ROGUE RIVER NATIONAL FOREST
Grants Pass
Medford
Jacksonville
SISKIYOU NATIONAL FOREST
Cave Junction
Oregon Caves Nat'l. Monument ⓱
Ashland ⓲
Mt. Ashland

Mt. Hood
Government Camp
MT. HOOD NATIONAL FOREST
Hood River
Mt. Jefferson
WILLAMETTE NATIONAL FOREST
Sisters
242 (closed in winter)
McKenzie Pass
Mt. Bachelor
DESCHUTES NATIONAL FOREST
Waldo Lake
Oakridge
Willamette Pass
Upper Klamath Lake
Klamath Falls

Rogue R.
Agness

0   30 miles
0   45 km
N

America's wealthiest man, who financed the original fur-trading colony here. Modern Astoria is a placid amalgamation of small town and hardworking port city. Settlers built sprawling Victorian houses on the flanks of **Coxcomb Hill.** Many of the homes have since been restored and are no less splendid as bed-and-breakfast inns. With so many museums, inns, and recreational offerings, Astoria should be one of the Northwest's prime tourist destinations. Yet the town remains relatively undiscovered, even by Portlanders.

★ ☾ The **Columbia River Maritime Museum,** on the downtown waterfront, is one of the two most interesting man-made tourist attractions on the Oregon coast (Newport's aquarium is the other). Beguiling exhibits at the facility range from the observation tower of the World War II submarine USS *Rasher* (complete with working periscopes) and the fully operational U.S. Coast Guard lightship *Columbia* to the personal belongings of some of the ill-fated passengers of the 2,000 ships that have foundered here since 1811. ⊠ *1792 Marine Dr., at 17th St.,* ☎ *503/ 325–2323.* ⊡ *$5.* ☾ *Daily 9:30–5.*

The **Astoria Column,** a 125-ft monolith atop Coxcomb Hill that was patterned after Trajan's Column in Rome, rewards the 164-step, spiral-stair climb with breathtaking views over Astoria, the Columbia River, the Coast Range, and the Pacific. ⊠ *From U.S. 30 downtown take 16th St. south 1 mi to the top of Coxcomb Hill.* ⊡ *Free.* ☾ *Daily 9– dusk.*

The prim and proper **Flavel House** was built between 1883 and 1885. Its Victorian-era furnishings, many selected by Captain George Flavel, yield insight into the lifestyle of a wealthy 19th-century shipping tycoon. The admission price also includes a visit to the **Heritage Museum.** Housed in the former City Hall, the museum surveys the history of Clatsop County, the oldest American settlement west of the Mississippi. ⊠ *441 8th St., at Duane St.,* ☎ *503/325–2203.* ⊡ *$5.* ☾ *May– Sept., daily 10–5; Oct.–Apr., daily 11–4.*

"Ocean in view! O! The joy!" recorded William Clark, standing on a spit of land south of present-day Astoria in the fall of 1805. After building a fort and wintering here, though, the explorers wrote "O! How horriable is the day waves brakeing with great violence against the ★ ☾ ➊ shore . . . all wet and confined to our shelters." **Fort Clatsop National Memorial** is a faithful replica of the log stockade depicted in Clark's journal. Park rangers, who dress in period garb during the summer and perform early-19th-century tasks like making fire with flint and steel, lend an air of authenticity, as does the damp and lonely ambience of the fort itself. ⊠ *Fort Clatsop Loop Rd. (5 mi south of Astoria; from U.S. 101 cross Youngs Bay Bridge, turn east on Alt. U.S. 101, and follow signs),* ☎ *503/861–2471.* ⊡ *$2.* ☾ *Mid-June–Labor Day, daily 8–6; Labor Day–mid-June, daily 8–5.*

☾ The earthworks of 37-acre **Fort Stevens,** at Oregon's northwestern tip, were mounded up during the Civil War to guard the Columbia against a Confederate attack. No such event occurred, but during World War II, Fort Stevens became the only mainland U.S. military installation to come under enemy (Japanese submarine) fire since the War of 1812. The fort's abandoned gun mounts and eerie subterranean bunkers are a memorable destination. The corroded skeleton of the *Peter Iredale,* a century-old English four-master ship, protrudes from the sand just west of the campground, a stark testament to the malevolence of the Pacific. ⊠ *Fort Stevens Hwy. (from Fort Clatsop, take Alt. U.S. 101 west past U.S. 101, turn north onto Main St.–Fort Stevens Hwy., and* *follow signs),* ☎ *503/861–2000.* 🖅 *$3 per vehicle; park tours in summer $2.50; underground Battery Mishler $2.* ☉ *Mid-May–Sept., daily 10–6; Oct.–mid-May, daily 10–4.*

Dining and Lodging

$–$$ ✕ **Cannery Cafe.** Bright and contemporary, this restaurant in a 100-year-old renovated cannery has windows that look out onto the Columbia River. Fresh salads, large sandwiches, clam chowder, and crab cakes are lunch staples. The varied dinner menu emphasizes fresh seafood, including cioppino and oyster stew, and homemade southern Italian pasta dishes. ⊠ *1 6th St.,* ☎ *503/325–8642. AE, D, MC, V. Closed Mon. No dinner Sun.*

$ ✕ **Columbian Cafe.** Locals love this unpretentious diner with a tongue-in-cheek south-of-the-border decor that's heavy on chili-pepper-shaped Christmas lights and religious icons. Fresh, simple food—crepes with broccoli, cheese, and homemade salsa for lunch; grilled salmon and pasta with a lemon-cream sauce for dinner—is served by a staff that usually includes the owner. Come early; this place always draws a crowd. ⊠ *1114 Marine Dr.,* ☎ *503/325–2233. Reservations not accepted. No credit cards. Closed Sun. No dinner Mon.–Tues.*

$$–$$$ 🏨 **Franklin Street Station Bed & Breakfast.** Ticking grandfather clocks and mellow marine light filtering through leaded-glass windows set the tone at this velvet-upholstered Victorian built in 1900 on the slopes above downtown Astoria. Breakfasts are huge, hot, and satisfying, and there's always a plate of goodies and a pot of coffee in the kitchen. ⊠ *1140 Franklin St., 97103,* ☎ *503/325–4314 or 800/448–1098. 5 rooms. AE, D, MC, V.*

$$ 🏨 **Red Lion Inn.** The reliable chain's property sits right on the Columbia River, near the Astoria Bridge; the room balconies have views of the river, marina, and bridge. The small rooms and public areas are decorated in soothing earth tones. ⊠ *400 Industry St., 97103,* ☎ *503/ 325–7373. 124 rooms. Restaurant, bar. AE, D, DC, MC, V.*

$–$$ 🏨 **Grandview Bed & Breakfast.** This turreted mansion lives up to its name—decks and telescopes look out over Astoria, with the Columbia River and Washington State beyond. The interior is bright, with scrubbed hardwood floors and lace-filled rooms. The breakfast specialty is bagels with cream cheese and smoked salmon from Josephson's (☞ *Shopping, below).* ⊠ *1574 Grand Ave., 97103,* ☎ *503/ 325–5555 or 800/488–3250. 9 rooms, 7 with bath. D, MC, V.*

Shopping

Josephson's (⊠ 106 Marine Dr., ☎ 503/325–2190) is one of the Oregon coast's oldest commercial smokehouses, preparing Columbia River chinook salmon in the traditional alder-smoked and lox styles. Smoked shark, tuna, oysters, mussels, sturgeon, scallops, and prawns are also available by the pound or in sealed gift packs.

Seaside

12 mi south of Astoria on U.S. 101.

For years, Seaside had a reputation as a garish arcade-filled town. But it cleaned up its act and now supports a bustling tourist trade with hotels, condominiums, and restaurants surrounding a long beach. A 2-mi boardwalk parallels the shore and stately old beachfront homes. Only 90 mi from Portland, Seaside is often crowded, so it's not the place to come if you crave solitude. Peak times include February, during the Trail's End Marathon; mid-March, when hordes of teenagers descend on the town during spring break; and July, when the annual Miss Oregon Pageant is in full swing.

Dining

$–$$ ✕ **Doogers.** The original branch of this Northwest chain is much loved by local families. The seafood is expertly prepared, and the creamy clam chowder may be the best on the coast. ⊠ *505 Broadway,* ☎ *503/738–3773. Reservations not accepted. AE, MC, V.*

En Route   A brisk 2-mi hike from U.S. 101 south of Seaside leads to the 1,100-ft-high viewing point atop **Tillamook Head.** The view from here takes in the **Tillamook Rock Light Station,** which stands a mile or so out to sea. The lonely beacon, built in 1881 on a straight-sided rock, towers 41 ft above the surrounding ocean. In 1957 the lighthouse was abandoned; it is now a columbarium.

Eight miles south of Seaside, U.S. 101 passes the entrance to **Ecola State Park,** a playground of sea-sculpted rocks, sandy shoreline, green headlands, and panoramic views. The park's main beach can be crowded in summer, but the **Indian Beach** area contains an often deserted cove and explorable tide pools. ☎ *503/436–2844.* 🛒 *$3 per vehicle.* ☉ *Daily dawn–dusk.*

Cannon Beach

10 mi south of Seaside on U.S. 101; 80 mi west of Portland on U.S. 26.

Cannon Beach is Seaside's refined, artistic alter ego, a more mellow yet trendy place (population 1,200) for Portlanders to take the sea air. One of the most charming hamlets on the coast, the town contains beachfront homes and hotels, and a weathered-cedar downtown shopping district. On the downside, the Carmel of the Oregon coast is expensive, crowded, and afflicted with a subtle, moneyed hauteur (such as the town's recently enacted ban on vacation-home rentals) that may grate on more plebeian nerves.

The town got its name when a cannon from the wrecked schooner USS *Shark* washed ashore in 1846 (the piece is on display a mile east of town on U.S. 101). Towering over the broad sandy beach is **Haystack Rock,** a 235-ft-high monolith that is supposedly the most-photographed feature of the Oregon coast. The rock is temptingly accessible during some low tides, but the coast guard regularly airlifts stranded climbers from its precipitous sides, and falls have claimed numerous lives over the years. Every May the town hosts the Cannon Beach Sandcastle Contest, for which thousands throng the beach to view imaginative and often startling works in this most transient of art forms.

Shops and galleries selling kites, upscale clothing, local art, wine, coffee, and gourmet food line **Hemlock Street,** Cannon Beach's main thoroughfare.

Dining and Lodging

$$ ✕ **The Bistro.** Flowers, candlelight, and classical music create a romantic
★   atmosphere at this 12-table restaurant. The three-course prix-fixe menu includes imaginative Continental-influenced renditions of fresh local seafood dishes; monstrous scampi and a Pacific seafood stew often appear as specials. ⊠ *263 N. Hemlock St.,* ☎ *503/436–2661. Reservations essential. MC, V. Closed Tues.–Wed. Nov.–Jan. No lunch.*

$$ ✕ **Blue Sky Cafe.** Stained glass, a jungle of plants, and butcher-paper-covered tables lend a quirky air to this hole-in-the-wall café that's 13 mi south of Cannon Beach in Manzanita. Specialties include crab and rock shrimp baked in parchment, Thai coconut-curry soup, feta-mushroom-rosemary soup, and memorably rich desserts. ⊠ *154 Laneda St., off U.S. 101, Manzanita,* ☎ *503/368–5712. No credit cards. Closed Mon.–Tues. Oct.–June. No lunch.*

$–$$ ✕ **Doogers.** Like the original Doogers in Seaside, the Cannon Beach branch serves superb seafood in a casual, contemporary setting. Don't pass up the clam chowder. ⊠ *1371 S. Hemlock St.,* ☎ *503/436–2225. Reservations not accepted. AE, MC, V.*

$ ✕ **Lazy Susan Cafe.** Entrées at this laid-back spot—*the* place to come for breakfast in Cannon Beach—include quiche, omelets, hot cereal, and a substantial order of waffles topped with fruit and orange syrup. Don't leave without tasting the fresh-baked scones and the home fries. ⊠ *Coaster Sq., 126 N. Hemlock St.,* ☎ *503/436–2816. Reservations not accepted. No credit cards. Closed Tues. No dinner Mon., Wed.*

$$$–$$$$ ✕⌂ **Stephanie Inn.** Superior service, luxurious rooms, and tastefully
★ decorated public areas make this three-story inn the premier ocean-front hotel in Cannon Beach. Impeccably maintained, with country-style furnishings, fireplaces, large bathrooms with whirlpool tubs, and balconies commanding outstanding views of Haystack Rock, the rooms are so comfortable you may never want to leave—except perhaps to enjoy the four-course prix-fixe dinners (reservations essential) of innovative Pacific Northwest cuisine. Generous country breakfasts are included in the tariff, as are evening wine and hors d'oeuvres. ⊠ *2740 S. Pacific, 97110,* ☎ *503/436–2221 or 800/633–3466,* ℻ *503/436–9711. 46 rooms. Dining room, in-room VCRs, minibars, refrigerators, massage, library. AE, D, DC, MC, V.*

$–$$$$ ⌂ **Hallmark Resort at Cannon Beach.** Large suites with fireplaces, whirlpool tubs, kitchenettes, and great views make this triple-decker oceanfront resort a good choice for families or couples looking for a romantic splurge. The rooms, all with spacious balconies and oak-tile baths, have soothing color schemes. The least expensive units do not have views. ⊠ *1400 S. Hemlock St., 97110,* ☎ *503/436–1566 or 800/ 345–5676,* ℻ *503/436–0324. 132 rooms, 5 rental homes, 24 units in town. Restaurant, bar, refrigerators, indoor pool, wading pool, sauna, exercise room, laundry service. AE, D, DC, MC, V.*

$–$$$ ⌂ **Webb's Scenic Surf.** Small and family-operated, this beachfront hotel is a throwback to simpler times in Cannon Beach, before trendiness translated into big resorts and $500 weekends. Many of the functional rooms have kitchens and fireplaces. For the budget traveler, this is the best deal in town, but reservations are a must. ⊠ *255 N. Larch St., 97110,* ☎ *503/436–2706 or 800/374–9322,* ℻ *503/436–1229. 14 rooms. MC, V.*

En Route South of Cannon Beach, U.S. 101 climbs 700 ft above the Pacific, providing dramatic views and often hair-raising curves as it winds along the flank of **Neahkahnie Mountain.** Cryptic carvings on beach rocks near here and centuries-old Native American legends of shipwrecked Europeans gave rise to a tale that the survivors of a sunken Spanish galleon buried a fortune in doubloons somewhere on the side of the 1,661-ft-high mountain.

Oswald West State Park

10 mi south of Cannon Beach on U.S. 101.

Adventurous travelers will enjoy a sojourn at one of the best-kept secrets on the Pacific coast, Oswald West State Park, at the base of Neahkahnie Mountain. Park in one of the two lots on U.S. 101 and use a park-provided wheelbarrow to trundle your camping gear down a ½-mi trail. An old-growth forest surrounds the 36 primitive camp-sites (reservations not accepted), and the spectacular beach contains caves and tide pools.

The trail to the summit, on the left about 2 mi south of the parking lots for Oswald West State Park (marked only by a HIKERS sign), rewards the intrepid with unobstructed views over surf, sand, forest, and mountain. Come in December or April and you might spot pods of gray whales. ☎ *503/368–5943; 800/551–6949 for campground information.* ⌂ *Day use free, campsite $10–$13.* ☉ *Day use year-round, daily dawn–dusk; camping Mar.–Oct.*

En Route   After passing through several small fishing, logging, and resort towns, U.S. 101 skirts around **Tillamook Bay,** where the Miami, Kilchis, Wilson, Trask, and Tillamook rivers enter the Pacific. The bay is a sport-fishing mecca where the quarry includes sea-run cutthroat trout, bottom fish, and silver, chinook, and steelhead salmon, along with mussels, oysters, clams, and the delectable Dungeness crab. Charter-fishing services operate out of the **Garibaldi** fishing harbor 10 mi north of Tillamook. For some of the best rock fishing in the state, try Tillamook Bay's North Jetty.

Tillamook

30 mi south of Oswald State Park and Neahkahnie Mountain on U.S. 101.

Tillamook County is something of a wet Wisconsin-on-the-Pacific. Though it lacks the sophisticated charm of Cannon Beach, the town of Tillamook, about 2 mi inland from the ocean, is a quiet, natural retreat. Surrounded by rich dairy land and blessed with abundant freshwater and saltwater fishing, it has some of the finest scenery on the Oregon coast.

The **Pioneer Museum** in Tillamook's 1905 county courthouse has an intriguing if old-fashioned hodgepodge of Native American, pioneer, logging, and natural-history exhibits, along with antique vehicles and military artifacts. ⊠ *2106 2nd St.,* ☎ *503/842–4553.* ⌂ *$2.* ☉ *Mid-Mar.–Sept., Mon.–Sat. 8–5, Sun. noon–5; Oct.–mid-Mar., Tues.–Sat. 8–5, Sun. noon–5.*

More than 600,000 visitors annually press their noses against the spotlessly clean windows at the **Tillamook County Creamery,** the largest cheese-making plant on the West Coast. Here the rich milk from the area's thousands of Holstein and brown Swiss cows becomes ice cream, butter, and cheddar and Monterey Jack cheeses. Exhibits at the visitor center, where free samples are dispensed, explain the cheese-making process. ⊠ *4175 Hwy. 101 N, 2 mi north of Tillamook,* ☎ *503/842–4481.* ⌂ *Free.* ☉ *Mid-Sept.–May, daily 8–6; June–mid-Sept., daily 8–8.*

The **Blue Heron French Cheese Company** specializes in French-style cheeses—Camembert, Brie, and others. There's a petting zoo for kids, a sit-down deli, and a gift shop that carries wines and jams, mustards, and other products from Oregon. ⊠ *2001 Blue Heron Dr. (watch for signs from U.S. 101),* ☎ *503/842–8281.* ⌂ *Free.* ☉ *Memorial Day–Labor Day, daily 8–8; Labor Day–Memorial Day, daily 9–5.*

Housed in the world's largest wooden structure, a former blimp hangar south of town, the **Naval Air Station Museum** displays one of the finest private collections of vintage aircraft from World War II, including a B-25 Mitchell and an ME-109 Messerschmidt. The 20-story building is big enough to hold a dozen football fields. ⊠ *6030 Hangar Rd. (½* *mi south of Tillamook; head east from U.S. 101 on Long Prairie Rd. and follow signs),* ☎ *503/842–1130.* 🎫 *$5.* ☉ *Apr.–Nov., daily 9–6; Dec.–Mar., daily 10–5.*

Outdoor Activities and Sports

Alderbrook Golf Club (✉ 7300 Alderbrook Rd., ☎ 503/842–6413) is an 18-hole, par-69 golf course. The greens fee is $20; an optional cart costs $20.

Three Capes Loop

★ ❷ *Starts south of downtown Tillamook off 3rd St.*

The **Three Capes Loop,** a 35-mi byway off U.S. 101, is one of the coast's most thrilling driving experiences. The loop winds along the coast between Tillamook and Pacific City, passing three distinctive headlands—Cape Meares, Cape Lookout, and Cape Kiwanda. Bayocean Road heading west from Tillamook passes what was the thriving resort town of Bay Ocean. More than 30 years ago, Bay Ocean washed into the sea—houses, a bowling alley, everything—during a raging Pacific storm.

Nine miles west of Tillamook, trails from the parking lot at the end of Bay Ocean Spit lead through the dunes to a usually uncrowded and highly walkable white-sand beach.

Cape Meares State Park is on the northern tip of the Three Capes Loop. Cape Meares was named for English navigator John Meares, who voyaged along this coast in 1788. The restored **Cape Meares Lighthouse,** built in 1890 and open to the public from May to September, provides a sweeping view over the cliff to the caves and sea-lion rookery on the rocks below. A many-trunked Sitka spruce known as the Octopus Tree grows near the lighthouse parking lot. ✉ *Three Capes Loop 10 mi west of Tillamook,* ☎ *503/842–3182.* 🎫 *Free.* ☉ *Park daily dawn–dusk; lighthouse May–Sept., daily 11–4; Mar., Apr., and Oct., weekends 11–4.*

Cape Lookout State Park lies south of the beach towns of Oceanside and Netarts. A fairly easy 2-mi trail—marked on the highway as WILDLIFE VIEWING AREA—leads through giant spruces, western red cedars, and hemlocks to views of Cascade Head to the south and Cape Meares to the north. Wildflowers, more than 150 species of birds, and migrating whales passing by in early April make this trail a favorite with nature lovers. The park has a picnic area overlooking the sea and a year-round campground. ✉ *Three Capes Loop 8 mi south of Cape Meares,* ☎ *503/842–4981.* 🎫 *Day use $3, campsites $16.* ☉ *Daily dawn–9 PM.*

Huge waves pound the jagged sandstone cliffs and caves at **Cape Kiwanda State Natural Area.** The much-photographed, 327-ft-high **Haystack Rock** juts out of Nestucca Bay just south of here. Surfers ride some of the longest waves on the coast, hang gliders soar above the shore, and beachcombers explore tide pools and take in unparalleled ocean views. ✉ *Three Capes Loop 15 mi south of Cape Lookout,* ☎ *503/842–3182.* 🎫 *Free.* ☉ *Daily dawn–dusk.*

Pacific City

1½ mi south of Cape Kiwanda on Three Capes Loop.

The beach at Pacific City, the town visible from Cape Kiwanda, is one of the only places in the state where fishing dories (flat-bottom boats with high, flaring sides) are launched directly into the surf instead of from harbors or docks. During the commercial salmon season in late summer, it's possible to buy salmon directly from the fishermen.

A walk along the flat white-sand beach at **Robert Straub State Park** leads down to the mouth of the Nestucca River, considered by many to be the best fishing river on the north coast. ⊠ *West from main intersection in downtown Pacific City across the Nestucca River (follow signs),* ☎ *800/551–6949.* 🎫 *Free.* ⊙ *Daily dawn–dusk.*

OFF THE
BEATEN PATH **NATURE CONSERVANCY CASCADE HEAD TRAIL** – The trail at one of the most unusual headlands on the Oregon coast winds through a rain forest where 250-year-old Sitka spruces and a dense green undergrowth of mosses and ferns is nourished by 100-inch annual rainfalls. After the forest comes grassy and treeless Cascade Head, a rare example of a maritime prairie. Magnificent views down to the Salmon River and west to the Coast Range open up as you continue along the headland, where black-tailed deer often graze and turkey vultures soar in the strong winds. You need to be in fairly good shape for the first and steepest part of the hike, which can be done in about an hour. ⊠ *Savage Rd., 6 mi south of Neskowin off U.S. 101 (turn west on Three Rocks Rd. and north on Savage),* ☎ *503/230–1221.* 🎫 *Free.* ⊙ *July–Dec., daily dawn–dusk.*

Lincoln City

16 mi south of Pacific City on U.S. 101; 78 mi west of Portland on Hwy. 99W and Hwy. 18.

Once a series of small villages, Lincoln City is a sprawling, suburbanish town without a center. But the endless tourist amenities make up for whatever it lacks in charm. Clustered like barnacles on the offshore reefs are fast-food restaurants, gift shops, supermarkets, candy stores, antiques markets, dozens of motels and hotels, a factory-outlet mall, and an ungainly looking casino. Lincoln City is the most popular destination city on the Oregon coast, but its only real claim to fame is the 445-ft-long **D River,** stretching from its source in Devil's Lake to the Pacific; the *Guinness Book of Records* lists the D as the world's shortest river.

Dining and Lodging

$$–$$$ ✕ **Bay House.** This restaurant inside a charming bungalow serves meals to linger over while you enjoy views across sunset-gilded Siletz Bay. The seasonal Northwest cuisine includes Dungeness crab cakes with roasted-chili chutney, fresh halibut Parmesan, and roast duckling with cranberry compote. The wine list is extensive, the service impeccable. ⊠ *5911 S.W. Hwy. 101, about 5 mi south of Lincoln City,* ☎ *541/996–3222. AE, D, MC, V. Closed Mon.–Tues. Nov.–Apr. No lunch.*

$–$$ ✕ **Kyllo's.** Light-filled Kyllo's rests on stilts beside the D River. It's one of the best places in Lincoln City to enjoy casual but well-prepared seafood, pasta, and meat dishes. ⊠ *1110 N.W. 1st Ct.,* ☎ *541/994–3179. AE, D, MC, V.*

$ ✕ **Lighthouse Brew Pub.** This westernmost outpost of the Portland-based McMenamin brothers' microbrewery empire has the same virtues as their other establishments: fresh local ales; good, unpretentious sandwiches, burgers, and salads; and cheerfully eccentric decor that includes psychedelic art by Northwest painters. Try the stout-ale milk shake. ⊠ *4157 N. Hwy. 101,* ☎ *541/994–7238. Reservations not accepted. MC, V.*

$$ ⛅ **Ester Lee Motel.** On a bluff overlooking the cold Pacific, this small whitewashed motel attracts much repeat business. The fine amenities include wood-burning fireplaces, cable TV, and, in most rooms, full kitchens. Request a unit in the older section; the rooms there are larger and have brick fireplaces and picture windows. ✉ *3803 S.W. Hwy. 101, 97367,* ☎ *541/996–3606 or 888/996–3606. 53 units. D, MC, V.*

Outdoor Activities and Sports

The greens fee at the 18-hole, par-66 course at the **Lakeside Golf & Racquet Club** (✉ 3245 Clubhouse Dr., ☎ 541/994–8442) is $30; an optional cart costs $25.

Gleneden Beach

7 mi south of Lincoln City on U.S. 101.

Salishan, the most famous resort on the Oregon coast, perches high above placid Siletz Bay. This expensive collection of guest rooms, vacation homes, condominiums, restaurants, golf fairways, tennis courts, and covered walkways blends into a forest preserve; if not for the signs, you'd scarcely be able to find it.

Dining and Lodging

$$$ ✕ **Chez Jeanette.** This country-French cottage nestles in the shore
★ pines between U.S. 101 and the ocean and seems a continent away from frenetic downtown Lincoln City. The atmosphere is quiet, with a fireplace, antiques, and tables set with linen and crystal. Try the carpetbagger steak, a thick fillet stuffed with tiny local oysters, wrapped in bacon, and sauced with crème fraîche, scallions, spinach, and bacon. The rest of the menu puts a Parisian spin on local products from the sea, sky, and pasture. ✉ *7150 Old Hwy. 101 (turn west from U.S. 101 at the Salishan entrance, then turn south and go ¼ mi), Gleneden Beach,* ☎ *541/764–3434. Reservations essential. AE, MC, V. Closed Sun.–Mon. Labor Day–June. No lunch.*

$$$ ✕ **Gourmet Dining Room at Salishan.** The Salishan resort's main din-
★ ing room, a multilevel expanse of hushed waiters, hillside ocean views, and snow-white linen, has built an enviable reputation for showy Continental cuisine. House specialties include fresh local fish, game, beef, and lamb; the fettuccine with fat scallops and salmon caviar is heavenly. By all means make a selection from the wine cellar, which at 20,000 bottles holds the largest collection in the state. ✉ *7760 N. Hwy. 101,* ☎ *541/764–2371. Reservations essential. Jacket and tie. AE, D, DC, MC, V. No lunch.*

$$$$ ⛅ **Salishan Lodge.** From the soothing, silvered-cedar ambience of its rooms, divided among eight units in a hillside forest preserve, Salishan embodies a uniquely Oregonian elegance. Each of the quiet rooms has a wood-burning fireplace, a balcony, and original works by Northwest artists. Given all this, plus fine dining (☞ *above*), you'll understand why the timeless atmosphere also carries what may well be the steepest price tag on the coast. ✉ *7760 N. Hwy. 101, 97388,* ☎ *541/ 764–2371 or 800/452–2300,* ℻ *541/764–3681. 205 rooms. Restaurant, bar, in-room modem lines, minibars, no-smoking rooms, room service, indoor lap pool, beauty salon, massage, sauna, driving range, 18-hole golf course, putting green, 4 tennis courts, exercise room, hiking, beach, billiards, piano, library, baby-sitting, playground, laundry service and dry cleaning, concierge. AE, D, DC, MC, V.*

Outdoor Activities and Sports

Salishan Golf Links (⊠ 7760 N. Hwy. 101, ☎ 541/764–3632) is an 18-hole, par-72, often windy seaside course. The greens fee is $60; an optional cart costs $26.

Depoe Bay

12 mi south of Lincoln City on U.S. 101.

The tiny harbor at Depoe Bay, the world's smallest, may look vaguely familiar: It was used as a setting for the film *One Flew Over the Cuckoo's Nest*. The bay, with a narrow channel and deep water, is one of the most protected on the coast; it supports a thriving fleet of commercial- and charter-fishing boats. The **Spouting Horn,** a natural cleft in the basalt cliffs on the waterfront, blasts seawater skyward during heavy weather.

Outdoor Activities and Sports

Tradewinds (⊠ U.S. 101 near Coast Guard Boat Basin Rd., ☎ 541/765–2345 or 800/445–8730) operates $10 whale-watching cruises on the hour, when conditions permit, from 10 AM until 5 or 6 PM. The ticket office is at the north end of the Depoe Bay Bridge. A few of the gigantic gray whales that migrate annually past the Oregon coast break away from their herd and linger year-round in Depoe Bay.

En Route   Five miles south of Depoe Bay off U.S. 101 (watch for signs), the **Otter Crest Loop,** another scenic byway, winds along the cliff tops. The road has been closed for a few years but should reopen sometime in 1998. British explorer Captain James Cook named the 500-ft-high **Cape Foulweather** on a blustery March day in 1778. Backward-leaning shore pines lend mute witness to the 100 mph winds that still strafe this exposed spot. At the viewing point at the **Devil's Punchbowl,** a mile south of Cape Foulweather, you can peer down into a collapsed sandstone sea cave carved out by the powerful waters of the Pacific. About 100 ft to the north in the rocky tide pools of the beach known as **Marine Gardens,** purple sea urchins and orange starfish can be seen at low tide. The Otter Crest Loop rejoins U.S. 101 about 4 mi south of Cape Foulweather near **Yaquina Head,** which has been designated an Outstanding Natural Area. Harbor seals, sea lions, cormorants, murres, puffins, and guillemots frolic in the water and on the rocks below **Yaquina Bay Lighthouse**—a gleaming white tower activated in 1873.

Newport

12 mi south of Depoe Bay on U.S. 101; 114 mi from Portland, south on I–5 and west on Hwy. 34 and U.S. 20.

Newport hasn't been the same since Keiko, the orca star of *Free Willy,* arrived at the Oregon Coast Aquarium in 1996. Suddenly this small harbor and fishing town with about 8,000 residents became one of the most visited places on the coast. The surge of tourists brought a new prosperity to a town feeling the pinch of federally imposed fishing restrictions, which had cut into its traditional economy.

Newport exists on two levels: the highway above, threading its way through the community's main business district, and the old **Bayfront** along Yaquina Bay below (watch for signs on U.S. 101). With its high-masted fishing fleet, well-worn buildings, seafood markets, and art galleries and shops, Newport's Bayfront is an ideal place for an afternoon stroll. So many male sea lions in Yaquina Bay loiter near crab pots and bark from the waterfront piers that locals call the area the Bachelor Club.

Nye Beach, a neighborhood to the east of the highway, preserves a few remnants of Newport's crusty past. Many old cottages have been gentrified, but you can still get an idea of the simple beach architecture that until very recently characterized most of the Oregon coast. The Sylvia Beach Hotel (☞ Dining and Lodging, *below*), built in 1913 on a sea wall above the beach, once was billed as the honeymoon capital of Oregon. The graceful **Yaquina Bay Bridge,** a Work Projects Administration structure completed in 1936, leads to Newport's southern section.

★ ☾ ❸ The **Oregon Coast Aquarium,** a 4½-acre complex, contains re-creations of offshore and near-shore Pacific marine habitats, all teeming with life: playful sea otters (rescued from the Exxon *Valdez* oil spill in Alaska), comical puffins, fragile jellyfish, and even a 60-pound octopus. A sequence of exhibits follows a drop of rain from the forested uplands of the Coast Range, through the tidal estuary, and out to sea. There's a salty hands-on interactive area for children, and North America's largest seabird aviary. The biggest attraction—literally—is Keiko, the 4-ton killer whale brought to the aquarium to be rehabilitated and, hopefully, released back into the wild. Underwater viewing windows provide a thrilling opportunity to watch this magnificent mammal, the star of the movie *Free Willy,* in his state-of-the-art pool. ⊠ *2820 S.E. Ferry Slip Rd. (heading south from Newport, turn right at southern end of Yaquina Bay Bridge and follow signs),* ☎ *541/867–3474.* ☞ *$8.* ☉ *Memorial Day–Labor Day, daily 9–6; Labor Day–Memorial Day, daily 10–5.*

Interactive and interpretive exhibits at Oregon State University's **Hatfield Marine Science Center,** which is connected by a trail to the Oregon Coast Aquarium, explain current marine research from a global, bird's-eye, eye-level, and microscopic perspective. The star of the show is a large octopus in a touch tank near the entrance. She seems as interested in human visitors as they are in her; guided by a staff volunteer, you can sometimes reach in to stroke her suction-tipped tentacles. ⊠ *2030 S. Marine Science Dr. (heading south from Newport, cross Yaquina Bay Bridge on U.S. 101 S and follow signs),* ☎ *541/867–0100.* ☞ *Suggested donation $3.* ☉ *Memorial Day–Labor Day, daily 10–6; Labor Day–Memorial Day, Thurs.–Mon. 10–4.*

Mariner Square (⊠ 250 S.W. Bay Blvd.) has a **Ripley's Believe It or Not** and **The Wax Works** (☎ 541/265–2206 for both) and, in a boat moored across the street, **Undersea Gardens** (☎ 541/265–2206), where divers put on underwater shows.

Dining and Lodging

$$–$$$ ✕ **Tables of Content.** The well-plotted prix-fixe menu at the restaurant of the outstanding Sylvia Beach Hotel (☞ *below*) changes nightly. Chances are the main dish will be fresh local seafood, perhaps a moist grilled salmon fillet in a sauce Dijonnaise, served with sautéed vegetables, fresh-baked breads, rice pilaf, and a decadent dessert. The interior is functional and unadorned, with family-size tables, but decor isn't the reason to come here. ⊠ *267 N.W. Cliff St. (from U.S. 101 head west on 3rd St.),* ☎ *541/265–5428. Reservations essential. AE, MC, V. No lunch.*

$$ ✕ **Canyon Way Restaurant and Bookstore.** Cod, Dungeness crab cakes, bouillabaisse, and Yaquina Bay oysters are among the specialties of this Newport dining spot up the hill from the center of the Bayfront. There's also a deli counter for take-out. The restaurant, which has an outdoor patio, is to one side of a well-stocked bookstore. ⊠ *S.W. Canyon Way off Bay Front Blvd.,* ☎ *541/265–8319. AE, DC, MC, V. Closed Sun. No dinner Mon.*

$–$$ ✕ **Don Petrie's Italian Food Co.** A little hole-in-the-sand eatery in Nye Beach, Don Petrie's serves some of the best seafood lasagna you'll ever eat. Get here early, especially on weekends. ⊠ *613 N.W. 3rd St.,* ☎ *541/265–3663. Reservations not accepted. MC, V.*

$ ✕ **Whale's Tale.** The atmosphere is casual and family-oriented at this Bayfront restaurant with a menu of fresh local seafood, thick clam chowder, fish-and-chips, burgers, and sandwiches. ⊠ *452 S.W. Bay Blvd.,* ☎ *541/265–8660. AE, D, DC, MC, V. Closed Wed. Nov.–Apr.*

$$–$$$ 🏨 **The Embarcadero.** This resort of condominium/vacation rentals at the east end of Bay Boulevard has great views of Yaquina Bay and its graceful bridge. The public areas have a casual ambience. Spacious suites have one or two bedrooms, with a bay-side deck, a fireplace, and a kitchen. ⊠ *1000 S.E. Bay Blvd., 97365,* ☎ *541/265–8521 or 800/547–4779,* FAX *541/265–7844. 100 units. Restaurant, bar, indoor pool, outdoor hot tub, sauna, dock, boating, fishing. AE, D, DC, MC, V.*

$$–$$$ 🏨 **Sylvia Beach Hotel.** Make reservations far in advance for this 1913-
★ vintage beachfront hotel, whose antiques-filled rooms are named for famous writers. A pendulum swings over the bed in the Poe room. The Christie, Twain, and Colette rooms are the most luxurious; all have fireplaces, decks, and great ocean views. The rooms have no phones or TVs. A well-stocked split-level upstairs library has decks, a fireplace, slumbering cats, and too-comfortable chairs. Complimentary mulled wine is served here nightly at 10. A breakfast buffet, included in the room rate, includes homemade pastries, cereals, and a hot entrée. ⊠ *267 N.W. Cliff St., 97365,* ☎ *541/265–5428. 20 rooms. Restaurant, library. AE, MC, V.*

Outdoor Activities and Sports

Fossils, clams, mussels, and other aeons-old marine creatures, easily dug from soft sandstone cliffs, make **Beverly Beach State Park,** 5 mi north of Newport, a favorite with young beachcombers. Agate hunters regularly comb **Agate Beach,** just north of Newport, for these colorful quartz treasures.

Shopping

On Newport's **Bay Boulevard** you'll find the finest group of fresh seafood markets on the coast. **Englund Marine Supply** (⊠ 424 S.W. Bay Blvd., ☎ 541/265–9275) carries nautical supplies. **Nature's Window** (⊠ 338 S.W. Bay Blvd., ☎ 541/265–3940) stocks interesting science- and nature-related gift items. **Wood Gallery** (⊠ 818 S.W. Bay Blvd., ☎ 541/265–6843) sells wood crafts and paintings.

En Route Chain-saw sculpture—a peculiar Oregon art form—reaches its dubious pinnacle at **Sea Gulch,** a full-size ghost town inhabited by more than 300 carved-wood figures. Ray Kowalski wields his Stihl chain saw to create cowboys, Indians, hillbillies, trolls, gnomes, and other humorous figures. ⊠ *U.S. 101, 10 mi south of Newport,* ☎ *541/563–2727.* 🎟 *$4.50.* ☉ *Apr.–Sept., daily 8–5; Oct.–Mar., weekdays 8–5.*

Waldport

15 mi south of Newport on U.S. 101; 67 mi west of Corvallis on Hwy. 34 and U.S. 20.

Long ago the base of the Alsi Indians, Waldport later became a gold-rush town and a logging center. In the 1980s it garnered national attention when local residents fought the timber industry and stopped the spraying of dioxin-based defoliants in the Coast Range forests. Waldport attracts many retirees and those seeking an alternative to the expensive beach resorts nearby.

The **Drift Creek Wilderness** east of Waldport holds some of the rare old-growth forest that has triggered battles between the timber industry and environmentalists. Hemlocks hundreds of years old grow in parts of this 9-square-mi area. The 2-mi **Harris Ranch Trail** winds through these ancient giants—you may even spot a spotted owl. The Siuslaw National Forest–Waldport Ranger Station provides directions and maps. ⊠ *Risely Creek Rd. (from Waldport, take Hwy. 34 east for 7 mi to the Alsea River crossing),* ☎ *541/563–3211.* ☉ *Daily 8–4.*

Lodging

$$$–$$$$ 🏨 **Cliff House Bed-and-Breakfast.** The view from Yaquina John Point, on which this B&B sits, is magnificent. An almost overwhelming assortment of Asian and European antiques—including a 500-year-old sleigh bed, lacquered screens, and Chinese porcelains—adorns the house, which in livelier days was a bordello. The plush rooms all have ocean views and color TVs and VCRs. Three have balconies and wood-burning stoves. A glass-fronted terrace looking out over 8 mi of white-sand beach leads down to the garden. Breakfasts are as sumptuous as the surroundings. ⊠ *1450 Adahi Rd., 1 block west of U.S. 101, 97394,* ☎ *541/563–2506,* 𝔽𝔸𝕏 *541/563–4393. 4 rooms. Hot tub, sauna. MC, V.*

Outdoor Activities and Sports

McKinley's Marina (⊠ Hwy. 34, ☎ 541/563–4656) rents boats and crab pots to those who want to take advantage of the excellent crabbing in Alsea Bay.

Yachats

8 mi south of Waldport on U.S. 101.

A tiny burg of 635 inhabitants, Yachats (pronounced Ya-*hots*) has acquired a reputation among Oregon beach lovers that is disproportionate to its size. A relaxed alternative to the more touristy communities to the north, Yachats has all the coastal pleasures: B&Bs, good restaurants, deserted beaches, tide pools, surf-pounded crags, fishing, and crabbing. The town's name is a Native American word meaning "foot of the mountain."

Dining and Lodging

$$ ✕ **The Adobe Restaurant.** The food at the dining room of the Adobe Hotel doesn't always measure up to the extraordinary ocean views, but if you stick to the fresh seafood, you'll come away satisfied. The Baked Crab Pot is a rich, bubbling casserole filled with Dungeness crab and cheese in a shallot cream sauce; best of all is the Captain's Seafood Platter, heaped with prawns, scallops, grilled oysters, and razor clams. ⊠ *1555 Hwy. 101,* ☎ *541/547–3141. AE, D, DC, MC, V.*

$$ ✕ **La Serre.** Don't be dismayed by the vaguely steak-and-salad-bar am-
★ bience at this skylit, plant-filled restaurant—the chef's deft touch with fresh seafood attracts knowledgeable diners from as far away as Florence and Newport. Try the tender geoduck clam, breaded with Parmesan cheese and flash-fried in lemon-garlic butter. A reasonably priced wine list and mouthwatering desserts complete the package. La Serre also serves Sunday brunch. ⊠ *2nd and Beach Sts.,* ☎ *541/547–3420. AE, MC, V. Closed Jan. and Tues. No lunch.*

$ ✕ **Rainforest Roadhouse.** Organic produce, grains, and other ingredients (even the coffee in the espresso is organic) and hormone- and antibiotic-free chicken and beef go into the eclectic cuisine—anything from stir-fries to tacos, including many vegetarian dishes—prepared at this folksy restaurant. ⊠ *4th St. and U.S. 101,* ☎ *541/547–3848. MC, V.*

$$$ 🏠 **Ziggurat.** You have to see this four-story cedar-and-glass pyramid 6½ mi south of Yachats to believe it. And you need to spend a night or two, serenaded by the wind and sea, to fully appreciate it. Odd angles, contemporary furnishings, and works of art gathered on the owners' world travels lend a discerning, sophisticated air. Two first-floor suites open out to grassy cliffs; the smaller fourth-floor bedroom has two balconies and dramatic views. There are a few rules: Pets, smoking, and children under 14 are not permitted. ⊠ *95330 Hwy. 101, 97498,* ☎ *541/547–3925. 3 rooms. No credit cards.*

$–$$$ 🏠 **The Adobe.** The knotty-pine rooms in this unassuming resort motel are on the smallish side but are warm and inviting. High-beam ceilings and picture windows frame majestic views. Many rooms have wood-burning fireplaces; all have cable TV and coffeemakers. ⊠ *1555 Hwy. 101, 97498,* ☎ *541/547–3141 or 800/522–3623,* 𝔽𝔸𝕏 *541/547–4234. 95 units, 6 suites. Restaurant, bar, in-room VCRs, refrigerators, hot tub, sauna. AE, D, DC, MC, V.*

Shopping

Sea Rose (⊠ 95478 Hwy. 101, 6 mi south of Yachats, ☎ 541/547–3005) sells seashells from Oregon and around the world at remarkably low prices.

Cape Perpetua

9 mi south of Yachats town on U.S. 101.

About 1 mi south of the bevy of upscale B&Bs at the southern boundary of Yachats (6 mi from the town itself), an easy trail leads down from the parking lot at **Devil's Churn State Park** (⊠ U.S. 101, east side, no phone) to the deep, tide-cut fissure for which the park was named. Surging waves funneled into this narrow cleft in the basaltic embankment explode into "spouting horns" and sea spray.

★ ❹ **Cape Perpetua,** which has the highest lookout point on the Oregon coast, towers 800 ft above the rocky shoreline. Named by Captain Cook on St. Perpetua's Day in 1778, the cape is part of a 2,700-acre scenic area popular with hikers, campers, beachcombers, and naturalists. General information and a map of 10 trails are available at the **Cape Perpetua Visitors Center,** on the east side of the highway, 2 mi south of Devil's Churn. The easy 1-mi **Giant Spruce Trail** passes through a fern-filled rain forest to an enormous 500-year-old Sitka spruce. Easier still is the marked Auto Tour; it begins about 2 mi north of the visitor center and winds through Siuslaw National Forest to the ¼-mi **Whispering Spruce Trail.** Views from the rustic rock shelter here extend 150 mi north and south and 37 mi out to sea. The **Cape Perpetua Interpretive Center,** in the visitor center, has educational movies and exhibits about the natural forces that shaped Cape Perpetua. ⊠ *U.S. 101,* ☎ *541/747–3289.* 🎫 *Visitor center free, interpretive center $3.* ☉ *Memorial Day–Labor Day, daily 9–5; Labor Day–Memorial Day, weekends 10–4.*

Heceta Head

10 mi south of Cape Perpetua on U.S. 101; 65 mi from Eugene, west on Hwy. 126 and north on U.S. 101.

A ½-mi trail from the beachside parking lot at **Devil's Elbow State Park** leads to **Heceta Head Lighthouse,** whose beacon, visible for more than 21 mi, is the most powerful on the Oregon coast. The trail passes **Heceta House,** a pristine white structure said to be haunted by the wife of a lighthouse keeper whose child fell to her death from the cliffs shortly after the beacon was lit in 1894. The house is one of Oregon's most remarkable bed-and-breakfasts (☞ Lodging, *below*). ⊠ *U.S. 101,* ☎ *541/997–3851.* ⌛ *Day use $3, lighthouse tours free.* ☉ *Lighthouse Mar.–Oct., daily noon–5; park daily dawn–dusk.*

In 1880 a sea captain named Cox rowed a small skiff into a fissure in a 300-ft-high sea cliff. Inside, he was startled to discover a vaulted chamber in the rock, 125 ft high and 2 acres in area. Hundreds of massive sea lions—the largest bulls weighing 2,000 pounds or more—covered every available horizontal surface. Cox had no way of knowing it, but

★ ☾ ❺ his discovery would eventually become one of the Oregon coast's premier tourist attractions, **Sea Lion Caves.** An elevator near the cliff-top ticket office descends to the floor of the cavern, near sea level, where Stellar and California sea lions and their fuzzy pups can be viewed from behind a wire fence. This is the only known hauling area (lair) and rookery for wild sea lions on the American mainland, and it's an awesome sight and sound. ⊠ *91560 U.S. 101N, 1 mi south of Heceta Head,* ☎ *541/547–3111.* ⌛ *$6.50.* ☉ *July–Aug., daily 8–dusk; Sept.–June, daily 9–dusk.*

Lodging

$$–$$$ 🏨 **Heceta House.** This unusual B&B perches on a windswept promontory in one of Oregon's most majestic settings. Surrounded by a white picket fence, the late-Victorian house, owned by the U.S. Forest Service, is managed by Mike and Carol Korgan, certified executive chefs who prepare a seven-course breakfast (included in the room rate) each morning. The nicest of the simply furnished rooms is the Mariner's, with a private bath and an awe-inspiring view. Filled with period detailing and antiques, the common areas are warm and inviting. If you're lucky, you may hear Rue, the resident ghost, in the middle of the night. ⊠ *Devil's Elbow State Park, U.S. 101,* ☎ *541/547–3696. 3 rooms, 1 with bath. MC, V.*

En Route South of Heceta Head, U.S. 101 jogs inland and the frowning headlands and cliffs of the north coast give way to the beaches, lakes, rivers, tidal estuaries, and rolling dunes of the south. Historic bridges span many of the famous fishing rivers that draw anglers from around the world. **Darlingtona Botanical Wayside** (⊠ Mercer Lake Rd., no phone), 6 mi south of Sea Lion Caves on the east side of U.S. 101, is an example of the rich plant life found in the marshy terrain near the coast. It's also a surefire child pleaser. A short paved nature trail leads through clumps of insect-catching cobra lilies, so named because they look like spotted cobras ready to strike. This wayside area is the most interesting in May, when the lilies are in bloom. Admission is free.

Florence

12 mi south of Heceta Head on U.S. 101; 63 mi west of Eugene on Hwy. 126.

Tourists and retirees have been flocking to Florence in ever greater numbers in recent years. Its restored waterfront Old Town holds restaurants, antiques stores, fish markets, and other diversions. But what really makes the town so appealing is its proximity to remarkable stretches of coastline.

☾ Florence is the gateway to the **Oregon Dunes National Recreation Area,** a 41-mi swath of undulating camel-color sand. The dunes, formed by eroded sandstone pushed up from the sea floor millions of years ago, have forests growing on them, water running through them, and rivers that have been dammed by them to form lakes. **Honeyman Memorial State Park,** 522 acres within the recreation area, is a base camp for dune-buggy enthusiasts, mountain bikers, hikers, boaters, horseback riders, and dogsledders (the sandy hills are an excellent training ground). The dunes are a vast and exuberant playground for children, particularly the slopes surrounding cool **Cleawox Lake.** ⊠ *Oregon Dunes National Recreation Area office, 855 Hwy. 101, Reedsport 97467, ☎ 541/271–3611.* ⌂ *Day use $3, campsites (☞ below).* ⊙ *Daily dawn–dusk.*

Dining and Lodging

$$–$$$ ✕ **Windward Inn.** One of the south coast's most elegant eateries, this tightly run ship prides itself on its vast menu, master wine list, home-baked breads and desserts, and fresh seafood. The chinook salmon fillets poached in Riesling and the shrimp and scallops sautéed in white wine are delectable. ⊠ *3757 Hwy. 101 N,* ☎ *541/997–8243. AE, D, DC, MC, V.*

$–$$ ✕ **Bridgewater Seafood Restaurant.** Freshly caught seafood—25 to 30 choices nightly—is the mainstay of this creaky-floored Victorian-era restaurant in Florence's Old Town. The cooking is plain and not exactly inspired, but the locals seem to like it that way. ⊠ *1297 Bay St.,* ☎ *541/997–9405. MC, V.*

$ ✕ **Mo's.** Come here for clear bayfront views and a creamy bowl of clam chowder. This coastal institution has been around for more than 40 years, consistently providing fresh seafood and down-home service. ⊠ *1436 Bay St.,* ☎ *541/997–2185. D, MC, V.*

$$–$$$ ▥ **Driftwood Shores Surfside Resort Inn.** The chief amenity of this resort is its location directly above Heceta Beach, one of the longest sand beaches on the south coast. The simple rooms have ocean views and kitchens; the three-bedroom suites have fireplaces and balconies. ⊠ *88416 1st Ave. (from U.S. 101 take Heceta Beach Rd. west about 3 mi north of Florence), 97439,* ☎ *541/997–8263 or 800/422–5091,* FAX *541/997–7301. 127 rooms, 26 suites. Restaurant, bar, indoor pool, hot tub, beach. AE, D, DC, MC, V.*

Camping

⚠ **Oregon Dunes National Recreation Area.** The facilities in the recreation area (☞ *above*) include a boat ramp and campgrounds for tents, RVs, and off-highway vehicles; all sites are available on a first-come, first-served basis, except the ones for off-highway vehicles, for which reservations are essential on weekends and holidays from mid-May to mid-September. ⊠ *U.S. 101 at Florence,* ☎ *541/271–3611; 800/280–2267 for reservations only. 381 sites (66 with full hookups). Flush toilets, potable water, showers.* ⌂ *$11–$15.* ⊙ *Year-round.*

Outdoor Activities and Sports

Ocean Dunes Golf Links (⊠ 3345 Munsel Lake Rd., ☎ 541/997–3232) is an 18-hole, par-71 course. The greens fee is $28; an optional cart costs $24. **Sandpines Golf Course** (⊠ 1201 35th St., ☎ 541/997–1940) is an 18-hole, par-72 course. The greens fee runs from $35 to $45; an optional cart costs $26.

Shopping

Incredible & Edible Oregon (⊠ 1350 Bay St., ☎ 541/997–7018) in Florence's Old Town is devoted to Oregon products: wine, fruit preserves, books, and gift items.

Reedsport

20 mi south of Florence on U.S. 101; 90 mi west of Eugene on I–5 and Hwy. 38.

The small town of Reedsport owes its existence to the Umpqua River, one of the state's great steelhead fishing streams. Exhibits at the

Umpqua Discovery Center in the waterfront area give a good introduction to the Lower Umpqua estuary and surrounding region. The center's chief attraction is the *Hero,* the laboratory ship Admiral Byrd used on his expeditions to the Antarctic. ⊠ *409 Riverfront Way,* ☎ *541/271–4816.* 🖭 *Museum $3, tour of the* Hero *$4.* ☉ *May–Sept., daily 9–5; Oct.–Apr., daily 10–4.*

The natural forces that created the towering sand dunes along this section of the Oregon coast are explained in interpretive exhibits at the **Reedsport Oregon Dunes National Recreation Area Visitors Center.** The center, which also sells maps, books, and gifts, is a good place to pick up free literature on the area. ⊠ *855 Highway Ave., south side of Umpqua River Bridge,* ☎ *541/271–3611.* 🖭 *Free.* ☉ *Memorial Day–Labor Day, daily 8:30–5; hrs vary rest of yr.*

☾ A herd of wild Roosevelt elk, Oregon's largest land mammal, roams within sight of the **Dean Creek Elk Viewing Area.** Abundant forage and a mild winter climate enable the elk to remain at Dean Creek year-round. The best viewing times are early morning and just before dusk. ⊠ *Hwy. 38, 3 mi east of Reedsport (watch for signs).* 🖭 *Free.* ☉ *Daily dawn–dusk.*

En Route   A public pier at **Winchester Bay's Salmon Harbor,** 3¼ mi south of Reedsport, juts out over the bay and yields excellent results for crabbers and fishermen (especially those after rockfish). There's also a full-service marina with a fish market.

Umpqua Lighthouse Park

6 mi south of Reedsport on U.S. 101.

Some of the highest sand dunes in the country are found in the 50-acre Umpqua Lighthouse Park. The first **Umpqua River Lighthouse,** built on the dunes at the mouth of the Umpqua River in 1857, lasted only four years before it toppled over in a storm. It took local residents 33 years to build another one. The "new" lighthouse, built on a bluff overlooking the south side of Winchester Bay and operated by the U.S. Coast Guard, is still going strong, flashing a warning beacon out to sea every five seconds. The **Douglas County Coastal Visitors Center** adjacent to the lighthouse has a museum and can arrange lighthouse tours. ⊠ *Umpqua Hwy., west side of U.S. 101,* ☎ *541/271–4631.* 🖭 *Donations appreciated.* ☉ *Lighthouse May–Sept., Wed.–Sat. 10–4, Sun. 1–4; closed Oct.–Apr.*

Coos Bay Area

27 mi south of Reedsport on U.S. 101; 116 mi southwest of Eugene, I–5 to Hwy. 38 to U.S. 101.

The Coos Bay–Charleston–North Bend metropolitan area, collectively known as the Bay Area (population 25,000), is the gateway to rewarding recreational experiences. The town of **Coos Bay** lies next to the largest natural harbor between San Francisco Bay and Seattle's Puget Sound. A century ago vast quantities of lumber cut from the Coast Range were milled in Coos Bay and shipped around the world. The mountainous piles of wood chips visible from the highway on the north side of town are Oregon's number one export. Coos Bay still has a reputation as a rough-and-ready port city, but with mill closures and dwindling lumber reserves it has begun to look in other directions, such as tourism, for economic prosperity. One former mill has even been converted into a casino.

To see the best of the Bay Area head west from Coos Bay on Newmark Avenue for about 7 mi to **Charleston.** Though it's a Bay Area community, this quiet fishing village at the mouth of Coos Bay is a world unto itself. As it loops into town the road becomes the Cape Arago Highway and leads to several oceanfront parks.

Sunset Bay State Park, a placid semicircular lagoon protected from the sea by overlapping fingers of rock and surrounded by reefs, is one of the few places along the Oregon coast where you can swim without worrying about the currents and undertows. Only the hardiest souls will want to brave the chilly water, however. ⊠ *2 mi south of Charleston off Cape Arago Hwy., no phone.* ☎ *Free.* ⊙ *Daily dawn–dusk.*

At **Shore Acres State Park,** an observation building on a grassy bluff overlooking the Pacific marks the site that held the mansion of lumber baron Louis J. Simpson. The view over the rugged wave-smashed cliffs is splendid, but the real glory of Shore Acres lies a few hundred yards to the south, where an entrance gate leads into what was Simpson's private garden. Beautifully landscaped and meticulously maintained, the gardens incorporate formal English and Japanese designs. From March to mid-October the grounds are ablaze with blossoming daffodils, rhododendrons, azaleas, roses, and dahlias. In December the entire garden is decked out with a dazzling display of holiday lights. ⊠ *10965 Cape Arago Hwy., 1 mi south of Sunset Bay State Park,* ☎ *541/888–3732.* ☎ *Day use $3 per vehicle.* ⊙ *Daily 8–dusk.*

The distant barking of seals echoes in the air at **Cape Arago State Park.** A trio of coves connected by short but steep trails, the park overlooks the **Oregon Islands National Wildlife Refuge,** where offshore rocks, beaches, islands, and reefs provide breeding grounds for seabirds and marine mammals. ⊠ *End of Cape Arago Hwy., 1 mi south of Shore Acres State Park,* ☎ *541/888–4902.* ☎ *Free.* ⊙ *Daily dawn–dusk.*

The mudflats and tidal estuaries of Coos Bay support everything from algae to bald eagles and black bears. More than 300 species of birds have been sighted at the **South Slough National Estuarine Research Reserve;** an interpretive center, guided walks (summer only), and nature trails will give you a chance to see things up close. ⊠ *Seven Devils Rd., 4 mi south of Charleston,* ☎ *541/888–5558.* ☎ *Free.* ⊙ *Trails daily dawn–dusk; interpretive center Memorial Day–Labor Day, daily 8:30–4:30; Labor Day–Memorial Day, weekdays 8:30–4:30.*

Dining and Lodging

$$ ✕ **Blue Heron Bistro.** You'll find subtle preparations of local seafood,
★ chicken, and homemade pasta at this busy bistro. There are no flat spots on the far-ranging menu; even the innovative soups and desserts are excellent. The skylit tile-floor dining room seats about 70 amid natural wood and blue linen. The seating area outside has blue awnings and colorful Bavarian window boxes that add a festive touch. Espresso and 18 microbrewery beers are available. ⊠ *100 W. Commercial St.,* ☎ *541/267–3933. D, MC, V. Closed Sun. Oct.–May.*

$$ ✕ **Portside Restaurant.** The fish at this gem of a restaurant overlooking the Charleston boat basin comes straight to the kitchen from the dock outside. Try the steamed Dungeness crab with drawn butter. On Friday night come for the all-you-can-eat seafood buffet. The nautical decor reinforces the view of the harbor through the restaurant's picture windows. ⊠ *8001 Kingfisher Rd. (follow Cape Arago Hwy. from Coos Bay),* ☎ *541/888–5544. AE, DC, MC, V.*

$ ✕ **Kum-Yon's.** The preparations at this small pan-Asian restaurant on Coos Bay's main drag are average, and the ambience resembles nothing so much as a Seoul Burger King, but the portions of sushi, kung-pao shrimp, and other dishes are satisfying, and the prices are ridiculously low. ⊠ *835 S. Broadway,* ☎ *541/269–2662. AE, MC, V.*

$$ ▣ **Coos Bay Manor**. Built in 1912 on a quiet residential street in Coos Bay, this 15-room Colonial Revival manor is listed on the National Register of Historic Places. Hardwood floors, detailed woodwork, high ceilings, and antiques and period reproductions offset the red-and-gold flocked wallpaper. An unusual open balcony on the second floor leads to the large rooms. Innkeeper Patricia Williams serves an extended Continental breakfast (included in the rates) in the wainscoted dining room or, if the weather is fine, on the upper balcony. ⊠ *955 S. 5th St., 97420,* ☎ *541/269–1224 or 800/269–1224,* ℻ *541/269–1224. 5 rooms, 3 with bath. Airport shuttle. MC, V.*

Outdoor Activities and Sports

Kentuck Golf Course (⊠ 675 Golf Course La., North Bend, ☎ 541/ 756–4464) is an 18-hole, par-70 course. The greens fee is $14 on weekdays, $16 on weekends; a cart costs $15. **Sunset Bay Golf Course** (⊠ 11001 Cape Arago Hwy., ☎ 541/888–9301) is a nine-hole, par-36 course. The greens fee ranges from $9 to $10, plus $11 for a cart.

OFF THE
BEATEN PATH

GOLDEN AND SILVER FALLS STATE PARK – Deep in old-growth forest sprinkled with delicate maidenhair ferns, this park is home to two of the region's natural wonders. Silver Falls is an arresting sight as it pours over a 200-ft-high semicircular rock ledge. One-quarter mile to the northwest, Golden Falls, another giant cataract formed by the thundering waters of Glenn Creek, is even more impressive, especially in the spring. ⊠ U.S. 101, 24 mi northeast of Coos Bay (follow signs), no phone. ▧ Free. ⊙ Daily dawn–dusk.

Bandon

25 mi south of Coos Bay on U.S. 101.

It may seem odd that tiny Bandon, built above a beach notable for its gallery of photogenic seastacks, bills itself as the Cranberry Capital of Oregon. But 10 mi north of town lie acres of bogs and irrigated fields where tons of the tart berries are harvested every year. Each October a Cranberry Festival, complete with a parade and a fair, takes place.

The town, almost entirely rebuilt after a devastating fire in 1936, has fine restaurants, resort hotels, and a busy boat basin on the Coquille River estuary. A few of the buildings in the Old Town area a block north of the boat basin hark back to the early 20th century, when Bandon was a booming port of call for passengers traveling from San Francisco to Seattle by steamship.

The **Bandon Historical Society Museum,** in the old City Hall building, documents the town's past. ⊠ *270 Fillmore St.,* ☎ *541/347–2164.* ▧ *$1.* ⊙ *Mon.–Sat. 10–4, Sun. noon–3.*

Follow the signs from Bandon south along Beach Loop Road to **Face Rock Wayside** and descend a stairway to the sand. Here you can gaze out to sea through a veritable gallery of natural sculptures, including Elephant Rock, Table Rock, and Face Rock.

The octagonal **Coquille Lighthouse** at **Bullards Beach State Park,** built in 1896 and no longer in use, stands lonely sentinel at the mouth of the Coquille River. From the highway the 2-mi drive to reach it passes through the Bandon Marsh, a prime bird-watching and picnicking area. The beach beside the lighthouse is a good place to search for jasper, agate, and driftwood. ⊠ *U.S. 101, 2 mi north of Bandon, no phone.* ☎ *Free.* ⊙ *Daily dawn–dusk.*

☺ **West Coast Game Park Safari** shelters 75 exotic species of animals, some of which children can pet. ⊠ *U.S. 101, 7 mi south of Bandon,* ☎ *541/ 347–3106.* ☎ *$7.* ⊙ *Jan.–Feb., weekends 9–5; Mar.–Sept., daily 9–7; Oct.–Nov., daily 9–5.*

Dining and Lodging

$$ ✕ **Bandon Boatworks.** A local favorite, this romantic jetty-side eatery serves up its seafood, steaks, and prime rib with a view of the Coquille River harbor and lighthouse. Try the panfried oysters flamed with brandy and anisette or the quick-sautéed seafood combination that's heavy on scampi and scallops. ⊠ *S. Jetty Rd. off 1st St.,* ☎ *541/347–2111. AE, D, MC, V.*

$$ ✕ **Lord Bennett's.** His lordship has a lot going for him: a cliff-top setting, modern decor, sunsets visible through picture windows overlooking Face Rock Beach, and musical performers on weekends. The rich dishes include prawns sautéed with sherry and garlic and steaks topped with shiitake mushrooms. A Sunday brunch is served. ⊠ *1695 Beach Loop Rd.,* ☎ *541/347–3663. AE, D, MC, V.*

$–$$ ✕ **Christophe.** The grilled duck breast and oysters with a chardonnay cream sauce and the rabbit in mustard sauce are among the Northwest dishes with French accents at this restaurant with Pacific views. Pasta dishes and a spicy jambalaya are other menu highlights. ⊠ *Inn at Face Rock, 3225 Beach Loop Rd.,* ☎ *541/347–9441 or 800/638–3092. AE, D, DC, MC, V.*

$$–$$$ ▥ **Inn at Face Rock.** This modern resort sits across Beach Loop Drive from Bandon's fabulous walking beach. The units, many suite-size and larger, are comfortably furnished in a cream and sand-color scheme; nearly half have ocean views, and some have kitchenettes and fireplaces. ⊠ *3225 Beach Loop Rd., 97411,* ☎ *541/347–9441 or 800/638–3092,* ⅲ *541/347–2532. 55 units. Restaurant, bar, hot tub, 9-hole golf course, horseback riding. AE, D, DC, MC, V.*

Shopping

Cranberry Sweets (⊠ 1st and Chicago Sts., ☎ 541/347–9475) specializes in delectable handmade candies—cranberry jellies, "lemon pies" (white chocolate around a lemon jelly center), and other delicacies.

Cape Blanco State Park

27 mi south of Bandon on U.S. 101.

Cape Blanco is the westernmost point in Oregon, and perhaps the windiest—gusts clocked at speeds as high as 184 mph have twisted and battered the Sitka spruces along the 6-mi road from U.S. 101 to the **Cape Blanco Lighthouse.** The lighthouse, atop a 245-ft headland, has been in continuous use since 1870, longer than any other in Oregon. No one knows why the Spaniards sailing past these reddish bluffs in 1603 called them *blanco* (white). One theory is that the name refers to the fossilized shells that glint in the cliff face. Campsites at the 1,880-acre Cape Blanco State Park are available on a first-come, first-served basis. ⊠ *Cape Blanco Rd. (follow signs from U.S. 101),* ☎ *541/332–6774.* ☎ *Day use free, campsites $13–$18.* ⊙ *Park daily dawn–dusk. Lighthouse Apr.–Oct., Thurs.–Mon. 10–3:30.*

En Route   U.S. 101 between Port Orford and Brookings, often referred to as the "fabulous fifty miles," soars up green headlands, some of them hundreds of feet high, and past an awesome seascape of cliffs and seastacks. The ocean is bluer and clearer—though not appreciably warmer—than it is farther north, and the coastal countryside is dotted with farms, grazing cattle, and small rural communities. As you round a bend between Port Orford and Gold Beach you'll see one of those sights that make grown-ups groan and kids squeal with delight: a huge, open-jawed Tyrannosaurus rex, with a green brontosaurus peering out from the forest beside it. **The Prehistoric Gardens** (⊠ 36848 Hwy. 101, ☎ 541/332–4463) is filled with life-size replicas of these primeval giants. The complex is open daily from 8 AM until dusk. Admission is $6.

Gold Beach

35 mi south of Cape Blanco on U.S. 101.

The fabled Rogue River, which empties into the Pacific at Gold Beach, has been luring anglers and outdoor enthusiasts for more than a century. Zane Grey, in books like *Rogue River Feud,* was among the writers who helped establish the Rogue's reputation as a world-class chinook salmon and steelhead stream. Celebrities as diverse as Winston Churchill, Clark Gable, George Bush, and Ginger Rogers, who had a home on the Rogue, have all fished here. It's one of the few U.S. rivers to merit Wild and Scenic status from the federal government.

From spring to late fall an estimated 50,000 visitors descend on the town to take one of the daily jet-boat excursions (☞ Outdoor Activities and Sports, *below*) that roar upstream from Wedderburn, Gold Beach's sister city across the bay, into the Rogue River Wilderness Area. Some of the boats go to Agness, 32 mi upstream, where the riverside road ends and the Wild and Scenic portions of the Rogue begin. Other boats penetrate farther, to the wet-knuckle rapids at Blossom Bar, 52 mi upstream. Black bears, otters, beavers, ospreys, egrets, and bald eagles are regularly seen on these trips. From Grave Creek to Watson Creek, along the 40-mi stretch classified as Wild, there is a National Recreation Trail granting access to this "vestige of primitive America."

Gold Beach is very much a seasonal town, thriving in the summer and nearly deserted the rest of the year. It marks the entrance to Oregon's banana belt, where mild, California-like temperatures take the sting out of winter and encourage a blossoming trade in lilies and daffodils.

Dining and Lodging

$$ ✕ **Captain's Table.** The ambience leaves something to be desired, but this eatery serves up good steaks and fresh seafood. Locals come for the sautéed mushrooms and steamed clams; the salmon teriyaki is also worth trying. ⊠ *29251 Ellensburg Rd. (U.S. 101),* ☎ *541/247–6308. Reservations not accepted. MC, V. No lunch.*

$$$$ ⌂ **Tu Tu Tun Lodge.** This well-known fishing resort (pronounced *Too*
★ *Tootin'*) sits right on the Rogue River, 7 mi upriver from Gold Beach. Salmon and steelhead fishing made the Tu Tu Tun's name, but jet-boat excursions, golf, and other activities take place. All the units in this small establishment are rustically elegant. Some have hot tubs, others have fireplaces, and a few have both; private decks overlook the river. Two deluxe rooms have tall picture windows, tile baths, and outdoor soaking tubs with river views. The restaurant (closed from November to April) serves breakfast, lunch, and dinner; the last, open to nonguests (though reservations are hard to come by), consists of a five-course prix-fixe meal that changes nightly. Portions are dauntingly huge. ⊠ *96550 N. Bank Rogue, 97444,* ☎ *541/247–6664,* ℻ *541/247–0672. 16 rooms, 2 suites, 3-bedroom house. Restaurant, bar, outdoor pool, 4-hole golf course, hiking, horseshoes, dock, boating, fishing. MC, V. Restaurant closed Nov.–Apr.*

$–$$ 🏨 **Ireland's Rustic Lodges.** Seven original one- and two-bedroom cabins filled with rough-hewn charm, plus 28 newer motel rooms and two new cabins, are available in a landscaped beachside setting. Some units have wood-burning fireplaces and decks overlooking the sea. For the price, you can't beat this accommodation. ⊠ *29330 Ellensburg Rd. (U.S. 101), 97444,* ☎ *541/247–7718,* 🖷 *541/247–0225. 40 units. No-smoking rooms. MC, V.*

Outdoor Activities and Sports

GOLF

Cedar Bend Golf Course (⊠ 34391 Squaw Valley Rd., ☎ 541/247–6911) is a nine-hole, par-36 course. The greens fee is $13; a cart costs $12.

JET-BOAT EXCURSIONS

Jerry's Rogue Boats (⊠ 29985 Harbor Way, ☎ 541/247–4571 or 800/451–3645) and **Rogue River Mail Boat Trips** (⊠ 94294 Rogue River Rd., ☎ 541/247–7033 or 800/458–3511) operate jet-boat excursions from May to October. Adult fares are between $30 and $75; some tours include a lunch stop at a riverside inn.

En Route Between Gold Beach and Brookings, you'll cross Thomas Creek Bridge, the highest span in Oregon. Take advantage of the off-road coastal viewing points along the 10-mi-long **Samuel H. Boardman State Park**—especially in summer, when highway traffic becomes heavy and rubbernecking can be dangerous.

Brookings

27 mi south of Gold Beach on U.S. 101.

A startling 90% of the pot lilies grown in the United States come from a 500-acre area inland from Brookings. Strangely enough, these white symbols of peace probably wouldn't be grown here in such abundance if not for the fact that in 1942 Brookings experienced the only wartime aerial bombing attack on the U.S. mainland. A Japanese air raid set trees ablaze and understandably panicked the local residents; the imminent ban on Japanese flowers set them to work cultivating the Easter lilies that appear in stores across the country every April. Mild temperatures along this coastal plain provide ideal conditions for flowering plants of all kinds—even a few palm trees, a rare sight in Oregon.

The town is equally famous as a commercial and sportfishing port at the mouth of the turquoise-blue Chetco River. If anything, the Chetco is more highly esteemed among fishermen and wilderness lovers than is the Rogue. A short jetty, used by many local crabbers and fishermen, provides easy and productive access to the river's mouth; salmon and steelhead weighing 20 pounds or larger swim here.

Brookings celebrates its horticultural munificence on Memorial Day weekend with an Azalea Festival in **Azalea State Park** (⊠ N. Bank Rd. off U.S. 101 downtown) amid blossoming wild azaleas, some of them hundreds of years old.

The **Chetco Valley Historical Museum,** inside a mid-19th-century stagecoach stop and trading post, has some unusual items and is worth a brief visit. An iron casting that bears a likeness to Queen Elizabeth I has led to speculation that it was left during an undocumented landing on the Oregon coast by Sir Francis Drake. On a hill near the museum stands the **World Champion Cypress Tree,** 99 ft tall and with a 27-ft circumference. ⊠ *5461 Museum Rd.,* ☎ *541/469–6651.* 🎫 *Free (donations appreciated).* ☉ *Mid-May–Oct., Tues.–Sat. 2–6, Sun. noon–6; Nov.–mid-May, Fri.–Sun. noon–5.*

Loeb State Park contains 53 riverside campsites and some fine hiking trails, including one that leads to a hidden redwood grove. There's also a grove of myrtlewood trees—impressive because the species grows nowhere else in the world. ⊠ *North bank of the Chetco River, 10 mi east of Brookings (follow signs from U.S. 101),* ☎ *541/469–2021.* ☉ *Daily dawn–dusk.* ✍ *Day use free, campsites $13–$16, reservations not accepted.*

Dining and Lodging

$$ ✕ **Starboard Tack.** Fishing vessels docked in the adjacent boat basin and picture windows looking out to the sea lend a salty ambience to this low-key restaurant. The daily seafood specials—usually halibut and salmon—are the best bets. For lunch try the fish-and-chips or the crab melt. ⊠ *16011 Boat Basin Rd.,* ☎ *541/469–6006. MC, V.*

$$–$$$ ▥ **Best Western Beachfront Inn.** The ocean is right outside your window at this inn with balconies closer to the water than those at any other hotel in southern Oregon. The large rooms have microwaves; some units also have kitchens, and 12 rooms have whirlpool tubs. ⊠ *16008 Boat Basin Rd., off Lower Harbor Rd. (south of Port of Brookings), 97415,* ☎ *541/469–7779 or 800/468–4081,* ℻ *541/469–0283. 78 rooms. Refrigerators, pool, outdoor hot tub, beach. AE, D, DC, MC, V.*

$$ ✕▥ **Chetco River Inn.** Thirty-five acres of private forest surround this
★ remote inn 17 mi up the Chetco River from Brookings. Guests come here to hike, hunt wild mushrooms, and relax in the library or in front of the fireplace in the common room. The host cooks delicious dinners that sometimes star a nickel-bright salmon fresh from the stream. Rooms have thick comforters and panoramic river and forest views. ⊠ *21202 High Prairie Rd., off N. Bank Rd., 97415,* ☎ *541/670–1645 (cell phone) or 800/327–2688,* ℻ *541/469–4341. 5 rooms. Restaurant. MC, V.*

The Oregon Coast Essentials

Arriving and Departing

BY BUS

Greyhound (☎ 800/231–2222) serves Astoria, Coos Bay, Newport, Florence, and other coastal cities.

BY CAR

U.S. 101 enters coastal Oregon from Washington State at Astoria and from California near Brookings. **U.S. 30** heads west from Portland to Astoria. **U.S. 20** travels west from Corvallis to Newport. **Highway 126** winds west to the coast from Eugene. **Highway 42** leads west from Roseburg toward Coos Bay.

Getting Around

BY CAR

U.S. 101 runs the length of the coast, sometimes turning inland for a few miles.

Visitor Information

Astoria-Warrenton Area Chamber of Commerce (⊠ 111 W. Marine Dr., Astoria 97103, ☎ 503/325–6311 or 800/875–6807). **Bay Area Chamber of Commerce** (⊠ 50 E. Central St., Coos Bay 97420, ☎ 541/269–0215 or 800/824–8486). **Brookings Harbor Chamber of Commerce** (⊠ 16330 Lower Harbor Rd., 97415, ☎ 541/469–3181 or 800/535–9469). **Cannon Beach Chamber of Commerce** (⊠ 2nd and Spruce Sts., 97110, ☎ 503/436–2623). **Florence Area Chamber of Commerce** (⊠ 270 Hwy. 101, 97439, ☎ 541/997–3128). **Greater Newport Cham-**

ber of Commerce (⊠ 555 S.W. Coast Hwy., 97365, ☎ 503/265–8801 or 800/262–7844). **Lincoln City Visitors Center** (⊠ 801 S.W. Hwy. 101, Suite 1, 97367, ☎ 541/994–8378 or 800/452–2151). **Seaside Visitors Bureau** (⊠ 7 N. Roosevelt Ave., 97138, ☎ 503/738–6391 or 800/444–6740). **Tillamook Chamber of Commerce** (⊠ 3705 Hwy. 101 N, 97141, ☎ 503/842–7525). **Yachats Area Chamber of Commerce** (⊠ U.S. 101 near 2nd St., 97498, ☎ 541/547–3530).

THE WILLAMETTE VALLEY AND THE WINE COUNTRY

During the 1940s and 1950s, researchers at Oregon State University concluded that the Willamette Valley—the wet, temperate trough between the Coast Range to the west and the Cascade Range to the east—had the wrong climate for the propagation of varietal wine grapes. The researchers' techniques were faulty, as has been proven by the success of Oregon's burgeoning wine industry. More than 60 wineries dot the Willamette (locals say "Wil-*lam*-it") and Yamhill valleys in the northern part of the state. Two dozen more wineries are scattered among the Umpqua and Rogue valleys (near Roseburg and Ashland, respectively) to the south. Their products—mainly cool-climate varietals like pinot noir, chardonnay, and Johannisberg Riesling—have won gold medals in blind tastings against the best wines of California and Europe.

Numbers in the margin correspond to points of interest on the Oregon Coast and Willamette Valley/Wine Country map.

Newberg

38 mi southwest of Portland on Hwys. 99 W and 18.

Newberg, a graceful pioneer town at a broad bend in the Willamette River, marks the starting point of the North Willamette Valley's wine country.

The oldest and most significant of Newberg's original structures is the **Hoover-Minthorne House,** the boyhood home of President Herbert Hoover. Built in 1881, the preserved frame house still contains many of the original furnishings. Outside is the woodshed that no doubt played an important role in shaping young "Bertie" Hoover's character. ⊠ *115 S. River St.,* ☎ *503/538–6629.* ▣ *$1.50.* ☉ *Mar.–Nov., Wed.–Sun. 1–4; Dec. and Feb., weekends 1–4.*

Rex Hill Vineyards, on a hill east of Newberg, produces some of the best pinot noir wines in Oregon, wines that more than hold their own against ones from California, France, and other high-profile locales. ⊠ *30835 N. Hwy. 99W,* ☎ *503/538–0666.* ☉ *Memorial Day–Labor Day, daily 11–5; Labor Day–Memorial Day, Mon.–Thurs. 11–5, Fri.–Sun. 10–5.*

Champoeg State Park

9 mi from Newberg, south on Hwy. 219 and east on Champoeg Rd.

Champoeg (pronounced *shampooey*) **State Park** is on the site of a Hudson's Bay Company trading post, granary, and warehouse that was built in 1813. This was the seat of the first provisional government in the Northwest. The settlement was abandoned after a catastrophic flood in 1861, then rebuilt and abandoned again after the flood of 1890. The park's wide-open spaces, groves of oak and fir, modern visitor center, museum, and historic buildings yield vivid insight into pioneer life. ⊠ *8239 Champoeg Rd. NE, St. Paul 97137, ☎ 503/678–1251. ☞ $3 per vehicle. ⊙ Memorial Day–Labor Day, daily 10–6; Labor Day– Memorial Day, weekdays 8–4, weekends noon–4.*

OFF THE BEATEN PATH
OLD AURORA COLONY – A fascinating slice of Oregon's pioneer past, the colony was the only major 19th-century communal society in the Pacific Northwest. Created by Germans in 1856, this frontier society espoused a "Love thy neighbor" philosophy, shared labor and property, and was known for its hospitality. Aurora retains many white frame houses dating from the 1860s and 1870s. Several structures have been incorporated into the Old Aurora Colony Museum (⊠ 2nd and Liberty Sts., ☎ 503/678–5754), which provides an overview of the colony's way of life. Follow an easy self-guided tour of the historic district, or take the guided walking tour given on weekends at 1 and 3 PM. ⊠ *About 14 mi from Champoeg State Park; take Champoeg Rd. east to Arndt Rd.; pass under I–5 and turn south onto Airport Rd., then east onto Ehlen Rd.*

Dundee and Yamhill

6 mi southwest of Newberg on Hwy. 99W.

The lion's share (up to 90%) of the U.S. hazelnut crop is grown in Dundee, a haven of produce stands and tasting rooms. The 25 mi of Highway 18 between Dundee and Grand Ronde, in the Coast Range, roll through the heart of the Yamhill Valley wine country; wide shoulders and relatively light traffic earned the route a "most suitable" rating from the "Oregon Bicycling Guide."

The tasting room of **Argyle Winery,** a producer of sparkling wines, is housed in a restored Victorian farmhouse in Dundee. ⊠ *691 Hwy. 99W, ☎ 503/538–8520. ⊙ Tasting room daily 11–5, tours by appointment.*

Sokol Blosser, one of Oregon's oldest and largest wineries, has a tasting room and walk-through vineyard with a self-guided tour that explains the grape varieties—pinot noir and chardonnay, among others. ⊠ *5000 Sokol Blosser La. (3 mi west of Dundee off Hwy. 99W), ☎ 503/864–2282 or 800/582–6668. ⊙ Daily 11–5.*

Willakenzie Estate began operation of its ultramodern gravity-feed system in 1995. Its two inaugural wines, the 1995 pinot gris and pinot blanc, have enjoyed critical acclaim. ⊠ *19143 N.E. Laughlin Rd. (12 mi from Newberg; head west on Hwy. 240 and north on Laughlin), Yamhill, ☎ 503/662–3280. ⊙ Memorial Day–Labor Day, daily 11– 5; Labor Day–mid-Oct., weekends 11–5.*

McMinnville

14 mi south of Newberg on Hwy. 99W.

McMinnville, the largest (population 20,000) and most sophisticated of the wine-country towns, has a fine collection of B&Bs, small hotels, and restaurants.

Linfield College (⊠ Linfield Ave. east of Hwy. 18), a perennial football powerhouse, is an oasis of brick and ivy amid McMinnville's farmers'-market bustle. The college, founded in 1849 and the second oldest in Oregon, hosts the **International Pinot Noir Celebration** (☎ 800/775–4762) on the first weekend in August.

The pinot noir and pinot gris wines produced on the 300-acre estate of **Yamhill Valley Vineyards** have won prestigious awards. ⊠ *16250*

S.W. Oldsville Rd. (5 mi from downtown McMinnville; take Hwy. 99W south to Hwy. 18 south to Oldsville Rd. and make a right), ☎ *800/ 825–4845.* ⊘ *Mid-Mar.–June, weekends 11–5; June–Thanksgiving, daily 11–5.*

Dining and Lodging

$$$ ✕ **Nick's Italian Cafe.** Modestly furnished but with a voluminous wine
★ cellar, Nick's is a favorite of area wine makers. The food is spirited and simple, reflecting the owner's northern Italian heritage. The five-course prix-fixe menu changes nightly. ⊠ *521 E. 3rd St.,* ☎ *503/434– 4471. Reservations essential. AE, DC, MC, V. Closed Mon. No lunch.*

$$–$$$ ✕ **Cafe Azul.** The regional Mexican cuisine at this McMinnville restaurant represents a startling departure from the traditional burritos and enchiladas. The chef, formerly of Chez Panisse in Berkeley, California, emphasizes fresh vegetables, handmade corn tortillas, wild herbs, salted fish, and salads. Unusual specialties include yellow and black moles (the latter with fiery charred peppers) and a spicy marinated pork that's wrapped in banana leaves and braised in the juice of Seville oranges. ⊠ *313 3rd St.,* ☎ *503/435–1234. Reservations essential. MC, V. Closed Sun.–Mon. No lunch.*

$$–$$$ 🏨 **Flying M Ranch.** A great log lodge, decorated in a style best described as Daniel Boone eclectic, is the centerpiece of the 625-acre Flying M Ranch, perched above the steelhead-filled Yamhill River. Choose between somewhat austere cabins (the cozy, hot-tub-equipped Honeymoon Cabin is the nicest) or riverside hotel units. In keeping with the rustic tone, there are no TVs or telephones. Book ahead for a Flying M specialty: the Steak Fry Ride, on which guests, aboard their choice of a horse or a tractor-drawn wagon, ride into the mountains for a feast of barbecued steak with all the trimmings. ⊠ *23029 N.W. Flying M Rd., Yamhill 97148; from McMinnville, off Hwy. 99W head north on North Baker Rd.—which becomes West Side Rd.—for 5 mi, head west on Meadowlake Rd., and follow signs,* ☎ *503/662–3222,* 🖷 *503/ 662–3202. 28 units, 7 cabins, more than 100 campsites. Restaurant, bar, tennis court, basketball, hiking, horseback riding, horseshoes, fishing. AE, D, DC, MC, V.*

$$ 🏨 **Mattey House Bed & Breakfast.** This 100-year-old Victorian-style
★ home was built by English immigrant Joseph Mattey, a prosperous local butcher. Its cheerful faux-marble fireplace and gourmet breakfasts (poached pears with raspberry sauce, frittatas, and Dutch-apple pancakes are typical fare) have made this B&B an area favorite. ⊠ *10221 N.E. Mattey La. (off Hwy. 99W, ¼ mi south of Lafayette), 97128,* ☎ *503/434–5058. 4 rooms. MC, V.*

$ 🏨 **Safari Motor Inn.** More functional than fancy, this motel on McMinnville's main drag has modest rates and clean accommodations with up-to-date furnishings. ⊠ *345 N. Hwy. 99W, at 19th St., 97128,* ☎ *503/472–5187 or 800/321–5543,* 🖷 *503/434–6380. 90 rooms. Restaurant, bar, hot tub, exercise room. AE, D, DC, MC, V.*

Outdoor Activities and Sports

Bayou Golf & Country Club (⊠ 9301 S.W. Bayou Dr., ☎ 503/472–4651), a nine-hole, par-36 course, has a $12 greens fee; a cart costs $10.

Shopping

A restored 1910 schoolhouse contains the **Lafayette Schoolhouse Antique Mall** (⊠ Hwy. 99W, 5 mi north of McMinnville, ☎ 503/864–2720), Oregon's largest permanent antiques show.

Salem

24 mi from McMinnville, south on Hwy. 99W, and east on Hwy. 22; 45 mi south of Portland on I–5.

Salem has a rich pioneer history, but before that it was the home of the Calapooyan Indians, who called it Chemeketa, which means "place of rest." The town was later settled by fur trappers, farmers, and missionaries. The Willamette River provided easy transport for lumber from nearby forests and produce grown on the fertile farmlands of the Central Valley. By 1842 the first university on the West Coast had been established; in 1862 the thriving river town of Salem became the capital of the new state of Oregon. The main attractions in the state's third-largest city are west of I–5 in and around the Capitol Mall.

Numbers in the text correspond to numbers in the margin and on the Salem map.

A Good Walk

Begin at Court Street and Oregon's **State Capitol complex** ⑥. Behind the capitol, just across State Street, is **Willamette University** ⑦. Cross over 12th Street to the **Mission Mill Village** ⑧. From there, stroll down 12th Street to **Deepwood Estate** ⑨, south of Salem's downtown district. West of here is **Bush's Pasture Park** ⑩.

TIMING

Without stopping for tours, this walk can be done in about two hours. Allot an additional half hour for a guided tour of the capitol building, two hours for a full tour of Mission Mill Village, and a half hour each for the house tours at Deepwood Estate and Bush's Pasture Park. If you're pressed for time, skip the capitol and university and begin your tour at Mission Mill Village.

Sights to See

❿ **Bush's Pasture Park.** These 105 acres of rolling lawn and formal English gardens include the remarkably well preserved **Bush House,** an 1878 Italianate mansion at the park's far western boundary. It has 10 marble fireplaces and virtually all of its original furnishings. The house and gardens are on the National Register of Historic Places. **Bush Barn Art Center,** behind the house, exhibits the work of Northwest artists and has a sales gallery. ⊠ *600 Mission St. SE,* ☎ *503/363–4714.* ⌸ *$1.50.* ⊙ *May–Sept., Tues.–Sun. noon–5; Oct.–Apr., Tues.–Sun. 2–5.*

❾ **Deepwood Estate.** This fanciful 1894 Queen Anne–style house has splendid interior woodwork and original stained glass. An ornate gazebo from the 1905 Lewis and Clark expedition graces the fine gardens created in 1929 by landscape designers Elizabeth Lord and Edith Schryver. The estate is on the National Register of Historic Places. ⊠ *1116 Mission St. SE,* ☎ *503/363–1825.* ⌸ *$3.* ⊙ *May–Sept., Sun.–Fri. noon–4:30; Oct.–Apr., Sun.–Mon. and Wed.–Fri. 1–4.*

❽ **Mission Mill Village.** The **Thomas Kay Woolen Mill Museum** complex (circa 1889), complete with working waterwheels and millstream, looks as if the workers have just stepped away for a lunch break. Teasel gigging, napper flock bins, and the patented Furber double-acting napper are but a few of the machines and processes on display. The **Jason Lee House,** the **John D. Boon Home,** and the **Methodist Parsonage** are also part of the village. There is nothing grandiose about these early pioneer homes, the oldest frame structures in the Northwest, but they reveal a great deal about domestic life in the wilds of Oregon in the 1840s. The adjacent **Marion County Historical Society Museum** (☎

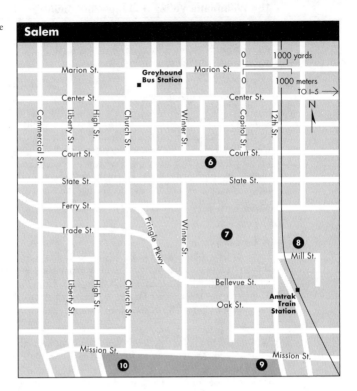

Salem

503/364–2128) displays pioneer and Calapooya Indian artifacts. ☒ *Museum complex, 1313 Mill St. SE,* ☎ *503/585–7012.* ☒ *$5 (includes tour).* ☺ *Daily 10–4. Guided tours of houses and woolen mill museum leave from mill's admission booth every hr on the hr.*

6 **Oregon State Capitol.** A brightly gilded bronze statue of the Oregon Pioneer stands atop the 140-ft-high capitol dome, looking north across the Capitol Mall. Built in 1939 with blocks of gray Vermont marble, Oregon's state capitol has an elegant yet austere neoclassical feel. New east and west wings were added in 1978. Relief sculptures and deft historical murals soften the interior. Tours of the rotunda, the house and senate chambers, and the governor's office leave from the information center under the dome. ☒ *900 Court St.,* ☎ *503/378–4423.* ☒ *Free.* ☺ *Weekdays 8–5, Sat. 9–4, Sun. noon–4. Guided tours Memorial Day–Labor Day, daily on the hr; rest of yr by appointment.*

OFF THE
BEATEN PATH

SCHREINER'S IRIS GARDENS – Some call the Willamette Valley near Salem the "Bulb Basket of the Nation." Irises and tulips create fields of brilliant color in near-perfect growing conditions. Schreiner's Iris Gardens, established in 1925, ships bulbs all over the world; during the short spring growing season (from mid-May to early June), the 10-acre display gardens are ablaze with fancifully named varieties such as Hello Darkness, Well Endowed, and Ringo. ☒ *3625 Quinaby Rd. NE (north from Salem take I-5's Exit 263, head west on Brooklake Rd., south on River Rd., and east on Quinaby),* ☎ *503/393-3232.* ☒ *Free.* ☺ *8–dusk during blooming season only.*

7 **Willamette University.** Behind the capitol building, just across State Street but half a world away, are the brick buildings and grounds of Willamette University, the oldest college in the West. Founded in 1842, Willamette has long been a mecca for aspiring politicians (former Oregon senators Mark O. Hatfield and Robert Packwood are alumni). **Hatfield Library,** built in 1986 on the banks of Mill Stream, is a handsome brick and glass building with a striking campanile; tall, prim **Waller Hall,** built in 1841, is one of the oldest buildings in the Pacific Northwest. ⊠ *Information Desk, Putnam University Center, Mill St.,* ☎ *503/ 370–6267.* ⊙ *Weekdays 9–5.*

Dining and Lodging

$$–$$$ ✕ **DaVinci.** Salem politicos flock to this two-story downtown restaurant for Italian-inspired dishes cooked in a wood-burning oven. No shortcuts are taken in the preparation, so don't come if you're in a rush. But if you're in the mood to linger over seafood and pasta (made on the premises), you'll be more than content. The wine list is one of the most extensive in the Northwest; the staff is courteous and extremely professional. ⊠ *180 High St.,* ☎ *503/399–1413. AE, DC, MC, V. No lunch Sun.*

$ ✕ **Gerry Frank's Konditorei.** Furnished in the style of a European sidewalk café, this is *the* place to go in Salem for rich desserts. Sandwiches, salads, soup, and other simple entrées are served, but most people head straight for the display cases of homemade cakes, tortes, and cheesecakes with tempting names like "Orange Cloud" and "Blackout." ⊠ *310 Kearney St. SE,* ☎ *503/585–7070. D, MC, V.*

$ ✕ **Thompson Brewery & Public House.** The intimate rooms at this pub are decked out in a funky mix of '60s rock-and-roll memorabilia and hand-painted woodwork. India Pale Ale and Terminator Stout are among the beers made in a tiny brewery enlivened by colorful original art. The food—mostly hearty sandwiches, salads, and pasta dishes— is remarkably cheap. ⊠ *3575 Liberty Rd. S,* ☎ *503/363–7286. Reservations not accepted on weekends. AE, MC, V.*

$$–$$$ 🏨 **Quality Inn.** The chief virtue of this clean, functional hotel is its location, about five minutes from the capitol. ⊠ *3301 Market St. NE, 97301,* ☎ *503/370–7888 or 800/248–6273,* ℻ *541/370–6305. 150 rooms. Restaurant, bar, no-smoking rooms, indoor pool, sauna, coin laundry, airport shuttle. AE, D, DC, MC, V.*

$$ 🏨 **State House Bed & Breakfast.** Twelve blocks from the Capitol Mall and Willamette University, this B&B has comfortable if smallish downstairs public areas and a hot tub that overlooks Mill Creek. The two simply furnished rooms on the second floor share a bath. The Grand Suite and the third-floor suite have kitchenettes. The noise level at this State Street property can be a bit high, but the convenient location and friendly proprietors are among the compensations. ⊠ *2146 State St., 97301,* ☎ *503/588–1340,* ℻ *503/585–8812. 2 rooms share 1 bath, 2 suites. MC, V.*

Nightlife and the Arts

A flamboyant Tudor Gothic vaudeville house dating from 1926, the **Elsinore Theatre** (⊠ 170 High St. SE, ☎ 503/375–3574) presents stage shows, concerts, and silent movies. The restored interior is worth seeing even if nothing is playing; call to arrange a tour.

Outdoor Activities and Sports

Battle Creek Golf Course (⊠ 6161 Commercial St. SE, ☎ 503/585– 1402) is an 18-hole, par-72 course. The greens fee ranges from $23 to $25; a cart costs $20. The greens fee at the 18-hole, par-72 course at the **Salem Golf Club** (⊠ 2025 Golf Course Rd., ☎ 503/363–6652) is $35 ($30 twilight); a cart costs $20.

Silver Falls State Park

★ ⓫ *26 mi east of Salem, Hwy. 22 to Hwy. 214.*

Hidden amid old-growth Douglas firs in the foothills of the Cascades, Silver Falls is the largest state park in Oregon (8,700 acres). South Falls, roaring over the lip of a mossy basalt bowl into a deep pool 177 ft below, is the main attraction here, but 13 other waterfalls—half of them more than 100 ft high—are accessible to hikers. The best time to visit is in the fall, when vine maples blaze with brilliant color, or early spring, when the forest floor is carpeted with trilliums and yellow violets. There are picnic facilities and a day lodge; during the winter you can cross-country ski. ⊠ *20024 Silver Falls Hwy. SE, Sublimity,* ☎ *503/873–8681.* ✆ *$3 per vehicle.* ☉ *Daily dawn–dusk.*

OFF THE BEATEN PATH	**MOUNT ANGEL ABBEY** – This Benedictine monastery atop a 300-ft-high butte was founded in 1882. It's the site of one of two American buildings designed by Finnish architect Alvar Aalto. A masterpiece of serene and thoughtful design, Aalto's library opened its doors in 1970 and has become a place of pilgrimage for students and aficionados of modern architecture. ⊠ *18 mi from Salem, east on Hwy. 213 and north on Hwy. 214,* ☎ *503/845–3030.*

Albany

46 mi south of Silver Springs State Park on I–5 and Hwy. 20; 20 mi from Salem, south on I–5 and west on U.S. 20.

To see what a quintessential Willamette Valley river town looked like before the major highways were built, explore Albany, a former wheat and produce center. The town's 700 historic buildings, scattered over a 100-block area in three districts, include every major architectural style in the U.S. from 1850. Eight covered bridges can also be seen on a half-hour drive from Albany. Pamphlets and maps for self-guided walking and driving tours are available from the **Albany Visitors Association** (⊠ 300 S.W. 2nd Ave., ☎ 541/928–0911 or 800/526–2256), open on weekdays from 9 to 5.

Dining

$–$$ ✕ **Novak's Hungarian Paprikas.** The Hungarian owners of this unpretentious restaurant turn out native specialties such as *kolbasz* (homemade sausages with sweet-and-sour cabbage) and beef *szelet* (crispy batter-fried cutlets) with virtuosity. The restaurant's only drawback is its lack of a liquor license. ⊠ *2835 Santiam Hwy. SE,* ☎ *541/967–9488. MC, V. No lunch Sat.*

Corvallis

10 mi southwest of Albany on U.S. 20; 35 mi from Salem, south on I–5 and west on Hwy. 34.

The pioneers who settled Corvallis in 1847 named their town for its location in the "heart of the valley." About halfway between Salem and Eugene, Corvallis is not so much a sightseeing mecca as it is a good place to stop for a meal or spend the night. Driving or strolling through its quiet neighborhoods, along streets lined with stately trees, it's easy to get the impression that time here stopped sometime in the 1950s.

The pace quickens around the 500-acre campus of **Oregon State University** (⊠ 15th and Jefferson Sts., ☎ 541/737–0123), west of the city center. Established as a land-grant institution in 1868, OSU (or "Moo U" as it's sometimes called) is home to more than 15,000 students, many of them studying the agricultural sciences and engineering. Exhibits at the **Horner Museum** (✉ Gill Coliseum, 26th and Washington Sts., ☎ 541/754–2951) detail Oregon's animal, mineral, and human history.

Dining and Lodging

$$–$$$ ✕ **The Gables.** The most romantic restaurant in Corvallis has dark wood paneling and a straightforward menu of steaks, seafood, local lamb, and prime ribs. The portions are huge and satisfying. ✉ *1121 N.W. 9th St.,* ☎ *541/752–3364. Reservations essential. AE, D, DC, MC, V. No lunch.*

$–$$ ✕ **Big River.** A former Greyhound bus depot holds one of Corvallis's most popular restaurants. The menu changes frequently but emphasizes foods from Oregon—pan-seared salmon, grilled chicken, and roasted lamb shanks. This is one of the few places in Corvallis to snag a good martini or single-malt Scotch. Musicians perform on Friday and Saturday night. ✉ *101 N.W. Jackson St.,* ☎ *541/757–0694. AE, MC, V. Closed Sun.*

$$ ▨ **Harrison House.** Maria Tomlinson runs this B&B in a 1939 Dutch Colonial–style home three blocks from the OSU campus. Chippendale, Queen Anne, and Colonial Williamsburg–era furniture fills the living and dining rooms. The three rooms on the second floor and one on the first are spacious and immaculate. The rates include a breakfast of Belgian waffles or eggs Benedict. ✉ *2310 N.W. Harrison Rd., 97330,* ☎ *541/752–6248 or 800/233–6248,* ▨ *541/754–1353. 4 rooms, 2 with bath. AE, D, DC, MC, V. Bicycles.*

Outdoor Activities and Sports

GOLF

Trysting Tree Golf Club (✉ 34028 Electric Rd., ☎ 541/752–3332) has an 18-hole, par-72 course. The greens fee is $27; a cart costs $22.

Brownsville

27 mi south of Corvallis off I–5.

Brownsville is another Willamette Valley town that has retained much of its original character. The **Linn County Historical Museum,** housed in Brownsville's 1890 railroad depot, has some noteworthy pioneer-era exhibits, including a covered wagon that arrived in 1865 after a trek along the Oregon Trail from Missouri. ✉ *101 Park Ave.,* ☎ *541/ 466–3390.* ⊙ *Mon.–Sat. 11–4, Sun. 1–5.*

Eugene

63 mi south of Corvallis on I–5.

Eugene was founded in 1846 when Eugene Skinner staked the first federal land-grant claim for pioneers. Back then it was called Skinner's Mudhole. Wedged between two landmark buttes—Skinner and Spencer—along the Willamette River, Eugene is the culinary, cultural, sports, and intellectual hub of the central Willamette Valley. The home of the University of Oregon is consistently given high marks for its "livability." A large student and former-student population lends Oregon's second-largest city a youthful vitality and countercultural edge. Full of parks and oriented to the outdoors, Eugene is a place where bike paths are used, pedestrians *always* have the right-of-way, and joggers are so plentiful that the city is known as the running capital of the world.

Past urban-renewal schemes to make downtown Eugene more pedestrian-friendly have left it the least interesting part of town. Shopping and commercial streets surround the Eugene Hilton and the world-class

Hult Center for the Performing Arts (☞ Nightlife and the Arts, *below*), the two most prominent downtown buildings. Stock up on maps and information about the Eugene area at the **Lane County Convention and Visitors Association** (⌧ 115 Olive St., between 7th and 8th Aves., ☎ 800/547–5445).

Numbers in the text correspond to numbers in the margin and on the Eugene map.

A Good Walk

From downtown Eugene, walk north across the Willamette River on the Autzen Footbridge and stroll through **Alton Baker Park.** Head north to the entertaining **Wistec** ⑫ science and technology museum, which is just outside the park to the west of Autzen Stadium. Or follow the path that leads west along the river. Walk back across the Willamette River via the Ferry Street Bridge to Gateway Park. Stay to the left at the end of the bridge and you'll eventually hit High Street. Head south on High to the **5th Street Public Market** ⑬ (which, despite its name, is on 5th Avenue). The market is a great place to have lunch. You'll need fortification for your next stop, **Skinner Butte Park** ⑭. From the market take 5th Avenue west and Lincoln Street north. If you're feeling hardy, you can climb to the top of Skinner Butte for a great view. The **Owen Rose Garden** ⑮ is west of the park. Follow the bike path west from Skinner Butte Park along the Willamette River to the garden.

TIMING

This tour takes more than half a day unless you drive it. Plan to spend an hour or so at each stop, and add an extra hour if you visit the science center.

Sights to See

Alton Baker Park. There's fine hiking and biking at Alton Baker, the largest of three adjoining riverside parks—Gateway and Skinner Butte are the other two—on the banks of the Willamette River. A footpath along the river runs the length of the park. ⌧ *Centennial Blvd. east of the Ferry St. Bridge.* ⊙ *Daily dawn–dusk.*

⑬ **5th Street Public Market.** A former chicken-processing plant houses this combination shopping mall and food court. The dining options range from sit-down restaurants to decadent bakeries (the Metropol Bakery on the building's lower level is especially fine) to the bewildering international diversity of the second-floor food esplanade. ⌧ *5th Ave. and High St.,* ☎ *541/484–0383.* ⊙ *Shops daily 10–6 (Fri. until 9); restaurants daily 7 AM–9 PM (weekends until 10).*

Hendricks Park. This quiet park east of the University of Oregon is at its most glorious in May, when its towering rhododendrons and azaleas blossom in shades of pink, yellow, red, and purple. From the university's Franklin Boulevard gate, head south on Agate Street, east on 19th Avenue, south on Fairmont Boulevard, and east on Summit Avenue. ⌧ *Summit and Skyline Aves.,* ☎ *541/682–4800.*

Maude Kerns Art Center. The oldest church in Eugene, two blocks east of the university, houses this arts facility that exhibits contemporary fine arts and crafts. ⌧ *1910 E. 15th Ave.,* ☎ *541/345–1571.* 🎫 *Free.* ⊙ *Mon.–Sat. 10–5, Sun. 1–5.*

⑮ **Owen Rose Garden.** Three thousand roses bloom from June to September at this garden west of Skinner Butte Park. Magnolia, cherry, and oak trees dot the grounds. ⌧ *300 N. Jefferson St.,* ☎ *541/682–4800.* 🎫 *Free.* ⊙ *Daily 6 AM–11 PM.*

Eugene

❿ **Skinner Butte Park.** Eugene's parks and gardens are wonderfully diverse and add to the outdoor fabric of the city. Skinner Butte Park, rising from the south bank of the Willamette River, has the most historical cachet, since it was here that Eugene Skinner staked the claim that put Eugene on the map. Skinner Butte Loop leads to the top of Skinner Butte, from which **Spencer Butte**, 4 mi to the south, can be seen. The two main trails to the top of Skinner Butte traverse a sometimes difficult terrain through a mixed-conifer forest. ⊠ *2nd Ave. and High St.,* ☎ *541/687–5333.* ⌸ *Free.* ☺ *Daily 10 AM–midnight.*

University of Oregon. The true heart of Eugene lies southeast of the city center at its university. Several fine old buildings can be seen on the 250-acre campus; **Deady Hall,** built in 1876, is the oldest. More than 400 varieties of trees grace the bucolic grounds, along with outdoor sculptures that include *Pioneer* and *Pioneer Mother.* The two bronze figures by Alexander Phimster Proctor were dedicated to the men and women who settled the Oregon Territory and less than a generation later founded the university. Track star Steve Prefontaine and Nike shoes founder Phil Knight attended school here and helped to establish Eugene's reputation as Tracktown, U.S.A.

Eugene's two best museums are affiliated with the university. The collection of Asian art at the **University of Oregon Museum of Art** (⊠ 1430 Johnson La., ☎ 541/346–3027), next to the library, includes examples of Chinese imperial tomb figures, textiles, and furniture.

Relics of a more localized nature are on display at the **University of Oregon Museum of Natural History** (⊠ 1680 E. 15th Ave., ☎ 541/ 346–3024). Devoted to Pacific Northwest anthropology and the natural sciences, its highlights include the fossil collection of Thomas Condon, Oregon's first geologist, and a pair of 9,000-year-old sagebrush sandals. ⊠ *University of Oregon main entrance: Agate St. and Franklin Blvd.,* ☎ *541/346–3111.* ⊑ *Art museum free, natural-history museum $1.* ☉ *Museums Wed.–Sun. noon–5.*

🐾 ⑫ **Wistec.** Eugene's imaginative, hands-on Willamette Science and Technology Center—Wistec to the locals—assembles rotating exhibits designed for curious young minds. The adjacent **planetarium,** one of the largest in the Pacific Northwest, presents star shows and entertainment events. ⊠ *2300 Leo Harris Pkwy.,* ☎ *541/682–3020 for museum, 541/687–7827 for planetarium.* ⊑ *$3.* ☉ *Wed.–Sun. noon–6.*

Dining and Lodging

$$$ ✕ **Chanterelle.** Some diners find the European cuisine at this romantic 14-table restaurant old-fashioned, but the chef, Rolf Schmidt, sees no reason to go nouvelle. He continues to prepare the region's beef, lamb, and seafood in a traditional Old World manner. Crystal and fresh flowers fill Chanterelle, which is in an old warehouse across from the 5th Street Public Market. ⊠ *207 E. 5th Ave.,* ☎ *541/484–4065. Reservations essential. AE, DC, MC, V. Closed Sun.–Mon., last 2 wks of Mar., 1st wk of Apr., last wk of Aug., 1st 2 wks of Sept. No lunch.*

$$–$$$ ✕ **Excelsior Café.** Its accomplished cuisine enhances the appealing European elegance of this restaurant, bar, and bistro-style café across from the University of Oregon. The chef uses only fresh local produce, some of it grown on the premises. The menu changes according to the season, but staples include delicious salads and soups, gnocchi, grilled chicken, broiled salmon, and sandwiches. The dining room, shaded by blossoming cherry trees in the spring, has a quiet, understated atmosphere. There's outdoor seating on the front terrace or under a grape arbor in the back; in good weather both are fine places to take Sunday brunch. ⊠ *Excelsior Inn, 754 E. 13th Ave.,* ☎ *541/342–6963. AE, D, DC, MC, V.*

$$ ✕ **Zenon Cafe.** You never know what you'll find on the menu here— Thai, Indian, Italian, South American, or down-home barbecue—but it's sure to be memorable and expertly prepared. Slate floors, picture windows, Parisian-style street lamps, marble-top tables, and café chairs lend this eatery the feel of a romantic, open-air bistro. The desserts are formidable—two full-time bakers produce 20 to 30 daily. Look for the *zuccotto Fiorentino,* a dove-shape Italian wedding cake with rum, orange, and flavored whipped cream. ⊠ *898 Pearl St.,* ☎ *541/343–3005. Reservations not accepted. MC, V.*

$–$$ ✕ **Mekala's.** The emphasis at this eatery in the Fifth Street Public Market is on healthful yet zippy Thai staples such as pad thai and curries. ⊠ *296 E. 5th Ave.,* ☎ *541/342–4872. AE, MC, V.*

$ ✕ **Poppi's Anatolia.** The moussaka and *kalamarakia* (fried squid) at this home-style Greek restaurant are great; wash them down with retsina or Aegean beer. Except on Sunday nights, when the chef prepares only Greek dishes, you can also sample East Indian specialties. ⊠ *992 Willamette St.,* ☎ *541/343–9661. MC, V. No lunch Sun.*

$$–$$$$ 🏨 **Campbell House.** Built in 1892 on the east side of Skinner Butte, Campbell House is one of the oldest structures in Eugene. Restored with fastidious care, the luxurious B&B is surrounded by an acre of landscaped grounds. The parlor, library, and dining rooms have their original hardwood floors and curved-glass windows. Their differing architectural details, building angles, and furnishings (a mixture of century-old antiques and reproductions) lend each of the rooms a distinctive personality. One suite has a Jacuzzi. The room rates include a breakfast of fresh-baked pastries and other items. ⊠ *252 Pearl St., 97401,* ☎ *541/343–1119 or 800/264–2519,* ℻ *541/343–2258. 12 rooms, 6 suites. No-smoking rooms, in-room VCRs. AE, D, MC, V.*

$$–$$$ ▨ **Eugene Hilton.** Location, amenities, service, and a room-by-room remodeling completed in 1997 make this downtown hotel Eugene's most convenient and comfortable. Sliding glass doors in each of the rooms open out to the city. The top-floor restaurant, Vistas, and CJ's, the adjacent bar, have the best butte-to-butte view in Eugene. The Hilton and its extensive convention facilities adjoin Eugene's Hult Center for the Performing Arts. Downtown shopping, the Willamette River, and more than 30 restaurants are within easy walking distance. ⊠ *66 E. 6th Ave., 97401,* ☎ *541/342–2000 or 800/937–6660,* ‖‖ *541/342–6661. 272 rooms. 2 restaurants, 2 bars, indoor pool, beauty salon, indoor hot tub, exercise room, free parking, airport shuttle. AE, D, DC, MC, V.*

$$–$$$ ▨ **Excelsior Inn.** This small hotel in a former frat house manifests a
★   quiet sophistication more commonly found in Europe than in America. Crisply detailed, with cherry-wood doors and moldings, it has rooms furnished in a refreshingly understated manner, each with a marble-and-tile bath. The rates include a delicious breakfast. The ground-level Excelsior Café is one of Eugene's best restaurants. ⊠ *757 E. 13th Ave., 97401,* ☎ *541/342–6963 or 800/321–6963,* ‖‖ *541/342–1417. 14 rooms. Restaurant, bar, café, in-room VCRs, in-room modem lines, no-smoking rooms, free parking. AE, D, DC, MC, V.*

$$ ▨ **New Oregon Best Western.** The plush furnishings and comprehensive amenities at this midsize motel near the University of Oregon come as a bit of a surprise, given the property's price range. ⊠ *1655 Franklin Blvd., 97403,* ☎ *541/683–3669,* ‖‖ *541/484–5556. 130 rooms. In-room modem lines, no-smoking floor, refrigerators, indoor pool, indoor hot tub, sauna, exercise room, racquetball, laundry service and dry cleaning, free parking. AE, D, DC, MC, V.*

Nightlife and the Arts

The **Hult Center For the Performing Arts** (⊠ 1 Eugene Centre, ☎ 541/342–5746), a spacious building of glass and native wood, is the locus of Eugene's cultural life. Renowned for the quality of their acoustics, the center's two theaters are home base for Eugene's symphony and opera companies (☞ *below*). There's nearly always something going on—ballets, major performers, traveling Broadway shows, and rock bands appear regularly.

Conductor Helmuth Rilling leads the internationally known **Oregon Bach Festival** (☎ 541/346–5666 or 800/457–1486) every summer. Concerts, chamber music, and social events—held mainly in Eugene at the Hult Center and the University of Oregon School of Music but also in Corvallis and Florence—are part of this 17-day event. In May and August, the **Oregon Festival of American Music** (☎ 541/687–6526 or 800/248–1615) presents concerts at the Hult Center and parks around Eugene. **Oregon Mozart Players** (☎ 541/345–6648), the state's premier professional chamber music orchestra, plays 20 concerts a year. The **Eugene Opera** (☎ 541/485–3985) produces three fully staged operas per season. The **Eugene Symphony** (☎ 541/687–9487) performs a full season of classical, family, and pops concerts.

Outdoor Activities and Sports

BASEBALL

The **Eugene Emeralds,** the Northwest League (Class A) affiliate of the Atlanta Braves, play at Civic Stadium (⊠ 2077 Willamette St., ☎ 541/342–5367).

BASKETBALL

The **University of Oregon Ducks** play at MacArthur Court (⊠ 1601 University St., ☎ 800/932–3668).

The **River Bank Bike Path,** originating in Alton Baker Park on the Willamette's north bank, is a level and leisurely introduction to Eugene's topography. It's one of 120 mi of trails in the area. **Prefontaine Trail,** used by area runners, travels through level fields and forests for 1½ mi. **Pedal Power** (⊠ 535 High St., ☎ 541/687–1775) downtown rents bikes.

FOOTBALL
The **University of Oregon Ducks** play their home games at Autzen Stadium (⊠ 2700 Centennial Blvd., ☎ 800/932–3668).

GOLF
Riveridge Golf Course (⊠ 3800 N. Delta Hwy., ☎ 541/345–9160) is an 18-hole, par-71 course. The greens fee is $30; a cart costs $20.

SKIING
Willamette Pass (⊠ Hwy. 58, 69 mi southeast of Eugene, ☎ 541/484–5030 or 800/444–5030), 6,666 ft high in the Cascades Range, packs an annual average snowfall of 300 inches atop 29 runs. The vertical drop is 1,563 ft. Four triple chairs and one double chair service the downhill ski areas, and 13 mi of Nordic trails lace the pass. Facilities here include a ski shop, day care, a bar, a restaurant, and Nordic and downhill rentals, repairs, and instruction.

Shopping

Every Saturday between April and Christmas, local craftspeople, farmers, and chefs come together from 10 to 5 to create the weekly **Eugene Saturday Market** (⊠ 8th and Oak Sts., ☎ 541/686–8885), a great people-watching event with cheap eats and nifty arts and crafts.

OFF THE
BEATEN PATH

HIGHWAY 126 WEST OF EUGENE – Westward toward the coast, Highway 126 curves past several wineries and the trout-filled Siuslaw River before ending in Florence (☞ The Oregon Coast, *above*). Two of the best-known wineries are Hinman Vineyards (⊠ 27012 Briggs Hill Rd., south of Hwy. 126, Eugene, ☎ 541/345–1945) and LaVelle Vineyards (⊠ 89697 Scheffler Rd., north of Hwy. 126, Elmira, ☎ 541/935–9406).

WALDO LAKE – Nestled in old-growth forest, Waldo Lake is thought by some to be the cleanest landlocked body of water in the world. The lake is only accessible after a short hike, so bring comfortable walking attire. ⊠ *From Eugene take Hwy. 58 to Oakridge and continue toward Willamette Pass (follow signs north to Waldo Lake).*

McKenzie River Highway

East of Eugene on Hwy. 126 (52 mi to town of McKenzie Bridge).

Highway 126 as it heads east from Eugene is known as the McKenzie River Highway. Following the curves of the river, it passes grazing lands, fruit and nut orchards, and the small riverside hamlets of the McKenzie Valley. From the highway you can glimpse the bouncing, bubbling, blue-green McKenzie River, one of Oregon's top fishing, boating, and white-water rafting spots, against a backdrop of densely forested mountains, splashing waterfalls, and jet-black lava beds. The small town of McKenzie Bridge marks the end of the McKenzie River Highway and the beginning of the 26-mi McKenzie River National Recreation Trail, which heads north through the Willamette National Forest along portions of the Old Santiam Wagon Road.

Dining and Lodging

$$ ✕⬜ **Log Cabin Inn.** This inn on the banks of the wild, fish-filled McKenzie River is equally appropriate for a fishing vacation or a romantic weekend getaway. Antique furniture decorates log-cabin-style buildings with new beds and baths; each room has a river view. Six riverfront tepees share a bath. Menu standouts at the delightful restaurant include wild boar, quail, salmon, a decadent homemade beer-cheese soup, and a locally famous marionberry cobbler. ⊠ *56483 McKenzie Hwy., 97413,* ☎ *541/822–3432 or 800/355–3432. 8 cabins, 6 tepees. Restaurant, bar, fishing. MC, V.*

Outdoor Activities and Sports

BOATING AND RAFTING

The 22-ft-long pontoons operated by **McKenzie Pontoon Trips** (⊠ 37855 Shenandoah Loop, Springfield, ☎ 541/741–1905) are a safe and relatively comfortable way to experience a guided float trip down the McKenzie River. **Oregon Whitewater Adventures** (⊠ 660 Kelly Blvd., Springfield, ☎ 541/746–5422 or 800/820–7238) operates half- to two-day rafting excursions on the river.

OFF THE
BEATEN PATH

McKENZIE PASS – Just beyond McKenzie Bridge, Highway 242 begins a steep, 22-mi eastward climb to McKenzie Pass in the Cascade Range. The scenic highway, which passes through the Mount Washington Wilderness Area and continues to the town of Sisters (☞ Central Oregon, *below*), is generally closed from October to June because of heavy snow.

Umpqua Valley

73 mi south of Eugene on I–5 (to town of Roseburg).

Roseburg is a name sacred to fishermen the world over. The town on the North Umpqua River is home to a dozen popular fish species, including bass, brown and brook trout, and chinook, coho and sockeye salmon.

The **Douglas County Museum,** one of the best county museums in the state, surveys 8,000 years of human activity in the region. Its fossil collection, which includes a million-year-old saber-toothed tiger, is worth a stop. ⊠ *Douglas County Fairgrounds (take Exit 123 from I–5 and follow signs),* ☎ *541/440–4507.* ▢ *Free.* ☉ *Tues.–Sat. 10–4, Sun. noon–4.*

Area Wineries

Callahan Ridge Winery, which has won prizes for its zinfandel and late-harvest Rieslings, hosts the Cure for the Summertime Blues Festival of music, crafts, food, and games each July. ⊠ *340 Busenbark La. (from I–5's Exit 125 head northwest on Garden Valley Rd. and west on Melrose Rd.), Roseburg,* ☎ *541/673–7901 or 800/695–4946.* ☉ *Apr.–Dec., daily 11:30–5; rest of yr by appointment.*

Girardet Wine Cellars has won gold medals for its Bacot Noir and other wines—its pinot noir and rare Maréchal Foch are two standouts. ⊠ *895 Reston Rd. (from I–5's Exit 119 head south on Hwy. 99 to the town of Winston, west on Hwy. 42, and north on Reston), Tenmile,* ☎ *541/679–7252.* ☉ *Mar.–Aug., daily 11–5; Sept.–Feb., Sat. 11–5.*

Henry Estate Winery, north of Roseburg along the Umpqua River, produces pinot noir, chardonnay, gewürztraminer, and Riesling wines. The vineyard's flower garden is perfect for summer picnics. ⊠ *678 Hubbard Creek Rd. (from I–5's Exit 136 head west ¼ mi on Hwy. 138* *and take the 1st left onto Fort McKay Rd.—on some maps the Suther-lin–Umpqua Rd. or County Rd. 9—which runs into Hubbard Creek), Umpqua,* ☎ *541/459–5120.* ☉ *Daily 11–5.*

An early (1960s) entrant in the Oregon wine-making industry, **Hillcrest Vineyard** specializes in dry Riesling and cabernet sauvignon wines but also produces zinfandels, unusual for these parts. The panoramic views of the countryside from here are splendid. ⊠ *240 Vineyard La. (from I–5's Exit 125, head west on Garden Valley Rd. to Melrose Rd. to Do-erner Rd. and north on Elgarose Loop Rd.), Roseburg,* ☎ *800/736–3709.* ☉ *Daily 11–5.*

La Garza Cellars, which is known for its cabernet sauvignon and chardonnay wines, has a covered deck for picnics and a shop that sells many regional wines. A restaurant, La Garza Gourmet, is open dur-ing the summer from 11 to 4. ⊠ *491 S.W. Winery La. (head south-west from I–5's Exit 119 to Winery La. and turn left), Roseburg,* ☎ *541/679–9654.* ☉ *June–Sept., daily 11–5; Oct.–May, Wed.–Sun. noon–4.*

Dining and Lodging

$–$$ ✕ **Tolly's.** You can go formal or informal at this restaurant in Oak-land, 18 mi north of Roseburg. Have an old-fashioned soda or malt downstairs in the Victorian ice-cream parlor, or head upstairs to the oak- and antiques-filled dining room for expertly prepared beef, chicken, seafood, and lamb. Try the grilled salmon or the grilled flank steak marinated and served with fiery chipotle chilies. ⊠ *115 Locust St. (take I–5's Exit 138 and follow the road north from the exit for 4 mi, cross the railroad tracks, and turn west on Locust),* ☎ *541/459–3796. AE, D, MC, V.*

$$–$$$ ✕🏠 **Steamboat Inn.** Oregon's most famous fishing lodge was first
★ brought to the world's attention in the 1930s in travel articles by the western writer Zane Grey. Every fall a Who's Who of the world's top fly fishermen converges here, high in the Cascades above the emerald North Umpqua River, in search of the 20-pound steelhead that haunt these waters. (Guide services are available, as are equipment rentals and sales.) Others come simply to relax in the reading nooks or on the broad decks of the riverside guest cabins. Another renowned attrac-tion is the nightly Fisherman's Dinner, a multicourse feast served around a massive 50-year-old sugar-pine dinner table. Lodging choices include riverside cabins, forest bungalows, and riverside suites; the bun-galows and suites have kitchens. Make reservations well in advance, especially for a stay between July and October, the prime fishing months. ⊠ *42705 N. Umpqua Hwy. (38 mi east of Roseburg on Hwy. 138, near Steamboat Creek), Steamboat 97447,* ☎ *541/498–2230,* 🅵🅰🅷 *541/498–2411. 8 cabins, 5 bungalows, 2 suites. Restaurant, library, meeting room. MC, V.*

Crater Lake National Park

★ ⓰ *85 mi east of Roseburg on Hwy. 138; 71 mi northeast of Medford on Hwy. 62.*

Oregon's only national park got its start 7,700 years ago, when Mount Mazama erupted in a volcanic explosion that spewed hot ash and pumice for hundreds of miles. Rain and snowmelt eventually filled the result-ing caldera, creating a sapphire-blue lake so clear that sunlight pene-trates to a depth of 400 ft. In 1902 this geological curiosity, the crown jewel of the Cascades and Oregon's most famous tourist attraction, was established as **Crater Lake National Park.** The park is closed most of the year because of heavy snows, but the north and south entrance roads are generally clear by early June. Peak visiting times are July and August, but even then you'll rarely encounter a traffic jam. Drive, bicycle, or hike Crater Lake's 25-mi rim; watch the chipmunks along either **Godfrey Glen Nature Trail** or the **Castle Crest Wildflower Trail;** or take a boat ride out to **Wizard Island,** a perfect miniature cinder cone protruding 760 ft above the surface of the lake. Private boats are not allowed on Crater Lake, so these tours ($12.50) provide a unique surface-level view of the caldera. Several times a day from June to early September, boat tours leave from Cleetwood Cove on the lake's north side. ⊠ *Steel Information Center: Munson Valley Rd. on south side of park (follow signs from entrances),* ☎ *541/594–2211.* ⌨ *Day use $10 per vehicle, campsites $10–$15.* ⊘ *Visitor center daily 9–5; Rim Dr. closed mid-Sept.–mid-May.*

Dining and Lodging

$$–$$$ ✕ **The Dining Room at Crater Lake Lodge.** Open for breakfast, lunch, and dinner, this restaurant serves ambitious fare in decidedly upscale surroundings. The room itself is magnificent, with a large stone fireplace and views out over the clear blue waters of Crater Lake. This is virtually the only place to dine well once you're in the park. The evening menu usually includes fresh Pacific Northwest seafood, a pasta dish, pork medallions, and steak Oscar. The wines are from Oregon and Washington. ⊠ *Crater Lake Lodge, Rim Village,* ☎ *541/594–2255. Reservations essential for dinner. MC, V. Closed mid-Sept.–mid-May.*

$$–$$$$ ⊟ **Crater Lake Lodge.** The historic 1917 lodge on the rim of the caldera was renovated in the mid-1990s yet retains a period ambience. Lodgepole pine columns, gleaming wood floors, and stone fireplaces grace the common areas, and the newer furnishings blend in perfectly. The lodge has only one telephone, in the lobby area, and there are no televisions or electronic diversions of any kind. ⊠ *Rim Village, Box 128, Crater Lake 97604,* ☎ *541/594–2255,* FAX *541/594–2622. 71 rooms. Restaurant, no-smoking rooms. MC, V. Closed mid-Sept.–mid-May.*

$$ ⊟ **Mazama Village Motor Inn.** This 40-room Forest Service complex south of the lake provides basic accommodations in 10 A-frame buildings. ⊠ *Rim Village, Box 128, Crater Lake 97604,* ☎ *541/594–2255,* FAX *541/594–2622. MC, V.*

Camping

⛺ **Mazama Campground.** All the sites here, along with 900 more in the surrounding national forests, are available on a first-come, first-served basis. ⛺ *Mazama Village near Annie Springs entrance station,* ☎ *541/594–2255. 198 sites.* ⌨ *$13. Flush toilets, potable water, showers, laundry facilities.* ⊘ *Mid-June–mid-Oct.*

Outdoor Activities and Sports

If you're an advanced-intermediate or expert downhill skier and crave solitude, **Mount Bailey Snocat Skiing** (☎ 541/793–3333 or 800/733–7593) is the ski-guide service for you. Heated Sno-Cats deliver you to the summit of Mount Bailey, an 8,300-ft peak not far from Crater Lake, where you can attack the virgin powder on 4 mi of runs, with a vertical drop of 3,000 ft. The excursions are limited to 12 skiers a day. Tours leave Diamond Lake Resort (⊠ Hwy. 138, 76 mi east of Roseburg and 25 mi north of Crater Lake) daily at 7 AM. The resort's facilities include three restaurants, a bar, lodging, Nordic trails, and downhill and Nordic ski rentals.

Crater Lake National Park

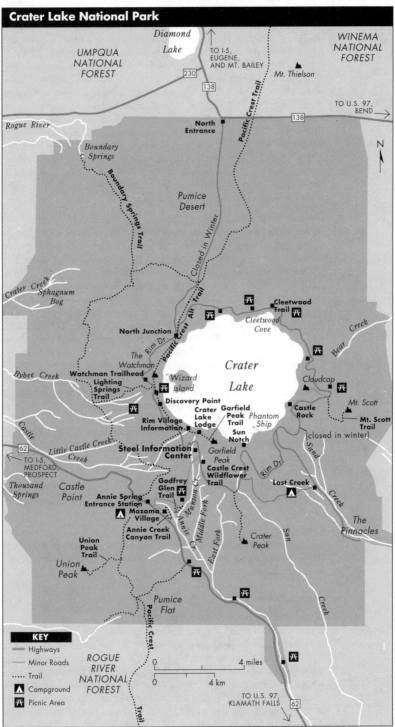

UMPQUA NATIONAL FOREST

Diamond Lake

WINEMA NATIONAL FOREST

TO I-5, EUGENE, AND MT. BAILEY

230

138

Mt. Thielson

TO U.S. 97, BEND

138

Rogue River

North Entrance

Pacific Crest Trail

Boundary Springs

Pumice Desert

N

Boundary Springs Trail

Closed in Winter

Crater Creek

Sphagnum Bog

Cleetwood Trail

Bear Creek

North Junction

Cleetwood Cove

Pacific Crest Alt Trail

Rim Dr.

The Watchman

Crater Lake

Cloudcap

Watchman Trailhead

Bybee Creek

Lighting Springs Trail

Wizard Island

Mt. Scott

Discovery Point

Castle Rock

Mt. Scott Trail

Castle

Rim Village Information

Crater Lake Lodge

Garfield Peak Trail

Phantom Ship

(closed in winter)

Little Castle Creek

Sun Notch

62

TO I-5, MEDFORD; PROSPECT

Steel Information Center

Garfield Peak

Rim Dr.

Creek

Thousand Springs

Castle Point

Castle Crest Wildflower Trail

Lost Creek

The Pinnacles

Godfrey Glen Trail

Annie Spring Entrance Station

Annie Creek

Mazama Village

Middle Fork

Crater Peak

Sun

Annie Creek Canyon Trail

East Fork

Creek

Union Peak Trail

Union Peak

Pacific Crest

Pumice Flat

KEY

— Highways
— Minor Roads
···· Trail
▲ Campground
🅿 Picnic Area

ROGUE RIVER NATIONAL FOREST

0   4 miles
0   4 km

TO U.S. 97, KLAMATH FALLS

62

Trail

OFF THE
BEATEN PATH

ROGUE RIVER VIEWS – Nature lovers who want a glimpse of the Rogue River's loveliest angle can take a side trip to the Avenue of the Boulders, Mill Creek Falls, and Barr Creek Falls, off Highway 62, near Prospect. Here the wild waters of the upper Rogue foam through volcanic boulders and the dense greenery of the Rogue River National Forest.

Medford

71 mi southwest of Crater Lake on Hwy. 62; 88 mi south of Roseburg on I–5.

Strip malls surround Medford, the commercial center of southern Oregon, though in recent years the town has restored most of its old downtown core.

Lodging

$$$
★

☎ **Under the Greenwood Tree.** Regular guests at this B&B between Medford and Ashland find themselves hard-pressed to decide what they like most: the luxurious and romantic rooms, the stunning 10-acre gardens, or the breakfasts cooked by the owner, a Cordon Bleu–trained chef. Gigantic old oaks hung with hammocks shade the inn, a 130-year-old farmhouse exuding genteel charm. There's a manicured 2-acre lawn and a creaky three-story barn for exploring; an outbuilding holds the buckboard wagon that brought the property's original homesteaders westward on the Oregon Trail. The interior is decorated in Renaissance splendor. ⊠ *3045 Bellinger La. (head west from I–5's Exit 27 on Barnett Rd., south briefly on Hwy. 99, west on Stewart Ave., south briefly on Hull Rd., and west on Bellinger), 97501,* ☎ *541/776–0000. 5 rooms. MC, V.*

$
☎ **Motel 6.** It's not the Savoy, but it's clean, cheap, and close to the Shakespeare Festival, the Mount Ashland ski area, and Crater Lake. ⊠ *950 Alba Dr. (Exit 27 off I–5), 97504,* ☎ *541/773–4290 or 800/466–8356 (central reservations),* FAX *541/857–9574. 167 units. Pool. AE, D, DC, MC, V.*

Nightlife and the Arts

The **Ginger Rogers Theatre** (⊠ 23 S. Central Ave., ☎ 541/779–3000), a restored vaudeville house named for the late Hollywood star, who became an area resident after her retirement, presents concerts, theater works, and touring shows.

Outdoor Activities and Sports

GOLF

Cedar Links Golf Club (⊠ 3155 Cedar Links Dr., ☎ 541/773–4373 or 800/853–2754), an 18-hole, par-70 public golf course, charges from $20 to $22, plus $9 per rider for an optional cart.

JET-BOAT EXCURSIONS

Hellgate Jetboat Excursions (⊠ 953 S.E. 7th St., Grants Pass, ☎ 541/479–7204) operates jet-boat trips down the Rogue River's Hellgate Canyon from May to September.

Shopping

Harry and David's/Jackson & Perkins (⊠ 2518 S. Pacific Hwy., ☎ 541/776–2121 or 800/345–5655) are two of the largest mail-order companies in the world: Harry and David's for fruit and gift packs, Jackson & Perkins for roses. Harry and David's Country Store in the complex is a retail outlet for their products, most of which are grown in the Bear Creek Orchards.

Jacksonville

5 mi west of Medford on Hwy. 238.

In many ways southern Oregon has become as important to the cultural life of the state as are Portland and Eugene. Tiny Jacksonville, once a stagecoach stop, hosts the **Britt Festivals** (☞ Nightlife and the Arts, *below*) of music and theater each summer. All of Jacksonville is on the National Register of Historic Places. Several of the 80 privately owned landmark buildings date from the town's gold-rush heyday of 1853. For free maps and guides to Jacksonville's many historic structures, stop by the **Jacksonville Visitor Information Center** (⊠ 185 N. Oregon St., ☎ 541/899–8118).

The **Jacksonville Museum,** inside the old Jackson County Courthouse, houses intriguing gold-rush-era artifacts. The "Jacksonville! Boomtown to Home Town" exhibit lays out the area's history. The **Children's Museum,** occupying the 80-year-old Jackson County Jail, contains hands-on exhibits about pioneer life and has a splendid collection of antique toys. ⊠ 206 N. 5th St., ☎ 541/773–6536. ☑ *$3 for each museum, $7 pass for both museums and other nearby attractions.* ☉ *Memorial Day–Labor Day, daily 10–5; Labor Day–Memorial Day, Tues.–Sun. 10–5.*

Dining and Lodging

$–$$ ✕ **Bella Union.** The menu is downright sophisticated at this unpretentious restaurant in an 1870s saloon. Fresh fish—familiar species and more exotic ones like Hawaiian opah and mako shark—is flown in daily, and the pastas are handmade on the premises. ⊠ *170 California St.,* ☎ *541/899–1770. AE, MC, V.*

$$$–$$$$ ✕🏠 **Jacksonville Inn.** The spotless period antiques and the host of well-
★   chosen amenities at this 1863-vintage inn evoke what the Wild West might have been had Martha Stewart been in charge. A block away are three larger and more luxurious cottages with fireplaces and saunas. The Continental fare and 600-label wine cellar in the basement dining room (reservations essential; no lunch on Monday) are among the best in southern Oregon—fresh razor clams and veal dishes are the house specialties. Book well in advance, particularly between late June and August, when the Britt Festivals draw thousands of visitors. The room rates include a full breakfast. ⊠ *175 E. California St., 97530,* ☎ *541/ 899–1900 or 800/321–9344,* FAX *541/899–1373. 8 rooms, 3 cottages. Restaurant, refrigerator. AE, D, DC, MC, V.*

$$ ✕🏠 **The McCully House Inn.** One of Jacksonville's six original homes, a gleaming white Gothic Revival mansion built in 1860, McCully House sits amid a fragrant rose garden. The period-decorated rooms, one with a fireplace and all of them filled with antiques, are on the second floor. One of the town's best restaurants (reservations essential; no lunch), on the ground level, specializes in seafood and has a Sunday brunch. The room rates include a full breakfast. ⊠ *240 E. California St., 97530,* ☎ *541/899–1942 or 800/367–1942,* FAX *541/899– 1560. 3 rooms. Restaurant. AE, MC, V.*

Nightlife and the Arts

Every summer some of the finest musicians in the world gather for the **Britt Festivals** (☎ 541/773–6077 or 800/882–7488), outdoor concerts and theater presentations lasting from mid-June to early September. Contemporary and classical performances are staged in an outdoor amphitheater on the estate of 19th-century photographer and painter Peter Britt.

Oregon Caves National Monument

⑰ *90 mi from Jacksonville, west on Hwy. 238, south on U.S. 199, and east on Hwy 46.*

The town of **Cave Junction** is the turn-off point for the Oregon Caves National Monument. The "Marble Halls of Oregon," high in the verdant Siskiyou Mountains, have enchanted visitors since local hunter Elijah Davidson chased a bear into them in 1874. Huge stalagmites and stalactites, the Ghost Room, Paradise Lost, and the River Styx are part of a ½-mi subterranean tour that lasts about 75 minutes. The tour includes more than 200 stairs and is not recommended for anyone who experiences difficulty in walking or has respiratory or coronary problems. Children over six must be at least 42 inches tall and pass a safety and ability test, because they cannot be carried. ⊠ *Hwy. 46, 20 mi southeast of Cave Jct.,* ☎ 541/592–3400. *A $6.* ☉ *May–mid-June, daily 9–5; mid-June–Sept., daily 9–7; Oct.–Apr., daily 8:30–4.*

Dining and Lodging

$$ ✕🏨 **Oregon Caves Lodge.** If you're looking for a quiet retreat in an unusual setting, consider this lodge on the grounds of the national monument. Virtually unchanged since it was built in 1934, it has a rustic authenticity you'll find nowhere else in the state. Rooms, all with their original furnishings, have canyon or waterfall views. The dining room serves the best regional fare in the vicinity. ⊠ *2000 Caves Hwy., Cave Junction 97523,* ☎ *541/592–3400,* 📠 *541/592–6654. 22 rooms, 3 suites. Restaurant, coffee shop, hiking. No smoking. MC, V.*

Ashland

⑱ *20 mi from Jacksonville, east on Hwy. 238 and southeast on I–5; 90 mi from Oregon Caves National Monument, west on Hwy. 46, northeast on U.S. 199, and southeast on I–5; 180 mi south of Eugene on I–5.*

★ Ashland, the home of the **Oregon Shakespeare Festival** (☞ Nightlife and the Arts, *below*), draws more than 100,000 theater lovers to the Rogue Valley each year. The greatest influx is between June and September.

At the Oregon Shakespeare Festival's **Exhibit Center** in the festival complex, theater fans can try on costumes and view displays that outline the history of the festival. A fascinating guided backstage tour includes peeks at production shops and the Angus Bowmer Theatre and a walk to the very heavens above the Elizabethan stage. ⊠ *S. Pioneer and Main Sts.,* ☎ 541/482–4331. 🎟 *Backstage tour $9.50 early June–mid-Oct., $8.50 at other times (under 5 not admitted); exhibit center $2.* ☉ *Late Feb.–early June, Tues.–Sun. 10:30–1:30; early June–mid-Oct., Tues.–Sun. 10–4. Tours: Feb.–mid-Oct., Tues.–Sun. 10 AM; last 2 wks of Oct., Tues.–Sun. 10:30 AM and 1:30 PM.*

The Elizabethan Theatre overlooks **Lithia Park,** a 99-acre swath of green in the center of the town. An old-fashioned band shell, a duck pond, a children's playground, nature trails, and **Ashland Creek** make this a perfect spot for a pretheater picnic. Each June the festival opens its outdoor season by hosting the Feast of Will in the park, complete with music, dancing, bagpipes, and food. Tickets (about $16) are available through the festival box office (☞ Nightlife and the Arts, *below*).

The **Pacific Northwest Museum of Natural History** emphasizes hands-on exploration of the natural world through "multisensory" exhibits that visitors can touch and manipulate. ⊠ *1500 E. Main St. (1 mi east* *of downtown),* ☎ *541/488–1084.* ✍ *$6.50.* ☉ *Apr.–Oct., daily 9–5; Nov.–Mar., daily 10–4.*

Dining and Lodging

The Oregon Shakespeare Festival has stimulated one of the most extensive networks of B&Bs in the country—more than 50 in all. High season for Ashland-area B&Bs is between June and October. Expect to pay from $90 to $150 per night, which includes breakfast for two; during the off-season the rates are between $60 and $100. The **Ashland B&B Clearinghouse** (☎ 541/488–0338 or 800/588–0338) and the **Ashland B&B Reservation Network** (☎ 541/482–2337) provide lodging referrals.

$$$ ✕ **Chateaulin.** One of southern Oregon's most romantic restaurants
★ occupies an ivy-covered storefront a block from the Oregon Shakespeare Festival center, where it dispenses French food, local wine, and impeccable service with equal facility. Try the pan-roasted rack of lamb with a white-wine demi-glace sauce of roasted garlic, fresh basil, black olives, and sun-dried tomatoes, accompanied by a bottle of Ken Wright Cellars pinot noir. ⊠ *50 E. Main St.,* ☎ *541/482–2264. Reservations essential. AE, DC, MC, V. No lunch.*

$$–$$$ ✕ **Il Giardino.** An orange Vespa parked in the front entrance sets the casually chic tone at this Italian-run restaurant with great food and a warm atmosphere. The dozen or so pasta dishes are based on traditional recipes but incorporate local ingredients; the remainder of the menu is divided between meat and fresh fish. ⊠ *5 Granite St.,* ☎ *541/ 488–0816. Reservations essential for dinner. MC, V. Closed Mon.*

$$ ✕ **Thai Pepper.** Spicy Thai-style curries and stir-fries are the specialties at this restaurant above Ashland Creek. With an interior filled with local art, rattan, linen, and crystal, the restaurant feels like a French café in downtown Bangkok. Try the coconut prawns or the Thai beef-salad appetizers, followed by the house curry. ⊠ *84 N. Main St.,* ☎ *541/482–8058. MC, V. No lunch Sat.–Thurs.*

$–$$ ✕ **Gepetto's.** Kids love this unpretentious eatery, open daily for breakfast, lunch, and dinner. The friendly and fast-moving staff serves pasta dishes and delicious and unusual sandwiches, salads, and soups. Try the fresh-grilled marinated turkey served on crispy cheese bread. ⊠ *345 E. Main St.,* ☎ *541/482–1138. MC, V.*

$ ✕ **Rogue Brewery & Public House.** Ashland's first brew pub, a no-smoking establishment, serves pizza and other comfort food. Among the rotating selection of four to six ales, brewed on the premises, are Rogue Golden, Ashland Amber, and Shakespeare Stout. Two decks overhang the creek, a pleasant venue for ale and conversation during Ashland's warm summer evenings. ⊠ *31 B Water St.,* ☎ *541/488–5061. Reservations not accepted. MC, V.*

$$$ ✕🏠 **Winchester Country Inn.** The menu is small but imaginative at the restaurant inside this inn built in 1886. High-windowed dining rooms, set among manicured gardens, radiate a feeling of casual elegance. The roast duck in a sauce of caramel, brandy, and fresh fruit is ambrosial; the homemade scones, crab Benedict, and duck hash with orange hollandaise, served for Sunday brunch, are equally memorable. The restaurant (no lunch) is closed on Monday between November and May. Overnight accommodations are available upstairs in the main building, in a cottage, or in two restored Victorian homes. The rates include a gourmet breakfast. ⊠ *35 S. 2nd St., 97520,* ☎ *541/488–1113 or 800/ 972–4991,* ℻ *541/488–1404. Restaurant. 14 rooms, 4 suites. AE, D, MC, V.*

$$–$$$ 🏨 **Best Western Bard's Inn.** Original local art hangs on the walls of this property close to the theaters. The rooms, decorated with oak and knotty pine furniture, are small but have Rogue Valley views. ✉ *132 N. Main St., 97520,* ☎ *541/482–0049 or 800/528–1234,* ⨳ *541/488–3259. 89 units. Restaurant, bar, refrigerators, outdoor pool, outdoor hot tub. AE, D, DC, MC, V.*

$$–$$$ 🏨 **Mt. Ashland Inn.** Close to the summit ski area on Mount Ashland,
★   15 mi south of Ashland, this 5,500-square-ft lodge, hand built of cedar logs, has magnificent views of Mount Shasta and the rest of the Siskiyou Mountains; the Pacific Crest Trail runs through the parking lot. A large stone fireplace, antiques, hand-stitched quilts, and natural wood provide welcoming warmth, and a sauna and outdoor hot tub overlooking the mountains add to the alpine splendor. The room rates include a three-course breakfast that's wonderfully prepared and gracefully served, and the owners plan bike trips and provide snowshoes for guests. ✉ *550 Mt. Ashland Rd. (take Exit 6 from I–5 and follow signs west toward ski area to just beyond milepost 5), 97520,* ☎ ⨳ *541/482–8707 or* ☎ *800/830–8707. 5 rooms. Hiking, mountain bikes, cross-country skiing. AE, D, MC, V.*

Nightlife and the Arts

From February to October, more than 100,000 Bard-loving fanatics descend on Ashland for the **Oregon Shakespeare Festival** (✉ 15 S. Pioneer St., 97520, ☎ 541/482–4331, ⨳ 541/482–8045), presented in three theaters. Its accomplished repertory company mounts some of the finest Shakespearean productions you're likely to see on this side of Stratford-upon-Avon—plus works by Ibsen, Williams, and contemporary playwrights. Between June and October, plays are staged in the 1,200-seat Elizabethan Theatre, an atmospheric re-creation of the Fortune Theatre in London. The festival generally operates close to capacity, so it's important to book ahead.

Ashland's after-theater crowd (including many of the actors) congregates in the bar at **Chateaulin** (✉ 50 E. Main St., ☎ 541/482–2264).

Outdoor Activities and Sports

Siskiyou Adventures, Inc. (✉ 358 E. Main St., ☎ 541/488–1632 or 800/250–4602) provides guides and basic equipment for all manner of outdoor recreational sports, including white-water rafting, kayaking, fishing, and skiing.

SKIING

Mount Ashland (✉ Mt. Ashland Access Rd., 18 mi southwest of downtown Ashland; follow signs 9 mi from I–5's Exit 6, ☎ 541/482–2897 or 800/547–8052), a cone-shape Siskiyou peak, has some of the steepest runs in the state. Two triple and two double chairlifts accommodate a vertical drop of 1,150 ft; the longest of the 22 runs is 1 mi. Facilities include rentals, repairs, instruction, a ski shop, a restaurant, and a bar.

The Willamette Valley and Wine Country Essentials

Arriving and Departing

BY BUS

Greyhound (☎ 800/231–2222) serves Eugene and many other towns along the I–5 corridor.

BY CAR

Interstate 5 runs north–south the length of the Willamette, Umpqua, and Rogue River valleys.

Eugene Airport (☎ 541/687–5430) is served by Horizon, Skywest, and United/United Express. Horizon and United Express serve the **Rogue Valley Airport** (☎ 541/772–8068) in Medford. *See* Air Travel *in* the Gold Guide for airline phone numbers.

Getting Around
BY CAR

Many Willamette, Umpqua, and Rogue River valley attractions lie not too far east or west of I–5. **Highway 22** travels west from the Willamette National Forest through Salem to the coast. **Highway 99** travels parallel to I–5 through much of the Willamette Valley. **Highway 34** leaves I–5 just south of Albany and heads west, past Corvallis and into the Coast Range, where it follows the Alsea River. **Highway 138** winds along the Umpqua River, east of Roseburg to the back door of Crater Lake National Park. **Highway 126** heads east from Eugene toward the Willamette National Forest; it travels west from town to the coast.

Visitor Information

Ashland Chamber of Commerce and Visitors Information Center (⌂ 110 E. Main St., 97520, ☎ 541/482–3486). **Corvallis Convention and Visitors Bureau** (⌂ 420 N.W. 2nd St., 97330, ☎ 541/757–1544 or 800/334–8118). **Eugene Convention & Visitors Bureau** (⌂ 115 W. 8th St., Suite 190, 97440, ☎ 541/484–5307 or 800/452–3670). **Grant's Pass Visitors & Convention Bureau** (⌂ 1501 N.E. 6th St., 97526, ☎ 541/476–7717 or 800/547–5927). **McMinnville Chamber of Commerce** (⌂ 417 N. Adams St., 97128, ☎ 503/472–6196). **Roseburg Visitors & Convention Bureau** (⌂ 410 S.E. Spruce St., 97470, ☎ 541/672–9731 or 800/444–9584). **Salem Convention & Visitors Center** (⌂ 1313 Mill St. SE, 97301, ☎ 503/581–4325 or 800/874–7012).

THE COLUMBIA RIVER GORGE AND THE OREGON CASCADES

There's only one reason to drive to the Columbia River Gorge and Oregon Cascades: pleasure. Sightseers, hikers, skiers, and waterfall lovers all find contentment in this rugged region east of Portland. The highlights of the Columbia River Gorge, where America's second largest river (after the Mississippi) slashes through the Cascade Range, include, from west to east, Multnomah Falls, Bonneville Dam, and the windsurfing hub and rich orchard land of Hood River. To the south of Hood River lie the skiing and other alpine attractions of the 11,245-ft-high Mount Hood.

From Portland, the **Columbia Gorge–Mount Hood Loop** is the easiest way to see the gorge and the mountain. Take I–84 east to Troutdale and follow U.S. 26 to Bennett Pass (near Timberline), where Highway 35 heads north to Hood River; then follow I–84 back to Portland. Or make the loop in reverse.

Winter weather in the Columbia Gorge and the Mount Hood area is much more severe than that in Portland and western Oregon. Even I–84 may be closed because of snow and ice. If you're planning a winter visit, be sure your car has traction devices. And carry plenty of warm clothes. At any time of year, if you stop to explore, take your valuables with you—in spite of the idyllic surroundings, car prowlers are not unknown in the gorge.

Numbers in the margin correspond to points of interest on the Columbia River Gorge, the Cascades, and Central Oregon map.

Troutdale Area

13 mi east of Portland on I–84.

★ The town of Troutdale is the gateway to the **Columbia River Gorge.** Here, the 22-mi-long **Historic Columbia River Highway** (U.S. 30, also known as the Columbia River Scenic Highway and the Scenic Gorge Highway) leaves I–84 and begins its climb to the forested riverside bluffs high above the interstate. Completed in 1915, the serpentine highway was the first paved road in the gorge built expressly for automotive sightseers.

⑲ East of Troutdale a few miles on U.S. 30 is **Crown Point State Park,** a 730-ft-high bluff with an unparalleled 30-mi view down the Columbia River Gorge. **Vista House,** the two-tier octagonal structure on the side of the cliff, opened its doors to visitors in 1918; the rotunda contains displays about the gorge and the highway. ⊠ *U.S. 30,* ☎ *503/695–2240.* ▧ *Free.* ⊙ *Mid-Apr.–mid-Oct., daily 9–6.*

Rooster Rock State Park, the most famous beach lining the Columbia River, is below Crown Point; access is from the interstate only. Nudists and conventional bathers soak up the sun here. ⊠ *I–84, 7 mi east of Troutdale,* ☎ *503/695–2261.* ▧ *Day use $3 per vehicle.* ⊙ *Daily 7 AM–10 PM.*

En Route   From Crown Point, the Columbia River Highway heads downhill over graceful stone bridges built by Italian immigrant masons and winds through quiet forest glades. More than a dozen waterfalls pour over fern- and lichen-covered cliffs in a 10-mi stretch. Latourell, Bridal Veil, Wahkeena, and Horsetail falls are the most impressive. All have parking areas and hiking trails.

Multnomah Falls

⑳ *20 mi east of Troutdale on I–84 or Historic Columbia River Hwy. (U.S. 30).*

Multnomah Falls, a 620-ft-high double-decker torrent, the fifth-highest waterfall in the nation, is by far the most spectacular of the cataracts east of Troutdale. The scenic highway leads down to a parking lot; from there, a paved path winds to a bridge over the lower falls. A much steeper trail climbs to a viewing point overlooking the upper falls.

Dining

$–$$ ✕ **Multnomah Falls Lodge.** The lodge, built in 1925, has vaulted ceilings and classic stone fireplaces. Freshwater trout, salmon, and a platter of prawns, halibut, and scallops are the specialties. The restaurant is justly famous for its wild-huckleberry daiquiris and desserts. ⊠ *Historic Columbia River Hwy. (or Exit 31 off I–84),* ☎ *503/695–2376. AE, MC, V.*

Oneonta Gorge

㉑ *2 mi east of Multnomah Falls on Historic Columbia River Hwy.*

Following the old highway east from Multnomah Falls, you come to a narrow, mossy cleft with walls hundreds of feet high. Oneonta Gorge is the most enjoyable during the summer, when you can walk up the stream bed through the cool green canyon, where hundreds of plant species—some found nowhere else—flourish under the perennially moist conditions. At other times of year, take the trail along the west side of the canyon. The clearly marked trailhead is 100 yards west of the gorge, on the south side of the road. The trail ends at Oneonta Falls,

Columbia River Gorge, the Cascades, and Central Oregon

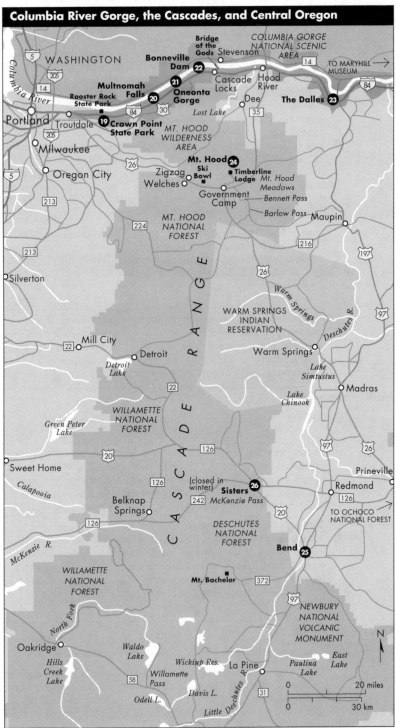

about ½ mi up the stream. You'll need boots or submersible sneakers—plus a strong pair of ankles—because the rocks are slippery. East of Oneonta Gorge, the scenic highway returns to I–84.

Cascade Locks

7 mi east of Oneonta Gorge on Historic Columbia River Hwy. and I–84; 30 mi east of Troutdale on I–84.

In pioneer days, boats needing to pass the bedeviling rapids near the town of Cascade Locks had to portage around them. The locks that gave the town its name were completed in 1896, allowing waterborne passage for the first time. Native Americans still use the locks for their traditional dip-net fishing.

㉒ **Bonneville Dam** is Oregon's most impressive man-made attraction. The first federal dam to span the Columbia, Bonneville was dedicated by President Franklin D. Roosevelt in 1937. Its generators (visible from a balcony during self-guided powerhouse tours) have a capacity of nearly a million kilowatts, enough to supply power to more than 200,000 single-family homes. There is a modern visitor center on Bradford Island, complete with underwater windows for viewing migrating salmon as they struggle up fish ladders. The best viewing times are between April and October. In recent years the dwindling runs of wild Columbia salmon have made the dam a subject of much environmental controversy. ⊠ *From I–84 take Exit 40, head northeast, and follow signs 1 mi to visitor center,* ☎ *541/374–8820.* ▨ *Free.* ☉ *Visitor center daily 9–5.*

Below the dam, the ponds at the **Bonneville Fish Hatchery** teem with fingerling salmon, fat rainbow trout, and 6-ft-long sturgeon. The hatchery raises chinook and coho salmon; from mid-October to late November, you can watch as staff members spawn the fish, beginning a new hatching cycle, or feed the trout with food pellets from a coin-operated machine. ⊠ *From I–84 take Exit 40 and follow signs northeast 1 mi to hatchery,* ☎ *541/374–8393.* ▨ *Free.* ☉ *Hatchery grounds daily 6 AM–10 PM, spawning room daily 7:30–4:30.*

Cascade Locks is the home port of the 600-passenger sternwheeler *Columbia Gorge.* Between mid-June and late September, the comfortable ship churns its way upriver, then back again, on two-hour excursions through some of the gorge's most awesome scenery. ⊠ *Cruises leave from Marine Park in Cascade Locks,* ☎ *541/374–8427.* ▨ *2-hr cruises (no meal) $14, longer cruises with meals $26–$36. Reservations essential for any cruise with meal.* ☉ *2-hr cruises (no meal) June–Sept., daily at 10, 12:30, and 3. Dinner cruise Fri. 7 PM, Sat. 6 PM. Brunch cruise weekends 12:30 PM. AE, MC, V.*

Dining and Lodging

$ ✕ **Char Burger Restaurant.** Arrowheads, rifles, and wagon-wheel chandeliers carry out the western motif of this dining room overlooking the Columbia River. Hamburgers, salmon, seafood, steaks, and breakfast favorites are served cafeteria-style. ⊠ *745 S.W. Wanapa St.,* ☎ *541/374–8477. Reservations essential for Sun. brunch. MC, V.*

$–$$$ ▥ **Best Western Columbia River Inn.** Most rooms in this comfortable inn have wonderful river views. Pale-blue carpeting, upholstered sofas and chairs, and oak tables decorate the soothing rooms, all of which have microwave ovens. Here's the downside: The inn sits above railroad tracks plied by numerous freight trains. Upper-floor rooms are a bit quieter than lower ones. ⊠ *735 Wanapa St., 97014,* ☎ *541/374–*

8777 or 800/595–7108, FAX *541/374–2279. 62 rooms. Refrigerators, indoor pool, indoor hot tub. AE, D, DC, MC, V.*

Stevenson, Washington

Across the river from Cascade Locks via the Bridge of the Gods and 4 mi east on Washington State Hwy. 14.

For a magnificent vista from high above the Columbia, pay the 75¢ toll and take the truss bridge, called the **Bridge of the Gods,** above Cascade Locks over to the Washington side.

The **Columbia Gorge Interpretive Center,** below the dramatic basaltic cliffs on the north bank of the Columbia River Gorge, contains exhibits that explain the volcanic forces that shaped the gorge landscape and the cultural history of the area. On display are a huge fish wheel and native dip nets used for salmon fishing, a Native American pit house, and artifacts pertaining to the explorers, missionaries, fur trappers, and soldiers who came through the gorge. ⊠ *990 S.W. Rock Creek Dr., Stevenson, WA (1 mi east of Bridge of the Gods on Hwy. 14),* ☎ *509/ 427–8211.* ⌷ *$6.* ⊙ *Daily 10–5.*

Dining and Lodging

$$$–$$$$ ✕ **The Dining Room at Skamania Lodge.** Windows in this cavernous dining room overlook the Columbia River Gorge. Fresh oysters, crab cakes, plank-roasted salmon, and succulent rack of lamb, all cooked in a wood-burning oven, are worth trying. The Friday-night Gorge Harvest Seafood Buffet and the Sunday brunch draw patrons from miles around. The dining room is open for breakfast daily. ⊠ *Skamania Lodge Way north of Hwy. 14, 2 mi east of the Bridge of the Gods,* ☎ *509/ 427–2508. Reservations essential for dinner. AE, D, DC, MC, V.*

$ ✕ **Big River Grill.** The fare at this appealing storefront grill on Stevenson's main street is simple—chili, soup, sandwiches, and burgers. High-back wooden booths line one side; photos and memorabilia provide insight into the local past. ⊠ *192 S.W. 2nd St.,* ☎ *509/427–4888. Reservations not accepted. MC, V.*

$$–$$$$ ✕▥ **Skamania Lodge.** The great Work Projects Administration lodges of the 1930s inspired this full-service resort that was built in the 1990s, high on a knoll overlooking the Columbia River. The Georgian pine floors, fir walls, and stone fireplace of the Gorge Room set a tone of rustic grandeur. The rooms, decorated with framed rubbings of petroglyphs and furnished with lodge-style furniture covered with handwoven fabrics, have views of the river and the surrounding gorge landscape. A restaurant (☞ *above*) and outstanding recreational facilities make this the premier resort on the Washington side of the Columbia. ⊠ *Skamania Lodge Way north of Hwy. 14, 2 mi east of the Bridge of the Gods, 98648,* ☎ *509/427–7700 or 800/221–7117,* FAX *509/427–2548. 195 rooms. 2 restaurants, bar, indoor pool, indoor and outdoor hot tubs, massage, sauna, 18-hole golf course, 2 tennis courts, exercise room, hiking, cross-country skiing, mountain bikes, library, business center. AE, D, DC, MC, V.*

$–$$ ▥ **Carson Mineral Hot Springs Resort.** People have been coming to this funky place for decades to soak in the hot mineral-laden water pumped up to the two bathhouses (virtually unchanged since they opened in 1923) from the Wind River. After a soak in an old claw-foot tub, you're wrapped in sheets and blankets for a blissful, sweaty snooze. The bathhouses are open daily from 8:45 AM to 7 PM. Call ahead if you want a massage; baths ($10) are available to nonguests on a first-come, first-served basis. The hotel, dating from 1897, is clean, if charmless, with spartan rooms and cabins. The restaurant, open for breakfast, lunch, and dinner, serves decent if generally uninspired old-fashioned cooking. ⊠ *372 St. Martin's Springs Rd., Carson, WA 98610 (4 mi east of Stevenson on Hwy. 14),* ☎ *509/427–8292 or 800/607–3678,* FAX *509/427–7242. 9 rooms share 4 baths; 1 suite; 14 cabins with ½ bath; 2 cabins with full bath and kitchen. Restaurant. AE, MC, V.*

Hood River

17 mi east of Cascade Locks on I–84.

For years the incessant easterly winds at the town of Hood River, where the Columbia Gorge widens and the scenery changes to tawny, wheat-covered hills, were nothing but a nuisance. Then somebody bolted a sail to a surfboard, and a new recreational craze was born. A fortuitous combination of factors—mainly the reliable gale-force winds blowing against the current—has made Hood River the self-proclaimed boardsailing capital of the world. Especially in the summer, this once-somnolent fruit-growing town swarms with colorful "boardheads," many of whom have journeyed from as far away as Europe and Australia.

🍂 **Mount Hood Railroad,** established in 1906 as a passenger and freight line, is a delightful way to take in the changing seasons and scenery of the Hood River valley. In operation from April to October, the train chugs alongside the Hood River through vast fruit orchards before climbing up steep forested canyons, providing views of Mount Hood along the way. Excursions include brunch, dinner, or no meal. ⊠ *Depot: 110 Railroad Ave.,* ☎ *541/386–3556.* ⊞ *$21.95–$67.50.* ☉ *July–Aug., Tues.–Sun. 10 AM, weekends 3 PM, Sat. 5:30 PM (dinner), Sun. 10:30 AM (brunch); Apr.–June and Sept.–Oct., Wed.–Sun. 10 AM, weekends 3 PM, Sat. 5:30 PM (dinner), Sun. 10:30 AM (brunch); Nov.–Dec., weekends 10 AM.*

Columbia Gorge Sailpark (⊠ Port Marina, Exit 64 off I–84, ☎ 541/386–1645), on the river downtown, has a boat basin, a swimming beach, jogging trails, picnic tables, and rest rooms.

Dining and Lodging

$$ ✕ **6th Street Bistro and Loft.** The menu here changes weekly but concentrates on Pacific Northwest flavors, right down to the coffees and salads. Try the grilled fresh fish and chicken or, in season, local fresh steamer clams and wild coral mushrooms. ⊠ *6th and Cascade Sts.,* ☎ *541/386–5737. MC, V.*

$–$$ ✕ **The Mesquitery.** Fresh herbs and tangy marinades supply added flavor to the fish, beef, chicken, and pork grilled over aromatic mesquite at this sunny restaurant. ⊠ *1219 12th St. (atop the hill south of downtown),* ☎ *541/386–2002. Reservations not accepted. MC, V.*

$ ✕ **Full Sail Tasting Room and Pub.** This glass-walled microbrewery with a windswept deck overlooking the Columbia has won major awards at the Great American Beer Festival. Savory snack foods complement the fresh ales. ⊠ *506 Columbia St. (in the old Diamond cannery overlooking downtown Hood River),* ☎ *541/386–2247. Reservations not accepted. MC, V.*

$$$$ ✕🏨 **Columbia Gorge Hotel.** The ambience at the grande dame of gorge hotels is a bit florid, but the major attraction—the 208-ft-high waterfall—is magnificent. Rooms with plenty of wood, brass, and antiques overlook the formal gardens. The rates include a seven-course breakfast dubbed the World Famous Farm Breakfast (nonguests pay $22.95).

While watching the sun set on the Columbia River, you can dine on breast of pheasant with pear wine, hazelnuts, and cream; grilled venison; breast of duck; Columbia River salmon; or sturgeon. ⊠ *4000 Westcliff Dr., off I–84's Exit 62, 97031,* ☎ *541/386–5566 or 800/345–1921,* FAX *541/387–5414. 46 rooms. Restaurant, bar. AE, D, DC, MC, V.*

$–$$$ ▦ **Best Western–Hood River Inn.** This modern hotel on the river within paddling distance of the Columbia Gorge Sailpark is the address of choice for visiting windsurfers. Ask for a room with a river view. ⊠ *1108 E. Marina Way, 97031,* ☎ *541/386–2200 or 800/828–7873,* FAX *541/386–8905. 149 rooms. Restaurant, bar, outdoor pool. AE, D, DC, MC, V.*

$$ ▦ **Hood River Hotel.** Public areas at this 1913 landmark are rich in beveled glass, warm wood, and tasteful jade-and-cream-color fabrics. Rooms have fir floors, Oriental carpets, four-poster beds, and skylights. The suites, all with kitchens, can sleep five. There's a lively lobby bar and a Mediterranean-inspired kitchen, plus—a thoughtful touch— plenty of locked storage for boardsailors. ⊠ *102 Oak St., 97031,* ☎ *541/386–1900,* FAX *541/386–6090. 33 rooms, 9 suites. Restaurant, bar, café, hot tub, sauna, exercise room. AE, D, DC, MC, V.*

$$ ▦ **Lakecliff Estate.** Architect A. E. Doyle, who designed the Mult- ★ nomah Falls Lodge and the Classic Revival public library and U.S. Bank Building in Portland, also designed the summer home that holds this small bed-and-breakfast inn. The 1908 house, built on a cliff overlooking the river, is beautifully maintained and exceptionally comfortable. A deck at the back of the house and wood-burning fireplaces in three of the rooms ensure a relaxing stay. ⊠ *3820 Westcliff Dr. (head east from I–84's Exit 62), 97031,* ☎ *541/386–7000,* FAX *541/386–1803. 4 rooms. No smoking. No credit cards. Closed Labor Day–Apr.*

OFF THE **LOST LAKE –** The waters of one of the most photographed sights in the
BEATEN PATH Pacific Northwest reflect towering Mount Hood and the thick forests that line the lakeshore. Cabins are available for overnight stays, and because no motorboats are allowed on Lost Lake, the area is blissfully quiet. ⊠ *Lost Lake Rd. (take Hood River Hwy. south from Hood River to town of Dee and follow signs),* ☎ *541/386–6366 for cabin reservations.*

The Dalles

㉓ *20 mi east of Hood River on I–84.*

The Dalles has a small-town, Old West feel, possibly because it's the traditional end of the Oregon Trail, where the wagons were loaded onto barges for the final leg of their 2,000-mi journey from western Missouri.

Outstanding exhibits at the 130-year-old **Wasco County Courthouse** illustrate the trials and tribulations of those who traveled the Oregon Trail. ⊠ *410 W. 2nd Pl.,* ☎ *541/296–4798.* ⛁ *Free (donation suggested).* ☾ *Apr.–May, Tues.–Sat. 11–3; June–Sept., Tues.–Sat. 10–4.*

The 1856-vintage Fort Dalles Surgeon's Quarters houses the **Fort Dalles Museum.** On display are the personal effects of some of the region's settlers and a collection of early automobiles. The entrance fee gains you admission to the **Anderson House museum** across the street, which also has pioneer artifacts. ⊠ *15th and Garrison Sts.,* ☎ *541/296–4547.* ⛁ *$2.* ☾ *Mar.–Oct., weekdays 10:30–5, weekends 10–5; Nov.–Feb., Wed.–Fri. noon–4, weekends 10–4.*

Dining and Lodging

$$ ✕ **Ole's Supper Club.** The fine western-style food at this restaurant with friendly, competent service has a Continental twist. It's hard to go wrong when choosing an entrée—try a thick slab of prime rib or the veal Oscar—especially when it's accompanied by a selection from the well-conceived wine list. ⊠ *2620 W. 2nd St.,* ☏ *541/296–6708. AE, MC, V. Closed Sun.–Mon. No lunch.*

$$ ⌸ **The Columbia House.** A period feel lingers at this enormous late-1930s house on a cliff overlooking the Columbia. The rooms, all with king-size beds, are decorated with original "Waterfall"-style furniture; two have river views. On a quiet wooded acre three blocks from downtown, the B&B has three decks out back, perfect for relaxing or, in good weather, enjoying the breakfast served up by the owner. ⊠ *525 E. 7th St., 97058,* ☏ *541/298–4686 or 800/807–2668. 4 rooms, 1 with shared bath. Airport shuttle. MC, V.*

OFF THE
BEATEN PATH

MARYHILL MUSEUM OF ART – One of the Columbia Gorge's most unusual cultural attractions, this museum in a castle-like mansion perches high on a cliff on the Washington side of the river. Built by a colorful character named Sam Hill as a private residence, the house was dedicated as a museum by Queen Marie of Romania in 1923. It contains the largest collection of Rodin sculptures and watercolors west of the Mississippi; prehistoric Native American tools and baskets; and the charming "Théâtre de la Mode," a miniature fashion show devised by French couturiers after World War II. Queen Marie's coronation gown and personal artifacts are also on display. Three miles east of the museum, just off Washington State Highway 14, is an even stranger landmark in this unpopulated high-desert country: a replica of Stonehenge, built by Sam Hill as a memorial to soldiers killed in World War I. ⊠ *35 Maryhill Museum Dr., Goldendale, Wa. (20 mi east of The Dalles on I–84, 2 mi north of Biggs on U.S. 97, about 1 mi west on Hwy. 14),* ☏ *509/773–3733.* ⛭ *$5.* ☉ *Mid-Mar.–mid-Nov., daily 9–5.*

Mount Hood

★ ㉔   *About 60 mi east of Portland on I–84 and U.S. 26; 65 mi from The Dalles, west on I–84 and south on Hwy. 35 and U.S. 26.*

Regal, snow-covered Mount Hood is believed to be an active volcano that is quiet now but capable of the same violence that decapitated nearby Mount St. Helens in 1980. The mountain is just one feature of the 1.1 million-acre **Mount Hood National Forest,** an all-season playground that attracts more than seven million visitors annually. Within the forest are 95 campgrounds and 50 lakes stocked with brown, rainbow, cutthroat, brook, and steelhead trout. The Sandy, Salmon, and other rivers are known for their fishing, rafting, canoeing, and swimming. Both forest and mountain are crossed by an extensive trail system for hikers, cyclists, and horseback riders. The **Pacific Crest Trail,** which begins in British Columbia and ends in Mexico, crosses here at the 4,157-ft-high Barlow Pass, the highest point on the highway. ⊠ *Information center 3 mi west of town of Zigzag on the north side of U.S. 26.* ☏ *503/622–7674.* ⛭ *Day use $3–$5, campsites $10–$12.* ☉ *Information center daily 8–6; most campgrounds open year-round.*

Government Camp

45 mi from The Dalles, south on Hwy. 35 and west on U.S. 26; 54 mi east of Portland on I–84 and U.S. 26.

Government Camp, an alpine resort village, holds an abundance of lodging and restaurants. It's a convenient drive from here to Mount Hood's five ski resorts or to Welches, which has restaurants and a resort. A road from U.S. 26 (follow signs) leads south to **Trillium Lake** (☎ 503/666–0771), a fine spot for picnicking, overnight camping, and fishing for brown and rainbow trout.

Dining and Lodging

$$–$$$ ✕⌂ **Falcon's Crest Inn.** The three common areas at this sophisticated cedar-and-glass chalet have different moods and styles, and the theme-oriented rooms run the gamut from safari to French provincial. A nightly six-course gourmet dinner (open to nonguests; reservations essential) includes entrées like chicken stuffed with shrimp in a sauce of champagne and Pernod. The room rates include a full breakfast. ⌂ 87287 *Government Camp Loop Hwy., 97028,* ☎ *503/272–3403 or 800/624–7384,* ⅁ *503/272–3454. 5 rooms. Restaurant. AE, D, DC, MC, V.*

$$–$$$ ✕⌂ **Timberline Lodge.** This National Historic Landmark has withstood
★   howling winter storms on an exposed flank of the mountain for more than 50 years—not to mention the maniacal behavior of Jack Nicholson (in *The Shining,* one of a number of films shot here). Everything at this Work Projects Administration structure has a handcrafted, rustic feel, from the wrought-iron chairs with rawhide seats to the massive hand-hewn beams. The expert cuisine at the Cascade Dining Room incorporates the freshest Oregon products. ⌂ *Timberline Rd. (north from U.S. 26; follow signs), Timberline 97028,* ☎ *503/272–3311 or 800/547–1406,* ⅁ *503/727–3710. 71 rooms. Restaurant, bar, pool, outdoor hot tub, sauna, downhill and cross-country skiing. AE, D, MC, V.*

$$$ ⌂ **Mount Hood Inn.** The Mount Hood National Forest is right outside the east windows of this comfortable contemporary inn; rooms facing the southwest have a remarkable view of Ski Bowl, which is across the street. Accommodations come in various sizes, from spacious standards to king-size suites with refrigerators and hot tubs. Among the amenities are complimentary ski lockers and a ski tuning room; the rates include a Continental breakfast. ⌂ 87450 *Government Camp Loop Hwy., 97028,* ☎ *503/272–3205 or 800/443–7777,* ⅁ *503/272–3307. 55 rooms. No-smoking rooms, indoor hot tub, coin laundry. AE, D, DC, MC, V.*

Outdoor Activities and Sports

CROSS-COUNTRY SKIING

Nearly 120 mi of cross-country ski trails lace the **Mount Hood National Forest**; try the trailheads at Government Camp, Trillium Lake, or the Cooper Spur Ski Area, on the mountain's northeast flank.

DOWNHILL SKIING

Cooper Spur Ski Area. This ski area on the eastern slope of Mount Hood caters to families and has two rope tows and a T-bar. The longest run is ⅔ mi, with a 500-ft vertical drop. Facilities and services include rentals, instruction, repairs, and a ski shop, day lodge, snack bar, and restaurant. ⌂ *Follow signs from Hwy. 35 for 3½ mi to ski area,* ☎ *541/352–7803.* ☺ *Call for hrs.*

Mount Hood Meadows Ski Resort. The resort, Mount Hood's largest, has more than 2,000 skiable acres, dozens of runs, seven double chairs, one triple chair, one quad chair, a top elevation of 7,300 ft, a vertical drop of 2,777 ft, and a longest run of 3 mi. Facilities include a day lodge, seven restaurants, two lounges, a ski school, and a ski shop; equipment rental and repair are also available. ⊠ *10 mi east of Government Camp on Hwy. 35,* ☎ *503/337–2222 or 800/929–2754.* ⊘ *Mon.–Tues. 9–4, Wed.–Sat. 9 AM–10 PM, Sun. 9–7.*

Mount Hood Ski Bowl. The ski area closest to Portland has 63 trails serviced by four double chairs and five surface tows, a top elevation of 5,050 ft, a vertical drop of 1,500 ft, and a longest run of 3½ mi. Night skiing is a major activity here. Visitors can take advantage of two day lodges, a mid-mountain warming hut, three restaurants, and two lounges. Sleigh rides are conducted, weather permitting. ⊠ *53 mi east of Portland, across U.S. 26 from Government Camp,* ☎ *503/272– 3206.* ⊘ *Mon.–Thurs. 9 AM–10 PM, Fri. 9 AM–11 PM, Sat. 8:30 AM–11 PM, Sun. 8:30 AM–10 PM.*

Summit Ski Area. The longest run at Summit is ½ mi, with a 400-ft vertical drop; there's one chairlift and one rope-tow. Facilities include instruction, a ski shop, a cafeteria, and a day lodge. Bike rentals are available in summer. ⊠ *Government Camp Loop Hwy., east end, Government Camp,* ☎ *503/272–0256.* ⊘ *Nov.–Apr., daily 9–5.*

Timberline Lodge Ski Area. The U.S. ski team conducts summer training at this full-service ski area that welcomes snowboarders. Timberline is famous for its Palmer chairlift, which takes skiers to a high glacier for summer skiing. There are five double chairs, two high-speed quad chairs; the top elevation is 8,500 ft, with a 3,600 ft vertical drop. The longest run is 3 mi. Facilities include a day lodge with fast food and a ski shop; lessons and equipment rental and repair are available. ⊠ *U.S. 26, Timberline,* ☎ *503/272–3311.* ⊘ *Sun.–Tues. 9–5, Wed.–Sat. 9 AM– 10 PM. Summer lift 7 AM–1:30 PM.*

SUMMER SPORTS

During the summer months, **Ski Bowl** has go-carts, mountain- and alpine-bike rentals, and pony rides. The **Alpine Slide** gives the intrepid a chance to whiz down the slopes on a European-style toboggan run. This is heady stuff, with a marvelous view. **Eastside Action Park,** ½-mi to the east, has more than 20 kids-oriented attractions, including something called the Rapid Riser, a sort of reverse bungee-jumping device that catapults riders 80 ft in the air. ⊠ *87000 E. Hwy. 26 (at milepost 53),* ☎ *503/272–3206.* 🎫 *Day pass $25.* ⊘ *June–Sept., weekdays 11– 6, weekends 10–7 (weather permitting).*

Welches and Zigzag

14 mi west of Government Camp on U.S. 26; 40 mi east of Portland, I–84 to U.S. 26.

These two small towns at the base of Mount Hood have restaurants and other services. Drop by the **Mount Hood Visitors Center** (⊠ 65000 E. Hwy. 26, ☎ 503/622–3017) in Welches for detailed information on all the area attractions.

Dining and Lodging

$$$$ ✕🏨 **Resort at the Mountain.** This sprawling complex in the burly Cascade foothills has the mountain's most complete resort facilities, with attractive public areas. Accommodations include standard rooms, huge deluxe rooms, and two-bedroom condos. The Northwest cuisine at the Highland Dining Room includes fillet of salmon with fresh herbs and red wine, venison with black-currant sauce, and quail sautéed with mustard. ⊠ *68010 E. Fairway Ave. (follow signs south from U.S.*

26 in Welches), 97067, ☎ 503/622–3101 or 800/669–7666, FAX 503/ 622–2222. 158 rooms. 2 restaurants, 2 bars, pool, indoor and outdoor hot tubs, 9- and 18-hole golf courses, 6 tennis courts, health club, bicycles, meeting rooms. AE, D, DC, MC, V.

The Columbia River Gorge and the Oregon Cascades Essentials

Arriving and Departing
BY BUS

Greyhound (☎ 800/231–2222) provides service from Portland to Troutdale, Hood River, The Dalles, and Government Camp.

BY CAR

Interstate 84 is the main east–west route into the Columbia River Gorge. **U.S. 26** heading east from Portland and northwest from Prineville is the main route into the Mount Hood area. The portions of I–84 and U.S. 26 that pass through the mountains can be difficult to maneuver in winter, though the state plows them regularly.

Getting Around
BY CAR

The **Historic Columbia River Highway** (U.S. 30) from Troutdale to just east of Oneonta Gorge passes Crown Point State Park and Multnomah Falls. **Interstate 84/U.S. 30** continues on to The Dalles. **Highway 35** heads south from The Dalles to the Mount Hood area, intersecting with U.S. 26 at Government Camp.

Visitor Information
Hood River County Chamber of Commerce (✉ Port Marina Park, 97031, ☎ 541/386–2000 or 800/366–3530). **Mount Hood National Forest Ranger Stations** (✉ 6780 Hwy. 35, Mount Hood 97041, ☎ 541/ 352–6002; ✉ Superintendent, 16400 Champion Way off Hwy. 26, Sandy 97055, ☎ 503/668–1771; ✉ Mount Hood Information Center, 65000 E. Hwy. 26, Welches 97067, ☎ 503/622–7674; ✉ 70220 W. Hwy. 26, Zigzag 97049, ☎ 503/662–3191). **Mount Hood Recreation Association** (65000 E. Hwy. 26, Welches 97067, ☎ 503/622–3162 or 503/622– 4822).

CENTRAL OREGON

The arid landscape east of the Cascades differs dramatically from that on the lush, wet western side. Crossing the mountains, you enter a high-desert plateau with scrubby buttes, forests of ponderosa pine, and mile after mile of sun-bleached earth. The booming resort town of Bend is the most prominent playground in central Oregon, but within the region are dozens of other outdoor recreational hubs, many of them blissfully uncrowded.

Numbers in the margin correspond to numbers on the Columbia River Gorge, the Cascades, and Central Oregon map.

Warm Springs

115 mi southeast of Portland on U.S. 26.

Warm Springs, in the southeastern corner of the 640,000-acre Warm Springs Indian Reservation, is not so much a town as a place to refuel, stretch your legs, and take a deep breath of the juniper-scented high-desert air.

The Confederated Tribes of the Warm Springs Reservation created the **Museum at Warm Springs** to preserve their traditions and keep their legacy alive. On display are tribal heirlooms, beaded artifacts, baskets, historic photographs, ceramics, and traditional dwellings. The museum's gift shop sells Native American crafts. ⊠ *U.S. 26,* ☎ *541/553–3331.* ☎ *$6.* ⊙ *Daily 10–5.*

Dining and Lodging

$$–$$$$ ✕⊡ **Kah-Nee-Tah Resort.** The culture of the native Wasco, Warm Springs, and Paiute tribes permeates this luxurious resort 11 mi north of Warm Springs. Traditional Indian salmon bakes, festivals, arts, and dances enliven an austerely beautiful setting in the middle of the Warm Springs Reservation. Mineral hot springs bubbling up from the desert floor fill baths and pools. The Warm Springs, Wasco, and Paiute suites, which cost a little extra, have tile fireplaces and hot tubs, big-screen TVs, king-size beds, and grand desert views. If you'd rather rough it (sort of) and don't mind bringing your own bedroll, check into one of the wood-frame, canvas-covered tepees. There's a casino on site, and the resort sets aside kayaks for guests to use. ⊠ *Hwy. 3 north of U.S. 26 (follow signs), 97761,* ☎ *541/553–1112 or 800/554–4786,* FAX *541/ 553–1015. 139 rooms, 21 tepees. 2 restaurants, bar, 2 pools, hot tubs, sauna, 18-hole golf course, tennis court, exercise room, hiking, horse-back riding, water slide, fishing, mountain bikes, casino, convention center. AE, D, DC, MC, V.*

Bend

㉕ *58 mi south of Warm Springs, U.S. 26 to U.S. 97; 160 mi from Port-land, east and south on U.S. 26 and south on U.S. 97.*

Bend, a city of 30,000 that very nearly sits in the center of Oregon, occupies a high-desert plateau perfumed with juniper and surrounded by 10,000-ft Cascade peaks. Called Bend because it was built on Farewell Bend in the Deschutes River—an easy-flowing river that be-comes a roaring cataract a few miles downstream—the city holds restaurants, dance bars, equipment-rental places, and reasonably priced hostelries. Because Bend is among Oregon's fastest-growing cities, its stretch of U.S. 20 has become one enormous strip mall and is frequently snarled with traffic. To see old Bend, turn off the highway and head downtown.

The intricately crafted walk-through dioramas at the **High Desert Mu-seum** include a stone-age Indian campsite, a pioneer wagon camp, a mine, and an Old West boardwalk. The displays capture the sights and even the smells of various historical periods. There are outstanding ex-hibits on local Native American cultures as well. In the 150-acre out-door section, fat porcupines, baleful birds of prey, and crowd-pleasing river otters play aboveground and underwater. ⊠ *59800 S. Hwy. 97, 3½ mi south of Bend,* ☎ *541/382–4754.* ☎ *$5.50.* ⊙ *Daily 9–5.*

OFF THE
BEATEN PATH

NEWBERRY VOLCANIC NATIONAL MONUMENT – The last time Newberry Volcano blew its top was about 13 centuries ago. Paulina Peak, up an unpaved road at the south end of the national monument, has the best view into the crater and its two lakes (Paulina and East). Lava Butte and Lava River Cave are at the north end of the monument near the visitor center. ⊠ *Visitor center: U.S. 97, 10 mi south of Bend,* ☎ *541/593– 2421.* ☎ *$5 per vehicle.* ⊙ *Memorial Day–Labor Day, daily 9:30–5; Labor Day–Memorial Day, Wed.–Sun. 9:30–5 (sometimes closed in bad weather and at other times).*

Dining and Lodging

$$ ✕ **Coho Grill.** Innovative Northwest dishes, geared to the season, are the hallmarks of this well-respected restaurant. Asparagus, fresh fish,

and Cascade morels are on the spring menu; in the fall expect Oregon crab and fruits from the Hood River valley, and in winter American classics like pot roast and braised lamb shanks. ⊠ *61535 Fargo La.,* ☎ *541/388–3909. AE, MC, V.*

$$ ✕ **Giuseppe's Ristorante.** This downtown restaurant has won awards for its ethnic Italian food—homemade pastas, chicken, seafood, veal, steak, and vegetarian dishes. ⊠ *932 N.W. Bond St.,* ☎ *541/389–8899. AE, DC, MC, V. Closed Mon. No lunch.*

$ ✕ **Deschutes Brewery & Public House.** Try the admirable Black Butte Porter, a local ale, at this brew pub that serves upscale Northwest cuisine. A blackboard above the open kitchen lists the many lunch and dinner specials. Portions are large. ⊠ *1044 N.W. Bond St.,* ☎ *541/382–9242. Reservations not accepted. MC, V.*

$$$–$$$$ 🏨 **Sunriver.** One of Oregon's premier outdoor resort destinations, Sunriver provides a slew of facilities and is convenient to skiing at Mount Bachelor; Class 4 white-water rafting on the Deschutes River (which flows right through the complex); and high-desert hiking and mountain biking. A former army base, the self-contained community has stores, restaurants, contemporary homes, condominiums, and even a private airstrip—all in a pine-scented desert landscape. Visitors can rent condos, hotel rooms, or houses; shops rent a host of outdoorsy paraphernalia. ⊠ *Center Dr. (west of U.S. 97, 15 mi south of Bend), Sunriver 97707,* ☎ *541/593–1000 or 800/547–3922,* ℻ *541/593–5458. 426 units. 8 restaurants, 2 pools, hot tubs, saunas, 2 18-hole golf courses, 28 tennis courts, horseback riding, racquetball, boating, fishing, bicycles. AE, D, DC, MC, V.*

$$–$$$ 🏨 **Lara House Bed & Breakfast Inn.** This restored 1910 Craftsman house sits on a huge sloping lot in a residential district overlooking Drake Park and Mirror Pond, a five-minute walk from downtown. The rooms, all on the second floor, have seating areas and private bathrooms, and the public areas are sunny and inviting. ⊠ *640 N.W. Congress St., west 1 mi on Franklin St. from U.S. 97, 97701,* ☎ ℻ *541/388–4064 or* ☎ *800/766–4064. 6 rooms. Outdoor hot tub. D, MC, V.*

$$ 🏨 **The Riverhouse.** A cut or two above what you'd expect given its very reasonable rates, this hotel within earshot of the rushing Deschutes River contains large rooms with contemporary oak furniture. Many have river views—well worth the extra $5 charge. ⊠ *3075 N. Hwy. 97, 97701,* ☎ *541/389–3111 or 800/547–3928,* ℻ *541/389–0870. 220 units. 3 restaurants, bar, indoor and outdoor pools, hot tub, sauna, 18-hole golf course, 2 tennis courts, exercise room, jogging. AE, D, DC, MC, V.*

$$ 🏨 **The Sather House Bed & Breakfast.** The Colonial Revival Sather House, built in 1911, occupies a prominent spot in Bend's oldest residential neighborhood. The exterior, glistening white with green trim, has a wraparound veranda and overhanging eaves; period furnishings and original Douglas fir woodwork fill the interior. Breakfast, included in the room rates and served in the formal dining room, typically consists of French toast with raspberries and almonds, or pecan pancakes; fireside teas are served in the winter, and lemonade and cookies are on the veranda in the summer. Smoking and pets are not allowed at the inn. ⊠ *7 N.W. Tumalo, 97701,* ☎ *541/388–1065. 4 rooms, 2 with bath. D, MC, V.*

Outdoor Activities and Sports

BICYCLING

U.S. 97 north to the Crooked River Gorge and the Smith Rocks provides bikers with memorable scenery and a good workout. **Sunriver** (☞ *Dining and Lodging, above*) has 26 mi of paved bike paths.

The **Deschutes River** flows north from the Cascades west of Bend, gaining volume and momentum as it nears its rendezvous with the Columbia River at The Dalles. Its upper stretches, particularly those near Sunriver and Bend, are placid and suitable for leisurely canoeing. Whitewater rafters flock to the stretch of the Deschutes between Madras and Maupin. You need a state marine boater pass to participate. For details contact the **Bureau of Land Management** (☎ 541/416–6700) in Prineville.

Rafting Guides: Cascade River Adventures (☎ 541/389–8370 or 541/593–3113). **Fantastic Adventures** (☎ 541/389–5640 or 800/449–5640). **Inn of the Seventh Mountain Whitewater Rafting** (☎ 541/382–8711).

The semi-private **Awbrey Glen Golf Club** (⊠ 2500 N.W. Awbrey Glen Dr., ☎ 541/388–8526 or 800/697–0052), an 18-hole, par-72 course, is open to the public daily between 11 and 4. The greens fee is $45; an optional cart costs $13. **Rivers Edge Golf Course** (⊠ 400 Pro Shop Dr., ☎ 541/389–2828) is an 18-hole, par-72 course. The greens fee ranges from $15 to $36; an optional cart costs $12.50.

Mount Bachelor Resort (⊠ 22 mi southwest of Bend off U.S. 97, ☎ 541/382–7888 or 800/829–2442), the Northwest's largest facility, is one of the best in the United States—60% of the downhill runs are rated expert. One of the 11 lifts takes skiers all the way to the mountain's 9,065-ft summit. The vertical drop is 3,265 ft; the longest of the 70 runs is 2 mi. Facilities and services include equipment rental and repair, a ski school, ski shop, Nordic skiing, weekly races, and day care; visitors can enjoy restaurants, bars, and six lodges. The 36 mi of trails at the **Mount Bachelor Nordic Center,** most of them near the base of the mountain, are by and large intermediate.

Many Nordic trails—more than 165 mi of them—wind through the **Deschutes National Forest.** For information abut conditions call 541/222–2211, 541/222–2695, or 541/227–7669.

Sisters

26 *18 mi northwest of Bend on U.S. 20.*

Sisters, with a population of about 3,000, provides an alternative to the frenetic pace and traffic tie-ups that plague Bend. The town was named for and sits in the lap of the stunning mountain peaks known as the "Sisters." To lure tourists, it has adopted a western look.

Dining and Lodging

$–$$ ✕ **Hotel Sisters Restaurant.** The most popular restaurant in Sisters first opened as a hotel in 1912. Broiled steaks, barbecued chicken and ribs, and Mexican dishes form the backbone of the extensive menu. The hamburgers, loaded with green chilies, guacamole, melted cheese, and salsa, have been voted Oregon's best. ⊠ *105 W. Cascade St.,* ☎ *541/549–7427. AE, MC, V.*

$ ✕ **Seasons.** Gourmet quiches, salads, and sandwiches are among the fare at this small café and wine shop with a streamside picnic area in the back. ⊠ *411 E. Hood St.,* ☎ *541/549–8911. MC, V. No dinner.*

$$$–$$$$ 🏠 **Metolius River Resort.** The wood-shake cabins in this upscale resort 14 mi from Sisters have fully equipped kitchens, river-rock fireplaces, and large riverside decks. The atmosphere resembles that of a 1930s alpine fishing village. All units are no-smoking and set up for at least four guests. From late spring to fall, there's dining at the resort's Kokanee Cafe. ⊠ *Forest Service Rd. 1419 (take U.S. 20 northeast 10 mi from Sisters, turn north on Camp Sherman Rd. and east on Forest Service Rd. 1419), Camp Sherman 97730,* ☎ *541/595–6281 or 800/818–7688,* FAX *541/595–6281. 11 cabins. Café, in-room VCRs, refrigerators, fishing. MC, V.*

$$ 🏨 **Cascade Country Inn.** This inn near Sisters is one of the few in America with an on-site runway for small aircraft. Part of the hangar has been fashioned into a two-level studio filled with flying memorabilia. The main inn, a contemporary structure, is modeled after a large country house. The theme-oriented rooms have queen- or king-size beds. Owner Judy Patterson cooks up delicious breakfasts (included in the rates); her whirlwind energy and sense of humor add a lively spark to the solitude of the surrounding high-desert landscape. ⊠ *15870 Barclay Dr., 97759,* ☎ *541/549–4666 or 800/316–0089. 6 rooms with bath, 1 suite. Mountain bikes. No smoking. D, MC, V.*

$$ 🏨 **Conklin Guest House.** When it comes to mountain views, this stylish B&B takes first prize. As you're sitting poolside or eating breakfast in the conservatory, the snowcapped Sisters rise up in almost hallucinatory splendor. Four large rooms are decorated in classic country style in deep plums, warm golds, and other colors; the dorm room, suitable for families with children, sleeps six. The rates include a full breakfast. ⊠ *69013 Camp Polk Rd., 97759,* ☎ *541/549–4909 or 800/700–1275. 5 rooms, 4 with bath. Pool. MC, V.*

Prineville

52 mi east of Sisters on Hwy. 126; 35 mi northeast of Bend on Hwy. 126 and U.S. 97; 146 mi southeast of Portland on U.S. 26.

Despite its rough-hewn reputation, Prineville, the oldest town in Oregon and the state's unofficial "cowboy capital," was once the most genteel place in central Oregon. Nearby Bend now takes the honors in the trendy department, but low-key Prineville still makes a good base for exploring the Crooked River and the Ochoco National Forest. The town is a worldwide mecca for rock hounds, who come seeking agate, obsidian, and other rocks.

Exhibits and artifacts at the **Bowman Museum** document Prineville's history as the booming cattle and logging center of Crook County. ⊠ *246 N. Main St.,* ☎ *541/447–3715.* 🎟 *$1 (suggested donation).* ⊙ *Mar.–Dec., weekdays 10–5, Sat. 11–4.*

Dining and Lodging

$$ ✕ **Crooked River Railroad Company Dinner Train.** On-board entertainment—hoedowns, western murder mysteries, simulated robberies at Sunday brunch—adds to the fun on this excursion train that winds through the rimrock-lined Crooked River valley between Redmond and Prineville. Call for reservations and departure times. ⊠ *525 S.W. 6th St., Redmond,* ☎ *541/548–8630. AE, D, MC, V.*

$ ✕ **Dad's Place.** A typical American diner, Dad's dishes out no-nonsense breakfasts and lunches at no-nonsense prices. If you're not afraid of fat and cholesterol, try the sandwich of ham, bacon, cheese, and egg on a toasted biscuit. ⊠ *229 N. Main St.,* ☎ *541/447–7059. No credit cards. Closed Sun. No dinner.*

$ 🏨 **Elliott House.** With its thick green lawns, wraparound porch, Tuscan columns, and bay windows, this B&B stands out like a well-groomed dowager in an otherwise undistinguished neighborhood. Century-old furnishings and accessories fill the house. One of the two rooms contains a double cast-iron bed and an embroidered quilt, and the large shared bathroom has original brass fixtures and a marble-top sink. Breakfast is served on antique china. ⊠ *305 W. 1st St., 97754,* ☎ *541/416–0423,* FAX *541/416–9368. 2 rooms share bath. No-smoking rooms. No credit cards.*

$ ▦ **Rustler's Roost.** From the old-style covered walkways to the large, antiques-furnished rooms, this motel is Old West all the way. Each room is decorated differently—if you call in advance, the managers will attempt to match your sleeping decor to your personality. Some rooms have kitchenettes. ⊠ *960 W. 3rd St./U.S. 26, 97754,* ☎ *541/447–4185. 20 rooms. AE, D, MC, V.*

Ochoco National Forest

East of the flat juniper-dotted countryside around Prineville the land-scape changes to forested ridges covered with tall ponderosa pines and Douglas firs. Sheltered by the diminutive Ochoco Mountains and with only about a foot of rain each year, the **Ochoco National Forest** manages to lay a blanket of green across the dry high desert of central Oregon. This arid landscape—marked by deep canyons, towering volcanic plugs, and sharp ridges—goes largely unnoticed except for the annual influx of hunters during the fall. The Ochoco is a great place for camping, hiking, biking, and fishing in relative solitude. In its three wilderness areas—Mill Creek, Bridge Creek, and Black Canyon—where cars, roads, and even bicycles are not allowed, it's possible to see elk, wild horses, eagles, and even cougars. ⊠ *Ochoco National Forest Headquarters/Prineville Ranger Station, 3160 N.E. 3rd St. (U.S. 26),* ☎ *541/ 416–6500.* ⏱ *Forest year-round (some sections closed during bad weather), ranger station weekdays 7:30–4:30.*

The **Ochoco Ranger Station** has trail maps and other information. ⊠ *County Rd. 23 (25 mi east of Prineville off U.S. 26),* ☎ *541/416–6645.* ⏱ *Daily 7–4:30.*

OFF THE
BEATEN PATH

BIG SUMMIT PRAIRIE LOOP – This 43-mi scenic route starts at the Ochoco Ranger Station (☞ *above*) and winds past Lookout Mountain, Round Mountain, Walton Lake, and Big Summit Prairie. The prairie abounds with trout-filled creeks and has one of the finest stands of ponderosa pines in the state; wild mustangs roam the area. The prairie can be glorious between late May and June, when wildflowers with evocative names like mules ear, wyethia, biscuit root, and yellow bells burst into bloom. ⊠ *Forest Service Rd. 22 east to Forest Service Rd. 30 (which turns into Forest Service Rd. 3010) south, to Forest Service Rd. 42 heading west, which loops back to Forest Service Rd. 22.*

Camping

Most of the area's developed campsites are open between May and September. All operate on a first-come, first-served basis. Phone 541/ 416–6500 for campground information.

⛺ **Ochoco Forest Camp.** Elk, wild horses, and mule deer thrive at this campground adjacent to the Ochoco Ranger Station and the trailhead for the Lookout Mountain Trail. The tent sites are along Ochoco Creek. ⊠ *Forest Service Rd. 2610, 25 mi east of Prineville. 6 sites.* ▨ *$8. Pit toilets, potable water.*

⛺ **Walton Lake Campground.** This developed setting on Walton Lake is a great place for an afternoon swim or a trek along the nearby Round Mountain Trail. The sites fill up early on weekends and holidays. ⊠ *Forest Service Rd. 22; from Prineville head northeast on U.S.*

26 for 15 mi, east on County Rd. 23 for 8 mi, and northeast on Forest Service Rd. 22 for 7 mi. 30 sites. 🚻 *$8. Pit toilets, potable water.*

🏕 **Wildcat Campground.** On the edge of the Mill Creek Wilderness amid ponderosa pines, Wildcat is the trailhead for the Twin Pillars Trail. ✉ *Mill Creek Rd./Forest Service Rd. 33; from Prineville head northeast on U.S. 26 for 10 mi and north on Mill Creek Rd. for 10 mi. 17 sites.* 🚻 *$8. Pit toilets, potable water. Closed Nov.–Mar., depending on weather.*

Outdoor Activities and Sports

BIKING

The Ochoco National Forest contains hundreds of miles of dirt roads and multiuse trails. The forest headquarters (☞ *above*) has a guide to 10 trails in the forest. Cougar Trail and the more harrowing Lone Mountain Trail, both about 25 mi east of Prineville, are two worthy options. **Road Top Bike Shop** (✉ 2164 E. 3rd St./U.S. 26, Prineville, ☎ 541/447–3182) provides equipment and repairs.

FISHING

Steelhead and rainbow trout pack the forest's rivers and streams, but serious fly fishers should head south of Prineville on Highway 27, which parallels Crooked River. Along the way are the bankside Bureau of Land Management campgrounds, where you can pull off and troll for fish. Walton Lake (☞ Camping, *above*) also has fishing. Most large supermarkets sell permits, as does **Prineville Sporting Goods** (✉ 346 N. Deer St., off U.S. 26, ☎ 541/447–6883).

HIKING

Pick up maps at the Prineville or Ochoco ranger station (☞ *above*) for the trails through the 5,400-acre **Bridge Creek Wilderness** and the demanding **Black Canyon Trail** (24 mi round-trip) in the Black Canyon Wilderness. The 1½₀-mi **Ponderosa Loop Trail** follows an old logging road through ponderosa pines growing on rolling hills. In early summer, wildflowers take over the open meadows. The trailhead begins at Bandit Springs Rest Area, 22 mi east of Prineville on U.S. 26. A 2½-mi, one-way trail winds through old-growth forest and mountain meadows to **Steins Pillar,** a giant lava column with panoramic views; be prepared for a workout on the trail's poorly maintained second half, and allow at least three hours for the hike. To get to the trailhead drive east 9 mi from Prineville on U.S. 26, head north (to the left) for 6½ mi on Mill Creek Road (also signed as Forest Service Road 33), and head east (to the right) on Forest Service Road 500.

ROCKHOUNDING

Stones in the area include agate, obsidian, fire obsidian, petrified wood, and red and green jasper. A free brochure from forest headquarters and the informative "Rockhound's Handbook," available from the Prineville/Crook County Chamber of Commerce (☞ Visitor Information, *below*), map out the best locations for prospecting.

Thundereggs—egg-shape rocks with crystalline interiors—can be found at **White Fir Springs** (✉ Forest Service Rd. 3350; from Prineville head east on U.S. 26 to milepost 41, turn left, and continue for about 5 mi).

SKIING

Two loops have recently been developed in the forest for cross-country skiers; both start at Bandit Springs Rest Area, 29 mi east of Prineville on U.S. 26. One loop is designed for beginners and the other for intermediate to advanced skiers. Both traverse the area near the Ochoco Divide and have great views. The forest headquarters (☞ *above*) has a handout on the trails and can provide the required Sno-Park permits, which are also available from the **Department of Motor Vehicles** (✉ Ochoco Plaza, 1595 E. 3rd St., Suite A-3, Prineville, ☎ 541/447–7855).

Central Oregon Essentials

Arriving and Departing

BY BUS

Greyhound (☎ 800/231–2222) serves Bend and Sisters from Portland.

BY CAR

U.S. 20 heads west from Idaho and east from the coastal town of Newport into central Oregon. **U.S. 26** travels southeast from Portland to Prineville, where it heads northeast into the Ochoco National Forest. **U.S. 97** heads north from California and south from Washington to Bend. **Highway 126** travels east from Eugene to Prineville; it connects with U.S. 20 heading south (to Bend) at Sisters.

BY PLANE

Bend-Redmond Municipal Airport (☎ 541/548–6059) is served by Horizon (☎ 800/547–9308) and United Express (☎ 800/241–6522).

Getting Around

BY BUS

See Getting Around *in* Oregon A to Z, *below.*

BY CAR

Roads throughout central Oregon (☞ Arriving and Departing, *above*) are well maintained and open throughout the winter season, though it's always advisable to carry chains.

Guided Tours

Oregon Llamas (☎ 541/595–2088 or 888/722–5262), north of Sisters in Camp Sherman, operates fully catered three- to five-day llama treks in the Sisters, Mount Jefferson, and Cascade wilderness areas.

Visitor Information

Central Oregon Visitors Association (✉ 63085 N. Hwy. 97, Suite 104, Bend 97701, ☎ 541/389–8799 or 800/800–8334). **Confederated Tribes of Warm Springs** (✉ Warm Springs 97761, ☎ 541/553–1161). **Deschutes National Forest** (✉ 1645 Hwy. 20 E, Bend 97701, ☎ 541/388–2715). **Ochoco National Forest Headquarters and Prineville Ranger Station** (✉ 3160 N.E. 3rd St., Prineville 97754, ☎ 541/416–6500). **Prineville/Crook County Chamber of Commerce** (✉ 390 N. Fairview St., 97754, ☎ 541/447–6304). **Sisters Chamber of Commerce** (✉ 222 Hood Ave., 97759, ☎ 541/549–0251).

EASTERN OREGON

Travel east from The Dalles, Bend, or any of the foothill communities blossoming in the shade of the Cascades, and a very different side of Oregon makes its appearance. The air is drier, clearer, and often pungent with the smell of juniper. The vast landscape of sharply folded hills, wheat fields, and mountains shimmering in the distance evokes the Old West. There is a lonely grandeur in eastern Oregon, a plain-spoken, independent spirit that can startle, surprise, and entrance.

Much of eastern Oregon consists of national forest and wilderness, and the people who live here lead very real, very rural lives. This is a world of ranches and rodeos, pickup trucks and country-western music. Some of the most important moments in Oregon's history took place in the towns of northeastern Oregon. The Oregon Trail passed through

Eastern Oregon

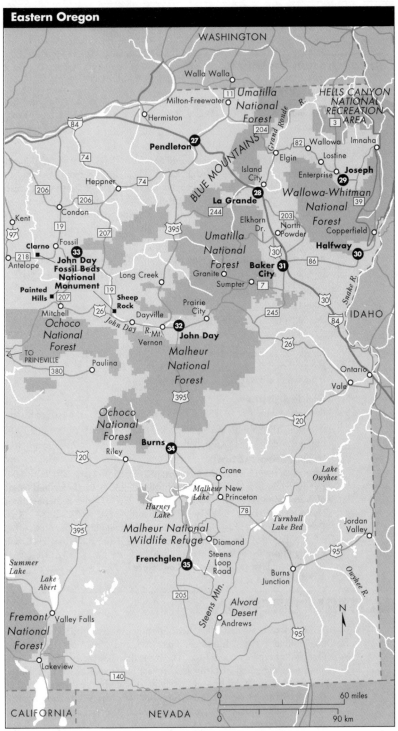

WASHINGTON

Walla Walla

Milton-Freewater

Umatilla National Forest

HELLS CANYON NATIONAL RECREATION AREA

11
204
3

Hermiston

84

Pendleton 27

74

Island City

82 Wallowa
Elgin
Lostine
Enterprise

Imnaha

Joseph 29

74

Heppner

BLUE MOUNTAINS

206

La Grande
28
244

Wallowa-Whitman National Forest

39

Kent

206

Condon

19

207

395

Elkhorn Dr.
North Powder
203
Copperfield

Halfway 30

97

Fossil

218 **Clarno**
Antelope

John Day Fossil Beds National Monument 33

Long Creek

Umatilla National Forest
Granite

30

Baker City 31

86

Snake R.

IDAHO

Painted Hills
207

19 **Sheep Rock**

Sumpter
7

245

30

Mitchell

26 John Day
Dayville

Prairie City

Ochoco National Forest

TO PRINEVILLE

R. Mt. Vernon
32
John Day

Paulina

380

Malheur National Forest

26

84

Ontario
Vale

395

Ochoco National Forest

Burns 34

20

Lake Owyhee

Riley

Crane

20

Malheur Lake New Princeton

78

Turnbull Lake Bed

Jordan Valley

Harney Lake

95

395

Malheur National Wildlife Refuge Diamond

Steens Loop Road

Frenchglen 35

Burns Junction

Summer Lake

Lake Abert

205

Steens Mtn.

Alvord Desert
Andrews

N

Onyhee R.

95

Fremont National Forest

Valley Falls

Lakeview

140

0   60 miles

0   90 km

CALIFORNIA   NEVADA

this corner of the state, winding through the Grande Ronde Valley between the Wallowa and Blue mountain ranges. The discovery of gold in the region in the 1860s sparked a second invasion of settlers and eventually led to the displacement of the Native American Nez Percé and Paiute tribes. Pendleton, La Grande, and Baker City were all beneficiaries of the gold fever that swept through the area.

Numbers in the margin correspond to points of interest on the Eastern Oregon map.

Pendleton

27 *211 mi east of Portland, 129 mi east of The Dalles on I–84.*

At the foot of the Blue Mountains amid vast wheat fields and cattle ranches, Pendleton is a quintessential western town with a rip-snorting history. The huge herds of wild horses that once thundered across this rolling landscape were at the center of the area's early Native American cultures. Later, Pendleton became an important pioneer junction and home to a sizable Chinese community. Lacking a sheriff until 1912, Pendleton was a raw and wild frontier town filled with cowboys, cattle rustlers, saloons, and bordellos. The many century-old homes still standing range in style from simple farmhouses to stately Queen Annes.

Given its raucous past, Pendleton, the largest city in eastern Oregon (population 15,900), looks unusually sedate. But all that changes in September when the **Pendleton Round-Up** (☞ Outdoor Activities and Sports, *below*) draws thousands for a rodeo and related events. Motels fill up, schools close down, and everybody goes hog-wild for a few days.

The **Pendleton Woolen Mills** produce superb Indian blankets and Pendleton shirts and sportswear. In days past the clothing of choice for cowboys, the western and Indian-inspired threads have gained popularity among urbanites for their colors, warmth, and durability. A free tour that lasts about 20 minutes describes the weaving process from start to finish. The mill's retail store stocks blankets and men's clothing; there are good bargains on factory seconds. ⊠ *1307 S.E. Court Pl.,* ☎ *541/276–6911.* ☉ *Mon.–Sat. 8–5; tours weekdays at 9, 11, 1:30, 3.*

The collection at the **Round-Up Hall of Fame Museum** spans the rodeo's history since 1910 with photographs—including some great ones of Rodeo Queens and the Happy Canyon Princesses (all Native American)—as well as saddles, guns, costumes, and even a stuffed championship bronco named War Paint. ⊠ *Round-Up Grounds, 1205 S.W. Court Ave., near S.W. 12th St.,* ☎ *541/278–0815.* ☜ *Free.* ☉ *May–Oct., daily 10–5; other times, call for appointment.*

The Underground, a 90-minute vividly guided tour, yields clues about life in Pendleton a century ago, when the town held 32 saloons and 18 brothels. The first half of the tour heads into a subterranean labyrinth that hid gambling rooms, an opium den, and other illegal businesses. Chinese laborers lived in a chilly jumble of underground rooms. The second half focuses on the life of Madame Stella Darby, the town's best-known madam, and includes a visit to her bordello. Tours leave at various times during the day; reservations are strongly recommended. ⊠ *37 S.W. Emigrant Ave.,* ☎ *541/276–0730 or 800/226–6398.* ☜ *$10; $5 for ½ tour.*

The **Tamustalik Cultural Institute** (⊠ 72777 Hwy. 331; head north from I–84's Exit 216), under construction at the Wildhorse Resort Hotel

(☞ *Dining and Lodging, below*) and scheduled for completion in mid-1998, will contain exhibits about Oregon from a Native American perspective. For information contact the Confederated Tribes of the Umatilla Indian Reservation (☎ 541/276–3873).

Displays and photographs at the **Umatilla County Historical Society Museum** outline Pendleton's story. The town's old railway depot houses the museum. ⌗ *108 S.W. Frazer Ave.,* ☎ *541/276–0012.* ☜ *$2.* ☉ *Tues.–Sat. 10–4.*

The **Pendleton Chamber of Commerce** (⌗ *501 S. Main St.,* ☎ *541/276–7411 or 800/547–8911*), open on weekdays between 8 and 5, has information about the town and surrounding area, including the Umatilla National Forest and the Blue Mountains.

Dining and Lodging

$$ ✕ **Raphael's.** Chef Raphael Hoffman serves traditional steaks, seafood, and fettuccine dishes, but she also specializes in adventurous seasonal cuisine—venison, elk, rattlesnake, blackened Cajun alligator, and Indian salmon topped with huckleberries. This may be the only place in eastern Oregon to get a huckleberry daiquiri. A garden out back is perfect for alfresco dining. ⌗ *233 S.E. 4th St.,* ☎ *541/276–8500. AE, D, DC, MC, V. Closed Sun.–Mon. No lunch.*

$–$$ ✕ **Cimmiyotti's.** Eat here just to enjoy the Old West decor, complete with chandeliers and flocked wallpaper. Well-prepared steaks and Italian food are the main fare. ⌗ *137 S. Main St.,* ☎ *541/276–4314. AE, DC, MC, V. Closed Sun. No lunch.*

$ ✕ **Great Pacific Wine and Coffee Company.** Yes, it is possible to get a decent cup of coffee—even a latte—in Pendleton. This downtown café, open until 6 PM, also serves bagels, muffins, and good deli sandwiches; dozens of gourmet beers and wines are available. ⌗ *403 S. Main St.,* ☎ *541/276–1350. AE, MC, V. Closed Sun.*

$ ✕ **Rainbow Cafe.** Even if you don't eat, drink, or pass out here, you owe it to yourself to step through the swinging door and into the past: The Rainbow is a glimpse of how the West was fun. Take a seat at the counter surrounded by crusty locals eating fried-egg sandwiches, tall stacks of hotcakes, and fried chicken. ⌗ *209 S. Main St.,* ☎ *541/276–4120. No credit cards.*

$$–$$$ ⬚ **Parker House.** Virtually unchanged since it was built in 1917, this
★ handsome pink stucco home in Pendleton's North Hill neighborhood is a very grand reminder that the Old West had its share of wealth and worldly sophistication. A hybrid blend of French neoclassical and Italianate styles, Parker House is a rarity among B&Bs: It still has its original Chinese wallpaper, custom fittings, and woodwork that is nothing less than astonishing. The rooms, furnished with period furniture, are quiet and comfortable. There's only one bathroom, but once you see it you'll understand why the owner has chosen to preserve everything as it was rather than adding modern "improvements." Breakfasts are delicious and filling. ⌗ *311 N. Main St., 97801,* ☎ *541/276–8581 or 800/700–8581. 5 rooms, 1 with bath. AE, MC, V.*

$$–$$$ ⬚ **Wildhorse Resort Hotel.** Owned and operated by the Cayuse, Umatilla, and Walla Walla tribes, this gaming resort is about 6 mi east of downtown Pendleton. The motel-like rooms, many with whirlpools, are large and comfortable, if not particularly luxurious. The rates include a Continental breakfast. The casino has 300 video slots, Keno, and poker tables. From July 4 to July 6 the resort sponsors a Pow-Wow that draws up to 1,000 dancers. An 18-hole golf course and the Tamustalik Cultural Institute are scheduled for completion in 1998. ⌗ *72777 Hwy. 331 (head north from I–84's Exit 216),* ☎ *541/276–*

0355 or 800/654–9453, FAX 541/276–0297. 100 rooms. Indoor pool, sauna, exercise room. AE, D, DC, MC, V.

$–$$ 🏨 **Working Girls Hotel.** This 1890s building in downtown Pendleton served time as a boarding house and a bordello—hence its name—before it became a B&B. The rooms are individually furnished with antiques dating from the early 1900s to the 1950s; ceilings are 18 ft high. The rates include a Continental breakfast. ⊠ *17 S.W. Emigrant Ave., 97801,* ☎ *541/276–0730 or 800/226–6398, FAX 541/276–0665. 5 rooms share 2 baths. MC, V.*

Camping

🏕 **Emigrant Springs State Park.** At this historical site that was part of the Oregon Trail, campers can stay in covered wagons or rustic totem cabins, pitch a tent, or hook up an RV. The full-service facility has exhibits, a nature trail, a horse camp, and a free day-use area. ⊠ *I–84 (Exit 234W), 26 mi east of Pendleton,* ☎ *541/983–2277; 800/452–5687 for reservations only. 33 tent campsites, 18 trailer hookups, 2 covered camper wagons, 2 totem cabins. Flush toilets, potable water, showers.* 🎫 *$25 covered wagons, $20 cabins, $17 RV sites, $13 tent sites.* ⊙ *Mid-Apr.–mid-Oct.*

Outdoor Activities and Sports

The Blue Mountains may be the area's largest attraction, but the **Pendleton Round-Up** is certainly the biggest; more than 50,000 people roll into town for this overwhelming event. Held on the second full week of September, it attracts rodeo performers and fans for four days of rodeo events, wild-horse races, barbecues, parades, and milking contests. Vendors line the length of Court Avenue and Main Street, selling beadwork and western-style curios while country bands twang in the background. Tickets for the various events—which include the Happy Canyon Pageant and Dance—cost between $6 and $12; make your reservations far in advance. ⊠ *Rodeo Grounds and ticket office: 1205 S.W. Court Ave., at S.W. 12th St. (mailing address for tickets: Box 609, Pendleton 97801),* ☎ *541/276–2553 or 800/457–6336.*

Shopping

Court Avenue downtown contains several antiques stores. The Chamber of Commerce (☞ *above*) has a detailed list.

Hamley's Western Store & Custom Saddlery (⊠ 30 S.E. Court Ave., ☎ 541/276–2321) carries authentic cowboy or cowgirl gear and quality leather products. On-site craftspeople fashion hand-tooled saddles that are considered the best in the world.

Murphy House (⊠ 1112 S.E. Emigrant Ave., ☎ 541/276–7020) is the only store in town that sells the women's line of Pendleton fashions.

La Grande

28 *56 mi southeast of Pendleton on I–84 at Hwy. 82.*

La Grande started life in the late 1800s as a farming community. It grew slowly while most towns along the Blue Mountains were booming or busting in the violent throes of gold-fueled stampedes. When the railroad companies were deciding where to lay their tracks through the valley, a clever local farmer donated 150 acres to ensure that the iron horse would run through La Grande. With the power of steam fueling a new boom, the town quickly outgrew its neighbors, claimed the title of county seat from fading Union City, and now sits at the urban center of the valley.

With a population of 12,000, La Grande isn't exactly a bustling metropolis, but the presence of Eastern Oregon State College—the only four-year college in the region—lends it some sophistication. La Grande is a convenient stop if you're heading to the nearby Wallowa Mountains. Stop by the **La Grande Chamber of Commerce** (⌧ 1912 4th St., Suite 200, ☎ 541/963–8588 or 800/848–9969) for information and brochures.

The **Wallowa Mountains** form a rugged U-shape fortress between Hells Canyon on the Idaho border and the Blue Mountains, west of the Grande Ronde Valley. Sometimes called the American Alps or Little Switzerland, the granite peaks in this range are between 5,000 and 9,000 ft in height. Dotted with crystalline alpine lakes and meadows, rushing rivers, and thickly forested valleys that fall between the mountain ridges, the Wallowas have a grandeur that can take your breath away. Bighorn sheep, elk, deer, and mountain goats populate the entire area.

The 358,441-acre **Eagle Cap Wilderness,** the largest in Oregon, encompasses most of the Wallowa range. Many of the more remote areas are accessible only to hard-core backpackers or horseback riders. From La Grande, the most scenic route through the area is Highway 82.

Dining and Lodging

$ ✕ **Lifeline Cafe.** The sophisticated Lifeline caters to the town's health-conscious college crowd with a low-fat menu of homemade soups, salads, and focaccia and baguette sandwiches. Fresh bagels, scones, and assorted pastries are on the breakfast menu. Espresso drinks are also available. ⌧ 111 Depot St., ☎ 541/962–9568. No credit cards. Closed Sun.

$ ✕ **Mamacita's.** This Mexican restaurant with hand-painted murals serves the best food in town. Daily lunch specials include enchiladas, tacos, tostadas, burritos, and salads. ⌧ 110 Depot St., ☎ 541/963–6223. No credit cards. Closed Mon. No lunch on weekends.

$$ 🍽 **Stang Manor Bed and Breakfast.** You'll get a feel for the luxury of
★   a bygone era at this 10,000-square-ft Georgian Revival mansion built in 1926 by a timber baron. Extraordinary features are found in every room of the house, which has remained unmodified except for its wallcoverings. Breakfast, included in the room rates, is a lavish affair served in the formal dining room by the charming and witty hosts. ⌧ 1612 Walnut St., 97850, ☎ FAX 541/963–2400 or ☎ 888/286–9463. 4 rooms with bath. MC, V.

Outdoor Activities and Sports

BICYCLING

Cyclers should check in with La Grande's Chamber of Commerce (☞ above), which actively touts the region's paths. Two short trails leave from **Spring Creek,** about 16 mi west of La Grande. Eight pairs of great grey owls—the largest concentration of the species in the world—live along the routes. To reach the trailhead from La Grande, take I–84 west 13 mi to the Spring Creek Exit and head south on Spring Creek Road/Forest Service Road 21 for 3⁷⁄₁₀ mi.

En Route   Heading north from La Grande, Highway 82 passes through the small towns of Elgin and Minam before looping south toward Wallowa, Lostine, Enterprise, and Joseph en route to Wallowa Lake, where it dead-ends. Packed with RVs and cars during the summer, the road sprouts diners, motels, and plenty of antiques shops in every town it passes. If you have only limited time for browsing, save it for Joseph.

For information about the Eagle Cap Wilderness, stop in at the **Wallowa Mountains Visitors Center** outside Enterprise. It has videos of the area, pamphlets, and topographical maps. ⌧ Hwy. 82, 1 mi west of Enterprise, ☎ 541/426–5546. ☉ Memorial Day–Labor Day, Mon.–Sat. 8–5; Labor–Memorial Day, weekdays 8–5.

Joseph

29 *80 mi east of La Grande on Hwy. 82.*

The area around Wallowa Lake was the traditional home of the Nez Percé Indians—the town of Joseph is named for Chief Joseph, their famous leader. The peaks of the Wallowa Mountains, snow-covered until July, tower 5,000 ft above the town and lake, which are the regional tourist hubs. Handicraft and antiques shops line Main Street; galleries exhibit the works of area artists and bronze castings from local metal foundries. Tours of the **Valley Bronze of Oregon** (⊠ 18 Main St., ☎ 541/432–7445) foundry facility leave from its showroom.

The **Four Corners Manuel Museum** displays a superb collection of Nez Percé clothing and artifacts. The museum, which also contains pioneer wagons, is one of the town's leading bronze foundries, with 25,000 square ft of facilities in separate buildings. ⊠ *400 N. Main St.,* ☎ *541/ 432–7235.* ⊡ *$5.* ☉ *June–Oct., daily 8–5; Nov.–May, Mon.–Sat. 10– 4; tours at 10:15 and 2:15.*

The **Wallowa County Museum** in Joseph has a small but poignant collection of artifacts and photographs chronicling the Nez Percé Wars, a series of battles against the U.S. Army that took place in the late 1870s. The building, originally built as a bank in 1888, was robbed in 1896, an event that is reenacted with full pageantry every Wednesday at 1 PM in the summer, complete with music, dancing girls, gunshots, and yelping. ⊠ *110 S. Main St.,* ☎ *541/432–6095.* ⊡ *Free.* ☉ *Memorial Day–Sept., daily 10–5.*

From Joseph, Highway 82 continues south and ends at sparkling, blue-green **Wallowa Lake** (⊠ Wallowa Lake Hwy.), the highest body of water in eastern Oregon (elevation 5,000 ft). Call the **Joseph Chamber of Commerce** (☎ 541/426–4622) for information about Wallowa Lake and its facilities.

The **Wallowa Lake Tramway,** the steepest gondola in North America, rises to the top of 8,150-ft Mount Howard in 15 minutes. Vistas of mountain peaks, forest, and Wallowa Lake far below will dazzle you on the way up and at the summit. ⊠ *59919 Wallowa Lake Hwy.,* ☎ *541/432–5331.* ⊡ *$13.50.* ☉ *May–June, daily 10–4; July–Aug., daily 9–5; Sept., daily 10–5.*

Dining and Lodging

$$–$$$ ✕⊡ **Wallowa Lake Lodge.** The rustic atmosphere at this fine and friendly 1920s lodge is tasteful and true to the period. Handmade replicas of the structure's original furniture fill a large common area that contains a massive fireplace. The lodge's rooms are simple yet appealing; the grandest have balconies facing the lake. The cabins, all with fireplaces and some with lake views, are small, old-fashioned havens of knotty pine. The on-site restaurant serves standard American fare for breakfast, lunch, and dinner. ⊠ *60060 Wallowa Lake Hwy., Wallowa Lake 97846,* ☎ *541/432–9821,* ⨳ *541/432–4885. 22 rooms, 8 cabins. Restaurant. No smoking. D, MC, V.*

$–$$ ⊡ **Chandler's Bed, Bread & Trail Inn.** An extensive deck surrounds this lodgelike modern house between Joseph and Wallowa Lake. The rooms have high, sloping, beamed ceilings and are furnished in an eclectic suburban style. The "bread" in the inn's name refers to Ethel Chandler's homemade loaves, a staple of the breakfasts (included in the room rates) she prepares daily. As for the "trail" part, Ethel and her husband, Jim, advise guests on the best places to hike or backpack and provide a shuttle service to nearby trailheads. Pets and smoking are not permitted at the inn. ✉ *700 S. Main St., 97846,* ☎ *541/432–9765 or 800/452–3781. 5 rooms, 3 with bath. Outdoor hot tub. MC, V.*

Outdoor Activities and Sports

BOATING AND FISHING

Rainbow trout, kokanee, and mackinaw are among the species of fish in 300-ft-deep, 4½-mi-long Wallowa Lake. You can picnic on the water at several moored docks. **Wallowa Lake Marina Inc.** (✉ Wallowa Lake, south end, ☎ 541/432–9115) rents paddleboats, motorboats, rowboats, and canoes by the hour or the day.

HORSEBACK RIDING

Eagle Cap Wilderness Pack Station (✉ 59761 Wallowa Lake Hwy., ☎ 541/432–4145 or 800/681–6222), at the south end of Wallowa Lake, conducts guided rides and leads summer pack trips into the Eagle Cap Wilderness.

En Route   The **Wallowa Mountain Loop** is a relatively easy way to take in the natural splendor of the Eagle Cap Wilderness and reach Baker City without backtracking to La Grande. The 3½-hour trip from Joseph to Baker City winds through the national forest and part of Hells Canyon Recreation Area, passing over forested mountains, creeks, and rivers. Before you travel the loop, check with the Joseph Chamber of Commerce (☞ *above*) about road conditions; in winter always carry chains. ✉ *From Joseph take Little Sheep Creek Hwy. east for 8 mi, turn south onto Forest Service Rd. 39, and continue until it meets Hwy. 86, which winds past the town of Halfway to Baker City.*

OFF THE
BEATEN PATH

HELLS CANYON AND THE SNAKE RIVER – The Snake River created Hells Canyon, the world's deepest river-carved gorge. Most travelers take a scenic peek from the overlook on the Wallowa Mountain Loop (☞ *above*). The more adventurous experience this dramatic and formidable landscape by following the Snake River segment of the Wallowa Mountain Loop. Following Highway 86 north from Copperfield, the 60-mi round-trip route winds along the edge of Hells Canyon Reservoir, crosses the Snake River to Hells Canyon Dam on the border of Oregon and Idaho, and continues on to Hells Canyon Creek Recreation Site. At places the canyon is 10 mi in width, with basalt rock walls more than 6,000 ft high. The trip is a memorable one, but be certain you have plenty of gas before starting out.

Halfway

㉚ *63 mi south of Joseph on Wallowa Mountain Loop.*

Halfway, the closest town to Hells Canyon, got its name because it was midway between the town of Pine and the gold mines of Cornucopia. On the southern flanks of the Wallowas, it's a straightforward, unpretentious community with a Main Street and a quiet rural flavor.

Dining and Lodging

$–$$ ✕⊞ **Pine Valley Lodge and Halfway Supper Club.** From the outside, this house on Main Street in "downtown" Halfway is styled like many others built in eastern Oregon during the timber boom of the late 1920s. Inside, the common area is artfully cluttered with a mixture of antique Florida fishing gear, Native American artifacts, and paintings. Accommodations include two eclectically furnished rooms upstairs and two suites next door. The rates include a full breakfast prepared by the inn's owner, Babette Beatty, a gourmet cook who runs the very fine Halfway Supper Club (no lunch; closed on Tuesday and Wednesday) and bakery across the street. ✉ *163 N. Main St., 97834,* ☎ *541/742–*

2027. 2 doubles share 1 bath, 2 suites share 1 bath. Restaurant, bicycles. No credit cards.

$ ⛺ **Clear Creek Farm Bed and Breakfast.** Set amid 160 acres of orchards, woods, and fields on the southeastern flank of the Wallowa Mountains, this 1880s Craftsman farmhouse is a simple but comfortable rural retreat. The main house has four rooms. Two bunkhouses with ceilings but no windows are available from May to October. Lakeview, with a balcony overlooking a small pond, is the better of the two. Breakfast, served in an outdoor kitchen in warm weather, includes eggs, buffalo sausage, Dutch babies, and home-grown raspberries and peaches in season. ⊠ *Fish Lake Rd., 5½ mi north of Halfway, 97834,* ☎ *541/742–2238 or 800/742–4992,* FAX *541/742–5175. 4 rooms share 1 bath, 2 2-room bunkhouses share 3 baths. Outdoor hot tub. MC, V.*

Outdoor Activities and Sports

Wallowa Llamas (⊠ Rte. 1, Box 84, 97834, ☎ 541/742–2961) conducts guided tours into the Eagle Cap Wilderness. The company's llamas can be easily led by those with no previous experience, including children. The company provides tents, eating utensils, and all meals on three- to seven-day pack trips.

Baker City

㉛ *53 mi west of Halfway on Hwy. 86; 44 mi south of La Grande on U.S. 30 off I–84.*

You'd never guess that quiet Baker City, positioned between the Wallowa Mountains and the Elkhorn Range of the Blue Mountains, was once bigger than Spokane and Boise. During the gold-rush era in the late 19th century, the town profited from the money that poured in from nearby mining towns. With the end of the gold rush, the city transformed itself into the logging and ranching town it is today. Remnants of its opulence are still visible in the many restored Victorian houses and downtown shops, but all this history seems minor when you consider the region's fascinating geography. The **Baker County Visitor and Convention Bureau** (⊠ 490 Campbell St., ☎ 541/523–3356 or 800/ 523–1235) operates a small pioneer museum and has information on area attractions.

The highlight of the gold display at the **U.S. Bank** (⊠ Washington and Main Sts.) is the 6¾-pound Armstrong Nugget, found in 1913.

★ The **National Historic Oregon Trail Interpretive Center,** a few miles outside Baker City, does a superb job of re-creating pioneer life in the mid-1800s. From 1841 to 1861 about 300,000 people made the 2,000-mi journey from western Missouri to the Columbia River and the Oregon coast, looking for agricultural land in the west. A simulated section of the Oregon Trail will give you a feel for camp life, the toll the trip took on marriages and families, and the settlers' impact on Native Americans; an indoor theater presents movies and plays. A 4-mi round-trip trail winds from the center to the actual ruts left by the wagons. ⊠ *Hwy. 86 E, east of I–84,* ☎ *541/523–1843.* ⛬ *Free.* ☉ *Apr.–Oct., daily 9–6; Nov.–Mar., daily 9–4.*

The **Oregon Trail Regional Museum** seems rather staid after the interpretive center. A covered wagon, an old fire-fighting wagon, and pioneer tools fill the back room. The museum has an enormous butterfly collection and one of the most impressive rock collections in the west, including thundereggs, glowing phosphorescent rocks, and a 950-pound hunk of quartz. ⊠ *2490 Grove St., at Campbell St.,* ☎ *541/523–9308.* ⛬ *$2.* ☉ *Mid-Apr.–Oct., daily 9–5; Nov.–Mar., by appointment.*

Dining and Lodging

$ ✕ **Baker City Cafe–Pizza à Fetta.** The gourmet pizzas here are made from hand-thrown dough; the pesto and three-tomato pies are particularly good. Also on the menu are pastas, salads, Italian sodas, and espresso. ⊠ *1915 Washington Ave., 1 block from Main St.,* ☎ *541/523–6099. MC, V. Closed Sun. No dinner Sat.*

$$–$$$$ ✕⊞ **Geiser Grand Hotel.** Considered for many years the finest hotel
★   between Portland and Salt Lake City, the Geiser Grand was built in 1889 during the height of the gold rush. The Italian Renaissance Revival gem reopened in 1997 after a meticulous restoration. The rooms, filled with period furnishings and every modern amenity, have 18-ft ceilings, enormous windows (many overlooking the nearby mountains), and large bathrooms. The striking Palm Court, with a suspended stained-glass ceiling, dominates the first floor. The hotel's Swan dining room, serving steaks, prime rib, fresh fish, and pasta dishes, is Baker City's finest restaurant. A breakfast coupon is provided upon check-in. ⊠ *1996 Main St., 97814,* ☎ *541/523–1889 or 888/434–7374,* FAX *541/523–1800. 30 rooms. Restaurant, bar, no-smoking floors, room service, beauty salon, exercise room, concierge, meeting rooms. AE, D, MC, V.*

$$ ⊞ **Best Western Sunridge Inn.** The inn's five well-maintained buildings surround a swimming pool. Rooms are large and decorated with pine and upholstered furniture. Poolside rooms are preferable—the mountain-view rooms overlook the parking lot. There's a good restaurant on the premises. ⊠ *1 Sunridge La. (off I–84's City Center exit), 97814,* ☎ *541/523–6444,* FAX *541/523–6446. 156 rooms. Restaurant, bar, no-smoking rooms, outdoor pool, indoor hot tub. AE, D, DC, MC, V.*

Camping

⚠ **Anthony Lake.** The premier camping spots near Baker City are the three campgrounds at Anthony Lake. These sites, which usually fill up early during summer weekends, are available on a first-come, first-served basis. ⊠ *Anthony Lakes Hwy., 20 mi west of North Powder off I–84. From Baker City take U.S. 30 (when it splits off from I–84) north 10 mi to the Haines exit, turn west on County Rd. 1146, and follow the Elkhorn Drive Scenic Byway signs about 24 mi to the lake;* ☎ *541/523–4476. 37 campsites. Pit toilets, potable water.* ▭ *$3–$5.* ☉ *Late June–Sept.*

....

OFF THE   **ELKHORN DRIVE AND THE SUMPTER VALLEY RAILROAD** – The 106-mi
BEATEN PATH   Elkhorn Drive winds from Baker City through the Elkhorn Range of the Blue Mountains. Only white-bark pine can survive on the Elkhorn Range's sharp ridges and peaks, which top 8,000 ft; spruce, larch, Douglas fir, and ponderosa pine thrive on the lower slopes. The well-marked drive starts on Highway 7 west of Baker City, turns onto County Road 24 toward Sumpter, goes by Granite on Forest Service Road 73, and then returns to Baker City along U.S. 30. The Sumpter Valley Railroad operates a restored steam engine on a stretch of track that formerly serviced trains bearing passengers, timber, and gold ore. ⊠ *Sumpter Valley Railroad Depot, Hwy. 7 near McEwen, 25 mi southwest of Baker City,* ☎ *541/894–2268.* ▭ *$6 one-way, $9 round-trip.* ☉ *2-hr round-trip excursions and 35-min one-way train rides Memorial Day–Sept., weekends and holidays; departures from Sumpter Depot at 11:15, 2, and 4:40 and from McEwen Depot at 10, 12:45, and 3:15.*

....

John Day

② *80 mi west of Baker City on U.S. 26.*

From Baker City, Highway 7 and then U.S. 26 wind west through mountain, high-desert, and forest terrain to the town of John Day, a central location for trips to the John Day Fossil Beds National Monument to the west or the Malheur National Wildlife Refuge and the towns of Burns, Frenchglen, and Diamond to the south.

★ The small restored building that houses the **Kam Wah Chung & Co. Museum** was a trading post on The Dalles Military Road in 1866 and 1867. It later served as a general store, a Chinese labor exchange for the area's mines, a Chinese doctor's shop, and an opium den. The museum contains a completely stocked Chinese pharmacy, items that would have been sold at the general store, and re-created living quarters. Adjacent to the City Park, the museum is an extraordinary testament to the early Chinese community in Oregon. ⊠ *Ing-Hay Way off Canton St.,* ☎ *541/575–0028.* ⌸ *$2.* ☉ *May–Oct., Mon.–Thurs. 9–noon and 1–5, weekends 1–5.*

Driving west through the dry, shimmering heat of the John Day Valley on U.S. 26, it may be hard to imagine this area as a humid subtropical forest filled with lumbering 50-ton brontosauruses and 50-ft-long crocodiles. But so it was, and the eroded hills and sharp, barren-looking ridges contain the richest concentration of prehistoric plant and animal fossils in the world.

★ ㉝ Formed as a result of volcanic activity during the Cenozoic era 5 to 50 million years ago, the geological formations that make up the **John Day Fossil Beds National Monument** cover hundreds of square miles but are divided into three "units"—**Sheep Rock, Painted Hills,** and **Clarno** (☞ *below*). If your time is limited, skip Clarno: It's the farthest from John Day and the least interesting. The park's headquarters is at the Sheep Rock unit. ☎ *541/987–2333.* ⌸ *Free.* ☉ *Year-round.*

Sheep Rock

40 mi from John Day, west 38 mi on U.S. 26 and north 2 mi on Hwy. 19.

Exhibits, a video, and handouts at the **Sheep Rock visitor center** outline the significance of the John Day Fossil Beds. Two miles north of the visitor center on Highway 19 lies the impressive **Blue Basin,** a badlands canyon with sinuous blue-green spires. Winding through this basin is the ½-mi **Island in Time Trail,** where trailside exhibits explain the area's 28-million-year-old fossils. The 3-mi **Blue Basin Overlook Trail** loops around the rim of the canyon, yielding some splendid views. ⊠ *Visitor center: Hwy. 19,* ☎ *541/987–2333.* ☉ *Memorial Day–Labor Day, daily 9–6; Labor Day–Memorial Day, weekdays 9–5; off-season hrs sometimes vary.*

Lodging

$ ⌸ **Fish House Inn.** The Piscean decor at this B&B 9 mi east of the Sheep Rock fossil beds includes fishing gear, nets, and framed prints of fish. The main house holds three rooms, and behind it is a cottage with two. The friendly hosts serve a huge country breakfast (on the lawn in good weather). While you're in town, stop by the Dayville Mercantile, a century-old general store on U.S. 26. ⊠ *110 Franklin St., Dayville 97825,* ☎ *541/987–2124 or 888/286–3474. 5 rooms, 3 with bath. AE, MC, V.*

Mitchell

37 mi from Sheep Rock, south 2 mi on Hwy. 19 and west 35 mi on U.S. 26; 70 mi east of John Day on U.S. 26.

Mitchell, an authentic homey desert town, has a small business district with food and basic services. From Mitchell, U.S. 26 continues southwest for 48 mi through the Ochoco National Forest to Prineville (☞ Central Oregon, *above*).

Dining and Lodging

$ ✕ **Blueberry Muffin Cafe.** A friendly glow envelops this sunny roadside café serving old standards: pancakes for breakfast, sandwiches for lunch, burgers and fried chicken with all the fixings for dinner. ⊠ *218 U.S. 26,* ☎ *541/462–3434. No credit cards.*

$ 🏨 **Sky Hook Motel.** This carefully tended inn surrounded by flower and vegetable gardens is a welcome comfort zone after a day's hike in the fossil beds. The owners are friendly and the rooms, two with kitchenettes, are homey and comfortably furnished. ⊠ *101 U.S. 26, 97750,* ☎ *541/462–3569. 6 rooms. MC, V.*

Painted Hills

9 mi from Mitchell; head west on U.S. 26 and follow signs north.

The fossils at Painted Hills date back about 33 million years and reveal a climate that had become noticeably drier than that of Sheep Rock's era. The eroded buff-color hills reveal striking red and green striations created by minerals in the clay. Come at dusk or just after it rains, when the colors are most vivid. Take the steep ¼-mi **Carroll Rim Trail** for a commanding view of the hills or sneak a peek from the parking lot at the trailhead, about 2 mi beyond the picnic area.

Clarno

67 mi from Mitchell, north 25 mi on Hwy. 207, north 21 mi on Hwy. 19 (to Fossil), and west 20 mi on Hwy. 218.

The 48-million-year-old beds in this small section have yielded the oldest fossils in the national monument. The drive to the beds traverses forests of ponderosa pines and sparsely populated valleys along the John Day River before turning through a landscape filled with spires and outcroppings that attest to the region's volcanic past. A short trail that runs between the two parking lots contains fossilized evidence of an ancient subtropical forest. Another trail climbs ¼ mi from the second parking lot to the base of the Palisades, a series of abrupt, irregular cliffs created by ancient volcanic mud flows.

Burns and Environs

34 *76 mi south of the town of John Day on U.S. 395.*

The stretch of U.S. 395 between John Day and Burns cuts a winding swath through the Malheur National Forest in the Blue Mountains. Black bears, bighorn sheep, elk, and wolverines inhabit thickly wooded stands of pine, fir, and cedar. Near Burns the trees dwindle in number and the landscape changes from mountainous forest to open areas covered with sagebrush and dotted with junipers.

Burns is the only place in Harney County—10,185 square mi of sagebrush, rimrock, and grassy plains—that has basic tourist amenities. Think of it as a rest stop or a jumping-off point for exploring the real poetry of the Malheur National Wildlife Refuge, Steens Mountain, and the Alvord Desert.

The Harney County Chamber of Commerce and the Bureau of Land Management office in Hines (☞ Visitor Information *in* Eastern Oregon Essentials, *below*) are good places to obtain information about the area.

Dining and Lodging

$ ✕ **Hilander Restaurant.** In 1997 the wood-panel Hilander began serving Chinese food in addition to its usual American dishes. Daily specials might include pork chops with apple sauce or roast beef with brown gravy, but spicy Szechuan chicken, curry beef, and various foo yungs and chow meins are also on the menu. ⊠ *195 N. Broadway,* ☎ *541/573–2111. MC, V. Closed Mon.*

$ ✕ **Mazatlan.** Part of a Northwest chain, this place on the main drag in Burns serves large portions of reliable Mexican food—enchiladas, tacos, tostadas, chilies rellenos, chimichangas, and tamales. ⊠ *293 N. Broadway,* ☎ *541/573–1829. MC, V.*

$ ▥ **Bontemps Motel.** The Bontemps is a throwback to the days when motels had personalities. The rooms, decorated with a funky mixture of old and new furnishings, still retain a 1930s charm. With old-fashioned tile showers, mirrored alcoves, cable TV, and coffeemakers, you can't beat this motel for the price. Everything in Burns is within walking distance. ⊠ *74 Monroe St., 97220,* ☎ *541/573–2037 or 800/229–1394,* ⛝ *541/573–2577. 15 units. Refrigerators. AE, D, DC, MC, V.*

Outdoor Activities and Sports

GOLF

Valley Golf Club (⊠ 345 Burns–Hines Hwy., ☎ 541/573–6251) has a challenging nine-hole, par-36 course open to the public; the clubhouse facilities are reserved for members. The greens fee is $11; a cart costs $10.

ROCKHOUNDING

Rockhounding enthusiasts flock to Harney County to collect fossils, jasper, obsidian, agates, and thundereggs. The Stinkingwater Mountains, 30 mi east of Burns, contain petrified wood and gemstones. Warm Spring Reservoir, just east of the mountains, is a good source for agates. At Charlie Creek, west of Burns, and at Radar, to the north, black, banded, and brown obsidians can be found. It is illegal to remove arrowheads and other artifacts from public lands. Check with the Harney County Chamber of Commerce (⊠ 18 W. D St., ☎ 541/573–2636) for more information.

Malheur National Wildlife Refuge

Highway 205 slices south from Burns through one of the most unusual desert environments in the West. The squat snow-covered summit of Steens Mountain is the only landmark in this area of alkali playas, buttes, scrubby meadows, and, most surprising of all, marshy lakes. The Malheur National Wildlife Refuge, bounded on the north by Malheur and Harney lakes, covers 185,000 acres. It's arid and scorchingly hot in the summer, but in the spring and early summer more than 320 species of migrating birds descend on the refuge's wetlands for their annual nesting and mating rituals. Following an ancient migratory flyway, they've been coming here for nearly a million years. The species include sandhill cranes, snowy white egrets, trumpeter swans, numerous hawks, golden and bald eagles, and white-faced ibis. The number of bird-watchers who turn up for this annual display sometimes rivals the number of birds.

The 30-mi Central Patrol Road, which runs through the heart of the refuge, is your best bet for viewing birds. But first stop at the **Malheur National Wildlife Refuge Headquarters,** where you can pick up leaflets and a free map. The staff will tell you where you're most likely to see the refuge's winged inhabitants. The refuge is a short way from local petroglyphs (ask at the headquarters); a remarkable pioneer structure called the **Round Barn** (head east from the headquarters on Narrows-Princeton Road for 9 mi; road turns to gravel and then runs into Diamond Highway, a paved road that leads south 12 mi to the barn); and **Diamond Craters,** a series of volcanic domes, craters, and lava tubes (continue south from the barn 6 mi on Diamond Highway). ⊠ *Malheur National Wildlife Refuge Headquarters: 32 mi southeast of Burns on Hwy. 205 (follow signs 26 mi south of Burns),* ☎ *541/493–2612.* ⊙ *Park dawn–dusk; headquarters Mon.–Thurs. 7–4:30, Fri. 7–3:30, also 8–3 weekends mid-Mar.–Oct.*

Diamond

54 mi from Burns, south on Hwy. 205 and east on Diamond–Grand Camp Rd.

The tiny town of Diamond has a few lodgings. It's not far from the **Kiger Mustang Lookout,** a wild-horse viewing area run by the Bureau of Land Management. With their dun-colored coats, zebra stripes on knees and hocks, and hooked ear tips, the Kiger Mustangs are thought to be one of the purest herds of wild Spanish mustangs in the world today. They may even be the ancestors of Barb horses brought by the Spanish to North America in the 16th century. The viewing area is accessible to high-clearance vehicles only and is passable only in dry weather. The road to it descends from Happy Valley Road 6 mi north of Diamond. ⊠ *11 mi from Happy Valley Rd.,* ☎ *541/573–4400.* ⊠ *Free.* ⊙ *Dry season (generally May–Oct.) dawn–dusk.*

Lodging

$–$$ ☒ **Hotel Diamond.** A hundred years ago the Hotel Diamond served the local population of ranchers, Basque sheepherders, and cowhands. Now it caters to the birders, naturalists, and high-desert lovers who flock to the Malheur refuge. The air-conditioned rooms are clean, comfortable, and pleasantly furnished with a mix of old-fashioned furniture. Family-style meals are served (to hotel guests only) downstairs. Adjacent to the hotel are a deli, a general store, and a post office. ⊠ *Diamond–Grand Camp Rd., 10 mi east of Hwy. 205, 97722,* ☎ *541/ 493–1898,* ℻ *541/493–2084. 1 room with bath, 5 rooms share 2 baths. Dining room. MC, V.*

$–$$ ☒ **McCoy Creek Inn.** Peaceful and well maintained, this B&B is on the grounds of a working ranch that was established in 1918. You can sit on the porch and watch cows grazing and peacocks strutting. Reproduction Victorian-style furnishings decorate the house. Prix-fixe dinners are available by reservation only; no smoking is permitted at the inn. ⊠ *HC 72, Box 11 (off Diamond–Grand Camp Rd., 10 mi east of Hwy. 205, 2 mi south down a gravel road), Diamond 97722,* ☎ ℻ *541/493–2131. 3 rooms with bath, 1 cabin. Restaurant, hot tub, hiking, swimming. No smoking. MC, V.*

Frenchglen

❸❺ *61 mi south of Burns on Hwy. 205.*

Frenchglen is the gateway to **Steens Mountain.** Amid the flat landscape of eastern Oregon, the mountain is hard to miss, but the sight of its

9,700-ft summit is more remarkable from the east, where its sheer face rises from the flat basin of the Alvord Desert. On the western side, Steens Mountain slopes gently upward over a space of about 20 mi and is less astonishing. Steens is not your average mountain—it's a huge fault block created when the ancient lava that covered this area fractured. Except for groves of aspen, juniper, and a few mountain mahogany, Steens is almost entirely devoid of trees and resembles alpine tundra. But starting in June, the wildflower displays are nothing short of breathtaking. As are the views: On Steens you'll encounter some of the grandest scenery in the West.

The mountain is a great spot for hiking over untrammeled and unpopulated ground, but you can also see it by car (preferably one with four-wheel drive) on the rough but passable 52-mi **Steens Loop Road,** open from mid-July to October. You need to take reasonable precautions; storms can whip up out of the blue, creating hazardous conditions.

On the drive up you might spot golden eagles, bighorn sheep, and deer. The view out over **Kiger Gorge,** on the southeastern rim of the mountain, includes a dramatic U-shape path carved out by a glacier. A few miles farther along the loop road, the equally stunning **East Rim viewpoint** is more than 5,000 ft above the valley floor. The view on a clear day takes in desolate Alvord Desert, which stretches into Idaho and Nevada. ⊠ *Northern entrance to Steens Loop Rd. leaves Hwy. 205 at the south end of Frenchglen and returns to Hwy. 205 about 9 mi south of Frenchglen.*

Frenchglen Mercantile (⊠ Hwy. 205, ☎ 541/493–2738), Frenchglen's only store, is packed with intriguing high-quality western merchandise, including Stetson hats, horsehair belts, antique housewares and horse bits, fossilized shark's teeth, silver and turquoise Native American jewelry, Navajo rugs, books, postcards, and maps. Cold drinks, film, sunscreen, good coffee, snacks, and canned goods are also for sale.

Dining and Lodging

$$ ✕ **Buckaroo Room.** In a region where the food is pretty basic, this tiny
★ restaurant adjoining the Frenchglen Mercantile serves sophisticated fare. The rustic but carefully furnished dining room has a sloping ceiling, rough-hewn timber walls, deer heads, period memorabilia, and kerosene lamps. Sandwiches only are served for lunch. Dinner entrées are few but expertly prepared: Basque chicken coated with olive oil and marinated in herbs and Greek wine, a succulent filet mignon, pasta, and (a rarity in meat-and-potato land) a vegetarian dish. There's a good selection of beer and wine, and the only full bar for miles around. ⊠ *Hwy. 205,* ☎ *541/493–2738. Reservations essential for dinner. AE, D, MC, V. Closed mid-Nov.–Mar.*

$$ ⌂ **Steens Mountain Inn.** Missy and Lance Litchy, the owners of this
★ small, sophisticated inn, combined and transformed two buildings— the home of Frenchglen's first schoolteacher and a two-story dance hall moved from a nearby ghost town—into a bright haven of handsome western furniture, art, and artifacts. From the starched sheets on the beds to the white-tile bathrooms with oversize towels, the attention to detail sets this place apart. The two second-floor bedrooms open out onto a large cedar deck with sweeping views eastward across the broad Blitzen Valley and up the sloping shoulders of Steens Mountain. Missy and Lance also operate the only full-scale guide service in the area— a perfect opportunity for eco-minded visitors to find out more about this fascinating region's natural history and archaeology. ⊠ *Hwy. 205, 97736,* ☎ *541/493–2738,* FAX *541/493–2835. 2 rooms with bath. Room service, laundry service. AE, D, MC, V.*

$ ⊞ **Frenchglen Hotel.** The ambience is simple and rustic at this state-owned hotel built in 1920. Every evening a family-style dinner (reservations essential) is prepared for guests and the public in the combination lobby-dining room; breakfast and lunch are also served. The smallish rooms are upstairs off a single hallway; pets and smoking are not permitted. ⊠ *Hwy. 205, 97736,* ☎ FAX *541/493–2825. 8 rooms share 2 baths. Restaurant. MC, V. Closed mid-Nov.–mid-Mar.*

Camping

⚠ **Page Springs.** A profusion of birds greets you as you set up camp at this idyllic oasis—easily the best campsite in the desert—next to the Blitzen River. ⊠ *4 mi east of Frenchglen on N. Steens Loop Rd.,* ☎ *541/573–4400. 30 sites.* ▨ *$4. Pit toilets, potable water.* ☉ *Apr.–Oct.*

OFF THE BEATEN PATH

ALVORD DESERT – With the eastern face of Steens Mountain in the background, the Alvord Desert conjures up western-movie scenes of parched cowboys riding through the desert—though today you're more likely to see wind sailors scooting across these hard-packed alkali flats and glider pilots using the basin as a runway. But once the wind jockeys and flyboys go home, this desert is deserted. Snowmelt from Steens Mountain can turn it into a shallow lake until as late as mid-July. ⊠ *From Frenchglen take Hwy. 205 south for about 33 mi until the road ends at a T-junction near the town of Fields; go left (north) to the Alvord Desert and the tiny settlement of Andrews.*

Eastern Oregon Essentials

Arriving and Departing

BY BUS

Greyhound (☎ 800/231–2222) buses traveling between Portland and Boise, Idaho, stop in Pendleton, Baker City, and La Grande.

BY CAR

Interstate 84 runs east along the Columbia River and dips down to Pendleton, La Grande, and Baker City. **U.S. 26** heads east from Prineville through the Ochoco National Forest, passing the three units of the John Day Fossil Beds. **U.S. 20** travels southeast from Bend in central Oregon to Burns. U.S. 20 and U.S. 26 both head west into Oregon from Idaho.

BY PLANE

Eastern Oregon Regional Airport (☎ 541/276–7754) in Pendleton is served by Horizon Air (☎ 800/547–9308).

Getting Around

BY BUS

Wallowa Valley Stage Line (⊠ La Grande Station, 2108 Cove Ave., ☎ 541/963–5165) operates buses between La Grande and Joseph. *See* also Getting Around *in* Oregon A to Z, *below.*

BY CAR

To reach Joseph take **Highway 82** east from La Grande. **Highway 86** loops down from Joseph to Baker City. From Baker City, **Highway 7** heading west connects to **U.S. 26** and leads to John Day. **U.S. 395** runs south from John Day to Burns. **Highway 205** heads south from Burns through the Malheur National Wildlife Refuge to Frenchglen, Steens Mountain, and the Alvord Desert (all accessed by local roads). In all these areas, equip yourself with chains for winter driving.

Guided Tours

Eagle Cap Fishing Guides (⊠ 110 S. River St., Enterprise 97828, ☎ 541/426–3493 or 541/432–9685) operates guided fishing trips on the

Grand Ronde, Wallowa, and Imnaha rivers. The company's customized tours (from $80 to $325) in air-conditioned vans explore the wildlife, wildflowers, and geology of Hells Canyon and the Eagle Cap Wilderness.

A trip by raft or jet boat on the Snake River is an exciting and unforgettable way to see Hells Canyon. **Hells Canyon Adventures** (⊠ Box 159, Oxbow 97840, ☎ 800/422–3568) operates jet-boat and other trips of varying lengths.

Visitor Information

Baker County Visitor and Convention Bureau (⊠ 490 Campbell St., Baker City 97814, ☎ 541/523–3356 or 800/523–1235). **Bureau of Land Management** (⊠ Hwy. 20 W., Burns 97220, ☎ 541/573–5241). **Harney County Chamber of Commerce** (⊠ 18 W. D St., Burns 97720, ☎ 541/573–2636. **La Grande Chamber of Commerce** (⊠ 1912 4th St., Suite 200, La Grande 97850, ☎ 541/963–8588 or 800/848–9969). **Pendleton Chamber of Commerce** (⊠ 501 S. Main St., 97801, ☎ 541/276–7411 or 800/547–8911).

OREGON A TO Z

Arriving and Departing

By Bus

Greyhound (☎ 800/231–2222) services the state with routes from elsewhere on the West Coast and from points east.

By Car

Interstate 5 and U.S. 101 enter Oregon heading north from California and south from Washington. **Interstate 84 and U.S. 26** head west from the Idaho border to Portland.

By Plane

Portland International Airport (☞ Portland A to Z *in* Chapter 2) is Oregon's main airport.

Getting Around

By Bus

Greyhound (☎ 800/231–2222) bus routes crisscross the state. **People Mover** (⊠ 229 N.E. Dayton St., John Day, ☎ 541/575–2370 or 800/527–2370) travels on U.S. 26 between Bend and John Day.

By Train

Amtrak's (☎ 800/872–7245) *Coast Starlight,* which runs between Seattle and Los Angeles, passes through western Oregon.

Contacts and Resources

Emergencies

In most parts of the state, calling 911 will summon **police, fire,** or **ambulance** services. In some rural areas, it may be necessary to dial the **Oregon State Police** (☎ 800/452–7888).

Guided Tours

ORIENTATION TOURS

Gray Line Sightseeing Tours (☎ 503/285–9845) conducts guided tours of Oregon. Regular destinations include the Mount Hood Loop and the Oregon coast.

WINERY

"Discover Oregon Wineries," the free map and guide published by the **Oregon Wine Winegrowers Association** (☎ 503/228–8336 or 800/242–

2363), provides profiles and service information about many Oregon wineries. It's available at many wine shops in the state.

Outdoor Activities and Sports

BIKING

The **Oregon Bikeway Program** (✉ Room 210, Transportation Bldg., 355 Capitol St. NE, Salem 97310, ☎ 503/986–3200 or 503/986–3555) has information about biking throughout the state. Call 503/986–3556 for a free bicycle map of the Coast/U.S. 101 route.

BOATING AND RAFTING

Boating and rafting permits are required for the Rogue and lower Deschutes rivers. Recreational access to the Rogue is limited; a lottery for permits is held each February. For more information, contact the Rand Visitor Center (☎ 541/479–3735) in Galice. Permits for the Deschutes can be obtained at the Bureau of Land Management (☎ 541/416–6700) office in Prineville.

Oregon Outdoors Association (☎ 541/683–9552) publishes a free directory of Oregon guides and will help you find a professional guide service—an absolute necessity on the McKenzie and Rogue rivers.

FISHING

To fish in most areas of Oregon, out-of-state visitors need a yearly (about $41), seven-day ($31), or daily ($7) nonresident angler's license. Additional tags are required for those fishing for salmon or steelhead ($11), sturgeon ($6), or halibut ($6); these tags are available from any local sporting-goods store. For more information, contact the **Sport Fishing Information Line** (☎ 800/275–3474).

SKIING

Sno-Park permits, distributed by the Oregon Department of Transportation (☎ 503/986–3006), are required for parking at winter recreation areas from mid-November to April. The permits may be purchased for one day ($2), three days ($3.50), or a full season ($10) at DMV offices and retail agents—sporting-goods stores, markets and gas stations, usually near the areas—which sometimes charge slightly more than the listed price. Permits can often be purchased upon arrival at a ski area, but it's best to call ahead.

Road Conditions

Road Conditions hot line (☎ 503/588–2941; 800/977–6368 in OR).

State Parks

The **Oregon State Park Information Center** (☎ 800/551–6949) has information about campsite availability, rental rates, and recreational activities. Its operators take calls on weekdays from 8 AM to 5 PM.

Visitor Information

Oregon tourist-information centers are marked with blue "I" signs from main roads. Opening and closing times vary, depending on the season and the individual office; call ahead for hours.

National Park Service Pacific Northwest Regional Office (☎ 206/470–4060). **Oregon Economic Development Tourism Division** (✉ 595 Cottage St. NE, Salem 97310, ☎ 800/547–7842). **Oregon State Parks Information Line** (☎ 800/551–6949). **Portland/Oregon Visitors Association** (✉ 2 World Trade Center, 26 S.W. Salmon St., 97204, ☎ 503/222–2223 or 800/345–3214).

4 Seattle

Coffeehouses, brew pubs, grunge music, and lots of rain—these are what many people associate with the hippest city in the U.S. Northwest. But Seattle has more to offer than steaming lattes and garage bands. You can wander historic neighborhoods, browse amid the sights and smells of the Pike Place Market, explore lakes and islands, or just eat, eat, eat—Seattle restaurants are among the nation's most innovative and diverse.

By Wier
Harman

SEATTLE IS DEFINED BY WATER. There's no use denying the city's damp weather, or the fact that its skies are cloudy for much of the year. Residents of Seattle don't tan, goes the joke, they rust. But Seattle is also defined by the rivers, lakes, and canals that bisect its steep green hills, creating a series of distinctive areas along the water's edge. Funky fishing boats, floating homes, swank yacht clubs, and waterfront restaurants exist side by side.

But a city is defined by its people as well as by its geography, and the people of Seattle—a half million within the city proper, another 2 million in the surrounding Puget Sound region—are a diversified bunch. Seattle has long had a vibrant Asian and Asian-American population, as well as well-established communities of Scandinavians, African-Americans, Jews, Native Americans, and Latinos. It's impossible to generalize about such a varied group, but the prototypical Seattleite was once pithily summed up by a *New Yorker* cartoon in which one arch-eyebrowed East Coast matron says to another, "They're backpacky, but nice."

Seattle's climate fosters an easygoing indoor lifestyle. Overcast days and long winter nights have made it a haven for moviegoers and book readers. Hollywood often tests new films here, and residents' per-capita book purchases are among the country's highest. The town that Sir Thomas Beacham once described as a "cultural wasteland" now has all the trappings of a metropolitan hub—two daily newspapers, a state-of-the-art convention center, professional sports teams, a diverse music-club scene, and top-notch ballet, opera, symphony, and theater companies. A major seaport, Seattle is a vital link in Pacific Rim trade. Evidence of this internationalism is everywhere, from the discreet Japanese script identifying downtown department stores—for example, "Nordstrom" written as "Katakana"—to the multilingual recorded messages at Seattle-Tacoma International Airport.

Seattle's expansion has led to the usual big-city problems: increases in crime, drug abuse, homelessness, poverty, and traffic congestion, along with a decline in the quality of the public schools. Many residents have fled to the nearby suburb of Bellevue, which has swollen from a quiet farming community to become Washington's fifth-largest city. But despite the growing pains they've endured, Seattleites as a whole manifest a great love for their city and a firm commitment to maintaining its reputation as one of the most livable areas in the country.

Pleasures and Pastimes

Dining
The best Seattle restaurants build their menus around local ingredients. The city has an invaluable resource in the Pike Place Market, which warehouses bountiful supplies of seafood and produce. A quick scan of the stalls will tell you what to expect on restaurant plates in any given season: strawberries in June; Walla Walla Sweets—a mild softball-size onion—in July; wild blackberries in August; and Washington's renowned apples during autumn. All year long, you'll find Washington wines and beer at Seattle eateries. This reliance on locally produced ingredients, along with the synthesis of European and Asian cooking techniques and a touch of irreverence, makes for what has come to be known as Pacific Northwest cuisine.

Nightlife and the Arts

Seattle achieved fleeting notoriety as the birthplace of grunge rock. Some of the better-known bands to emerge from the local scene include Nirvana, Pearl Jam, and Soundgarden. But jazz, blues, and R&B have been perennial favorites, and you'll find clubs that showcase everything from tinny garage bands to subtle stylists. Beyond music, you can catch a comedian or a movie—or just have a drink while watching the lights flicker on the water. On any given night there are usually several worthwhile dance or theater offerings. Seattle's galleries support an active community of painters, sculptors, woodworkers, and glass artists. The annual Northwest Folklife Festival on Memorial Day weekend celebrates their creativity.

Parks and Gardens

"Seattle possesses extraordinary landscape advantages. . . . In designing a system of parks and parkways the primary aim should be to secure and preserve for the use of the people as much as possible of these advantages of water and mountain views and of woodlands . . . as well as some fairly level land for field sports and the enjoyment of scenery." These words appeared in a surveyors report prepared in 1903 for Seattle's fledgling parks commission and established the foundation for an ambitious master plan, the spirit of which has been maintained to this day. Seattle's extensive parks system retains that delicate (and often elusive) balance between the fanciful and functional—from the primeval growth of West Seattle's Schmitz Park to the manicured ball fields around Green Lake, from the epic sprawl of the Washington Park Arboretum to Parson's Garden, a prim urban oasis.

EXPLORING SEATTLE

Seattle, like Rome, is built on seven hills. As a visitor, you're likely to spend much of your time on just two of them (Capitol Hill and Queen Anne Hill), but the seven knobs are indeed the most definitive element of the city's natural and spiritual landscape. Years of largely thoughtful zoning practices have kept tall buildings from obscuring the lines of sight, maintaining vistas in most directions and around most every turn. The hills are lofty, privileged perches from which Seattleites are constantly reminded of the beauty of the forests, mountains, and water lying just beyond the city. That is, when it stops misting long enough to see your hand in front of your face.

To know Seattle is to know its distinctive neighborhoods. Below is a thumbnail sketch of the major ones. Because of the hills, comfortable walking shoes are a must.

Ballard, home to Seattle's fishing industry and fun-to-tour locks, is at the mouth of Salmon Bay, northwest of downtown.

Capitol Hill, northeast of downtown on Pine Street, east of Interstate 5 (I–5), is the center of youth culture in this very young city.

Downtown is bounded on the west by **Elliott Bay,** on the south by **Pioneer Square** (the city's oldest neighborhood) and the **International District,** on the north by the attractive residences lining the slopes of **Queen Anne Hill,** and by I–5 to the east. You can reach most points of interest by foot, bus, trolley, or the monorail that runs between the Seattle and Westlake centers.

Fremont, Seattle's eccentric and artsy hamlet, is just north of **Lake Union** and the **Lake Washington Ship Canal,** east of Ballard, west of **Wallingford,** and south of **Woodland Park.**

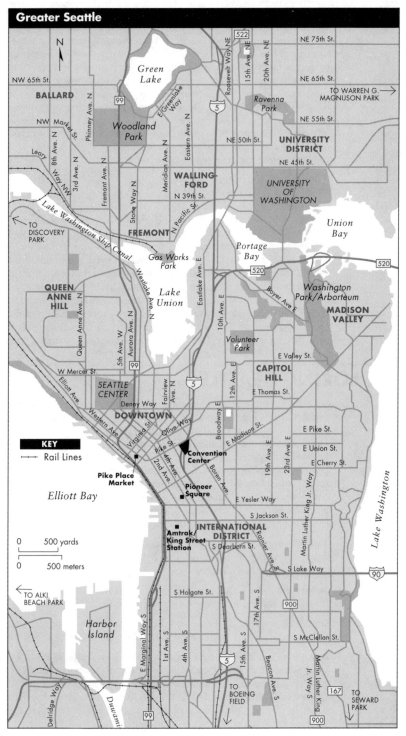

Greater Seattle

N

NW 65th St.

Green Lake

BALLARD

Roosevelt Way NE

15th Ave. NE

20th Ave. NE

NE 75th St.

NE 65th St.

TO WARREN G. MAGNUSON PARK

Ravenna Park

NE 55th St.

Phinney Ave. N

Woodland Park

E Greenlake Way N

Eastern Ave. N

Meridian Ave. N

NE 50th St.

UNIVERSITY DISTRICT

NW Market St.

8th Ave. NW

3rd Ave. N

Fremont Ave. N

Stone Way N

WALLING-FORD

N 39th St.

N Pacific St.

NE 45th St.

UNIVERSITY OF WASHINGTON

Leary Way NW

Lake Washington Ship Canal

FREMONT

Gas Works Park

Portage Bay

Union Bay

TO DISCOVERY PARK

QUEEN ANNE HILL

Queen Anne Ave. N

5th Ave. W

Aurora Ave. N

Westlake Ave. N

Lake Union

Eastlake Ave. E

10th Ave. E

520

Boyer Ave. E

520

Washington Park/Arboretum

MADISON VALLEY

Volunteer Park

W Mercer St.

Fairview Ave. N

SEATTLE CENTER

Denny Way

12th Ave. E

E Valley St.

CAPITOL HILL

E Thomas St.

Elliott Ave.

Western Ave.

DOWNTOWN

Virginia St.

Olive Way

Pike St.

Broadway E

E Madison St.

19th Ave. E

23rd Ave. E

E Pike St.

E Union St.

E Cherry St.

KEY

Rail Lines

2nd Ave.

4th Ave.

Convention Center

Boren Ave.

Pike Place Market

Pioneer Square

E Yesler Way

Martin Luther King Jr. Way

Elliott Bay

S Jackson St.

INTERNATIONAL DISTRICT

Amtrak/ King Street Station

S Dearborn St.

0   500 yards

0   500 meters

Rainier Ave.

S Lake Way

90

TO ALKI BEACH PARK

S Holgate St.

17th Ave. S

900

Harbor Island

E Marginal Way S

1st Ave. S

4th Ave. S

15th Ave. S

Beacon Ave. S

S McClellan St.

Martin Luther King Jr. Way S

Lake Washington

Delridge Way

Duwamish

5

TO BOEING FIELD

167

900

TO SEWARD PARK

99

Magnolia, dotted with expensive (and precariously perched) homes, is at the northwestern edge of Elliott Bay, west of Queen Anne Hill.

University District, the area around the University of Washington, is north of Capitol Hill and Union Bay.

Great Itineraries

IF YOU HAVE 1 DAY

If you've come to Seattle on business or for another reason only have a day for sightseeing, focus your energy on downtown. Weather permitting, an after-dinner ferry ride to Bainbridge Island (☞ Chapter 3) and back is a perfect way to conclude your day.

IF YOU HAVE 3 DAYS

Get a feel for what makes Seattle special at Pike Place Market and then explore more of downtown and the waterfront. Start your second day at the Ballard Locks, reaching Fremont in time for lunch. After a stroll through the neighborhood's galleries and shops, grab a beer at the Redhook Brewery before heading to the Space Needle, where the views are the most spectacular as sunset approaches. Venture outside the city on I–90 to Snoqualmie Falls (☞ Chapter 3) on day three. Hike to the falls and lunch at Salish Lodge. To get a true sense of the pace of life in the Northwest, on your return to Seattle, detour north from I–90 on Highway 203 and stop in tiny Duvall, home to antiques shops, boutiques, and cafés. You can easily make it back to Seattle in time for dinner or a night on the town.

IF YOU HAVE 5 TO 7 DAYS

Follow the three-day itinerary above. Take a morning bay cruise on day four and spend the afternoon at the Washington Park Arboretum before heading to Capitol Hill for dinner and some nightclubbing. If you can only stay in the Seattle area one more day, take the ferry to Port Townsend on day five. If you have a few days, take the ferry to one or more of the San Juan Islands.

Pike Place Market, the Waterfront, and Seattle Center

Numbers in the text correspond to numbers in the margin and on the Downtown Seattle map.

A Good Tour

Spend some time at **Pike Place Market** ① before walking south a block on 1st Avenue to the **Seattle Art Museum** ②, whose postmodern exterior is worth a look even if you're not going inside. From the museum, walk west across 1st Avenue and descend the **Harbor Steps.** At the bottom of the steps is the waterfront. Head north (to the right). At Pier 59, you'll find the **Seattle Aquarium** ③ and the **Omnidome Film Experience** ④. You can walk out on Piers 62 and 63 for a good view of Elliott Bay. The newly refurbished **Bell Street Pier** (Pier 66) contains a marina, several restaurants, and **Odyssey: The Maritime Discovery Center** ⑤, which is scheduled to open in July 1998.

Continue up the waterfront to **Myrtle Edwards Park,** just past Pier 70. It's a good place to rest a moment before making the several-block walk up **Broad Street** through the northern part of the Belltown neighborhood (be forewarned: the first three blocks are a tad steep) to the **Seattle Center** and the **Space Needle** ⑥. Especially if you've got kids in tow, you'll want to arrive here before the **Pacific Science Center** ⑦ and **Seattle Children's Museum** ⑧ close. Take the **Seattle Center Monorail** to return to downtown. The monorail stops at **Westlake Center** ⑨, at the corner of 5th Avenue and Pine Street. To get to the **Washington State Convention and Trade Center** ⑩, walk one block southeast to Pike

Street and east to 8th Avenue. Seattle's main **Visitor Information Center** is inside the street-level mall at Convention Place.

TIMING

It would take about half the day to complete the above route stopping only a little, but you'll need to devote the whole day or more to fully appreciate the various sights. A visit to Pike Place Market can easily fill two hours. Plan on an hour for the art museum. The aquarium is a two-hour stop at most. You could spend half a day or more in Seattle Center. The Space Needle is especially fun at sunset. Most of the sights listed below are open daily; the Frye Art Museum and the Seattle Art Museum are closed Monday and open until 9 PM on Thursday.

Sights to See

Frye Art Museum. Among the pivotal late-19th- and early-20th-century American and European realist works at this gallery east of downtown are German artist Franz von Stuck's *Sin,* a painting with Impressionist leanings that predates the movement, and Alexander Koester's *Ducks,* an example of the Academy school of German painting. The Frye, which opened in 1952, underwent a mid-1990s redesign that has added more exhibition space, an outdoor garden courtyard, and a reflecting pool. ⊠ *704 Terry Ave.,* ☏ *206/622–9250.* ⌦ *Free.* ☉ *Tues.–Sat. 10–5 (Thurs. until 9), Sun. noon–5.*

Myrtle Edwards Park. Sandwiched between the Burlington Northern Railroad to the east and the gently lapping waters of Elliott Bay to the west, this sliver of a park just north of Pier 70 is popular with Seattleites for jogging, walking, and picnicking. As a place to catch the sunset in the city, it's rivaled only by the deck of a westbound Bainbridge Island ferry. ⊠ *Alaskan Way between W. Bay and W. Thomas Sts.*

❺ **Odyssey: The Maritime Discovery Center.** Cultural and educational maritime exhibits on Puget Sound and ocean trade will be the focus of this facility that is scheduled to open in July 1998 (though its debut has already been delayed a couple of times). Already open at the center are a conference center, a short-stay boat basin, fish-processing terminals, a gourmet fish market, and a restaurant. ⊠ *Pier 66 off Alaskan Way,* ☏ *206/623–2120.* ⌦ *$6.50.* ☉ *Daily 10–6.*

❹ **Omnidome Film Experience.** The theater next to the aquarium shows short films on a large, curved screen about the eruption of Mount St. Helens, mountain gorillas, real-life storm chasers, and the Great Barrier Reef. ⊠ *Pier 59 off Alaskan Way,* ☏ *206/622–1868.* ⌦ *$6.95; combination tickets including aquarium admission $12.75.* ☉ *Daily 10–5.*

☾ ❼ **Pacific Science Center.** An excellent stop for children and adults, the Pacific Science Center has 200 hands-on exhibits. The large, brightly colored machines of Body Works amusingly analyze cardiovascular activity, the motion of limbs, and other aspects of physiology. Text Zones contains robots and virtual-reality diversions that participants can control. The dinosaurs exhibit is wildly popular. IMAX screenings and laser light shows take place daily. A *Jetsons*-style outdoor plaza, with fountains and concrete towers, dates from the 1962 World's Fair. ⊠ *200 2nd Ave. N,* ☏ *206/443–2001.* ⌦ *$7.50.* ☉ *Weekdays 10–5, weekends 10–6.*

★ ❶ **Pike Place Market.** The heart of the Pike Place Historical District, this Seattle institution began in 1907 when the city issued permits to farmers allowing them to sell produce from their wagons parked at Pike Place. Later the city built stalls for the farmers. At one time the market was a madhouse of vendors hawking their produce and haggling over prices; some of the fishmongers still carry on this kind of frenzied banter, but chances are you won't get them to waver on their prices.

Urban renewal almost killed the market, but city voters, led by the late architect Victor Steinbreuck, rallied and voted it a historical asset. Many buildings have been restored, and the project is now connected to the waterfront by stairs and elevators. Besides a number of restaurants, you'll find booths selling fresh seafood—which can be packed in dry ice for your flight home—produce, cheese, Northwest wines, bulk spices, tea, coffee, and arts and crafts.

If the weather is nice, gather a picnic of market foods—fresh fruit and smoked salmon, of course, but soups, sandwiches, pastries, and various ethnic snacks are also available in the market or from the small shops facing it along Pike Place. Carry your bounty north, past the market buildings, to **Victor Steinbreuck Park,** a small green gem named for Pike Place's savior. ⊠ *Pike Pl. at Pike St., west of 1st Ave.,* ☎ *206/ 682–7453.* ☺ *Mon.–Sat. 9–6, Sun. 11–5.*

NEED A
BREAK?

Three Girls Bakery (⊠ Pike Pl. Market, 1514 Pike Pl., ☎ 206/622–1045), a 13-seat glassed-in lunch counter that's tucked behind a bakery outlet, serves sandwiches, soups, and pastries to hungry folks in a hurry. Go for the chili and a hunk of Sicilian sourdough, or buy a loaf at the take-out counter, pick up some smoked salmon at the fish place next door, and head for a picnic table in Waterfront Park.

☺ ❸ **Seattle Aquarium.** Pacific Northwest marine life is the emphasis at this waterfront facility. At the Discovery Lab you'll see baby barnacles, minute jellyfish, and other "invisible" creatures through high-resolution video microscopes. The "Tide Pool" exhibit re-creates Washington's rocky coast and sandy beaches at low tide; there's even a 6,000-gallon wave that sweeps in over the underwater life—spectators standing close by may get damp from the simulated sea spray. Sea otters and seals swim and dive in their pools, and the "State of the Sound" exhibit shows the aquatic life and ecology of Puget Sound. ⊠ *Pier 59 off Alaskan Way,* ☎ *206/386–4320.* ☜ *$7.50.* ☺ *Memorial Day–Labor Day, daily 10–8, Labor Day–Memorial Day, daily 10–6.*

❷ **Seattle Art Museum.** Postmodern architect Robert Venturi designed this five-story museum, which is a work of art in itself. The 1991 building has a limestone exterior with large-scale vertical fluting accented by terra-cotta, cut granite, and marble. Sculptor Joseph Borofsky's several-stories-high *Hammering Man* pounds away outside the front door. The museum displays an extensive collection of Asian, Native American, African, Oceanic, and pre-Columbian art and has a café and gift shop. A ticket to the Seattle Art Museum is valid for admission to the Seattle Asian Art Museum (☞ *below*) in Volunteer Park if used within one week. ⊠ *100 University St.,* ☎ *206/654–3100.* ☜ *$6; free 1st Thurs. of month.* ☺ *Tues.–Sun. 10–5 (Thurs. until 9).*

Seattle Center. The 74-acre Seattle Center complex was built for the 1962 World's Fair. A rolling green campus organized around the massive International Fountain, the center includes an amusement park, theaters, exhibition halls, museums, shops, a skateboard park, Key Arena, the Pacific Science Center (☞ *above*), and the Space Needle (☞ *below*). Among the arts groups headquartered here are Seattle Repertory Theatre, Intiman Theatre, the Seattle Opera, and the Pacific Northwest Ballet. (The Seattle Symphony will perform here until the opening of Benaroya Hall downtown in 1998.) The center hosts several professional sports teams: the Seattle Supersonics (NBA basketball), Reign

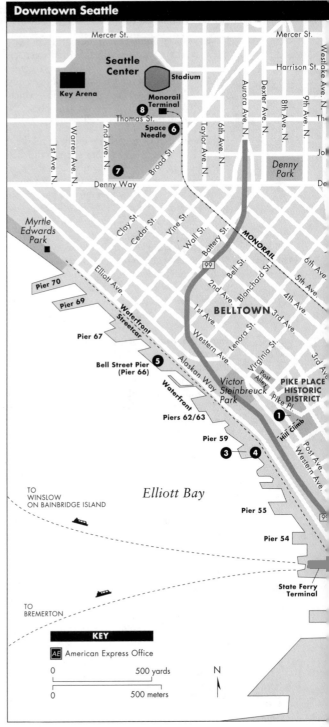

Downtown Seattle

Mercer St.

Mercer St.

Harrison St.

Seattle Center

Stadium

Key Arena

Monorail Terminal

Thomas St.

Space Needle **6**

8

6

Denny Park

7

Denny Way

Westlake Ave. N.

Dexter Ave. N.

Aurora Ave. N.

8th Ave. N.

9th Ave. N.

6th Ave. N.

Taylor Ave. N.

Warren Ave. N.

2nd Ave. N.

1st Ave. N.

Myrtle Edwards Park

Clay St.

Cedar St.

Vine St.

Wall St.

Battery St.

99

Bell St.

Blanchard St.

MONORAIL

6th Ave

5th Ave

4th Ave

3rd Ave

BELLTOWN

2nd Ave.

3rd Ave.

Elliott Ave.

Pier 70

Pier 69

Waterfront Streetcar

1st Ave.

Lenora St.

Virginia St.

Pier 67

Western Ave.

Bell Street Pier (Pier 66)

5

Alaskan Way

Victor Steinbrueck Park

Post Alley

PIKE PLACE HISTORIC DISTRICT

Pike Pl.

1

Waterfront

Piers 62/63

Pier 59

3

4

Hill Climb

Post Ave.

Western Ave.

Elliott Bay

TO WINSLOW ON BAINBRIDGE ISLAND

Pier 55

Pier 54

9

TO BREMERTON

State Ferry Terminal

KEY

AE American Express Office

0   500 yards

0   500 meters

N

TO CENTER
FOR WOODEN
BOATS

Republican St.

E. Mercer St.

CAPITOL HILL

⑮ ⑯

Bellevue Ave. E.

Summit Ave. E.

E. Republican St.

E. Harrison St.

E. Thomas St.

⑭

E. John St.

E. Olive Way

E. Denny Way

E. Howell St.

**Seattle
Central
Community
College**

*Broadway
Playfield*

E. Olive St.

E. Pine St.

⑬

E. Pike St.

Broadway

10th Ave.

11th Ave.

12th Ave.

E. Union St.

Boylston Ave.

Summit Ave.

13th Ave.

14th Ave.

15th Ave.

**Seattle
University**

Cherry St.

Boren Ave.

Terry Ave.

Howell St.

8th Ave.

9th Ave.

7th Ave.

Stewart St.

Olive Way

AE

⑨
**Monorail
Terminal**

Pine St.

7th Ave.

6th Ave.

5th Ave.

4th Ave.

⑩

Pike St.

Union St.

*Freeway
Park*

8th Ave.

9th Ave.

Terry Ave.

Boren Ave.

Minor Ave.

Boylston Ave.

Summit Ave.

DOWNTOWN

FIRST HILL

② University

Seneca St.

Spring St.

Madison St.

**Frye Museum
of Art** ■

Boren Ave.

11th Ave.

10th Ave.

2nd Ave.

1st Ave.

Marion St.

Columbia St.

Cherry St.

James St.

E. Jefferson St.

**Pioneer
Place** ■

Yesler Way

**PIONEER
SQUARE**

Washington St.

Waterfall Garden ■

Main St.

⑪

S. Jackson St.

2nd Ave. S.

**INTERNATIONAL
DISTRICT**

⑫

Maynard Ave. S.

7th Ave. S.

8th Ave. S.

10th Ave. S.

12th Ave.

S. King St.

Uwajimaya ■

S. Weller St.

S. Lane St.

S. King St.

S. Dearborn St.

Occidental Ave. S.

Kingdome

4th Ave. S.

Airport Way S.

1st Ave. S.

TO
MUSEUM OF
FLIGHT

(women's basketball), Sounders (soccer), Seadogs (indoor soccer), and Thunderbirds (hockey). It's a bit cramped, and parking can be a nightmare, but Seattle Center is the undisputed hub of the city's leisure life. It's also the site of three of the area's largest summer festivals: the Northwest Folklife Festival, Bite of Seattle, and Bumbershoot. *See* Festivals and Seasonal Events *in* Chapter 1 for details about these. The Experience Music Project, a music museum financed by a nonprofit organization started by Microsoft cofounder Paul Allen and designed by architect Frank Gehry, will open near the Space Needle in 1999. The **Seattle Center Monorail** (☞ Getting Around *in* Seattle A to Z, *below*) travels between the center and Westlake Center. ☒ *Between 1st and 5th Aves. N and Denny Way and Mercer St.,* ☎ *206/684–8582.*

☾ **⑧ Seattle Children's Museum.** The global village at this colorful and spacious facility introduces children to everyday life in Ghana, the Philippines, and other lands. A mountain wilderness area (including a slide and waterfall) educates kids about climbing, camping, and understanding the Northwest environment. Cog City is a giant maze of pipes and pulleys. A pretend neighborhood contains a post office, café, fire station, and grocery store. An infant/toddler area is well padded for climbing and sliding. Arts-and-crafts activities, special exhibits, and workshops are also offered. ☒ *Seattle Center House, fountain level, 305 Harrison St.,* ☎ *206/441–1768.* ☒ *$4.* ☾ *Weekdays 10–5, weekends 10–6.*

★ **⑥ Space Needle.** The distinctive exterior of the 520-ft-high Space Needle can be seen from almost any spot in the downtown area. The view from the inside out is even better—the observation deck, a 42-second elevator ride from street level—yields vistas of the entire region. Have a drink at the Space Needle Lounge or a latte at the adjacent coffee bar and take in Elliott Bay, Queen Anne Hill, and on a clear day the peaks of the Cascade Range. (If it's stormy, have no fear: 25 lightning rods protect the tower.) The needle's rotating restaurants, one family style and the other more formal, are not known for their innovative cuisine. ☒ *5th Ave. and Broad St.,* ☎ *206/443–2111.* ☒ *Observation deck $8.50.* ☾ *Daily 8 AM–midnight.*

⑩ Washington State Convention and Trade Center. Seattle's vine-covered exhibition hall straddles I–5. The design of verdant **Freeway Park** south of here is intended to convey the spirit and flavor of the Pacific Northwest, which it does fairly well, considering the urban location. The street-level **Visitor Information Center** has maps, brochures, and events listings. ☒ *Visitor center: 800 Convention Pl., at 8th Ave. and Pike St.,* ☎ *206/461–5840.* ☾ *Memorial Day–Labor Day, daily 10–4; Labor Day–Memorial Day, weekdays 8:30–5, Sat. 10–4.*

⑨ Westlake Center. This three-story mall (☞ Shopping, *below*) is also a major terminus for buses and the Seattle Center Monorail, which was built for the 1962 World's Fair and connects downtown to Seattle Center. The ground-level Made in Washington store showcases the state's products. ☒ *1601 5th Ave.,* ☎ *206/467–1600.* ☾ *Mon.–Sat. 9:30–8, Sun. 11–6.*

Pioneer Square and the International District

A walk through Seattle's Pioneer Square and International districts provides a glimpse into the city's days as a logging and shipping center and a haven for immigrants from Asia and the Pacific Islands.

Numbers in the text correspond to numbers in the margin and on the Downtown Seattle map.

A Good Walk

Begin at **Pioneer Place,** at 1st Avenue and Yesler Way in the **Pioneer Square District.** Explore the shops and historic buildings along 1st Avenue before heading to the **Klondike Gold Rush National Historical Park** ⑪, on Main Street two blocks south and one block east of Pioneer Place. A restful stop along Main Street heading east to the **International District** is **Waterfall Garden** park, designed by Masao Kinoshita on the site where the messenger service that became United Parcel Service began operations.

Head south (right) on 2nd Avenue South and east (left) at South Jackson Street. You'll see the **Kingdome** sports stadium and Amtrak's **King Street Station** on your right as you head up South Jackson to 7th Avenue, where the **Wing Luke Museum** ⑫ surveys the past and present of immigrants from Asia and the Pacific Islands and their descendants. The museum has walking-tour maps of historic buildings and businesses; one intriguing stop is the **Uwajimaya** store at 6th Avenue South and South King Street (head south one block on 7th Avenue South and turn right on South King Street). You can return to the harbor in one of the vintage **Waterfront Streetcar** trolleys—the southern terminus is at 5th Avenue South and Jackson Street. You can also catch a bus to downtown at the same corner.

TIMING

You can explore Pioneer Square and the International District in one to two hours unless you stop for lunch or like to shop. The Wing Luke Museum is closed Monday.

Sights to See

International District. The 40-block "I.D.," as it's locally known, began as a haven for Chinese workers who came to the United States to work on the transcontinental railroad. The community has remained largely intact despite anti-Chinese riots and the forcible eviction of Chinese residents during the 1880s and the internment of Japanese-Americans during World War II. About one-third of the I.D.'s residents are Chinese, one-third are Filipino, and another third come from elsewhere in Asia or the Pacific Islands. The district, which includes many Chinese, Japanese, and Korean restaurants, also contains herbalists, massage parlors, acupuncturists, antiques shops, and private clubs for gambling and socializing. Among the I.D.'s many great markets is the huge Uwajimaya Japanese supermarket and department store (☞ Shopping, *below*). ⊠ *Between Main and S. Lane Sts. and 4th and 8th Aves.*

⓫ **Klondike Gold Rush National Historical Park.** This indoor center provides insight into Seattle's role in the 1897–98 gold rush in northwestern Canada's Klondike Region through film presentations, permanent exhibits, and gold-panning demonstrations. ⊠ *117 S. Main St.,* ☎ *206/ 553–7220.* ▧ *Free.* ⏱ *Daily 9–5.*

Pioneer Square District. The ornate iron-and-glass pergola at **Pioneer Place,** at 1st Avenue and Yesler Way, marks the site of the pier and sawmill owned by Henry Yesler, one of Seattle's first businessmen. Timber logged off the hills was sent to the sawmill on a "skid road"—now Yesler Way—made of small logs laid crossways and greased so that the freshly cut trees would slide down to the mill. The area grew into Seattle's first business center; in 1889, a fire destroyed many of the district's wood-frame buildings, but the industrious residents and businesspeople rebuilt them with brick and mortar.

With the 1897 Klondike gold rush, however, this area became populated with saloons and brothels; businesses gradually moved north, and the old pioneering area deteriorated. Eventually, only drunks and bums hung out in the neighborhood that had become known as Skid Row, and the name became synonymous with "down and out." The Pioneer Square District encompasses about 18 blocks and includes restaurants, bars, shops, and the city's largest concentration of art galleries, but it is once again known as a hangout for those down on their luck. Incidents of crime in the neighborhood have increased lately, especially after dark, but few find it intimidating during the day.

⑫ Wing Luke Museum. The small but well-organized museum named for the first Asian-American elected official in the Northwest surveys the history and cultures of people from Asia and the Pacific Islands who have settled in the Pacific Northwest. The emphasis here is on how immigrants and their descendants have transformed and been transformed by American culture. The permanent collection includes costumes, fabrics, crafts, basketry, photographs, and Chinese traditional medicines. ⊠ *407 7th Ave. S,* ☎ *206/623–5124.* ▨ *$2.50.* ☺ *Tues.– Fri. 11–4:30, weekends noon–4.*

Capitol Hill Area

With its mix of theaters and churches, coffeehouses and nightclubs, stately homes and student apartments, Capitol Hill demonstrates Seattle's diversity better than any other neighborhood. There aren't many sights in the traditional sense, but you can while away an enjoyable day here and perhaps an even more pleasurable evening.

Numbers in the text correspond to numbers in the margin and on the Downtown Seattle and North Seattle maps.

A Good Walk

If you're prepared for some hills, this walk will give you a great overview of the area. From downtown, walk up Pine Street to the corner of Melrose Avenue, where you can fortify yourself with a jolt of java at the **Bauhaus** coffeehouse. This hip area of the hill is known as the **Pike–Pine corridor** ⑬. Continue east on Pine Street to Broadway and turn left (but don't miss the art deco Egyptian Theater to the right). Passing Seattle Central Community College, you'll cross Denny Way, the unofficial threshold of the **Broadway shopping district** ⑭. After six energetic blocks, the road bears to the right, becoming 10th Avenue East.

You'll notice many beautiful homes on the side streets off 10th Avenue East in either direction as you continue north to Prospect Street. Turn right at Prospect and gird yourself for another hill. Continue on to 14th Avenue East and turn left (north) to enter **Volunteer Park** ⑮. After walking around a picturesque water tower (with a good view from the top), you'll see the **Volunteer Park Conservatory** straight ahead, the **reservoir** to your left, and the **Seattle Asian Art Museum** to your right. Leave the park to the east via Galer Street. At 15th Avenue East, you can turn left (north) to visit **Lakeview Cemetery** (where Bruce Lee lies in repose), or turn right (south) and walk four blocks to shops and cafés. To return to downtown, continue walking south on 15th Avenue East and west on Pine Street (if you've had enough walking, catch Metro Bus 10 at this intersection; it heads toward Pike Place Market). At Broadway, cut one block south to Pike Street for the rest of the walk.

The above tour is a good survey of Capitol Hill, but it's by no means complete. The area's best attraction, the **Washington Park Arboretum** ⑯, is too far to walk; you'll need to take the bus (catch Metro Bus 11 heading northeast along East Madison Street) or drive.

TIMING

Simply walking this tour, which is a bit strenuous, requires about four hours—two if you start and end in the Broadway shopping district. You'll want to allow at least one to two hours for shopping the Pike–Pine corridor and Broadway, one to two hours for the Asian Art Museum, and a half hour for the conservatory. Any time you spend at Bruce Lee's grave site is between you and Mr. Lee. Plan on at least a few hours for a visit to the arboretum, where losing track of time, and yourself, is pretty much the point.

Sights to See

⓮ Broadway shopping district. Seattle's youth-culture, old-money, and gay scenes all converge on the lively stretch of Broadway East between East Denny Way and East Roy Street. A great place to stroll and sip coffee or have a brew, the strip contains the obligatory art-house movie theater (☞ Harvard Exit *in* Nightlife and the Arts, *below*), record shops and new and vintage clothing stores, and plenty of cafés. The three-story Broadway Market (⊠ 401 Broadway E) has the Gap, Urban Outfitters, and other slick merchandisers, along with some smaller boutiques. You won't be able to miss the glaring sign for the open-air **Dick's Drive-In** (⊠ 115 Broadway E). Dropping in for a Dick's Deluxe Burger and a shake at 1 AM is a quintessential Seattle experience.

Lakeview Cemetery. Kung-fu star **Bruce Lee's grave** is the most-visited site at this cemetery directly north of Volunteer Park. Inquire at the office for a map. ⊠ *1554 15th Ave. E,* ☎ *206/322–1582.* 🎟 *Free.* ☉ *Weekdays 9–4:30.*

⓭ Pike–Pine corridor. A hip new center of activity, this strip that runs toward downtown from the south end of the Broadway shopping district holds galleries, thrift shops, music stores, restaurants, and rock clubs.

Seattle Asian Art Museum. This facility in the former Seattle Art Museum holds thousands of paintings, sculptures, pottery, and textiles from China, Japan, India, Korea, and several other southeast Asian countries. You can sip any of nearly three dozen distinctive teas at the tranquil **Kado Tea Garden.** A ticket to the Asian Art Museum is valid for admission to the Seattle Art Museum (☞ Pike Place Market, the Waterfront, and Seattle Center, *above*) if used within one week. ⊠ *Volunteer Park, 1400 E. Prospect St.,* ☎ *206/654–3100.* 🎟 *$6; free 1st Thurs. of month.* ☉ *Tues.–Sun. 10–5 (Thurs. until 9) and some Mon. holidays; call for tour schedule.*

⓯ Volunteer Park. High above the mansions of North Capitol Hill sits 45-acre Volunteer Park, a grassy affair perfect for picnicking, sunbathing, reading, and strolling. It's a mere 108 steps to some great views at the top of the water tower near the main entrance. Beside the lake in the center of the park is the **Seattle Asian Art Museum** (☞ *above*), and across from the museum is the romantic **Volunteer Park Conservatory** (☎ 206/684–4743). The greenhouse, which was completed in 1912, has accumulated its inhabitants largely by donation, including an extensive collection of orchids begun in 1919. Rooms here are dedicated to ferns, palms, cacti, and exotic flowers. Admission is free; hours are seasonal, so call ahead. ⊠ *Park entrance: 14th Ave. E at Prospect St.*

⓰ Washington Park Arboretum. The 200-acre arboretum's Rhododendron Glen and Azalea Way are in full bloom from March through June. During the rest of the year, other plants and wildlife flourish. From March through October, visit the peaceful **Japanese Garden,** a compressed world of mountains, forests, rivers, lakes, and tablelands. The **Graham Visitors Center** at the north end provides explanations of the

North Seattle

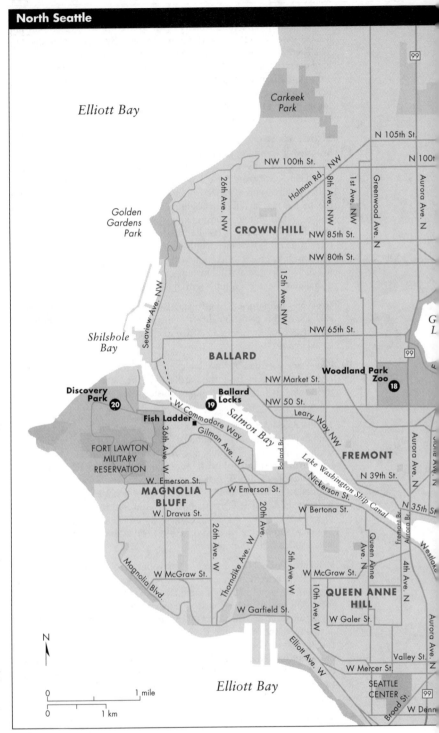

Elliott Bay

Carkeek Park

N 105th St.

NW 100th St.

N 100t

Holman Rd. NW

26th Ave. NW

8th Ave. NW

1st Ave. NW

Greenwood Ave. N

Aurora Ave. N

99

Golden Gardens Park

CROWN HILL

NW 85th St.

NW 80th St.

15th Ave. NW

Seaview Ave. NW

NW 65th St.

Shilshole Bay

BALLARD

G L

99

NW Market St.

Woodland Park Zoo 18

Ballard Locks 19

NW 50 St.

Leary Way NW

Discovery Park 20

Fish Ladder ■

W. Commodore Way

Salmon Bay

36th Ave. W.

Gilman Ave. W.

Ballard Br.

FREMONT

Aurora Ave. N

.uole Ave. N

FORT LAWTON MILITARY RESERVATION

Lake Washington Ship Canal

Nickerson St.

N 39th St.

W. Emerson St.

W Emerson St.

20th Ave.

Fremont Br.

Aurora Br.

Westlake

N 35th St

MAGNOLIA BLUFF

W. Dravus St.

26th Ave. W.

Thorndike Ave. W

W Bertona St.

Queen Anne Ave. N

Magnolia Blvd.

W McGraw St.

5th Ave. W

W McGraw St.

4th Ave. W

10th Ave. W

QUEEN ANNE HILL

Aurora Ave. N

W Garfield St.

W Galer St.

N

Elliott Ave. W

Valley St.

W Mercer St.

Aurora Ave. N

0   1 mile

0   1 km

Elliott Bay

SEATTLE CENTER

99

Broad St.

W Denn

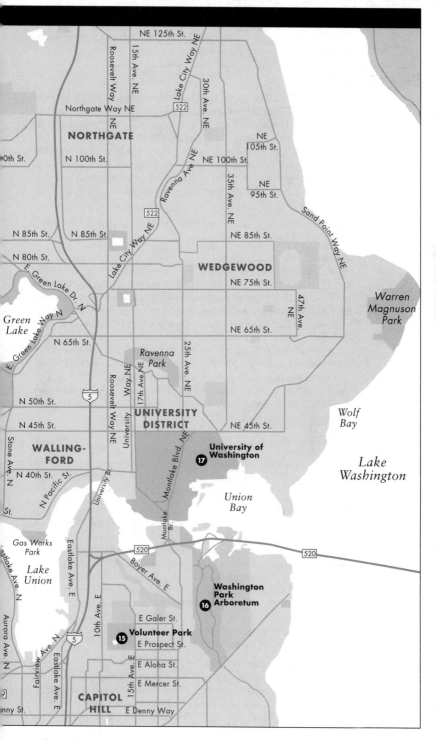

arboretum's flora and fauna and has brochures with self-guided walking tours. Or you can dispense with maps and follow your bliss. ⊠ *2300 Arboretum Dr. E,* ☎ *206/325–4510.* ▧ *Free.* ☉ *Park daily 7 AM–sunset, visitor center daily 10–4.*

University District

The U District, as the University District is known locally, is bounded by Ravenna Boulevard to the north, the Montlake Cut waterway (connecting Lake Union and Lake Washington) to the south, 25th Avenue Northeast to the east, and I–5 to the west. A stroll through the sprawling University of Washington campus can include stops at its museums and other cultural attractions. To get a whiff of the slightly anarchic energy that fuels this part of town, head off campus to "the Ave," the student-oriented shopping area along University Way Northeast.

Numbers in the text correspond to numbers in the margin and on the North Seattle map.

A Good Walk

Start at the corner of Northeast 45th Street and University Way Northeast. Turn left at Northeast Campus Parkway, stopping by the visitor center at the **University of Washington** ⑰. Straight ahead at the end of the block is the **Henry Art Gallery.** Continue east to Central Plaza, better known as **Red Square.** On clear days, you'll be rewarded with views of Mount Rainier to the southeast. Walk down Rainier Vista (past the Frosh Pond and fountain) to Stevens Way, turning left into **Sylvan Grove,** a gorgeous outdoor theater. Return via Rainier Vista to Red Square and strike out due north. A walk along shady Memorial Way past the commuter lot deposits you at the **Burke Museum of Natural History.** From the Burke step out onto Northeast 45th Street, walking two longish blocks to the left to return to University Way Northeast.

TIMING
The route above should only take about two hours, but factor in an hour or so each for the Henry gallery and Burke museum and an additional hour if you want to shop along the Ave. It's quite possible to tour the U District in a long morning or a short afternoon.

Sights to See

The Ave. University Way Northeast, the hub of University of Washington social life, has all the activities (and the grungy edge) one expects in a student-oriented district—great coffeehouses, cinemas (☞ the Grand Illusion *and* Varsity theaters *in* Nightlife and the Arts, *below*), clothing stores, and cheap restaurants, along with panhandlers and pockets of grime. The major action along the Ave is between 42nd and 50th streets, though there are more shops and restaurants as University Way continues north to 58th Street and the entrance to Ravenna Park. Stop in the **Big Time Brewery** (☞ Brew Pubs *in* Nightlife and the Arts, *below*) for a pint of ale and a gallon of local color.

☺ **Museum of History and Industry.** An 1880s-era room and a Seattle time line at this museum depict the city's earlier days. Other displays from the permanent collection are shown on a rotating basis—a recent one surveyed Pacific Coast League baseball teams—along with traveling exhibits. ⊠ *2700 24th Ave. E,* ☎ *206/324–1125.* ▧ *$5.50.* ☉ *Daily 10–5.*

⑰ **University of Washington.** Locals know this university with 35,000 students as "U-Dub." Founded in 1861 downtown, the university moved in 1895 to Denny Hall, the first building on the present campus. The

Alaska-Yukon-Pacific Exposition, which the school hosted in 1909, brought the Northwest national attention. The University of Washington is respected for its research and graduate programs in medicine, nursing, oceanography, drama, physiology, and social work, among many others. Its athletic teams—particularly football and women's basketball—have strong regional followings. A **Visitor Information Center** (⊠ 4014 University Way NE, ☎ 206/543–9198) is open daily from 8 to 5.

Red Square is the nerve center for student activity and politics. The "red" refers to its brick paving, not students' political inclinations—this is a decidedly nonactivist campus, though it's in the square that you'll see animal-rights, environmental, and other advocates attempting to rouse the masses. On sunny days the steps are filled with students sunbathing, studying, or hanging out.

The extensive collection of works by Northwest artists in the **Henry Art Gallery** (⊠ 15th Ave. NE and N.E. 41st St., ☎ 206/543–2280) on the west side of campus includes photography, 19th- and 20th-century paintings, and textiles; the facility often presents important touring exhibitions. Among the improvements that were part of a redesign completed in 1997 were added gallery space and a light-filled central atrium. The Henry is open Tuesday through Sunday from 11 to 5 (Thursday until 8). Admission is $5.

Exhibits at the **Burke Museum of Natural History** (⊠ 17th Ave. NE and N.E. 45th St., ☎ 206/543–5590), on the northwest edge of campus, survey the cultures of the Pacific Northwest and Washington State's 35 Native American tribes. The museum is open daily from 10 until 5 (Thursday until 8). Admission is $3.

OFF THE
BEATEN PATH

WARREN MAGNUSON PARK – Jutting into Lake Washington northeast of the University District, "Sand Point" (as it's called by locals) is one of the best beaches in the city for quiet sunbathing. The sound garden, a grassy area filled with metal sculptures that emit tones when the wind blows, is in the northern part of the park, through the turnstile and across *Moby Dick* Bridge (embedded with quotes from Melville's novel). ⊠ *Park entrance: Sand Point Way NE at 70th St.*

Fremont and Environs

Around Seattle, the word "Fremont" is invariably preceded by the word "funky," "artsy," or "eclectic." And why not? The neighborhood's residents—largely artists—do little to challenge the image. "The Artists Republic of Fremont," as many prefer to call it, brims with sass and self-confidence. Signs on the outskirts proclaim it THE CENTER OF THE UNIVERSE and instruct visitors to set their watches back five minutes, or to throw them away entirely. Given the area's many assets—galleries, restaurants, coffeehouses, brew pubs, antiques shops, and the like—dispensing with time can be a very good idea. To the east of Fremont is Wallingford, an inviting neighborhood of bungalow homes and boutique shopping. You'll find Phinney Ridge and the Woodland Park Zoo to the north of Fremont. Ballard, a neighborhood with a strong Scandinavian flavor, and the center of Seattle's fishing industry, lies to the west.

Numbers in the text correspond to numbers in the margin and on the North Seattle map.

A Good Tour

Coming from downtown, you'll probably enter Fremont via the **Fremont Bridge,** one of the busiest drawbridges in the world. Central Fremont is tiny and can easily be explored by intuition. Here's one strategy: Proceed north on Fremont Avenue North, turning right at North 35th Street. Walk two blocks to the **Aurora Bridge** (you'll be standing underneath it). Turn left and walk one block, but approach with care: The "Fremont troll"—a whimsical concrete monster that lurks beneath the bridge—jealously guards his Volkswagen Beetle. Head back along North 36th Street, making a hard left at the **statue of Lenin** (seriously) at Fremont Place, the first street after you cross Fremont Avenue North. Walk a half block southeast, go right at the crosswalk, and then make a right onto North 35th Street. At the end of the block is the 53-ft **Fremont Rocket,** officially designating the center of the universe. Walk straight ahead one long block to Phinney Avenue to **Redhook Brewery** (tours are conducted daily) and the **Trolleyman** (☞ Brew Pubs *in* Nightlife and the Arts, *below*). Turn left and continue one block to the **Ship Canal.** On the right is **Canal Park.** Linger there, or turn left onto North 34th Street and return to the Fremont Bridge. On the way you'll pass a parking lot that hosts two important Fremont traditions: the Sunday Flea and Crafts Market (spring to fall, weather permitting) and the Outdoor Cinema (bring a chair on Saturdays after dusk in the summer).

The major Fremont-area attractions are best reached by car, bus, or bike. The **Woodland Park Zoo** ⑱ is due north of Fremont via Fremont Avenue North (catch Bus 5 heading north from the northeast corner of Fremont Avenue North and North 39th Street). The **Ballard Locks** ⑲ are west of Fremont (take Bus 28 from Fremont Avenue North and North 35th Street to Northwest Market Street and 8th Avenue North and transfer to Bus 44 or, on weekdays only, Bus 46, heading west). **Discovery Park** ⑳ is a walk of less than a mile from the south entrance to the Ballard Locks. Head west (right) on Commodore Way and south (left) on 40th Street.

TIMING

The walk above takes an hour at most, but Fremont is meant for strolling, browsing, sipping, and shopping. Plan to spend a full morning or a good part of an afternoon. You could easily spend two hours at the Ballard Locks and several hours at Discovery Park or the zoo.

Sights to See

★ ⓒ ⑲ **Ballard Locks.** Officially the Hiram M. Chittenden Locks, this part of the 8-mi Lake Washington Ship Canal connects Lake Washington and Lake Union with the salt water of Shilshole Bay and Puget Sound. The locks, which were completed in 1917, service 100,000 boats yearly by raising and lowering water levels anywhere from 6 to 26 ft. On the north side of the locks is a 7-acre **ornamental garden** of native and exotic plants, shrubs, and trees. Also on the north side are a staffed visitor center with displays on the history and operation of the locks as well as several fanciful sculptures by local artists. Along the south side is a 1,200-ft promenade with a footbridge, a fishing pier, and an observation deck.

Take some time to watch the progress of fishing boats and pleasure craft through the locks, and then observe how the marine population makes the same journey from salt water to fresh: on the **fish ladder,** whose 21 levels form a gradual incline that allows an estimated half-million salmon and trout each year to swim upstream. Several windows at the waterline afford views of the fish struggling against the current as they migrate to their spawning grounds. Most of the migration takes place from late June through October. (The fish ladder, by the way, is where various attempts are being carried out to prevent sea lions, including the locally notorious Herschel, from depleting the salmon population.)

If you're coming via bus from downtown, take Bus 15 or 18 to the stop at Northwest Market Street and 15th Avenue Northwest and transfer to Bus 44 or (weekdays only) 46 heading west on Market. ⊠ *3015 N.W. 54th St.; from Fremont, head north on Leary Way NW, west on N.W. Market St., and south on 54th St.,* ☎ *206/783–7059.* ☎ *Free.* ☉ *Locks daily 7 AM–9 PM, visitor center June–Sept., daily 10–7; Oct.– May, Thurs.–Mon. 11–5; call for tour information.*

Center for Wooden Boats. Though slightly off the main drag at the south end of Lake Union, the center is a great place to launch your expedition if you're interested in exploring the water (or just the waterfront). You can check out the 1897 schooner *Wawona* and the other historic vessels on display, watch the staff at work on a restoration, or rent a boat at the Oarhouse for a sail around the lake. Picnic facilities are also available. ⊠ *1010 Valley St.,* ☎ *206/382–2628.* ☎ *Free.* ☉ *Memorial Day–Labor Day, daily 11–6 (boat rentals until 7); Labor Day–Memorial Day, daily 11–5 (museum and rentals).*

⓴ Discovery Park. Formerly a military base, Seattle's largest park (520 acres) now serves as a sprawling wildlife sanctuary. Visitors can hike through cool forests, explore saltwater beaches, or take in views of Puget Sound and Mount Rainier. A 2.8-mi trail traverses this urban wilderness. From Fremont, take Leary Way Northwest to 15th Avenue Northwest, turn left, and head south on 15th Avenue over the Ballard Bridge. Turn right onto West Emerson Street, right onto Gilman Avenue West, left onto West Fort Street, and right onto East Government Way. From downtown, take Elliott Avenue north until it becomes 15th Avenue Northwest, turn left onto West Emerson, and follow the previous directions the rest of the way. ⊠ *3801 E. Government Way,* ☎ *206/386– 4236.* ☎ *Free.* ☉ *Park daily 6 AM–11 PM, visitor center daily 8:30–5.*

Fremont Center. The self-styled Republic of Fremont is one of Seattle's most distinctive neighborhoods. The center is an eclectic strip of Fremont Avenue stretching from the Ship Canal at the south end to North 36th Street, with shops and cafés two blocks to either side. The area also contains many lighthearted "attractions," including a statue of Lenin, a 53-ft rocket, and the Fremont troll.

Gasworks Park. Summer afternoons at Gasworks Park, on the north end of Lake Union, bring colorful displays of kites in the air and spinnakers on the water. Get a glimpse of your future (and downtown Seattle) from the locally famous zodiac sculpture at the top of the hill, or feed the ducks at sea (make that *lake*) level. In the summer, Gasworks is the site of outdoor concerts, including an annual Independence Day fireworks display and a performance by the Seattle Symphony with fireworks. ⊠ *N. Northlake Way and Meridian Ave. N.*

Green Lake. Just across Highway 99 (Aurora Avenue North) from the Woodland Park Zoo (☞ *below*), Green Lake is the recreational hub of the city's park system. A 3-mi jogging and bicycling trail rings the lake, and there are facilities for basketball, tennis, baseball, and soccer. The park is generally packed (and the facilities overbooked) on weekday evenings, which has made this the best time for active Seattleites to see and be seen (truth be told, it's something of a young-singles' scene). ⊠ *E. Green Lake Dr. N and W. Green Lake Dr. N.*

☾ ⓲ Woodland Park Zoo. Many of the 300 species of animals in this 92-acre botanical garden roam freely in habitat areas that have won several design awards. The African Savanna, the elephant forest, and the Northern Trail (which shelters brown bears, wolves, mountain goats, and otters) are of particular interest. Wheelchairs and strollers can be rented. A memorial to musician Jimi Hendrix, a Seattle native, overlooks the African Savanna exhibit; appropriately enough, it's a big rock. ⊠ *5500 Phinney Ave. N,* ☎ *206/684–4800.* 🖭 *$8.* ☾ *Mid-Mar.–mid-Oct., daily 9:30–6; mid-Oct.–mid-Mar., daily 9:30–4.*

On Seattle's Outskirts and Beyond

Chateau Ste. Michelle Winery. One of the oldest wineries in the state is 15 mi northeast of Seattle on 87 wooded acres that were once part of the estate of lumber baron Fred Stimson. Trout ponds, a carriage house, a caretaker's cottage, formal gardens, and the 1912 family manor house—which is on the National Register of Historic Places—are part of the original estate. Visitors are invited to picnic and explore the grounds; the wine shop sells delicatessen items. During the summer, Chateau Ste. Michelle hosts nationally known performers and arts events in its amphitheater. ⊠ *14111 N.E. 145th St., Woodinville,* ☎ *206/488–1133. From downtown Seattle take I–90 east to north I–405. Take Exit 23 east (S.R. 522) to the Woodinville exit. Complimentary wine tastings and cellar tours daily 10–4:30, except holidays.*

Jimi Hendrix Grave Site. The famed guitarist's grave is in Greenwood Cemetery in Renton. From Seattle, take I–5 south to the Renton exit, then I–405 past Southcenter to Exit 4B. Bear right under the freeway. Take a right onto Sunset Boulevard and another right one block later at 3rd Street. Continue 1 mi, turning right at the third light. ⊠ *Corner of 3rd and Monroe Sts.,* ☎ *206/255–1511.* ☾ *Daily until dusk. Inquire at the office; a counselor will direct you to the site.*

★ ☾ **Museum of Flight.** Boeing, the world's largest builder of aircraft, is based in Seattle, so it's not surprising that this facility at Boeing Field is one of the city's best museums, and one that kids particularly enjoy. The Red Barn, Boeing's original airplane factory, houses an exhibit on the history of human flight. The Great Gallery, a dramatic structure designed by Seattle architect Ibsen Nelson, contains more than 20 vintage airplanes. ⊠ *9404 E. Marginal Way S (take I–5 south to exit 158; turn right on Marginal),* ☎ *206/764–5720.* 🖭 *$8.* ☾ *Daily 10–5 (Thurs. until 9).*

DINING

See the Downtown Seattle and Capitol Hill Dining map to locate restaurants in those areas and the North Seattle Dining map for establishments north of the Lake Washington Ship Canal and Union Bay.

CATEGORY	COST*
$$$$	over $35
$$$	$25–$35
$$	$15–$25
$	under $15

per person for a three-course meal, excluding drinks, service, and sales tax (about 9.1%; varies slightly by community)

Downtown Seattle and Capitol Hill

American

$$$ ✕ **Metropolitan Grill.** Meals at this favorite lunching spot of the white-
★ collar crowd are not for timid eaters: Custom-aged mesquite-broiled steaks—the best in Seattle—are huge and come with baked potatoes or pasta. Even the veal chop is extra thick. Lamb, chicken, and seafood entrées are also on the menu. Among the accompaniments, the onion rings and the sautéed mushrooms are tops. ⊠ *818 2nd Ave.,* ☎ *206/ 624–3287. AE, D, DC, MC, V. No lunch weekends.*

$$–$$$$ ✕ **Wolfgang Puck Cafe.** A laid-back, amiable staff serves postmodern
★ comfort food—barbecued-duck quesadillas, jerk-chicken Caesar salads, linguine with seared jumbo sea scallops—at this vivacious Puck enterprise across 1st Avenue from the Seattle Art Museum. You can slurp down some oyster shooters or "sip" a jumbo gulf-shrimp "martini" at the seafood bar. ⊠ *1225 1st Ave., ☎ 206/621–9653. AE, D, DC, MC, V.*

Asian

$$$ ✕ **Wild Ginger.** The seafood and Southeast Asian fare at this restaurant near Pike Place Market ranges from mild Cantonese to spicier Vietnamese, Thai, and Korean dishes. House specialties include *satay* (chunks of beef, chicken, or vegetables skewered and grilled, and usually served with a spicy peanut sauce), live crab, sweetly flavored duck, wonderful soups, and some fine vegetarian options. The satay bar, where you can sip local brews and eat skewered tidbits until 2 AM, is a local hangout. The clubby, old-fashioned dining room has high ceilings and lots of mahogany and Asian art. ⊠ *1400 Western Ave., ☎ 206/623–4450. AE, D, DC, MC, V. No lunch Sun.*

$ ✕ **Noodle Ranch.** Tongue planted firmly in cheek, Noodle Ranch bills itself as Belltown's purveyor of "Pan-Asian vittles." Standouts on the inexpensive menu include sugar-cane shrimp, Japanese eggplant in ginger, and a spicy basil stir-fry. The sense of humor evident in the name is borne out in the freewheeling decor. ⊠ *2228 2nd Ave., ☎ 206/728–0463. AE, MC, V. Closed Sun.*

Chinese

$ ✕ **Chau's Chinese Restaurant.** This small, very plain place on the northwest edge of Seattle's International District near Pioneer Square serves great seafood—steamed oysters in garlic sauce, Dungeness crab with ginger and onion, and geoduck. Avoid the standard Cantonese dishes and stick to the seafood and specials. ⊠ *310 4th Ave. S, ☎ 206/621–0006. MC, V. No lunch weekends.*

Deli

$ ✕ **Bakeman's Restaurant.** Low on frills but high on atmosphere, this well-lighted lunchery attracts a steady stream of business suits with its signature turkey and meat-loaf sandwiches, served on fluffy white bread. Bakeman's, open weekdays from 10 to 3, is within easy striking distance of Pioneer Square, but the feel here is far from touristy. ⊠ *122 Cherry St., ☎ 206/622–3375. Reservations not accepted. No credit cards. Closed weekends. No dinner.*

Eclectic

$$$$ ✕ **Fullers.** Consistently ranked at or near the top of Seattle's restau-
★ rants in local and national publications, Fullers delivers a rare commodity: a dining experience of exceptional poise and restraint born of unconventional, even visionary, risk-taking. The menu, a playground for acclaimed chef Monique Andrée Barbeau, is a perpetual work-in-progress that always seems exquisitely finished; with evident humor, Barbeau calls her cuisine "Americanized Northwest gourmet with French techniques, Pacific Rim influences, and some rustic touches." Among the signature dishes are Moroccan-spiced quail with preserved lemons and oregano, house-marinated kasu salmon with gingered Asian slaw, and herb-encrusted sea scallops with curried pesto broth. Works by Northwest artists adorn an otherwise austere dining room. ⊠ *Seattle Sheraton Hotel and Towers, 1400 6th Ave., ☎ 206/447–5544. Reservations essential. AE, D, DC, MC, V. Closed Sun. No lunch Sat.*

$$$–$$$$ ✕ **Axis.** Restaurant as theater is the angle at this Belltown restaurant with a wood-fire grill—diners can view the kitchen from just about every

Downtown Seattle and Capitol Hill Dining

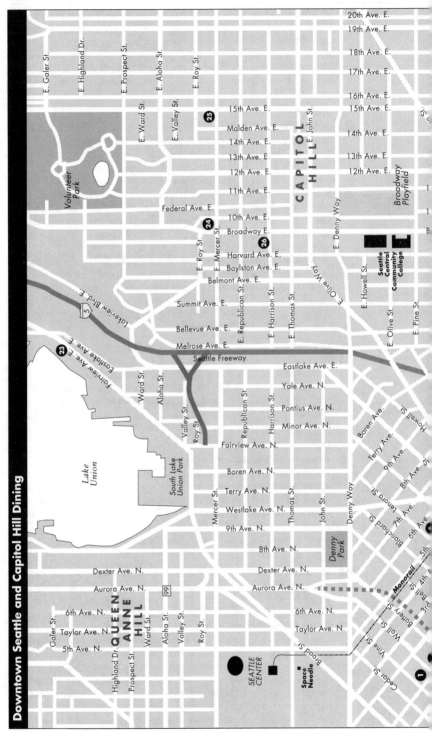

20th Ave. E.
19th Ave. E.
18th Ave. E.
17th Ave. E.
16th Ave. E.
15th Ave. E.
14th Ave. E.
13th Ave. E.
12th Ave. E.

E. Galer St.
E. Highland Dr.
E. Prospect St.
E. Aloha St.
E. Roy St.

E. Ward St.
E. Valley St.

CAPITOL HILL

John St.

Broadway
Playfield

15th Ave. E.
Malden Ave. E.
14th Ave. E.
13th Ave. E.
12th Ave. E.
11th Ave. E.

Volunteer
Park

Federal Ave. E.

10th Ave. E.
Broadway E.
Harvard Ave. E.
Boylston Ave. E.
Belmont Ave. E.

E. Denny Way

Seattle
Central
Community
College

E. Roy St.
E. Mercer St.

Summit Ave. E.

E. Republican St.
E. Harrison St.
E. Thomas St.

E. Olive Way

E. Howell St.

Lakeview Blvd. E.

5

Bellevue Ave. E.

Melrose Ave. E.

Seattle Freeway

E. Olive St.
E. Pine St.

Fairview Ave. E.
Eastlake Ave. E.

Eastlake Ave. E.
Yale Ave. N.
Pontius Ave. N.
Minor Ave. N.

Ward St.
Aloha St.

Valley St.
Roy St.

Republican St.
Harrison St.

Fairview Ave. N.

Boren Ave. N.

Boren Ave.
Terry Ave.
9th Ave.

Howell St.

**Lake
Union**

South Lake
Union Park

Mercer St.
Terry Ave. N.
Westlake Ave. N.
9th Ave. N.

Thomas St.
John St.

Denny Way

8th Ave.
Lenora St.

7th Ave.
Blanchard St.

8th Ave. N.

Denny
Park

6th Ave.
Bell St.
Battery St.

Dexter Ave. N.
Aurora Ave. N.

Dexter Ave. N.
Aurora Ave. N.

Aurora Ave. N.

Monorail

Wall St.

Galer St.
Taylor Ave. N.
5th Ave. N.

6th Ave. N.
Taylor Ave. N.

Vine St.
Cedar St.

Highland Dr.
Prospect St.
Ward St.
Aloha St.
Valley St.
Roy St.

**QUEEN
ANNE
HILL**

99

6th Ave. N.

Broad St.

**SEATTLE
CENTER**

Space
Needle

23
24
25
26
1

167

Andaluca, **10**
Axis, **5**
Bakeman's Restaurant, **21**
Betay Avone, **4**
Campagne, **13**
Chau's Chinese Restaurant, **28**

Dahlia Lounge, **9**
Chutney's, **25**
Emmett Watson's Oyster Bar, **12**
Etta's Seafood, **7**
Fullers, **14**
Gravity Bar, **26**

Hunt Club, **18**
Il Terrazzo Carmine, **22**
Lampreia, **2**
Marco's Supper Club, **1**
Metropolitan Grill, **20**

Nikko, **8**
Noodle Ranch, **3**
Painted Table, **19**
Palace Kitchen, **6**
The Pink Door, **11**
Place Pigalle, **16**
Saigon Gourmet, **29**
Siam, **23, 24**

Takara, **15**
Wild Ginger, **17**

seat in the house. But the cuisine proves worthy of the show, with appetizers like crispy eggplant wonton and an entrée of oven-roasted Dungeness crab with Cajun seasonings. ⊠ *2214 1st Ave.,* ☎ *206/441–9600. Reservations essential. AE, DC, MC, V. No lunch.*

$$$ ✕ **Andaluca.** Chef Don Curtiss oversees the kitchen at this secluded spot downstairs at the Mayflower Park Hotel. A synthesis of fresh local ingredients and Mediterranean techniques, the fare includes small plates that can act as starters or be combined to make a satisfying meal. A Dungeness crab tower with avocado, hearts of palm, and gazpacho salsa is cool and light, while the Cabrales crusted beef tenderloin with pears and blue cheese is neither. ⊠ *407 Olive Way,* ☎ *206/382–6999. AE, D, DC, MC, V.*

$$$ ✕ **Palace Kitchen.** The latest venture of Tom Douglas, who's also the
★ chef-owner of Dahlia Lounge and Etta's Seafood (☞ *below*), is simultaneously chic and convivial. The star of the stylish room may be the 45-ft bar, but the real show takes place within the giant open kitchen at the back. Sausages, sweet-pea ravioli, salmon carpaccio, and a nightly selection of exotic cheeses vie for your attention on an ever-changing menu of small plates, a few entrées, and 10 fantastic desserts. There's always a rotisserie special from the apple-wood grill as well. Especially rare for early-to-bed Seattle, dinner is served until 1 AM. ⊠ *2030 5th Ave.,* ☎ *206/448–2001. AE, D, DC, MC, V. No lunch.*

$$ ✕ **Marco's Supper Club.** Multiregional cuisine is the specialty of this casual former tavern with shrimp-color walls and mismatched flatware. Start with the fried sage-leaf appetizer with garlic aioli and salsa, and then move on to sesame-crusted ahi tuna, Jamaican jerk chicken, or a pork porterhouse in an almond mole sauce. ⊠ *2510 1st Ave.,* ☎ *206/ 441–7801. AE, MC, V. No lunch weekends.*

French

$$$$ ✕ **Campagne.** The white walls, picture windows, snowy linens, candles, and fresh flowers at this intimate and urbane restaurant evoke Provence, as does the menu—French cuisine here means the robust flavors of the Midi, not the more polished tastes of Paris. To start, try the seafood sausage or the calamari fillets with ground almonds. Main plates include panfried scallops with a green-peppercorn and tarragon sauce, cinnamon-roasted quail served with carrot and orange essence, and Oregon rabbit accompanied by an apricot-cider and green-peppercorn sauce. Campagne, which overlooks Pike Place Market and Elliott Bay, is open only for dinner, but its sister café serves breakfast and lunch daily. ⊠ *Inn at the Market, 86 Pine St.,* ☎ *206/728–2800. Reservations essential. AE, DC, MC, V. No lunch.*

Indian

$ ✕ **Chutney's.** The local chain (☞ Indian *in* North Seattle Dining, *below*) has a Capitol Hill branch. The outstanding dishes include tandoori halibut and prawns, chicken kabobs, five curries, and rack of lamb. ⊠ *605 15th Ave. E,* ☎ *206/726–1000. AE, D, DC, MC, V.*

Italian

$$$ ✕ **Il Terrazzo Carmine.** On the ground floor of a Pioneer Square office building, this restaurant owes its comfortable but refined ambience to ceiling-to-floor draperies, genteel service, and quiet music. Chef-owner Carmine Smeraldo prepares flavorful chicken dishes with prosciutto and fontina, and his veal baked with spinach and scallops is simply excellent. The pasta dishes are superb. In the summer, you can eat outdoors on a patio that faces a large fountain. ⊠ *411 1st Ave. S,* ☎ *206/ 467–7797. AE, D, DC, MC, V. Closed Sun. No lunch Sat.*

$$ ✕ **The Pink Door.** This restaurant with a "secret" entrance off Post Alley dishes up a generous portion of atmosphere along with solid Italian

fare. The roasted garlic and *tapenada* (a caper, anchovy, and black-olive spread) are eminently sharable appetizers; spaghetti *alla puttanesca* (with anchovies, capers, and tomatoes) and cioppino are the standout entrées. The quirky bar is often crowded with young people, and cabaret acts regularly perform on a small stage in the corner. But the real draw here is the outdoor deck, rimmed in flowers, topped with a canopy of colored lights, and perched perfectly over Pike Place Market, with a terrific view of the water beyond. ⊠ *1919 Post Alley,* ☎ *206/443–3241. AE, MC, V. Closed Sun.–Mon.*

Japanese

$$$ ✕ **Nikko.** Given that the sushi bar is the architectural centerpiece of this restaurant's low-light and black-lacquer decor, it's not surprising that Nikko serves some of the best sushi and sashimi in Seattle. The Kasuzuke cod and teriyaki salmon are also both highly recommended. ⊠ *Westin Hotel, 1900 5th Ave.,* ☎ *206/322–4641. AE, D, DC, MC, V. Closed Sun. No lunch Sat.*

$$ ✕ **Takara.** In full action, the sushi chef here can look like a character from a Japanese wood-block print, perhaps a master swordsman preparing to fight heaven and earth. His real calling, however, is carving up the freshest of seafood for sushi and sashimi. No wonder Japanese businessmen flock here for lunch. The dining room serves classic Japanese dishes using Northwest ingredients. The salmon teriyaki is top-notch, as is the steamed black cod. ⊠ *Pike Pl. Market Hillclimb, 1501 Western Ave.,* ☎ *206/682–8609. AE, MC, V. Closed Sun. in winter.*

Kosher

$$$ ✕ **Betay Avone.** The Mediterranean-inspired dishes at this restaurant inside an unassuming Belltown storefront are administered under rabbinical supervision. Moroccan *bysteeyas* (braised chicken with scallions, cinnamon, cayenne, and cumin wrapped in phyllo) are a fantastic starter, and the salmon fillet with caramelized onions and tahini over couscous is an imaginative spin on a Northwest staple. ⊠ *113 Blanchard St.,* ☎ *206/448–5597. AE, MC, V. No dinner Fri.–Sat., no lunch Fri.–Mon.*

Pacific Northwest

$$$ ✕ **Dahlia Lounge.** Romantic Dahlia worked its magic on Tom Hanks
★ and Meg Ryan in *Sleepless in Seattle*—with valentine-red walls lighted so dimly that you can't see much farther than your dinner companion's eyes, this place is cozy and then some. But the food plays its part, too. Locally legendary crab cakes, served as an entrée or an appetizer, lead an ever-changing regionally oriented menu. Other standouts are seared ahi tuna and near-perfect gnocchi. Desserts that include coconut cream pie and fresh cobblers are among the best in town. Chef-owner Tom Douglas is Seattle's most energetic restaurateur. He also owns Etta's Seafood in Pike Place Market, and the excellent Palace Kitchen on 5th Avenue, but Dahlia is the one to make your heart go pitter-pat. ⊠ *1904 4th Ave.,* ☎ *206/682–4142. Reservations essential. AE, D, DC, MC, V. No lunch weekends.*

$$$ ✕ **Hunt Club.** Dark wood and plush seating provide a comfortable if surprisingly traditional setting for chef Eric Leonard's interpretations of Pacific Northwest meat and seafood. The potato pancakes with caviar and the squash ravioli are excellent starters. Entrées on the seasonal menu include swordfish with an almond-herb crust, pork chops stuffed with artichokes and sun-dried tomatoes, and roast venison with a peppercorn-and-cranberry game-based demi-glace, served with candied yams. ⊠ *Sorrento, 900 E. Madison St.,* ☎ *206/622–6400. AE, DC, MC, V.*

$$$ ✕ **Lampreia.** The beige-and-gold interior of this Belltown restaurant
★   is the perfect backdrop for chef-owner Scott Carsberg's sophisticated
      cuisine. After an appetizer of cream of polenta with shiitake mushrooms,
      try one of the seasonal menu's intermezzo or light main courses—per-
      haps squid and cannelloni filled with salmon—or a full entrée such as
      pheasant with apple-champagne sauerkraut or lamb with pesto and
      whipped potatoes. The clear flavors of desserts like lemon mousse with
      strawberry sauce bring a soothing conclusion to an exciting experience.
      ✉ 2400 1st Ave., ☎ 206/443–3301. Reservations essential. AE, MC,
      V. Closed Sun.–Mon. No lunch.

$$$ ✕ **Painted Table.** Chef Tim Kelly selects the freshest regional ingredi-
      ents for dishes that are served on hand-painted plates. His seasonal menu
      might include spicy rock-shrimp linguine, wild-mushroom risotto, or
      herb-crusted lamb with grilled Japanese eggplant, fennel, and polenta.
      Desserts include a frozen banana soufflé and a jasmine-rice custard made
      with coconut milk. The restaurant's sand-color hues and local artwork
      make for an all-around stylish experience. ✉ Alexis Hotel, 1007 1st
      Ave., ☎ 206/624–3646. Reservations essential. AE, D, DC, MC, V.
      No lunch weekends.

$$$ ✕ **Place Pigalle.** Large windows look out onto Elliott Bay from this
      intimate restaurant tucked behind a meat vendor in Pike Place Mar-
      ket's main arcade; in nice weather, they're left ajar to admit the fresh
      salt breeze. Bright flower bouquets lighten up the café tables, and the
      friendly staff makes you feel right at home. Despite its French name,
      this is a very American restaurant. Seasonal meals showcase seafood
      and regional ingredients. Go for the rich oyster stew, the Dungeness
      crab (available only when it is truly fresh), or the fish of the day baked
      in hazelnuts. ✉ 81 Pike Pl. Market, ☎ 206/624–1756. AE, MC, V.
      Closed Sun.

Seafood

$$$ ✕ **Etta's Seafood.** Tom Douglas's restaurant near Pike Place Market
      has a sleek and slightly whimsical design and views of Victor Stein-
      breuck Park. In season try the Dungeness crab cakes, roasted king salmon
      with cornbread pudding, or the various Washington oysters on the half
      shell. Brunch, served on weekends, always includes zesty seafood
      omelets, but the chef also does justice to French toast, eggs and bacon,
      and Mexican-influenced breakfast fare. ✉ 202 Western Ave., ☎ 206/
      443–6000. AE, D, DC, MC, V.

  $ ✕ **Emmett Watson's Oyster Bar.** This unpretentious spot can be hard
      to find—it's in the back of the Pike Place Market's Soames-Dunn
      Building, facing a small flower-bedecked courtyard—but for Seattleites
      and visitors who know their oysters, it's worth the special effort. Not
      only are the oysters very fresh and the beer icy cold, but both are in-
      expensive and available in any number of varieties. If you don't like
      oysters, try the salmon soup or the fish-and-chips—flaky pieces of fish
      with very little grease. ✉ 1916 Pike Pl., ☎ 206/448–7721. Reserva-
      tions not accepted. No credit cards.

Thai

  $ ✕ **Siam.** Thai cooking is ubiquitous in Seattle—it can almost be con-
      sidered a mainstream cuisine. Start your meal at popular Siam with a
      satay skewer or the city's best tom kah gai, a soup of coconut, lemon-
      grass, chicken, and mushrooms. Entrées include curries, noodle dishes,
      and many prawn, chicken, and fish preparations. You can specify one
      to five stars according to your tolerance for heat. The location on Fairview
      Avenue near Lake Union has a more relaxed atmosphere than the en-
      ergetic Capitol Hill original on Broadway. ✉ 616 Broadway, ☎ 206/

324–0892; 1880 Fairview Ave. E, ☎ *206/323–8101. AE, MC, V. No lunch weekends.*

Vegetarian

$ ✕ **Gravity Bar.** Sprouty sandwiches and other "modern food," all healthful and then some, are dished up at this congenial juice bar with a sci-fi–industrial ambience at its Capitol Hill location. The juices—from all number of fruits and vegetables, solo or in combo form—are often zippier than the solid food, which in the old days would have been called "bland but grand." ✉ *Capitol Hill: 415 Broadway E,* ☎ *206/325–7186. No credit cards.*

Vietnamese

$ ✕ **Saigon Gourmet.** This small café in the International District is
★ about as plain as they get, but the food is superb and incredibly inexpensive. Aficionados make special trips for the Cambodian soup and the shrimp rolls, but also consider the unusual papaya with beef jerky. Parking can be a problem, but the food rewards your patience. ✉ *502 S. King St.,* ☎ *206/624–2611. Reservations not accepted. MC, V. Closed Mon.*

North Seattle

American

$$$$ ✕ **Canlis.** Little has changed at this Seattle institution since the '50s, when steak served by kimono-clad waitresses represented the pinnacle of high living. Recent renovations have made for a less old-boy clubby feel than before, but the restaurant is still very expensive, very good at what it does, and very popular. The view across Lake Union is almost as good as ever, though it now includes a forest of high-rises. Besides the famous steaks, there are equally famous oysters from Quilcene Bay and fresh fish in season. In 1997 the restaurant was one of only five restaurants in the United States to earn a Grand Award from *Wine Spectator* magazine for its wine list and service. ✉ *2576 Aurora Ave. N,* ☎ *206/283–3313. Reservations essential. AE, DC, MC, V. Closed Sun. No lunch.*

$$$ ✕ **Kaspar's.** A decidedly unglamorous atmosphere and its location amid lower Queen Anne Hill's low-rise office buildings and light industry shift the attention at this restaurant where it belongs—on chef-owner Kaspar Donier's finely wrought contemporary cuisine. Seafood, steak, and poultry options abound—the five-course Northwest seafood dinner will prove a lifeline to the indecisive. Its proximity to Seattle Center makes Kaspar's a natural destination before or after your evening's entertainment, but the food insists that you take your time. ✉ *19 W. Harrison St., west of Queen Anne Ave. N,* ☎ *206/298–0123. AE, MC, V. Closed Sun.–Mon. No lunch.*

$$ ✕ **Five Spot.** Just up the hill from Seattle Center, the Five Spot is comfortable and unpretentious. Its regional American menu makes a new stop every four months or so—Little Italy, New Orleans, and Florida are previous ones. The Five Spot is also popular for Sunday brunch. At the restaurant's kitchen cousins, Jitterbug in Wallingford and the Coastal Kitchen in Capitol Hill, the same rotating menu strategy, with more international flavor but equally satisfying results, applies. ✉ *1502 Queen Anne Ave. N,* ☎ *203/285–7768. MC, V. Jitterbug:* ✉ *2114 N. 45th St.,* ☎ *206/547–6313. MC, V. Coastal Kitchen:* ✉ *429 15th Ave. E,* ☎ *206/322–1145. MC, V.*

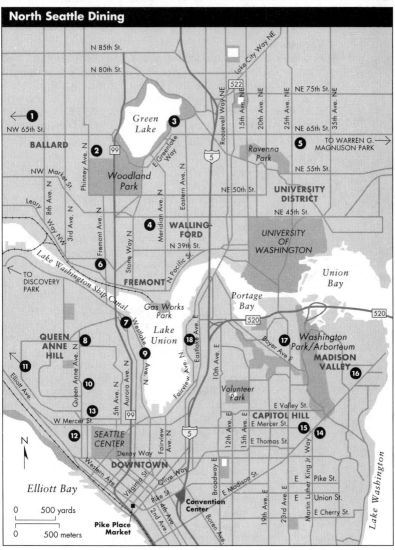

North Seattle Dining

Adriatica, **9**
Bandoleone, **18**
Cactus, **16**
Cafe Flora, **14**
Cafe Lago, **17**
Canlis, **7**
Chutney's, **4, 13**
El Camino, **6**

Five Spot, **10**
Kaspar's, **12**
Palisade, **11**
Pirosmani, **8**
Ray's Boathouse, **1**
Rover's, **15**
Saleh Al Lago, **3**
Santa Fe Cafe, **2, 5**

Eclectic

$$–$$$ ✕ **Bandoleone.** Here's a place that leads a double life. The dining room is simple and austere, even rustic, but the deck out back is festive and fun, decorated with colorful Mexican paper cutouts. Both spaces are perfect for a romantic dinner. Though the prevailing atmosphere at Bandoleone is decidedly unpretentious, the sophisticated menu of large and small plates roams Spain, the Caribbean, and Central and South America. A sweet and clean grilled ahi tuna entrée comes with papaya black-bean salsa; the eggplant relleno is a swampy blend of squash, summer corn, sweet onions, and goat cheese. Tequila-cured salmon gravlax and a banana-macadamia empanada with a tamarind dipping sauce are two of several outstanding tapas. The gravlax also appears on the imaginative and inexpensive menu for Saturday and Sunday brunch (served between 9 AM and 2 PM). ✉ *2241 Eastlake Ave. E,* ☎ *206/329–7559. MC, V. No lunch.*

French

$$$$ ✕ **Rover's.** The restaurant of Thierry Rautereau, one of the Northwest's
★ most imaginative chefs, is an essential destination on any culinary tour of Seattle. Most patrons order off a multicourse tasting menu (vegetarian selections available) of Rautereau's latest creations; sea scallops, venison, squab, lobster, and rabbit are frequent offerings. The incomparable sauce work and reliance on delicacies such as foie gras and truffles pay homage to Rautereau's French roots, but bold combinations of ingredients are evidence of his wanderlust. The service at Rover's is excellent—friendly but unobtrusive—the setting romantic, and the presentation stunning. ✉ *2808 E. Madison St.,* ☎ *206/325–7442. Reservations essential. AE, MC, V. Closed Sun.–Mon. No lunch.*

Georgian

$$$$ ✕ **Pirosmani.** This restaurant in a 1906 house on Queen Anne Hill is named for folk painter Niko Pirosmani. The Georgian dishes are notable for their clever use of herbs and lack of heavy sauces: Duck is seared, then braised with coriander and savory. Skewered lamb is grilled with basil, garlic, and cilantro and served with a plum sauce. Other entrées have their origins in North Africa or the south of France. The signature dessert is a walnut-date rosewater tart, but you wouldn't go wrong with the baklava-ricotta cheesecake either. ✉ *2220 Queen Anne Ave. N,* ☎ *206/285–3360. AE, MC, V. Closed Sun.–Mon. No lunch.*

Indian

$ ✕ **Chutney's.** The aromas of cardamom, cumin, and jasmine wafting through the air may make you feel like you've been transported to another continent. The outstanding dishes include tandoori halibut and prawns, chicken kabobs, five different curries, and rack of lamb. Consistently rated as one of Seattle's top restaurants, Chutney's has a flagship location in Queen Anne, a branch in Wallingford, and another in Capitol Hill (☞ Downtown Seattle and Capitol Hill Dining, *above*). ✉ *Queen Anne: 519 1st Ave. N,* ☎ *206/284–6799.* ✉ *Wallingford: 1815 N. 45th St.,* ☎ *206/634–1000. AE, D, DC, MC, V.*

Italian

$$$ ✕ **Saleh Al Lago.** Some of the best Italian fare in the city can be found north of downtown. The well-lighted dining room here is done in soft colors and, with its view of Green Lake and Woodland Park, invites slow-paced dining. The antipasti, fresh pasta, and veal dishes are always excellent, as is the chef's special ravioli. Even deceptively plain fare like grilled breast of chicken with olive oil and fresh herbs is su-

perb. ⊠ *6804 E. Greenlake Way N,* ☎ *206/522–7943. AE, DC, MC, V. Closed Sun.–Mon. No lunch Sat.*

$$ ✕ **Cafe Lago.** Hugely popular with locals, Cafe Lago specializes in wood-fired pizzas and light handmade pastas. The lasagna—ricotta, béchamel, and cherry-tomato sauce amid paper-thin pasta sheets—perfectly represents the menu's inclination toward the simply satisfying. Spare table settings, high ceilings, and a friendly atmosphere make the restaurant suitable for a night out with friends or a romantic getaway. ⊠ *2305 24th Ave. E,* ☎ *206/329–8005. D, MC, V. Closed Mon. No lunch.*

Mediterranean

$$$ ✕ **Adriatica.** This place gathered a loyal local following, became a virtual Seattle institution, and then was discovered by visitors who spread the word. The dining room and upstairs bar in this hillside Craftsman-style house have terrific views of Lake Union. The fare here could best be described as Pacific Northwest–influenced Greek and Italian cuisine. Regular offerings include fresh fish, pasta, risotto, and seafood souvlaki. Phyllo pastries with honey and nuts are among the tasty dessert choices. ⊠ *1107 Dexter Ave. N,* ☎ *206/285–5000. Reservations essential. AE, DC, MC, V. No lunch.*

Mexican

$$ ✕ **El Camino.** The atmosphere at this loose, loud, and funky Fremont storefront perfectly mirrors El Camino's irreverent Northwest interpretation of Mexican cuisine. Rock-shrimp quesadillas, chipotle-pepper and garlic sea bass, and duck with a spicy green sauce are typical of the gentle spin applied by chef Joe Curry. Even a green salad becomes transformed with toasted pumpkin seeds on crispy romaine with a cool dressing of garlic, lime juice, and cilantro. As for cool, there's no better place to chill on a summer afternoon than El Camino's deck. A tart scratch margarita, served in a pint glass with plenty of ice, makes the perfect accessory. ⊠ *607 N. 35th St.,* ☎ *206/632–7303. AE, DC, MC, V. No lunch weekdays.*

Seafood

$$$ ✕ **Ray's Boathouse.** The view of Puget Sound may be the big draw here, ★ but the seafood is impeccably fresh and well prepared. Perennial favorites include broiled salmon, kasu sake cod, Dungeness crab, and regional oysters on the half shell. Ray's has a split personality: There's a fancy dining room downstairs and a casual café and bar upstairs. In warm weather, you can sit on the deck outside the café and watch the parade of fishing boats, tugs, and pleasure craft floating past, almost right below your table. ⊠ *6049 Seaview Ave. NW,* ☎ *206/789–3770. Reservations essential for dining room; reservations not accepted for café. AE, DC, MC, V.*

$$ ✕ **Palisade.** The short ride to the Magnolia neighborhood yields a stunning view back across Elliott Bay to the lights of downtown. And there's no better place to take in the vista than this restaurant at the Elliott Bay Marina. Palisade scores points for its playfully exotic ambience—complete with a burbling indoor stream. As for the food, the simpler preparations, especially a signature plank-broiled salmon, will prove most satisfying. Maggie Bluffs, an informal café downstairs, is a great spot for lunch on a breezy summer afternoon. ⊠ *2601 W. Marina Pl.; from downtown, take Elliott Ave. northwest across Magnolia Bridge to Elliott Bay Marina exit,* ☎ *206/285–1000. AE, D, DC, MC, V.*

Southwestern

$$ ✕ **Cactus.** It's worth the drive to Madison Park to experience the rich flavors and colorful atmosphere of Cactus. The food, which displays Native American, Spanish, and Mexican influences, will satisfy wide-ranging palates, from the sensibly vegetarian to the utterly carnivorous. From the tapas bar, sample the marinated eggplant, garlic shrimp, or the tuna *escabeche* (spicy cold marinade). Larger plates include the vegetarian chili relleno, the grilled pork with orange and chipotle peppers, and a flavorful ancho-chili and cinnamon roasted chicken. ⊠ *4220 E. Madison St.,* ☎ *206/324–4140. D, DC, MC, V.*

$$ ✕ **Santa Fe Cafe.** Visitors from New Mexico say that this is about as authentic as southwestern fare gets in these parts—maybe because that's where the restaurant buys the red and green chilies for its sauces. Interesting brews on tap help mitigate the heat of such delicious dishes as green-chili burritos made with blue-corn tortillas. Try the red or green enchiladas or house specialties like the artichoke ramekin, the chili-relleno torte, and a roast-garlic appetizer. Of Santa Fe's locations, the 65th Street one, with its woven rugs and dried flowers, is cozier. The Phinney Avenue restaurant is slicker and more chic; skylights bring in rays that further brighten a pink-and-mauve color scheme. ⊠ *2255 N.E. 65th St.,* ☎ *206/524–7736. MC, V. No lunch Sat.–Mon.* ⊠ *5910 Phinney Ave. N,* ☎ *206/783–9755. MC, V. No lunch Sun.–Fri.*

Vegetarian

$$ ✕ **Cafe Flora.** This sophisticated Madison Valley café attracts vegetarians and meat eaters for artistically presented, full-flavored meals. An adventurous menu includes Portobello mushroom Wellington, fajitas, and polenta topped with onion, rosemary, and mushrooms. Sunday brunch draws a crowd. ⊠ *2901 E. Madison St.,* ☎ *206/325–9100. MC, V. Closed Mon. No dinner Sun.*

LODGING

By Julie Fay

Seattle has lodgings to suit most budgets, but though the city has many rooms, you need to book as far in advance as possible if you're coming between May and September. The most elegant properties are downtown; less expensive but still tasteful options, usually smaller in size (and with more of a Seattle feel), can be found in the University District. Many of the lower-price motels along Aurora Avenue North (Highway 99) were built for the 1962 World's Fair. Air travelers often stay along Pacific Highway South (also Highway 99), near Seattle-Tacoma International Airport. Always inquire about special rates based on occupancy or weekend stays; many hotels below give discounts to AARP or AAA members.

CATEGORY	COST*
$$$$	over $170
$$$	$110–$170
$$	$60–$110
$	under $60

All prices are for a standard double room, excluding 15.2% combined hotel and state sales tax.

Downtown

$$$$ ⊞ **Alexis Hotel.** The intimate, European-style Alexis occupies two re-
★ stored buildings near the waterfront. Complimentary sherry awaits you in the lobby bar upon your arrival, a prelude to the attentive service you'll receive throughout your stay at this property managed by the Kimpton Group. Rooms are decorated in subdued colors and imported Italian and French fabrics, with at least one piece of antique furniture. Some suites have whirlpool tubs or wood-burning fireplaces and some have marble fixtures. Unfortunately, views are limited and rooms facing 1st Avenue can be noisy. Amenities include complimen-

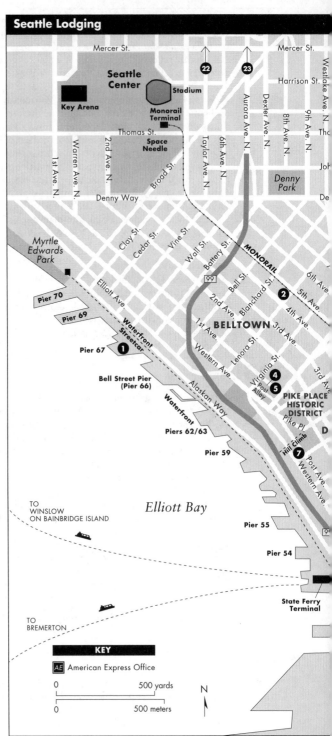

Seattle Lodging

E. Mercer St.

Republican St.

CAPITOL HILL

E. Republican St.

24

25 — 28

E. Harrison St.

E. Thomas St.

E. John St.

29

E. Olive Way

E. Denny Way

Boren Ave.

E. Howell St.

Seattle
Central
Community
College

Broadway
Playfield

30

E. Olive St.

E. Pine St.

E. Pike St.

11

E. Union St.

Washington
State Convention
and Trade
Center

Seattle
University

Freeway
Park

DOWNTOWN

FIRST HILL

Cherry St.

31

Frye Museum
of Art

Madison St.

Marion St.

Columbia St.

E. Jefferson St.

Cherry St.

James St.

Pioneer
Place

15 PIONEER
SQUARE

Yesler Way

Washington St.

Waterfall Garden

Main St.

S. Jackson

INTERNATIONAL
DISTRICT

S. King

Uwajimaya

S. King St.

S. Weller

S. Lane

Kingdome

Airport Way S.

S. Dearborn St.

36 — 42

32 — 35

tary Continental breakfast, shoe shines, the morning newspaper, and access to workout facilities. Pets are welcome. ✉ *1007 1st Ave., 98104,* ☎ *206/624–4844 or 800/426–7033,* ℻ *206/621–9009. 65 rooms, 44 suites. Restaurant, bar, in-room modem lines, minibars, room service, spa, steam room, exercise room, laundry service, meeting rooms, parking (fee). AE, DC, MC, V.*

$$$$ ▦ **Four Seasons Olympic Hotel.** The 1920s Renaissance Revival–style
★ Olympic is the grande dame of Seattle hotels. Marble, wood paneling, potted plants, thick rugs, and plush armchairs adorn the public spaces. Palms and skylights in the Garden Court provide a relaxing background for lunch, afternoon tea, or dancing to a live swing band on the weekends. The Georgian Room, the hotel's premier dining room, exudes Italian Renaissance elegance. The Shuckers oyster bar is more casual. Guest rooms, decorated with period reproductions and floral print fabrics, are less luxurious than the public areas but have a homey feel. All have sofas, comfortable reading chairs, and desks. Amenities include valet parking, chocolates on your pillow, complimentary shoe shines, the morning newspaper, and a bathrobe. ✉ *411 University St., 98101,* ☎ *206/621–1700 or 800/223–8772,* ℻ *206/682–9633. 450 rooms. 3 restaurants, lounge, room service, indoor pool, health club, children's programs, laundry service, concierge, meeting rooms, parking (fee). AE, DC, MC, V.*

$$$$ ▦ **Hotel Monaco.** Seattle's newest luxury hotel, a Kimpton Group
★ property, opened inside a former office building in 1997. The redesign by Cheryl Rowley, who was also responsible for the equally playful Monaco in San Francisco, has a nautical theme. Rooms are plush but have amenities such as voice mail and fax machines that business travelers will appreciate. All rooms have stereos with compact disc players, irons, hair dryers, coffeemakers. The hotel welcomes pets. ✉ *1101 4th Ave., 98101,* ☎ *206/621–1770 or 800/845–2240,* ℻ *206/621–7779. 144 rooms, 45 suites. Restaurant, bar, in-room modem lines, no-smoking rooms, room service, exercise room, dry cleaning, laundry service, concierge, business services, meeting rooms, airport shuttle, parking (fee).*

$$$$ ▦ **Hotel Vintage Park.** As a tribute to the state's growing wine industry, each accommodation in this small hotel is named for a Washington winery or vineyard. The theme is extended to complimentary servings of local wines each evening in the lobby, where patrons can relax on richly upholstered sofas and chairs arranged around a marble fireplace. The rooms, which are decorated in color schemes of dark green, plum, deep red, taupe, and gold, are furnished with custom-made cherry-wood pieces and original works by San Francisco artist Chris Kidd. For literary-minded guests, hotel staff will check out and deliver your choice of titles from the nearby Seattle Public Library. The more athletically inclined can have exercise equipment brought to their rooms. ✉ *1100 5th Ave., 98101,* ☎ *206/624–8000 or 800/624–4433,* ℻ *206/623–0568. 126 rooms. Restaurant, in-room modem lines, minibars, no-smoking floors, refrigerators, room service, spa, laundry service, concierge, meeting rooms, parking (fee). AE, D, DC, MC, V.*

$$$$ ▦ **Sorrento.** The Sorrento, built in 1909 for the Alaska-Yukon Expo-
★ sition, was designed to look like an Italian villa. The dramatic entrance is along a circular driveway around a fountain ringed by palm trees. Sitting high on First Hill, the hotel has views overlooking downtown and Elliott Bay. The rooms, smaller than those in more modern hotels, are nevertheless quiet and comfortable. The largest are the corner suites, which have some antiques and spacious baths. The Hunt Club (☞ Dining, *above*) serves Pacific Northwest dishes. The dark-paneled Fireside Lounge in the lobby is an inviting spot for coffee, tea, or cocktails. Other amenities include complimentary limousine service

within the downtown area and privileges at a nearby athletic club. ⊠ *900 Madison St., 98104,* ☎ *206/622–6400 or 800/426–1265,* 𝔽𝔸𝕏 *206/ 343–6155. 76 rooms, 42 suites. Restaurant, bar, in-room modem lines, minibars, room service, laundry service, concierge, meeting rooms, parking (fee). AE, DC, MC.*

$$$$ ⚏ **Warwick Hotel.** Despite its size, the Warwick has an intimate feel. Service is friendly and leisurely (but not slow), and the rooms are understated without being bland. Most have small balconies with views of downtown. There is live entertainment in the Liaison restaurant and lounge, and 24-hour courtesy transportation within downtown. ⊠ *401 Lenora St., 98121,* ☎ *206/443–4300 or 800/426–9280,* 𝔽𝔸𝕏 *206/448– 1662. 225 rooms, 4 suites. Restaurant, bar, in-room modem lines, no-smoking rooms, room service, indoor pool, hot tub, sauna, exercise room, concierge, parking (fee). AE, D, DC, MC, V.*

$$$$ ⚏ **Westin Hotel.** The flagship of the Westin chain often hosts visiting dignitaries, including U.S. presidents. Just north and east of Pike Place Market, the hotel is easily recognizable by its twin cylindrical towers. With this design, all rooms have terrific views of Puget Sound, Lake Union, the Space Needle, or the city. Airy rooms are furnished in a plain but high-quality style. A number have been turned into guest office rooms equipped with fax machines, speakerphones, and modem hookups. ⊠ *1900 5th Ave., 98101,* ☎ *206/728–1000 or 800/228–3000,* 𝔽𝔸𝕏 *206/ 728–2259. 822 rooms, 43 suites. 3 restaurants, 2 bars, in-room safes, minibars, no-smoking floors, room service, indoor pool, beauty salon, massage, exercise room, children's programs, laundry service, concierge, business services, convention center, car rental, parking (fee). AE, D, DC, MC, V.*

$$$–$$$$ ⚏ **Edgewater.** The spacious accommodations on the waterfront side of the only hotel on Elliott Bay have views of ferries, barges, and the Olympic Mountains. Rooms are decorated in rustic Northwest plaids and light-color unfinished wood furniture. From the lobby's comfortable sofas and chairs, you can sometimes see sea lions frolicking in the bay. A courtesy van shuttles patrons to the downtown area on a first-come, first-served basis. ⊠ *Pier 67, 2411 Alaskan Way, 98121,* ☎ *206/ 728–7000 or 800/624–0670,* 𝔽𝔸𝕏 *206/441–4119. 237 rooms. Restaurant, bar, in-room modem lines, minibars, no-smoking rooms, room service, exercise room, bicycles, laundry service, concierge, meeting rooms, parking (fee). AE, DC, MC, V.*

$$$–$$$$
★ ⚏ **Inn at the Market.** This sophisticated yet unpretentious property just up the street from Pike Place Market is perfect for travelers who prefer originality, personality, and coziness. The good-size rooms are decorated with comfortable modern furniture and small touches such as fresh flowers and ceramic sculptures. Ask for a room with views of the market and Elliott Bay. Coffee and the morning newspaper are complimentary each morning. An added plus is the fifth-floor 2,000-square-ft deck, furnished with Adirondack chairs and overlooking the water and market. Guests have access to a health club and spa. The restaurants here include Campagne (☞ Dining, *above*), its less formal yet equally romantic café spin-off, and Bacco, which serves tasty variations on breakfast classics. ⊠ *86 Pine St., 98109,* ☎ *206/443–3600 or 800/446–4484,* 𝔽𝔸𝕏 *206/448–0631. 55 rooms, 10 suites. 3 restaurants, in-room modem lines, no-smoking rooms, refrigerators, room service, laundry service, concierge, meeting room, parking (fee). AE, D, DC, MC, V.*

$$$–$$$$ ⚏ **Paramount Hotel.** The château-style Paramount opened in 1996 as a companion to the high-tech entertainment sites one block away, including Planet Hollywood, Gameworks, NikeTown, and a 16-screen Cineplex Odeon multiplex. Neither the Paramount nor these facilities have a particularly Seattle feel, but the hotel's lobby is cozy, with a fireplace, bookshelves, and period reproductions lending it the feel of a country gentleman's smoking parlor. Guest rooms, quiet but small, are decorated in hunter green and beige with gray accents. All have work areas, lounge chairs, large bathrooms, and state-of-the-art movie and game systems. ⊠ *724 Pine St., 98101,* ☎ *206/292–9500 or 800/426–0670,* 𝔽𝔸𝕏 *206/292–8610. 146 rooms, 2 suites. Restaurant, in-room modem lines, no-smoking rooms, room service, exercise room, laundry service, concierge, meeting rooms, parking (fee). AE, D, DC, MC, V.*

$$$–$$$$ 🏨 **Seattle Sheraton Hotel and Towers.** Business travelers are the primary patrons of this large hotel near the Washington State Convention & Trade Center. Rooms on the top five floors, larger and more elegant than those on lower floors, include concierge service and complimentary Continental breakfast. Dining options within the complex include Fullers (☞ Dining, *above*), one of Seattle's best restaurants. The Pike Street Cafe serves all-American cuisine in a casual atmosphere. The lobby features an art-glass collection by well-known Northwest artist Dale Chihuly. ⊠ *1400 6th Ave., 98101,* ☎ *206/621–9000 or 800/325–3535,* 𝔽𝔸𝕏 *206/621–8441. 800 rooms, 40 suites. 4 restaurants, 2 bars, in-room modem lines, minibars, room service, indoor pool, health club, laundry service, concierge, meeting rooms, parking (fee). AE, D, DC, MC, V.*

$$$ 🏨 **Crowne Plaza.** This favorite of business travelers is directly off I–5, midway between First Hill and the Financial District. The lobby is small and plainly appointed in teal and cream with brass accents and houseplants. Rooms are quiet and spacious, with views of the Kingdome and Harbor Island to the south and Elliott Bay and the Space Needle to the north; all have lounge chairs and work areas. The relaxed and friendly staff is very attentive. ⊠ *1113 6th Ave., 98101,* ☎ *206/464–1980 or 800/521–2762,* 𝔽𝔸𝕏 *206/340–1617. 415 rooms, 28 suites. Restaurant, bar, in-room modem lines, no-smoking rooms, room service, sauna, health club, laundry service, concierge, business services, meeting rooms, parking (fee). AE, D, DC, MC, V.*

$$$ 🏨 **Madison.** Rooms at this high-rise between downtown and I–5 are decorated in deep green, burgundy, and brown, with metal accents and dark wood furniture. Good views of downtown, Elliott Bay, and the Cascade Range can be had from above the 10th floor—above the 20th they're excellent. Guests on club-level floors (25, 26, and 27) receive complimentary Continental breakfast and have their own concierge. Amenities on other floors include complimentary coffee, the morning newspaper, and shoe shines. The health club has a 40-ft rooftop pool and a hot tub. ⊠ *515 Madison St., 98104,* ☎ *206/583–0300 or 800/278–4159,* 𝔽𝔸𝕏 *206/622–8635. 466 rooms, 88 suites. 2 restaurants, bar, in-room modem lines, minibars, room service, laundry service, concierge, meeting rooms, parking (fee). AE, D, DC, MC, V.*

$$$ 🏨 **Seattle Hilton.** This hotel west of I–5 hosts many conventions and meetings. Tastefully nondescript rooms have soothing color schemes. The Top of the Hilton serves well-prepared salmon dishes and other local specialties and has excellent views of the city. An underground passage connects the Hilton with the Rainier Square shopping concourse, the 5th Avenue Theater, and the Washington State Convention Center. ⊠ *1301 6th Ave., 98101,* ☎ *206/624–0500, 800/542–7700, or 800/426–0535;* 𝔽𝔸𝕏 *206/682–9029. 237 rooms, 3 suites. 2 restaurants, piano bar, in-room modem lines, no-smoking floors, room service, exercise room, laundry service, concierge, meeting rooms, parking (fee). AE, D, DC, MC, V.*

$$$ ⛆ **WestCoast Roosevelt Hotel.** An older hotel near the convention center and the shopping district, the Roosevelt has an elegant lobby with a grand piano, a fireplace, a Chinese lacquered screen, and walls of windows—a great place to relax and watch the foot traffic outside. Small-ish rooms are furnished with period reproduction furniture upholstered in mellow pinks and greens. Thanks to the insulated windows you can enjoy city views without hearing street noise. Some bathrooms have their original tile work, though there isn't much counter space. ⌧ *1531 7th Ave.,* ☎ *206/621–1200 or 800/426–0670,* ℻ *206/233–0335. 138 rooms, 13 suites. Restaurant, bar, in-room modem lines, no-smoking rooms, room service, exercise room, laundry service, meeting rooms, parking (fee). AE, D, DC, MC, V.*

$$–$$$ ⛆ **Mayflower Park Hotel.** The brass fixtures and antiques at this older property near the Westlake Center lend its public and private spaces a muted Asian feel. The service here is unobtrusive and smooth. Rooms are on the small side, but the Mayflower Park is so sturdily constructed that it is much quieter than many modern downtown hotels. Guests have privileges at a nearby health club. ⌧ *405 Olive Way, 98101,* ☎ *206/623–8700 or 800/426–5100,* ℻ *206/382–6997. 159 rooms, 13 suites. Restaurant, bar, no-smoking rooms, room service, exercise room, laundry service, business services, meeting rooms, parking (fee). AE, D, DC, MC, V.*

$$–$$$ ⛆ **Pioneer Square Hotel.** This landmark building was built in 1914 as a workmen's hotel. A mid-1990s renovation trimmed the property down to 75 generously sized rooms, all with private bathrooms. Furnishings are standard issue; the color scheme is predominantly pink. The rooms on the back of the hotel face an air shaft, creating a dark but peaceful refuge. Guests have access to a nearby health club. Room rates include a Continental breakfast. ⌧ *77 Yesler Way, 98104,* ☎ *206/340–1234,* ℻ *206/467–0707. 75 rooms, 3 suites. Coffee shop, pub, in-room modem lines, no-smoking rooms, room service, laundry service, concierge, business services, meeting rooms, parking (fee). AE, D, DC, MC, V.*

$$ ⛆ **Pacific Plaza.** This 1929 property that retains a '20s–'30s feel is a good bargain for singles or couples; families may find the nondescript rooms too small to accommodate them. A renovation of the hotel is scheduled for 1998. Room rates include a Continental breakfast. ⌧ *400 Spring St., 98104,* ☎ *206/623–3900 or 800/426–1165,* ℻ *206/623–2059. 159 rooms. Restaurant, coffee shop, pizzeria, no-smoking rooms, concierge, parking (fee). AE, D, DC, MC, V.*

$$ ⛆ **Pensione Nichols.** The bad news first: This eclectic B&B occupies the top two floors above an adult movie theater. But the location one block from Pike Place Market can't be beat, and this stretch of 1st Avenue is hardly run-down; the unobtrusive theater is almost out of place. Suites on the second floor have enclosed balconies, full-size kitchens, private baths, separate bedrooms, and large open living rooms. Most rooms on the third floor have skylights rather than windows and are decorated in light colors with antique and contemporary furnishings. ⌧ *1923 1st Ave., 98101,* ☎ *206/441–7125 or 800/440–7125. 10 rooms share 4 baths, 2 suites. AE, D, DC, MC, V.*

$$ ⛆ **WestCoast Camlin Hotel.** The lobby of this 1926 apartment-hotel on the edge of downtown but near the convention center has Oriental carpets, large mirrors, and lots of marble. Rooms ending with the number 10 are the best—they have windows on three sides. All rooms have work spaces with a chair and a table, and a cushioned chair to relax in. One drawback here is the noisy heating, air-conditioning, and ventilation system, but these along with the rest of the hotel are slated for upgrading in 1998. ⌧ *1619 9th Ave., 98101,* ☎ *206/682–0100* or 800/426–0670, FAX 206/682–7415. *132 rooms, 4 suites. Restaurant, bar, in-room modem lines, room service, outdoor pool, dry cleaning, concierge, meeting rooms. AE, D, DC, MC, V.*

$ 🏨 **Seattle YMCA.** Rooms at this member of the American Youth Hostels Association are clean and plainly furnished with a bed, a phone, a desk, and a lamp—all for about $40. Three bunk units, designed to accommodate four people each, cost about $20. ⊠ *909 4th Ave., 98104,* ☎ *206/382–5000. 3 rooms with private bath, 186 rooms with shared baths. Pool, health club, coin laundry. D, MC, V.*

$ 🏨 **Youth Hostel: Seattle International.** You can bed down in dormitory style for about $20 a night at this hostel near Pike Place Market. Guests have kitchen and dining-room access. ⊠ *84 Union St., 98101,* ☎ *206/622–5443. 3 rooms, 191 dormitory beds share baths. Library, coin laundry. AE, MC, V.*

Capitol Hill

$$–$$$ 🏨 **Gaslight Inn.** The Capitol Hill district contains many trendy shop-
★   ping, restaurant, and night-life establishments, all of which are within walking distance of this B&B. Rooms range from a cozy crow's nest with peeled-log furniture and Navajo-print fabrics to suites with gas fireplaces and antique carved beds. There's also an apartment with a blown-glass chandelier and an expansive view of downtown and Elliott Bay. The large common areas have a masculine feel, with oak wainscoting, animal statuary, high ceilings, and hunter-green carpeting. One owner's past career as a professional painter is evident in the impeccable custom-mixed finishes throughout the inn. Room rates include a Continental breakfast and use of a laundry room; suite rates include the same amenities and off-street parking. ⊠ *1527 15th Ave., 98122,* ☎ *206/325–3654,* FAX *206/328–4803. 9 rooms, 7 suites. No-smoking rooms, pool. AE, MC, V.*

$–$$ 🏨 **Hill House.** Ken Hayes and Eric Lagasca operate this Capitol Hill B&B in an impeccably restored 1903 Victorian. Rooms, painted in rich colors, contain a mix of antique and contemporary furnishings. Two suites have phones and televisions. That the rates here include a filling breakfast and free off-street parking makes this one of the city's best bargains. Book well in advance for summer weekends. ⊠ *1113 E. John St.,* ☎ *206/720–7161 or 800/720–7161,* FAX *206/323–0772. 5 rooms, 3 with private bath. Free parking. AE, D, MC, V.*

Queen Anne Hill and Fremont

$$$ 🏨 **Williams House.** Something is usually in bloom year-round in the beautiful garden that surrounds this Queen Anne Hill mansion. Carved lions with fangs said to bring good luck to those who rub them flank the entryway fireplace. The living and dining rooms have high ceilings, antique furnishings, hardwood floors, and plush carpeting. Guest rooms are small but have good views. The Brass and Satin Room overlooking the rose arbor has a romantic view of the city beyond. The Skyline Room has an unusually good angle on the Space Needle. Room rates include a Continental breakfast. Children are welcome with prior notice. ⊠ *1505 4th Ave. N, 98109,* ☎ *206/285–0810 or 800/880–0810,* FAX *206/285–8526. 5 rooms. Free parking. AE, D, MC, V.*

$$ 🏨 **Chelsea Station.** The feel is very Seattle at this B&B across the street from the Woodland Park Zoo. The parlor and breakfast rooms are decorated in sage green with mission-oak furniture, brocade upholstery, lace curtains, and works by local artists. Spacious guest rooms, each with a phone and a writing desk, have antique and contemporary furnishings. The accommodations in front have views of the

Cascade Range. One suite has an 1800s pump organ, another a kitchen. Several rooms have adjoining doors, useful for families or larger groups. Room rates include a full breakfast, tailored to your special dietary needs upon request. ✉ *4915 Linden Ave. N, 98103,* ☎ *206/547–6077 or 800/400–6077,* FAX *206/632–5107. 2 rooms, 6 suites. In-room modem lines. AE, D, DC, MC, V.*

University District and Lake Union

$$$ 🖭 **Marriott Residence Inn.** An extended-stay hotel on scenic Lake Union, the Marriott is a perfect choice for families. All rooms are either one- or two-bedroom suites, each with a living room, a fully equipped kitchen, and a breakfast bar. Decorated in greens and blues, the comfortable suites get plenty of natural light. The lobby is within a seven-story atrium with a waterfall and many areas to relax, watch TV, play games, or look up recipes in cookbooks displayed on bookshelves. Room rates include Continental breakfast and complimentary shuttle service within a 2½-mi radius of the hotel. ✉ *800 Fairview Ave. N, 98109,* ☎ *206/624–6000 or 800/331–3131 (central reservations),* FAX *206/223–8160. 234 suites. Room service, no-smoking rooms, indoor pool, sauna, spa, exercise room, children's programs, parking (fee). AE, D, DC, MC, V.*

$$ 🖭 **Chambered Nautilus.** A resident teddy bear will keep you company at this Georgian Colonial B&B that was built in 1915 by a professor of Asian studies at the University of Washington. Rooms all have private baths, some with antique dressers converted to serve as sinks and counters. Most rooms have private porches, and all come with robes and a well-stocked bookshelf. Breakfast might include stuffed French toast with orange syrup, rosemary buttermilk biscuits, or a breakfast pie made with salmon, dill, and Swiss cheese. ✉ *5005 22nd Ave. NE, 98105,* ☎ *206/522–2536,* FAX *206/528–0898. 6 rooms. AE, MC, V.*

$$ 🖭 **Edmond Meany Tower Hotel.** This 1931 property within blocks of the University of Washington underwent a $5.5 million restoration in 1997. Though the results were mixed, the hotel remains an important neighborhood landmark. Large-size rooms have fine views of the university campus, Mount Rainier, Green Lake, or Lake Union. Soothing shades of white bathe the rooms—green upholstered headboards and bright-red lounge chairs provide a striking contrast. The hallways are painted a none-too-subtle traffic-sign yellow. Our visit came while construction was still under way—the staff appeared stressed and the service was uneven. ✉ *4507 Brooklyn Ave. NE, 98105,* ☎ *206/634– 2000 or 800/899–0251,* FAX *206/547–6029. 155 rooms. Restaurant, bar, in-room modem lines, no-smoking rooms, room service, exercise room, laundry service, concierge, meeting rooms, free parking. AE, DC, MC, V.*

$$ 🖭 **University Inn.** The no-nonsense accommodations at this modern hotel have writing desks and are decorated in light wood and floral patterns. Some rooms have decks. Units in back are quieter. The rates include a Continental breakfast. Enjoy the hot tub year-round and the outdoor pool in season. ✉ *4140 Roosevelt Way NE, 98105,* ☎ *206/ 632–5055 or 800/733–3855,* FAX *206/547–4937. 102 rooms. Restaurant, in-room modem lines, in-room safes, no-smoking floors, outdoor pool, hot tub, exercise room, coin laundry, dry cleaning, meeting rooms, free parking. AE, D, DC, MC, V.*

$$ 🖭 **University Plaza Hotel.** Families and business travelers like this full-service motor hotel just across I–5 from the University of Washington campus. The mock-Tudor decor gives the place a dated feel, but the service is cheerful and the rooms are spacious and pleasantly decorated in teak furniture. Ask for a room away from the freeway. ✉ *400 N.E.*

45th St., 98105, ☎ 206/634–0100 or 800/343–7040, ⁛ 206/633–2743. 135 rooms. Restaurant, bar, no-smoking rooms, room service, pool, beauty salon, exercise room, meeting rooms, free parking. AE, D, DC, MC, V.

Seattle-Tacoma International Airport

$$$ ⌂ **Doubletree Hotel Seattle Airport.** The Doubletree is a full-service convention hotel. Rooms, large and bright, all have balconies—corner "King Rooms" have wraparound ones with great views. Furnishings include chests of drawers, comfortable chairs, a dining table, and a desk. ✉ *18740 Pacific Hwy. S, 98188, ☎ 206/246–8600, ⁛ 206/431–8687. 837 rooms, 13 suites. 3 restaurants, 2 bars, in-room modem lines, room service, outdoor pool, beauty salon, exercise room, laundry service, meeting rooms, airport shuttle, parking (fee). AE, D, DC, MC, V.*

$$$ ⌂ **Marriott Sea-Tac.** The luxurious Marriott has a five-story, 21,000-★ square-ft tropical atrium that's complete with a waterfall, a dining area, an indoor pool, and a lounge. Rooms are decorated in greens and mauve with dark wood and brass furnishings. ✉ *3201 S. 176th St., 98188, ☎ 206/241–2000 or 800/643–5479, ⁛ 206/248–0789. 459 rooms. Restaurant, lobby lounge, in-room modem lines, no-smoking rooms, room service, indoor pool, hot tubs, sauna, health club, video games, laundry service, concierge, meeting rooms, airport shuttle, free parking. AE, D, DC, MC, V.*

$$$ ⌂ **Seattle Airport Hilton.** With its cozy lobby fireplace and paintings of Northwest scenery, this hotel, only a half-hour drive from downtown, has a surprisingly intimate feel. Large rooms are bright and decorated in pastel colors. ✉ *17620 Pacific Hwy. S, 98188, ☎ 206/244–4800, ⁛ 206/248–4499. 175 rooms, 3 suites. Restaurant, bar, in-room modem lines, pool, exercise room, coin laundry, laundry service, concierge, business services, meeting rooms, airport shuttle, free parking. AE, D, DC, MC, V.*

$$$ ⌂ **Wyndham Garden Hotel.** This hotel has the most convenient airport access. The elegant lobby has a fireplace, a marble floor, and comfortable furniture. Rooms have large desks, overstuffed chairs, irons and boards, coffeemakers, and hair dryers. ✉ *18118 Pacific Hwy. S, 98188, ☎ 206/244–6666, ⁛ 206/244–6679. 180 rooms, 24 suites. Restaurant, lobby lounge, in-room modem lines, no-smoking floors, room service, indoor pool, exercise room, coin laundry, laundry service, meeting rooms, airport shuttle, free parking. AE, D, DC, MC, V.*

$$–$$$ ⌂ **Doubletree Inn, Doubletree Suites.** These two hotels across the street from each other are adjacent to the Southcenter shopping mall and convenient to business-park offices. The Inn is a classic Pacific Northwest–style lodge—its rooms are smaller and less lavish than those at the Suites, but they're perfectly fine and cost at least $25 less. Accommodations at the Suites all have a sofa, a table and chairs, and a wet bar. The vanity area includes a full-size closet with mirrored doors. ✉ *Doubletree Inn, 205 Strander Blvd., 98188, ☎ 206/575–8220 or 800/325–8733, ⁛ 206/575–4743. 193 rooms, 5 suites. Bar, coffee shop, dining room, indoor pool, outdoor pool, meeting rooms, airport shuttle, free parking. ✉ Doubletree Suites, 16500 Southcenter Pkwy., 98188, ☎ 206/575–8220 or 800/325–8733, ⁛ 206/575–4743. 221 suites. Restaurant, bar, refrigerators, indoor pool, hot tub, sauna, health club, racquetball, meeting rooms, airport shuttle, free parking. AE, D, DC, MC, V.*

$$ ⌂ **WestCoast Gateway Hotel.** Perfect for the traveler catching an early flight, this hotel contains quiet rooms in shades of burgundy and gray. All have coffeemakers; rates include a Continental breakfast. ✉ *18415*

Pacific Hwy. S, 98188, ☎ *206/248–8200 or 800/426–0670,* FAX *206/ 244–1198. 145 rooms. Breakfast room, in-room modem lines, no-smoking floors, room service, exercise room, dry cleaning, meeting room, airport shuttle, free parking. AE, D, DC, MC, V.*

$$ ⌂ **WestCoast Sea-Tac Hotel.** The enthusiastic and helpful staff at this conveniently located property make it attractive to the business or leisure traveler. Guests are welcome to play the baby grand piano in the small but comfortable lobby. All rooms come equipped with Nintendo systems. Rooms in the rear have views of Bow Lake. ⌧ *18220 International Blvd., 98188,* ☎ *206/246–5535 or 800/426–0670,* FAX *206/ 246–9733. 146 rooms. Restaurant, bar, room service, outdoor pool, hot tub, sauna, exercise room, business services, meeting rooms, airport shuttle, free parking. AE, D, DC, MC, V.*

Bellevue/Kirkland

$$$–$$$$ ⌂ **Doubletree Hotel Bellevue.** The 10-story Doubletree has an airy atrium filled with trees, shrubs, and flowering plants. The property also has a formal dining room, a lounge with two dance floors, and oversize guest rooms decorated in hunter green, burgundy, and beige. Rooms have either king- or queen-size beds. Two-room suites contain wet bars and whirlpool tubs. ⌧ *300 112th Ave. SE, Bellevue 98004,* ☎ *425/ 455–1300 or 800/733–5466,* FAX *425/455–0466. 348 rooms, 5 suites. 2 restaurants, bar, in-room modem lines, room service, outdoor pool, exercise room, laundry service, concierge, business services, meeting rooms, free parking. AE, D, DC, MC, V.*

$$$–$$$$ ⌂ **Hyatt Regency Bellevue.** This deluxe high-rise complex is in the heart of downtown Bellevue, within a few blocks of Bellevue Square and other shopping centers. The exterior looks pretty much like any other sleek high-rise, but the interior has Asian touches such as antique Japanese chests and huge displays of fresh flowers. The rooms are decorated in similarly understated ways, with floor-to-ceiling windows and dark wood and earth tones predominating. The service is impeccable. Deluxe suites include two bedrooms, bar facilities, and meeting rooms with desks and full-length tables; business-plan rooms have modem lines. Guests have access to a health club and pool. The restaurant serves excellent and reasonably priced breakfast, lunch, and dinner; an English-style pub and sports bar serves lunch and dinner. ⌧ *900 Bellevue Way NE, 98004,* ☎ *425/462–2626,* FAX *425/646–7567. 353 rooms, 29 suites. Restaurant, sports bar, no-smoking rooms, room service, concierge, meeting rooms, parking (fee). AE, D, DC, MC, V.*

$$$–$$$$ ⌂ **Woodmark Hotel.** Only steps away from downtown Kirkland, 7 mi
★ east of Seattle, this hotel is the only one on the shores of Lake Washington. Its contemporary-style rooms, which face the water, a courtyard, or the street, are done in exquisite shades of café au lait, taupe, and ecru. The numerous amenities include terry-cloth bathrobes, coffeemakers, irons, hair dryers, complimentary shoe shines, and the morning paper. Guests have privileges at the health club in the hotel complex. A circular staircase descends from the lobby to the Library Lounge, passing a huge bay window with a vast view of Lake Washington. Waters bistro serves Pacific Rim cuisine, dishes such as lemongrass steamed clams or grilled halibut with roasted onion-ginger relish. ⌧ *1200 Carillon Pt., Kirkland 98033,* ☎ *425/822–3700 or 800/822– 3700,* FAX *425/822–3699. 79 rooms, 21 suites. Restaurant, bar, in-room modem lines, in-room safes, minibars, refrigerators, room service, exercise room, laundry service, concierge, business services, meeting rooms, parking (fee). AE, DC, MC, V.*

$$ 🖭 **WestCoast Bellevue Hotel.** This hotel–motor inn has a number of town house suites, suitable for two to four people, with sleeping lofts and wood-burning fireplaces. Rooms are clean; those facing the courtyard are larger and quieter than the others. The hotel is a 20-minute walk from Bellevue Square. A substantial, complimentary appetizer buffet, served in the lounge weekdays between 5 and 7 PM, includes seafood and roast beef. ⊠ *625 116th Ave. NE, Bellevue 98004,* ☎ *425/455–9444,* 𝔽𝔸𝕏 *425/455–2154. 160 rooms, 16 suites. Restaurant, bar, room service, outdoor pool, exercise room, laundry service, business services, meeting rooms, free parking. AE, D, DC, MC, V.*

NIGHTLIFE AND THE ARTS

The Thursday edition of the *Seattle Times* and the Friday *Seattle Post-Intelligencer* include pullout weekend sections that detail upcoming arts and entertainment events. *Seattle Weekly,* which hits most newsstands on Wednesday, has even more detailed coverage and reviews. *The Stranger,* a provocative free weekly, provides broad, though not necessarily deep, coverage of the city's cultural activities and is the unofficial bible of the music and club scenes.

Ticketmaster (☎ 206/628–0888) provides tickets to most arts, entertainment, and sports events in the Seattle area; for a rather steep fee, you can charge by phone. The two locations of **Ticket/Ticket** (⊠ Broadway Market, 401 Broadway E, 2nd floor, ☎ 206/324–2744; ⊠ Pike Pl. Market Information Booth, 1st Ave. and Pike St., ☎ 206/682–7453, ext. 26) sell half-price tickets to many events on the day of the performance (or previous day for matinees). Sales are cash and in-person only.

Nightlife

Neighborhoods with high concentrations of clubs and bars include **Ballard, Pioneer Square, Capitol Hill, and Belltown** (also known as the Denny Regrade, just north of Pike Place Market). The opening of **Planet Hollywood** (⊠ 6th Ave. and Pike St., ☎ 206/287–0001) and the Steven Spielberg–Sega collaboration **GameWorks** (⊠ 7th Ave. and Pike St., ☎ 206/521–0952) amusement center on the same block with Nike-Town (⊠ 6th Ave. and Pike St., ☎ 206/447–6453) instantly livened things up in the area around the convention center.

Bars and Lounges

Bars with waterfront views are plentiful—you just have to pick your body of water. **Anthony's Home Port** (⊠ 6135 Seaview Ave. NW, ☎ 206/783–0780) overlooks Shilshole Bay. **Arnie's Northshore** (⊠ 1900 N. Northlake Way, ☎ 206/547–3242) has a great view of downtown from north Lake Union. **Duke's at Chandler's Cove** (⊠ 901 Fairview Ave. N, 206/382–9963) surveys south Lake Union. **Ernie's Bar & Grill** (⊠ Edgewater, 2411 Alaskan Way, Pier 67, ☎ 206/728–7000) has great views of Elliott Bay and the Olympic Mountains. The intimate deck at **Ponti** (⊠ 3014 3rd Ave. N, ☎ 206/284–3000) overlooks the Ship Canal.

If the view's not important, check out three of Seattle's hipper venues, all near Pike Place Market. The **Alibi Room** (⊠ 85 Post Alley, ☎ 206/623–3180) is the unofficial watering hole of the city's film community. The romantic **Il Bistro** (⊠ 93A Pike St., ☎ 206/682–3049) has low lights, low ceilings, and stiff drinks. Installations by local artists adorn the **Virginia Inn** (⊠ 1937 1st Ave., ☎ 206/728–1937).

In Pioneer Square check out **F. X. McRory's** (⊠ 419 Occidental Ave. S, ☎ 206/623–4800), near the Kingdome, which is famous for its huge selection of single-malt whiskeys and fresh oysters. The **Garden Court** (⊠ 411 University St., ☎ 206/621–1700) is without a doubt downtown's most elegant lounge. **Pioneer Square Saloon** (⊠ 77 Yesler Way, ☎ 206/340–1234) is a great, easygoing, no-frills tavern.

Brew Pubs

Seattle brew pubs—as drinking establishments attached to actual breweries are called—churn out many high-quality beers made for local distribution. All the pubs listed below serve food and nonalcoholic beverages. If live music is performed, a cover charge may be required; otherwise admission is free. Unless noted, the establishments listed below are open daily from at least noon to 11 PM; call ahead if you're planning a visit at other hours.

Big Time Brewery (⊠ 4133 University Way NE, ☎ 206/545–4509) caters to the U District crowd and resembles an archetypal college-town pub, with the obligatory moose head on the wall and vintage memorabilia scattered about. Pale ale, amber, and porter are always on tap; the imaginative specialty brews change monthly.

Hales Ales Brewery and Pub (⊠ 4301 Leary Way NW, ☎ 206/782–0737) serves up nine regular and seasonal taps in a cheerful Fremont setting. The pub's signature brews are its Honey Wheat and Moss Bay Amber ales; order a taster's "flight" to test the rest as well.

Pike Pub and Brewery (⊠ 1415 1st Ave., ☎ 206/622–6044), a dandy downtown establishment, is operated by the brewers of the award-winning Pike Place Pale Ale. Proudly proclaiming itself Beer Central, the Pike also houses the Seattle Microbrewery Museum and an excellent shop with supplies for home brewing.

Pyramid Alehouse (⊠ 91 S. Royal Brougham Way, at 1st Ave. S, ☎ 206/682–3377), just south of the Kingdome, brews the varied Pyramid Line—including a top-notch Hefeweizen and an Apricot Ale that tastes much better than it sounds—and Thomas Kemper Lagers. A loud, festive atmosphere makes Pyramid the perfect place to gather after a Mariners baseball game.

Redhook Brewery has an in-town location (☞ Trolleyman, *below*) and a larger complex—with a pub, a beer garden, and a gift shop in addition to brewing facilities ($1 tours available daily; call for hours and directions)—in Woodinville (⊠ 14300 N.E. 145th St., ☎ 206/483–3232).

Six Arms (300 E. Pike St., ☎ 206/223–1698) features the same comfortably eccentric decor that has become the trademark of the chain of pubs operated by the McMenamin family of Portland, Oregon. The beer is equally memorable, especially the challenging Terminator Stout. The Six Arms displays considerably more charm than her Seattle cousins, McMenamin's (⊠ 200 Roy St., ☎ 206/285–4722) and Dad Watson's (⊠ 3601 Fremont Ave., ☎ 206/632–6505), though the beer at all three tastes the same.

The Trolleyman (⊠ 3400 Phinney Ave. N, ☎ 206/548–8000), found near the north end of the Fremont Bridge, is the birthplace of local favorites Ballard Bitter and Redhook Ale. The pub mixes Northwest style (whitewashed walls and a no-smoking policy) with a relaxed atmosphere that includes a fireplace and ample armchairs. The original Redhook Brewery is right next door—take a 45-minute tour before you pop in for a pint. The pub opens at 8:30 AM except Sunday, when it opens at noon (and closes at 7). Call for tour times.

Coffeehouses

Unlike the city's brew pubs, Seattle's coffeehouses are defined as much by the people they serve as the beverages they pour. Most cafés serve the same drinks, but some Seattleites will linger for hours over their latte, while others prefer a cup to go from a drive-through espresso stand. Every neighborhood has its own distinctive coffee culture—usually three or four, actually. Below are a few of the options on Capitol Hill and downtown.

CAPITOL HILL

Local favorite **B&O Espresso** (✉ 204 Belmont Ave. E, ☎ 206/322–5028) lures Capitol Hill hipsters and solitary types. The on-site bakery turns out gorgeous wedding cakes. A youngish crowd browses through the art and architecture books on the shelves of **Bauhaus** (✉ 301 E. Pine St., ☎ 206/625–1600). Scribble and brood with the poetry set at **Cafe Paradiso** (✉ 1005 E. Pike St., ☎ 206/322–6960). Take a trip to Paris when you enter **Septième** (✉ 214 Broadway E, ☎ 206/860–8858), which, despite its white-linen tablecloths, has a calculatedly seedy feel. In back is an open patio, where during the summer you can listen to rhumba and salsa music and sip by the light of tiki torches. Exceptional, no-nonsense **Vivace Roasteria** (✉ 901 E. Denny Way, ☎ 206/860–5869) roasts its own coffee and sells to other coffeehouses.

DOWNTOWN

The rich smell of the roaster as you step through the door of tiny **Caffé Vitta** (✉ 2621 5th Ave., ☎ 206/441–4351) is intoxicating; the café also supplies the bean to a number of Seattle restaurants. **Lux** (✉ 2226 1st Ave., ☎ 206/443–0962) has a thrift-store opulence that's right at home among the fashionable boutiques of 1st Avenue and the Belltown arts scene. The **Sit & Spin** (✉ 2219 4th Ave., ☎ 206/441–9484) café has a full-service laundromat on one side. Sit & Spin's rival for the award for the coffeehouse most likely to improve your time management is **Speakeasy** (✉ 2304 2nd Ave., ☎ 206/728–9770), where you can download your e-mail along with your caffeine. Both cafés also double—or is it triple?—as performance spaces in the evening. **Zio Ricco** (✉ 1415 4th Ave., ☎ 206/467–8616) is downtown's most elegant coffee bar, with a well-stocked newsstand and inviting leather couches.

Comedy Clubs

Comedy Underground (✉ 222 S. Main St., ☎ 206/628–0303), a Pioneer Square club that's literally underground, beneath Swannie's sports bar and restaurant, presents stand-up comedy nightly. Monday and Tuesday are open-mike nights.

Giggles (✉ 5220 Roosevelt Way NE, ☎ 206/526–5653) in the University District books local and nationally known comedians from Thursday to Sunday, with late shows on Friday and Saturday.

Music

For $8 you can purchase the Pioneer Square joint cover charge, which will admit you to up to 10 area clubs; contact the New Orleans Restaurant (☞ Jazz, *below*) for details.

BLUES AND R&B

Ballard Firehouse (✉ 5429 Russell St. NW, ☎ 206/784–3516), Ballard's music mecca, books local and national blues acts.

Larry's (✉ 209 1st Ave. S, ☎ 206/624–7665) presents live blues and rhythm and blues nightly in an unpretentious, friendly, and usually jam-packed tavern-restaurant in Pioneer Square.

Old Timer's Cafe (✉ 620 1st Ave., ☎ 206/623–9800), a popular Pioneer Square restaurant and bar, has live music—mostly rhythm and blues—nightly.

Scarlet Tree (✉ 6521 Roosevelt Way NE, ☎ 206/523–7153), a neighborhood institution just north of the University District, serves up great burgers and live rhythm and blues most nights.

DANCE CLUBS

The local chapter of the **U.S. Amateur Ballroom Dancing Association** (☎ 206/822–6686) holds regular classes and dances throughout the year at the Avalon Ballroom (✉ 1017 Stewart St.). The **Washington Dance Club** (✉ 1017 Stewart St., ☎ 206/628–8939) sponsors nightly workshops and dances in various styles.

Downunder (✉ 2407 1st Ave., ☎ 206/728–4053) is an old-school disco with a packed floor. Top 40 music is the lure at **Iguana Cantina** (✉ 2815 Alaskan Way, at Broad St., ☎ 206/728–7071). The moody **Romper Room** (✉ 106 1st Ave. N, ☎ 206/284–5003) specializes in '70s soul. **Re-Bar** (✉ 1114 Howell St., ☎ 206/233–9873) presents an eclectic mix of music nightly, including acid jazz, rock, and soul. The **Vogue** (✉ 2018 1st Ave., ☎ 206/443–0673) hosts reggae, industrial, and gothic dance nights. Several rock clubs (☞ *below*) have dance floors.

FOLK

Backstage (✉ 2208 N.W. Market St., ☎ 206/781–2805) is a basement venue in Ballard that hosts national and local acts, with the emphasis on world music, offbeat rock, and new folk.

Kells (✉ 1916 Post Alley, ☎ 206/728–1916), a snug Irish-style pub near Pike Place Market, books Celtic-music artists from Wednesday to Saturday.

Murphy's Pub (✉ 2110 45th St. NE, ☎ 206/634–2110), a cozy neighborhood bar, has Irish and other folk music on Friday and Saturday.

JAZZ

Dimitriou's Jazz Alley (✉ 2037 6th Ave., ☎ 206/441–9729), a downtown club, books nationally known, consistently high-quality performers every night but Sunday. Excellent dinners are served before the first show.

Latona Pub (✉ 6423 Latona Ave. NE, ☎ 206/525–2238) is a funky, friendly neighborhood bar at the south end of Green Lake that presents local folk, blues, or jazz musicians nightly.

New Orleans Restaurant (✉ 114 1st Ave. S, ☎ 206/622–2563), a popular Pioneer Square restaurant, has good food and live jazz nightly—mostly top local performers but occasionally national acts as well.

ROCK

The **Moore Theater** (✉ 1932 2nd Ave., ☎ 206/443–1744) and the **Paramount** (✉ 907 Pine St., ☎ 206/682–1414, or Ticketmaster, ☎ 206/628–0888) are elegant structures from the early 20th century that now host visiting big-name acts.

Crocodile Café (✉ 2200 2nd Ave., ☎ 206/448–2114), one of Seattle's most successful rock clubs, books alternative music acts nightly except Monday.

The Fenix (✉ 315 2nd Ave. S, ☎ 206/467–1111) is a crowded Pioneer Square venue with an ever-changing roster of local and national acts.

Off-Ramp (✉ 109 Eastlake Ave. E, ☎ 206/628–0232) presents a rock band nightly, often the loud and alternative kind.

O.K. Hotel (✉ 212 Alaskan Way S, ☎ 206/621–7903) hosts rock, folk, and jazz nightly in a small venue near Pioneer Square.

Showbox (✉ 1426 1st Ave., ☎ 206/628–3151) presents locally and nationally acclaimed artists near Pike Place Market.

The Arts

On any given night in Seattle, you can attend first-rate symphony or ballet performances, or catch the world premiere of a play or a Hollywood blockbuster. Galleries and museums of every mission and description flourish here; scan the arts listings and see what catches your eye. With Seattle's often misty skies, it stands to reason that a city that spends this much time indoors has figured out how to make the best of it.

THE ARTS FOR FREE

Seattle's summer concerts, the **Out to Lunch Series** (☎ 206/623–0340), happen every weekday at noon from mid-June to early September in various parks, plazas, and atriums downtown. Concerts showcase local and national musicians and dancers. Call ahead for schedules and locations. **First Thursday Gallery Walk** (☎ 206/587–0260), an open house hosted by Seattle's art galleries, visits new local exhibits the first Thursday of every month, starting at 5.

Dance

Meany Hall for the Performing Arts (⊠ University of Washington campus, ☎ 206/543–4880) hosts important national and international companies, from September to May, with an emphasis on modern and jazz dance.

On the Boards (⊠ Washington Performance Hall, 153 14th Ave., ☎ 206/325–7901) presents and produces contemporary performances including not only dance but theater, music, and multimedia events by local, national, and international artists. Although the main subscription series runs from October to May, events are scheduled nearly every weekend year-round. In fall 1998, OTB will take up residence in a larger space on lower Queen Anne Hill (⊠ 100 W. Roy St.) near the Seattle Center.

Pacific Northwest Ballet (⊠ Opera House at Seattle Center, Mercer St. at 3rd Ave., ☎ 206/441–2424) is a resident company and school that presents 60 to 70 performances annually. Attending its Christmastime production of *The Nutcracker,* with choreography by Kent Stowell and sets by Maurice Sendak, is a Seattle tradition.

Film

The strongest evidence of Seattle's passion for the flickers is the wildly popular **Seattle International Film Festival** (☎ 206/324–9996), held each May. For show times and theater locations of current releases, call the **Seattle Times InfoLine** (☎ 206/464–2000, ext. 3456).

The Egyptian Theater (⊠ 801 E. Pine St., at Broadway, ☎ 206/323–4978), an art deco movie palace that was formerly a Masonic temple, screens first-run films and is the prime venue of Seattle's film festival. **Grand Illusion Cinema** (⊠ 1403 N.E. 50th St., at University Way, ☎ 206/523–3935) in the U District was a tiny screening room for exhibitors in the '30s. A venue for independent and art films, it has a terrific espresso bar. **Harvard Exit** (⊠ 807 E. Roy St., ☎ 206/323–8986), a first-run and art-film house, has Seattle's most inviting theater lobby—complete with couches and a piano. **U.A. 150 Cinemas** (⊠ 2131 6th Ave., ☎ 206/443–9591) screens second-run and classic films for the bargain price of $2. **Varsity Theater** (⊠ 4329 University Way NE, ☎ 206/632–3131), in the U District, usually dedicates two of its three screens to classic films.

Music

ORCHESTRAS

Northwest Chamber Orchestra (⊠ 1305 4th Ave., ☎ 206/343–0445) presents a full spectrum of music, from baroque to modern, at the University of Washington's Kane Hall. The subscription series, generally from September to May, includes a baroque-music festival every fall. **Seattle Symphony** (⌂ Opera House at Seattle Center and other locations, ☎ 206/215–4747) performs under the direction of Gerard Schwartz from September to June. The symphony is scheduled to move into its new home, Benaroya Hall (⌂ 2nd Ave. and University St.) in September 1998.

Opera

Seattle Opera (⌂ Opera House at Seattle Center, Mercer St. at 3rd Ave., ☎ 206/389–7676), considered among the top operas in the United States, presents five productions during its season, which runs from August to May.

Performance Venues

Broadway Performance Hall (⌂ Seattle Central Community College, 1625 Broadway, ☎ 206/323–2623), small but acoustically outstanding, often hosts dance and music concerts.

Cornish College of the Arts (⌂ 710 E. Roy St., ☎ 206/323–1400) serves as headquarters for distinguished jazz, dance, and other groups.

Fifth Avenue Theater (⌂ 1308 5th Ave., ☎ 206/625–1900) is the home of the Fifth Avenue Musical Theater Company (☞ Theater Companies, *below*). When the company is on hiatus, this chinoiserie-style historic landmark, carefully restored to its original 1926 condition, hosts traveling musical and theatrical performances.

Moore Theater (⌂ 1932 2nd Ave., ☎ 206/443–1744), a 1908 music hall, now presents dance concerts and rock shows.

Paramount Theatre (⌂ 907 Pine St., ☎ 206/682–1414), a 3,000-seat building from 1929 that has seen duty as a music hall and a movie palace, hosts Best of Broadway touring shows and national pop-music acts.

Seattle Center (⌂ 305 Harrison St., ☎ 206/684–8582) contains several halls that present theater, opera, dance, music, and performance art.

Theater Companies

Annex Theatre (⌂ 1916 4th Ave., ☎ 206/728–0933), run by a collective of artists, presents avant-garde works year-round.

Bathhouse Theater (⌂ 7312 W. Greenlake Dr. N, ☎ 206/524–9108) produces six productions per year, often innovative updates of classics.

A Contemporary Theater (⌂ Eagle Auditorium, 700 Union St., ☎ 206/292–7676) specializes in regional premieres of new works by established playwrights. Every December the theater revives its popular production of *A Christmas Carol*.

Crêpe de Paris (⌂ 1333 5th Ave., ☎ 206/623–4111), a restaurant in the Rainier Tower building downtown, books sidesplitting cabaret theater and musical revues.

Empty Space Theater (⌂ 3509 Fremont Ave., ☎ 206/547–7500) has a reputation for introducing Seattle to new playwrights. Its season generally runs from November to June, with five or six main-stage productions and several smaller shows.

Fifth Avenue Musical Theater Company (⌂ Fifth Avenue Theater, 1308 5th Ave., ☎ 206/625–1900) is a resident professional troupe that mounts four lavish musicals between October and May.

Group Theater (⌂ Seattle Center, fountain level of Center House, 305 Harrison St., ☎ 206/441–1299) is a multicultural troupe that prides itself on presenting socially provocative works—old and new—from September to June. A constant is the annual Voices of Christmas, a look at the holidays from various ethnic and cultural perspectives.

Intiman Theater (⌂ Playhouse at Seattle Center, 2nd Ave. N and Mercer St., ☎ 206/626–0782) presents classics of the world stage in an intimate setting. The season generally runs from May to November.

New City Theater and Arts Center (⌧ 1634 11th Ave., ☎ 206/323–6800) hosts experimental performances by local, national, and international artists.

Seattle Children's Theatre (⌧ Charlotte Martin Theatre at Seattle Center, 2nd Ave. N and Thomas St., ☎ 206/441–3322), the second-largest resident professional children's theater company in the United States, has commissioned several dozen new plays, adaptations, and musicals. The theater's six-play season runs from September to June.

Seattle Repertory Theater (⌧ Bagley Wright Theater at Seattle Center, 155 Mercer St., ☎ 206/443–2222) performs six new or classic plays on its main stage from October to May, along with three smaller shows at an adjoining smaller venue.

Village Theater (⌧ 303 Front St. N, Issaquah, ☎ 206/392–2202) produces high-quality family musicals, comedies, and dramas from September to May in Issaquah, a town east of Seattle. The main stage is at 303 Front Street; the theater's original venue, at 120 Front Street, is now known as First Stage.

OUTDOOR ACTIVITIES AND SPORTS

Beaches

If you happen to be in town on a sunny day, catch those precious rays at Golden Gardens (⌧ Seaview Ave. NW, ☎ 206/684–4075), a bit north of the Ballard Locks, or at Alki Beach (⌧ Alki Ave. SW; from downtown, take Hwy. 99 west, then head north on Harbor Ave. SW, ☎ 206/684–4075) in West Seattle. Another option is Warren Magnuson Park (☞ University District *in* Exploring Seattle, *above*). Be forewarned that the water stays pretty cold in Seattle year-round.

Participant Sports

Seattle Parks and Recreation (☎ 206/684–4075) has information about participant sports and facilities.

Bicycling

The Burke-Gilman Trail and the trail that circles Green Lake are popular among recreational bicyclists and children, but at Green Lake joggers and walkers tend to impede fast travel. The city-maintained Burke-Gilman Trail extends 12.1 mi along Seattle's waterfront from Lake Washington nearly to Salmon Bay along an abandoned railroad line; it is a much less congested path. Myrtle Edwards Park, north of Pier 70, has a two-lane path for jogging and bicycling.

Many shops rent mountain bikes and standard touring or racing bikes and equipment. Call **Gregg's Greenlake Cycle** (⌧ 7007 Woodlawn Ave. NE, ☎ 206/523–1822) in North Seattle. **Mountain Bike Specialists** (⌧ 5625 University Way NE, ☎ 206/527–4310) serves the U District.

Boating and Sailboarding

On sunny days, a virtual fleet of boats dots the Puget Sound waterways. Because of the region's mild climate, boating is a year-round endeavor. Charters, which are available with or without a skipper and crew, can be rented for a few hours or several days. Sea kayaking is another appealing way to explore the intertidal regions.

Sailboat Rentals & Yachts (⌧ 301 N. Northlake Way, ☎ 206/632–3302), on the north side of Lake Union near the Fremont area, rents sailboats with or without skippers by the hour or day. **Seacrest Boat House** (⊠ 1660 Harbor Ave. SW, ☎ 206/932–1050), in West Seattle, rents aluminum fishing boats by the hour or day. **Wind Works Rentals** (⊠ 7001 Seaview Ave. NW, ☎ 206/784–9386), on Shilshole Bay, rents sailboats with or without skippers by the half day, day, or week.

Lake Union and Green Lake are Seattle's prime sailboarding spots. Sailboards can be rented year-round at **Urban Surf** (⊠ 2100 N. Northlake Way, ☎ 206/545–9463) on Lake Union.

Fishing

There are plenty of good spots for fishing on Lake Washington, Green Lake, and Lake Union, and there are several fishing piers along the Elliott Bay waterfront. Companies operating from Shilshole Bay operate charter trips for catching salmon, rock cod, flounder, and sea bass. **Ballard Salmon Charter** (☎ 206/789–6202) is a recommended local firm. Like most companies, **Pier 54 Adventures** (☎ 206/623–6364) includes the cost of a two-day fishing license ($3.50) in its fee.

Golf

The city-run **Jackson Park** (⊠ 1000 N.E. 135th St., 206/301–0472 or 206/363–4747) and **Jefferson Park** (⊠ 4101 Beacon Ave. S, ☎ 206/762–4513 or 206/301–0472) golf facilities each have an 18-hole course (greens fee: $18.50, plus $20 for optional cart) and a 9-hole executive course ($8, plus $13 for optional cart).

Jogging, Skating, and Walking

Green Lake is far and away Seattle's most popular spot for jogging, and the 3-mi circumference of this picturesque lake is custom-made for it. Walking, bicycling, roller-skating, fishing, lounging on the grass, and feeding the plentiful waterfowl are other possibilities. Several outlets clustered along the east side of the lake have skate and cycle rentals.

Other good jogging locales are along the Burke-Gilman Trail (☞ Bicycling, *above*), around the reservoir at Volunteer Park (☞ Capitol Hill Area *in* Exploring Seattle, *above*), and at Myrtle Edwards Park, north of Pier 70 downtown.

Kayaking

Kayaking—around the inner waterways (Lake Union, Lake Washington, the Ship Canal) and open water (Elliott Bay)—affords some singular views of Seattle. The **Northwest Outdoor Center** (⊠ 2100 Westlake Ave. N, ☎ 206/281–9694), on the west side of Lake Union, rents one- or two-person kayaks and equipment by the hour or week and provides both basic and advanced instruction.

Skiing

There's fine downhill skiing in and around Snoqualmie (☞ Chapter 3). For Snoqualmie ski reports and news about conditions in the more distant White Pass, Crystal Mountain, and Stevens Pass, call 206/634–0200 or 206/634–2754. For recorded messages about road conditions in the passes, call 888/766–4636.

Tennis

There are public tennis courts in many parks around the Seattle area. Many are located in the U District, and several are near Capitol Hill. For information, contact the athletics office of the **King County Parks and Recreation Department** (☎ 206/684–7093).

Spectator Sports

Ticketmaster (☎ 206/628–8888) sells tickets to many local sporting events.

Baseball

The **Seattle Mariners** (☎ 206/622–4487) of the American League play at the Kingdome (✉ 201 S. King St.).

Basketball

The **Seattle SuperSonics** (☎ 206/283–3865) of the National Basketball Association play at Key Arena (✉ 1st Ave. N and Mercer St.) in the Seattle Center.

The women of the American Basketball League's **Seattle Reign** (☎ 206/285–5225) play their games at Seattle Center's Mercer Arena (4th Ave. N. and Mercer St.).

Boat Racing

The **unlimited hydroplane races** (☎ 206/628–0888) are a highlight of Seattle's Seafair festivities from mid-July to the first Sunday in August. The races are held on Lake Washington near Seward Park. Tickets cost from $10 to $20. Weekly sailing regattas are held in the summer on Lakes Union and Washington. Call the Seattle Yacht Club (☎ 206/325–1000) for schedules.

Football

Seattle Seahawks (☎ 206/827–9777) National Football League games take place in the Kingdome (✉ 201 S. King St.). The **University of Washington Huskies** (☎ 206/543–2200), every bit as popular as the Seahawks, play out their fall slate at Husky Stadium, off Montlake Boulevard Northeast on the UW campus.

Horse Racing

Take in Thoroughbred racing from April to September at **Emerald Downs** (✉ 2300 Emerald Downs Dr., Auburn, ☎ 206/288–7000), a 166-acre track about 15 mi south of downtown, east of I–5.

Soccer

For outdoor soccer, catch the A-League **Seattle Sounders** at Memorial Stadium (✉ Seattle Center, 5th Ave. N and Harrison St., ☎ 800/796–54250).

SHOPPING

Most Seattle stores are open daily. Mall hours are generally from 9:30 to 9 Monday through Saturday and from 11 to 6 on Sunday. Some specialty shops keep shorter evening and Sunday hours.

Shopping Districts

Broadway in the Capitol Hill neighborhood is lined with clothing stores selling new and vintage threads and high-design housewares shops.

Fremont Avenue contains a funky mix of galleries, thrift stores, and boutiques around its intersection with North 35th Street, just above the Fremont Bridge. At **Armadillo & Co.** (✉ 3510 Fremont Pl. N, ☎ 206/633–4241), you'll find jewelry, T-shirts, and other armadillo-theme accessories and gifts. The eclectic **Bitters Co.** (✉ 513 N. 36th St., ☎ 206/632–0886), a general store, has a wine bar. **Dusty Strings** (✉ 3406 Fremont Ave. N, ☎ 206/634–1656) is the place to pick up hammered dulcimers. **Frank & Dunya** (✉ 3418 Fremont Ave. N, ☎ 206/547–6760) carries unique art pieces, from furniture to jewelry. **Guess**

Where (⊠ 615 N. 35th St., ☎ 206/547–3793) stocks vintage men's and women's clothing and antiques.

The **International District,** bordered roughly by South Main and South Lane streets and 4th and 8th avenues, contains many Asian herb shops and groceries. **Uwajimaya** (⊠ 519 6th Ave. S, ☎ 206/624–6248), one of the largest Japanese stores on the West Coast, sells Asian foods and affordable china, gifts, fabrics, and housewares. Okazuya, the snack bar in Uwajimaya, prepares noodle dishes, sushi, tempura, and other Asian dishes to take out or to eat in.

University Way Northeast, in the University District between Northeast 41st and Northeast 50th streets, has a few upscale shops, many bookstores, and businesses that carry such student-oriented imports as ethnic jewelry and South American sweaters.

Shopping Centers and Malls

Bellevue Square (⊠ N.E. 8th St. and Bellevue Way, ☎ 425/454–8096), an upscale shopping center about 8 mi east of Seattle, holds more than 200 shops and includes a children's play area, the Bellevue Art Museum, and covered parking.

Northgate Mall (⊠ I–5 and Northgate Way, ☎ 206/362–4777), 10 mi north of downtown, houses 118 stores, including Nordstrom, the Bon Marché, Lamonts, and JCPenney.

Southcenter Mall (⊠ I–5 and I–405 in Tukwila, ☎ 206/246–7400) contains 140 shops and department stores.

Westlake Center (⊠ 1601 5th Ave., ☎ 206/467–1600), in downtown Seattle, has 80 upscale shops and covered walkways to Seattle's two major department stores, Nordstrom and the Bon Marché.

Specialty Shops

Antiques
Antique Importers (⊠ 640 Alaskan Way, ☎ 206/628–8905), a large warehouselike structure, carries mostly English oak and Victorian pine antiques.

Art Dealers
Foster/White Gallery (⊠ 311 Occidental Ave. S, ☎ 206/622–2833) represents many Northwest painters and sculptors, as well as glass artists of the Pilchuck School outside Seattle.

Stonington Gallery (⊠ 2030 1st Ave., ☎ 206/443–1108) specializes in contemporary Native American and other Northwest works.

Art Glass
The Glass House (⊠ 311 Occidental Ave. S, ☎ 206/682–9939) has one of the largest displays of glass artwork in the city.

Books and Maps
Bailey/Coy Books (⊠ 414 Broadway, ☎ 206/323–8842), on Capitol Hill, stocks contemporary and classic fiction and nonfiction and has a magazine section.

Elliott Bay Book Company (⊠ 101 S. Main St., ☎ 206/624–6600), a mammoth general independent bookstore in Pioneer Square, hosts lectures and readings by local and international authors and hosts a children's story hour at 11 AM on the first Saturday of the month.

M. Coy Books (⊠ 117 Pine St., ☎ 206/623–5354), in the heart of downtown, carries a large selection of contemporary literature and has a small espresso bar.

Metsker Maps (⊠ 702 1st Ave., ☎ 206/623–8747), on the edge of Pioneer Square, stocks many regional maps.

University of Washington Bookstore (⊠ 4326 University Way NE, ☎ 206/634–3403), which carries textbooks and general-interest titles, is one of Seattle's best bookshops.

Wide World Books and Maps (⊠ 1911 N. 45th St., ☎ 206/634–3453), north of downtown in the Wallingford neighborhood, carries travel books and maps.

Chocolates

Cafe Dilettante (⊠ 416 Broadway E, ☎ 206/329–6463) is well known for its mouthwatering dark chocolates, whose recipe comes from the imperial court of Russia.

Clothing

Alhambra (⊠ 101 Pine St., ☎ 206/621–9571) specializes in imported women's apparel, jewelry, and accessories.

Baby and Co. (⊠ 1936 1st Ave., ☎ 206/448–4077) sells stylish, contemporary fashions and accessories for women.

Butch Blum (⊠ 1408 5th Ave., ☎ 206/622–5760) carries contemporary menswear.

C. C. Filson (⊠ 1246 1st Ave. S, ☎ 206/622–3147) is a nationally renowned outdoor outfitter.

Ebbets Field Flannels (⊠ 406 Occidental Ave. S, ☎ 206/623–0724) specializes in replicas of vintage athletic apparel.

Littler (⊠ Rainier Sq., ☎ 206/223–1331) stocks classic fashions for women.

Local Brilliance (⊠ 1535 1st Ave., ☎ 206/343–5864) is a showcase for fashions from local designers.

Crafts

Hands of the World (⊠ 1501 Pike Pl., ☎ 206/622–1696) carries textiles, jewelry, and art from around the world.

Ragazzi's Flying Shuttle (⊠ 607 1st Ave., ☎ 206/343–9762) displays handcrafted jewelry, whimsical folk art, hand-knit items, and hand-woven garments.

Gifts

Ruby Montana's Pinto Pony (⊠ 603 2nd Ave., ☎ 206/721–7669) is kitsch heaven. You'll find furniture, housewares, T-shirts, books, and other postmodern accessories here.

Jewelry

Fireworks Gallery (⊠ 210 1st Ave. S, ☎ 206/682–8707; ⊠ 400 Pine St., ☎ 206/682–6462) sells handmade gifts, along with whimsical earrings and pins.

Newspapers and Magazines

Read All About It (⊠ 93 Pike Pl., ☎ 206/624–1040) serves downtown.

Steve's Broadway News (⊠ 204 Broadway E, ☎ 206/324–7323) covers Capitol Hill.

Steve's Fremont News (⊠ 3416 Fremont Ave. N, ☎ 206/633–0731) is just north of the bridge in Fremont Center.

Outdoor Wear and Equipment

Recreational Equipment, Inc. (⊠ 222 Yale Ave. N, ☎ 206/223–1944)—which everybody calls REI—has Seattle's most comprehensive selection of gear for the great outdoors at its state-of-the-art downtown facility. The nearly 80,000-square-ft store contains a mountain-bike test trail, a simulated rain booth for testing outerwear, and the REI Pinnacle, an enormous, freestanding indoor climbing structure. It's unbelievable, but there's room left over for a wildlife art gallery, a café, and a 250-seat meeting room for how-to clinics.

In case you want to be welcomed there.

We're here to see that you're always welcomed at establishments everywhere. That's why millions of people carry the American Express® Card — for peace of mind, confidence, and security, around the world or just around the corner.

do more

In case you're running low.

We're here to help with more than 118,000 Express Cash locations around the world. In order to enroll, just call American Express before you start your vacation.

do more

AMERICAN EXPRESS

Express Cash

And just in case.

We're here with American Express® Travelers Cheques
and Cheques *for Two.*® They're the safest way to carry
money on your vacation and the surest way to get a
refund, practically anywhere, anytime.
Another way we help you...

do more

AMERICAN EXPRESS

Travelers Cheques

Toys

Archie McPhee (⊠ 3510 Stone Way N, ☎ 206/545–8344), Seattle's self-proclaimed "outfitters of popular culture," specializes in bizarre toys and novelties.

Magic Mouse Toys (⊠ 603 1st Ave., ☎ 206/682–8097) has two floors of toys, from small windups to giant stuffed animals.

Wine

Delaurenti Wine Shop (⊠ 1435 1st Ave., ☎ 206/340–1498) has a knowledgeable staff and a large selection of Northwest Italian–style wines.

Pike & Western Wine Merchants (⊠ Pike Pl. and Virginia St., ☎ 206/441–1307 or 206/441–1308) carries Northwest wines from small wineries.

SEATTLE A TO Z

Arriving and Departing

By Bus

Greyhound Lines (☎ 800/231–2222) serves Seattle at 8th Avenue and Stewart Street (☎ 206/628–5508).

By Car

Seattle is accessible by I–5 and Highway 99 from Vancouver (three hours north) and Portland (three hours south), and by I–90 from Spokane (six hours east).

By Plane

Among the carriers serving **Seattle–Tacoma International Airport** (☎ 206/431–4444), also known as Sea-Tac, are Air Canada, Alaska, American, America West, British Airways, Continental, Delta, EVA Airways, Hawaiian, Horizon, Japan, Northwest, Southwest, Thai, TWA, United, United Express, and US Airways. *See* Air Travel *in* the Gold Guide for airline phone numbers.

Between the Airport and the City: Sea-Tac is about 15 mi south of downtown on I–5; a taxi costs about $30. **Gray Line Airport Express** (☎ 206/626–6088) service to downtown hotels costs $7.50. **Super Shuttle** (☎ 206/622–1424; 800/487–7433 in WA only) has 24-hour door-to-door service from $16 to $30, depending on the location of your pickup. **Metro Transit** (☎ 206/553–3000 or 800/542–7876) city buses (Express Tunnel Bus 194 and regular Buses 174 and 184) pick up passengers outside the baggage claim areas.

By Train

Amtrak (800/872–7245) trains service downtown's King Street Station (⊠ 303 S. Jackson St., ☎ 206/382–4125). The *Mt. Baker International* runs once daily to Vancouver, British Columbia, in about four hours. Three trains make the four-hour trip each day from Seattle to Portland, Oregon. Seattle is also the terminus for Amtrak's daily *Empire Builder* from Chicago and *Coast Starlight* from Los Angeles.

Getting Around

By Bus and Streetcar

Metropolitan Transit (⊠ 821 2nd Ave., ☎ 206/553–3000) is convenient, inexpensive, and fairly comprehensive. For questions about specific destinations, call the Automated Schedule Line (☎ 206/287–8463). Most buses run until around midnight to 1 AM; some run all night. All buses are wheelchair accessible. The visitor center at the Washington State Convention and Trade Center has maps and schedules.

Between 6 AM and 7 PM, all public transportation is free within the **Metro Bus Ride Free Area,** bounded by Battery Street to the north, 6th Avenue to the east (and over to 9th Avenue near the convention center), South Jackson Street to the south, and the waterfront to the west; you'll pay as you disembark if you ride out of this area. At other times (or in other places), fares range from 85¢ to $1.60, depending on how far you travel and at what time of day. Onboard fare collection boxes have prices posted on them. On weekends and holidays you can purchase a **Day Pass** from bus drivers for $1.70, a bargain if you're doing a lot of touring.

The **Waterfront Streetcar** line of vintage 1920s-era Australian trolleys runs south along Alaska Way from Pier 70, past the Washington State Ferries terminal at Piers 50 and 52, turning inland on Main Street, and passing through Pioneer Square before ending in the International District. It runs at about 20-minute intervals daily from 7 AM to 9 or 10 PM (less often and for fewer hours in the winter). The fare is 85¢. The stations and streetcars are wheelchair accessible.

By Car
Parking downtown is scarce and expensive. Metered parking is free after 6 PM and on Sunday. Be vigilant during the day—the parking enforcement officers here are notoriously efficient.

If you plan to be downtown longer than two hours (the maximum time allowed on the street), you may find parking in a garage easier. The Bon Marché garage (entrance on 3rd Avenue between Stewart and Pine streets) is centrally located. Many downtown retailers participate in the Easy Streets discount parking program. Tokens are good for $1 off parking in selected locations, and you receive more substantial reductions at the Shopper's Quick Park garages at 2nd Avenue and Union Street and at Rainier Square on Union Street between 4th and 5th avenues.

Right turns are allowed on most red lights after you've come to a full stop.

By Ferry
Washington State Ferries (☎ 206/464–6400; 800/843–3779 in WA only) serves the Puget Sound and San Juan Islands area. For more information about the ferry system, *see* Ferry Travel *in* the Gold Guide.

By Monorail
The **Seattle Center Monorail** (☎ 206/441–6038 or 206/684–7200), built for the 1962 World's Fair, shuttles between its terminals in Westlake Center and the Seattle Center daily from 9 AM to 11 PM every 15 minutes; the trip takes less than three minutes. The adult fare is $1.

By Taxi
It's difficult but not impossible to flag a taxi on the street, though it's usually easier to call for a ride. **Orange Cab** (☎ 206/522–8800) is Seattle's friendliest company. **Graytop Cab** (☎ 206/622–4800) is the oldest. Taxis are readily available at most downtown hotels, and the stand at the **Westin Hotel** (⊠ 1900 5th Ave.,☎ 206/728–1000) is generally attended all night.

Contacts and Resources

B&B Reservation Agencies
For information about bed-and-breakfast arrangements in western Washington, contact the **Bed & Breakfast Association of Seattle** (☎ 206/547–1020).

Car Rental

Most major rental agencies have offices downtown as well as at Sea-Tac Airport, including **Avis** (⌂ 1919 5th Ave., ☏ 800/331–1212), **Dollar** (⌂ 7th Ave. and Stewart St., ☏ 800/800–4000), **Hertz** (⌂ 722 Pike St., ☏ 800/654–3131), and **National** (⌂ 1942 Westlake Ave. N, ☏ 206/448–7368).

Consulates

Canada (⌂ Plaza 600 Bldg., 6th Ave. and Stewart St., 4th floor, ☏ 206/443–1777). **United Kingdom** (⌂ First Interstate Center, 999 3rd Ave., Suite 820, ☏ 206/622–9255).

Emergencies

Ambulance (☏ 911). **Fire** (☏ 911). **Police** (☏ 911).
Doctors, Inc. (⌂ 1215 4th Ave., ☏ 206/622–9933) gives referrals of physicians and dentists in the Seattle area.

Guided Tours

Three companies offer orientation tours of Seattle. The price of most tours is between $18 and $29, depending on the tour's length and mode of transportation. Custom packages cost more.

Gray Line of Seattle (☏ 206/626–5208 or 800/426–7532) operates bus and boat tours, including a six-hour Grand City Tour ($33) that includes many sights, lunch in Pike Place Market, and admission to the Space Needle observation deck.

Show Me Seattle (☏ 206/633–2489) surveys the major Seattle sights and also operates a tour that takes in the *Sleepless in Seattle* floating home, "the world's loveliest outdoor Jell-O mold collection," and other offbeat stops.

Seattle Tours (☏ 206/860–8687) conducts three-hour tours in customized vans. The tours cover about 50 mi, with plenty of stops for picture-taking.

BALLOON

Over the Rainbow (☏ 206/364–0995) operates balloon tours in the spring and summer only, weather permitting. The cost ranges from $120 to $160.

BICYCLING

Terrene Tours (☏ 206/325–5569) operates day and overnight bicycling and other tours of Seattle, the wine country surrounding the city, and points farther afield. The prices vary, depending on the destination and length of the tour.

BOAT

Argosy Cruises (☏ 206/623–4252) sail around Elliott Bay (one hour, from Pier 55 several times daily, $14.50), the Ballard Locks (2½ hours, from Pier 57, twice daily, $23.75), and other area waterways.

Pier 54 Adventures (☏ 206/623–6364) arranges speedboat rides, and sailboat excursions around Elliott Bay, along with guided kayak and bicycle tours. Salmon-fishing and seaplane charters are also available, as well as custom packages. The rates vary.

CARRIAGE

Sealth Horse Carriages (☏ 206/277–8282) offers narrated tours ($60 per hour) that trot away from the waterfront and Westlake Center.

PLANE

Galvin Flying Service (☏ 206/763–9706) departs from Boeing Field in southern Seattle on excursions as near as downtown or as far away as the San Juan Islands and Snoqualmie Falls. Prices begin at $89 ($10 for a second person).

Seattle Seaplanes (☎ 800/637–5553) operates a 20-minute scenic flight that takes in views of the Woodland Park Zoo, downtown Seattle, and the Microsoft "campus." Custom tours are also available. Prices begin at $42.50.

Sound Flight (☎ 206/255–6500) offers a 30-minute scenic flight for $59, custom sightseeing packages, and flights to secluded fishing spots.

SAILING

Let's Go Sailing (☎ 206/624–3931) permits passengers to take the helm, trim the sails, or simply enjoy the ride aboard the *Obsession,* a 70-ft ocean racer. Three 1½-hour excursions ($20) depart daily from Pier 56. A 2½-hour sunset cruise ($35) is also available. Passengers can bring their own food on board. Private charters can also be arranged.

WALKING

Chinatown Discovery Tours (☎ 206/236–0657) include two culinary excursions—one a light sampler, the other an eight-course banquet. The rates range from $9.95 to $34.95, based on a minimum of four participants.

Seattle Walking Tours (☎ 206/885–3173) through the city's historic areas, including the International District and Pioneer Square, cost $10.

Underground Seattle (☎ 206/682–4646) tours ($6.50) of the now-buried original storefronts and sidewalks of Pioneer Square are extremely popular, though many locals can't fathom why—they're somewhat like spending an hour and a half exploring your grandmother's extremely large basement. Then again, Underground Seattle does offer an effective primer on early Seattle history, and it may be a good place to take cover if your above-ground tour starts to get soggy.

Late-Night Pharmacies

Bartell Drugs (✉ 600 1st Ave. N, at Mercer St., ☎ 206/284–1353) is a 24-hour pharmacy.

Travel Agencies

AAA Travel (✉ 330 6th Ave. N, ☎ 206/455–9905). **American Express Travel Office** (✉ 600 Stewart St., ☎ 206/441–8622). **Doug Fox Travel** (✉ 1321 4th Ave., ☎ 206/628–6171).

Visitor Information

Seattle/King County Convention and Visitors Bureau (✉ 520 Pike St., Suite 1300, 98101, ☎ 206/461–5800). **Seattle Visitor Center** (✉ 800 Convention Pl., ☎ 206/461–5840). **Washington State Convention & Trade Center** (✉ 800 Convention Pl., ☎ 206/447–5000). **Washington Tourism Development Division** (✉ Box 45213, Olympia, WA 98504, ☎ 360/753–5600).

5 Washington

Long before outdoor adventures became popular in the rest of the country, they were a way of life for Washington residents—for northwesterners, adventuring isn't so much the "in" thing to do as it is the expression of a yearning to join with the mighty and majestic forces of nature.

WASHINGTON'S SCENIC ATTRACTIONS beckon the sightseer as well as the adventurer. To the west, the Olympic Peninsula's rain forest drips with moss, waterfalls, and sprawling greenery. The 5,200-ft-high Hurricane Ridge affords views of the Olympic Mountains and the Strait of Juan de Fuca. Inlets, coves, and secluded harbors puncture the western shoreline of the Olympic and the Long Beach peninsulas.

Revised by
Alex Aron

In and around the coastal region are many waterfront communities; outlying islands such as the San Juans, Whidbey, and Bainbridge; and the state's major urban areas, including Seattle, Bellingham, Tacoma, and Olympia. Across Puget Sound, Mount Rainier reigns over the Cascade Range. The mild climate and regular rainfall of western Washington sustain lush stands of Douglas fir; springtime brings Renoiresque washes of color as rhododendrons and azaleas come into bloom.

High in the mountains are Leavenworth and the towns of the North Cascades, where the snow in winter is as plentiful as the flowers in spring. Crossing the Cascades into central and eastern Washington, patchwork quilts of irrigated fruit orchards, miles of treeless prairie, and fields of golden grain prevail. On the eastern side of the Cascades in the Yakima Valley, gentle rolling hills, plenty of sunshine, and extremely fertile soil are the rule. Spokane, Washington's second-largest city, and the Coulee Dam are among the attractions in the part of the state due west of Idaho.

Pleasures and Pastimes

Boating
The sheltered waters of Puget Sound and the Inside Passage as well as Washington's many freshwater lakes make boating a popular activity. The calm waterways are rated among the best in the world for sea kayaking, an appealing way to explore the intertidal regions. For charters and outfitters, *see* the Outdoor Activities and Sports sections within each town or area's listings.

Dining
Washington's abundant seafood, especially salmon, shows up on menus throughout the state, and spicy yet subtle flavorings testify to the strong Asian influences on the cuisine here. Sweet, meaty Dungeness crab is the local delicacy on the Olympic Peninsula. Oysters are the specialty on Long Beach, mussels on Whidbey Island. Inland Ellensburg is famous for beef and lamb, and the Yakima Valley can't be beat for produce.

CATEGORY	COST*
$$$$	over $35
$$$	$25–$35
$$	$15–$25
$	under $15

per person for a three-course meal, excluding drinks, service, and sales tax (about 8.1%, varies slightly by community)

Lodging
First-rate hotels and moderately priced lodgings can be found throughout the state, and though most of Washington's smaller accommodations lack the old-fashioned charm and historical ties of their counterparts in New England or the South, they're often equipped with hot tubs and in-room fireplaces that take the edge off the crisp coastal air.

CATEGORY	COST*
$$$$	over $170
$$$	$110–$170
$$	$60–$110
$	under $60

All prices are for a standard double room, excluding 14.1% combined hotel and state sales tax.

Exploring Washington

Washington is divided in two by the Cascade Range, which sweeps from the northern to southern boundaries of the state. The ecosystems of Washington's moist, mountainous, western side vary dramatically. Much of the arid, flat landscape of eastern Washington resembles the Great Plains.

Numbers in the text correspond to numbers in the margin and on the Puget Sound, Tacoma, Olympic Peninsula, Long Beach Peninsula, San Juan Islands, Whatcom and Skagit Counties, and Crossing the Cascades maps.

Great Itineraries

IF YOU HAVE 4 DAYS

In four days, you can tour the northern section of the Olympic Peninsula, visit one of the coastal islands, and roam through a bit of the Cascade Range. ⛴ **Port Townsend** ㉔ is an ideal base for exploring the **Olympic Peninsula**'s crowning jewel—**Hurricane Ridge** ㉓. Depart for the **San Juan Islands** the next day. Take the ferry to **Whidbey Island** ①, where you can have lunch in Coupeville and visit **Deception Pass State Park** on the way up to **Anacortes,** on **Fidalgo Island** ②, the point of departure for the three largest San Juan Islands. Choose between ⛴ **Orcas** ④ and ⛴ **San Juan Island** ⑤; for either you'll need two full days to experience the exquisite natural surroundings. On the fourth day, head back to the mainland early and, from Anacortes, take in **Mount Rainier,** a towering volcanic peak with walking trails.

IF YOU HAVE 10 DAYS

From Seattle, drive to **Mount Rainier** and spend most of the day before heading south to ⛴ **Tacoma** ⑪–⑱—you'll find interesting dining and lodging options here. On day two stop briefly in **Olympia** ⑲, the state's capital, before venturing out to the **Olympic Peninsula.** Head west toward the Pacific Ocean and stay in the seaside town of ⛴ **Copalis Beach** or ⛴ **Moclips.** Drive up the coastline on the third day alongside the old-growth forests of the Olympic National Park. Spend a few hours at either the Hoh or Quinault rain forest and walk among the enormous moss-covered trees and plants. If you stay overnight in ⛴ **Port Angeles** ㉒, you'll be near your day-four destination: **Hurricane Ridge** ㉓. The ridge, part of the Olympic Range, has unparalleled views. Late in the day head to ⛴ **Port Townsend** ㉔. Visit Fort Worden State Park and the waterfront shops and eateries. Depart from the peninsula by ferry on the fifth day for **Whidbey Island** ①, where you can tour ⛴ **Coupeville** or ⛴ **Langley,** spending the night in either place. In the morning, head up to Anacortes and visit the Majestic Hotel before catching the ferry to the San Juan Islands, where you'll stay for two days. Choose between quiet ⛴ **Orcas Island** ④ and the more lively Friday Harbor, on ⛴ **San Juan Island** ⑤, for your base of operations. Interisland day trips are easy. On the seventh day head north from Anacortes to ⛴ **Bellingham** ⑥. Explore the town and **Lummi Island** for the next day and a half. Bellingham is the gateway to the North Cascades Range, which you

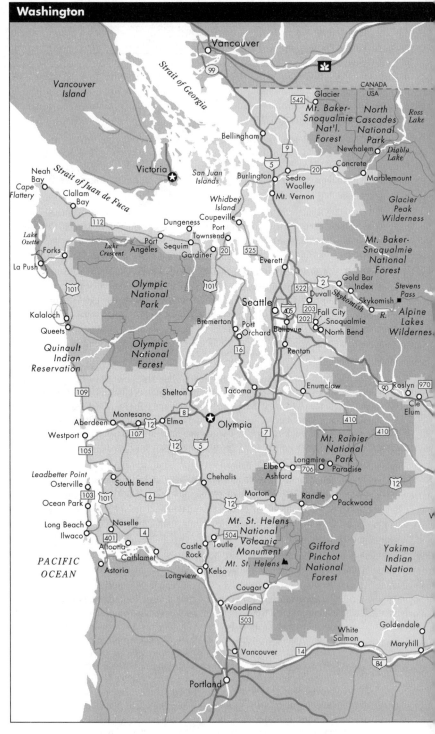

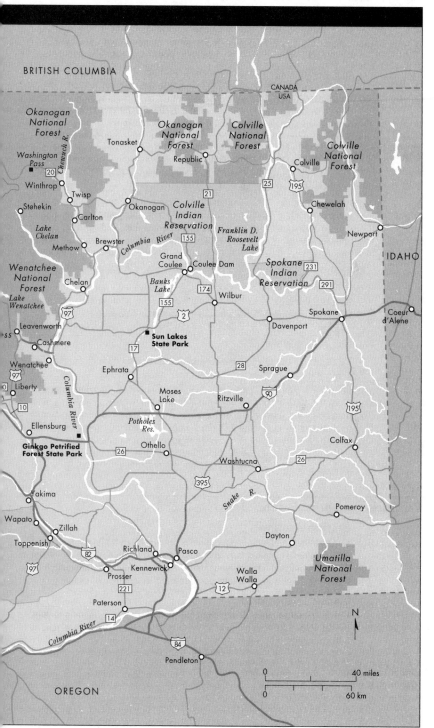

BRITISH COLUMBIA

CANADA
USA

Okanogan
National
Forest

Okanogan
National
Forest

Colville
National
Forest

Colville
National
Forest

Tonasket

Republic

Colville

Chewelah

Washington
Pass

Winthrop

[20]

Twisp

Stehekin

Carlton

Okanogan

Colville
Indian
Reservation

[21]

[25]

[195]

Newport

IDAHO

Lake
Chelan

Methow

Brewster

Columbia River

[155]

Franklin D.
Roosevelt
Lake

Grand
Coulee

Coulee Dam

Wenatchee
National
Forest

Chelan

Banks
Lake

[174]

Wilbur

Spokane
Indian
Reservation

[231]

[291]

Lake
Wenatchee

[97]

[155]

[2]

Davenport

Spokane

Coeur
d'Alene

Leavenworth

ss

Cashmere

Sun Lakes
State Park

Wenatchee

[97]

Liberty

[17]

Ephrata

[28]

Sprague

[10]

Columbia River

Moses
Lake

Ritzville

[90]

[195]

Ellensburg

Potholes
Res.

Ginkgo Petrified
Forest State Park

[26]

Othello

Washtucna

[26]

Colfax

[395]

Yakima

Snake R.

Pomeroy

Wapato

Zillah

Dayton

Umatilla
National
Forest

Toppenish

[82]

Richland

Pasco

Walla
Walla

[97]

Prosser

Kennewick

[221]

[12]

Paterson

[14]

Columbia River

[84]

Pendleton

N

OREGON

0   40 miles
0   60 km

can begin to tour on day nine. A scenic highway winds through the region. Stay the night in 🏨 **Glacier,** near **Mount Baker** ⑩.

When to Tour Washington

Summer is the best time for hiking and enjoying the coastal waters. Skies are generally clear and the temperatures mild. Spring can be overcast but is the best time to catch the flowers, especially the tulips in the Skagit Valley. Leavenworth and other mountain towns see more tourists in winter; the opposite is true in the coastal areas, where many of the activities geared toward travelers shut down.

BAINBRIDGE ISLAND

Take the half-hour ride on the **Bainbridge Island ferry** (☞ *below*) for great views of the city skyline and the surrounding hills. The ferry trip itself lures most of the island's visitors—this is the least expensive way to cruise Puget Sound—along with Bainbridge's small-town atmosphere and scenic countryside. From the Bainbridge Island terminal, continue north up a short hill on Olympic Drive to Winslow Way. If you turn west (left), you'll find yourself in **Winslow,** where there are several blocks of antiques shops, clothing boutiques, galleries, bookstores, and restaurants.

Pass the Winslow Way turnoff and head about ¼ mi farther north on Olympic to the **Bainbridge Island Vineyard and Winery** (✉ 682 Hwy. 305, ☎ 206/842–9463), which is open for tastings and tours Wednesday–Sunday noon–5.

You'll need a car to get to the **Bloedel Reserve,** whose grounds, the 150-acre estate of Vancouver, B.C., lumber baron Prentice Bloedel, were designed to recapture the natural, untamed look of the island. Within the park are ponds with ducks and trumpeter swans, Bloedel's grand mansion, and 2 mi of trails. Dazzling displays of rhododendrons and azaleas bloom in spring, and the leaves of Japanese maples and other trees colorfully signal the arrival of autumn. Reservations are essential, and picnicking is not permitted. ✉ *7571 N.E. Dolphin Dr. (from ferry follow signs on Hwy. 305),* ☎ *206/842–7631.* 🎫 *$6.* ☺ *Wed.–Sun. 10–4.*

Bainbridge Island Essentials

Getting Around

The **Bainbridge Island ferry** (☎ 206/464–6400), which takes cars and walk-on passengers, leaves Seattle once an hour during the day from Pier 52 (Colman Dock), south of Pike Place Market, and stops at Winslow. Highway 305 is the main road through the island.

Visitor Information

The **Bainbridge Island Chamber of Commerce** (✉ 590 Winslow Way, ☎ 206/842–3700), two blocks from the ferry dock, has maps and tourist information.

WHIDBEY ISLAND AND FIDALGO ISLAND

On a nice day there's no better short excursion from Seattle than a ferry trip across Puget Sound to **Whidbey Island.** It's a great way to watch the seagulls, sailboats, and massive container vessels in the sound—not to mention the surrounding scenery, which takes in the Kitsap Peninsula and the Olympic Mountains, Mount Rainier, the Cascade Range, and the Seattle skyline. Even when the weather isn't all that terrific,

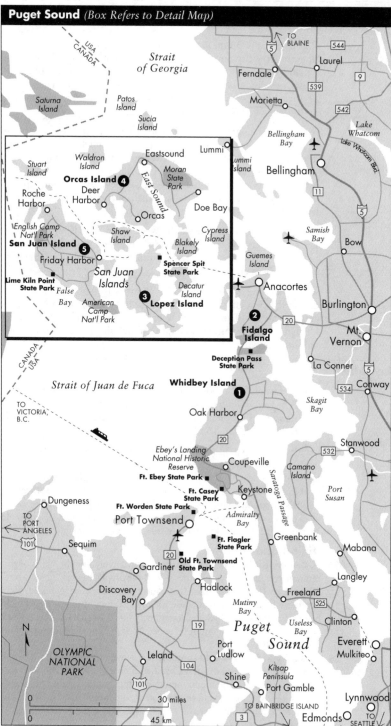

Puget Sound *(Box Refers to Detail Map)*

travelers can stay snug inside the ferry, have a snack, and listen to folk musicians.

Whidbey Island, 30 mi northwest of Seattle, is one of the nearest escapes from the city. Some folks escape to it nightly—they live on Whidbey and commute to work. The island is a blend of bucolic hills, forests, meadows, sandy beaches, and dramatic cliffs. It's a great place for driving in the country, viewing sunsets, riding bicycles, and exploring the shoreline by boat or kayak.

The best beaches are on the west side, where the sand stretches out to the sea and you have a view of the shipping lanes and the Olympic Mountains. Maxwelton Beach (⊠ Maxwelton Beach Rd.) is popular with the locals. Possession Point (⊠ Off Coltas Bay Rd.) includes a park, a beach, and a boat launch. Fort Ebey in Coupeville has a sandy spread, and West Beach is a stormy patch north of the fort with mounds of driftwood.

Whidbey is easily accessible via the Washington State Ferry from Mukilteo (pronounced muck-ill-*tee*-oh) to Clinton on the southern part of the island. Or you can drive across from the mainland on Highway 20 at the northern end of the island.

Sixty miles long and 8 miles wide, Whidbey is the second-longest island in the contiguous United States; only Long Island in New York stretches farther. The tour below begins at the island's southern tip, which has a mostly rural landscape of undulating hills, gentle beaches, and little coves.

Langley

From Seattle, take I–5 north 21 mi to Exit 189 (Whidbey Island–Mukilteo Ferry) and follow signs 7 mi to ferry landing; from Clinton (Whidbey Island ferry terminal), take Hwy. 525 north 2 mi to Langley Rd., turn right, and follow road 5 mi.

Langley sits atop a 50-ft-high bluff overlooking the Saratoga Passage on the southeastern shore. It's a great vantage point for viewing wildlife on land and sea. Upscale boutiques selling art, glass, jewelry, and clothing line 1st and 2nd streets in the heart of town. The **South Whidbey Historical Museum** (⊠ 312 2nd St., ☎ 360/579-4696), open on weekends from 1 to 4 in a former one-room schoolhouse, displays old Victrolas, farm tools, kitchen utensils, and antique toys.

Dining and Lodging

$$$ ✕ **Country Kitchen.** Tables for two unobtrusively line the walls of this intimate restaurant. On the other side of the fireplace is the "great table," which seats 10. The prix-fixe, five-course seasonal menu highlights local produce. Dinners might include locally gathered mussels in a black-bean sauce, breast of duck in a loganberry sauce, or rich Columbia River salmon. ⊠ *Inn at Langley, 400 1st St.,* ☎ *360/221–3033. Reservations essential. MC, V.*

$$ ✕ **Garibyan Brothers Café Langley.** Terra-cotta tile floors, antique oak tables, and the aroma of garlic, basil, and oregano set the mood at this Greek restaurant. The menu includes eggplant moussaka, Dungeness crab cakes, Mediterranean seafood stew, and lamb kabobs. Greek salads accompany all entrées. ⊠ *113 1st St.,* ☎ *360/221–3090. MC, V. Closed Tues. in winter. No lunch Tues.*

$$ ✕ **Star Bistro.** This slick 1980s-vintage bistro atop the Star Store serves Caesar salads, shrimp-and-scallop linguine, and gourmet burgers. Popular for lunch, it remains crowded well into the late afternoon. ⊠ *201½*

1st St., ☎ 360/221–2627. Reservations not accepted. AE, MC, V. No dinner Mon.

$ ✕ **Dog House Backdoor Restaurant.** Friendly and relaxed, this waterfront tavern and family restaurant, a recent addition to the National Register of Historic Places, is filled with collectibles that include a 1923 nickelodeon. Juicy burgers, homemade chili, and vegetarian entrées are made from low-salt recipes. The restaurant has a fine view of the Saratoga Passage. ✉ *230 1st St., ☎ 360/221–9996. Reservations not accepted. No credit cards.*

$$$$ ⌂ **Inn at Langley.** Langley's classiest inn, a concrete-and-wood Frank
★   Lloyd Wright–inspired structure, perches on the side of a bluff that descends to the beach. The Asian-style guest rooms have dramatic views of the Saratoga Passage and the Cascade Range. All have whirlpool tubs, fireplaces, outdoor terraces, and TVs. Meals are served in the inn's acclaimed restaurant, the Country Kitchen (☞ *above*). Dinner starts at 7 with a glass of sherry and a tour of the wine cellar. ✉ *400 1st St., 98260, ☎ 360/221–3033. 24 rooms. Restaurant. MC, V.*

$–$$ ⌂ **Drake's Landing.** Langley's most affordable lodging has humble but clean rooms with quilts on the beds and fine views. It's at the edge of town, across the street from the harbor off 1st Street. ✉ *203 Wharf St., 98260, ☎ 360/221–3999. 3 rooms. MC, V.*

Outdoor Activities and Sports

BICYCLING

In the Bayview area of Whidbey Island, off Highway 525 near Langley, **The Pedaler** (✉ 5603½ S. Bayview Rd., ☎ 360/321–5040) rents mountain bikes and hybrids year-round.

BOATING AND FISHING

Langley's small **boat harbor** (☎ 360/221–6765) provides moorage for 35 boats, plus utilities and a 160-ft fishing pier, all protected by a timber-pile breakwater. You can catch salmon, perch, and cod from the Langley pier. Supplies are available from the **Langley Marina** (✉ 202 Wharf St., ☎ 360/221–1771).

Shopping

Childers/Proctor Gallery (✉ 302 1st St., ☎ 360/221–2978) exhibits and sells paintings, jewelry, pottery, and sculpture. The **Cottage** stocks vintage and imported women's clothing (✉ 210 1st St., ☎ 360/221–4747). You can meet glass and jewelry artist Gwenn Knight at her shop, the **Glass Knight** (✉ 214 1st St., ☎ 360/221–6283). The **Museo Piccolo** (✉ 215 1st St., ☎ 360/221–7737), a gallery and gift shop, carries contemporary art by recognized and emerging artists.

Outside Langley at the **Blackfish Studio** (✉ 5075 S. Langley Rd., ☎ 360/221–1274), you can see works-in-progress and finished pieces by Kathleen Miller, who produces enamel jewelry and hand-painted clothing and accessories; and Donald Miller, whose photographs depict the land and people of the Northwest.

Freeland

7 mi north of Langley on Hwy. 525.

Unincorporated Freeland is home to two parks. You'll find picnic spots and a sandy beach at **Freeland Park** on Holmes Harbor. Bush Point Lighthouse is the main attraction at **South Whidbey State Park,** which has hiking trails, camping, and swimming.

Lodging

$$$–$$$$ ⌂ **Cliff House.** A winding drive through the woods leads to this secluded three-story house overlooking Admiralty Inlet. The award-winning architectural design is uncompromisingly modern; one side is nearly all glass and provides sweeping views. Rain and occasionally snow whisk through the open-air atrium in the middle of the house. An adjacent cottage also has sea views. Guests in both accommodations are pampered with fresh flowers, every modern amenity, and miles of driftwood beach. ⊠ *5440 Windmill Rd., 98249,* ☎ *360/221–1566. 2 rooms. No credit cards.*

Greenbank

11 mi north of Freeland on Hwy. 525.

About halfway up Whidbey is the town of Greenbank, home to the 125-acre **Greenbank Farm Winery,** which Island County purchased in late 1997. The vineyard here produces a small portion of the loganberries used for production of the island's unique spirit, Whidbey's Liqueur (available at the gift shop). Picnic tables are scattered throughout the farm. ⊠ *657 Wonn Rd.,* ☎ *360/678–7700.* 🎟 *Free.* ⏰ *Gift shop 10–5.*

The 53-acre **Meerkerk Rhododendron Gardens** contain 1,500 native and hybrid species of rhododendrons, numerous walking trails, and ponds. The flowers are in full bloom in April and May. ⊠ *Resort Rd.,* ☎ *360/678–1912.* 🎟 *$2.* ⏰ *Daily 9–4.*

Lodging

$$$ ⌂ **Guest House Cottages.** The very private log cabins here, surrounded
★ by 25 forested acres, have feather beds, VCRs, whirlpool tubs, country antiques, and fireplaces. Fresh flowers, robes, and a fine Continental breakfast are among the other draws, along with an enormous two-story lodge filled with collectibles that include a working pump organ. ⊠ *835 E. Christianson Rd., 98253,* ☎ *360/678–3115. 6 units. Pool, exercise room. No credit cards.*

Coupeville

15 mi north of Greenbank, Hwy. 525 to Hwy. 20.

Restored Victorian houses grace many of the streets in quiet Coupeville, which has one of the largest national historic districts in Washington. Stores along the waterfront have maintained their second-story false fronts and old-fashioned character. Captain Thomas Coupe founded the town in 1852; his house, built in 1853, is one of the state's oldest.

The **Island County Historical Museum** has exhibits on the history of the island's fishing, timber, and agricultural industries and conducts tours and walks. ⊠ *908 N.W. Alexander St.,* ☎ *360/678–3310.* 🎟 *$2.* ⏰ *May–Oct., daily 10–5; Nov.–Apr., Fri.–Mon. 11–4.*

Ebey's Landing National Historic Reserve encompasses two state parks and some privately held farmland. The reserve, the first and largest of its kind, holds nearly 100 nationally registered historic structures, most of them from the 19th century. A 22-acre beach area is the highlight of **Fort Ebey State Park**—the best view over Ebey's prairie can be had from the park's Sunnyside Cemetery. **Fort Casey State Park,** set on a bluff overlooking the Strait of Juan de Fuca, was one of three forts built in 1890 to protect Puget Sound. The park contains a small interpretive center, picnic sites, fishing spots, and a boat launch. ⊠ *Fort Ebey State Park: 2 mi west of Hwy. 20,* ☎ *360/678–4636. Fort Casey*

State Park: 3 mi west of Hwy. 20, ☎ 360/678–4519. Follow signs from Hwy. 20 to each park. ⌷ Day use free, campsites $11–$16. ⊙ 8 AM–dusk.

Dining and Lodging

$$–$$$ ✕ **Rosi's.** Deceptively simple-looking Rosi's is inside the Victorian
★ home of its chef-owners, who serve outstanding Italian and Pacific Northwest cuisine. Chicken mascarpone, osso buco, scallops pesto, prime rib, and Penn Cove mussels are among the entrées. ✉ *606 N. Main St., ☎ 360/678–3989. AE, MC, V. No lunch.*

$$ ✕ **Christopher's.** The ambience is warm and casual at this eclectically furnished restaurant whose tables are set with linens, fresh flowers, and candles. Penn Cove oysters broiled on the half shell with garlic, capers, and lemon butter are among the appealing appetizers; for the main course, try the pork medallions with blackberry-almond sauce or a daily vegetarian entrée such as curried lentils tossed with roasted vegetables and served on a bed of couscous. The wine list here is extensive. ✉ *23 Front St., ☎ 360/678–5480. AE, MC, V.*

$$ ⌂ **Fort Casey Inn.** The inn's two-story Georgian Revival structures, which served as officers' quarters, rest on a hillside overlooking Ebey's prairie. Each accommodation has a fireplace, two bedrooms, a living room, and a full country kitchen (with breakfast fixings on hand). Owners Gordon and Victoria Hoenig restored the house's tin ceilings and decorated the units with rag rugs, old quilts, hand-painted furniture, and sundry Colonial touches. Children are welcome here. ✉ *1124 S. Engle Rd., 98239, ☎ 360/678–8792. 9 units. Bicycles. AE, MC, V.*

Oak Harbor

10 mi north of Coupeville on Hwy. 20.

Oak Harbor gets its name from the Garry oaks that grow in the area. Dutch and Irish immigrants settled the town in the mid-1800s; several windmills are still in existence. Unfortunately, suburban sprawl has overtaken Whidbey Island's largest city in the form of multiple strips of fast-food restaurants and service stations.

★ **Deception Pass State Park** hosts more than 4 million visitors each year. With 19 mi of saltwater shoreline, three freshwater lakes, and more than 38 mi of madrona-forest trails, it's easy to see why. Summertime picnickers blanket the secluded inlet and long, sandy beach. The park is at the northernmost point of Whidbey Island, just over Deception Pass Bridge. If you walk across the bridge, you won't be able to miss the dramatic gorge below, well known for its swift tidal currents. ✉ *Hwy. 20, 7 mi north of Oak Harbor, ☎ 360/675–2417. ⌷ Park free, campsite fees vary. ⊙ Apr.–Sept., daily 6:30 AM–dusk; Oct.–Mar., daily 8 AM–dusk.*

Anacortes

15 mi north of Oak Harbor on Hwy. 20; 76 mi from Seattle, north on I–5 (to Exit 230) and west on Hwy. 20.

❷ Deception Pass Bridge links Whidbey to **Fidalgo Island.** From the bridge it's just a short distance to Anacortes, Fidalgo's main town and the terminus for ferries to the San Juan Islands. Anacortes consists mostly of strip malls and chain stores, but a small section of the waterfront contains some well-preserved redbrick buildings. The frequently changing exhibits at the **Anacortes Museum** (✉ 1305 8th St., ☎ 360/293–1915) focus on the cultural heritage of Fidalgo and nearby Guemes Island.

Lodging

$$$–$$$$ 🏨 **Majestic Hotel.** One of the finest small hotels in the Northwest
   ★   began life in 1889 as a mercantile building. From the Victorian-style
two-story lobby, you can enter the Rose & Crown pub and the ban-
quet rooms or ascend a sweeping staircase to your room or the En-
glish-style library. The top-floor gazebo has views of the marina,
Mount Baker, and the Cascades. The rooms are decorated with Euro-
pean antiques and down comforters; several contain whirlpool tubs.
A complimentary Continental breakfast is served in the dining room.
✉ *419 Commercial Ave., 98221,* ☎ *360/293–3355,* 𝕱 *360/293–
5214. 23 rooms. Restaurant, pub, library. MC, V.*

Whidbey Island and Fidalgo Island Essentials

Getting Around

BY CAR

Whidbey Island can be reached by heading north from Seattle or south
from the Canadian border on I–5, west on Highway 20 onto Fidalgo
Island, and south across Deception Pass Bridge.

BY FERRY

Washington State Ferries (☎ 206/464–6400) operates a ferry to Whid-
bey Island that leaves from Mukilteo, off I–5's Exit 189, 20 mi north
of Seattle. Walk-on passengers pay only for the westward leg of the
trip. Ferries leave roughly every half hour, more erratically off-season.
To reach Mukilteo from Seattle, take I–5 north to Exit 189. Ferries also
run from Port Townsend to Keystone (at Whidbey's midpoint). The
ride is 30 minutes one-way.

BY PLANE

Harbor Airlines (☎ 800/359–3220) flies to Whidbey Island from Fri-
day Harbor and Sea-Tac Airport. **Kenmore Air** (☎ 206/486–1257 or
800/543–9595) can arrange charter floatplane flights to Whidbey Is-
land.

Visitor Information

Anacortes Chamber of Commerce (✉ 819 Commercial Ave., Suite G,
98221, ☎ 360/293–7911). **Central Whidbey Chamber of Commerce**
(✉ 5 S. Main St., Coupeville 98239, ☎ 360/678–5434). **Langley
Chamber of Commerce** (✉ 124½ 2nd St., 98260, ☎ 360/221–6765).

THE SAN JUAN ISLANDS

The San Juan Islands beckon souls longing for quiet, whether it be kayak-
ing in a cove, walking a deserted beach, or nestling by the fire in an
old farmhouse. Unfortunately, solitude becomes a precious commod-
ity in the summer, when tourists descend on the region. Not surpris-
ingly, tourism and development are hotly contested issues among
locals.

There are 176 named islands in the San Juan archipelago, although the
islands total 743 at low tide and 428 at high tide. Sixty are populated
and 10 are state marine parks. Ferries stop at the four largest: Lopez,
Shaw, Orcas, and San Juan; other islands, many privately owned, must
be reached by private plane or boat. Naturalists love the San Juans be-
cause they are home to three pods of orca and a few minke whales,
plus seals, dolphins, otters, and more than 80 active pairs of breeding
bald eagles. The San Juans average more than 250 days of sunshine a
year. Temperatures hover around 70°F in the summer and between 40
and 60°F during the off-season.

San Juans residents are a blend of highly educated sophisticates and '60s-era (or thusly inspired) folk who have sought alternative lifestyles in a rustic setting. Fishing, farming, and tourism are the only industries. Creative chefs operate small restaurants here, but though the food is as contemporary as anything in Seattle, other aspects of island life haven't changed substantially in 30 years. Each of the islands has a distinct character, yet all share basic features: serene farmland, mysteriously charmed light, the velvet-green waters of the Strait of Juan de Fuca, and vistas framed by either Mount Baker and the Cascade Range to the east or the Olympics to the south.

Lopez Island

❸ *45 mins by ferry from Anacortes.*

The first ferry stop is at quiet and relatively flat Lopez Island, a favorite of bicyclists. Of the three islands that accommodate visitors, Lopez has the smallest population (approximately 1,800), and with its old orchards, weathered barns, and pastures of sheep and cows it's the most rustic. There is only one main town, Lopez Village, which has a few shops, some galleries that exhibit local artists' works, and the post office.

The **Lopez Island Historical Museum,** across the street from the island's only bank, has some impressive ship and small-boat models. The museum also has maps of local landmarks. ⌂ *Weeks and Washburn Rds.,* ☎ *360/468–2049.* ▨ *Donations accepted.* ⊙ *July–Aug., Wed.–Sun. noon–4; May–June and Sept., Fri.–Sun. noon–4.*

Beaches, trails, and wildlife are the draws at 130-acre **Spencer Spit State Park** (⌂ Rte. 2, ☎ 360/468–2251), on the northeast shore about 2 mi from Lopez Village. Popular **Odlin County Park** (⌂ Rte. 2, ☎ 360/468–2496) is 1 mi from the ferry landing. You'll probably spot marine life—perhaps seals, sea otters, and heron, or smaller creatures among the tide pools—at craggy, isolated **Shark Reef.** Park in the lot south of Lopez Village on Shark Reef Road and follow the unmarked trail (it begins next to the outhouse) for about 15 minutes through a thick forest to the water's edge.

The **Lopez Island Vineyard** (⌂ Fisherman Bay Rd. north of Cross Rd., ☎ 360/468–3644), the only vineyard on the San Juans, has a tasting room that is open between Memorial Day and Labor Day, from Wednesday to Sunday between noon and 5 (call for the hours during rest of the year).

Dining and Lodging

$$ ✕ **Bay Café.** At this colorful restaurant, you'll find everyone from locals and vacationers to movie stars filming on the island; many customers dock their boats at the restaurant's edge. Menu highlights include the seafood tapas: basil-and-goat-cheese stuffed prawns with saffron rice, a ricotta corn cake with smoked salmon and blackberry ketchup, and sea scallops with sun-dried tomatoes. All entrées include soup and salad. Homemade sorbet and a fine crème caramel are among the desserts. ⌂ *Lopez Village,* ☎ *360/468–3700. MC, V. Closed Mon.– Thurs. in winter. No lunch.*

$$$ ▤ **Edenwild.** A gray Victorian-style farmhouse surrounded by gardens and framed by Fisherman's Bay looks as if it has been restored, but it dates from 1990, not 1890. The rooms at the handsome, orderly Edenwild are airy, each painted in a bold color. Some rooms have fireplaces; all are furnished with simple antiques. Tiny roses fill the trellis on the wraparound ground-floor veranda. Well-selected contemporary

The San Juan Islands

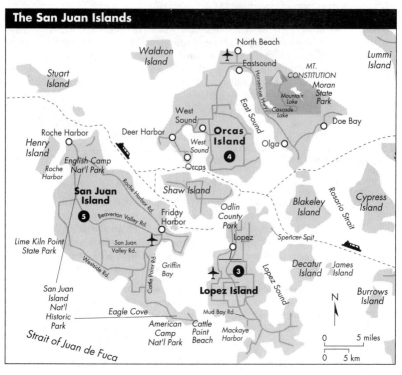

art adorns the ocher-color hallways, bright lobby, and dining room. Rates here include a full breakfast. The inn welcomes children. ✉ *Eades La. at Lopez Village Rd., 98261,* ☎ *360/468–3238,* FAX *360/468–4080. 8 rooms. AE, D, MC, V.*

$$–$$$ 🏠 **Inn at Swifts Bay.** New owners Rob Aney and Mark Adcock are continuing this inn's tradition of mellow hospitality. Their Tudor-style house has eclectic furnishings, a fascinating collection of books, and an exhaustive video library. Bay windows in the living and dining areas overlook well-kept gardens, and a crackling fire warms the living room on winter evenings. Robes, flip-flops, and flashlights are available for your walk through the garden to a hot tub under the stars. The rooms downstairs have heavy floral drapes and elaborate bed dressings but are small and share baths. The downstairs suite has more space and a private entrance, but even nicer are the two upstairs suites, which are long and narrow, with high, sloping ceilings. Gourmet breakfasts include exotic creations like pumpkin eggnog muffins. ✉ *Rte. 2, Box 3402, 98261,* ☎ *360/468–3636,* FAX *360/468–3637. 2 rooms, 3 suites. Hot tub, beach. AE, D, MC, V.*

$$ 🏠 **Mackaye Harbor Inn.** This two-story inn, a frame 1920s sea captain's house with ½ mi of beach, is at the south end of Lopez Island. Rooms have golden-oak and brass details and wicker furniture; three have views of Mackaye Harbor. Breakfast often includes Finnish pancakes and other Scandinavian specialties. Three rooms share 2½ baths; two suites have private baths, small decks, and fireplaces. A new carriage house has a two-bedroom suite with a steam room and a full kitchen; a small studio here also has a kitchen. Breakfast is not included for guests in the carriage house. Boats and mountain bikes are available for rent. ✉ *Rte. 1, Box 1940, 98261,* ☎ *360/468–2253,* FAX *360/468–3293. 5 rooms, 2 suites. Beach. MC, V.*

Outdoor Activities and Sports

BICYCLING

Cycle San Juans Tours and Rentals (⊠ Rte. 1, ☎ 360/468–3251) advertises this tour: "Cycle with bald Lopezian to discover island curiosities." **Lopez Bicycle Works** (⊠ Fisherman Bay Rd., ☎ 360/468–2847) provides free bicycle delivery all year.

MARINAS

Islands Marine Center (⊠ Fisherman Bay Rd. north of Hummel Lake Rd., ☎ 360/468–3377), near Lopez Village, has standard marina amenities, repair facilities, and transient moorage.

Shopping

The **Chimera Gallery** (⊠ Lopez Village, ☎ 360/468–3265), a local artists' cooperative, exhibits crafts, jewelry, and fine art. **Grayling Gallery** (⊠ 3630 Hummel Lake Rd., ☎ 360/468–2779) displays the paintings, prints, sculptures, and pottery of nearly a dozen artists from Lopez Island, some of whom live and work on the gallery's premises. The gallery is open on Friday and weekends from 10 to 5.

Shaw Island

20 mins on ferry from Lopez; 65 mins from Anacortes.

At tiny Shaw Island, local nuns wear their traditional habits while running the ferry dock. Few tourists get off here; the island is mostly residential. **King Salmon Charters** (☎ 360/468–2314) operates saltwater fishing excursions.

Orcas Island

❹ *10 mins from Shaw Island by ferry, 75 mins from Anacortes.*

The roads on horseshoe-shape Orcas Island sweep down through wide valleys and rise to marvelous hilltop views. The wealthy landowners on this mostly privately owned island mix with a visible, arts-oriented, countercultural community. Public access to the waterfront is limited.

Shops in **Eastsound Village,** in the middle of the horseshoe and the island's business and social center, showcase the jewelry, pottery, and other crafts of local artisans. Along Prune Alley you'll find a handful of small shops and restaurants. Pick up free maps and brochures at the unstaffed **Travel Infocenter** (⊠ Main St., ☎ 360/376–2273), next to the Orcas Island Museum (worth a stop if you're a history buff). Nearby is the simple yet stately **Emmanuel Church,** built in 1886 to resemble an English countryside chapel. The church's **Brown Bag Concerts** (☎ 360/376–2352)—you'll hear anything from a piano sonata to the vocalizing of a barbershop quartet—take place on summer Thursdays at noon.

Moran State Park contains 151 campsites, 14 hiking trails, some sparkling lakes, 5,000 acres of old-growth forests, and **Mount Constitution.** Exhilarating views of the San Juan Islands, the Cascades, the Olympics, and Vancouver Island can be had from the mountain's 2,400-ft summit, the tallest on all the islands. ⊠ *Star Rte. 22; from Eastsound, head northeast on Horseshoe Hwy. and follow signs (mailing address: Box 22, Eastsound 98245),* ☎ *360/376–2326.* ▣ *Camping $11 fee, plus $6 per night;* ☎ *800/452–5678 for reservations.*

Dining and Lodging

$$$ ✕ **Christina's.** The modern decor at the premier Orcas restaurant includes original works of art and copper-top tables. The seasonal menu changes daily but generally emphasizes local fish and seafood. You're

almost certain to encounter a salmon entrée, delicately prepared and served with grilled vegetables. Other possibilities include a seafood stew with a saffron broth and rouille (a peppery garlic sauce), and lamb shank with white beans, rosemary, and root vegetables. Expect a wait in-season at Christina's, which has fine views from its rooftop terrace and enclosed porch. ⊠ *N. Beach Rd. and Horseshoe Hwy., Eastsound,* ☎ *360/376–4904. AE, DC, MC, V. Closed Tues. Oct.–mid-June. No lunch.*

$–$$ ✕ **Bilbo's Festivo.** Stucco walls, Mexican tiles, wood benches, and weavings from New Mexico betray this restaurant's culinary inclinations. Munch on burritos, enchiladas, and other Mexican favorites like orange-marinated chicken grilled over mesquite and served with asparagus, potatoes, and salad. In warm weather, it's pleasant to sip lime margaritas in the courtyard. ⊠ *N. Beach Rd. and A St., Eastsound,* ☎ *360/376–4728. Reservations not accepted. AE, MC, V. No lunch Oct.–May.*

$$$–$$$$ ⊞ **Rosario Spa & Resort.** Shipbuilding magnate Robert Moran built this Mediterranean-style mansion on Cascade Bay in 1906. Told he had six months to live, Moran pulled out all the stops on his last extravagance—then lived another 30 years. Now his mansion is on the National Register of Historic Places. The original Mission-style furniture, displayed for the public, is worth a look even if you're not staying here. The house's centerpiece, an Aeolian pipe organ with 1,972 pipes, is used for summer music concerts. The resort is renovating the villas and hotel units that were added in 1960 when Rosario was converted from a private residence. The rooms completed so far are comfortable, with gas fireplaces and other modern amenities. The spa offers everything from aerobic instruction to herbal wraps and massage. A shuttle meets every ferry and provides transportation into Eastsound. ⊠ *Horseshoe Hwy., Eastsound 98245,* ☎ *360/376–2222 or 800/562–8820. 131 rooms. Dining room, indoor pool, 2 outdoor pools, hot tub, sauna, spa, 2 tennis courts, hiking, dock, boating, fishing. AE, DC, MC, V.*

$$$–$$$$ ⊞ **Spring Bay Inn.** Sandy Playa and Carl Burger, former park rangers, ★ run this bed-and-breakfast on acres of woodland surrounding private Spring Bay. All rooms have bay views (this is the only Orcas B&B actually on the water), wood-burning fireplaces, feather beds, and private sitting areas; one room has an outdoor hot tub. Walking trails meander through the property. Mornings begin with coffee, fresh muffins, and croissants outside your door—fortification for a two-hour kayaking experience, should you care to partake. While one of your hosts is out on the water—expect to see bald eagles, herons, or other wildlife—the other is preparing a full breakfast that includes fresh-squeezed orange juice and smoothies. ⊠ *Obstruction Pass Trailhead Rd. off Obstruction Pass Rd., Olga 98279,* ☎ *360/376–5531,* ℻ *360/376–2193. 5 rooms. Refrigerators, hot tub, kayaking. D, MC, V.*

$$$ ⊞ **Deer Harbor Inn.** The original 1915 log lodge here, on a knoll overlooking Deer Harbor, was the island's first resort. The lodge is now the inn's dining room. A log cabin built later holds eight rooms with peeled-log furniture and meadow views from balconies. Three newer cottages have whirlpool tubs and propane fireplaces. A complimentary Continental breakfast is delivered to your door in a picnic basket. The large but cozy dining room, which serves seafood, has an adjoining deck for outdoor eating. ⊠ *Box 142, Deer Harbor 98243,* ☎ *360/376–4110,* ℻ *360/376–2237. 11 units. Restaurant. AE, MC, V.*

$$–$$$ ⊞ **Orcas Hotel.** Construction began in 1900 on this three-story red-roof Victorian hotel on a hill across from the Orcas ferry landing. The building, complete with a wraparound porch and a white picket fence, is on the National Register of Historic Places. Guest rooms have feather beds, down comforters, and wicker, brass, and antique furnishings; many rooms have water views. All second-floor rooms share baths. Two suites have whirlpool tubs. The dining room—open in season (from June to October) to guests and nonguests—overlooks gardens and the ferry landing. In-season room rates include a full breakfast; lower off-season rates do not, but you can grab an espresso or baked goods at the on-site café. ⊠ *Horseshoe Hwy., Box 155, Orcas 98280,* ☎ *360/376–4300,* FAX *360/376–4399. 12 rooms, 2 with bath, 3 with ½ bath. Restaurant, bar, café. AE, D, MC, V.*

$$–$$$ 🖻 **Turtleback Farm Inn.** Eighty acres of meadow, forest, and farmland in the shadow of Turtleback Mountain surround this forest-green inn that dates from the late 1800s. The rooms have easy chairs, good beds with woolen comforters made from the fleece of resident sheep, some antiques, and views of meadows and forest. Breakfast can be taken in the dining room or on the deck overlooking the valley. ⊠ *R.R. 1, Box 650, Eastsound 98245,* ☎ *360/376–3914 or 800/376–4914. 7 rooms. MC, V.*

$–$$ 🖻 **Doe Bay Village Resort.** A haven for neohippies and outdoorsy families, this property at the eastern tip of Orcas morphed from a nudist colony into a commune, a youth hostel, and finally a resort. Prices for the patchwork of accommodations—campsites, yurts, a hostel, and cabins tucked between two forested hills—start as low as $12, and there's a mostly vegetarian café on site. The resort's small beach is perfect for kayak launches. Guests staying in the cabins may also use the resort's mineral baths and sauna for free ($3 fee for hostel guests and campers). ⊠ *Star Rte. 86 off Pt. Lawrence Rd. near Olga, 98279,* ☎ *360/376–2291,* FAX *360/376–4755. 30 cabins and structures, 24 campsites. Café, hot tubs, massage, mineral baths, sauna, volleyball, beach. AE, MC, V.*

Outdoor Activities and Sports

BICYCLING

Dolphin Bay Bicycles (☎ 360/376–3093) is at the ferry landing. **Key Moped Rental** (⊠ Eastsound, ☎ 360/376–2474) rents mopeds during the summer. **Wildlife Cycles** (⊠ Eastsound, ☎ 360/376–4708) also has bikes for rent.

FISHING

Three lakes at **Moran State Park** (☞ *above*) are open for fishing from late April to October.

MARINAS

Deer Harbor Resort & Marina (☎ 360/376–3037) and **West Sound Marina** (☎ 360/376–2240) have standard marina facilities. **Island Petroleum** (⊠ Orcas, ☎ 360/376–3883) has gas and diesel at the ferry landing. **Rosario Resort** (⊠ Eastsound, ☎ 360/376–2222) has boat slips.

Shopping

Darvill's Rare Print Shop (⊠ Eastsound, ☎ 360/376–2351) specializes in maps and bird and floral prints.

San Juan Island

⑤ *45 mins by ferry from Orcas; 75 mins from Anacortes on express ferries.*

The story goes that Friday Harbor got its name when an explorer rounding San Juan Island called from the boat "What bay is this?" A man on shore heard "What day is this?" and called back "Friday." The islands' county seat and the only incorporated town on San Juan Island is the most convenient destination for visitors without cars or bicycles.

Standing at the ferry dock, facing the bluff and downtown, you'll recognize the modest **Whale Museum** by the whale mural painted on its exterior. To reach the entrance, walk up Spring Street and turn right on 1st Street. Models of whales and whale skeletons, recordings of whale sounds, and videos of whales are the attractions. Workshops survey marine-mammal life and San Juan ecology. ⊠ *62 1st St. N,* ☎ *360/378–4710.* 🎫 *$3.* ⊙ *June–Sept., daily 10–5; Oct.–May, daily 11–4.*

For an opportunity to see whales cavorting in the Strait of Juan de Fuca, head to **Lime Kiln Point State Park,** on San Juan's west side just 6 mi from Friday Harbor. The best months for sighting whales are from the end of April through August. ⊠ *6158 Lighthouse Rd.,* ☎ *360/378–2044.* 🎫 *Free.* ⊙ *Daily 8 AM–10 PM.*

San Juan Island National Historic Park (☎ 360/468–3663) is a remnant of the "Pig War," a prolonged scuffle between American and British troops that were brought in after a Yank killed a Brit's pig in 1859. The mere presence of the soldiers was pretty much the extent of the hostilities (no gunfire was ever exchanged), although troops from both countries remained on the island until 1872. The park encompasses two separate areas: **British Camp** on the west side of the island (follow Roche Harbor Road north from Friday Harbor), containing a blockhouse, a commissary, and barracks; and **American Camp** (follow Cattle Point Road south from Friday Harbor), with a laundry, fortifications, and a visitor center. From June to August, the park conducts hikes and reenacts 1860s-era military life.

Snazzy **Roche Harbor** at the northern end of San Juan began as a limestone quarrying village. The Roche Harbor Lime and Cement Company, the oldest incorporated company in Washington, still maintains its original location on the docks. Painted like a Mississippi River boat, it's hard to miss. With its rose gardens, cobblestone waterfront, and well-manicured lawns, Roche Harbor retains the flavor of its days as a hangout for the world's elite—Teddy Roosevelt and many other notables stopped here.

The **Hotel de Haro** (☞ Roche Harbor Resort, *below*) displays period photographs and artifacts in its lobby. If you're interested, ask the staff for a map that points out remnants of the quarrying industry and the **Mausoleum,** an eerie Greek-inspired memorial to businessman and Roosevelt confidant John S. McMillin.

Dining and Lodging

$$$ ✕ **Duck Soup Inn.** Everything the Duck Soup Inn serves is made from scratch daily—fresh bread, Mediterranean-inspired entrées, vegetarian dishes, and delicious ice cream. Start with apple-wood-smoked Westcott Bay oysters, followed by pan-seared sea scallops in a red-curry coconut sauce on a bed of cashews and greens. Northwest, California, and European wines are on the list here. ⊠ *3090 Roche Harbor Rd., near town of Roche Harbor,* ☎ *360/378–4878. MC, V. Closed Mon.–Tues. Apr.–Oct.; closed entirely Nov.–Mar. No lunch.*

$$–$$$ ✕ **Springtree Café.** Chef James Boyle devises his daily menu around fresh seafood and Waldron Island organic produce and herbs, creating savory dishes that you won't soon forget. Begin with the Caesar salad—made with tofu instead of eggs—and continue with the king salmon in pesto sauce, the ginger shrimp with mango and dark rum, or other fish and meat entrées. Vegetarian options abound, and there's a full bar and an extensive wine selection. ⊠ *310 Spring St., Friday Harbor,* ☎ *360/378–4848. MC, V. Closed Sun.–Mon. mid-Oct.–Apr.*

$ ✕ **Front Street Ale House.** The English-style ale house serves sandwiches, salads, and traditional pub fare—lamb stew, meat pasties, steak-and-kidney pie, and the like. For vegetarians there's a vegetable patty lightly sautéed, then stacked with cheese, mushrooms, lettuce, tomato, and onions. On-tap brews from the San Juan Brewing Company carry such locally inspired names as Pig War Stout. ⊠ *1 Front St., Friday Harbor,* ☎ *360/378–2337. Reservations not accepted. MC, V.*

$$$–$$$$ ✕⛭ **Mariella Inn & Cottages.** This impeccably maintained property sits on 8 acres on a cove just outside Friday Harbor. Rooms inside a 100-year-old country house have English antique furniture. Each room has a private bath and a view of either the water or the exquisite gardens, but some are small. Some of the private cottages and waterfront suites scattered throughout the grounds have modern amenities such as VCRs and kitchenettes. Especially romantic are the contemporary solarium suites with private whirlpool tubs inside glass-enclosed atriums. Breakfast and the newspaper are delivered to the cottages each morning. Dinner might include lamb chops, pancetta-wrapped filet mignon, or oven-roasted Pacific salmon. ⊠ *630 Turn Point Rd., Friday Harbor 98250,* ☎ *360/378–6868 or 800/700–7668,* ⅁ *360/378–6822. 8 rooms, 3 suites, 12 cottages. Restaurant, bicycles. AE, MC, V.*

$$$ ✕⛭ **Friday Harbor House.** The ceiling-to-floor windows of this contemporary bluff-top villa hotel were designed to take advantage of its views of the marina, ferry landing, and San Juan Channel—as was the placement of whirlpool tubs in the center of each room. Slate tiles, fireplaces, cable TV, and sleek modern wood wall units all contribute to the casually upscale atmosphere. Dinners, primarily local seafood, include greens from San Juan's Zion Farm. Guests take their elaborate complimentary Continental breakfasts in the intimate harbor-view dining room. ⊠ *130 West St., Friday Harbor 98250,* ☎ *360/378–8455,* ⅁ *360/378–8453. 20 rooms. Restaurant, refrigerators. MC, V.*

$$–$$$ ⛭ **Hillside House.** This split-level house less than a mile from Friday Harbor has views of the waterfront and Mount Baker from a large deck. Rooms have either sophisticated or more whimsical decor. Some overlook the 10,000-square-ft full-flight aviary. Breakfast—made with residents hens' eggs, island jams, and fresh berries—is often served on the large deck that rings the house. ⊠ *365 Carter Ave., Friday Harbor 98250,* ☎ *360/378–4730 or 800/232–4730,* ⅁ *360/378–4715. 6 rooms, 1 suite. AE, D, MC, V.*

$$–$$$ ⛭ **Roche Harbor Resort.** The choice here is between nondescript cottages and condominiums or rooms in the 1886 restored Hotel de Haro. The old hotel building is better to look at than to stay in; its guest rooms are somewhat shabby (or rustic, depending on your point of view). On the other hand, the resort has slips for a few hundred boats, a full-service marina, and a 4,000-ft airstrip. Whale-watching and day cruises, plus kayaking tours, are available. ⊠ *4950 Tarte Memorial Dr., 10 mi northwest of Friday Harbor off Roche Harbor Rd., Roche Harbor 98250,* ☎ *360/378–2155 or 800/451–8910,* ⅁ *360/378–6809. 59 rooms, 5 with bath. Restaurant, grocery, pool, tennis court, boating, motorbikes. AE, MC, V.*

$$ ⛭ **San Juan Inn.** Rooms in this restored 1873 property less than a block from the ferry landing may be smallish, but there's an air of authenticity here that most island accommodations can't match: This site has been operated as an inn for more than 100 years. All rooms have brass, iron, or wicker beds, Queen Anne eyelet bedspreads, and some antiques. A breakfast of muffins, coffee, and juice is served each morning in a parlor overlooking the harbor. The garden suite behind the inn has a

TV and VCR, a full kitchen, and a fireplace. ⊠ *50 Spring St., Box 776, Friday Harbor 98250,* ☎ *360/378–2070 or 800/742–8210,* ℻ *360/ 378–6437. 9 rooms, 4 with bath; 1 suite. Outdoor hot tub, car rental. MC, V.*

Outdoor Activities and Sports

BEACHES
American Camp (☞ San Juan Island National Park, *above*) has 6 mi of public beach. You'll find 10 acres of beachfront at **San Juan County Park** (⊠ 380 Westside Rd. N, Friday Harbor, ☎ 360/378–2992).

BICYCLING
San Juan Island Bicycles (⊠ 380 Argyle St., Friday Harbor, ☎ 360/ 378–4941) has a reputation for good service and equipment. **Susie's Mopeds** (⊠ Friday Harbor, ☎ 360/378–5244 or 800/532–0087), at the top of the hill behind the line to board the ferry, rents mopeds.

BOATING
Port of Friday Harbor (☎ 360/378–2688), **Roche Harbor Resort** (☎ 360/378–2155), and **Snug Harbor Resort Marina** (☎ 360/378–4762) have standard marina facilities.

FISHING
You can fish year-round for bass and trout at Egg and Sportsman lakes, both north of Friday Harbor off Roche Harbor Road. **Buffalo Works** (☎ 360/378–4612) arranges saltwater fishing trips. Licenses are required.

WHALE-WATCHING
San Juan Excursions (☎ 360/378–6636 or 800/809–4253) cruises the waters around the islands. **Western Prince Cruises** (☎ 360/378–5315 or 800/757–6722) operates a four-hour narrated tour.

Shopping
Boardwalk Bookstore (⊠ 5 Spring St., Friday Harbor, ☎ 360/378– 2787) is strong in the classics and has a good collection of popular literature. **Dan Levin** (⊠ 50 1st St., ☎ 360/378–2051) stocks original jewelry. **Island Wools & Weaving** (⊠ 30 1st St. S, Friday Harbor, ☎ 360/ 378–2148) carries yarns, imaginative buttons, quilting supplies, and some hand-knit items. **Napier Sculpture Gallery** (⊠ 232 A St., ☎ 360/ 378–2221) exhibits many bronze and steel sculptures. **Waterworks Gallery** (⊠ 315 Argyle St., Friday Harbor, ☎ 360/378–3060) represents eclectic contemporary artists.

San Juan Islands Essentials

Arriving and Departing

BY CAR
To reach the San Juan Islands from Seattle, drive north on I–5 to Mount Vernon; at Exit 230 head west on Highway 20 and follow signs to Anacortes, where you can pick up the Washington State Ferry (☞ *below*). It is convenient to have a car in the San Juan Islands, but taking your car with you may mean waiting in long lines at the ferry terminals. With prior arrangement, most B&B owners will pick up guests without cars at the ferry terminals.

BY FERRY
The vessels of the **Washington State Ferries** (☎ 206/464–6400; 800/ 843–3779 in WA) range from one that holds 40 cars to jumbo craft capable of carrying more than 200 cars and 2,000 passengers each. The boats connect points all around Puget Sound and the San Juan Islands. Ferries depart from Anacortes, about 76 mi north of Seattle, to the San Juan Islands.

Sunny weekends are heavy traffic times all around the San Juan Islands, and weekday commuting hours for ferries headed into or out of Seattle are also crowded. Peak times on the Seattle runs are on sunny weekends, eastbound in the morning and Sunday nights, and westbound on Saturday morning and weekday afternoons. Since no reservations are accepted on Washington State Ferries (except for the Sidney-to-Anacortes run during the summer), arriving at least a half hour before a scheduled departure—even more at peak times—is always advised. Prior to boarding, lower your antenna. Only parking lights should be used at night, and it is considered bad form to start your engine before the ferry docks. Passengers and bicycles always load first unless otherwise instructed.

San Juan Islands Shuttle Express (✉ Alaska Ferry Terminal, 355 Harris Ave., No. 105, Bellingham 98225, ☎ 360/671–1137) takes passengers from Bellingham to Orcas Island and Friday Harbor.

BY PLANE

West Isle Air (☎ 800/874–4434) flies to Friday Harbor on San Juan Island from Sea-Tac and Bellingham airports. **Kenmore Air** (☎ 206/486–1257 or 800/543–9595) flies floatplanes from Lake Union in Seattle to the San Juan Islands.

Contacts and Resources

CAMPING

Marine State Parks (☎ 360/753–2027) are accessible by private boat only. No moorage or camping reservations are available, and fees are charged at some parks from May through Labor Day. Fresh water, where available, is limited. Island parks are Blind, Clark, Doe, James, Jones, Matia, Patos, Posey, Stuart, Sucia, and Turn. All have a few campsites; there are no docks at Blind, Clark, Patos, Posey, or Turn islands.

CHARTERS

Amante Sail Tours (☎ 360/376–4231). **Charters Northwest** (☎ 360/378–7196). **Harmony Sailing Charters** (☎ 360/468–3310). **Kismet Sailing Charters** (☎ 360/468–2435). **Nor'wester Sailing Charters** (☎ 360/378–5478).

KAYAKING

If you are kayaking on your own, beware of the ever-changing conditions, ferry and shipping landings, and the strong tides and currents. Go ashore only on known public property. **Shearwater Sea Kayak Tours** (☎ 360/376–4699), **Doe Bay Resort** (☎ 360/376–2291), **San Juan Kayak Expeditions** (☎ 360/378–4436), and **Seaquest** (☎ 360/378–5767) conduct day trips and longer expeditions.

VISITOR INFORMATION

San Juan Island Chamber of Commerce (✉ Friday Harbor 98250, ☎ 360/378–5240). **San Juan Islands Tourism Cooperative and Visitors Information Service** (✉ Lopez 98261, ☎ 360/468–3663).

WHATCOM AND SKAGIT COUNTIES

North of Seattle on the way to Vancouver, British Columbia, I–5 passes through the Skagit River valley and Skagit and Whatcom counties. The Skagit Valley connects the Cascade Range with Puget Sound. The valley is famous for its tulips, which blossom in spring into astounding colors. The small towns of the Skagit Valley are fun to stroll through. The gentle farmlands and low foothills in and around the valley are often wrapped in mist, resembling a delicate Japanese pen-and-ink landscape drawing. To the east, rising sharply from the foothills, is the anything-but-delicate Cascade Range.

Bellingham, in Whatcom County, is the largest town in the region. Lummi Island is a ferry ride due west of Bellingham. Ferndale and Blaine are easy day trips to the north. Bow and La Conner, both in Skagit County, are south of Bellingham. Sedro Woolley is east of La Conner; from Sedro Woolley you can loop back north into Whatcom County and connect with Highway 542, which leads into the Mount Baker National Recreation Area.

Bellingham

⑥ *90 mi north of Seattle on I–5.*

College students from Western Washington University and workers in the fishing and lumber industries are among the most visible residents of lush and beautiful Bellingham. The town, a bizarre jumble of industrial parks and commercial and residential buildings, is the sort of place that becomes more interesting as you get to know it.

The impressive four-building **Whatcom Museum of History and Art** has as its centerpiece Bellingham's first city hall, an 1892 redbrick structure that was converted into the original museum in 1940. Victorian clothing, toys, games, and clocks are on display, and there are art exhibits as well. The other buildings in the Whatcom complex include a natural-history gallery (with a permanent stuffed-bird collection) and a children's museum. ⊠ *121 Prospect St.,* ☎ *360/676–6981.* ⌦ *Free (children's museum $2).* ⊘ *Tues.–Sun. noon–5.*

Stairs at the back of the Whatcom Museum of History and Art lead down into **Maritime Heritage Park,** which pays tribute to Bellingham's fishing industry. On self-guided tours at the **Marine Heritage Center,** you can learn about hatcheries and salmon life cycles, see salmon-rearing tanks and fish ladders, and watch salmon spawning. You can go fishing for salmon and trout at Whatcom Creek within the park. ⊠ *1600 C St.,* ☎ *360/676–6806.* ⌦ *Free.* ⊘ *Weekdays 9–5.*

Boulevard Park (⊠ S. State St. and Bayview Dr.), midway between downtown and Old Fairhaven, is an excellent park with 14 acres and ½ mi of shoreline. You can play volleyball or Frisbee, search for starfish and other sea creatures when the tide is low, and go crabbing in the summer.

A good place to fish, lounge, picnic, or walk is the **Squalicum Harbor Marina** (⊠ Roeder Ave. and Coho Way), which holds more than 1,900 commercial and pleasure boats. **Pete Zuanich Park,** at the end of the spit, has a telescope for close-up views of the water, and there's a marine-life center with touch tanks.

On Railroad Avenue between Chestnut and Magnolia streets, you'll find cafés, vintage clothing and consignment shops, a batik boutique, and the narrow but engaging **Bellingham Antique Radio Museum** (⊠ 1515 Railroad Ave., no phone). A statue of the RCA dog keeps watch on the museum, whose friendly operator has been collecting radios for a half-century.

Western Washington University sits on a hill overlooking downtown and Bellingham Bay. The visitor center has maps and an audio tour of the nearly two dozen outdoor sculptures scattered about campus, including works by Mark DiSuvero, Isamu Noguchi, Richard Serra, and George Rickey. Take Garden Street to get to the university from the north, and College Drive if you're coming from the south. ⊠ *Visitor Center: S. College Dr. off Bill McDonald Pwky.,* ☎ *360/650–3000.*

Whatcom and Skagit Counties

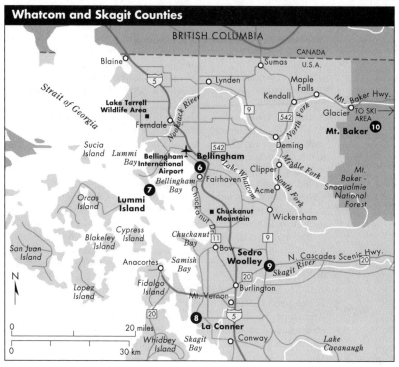

Fairhaven, the historic district to the south of Bellingham, at the beginning of Chuckanut Drive (Highway 11), retains a distinct identity as an intellectual and artistic center. The beautifully restored 1890s red-brick buildings of the **Old Fairhaven District,** especially around Harris Street between 10th and 12th streets, house restaurants, taverns, galleries, and specialty boutiques. In the early 1900s, the American Rose Society developed **Fairhaven Park** (⊠ 107 Chuckanut Dr., ☎ 360/671–1570) as a testing site. The roses in the garden here are at their best from June to September. The park, which is open daily from 10 to 5, also contains trails and picnic grounds, a playground, tennis courts, playing fields, a wading pool, and a youth hostel.

OFF THE
BEATEN PATH

CHUCKANUT DRIVE – Highway 11, also known as Chuckanut Drive, was once the only highway heading south from Bellingham and Fairhaven. The 23-mi road passes alongside beautiful Chuckanut Bay. On one side is the steep and heavily wooded Chuckanut Mountain; on the other are stunning westward views over Puget Sound and the San Juan Islands. Many attractive houses have been built along this stretch of road. The drive begins in Fairhaven Park (☞ *above*) and joins up with I–5 in the flat farmlands near Bow (☞ *below*), in Skagit County; the full loop can be made in a couple of hours. Several good restaurants are located toward the southern end of the drive.

Dining and Lodging

$$–$$$ ✕ **Il Fiasco.** The ambitious northern Italian fare at this sophisticated restaurant (the name means "the flask") is tasty but not light. Entrées include veal served with hazelnut topping in a flavorful reduction sauce with squash and carrot puree, and steamers in tomato bouillabaisse with orange essence. ⊠ *1309 Commercial St.,* ☎ *360/676–9136. MC, V. No lunch on weekends.*

$$–$$$ ✕ **Pacific Café.** The understated decor at this restaurant next door to the Mount Baker Theatre (☞ Nightlife and the Arts, *below*) is Asian-inspired: white walls, rice-paper screens, and wood shutters. The Asian influence extends to dishes like Alaska spot prawns in a garlicky black-bean sauce and grilled king salmon in hoisin sauce. The portions are large, but save room for wickedly good desserts like the chocolate éclairs. ⊠ *100 N. Commercial St.,* ☎ *360/647–0800. AE, MC, V. Closed Sun. No lunch Mon.*

$$ ✕ **Orchard Street Brewery.** The purple floor, orangish walls, and red tables of this upscale contemporary restaurant complement the industrial ambience—it's in a former manufacturing complex. Among the menu highlights are a crab turnover appetizer and a salmon entrée with shi-itake and oyster mushrooms in puff pastry. You can also order pizza baked in a wood oven. ⊠ *709 W. Orchard Dr., No. 1,* ☎ *360/647–1614. Reservations not accepted. AE, MC, V. Closed Sun.*

$ ✕ **Archer Ale House.** "Fresh air, fresh ale" is the slogan of this no-smok-ing pub in the renovated cellar of the 1903 Shering Block in Fairhaven. A 20-ft oak bar, stained-glass windows, an embossed-tin ceiling, and a dartboard create an English-pub atmosphere. The food is publike, too: pasties, robust soups, and deep-dish pizzas, plus a few vegetarian dishes. Ten taps dispense everything from pilsners to stouts. ⊠ *1212 10th St.,* ☎ *360/647–7002. Reservations not accepted. MC, V.*

$ ✕ **Colophon Café.** The restaurant inside the Village Bookstore serves African peanut soup, quiches, deli sandwiches, and other hearty fare. Homemade desserts and ice cream are also on the menu. ⊠ *1208 11th St., Old Fairhaven,* ☎ *360/647–0092. Reservations not accepted. MC, V.*

$$$–$$$$ 🛏 **Schnauzer Crossing.** Meticulously maintained gardens surround this contemporary B&B in a peaceful residential neighborhood over-looking Lake Whatcom. The original 1920s house was extended in the 1970s; the modern living room has extremely high ceilings. One of the two rooms in the house has a lake view; the other, a large suite, has a glass-enclosed atrium, a fireplace, and a whirlpool tub. A cottage unit, whose cost may leave you expecting something more lavish, has a kitchen, a gas fireplace, and a whirlpool tub. Friendly owners Donna and Ver-mont McAllister serve ample, unusual breakfasts like triple-sec French toast. ⊠ *4421 Lakeway Dr.,* ☎ *360/733–0055 or 800/562–2808,* ℻ *360/734–2808. 1 room, 1 suite, 1 cottage. Outdoor hot tub, boating. MC, V.*

$$ 🛏 **Best Western Lakeway Inn.** The bustling Lakeway is just off the in-terstate in downtown Bellingham. Its four floors surround an open-air courtyard with a clover-shape indoor pool and a hot tub. Rooms are functional; the rates include a hot breakfast. Children under 12 stay for free when sharing a room with their parents. ⊠ *714 Lakeway Dr., east of I–5's Exit 253, 98225,* ☎ *360/671–1011,* ℻ *360/676–8519. 132 rooms. Restaurant, bar, indoor pool, hot tub, sauna, exercise room, airport and ferry shuttle. AE, D, DC, MC, V.*

$$ 🛏 **North Garden Inn.** This B&B in a noteworthy Queen Anne–style mansion near Western Washington University is on the National Reg-ister of Historic Places. Some rooms have views of Bellingham Bay. The Steinway grand piano in the entryway is occasionally used for concerts; guests may play it, too. ⊠ *1014 N. Garden St., 98225,* ☎ *360/671–7828 or 800/922–6414. 10 rooms. MC. V.*

Nightlife and the Arts

Boundary Bay Brewery & Bistro (⊠ 1107 Railroad Ave., ☎ 360/647–5593), a warehouse turned classy brewery, pours five beers, displays eclectic local art, and serves good food. The mellowest place in Bellingham for a beer is the **Up and Up** (⊠ 1234 N. State St., ☎ 360/733–9739).

In late August and early September, the **Bellingham Festival of Music** (☎ 360/676–5997) presents nearly 20 orchestral, chamber-music, and jazz concerts at Western Washington University and other nearby locations. Informative talks are given an hour prior to the chamber and symphony performances.

The **Mount Baker Theatre** (⊠ 104 N. Commercial St., ☎ 360/734–6080), a restored theater from the vaudeville era, has a 110-ft Moorish tower and a lobby fashioned after a Spanish galleon. The theater, home to the Whatcom Symphony Orchestra, presents movies and touring performances. **Western Washington University** (⊠ 516 High St., ☎ 360/650–6146) presents classical music concerts and theatrical productions. The **Whatcom Museum of History and Art** (⊠ 121 Prospect St., ☎ 360/676–6981) sponsors downtown gallery walks.

Outdoor Activities and Sports

CLIMBING

The **American Alpine Institute** (⊠ 1515 12th St., ☎ 360/671–1505) is a prestigious mountain- and rock-climbing school.

GOLF

Lake Padden Golf Course (⊠ 4882 Samish Way, ☎ 360/738–7400), an 18-hole, par-72 municipal course, is carved out of second-growth forest. The greens fee runs from $15 to $20; an optional cart costs $22.

KAYAKING

Elakah! Expeditions (☎ 360/734–7270 or 800/434–7270) is dedicated to sensitive low-impact travel. **Moondance Kayak Tours and Sales** (⊠ 2448 Yew Street Rd., ☎ 360/738–7664) conducts tours that range in length from a half day to five.

WHALE-WATCHING

Island Mariner Cruises (⊠ 5 Harbor Esplanade, ☎ 360/734–8866) conducts whale-watching and nature cruises to the Queen Charlotte Islands and Alaska and sunset cruises around Bellingham Bay. **San Juan Islands Shuttle Express** (⊠ Alaska Ferry Terminal, 355 Harris Ave. at railroad tracks, ☎ 360/671–1137) operates summer whale-watching trips from Bellingham to the San Juan Islands.

Shopping

Along lower Holly Street in Bellingham's Old Town, you'll find antiques shops, secondhand stores, fish markets, hobby shops, and suppliers of outdoor-recreation equipment. Try the **Old Town Antique Mall** (⊠ 427 W. Holly St., ☎ 360/671–3301) for antiques and collectibles.

The glossy **Bellis Fair** (⊠ I–5, Exit 256B, ☎ 360/734–5022), a regional shopping mall a few miles north of downtown, has major department stores, several restaurants, shops, and a multiplex movie theater.

Lummi Island

➐ *10 mi west of Bellingham; board ferry at Gooseberry Point, or drive to I–5's Exit 260 and follow signs 3½ mi west on Slater Rd. and 6½ mi south on Haxton Way.*

Mountainous and largely uninhabited Lummi Island is a fine day trip from Bellingham, especially if you like to bike or hike. Often called the forgotten island of the San Juan chain, Lummi, named for the Lummi Indians who lived here until the 19th century, is a 10-mi stretch of tranquillity. Sweeping views of the San Juan Islands unfold from Puget Road and West Shore Drive, and you'll sometimes see reef-net fishermen hauling in salmon on Legoe Bay.

Ferndale

10 mi north of Bellingham on I–5.

The dairy-farming community of Ferndale lies in the Nooksack Valley north of Bellingham. In the town's **Pioneer Park** you can wander through log buildings from the 1870s—including Whatcom County's first church—that have been restored and converted into museums. ⊠ *1st and Cherry Sts. (2 blocks south of Main St.),* ☎ *360/384–6461.* ▧ *Free.* ⊗ *May–Sept., Tues.–Sun. 11:30–4:30.*

Hovander Homestead Park, a National Historic Site, contains a model farm complete with a Victorian-era farmhouse, barnyard animals, a water tower, vegetable gardens, and antique farm equipment. Surrounding it are 60 acres of walking trails, picnic grounds, and access to fishing in the Nooksack. ⊠ *5299 Nielsen Rd.,* ☎ *360/384–3444.* ▧ *Free.* ⊗ *Daily dawn–dusk.*

The **Tennant Lake Natural History Interpretive Center,** within the **Nielsen House,** an early homestead, has exhibits and information about nature walks. The lake is part of a 200-acre marshy habitat where eagles and other wildlife can be seen. The unusual **Fragrance Garden**— with herbs and flowers—is designed for the sight-impaired and can be explored by following Braille signs. ⊠ *5236 Nielsen Rd.,* ☎ *360/384–3444.* ▧ *Free.* ⊗ *Daily dawn–dusk.*

Many species of waterfowl live within the 11,000-acre **Lake Terrell Wildlife Preserve.** You can hunt pheasants and western Washington waterfowl in the fall, or try to catch perch, catfish, bass, and cutthroat year-round. ⊠ *5975 Lake Terrell Rd.,* ☎ *360/384–4723.* ▧ *Free.* ⊗ *Weekdays 8–5.*

Blaine

16 mi north of Ferndale on I–5.

Fishing boats ply the waters around Blaine, a casual town on Washington's border with Canada. Drayton Harbor, which dominates Blaine's shoreline, sweeps into the Semiahmoo Spit. "Semiahmoo" is the coastal Native American word for "clam eaters," and indeed, the miles of shoreline along the spit are good for clamming and fishing as well as swimming, beachcombing, and strolling.

Lodging

$$$ 🏠 **Inn at Semi-ah-moo.** A dramatic waterside location and many outdoor activities are the chief lures of the hostelry inside the old Semi-ahmoo Salmon Cannery building. The rooms range from motel-like accommodations to suites with fireplaces, balconies, and expansive views. You can join a fishing charter or sightseeing cruise, play golf on a course designed by Arnold Palmer, work out at the health club or indoor track, swim in heated pools indoors or out, and bike, jog, or hike around the nearby nature trails. ⊠ *9565 Semiahmoo Pkwy., 98230,* ☎ *360/371–2000 or 800/770–7992,* ℻ *360/371–5490. 188 rooms, 12 suites. 2 restaurants, bar, indoor pool, outdoor pool, golf course, tennis court, health club, jogging, racquetball, squash, dock, boating, bicycles. AE, MC, V.*

Bow

18 mi south of Bellingham on Chuckanut Dr. (Hwy. 11) or I–5.

Bow, at the southern end of Chuckanut Drive, is just east of Samish Bay, where oysters and other seafood are harvested. The town is a great place to stop for a bite to eat.

Dining

$$–$$$ ✕ **The Oyster Bar.** Nestled into a hillside, this intimate two-story restaurant has views of the creek below. Linens grace the tables, but the ambience is casual; an outdoor porch is especially popular in the summer. Try any of the Samish Bay oyster entrées or specials like tiger prawns stuffed with garlic and pecans or crab cakes with a mango-ginger chutney sauce. ⊠ *240 Chuckanut Dr.,* ☎ *360/766–6185. AE, MC, V.*

$$–$$$ ✕ **Oyster Creek Inn.** Window tables at this small restaurant overlook the creek below. Oysters prepared in traditional and imaginative ways are the menu highlights; excellent Washington State vintages make up the entire wine list. Dishes like salmon omelets and fries are served at Sunday brunch. ⊠ *190 Chuckanut Dr.,* ☎ *360/766–6179. AE, MC, V.*

$–$$ ✕ **Rhododendron Café.** Seafood, homemade soups, and fresh salads are the mainstays of this unpretentious café's ever-changing menu. Seasonal offerings might include mussel-vegetable soup or marinated snapper. The pies are locally famous. ⊠ *553 Chuckanut Dr.,* ☎ *360/ 766–6667. MC, V.*

La Conner

❽ *39 mi from Bellingham, south on I–5 and west on Hwy. 534; 65 mi from Seattle, north on I–5 and west on Hwy. 534.*

Morris Graves, Kenneth Callahan, Guy Anderson, Mark Tobey, and other painters set up shop in La Conner in the 1940s, and the small fishing village at the mouth of the Skagit River has been a haven for artists ever since. A concerted effort in recent years to make La Conner a tourist destination has had mixed results. The town borders on being too precious, and though the number of good shops and restaurants has increased, so too has the traffic—in summer the usually sleepy enclave becomes congested with people and cars.

Roozengaarde (⊠ 1587 Beaver Marsh Rd., ☎ 360/424–8531) is one of the largest growers of tulips, daffodils, and irises in the United States—200 or so varieties in all. It's open daily from 9 to 5 during the blooming season (from March to May) and is closed on Sundays the rest of the year.

The flat land around La Conner makes for easy bicycling, and there are historic buildings to view as you ride. The **Volunteer Fireman's Museum** (⊠ 611 S. 1st St., no phone) contains turn-of-the-century equipment that you can see from the street through the building's large windows. Historic furnishings are on display at the Victorian **Gaches Mansion** (⊠ 2nd and Calhoun Sts., 360/466–4288). Admission is $3; the house is open on Friday, Saturday, and Sunday from 1 to 4 (and until 5 in summer).

The **Museum of Northwest Art** (⊠ 121 S. 1st St. ☎ 360/466–4446) presents the works of regional artists past and present. Admission is $3; the museum is open daily except Monday between 10 and 5. The **Skagit County Historical Museum** (⊠ 501 4th St., ☎ 360/466–3365) surveys domestic life in early Skagit County and Northwest Coastal

Indian history. Admission is $2; the museum is open daily except Monday between 11 and 5.

Dining and Lodging

$$$–$$$$ ✕ **Palmer's Restaurant and Pub.** There's a distinctly French influence to the seasonally changing menu at this restaurant near the water. The chef's signature dish is a braised lamb shank, but you'll find salads, pastas, and other lighter fare as well. The adjacent pub (with much stained glass) serves bistro fare. ⊠ *205 E. Washington St.,* ☎ *360/466–4261. AE, MC, V. No lunch Mon.–Thurs. Sept.–Mar.*

$$$–$$$$ ⌂ **La Conner Channel Lodge.** La Conner's only waterfront hotel is an understated modern facility overlooking the narrow Swinomish Channel. Each room has a private balcony and a gas fireplace and is decorated in subdued gray tones with wooden trim; 12 rooms have whirlpool baths. Room rates include a Continental breakfast. Many corporations hold retreats at the lodge. ⊠ *205 N. 1st St., 98257,* ☎ *360/466–1500,* FAX *360/466–5902. 29 rooms, 12 suites. Business services, meeting rooms. AE, D, DC, MC, V.*

$$ ⌂ **Hotel Planter.** This renovated hotel, the oldest in La Conner, is on the National Register of Historic Places. Handmade furniture fills the rooms, which have fine views of La Conner's main street or the waterfront. No smoking is allowed within the hotel. ⊠ *715 1st St., 98257,* ☎ *360/466–4710 or 800/488–5409,* FAX *360/466–1320. 12 rooms. Hot tub. AE, MC, V.*

$$ ⌂ **Rainbow Inn.** A white picket fence surrounds this stately three-story, century-old country house outside town. The large rooms are furnished with antiques; one room has a whirlpool tub. All guests have access to the hot tub in the gazebo behind the house, from which Mount Baker can be seen. Breakfast, included in the room rates, is served in an enclosed porch with views of farmland. Smoking is not permitted at the inn. ⊠ *1075 Chilberg Rd., 98257,* ☎ *360/466–4578 or 800/888–8879,* FAX *360/466–3844. 5 rooms with bath, 3 rooms share 1 bath. Hot tub. MC, V.*

Sedro Woolley

❾ *14 mi northeast of La Conner; follow signs from I–5's Exit 232.*

Railroad tracks crisscross Sedro Woolley, the former hub of the logging industry in the North Cascades and the sort of town where, say, the old-timers, "you'd lock your wife and daughters inside on the weekends, when the loggers came in from the mountains." Public murals and carved log statues outside shops along the main streets give testament to the town's past, as does the **Sedro Woolley Museum** (⊠ 725 Murdock St., ☎ 360/855–2390), open on Saturday from 9 to 4 and Sunday from 1:30 to 4:30.

OFF THE
BEATEN PATH   **NORTH CASCADES SCENIC HIGHWAY** – Highway 20, known east of Sedro Woolley as the North Cascades Scenic Highway, is an ethereal drive through a region of craggy peaks and subalpine meadows filled with wildflowers and lakes. The highway, which is closed during the winter, leads to Ross and Diablo dams. A tugboat operated from June to September by Seattle City Light takes passengers from Diablo Dam to the base of Ross Dam. Four-hour tours operated by Seattle City Light's Skagit Tours include a ride up an antique incline lift, a boat cruise on Diablo Lake, a tour of the Ross Power House, and a meal of chicken and vegetarian spaghetti. Ninety-minute tours include a ride on the lift, a walk to Diablo Dam, and a tour of Diablo Power House. ⊠ *Seattle City Light, 500 Newhalem St., Rockport, WA 98283,* ☎ *206/684–3030.*

⌨ *$25 plus tax for 4-hr tour, $5 plus tax for 90-min tour, $2.50 each way for tugboat ride.* ☺ *Tours June–Sept. (hrs vary). Tugboat ride leaves Diablo Dam at 8:30 and 3.*

En Route   Highway 9 travels north from Sedro Woolley past the towns of Wickersham, Acme, and Clipper on the way to Highway 542, which leads to Mount Baker. At Wickersham, a detour west to Lake Whatcom makes for a splendid afternoon's drive. On Saturdays in July and August at 11 AM and 1 PM, you can ride through the woods on the vintage **Lake Whatcom Steam Train** (⊠ Lake Whatcom, south end, ☎ 360/595–2218). **Everybody's Store** (⊠ Hwy. 9, Van Zandt, ☎ 360/592–2297) in the town of Van Zandt is a good place to stock up on sandwiches and exotic foods. The store sells everything from dill pickles to homemade sausages, cheeses, and bialys—not to mention toys, imported clothes, and regular groceries. You can picnic on the store's grounds on tables underneath fruit trees.

Glacier

44 mi from Sedro Woolley, north on Hwy. 9 and east on Hwy. 542.

The mountain town of Glacier, just inside the Mount Baker–Snoqualmie National Forest boundary, has a few shops, cafés, and lodgings.

Lodging

$$ ▦ **Mt. Baker Lodging & Travel.** Cabins nestled in a wooded setting range from snug hideaways suitable for couples to larger chalets for families or groups. All the accommodations are clean and charming, if rustic, with wood-burning stoves or fireplaces. Some units are equipped with VCRs. ⊠ *7500 Mt. Baker Hwy., 98244,* ☎ *360/599–2453 or 800/709–7669. 19 units. Hot tub, sauna. AE, MC, V.*

$–$$$ ▦ **Mt. Baker Chalet.** The privately owned units here are available for one-night or longer rentals. Smallish two-person cabins are more in the rustic vein, but you can opt for upscale condominiums—some with several bedrooms—that have access to a hot tub, a sauna, and tennis, squash, and racquetball courts. All the units are in secluded wooded locations and have wood-burning stoves or fireplaces. Jogging and walking trails are right outside the door. Weekly rates are quite reasonable. ⊠ *9857 Mt. Baker Hwy., 98244,* ☎ *360/599–2405 or 800/258–2405,* ⚏ *360/599–2255. 25 units. Indoor pool, outdoor pool, MC, V.*

En Route   Highway 542 winds east from Glacier through the Mount Baker–Snoqualmie National Forest. The 170-ft-high **Nooksack Falls,** about 5 mi east of Glacier, are only a short walk from the highway.

Mount Baker

❿   *69 mi from Sedro Woolley, north on Hwy. 9 and east on Hwy. 542 (Mount Baker Hwy.); 61 mi east of Bellingham on Hwy. 542.*

At 10,778 ft high, the sharp peak of Mount Baker is visible from much of Whatcom County. The **Mount Baker–Snoqualmie National Forest** attracts hikers, mountain bikers, and skiers. The adjacent, photogenic Mount Shuksan, just east of the national forest, stands at an elevation of 9,038 ft.

Skiing

You can snowboard and ski downhill or cross-country at the **Mount Baker Ski Area** (⊠ Mount Baker Hwy. 542, ☎ 360/734–6771), 17 mi east of Glacier. The facility has the longest season in the state, lasting from roughly November to the end of April. Call 360/671–0211 for snow reports.

Whatcom and Skagit Counties Essentials

Arriving and Departing

BY BUS
Greyhound (☎ 800/231–2222 or 360/733–5251) serves Fairhaven Station daily from downtown Seattle and Vancouver.

BY CAR
The entire region is easily accessible by driving north from Seattle on **I–5.**

BY PLANE
Horizon Air and United Express service **Bellingham International Airport** (⊠ 4255 Mitchell Way; Bakerview Exit off I–5, ☎ 360/676–2500). *See* Air Travel *in* the Gold Guide for airline phone numbers.

BY TRAIN
Amtrak (☎ 800/872–7245) connects Seattle, Bellingham, and Vancouver.

Getting Around

BY CAR
Interstate 5 is the main north–south route through western Whatcom and Skagit counties. **Highway 542** travels east from Bellingham to Mount Baker. **Highway 20** heads east from Burlington to Sedro Woolley and continues on through the entire Cascade Range.

Visitor Information

BABS (⊠ Bed and Breakfast Service, ☎ 360/733–8642). **Bellingham/Whatcom County Convention and Visitors Bureau** (⊠ 904 Potter St., Bellingham 98227, ☎ 360/671–3990 or 800/487–2032). **La Conner Chamber of Commerce** (⊠ Lime Dock, 109 N. 1st St., 98257, ☎ 360/466–4778). **North Cascades National Park** (⊠ 2105 Hwy. 20, Sedro Woolley 98264, ☎ 360/856–5700).

TACOMA AND VICINITY

Tacoma's history, like that of many other towns in the Northwest, is linked inextricably to lumber and fishing, and with the two-fisted men and women who did the labor. The largely blue-collar town's reputation (especially with Seattleites) as a smelly place—pulp mills and smelters in the area generate at times malodorous pollution—is partly deserved, but civic leaders are doing much to clean up Tacoma's image. And with some success: The self-proclaimed "City of Destiny" frequently appears on most-livable-cities lists.

Among the many assets of this city of 184,500 are its handsome brick buildings, fine views of Commencement Bay, world-class state-history museum, impressive zoo, and active port. Tacoma is a convenient jumping-off point for exploring south-central Washington, particularly Mount Rainier and, across the Tacoma Narrows Bridge, the small fishing villages of the Kitsap Peninsula.

Tacoma

36 mi south of Seattle on I–5.

A Good Walk
Begin your tour in the Waterfront District at **Union Station** ⑪, on Pacific Avenue between East 18th and 19th streets. Next door is the state-of-the-art **Washington State History Museum** ⑫. After lunch at one of

the district's funky eateries, head north on Pacific to the **Tacoma Art Museum** ⑬. From the museum, head west on 11th Street to Broadway. Walk north on Broadway past the **Broadway Center for the Performing Arts** ⑭ and the **Children's Museum of Tacoma** ⑮. At 9th Street begins **Antique Row,** a collection of shops that are fun to browse through. Continue north along Tacoma Avenue to **Wright Park** ⑯ and the **Stadium Historic District** ⑰. No tour of Tacoma is complete without a visit to **Point Defiance Park** ⑱, which is at the most northern end of the city and best reached by car or bus.

TIMING

Union Station requires only a brief look, but you could easily spend one or two hours in the Washington State History Museum. The Tacoma Art Museum and Children's Museum each require about an hour. Antique Row and Wright Park are half-hour stops at most. A full day is necessary to take in all the attractions at Point Defiance Park, but the highlights can be visited in a few hours.

Sights to See

⑭ Broadway Center for the Performing Arts. Cultural activity in Tacoma centers on this complex of historic and new theaters. The famous theater architect B. Marcus Pritica designed the **Pantages** at 901 Broadway, a 1918 Greco-Roman–influenced music hall with classical figures, ornate columns, arches, and reliefs. W. C. Fields, Mae West, Charlie Chaplin, Bob Hope, and Stan Laurel all performed here. The Tacoma Symphony and BalleTacoma perform at the Pantages, which also presents touring musicals and other shows. Adjacent to the Pantages, the very contemporary **Theatre on the Square** (⊠ Broadway between 10th and 11th Sts.) is the home of the Tacoma Actors Guild, one of Washington's largest professional theater companies. In its early days, the **Rialto Theater** (⊠ 301 S. 9th St.), up Broadway a few blocks, presented vaudeville performances and silent films. The Tacoma Youth Symphony performs in the 1918 structure. ☎ *253/591–5890 for all theaters.*

⑮ Children's Museum of Tacoma. Many of the hip and fun cultural, historical, and science exhibits at this new facility are interactive, but you'll also find displays such as old board games or the artifacts of civilizations past and present. ⊠ *936 Broadway,* ☎ *253/627–6031.* ⌷ *$3.75.* ☉ *Tues.–Sat. 10–5, Sun. noon–5.*

★ **⑱ Point Defiance Park.** This 698-acre park that juts into Commencement Bay contains several museums and historical sites, extensive footpaths and hiking trails, picnic areas, a wide beachfront, and rose, dahlia, rhododendron, and other gardens. **Five Mile Drive,** which loops around the park past its major attractions, yields fine views of Tacoma's waterfront through moss-covered trees.

One of the first stops heading west on Five Mile Drive south of the zoo is the 15-acre **Camp Six Logging Museum** (☎ 253/752–0047), whose exhibits—restored bunkhouses, hand tools, and other equipment—illustrate the history of steam logging from 1880 to 1950. A steam-train ride ($2) operates from here on weekends between noon and 4.

A bit farther west is **Fort Nisqually** (☎ 253/591–5339), a restored Hudson's Bay Trading Post. A British outpost on the Nisqually Delta in the 1830s, it was moved to Point Defiance in 1935. A spiked wooden fence and two fun-to-climb lookout towers surround the compound. Inside are the original granary and officers' quarters. Within the main house are a small exhibition on the fur trade and a gift shop. Admission to the fort is $1; it's open from Memorial Day to Labor Day daily from 11 to 4 and the same hours from Wednesday to Sunday during the rest of the year. **Never Never Land** (☎ 253/591–6117), a children's

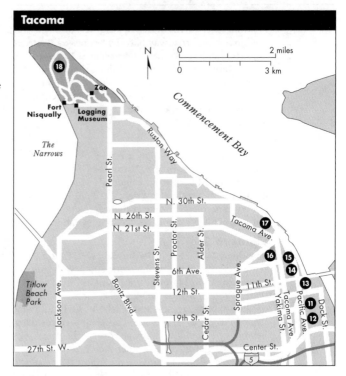

fantasy world of sculptured storybook characters, is across the parking lot from Fort Nisqually.

From Fort Nisqually, Five Mile Drive loops past several lookouts with views of the Narrows waterway. As it heads back toward the park entrance the drive passes viewing points that look onto lower Puget Sound and later onto Commencement Bay. Just past the road to Owen Beach is the rhododendron garden.

The natural habitats at the **Point Defiance Zoo and Aquarium** (☎ 253/591–5335) bring you close to whales, walruses, sharks, polar bears, octopuses, apes, reptiles, and birds. The zoo specializes in species of the Pacific Northwest. The zoo and the aquarium have gained an international reputation for their expert caretakers who treat injured wildlife.

Near the zoo are bus stops, several gardens, a marina, the ferry landing, and other facilities. ⊠ *Point Defiance Park: 5400 N. Pearl St.,* ☎ *253/305–1000.* ⊑ *Park free; zoo $6.75.* ⊘ *Park daily dawn–dusk; zoo June–Aug., daily 10–7; Sept.–May, weekdays 10–4, weekends 10–5.*

⑰ Stadium Historic District. Many of the Victorian homes in this charming neighborhood, high on a hill overlooking Commencement Bay, have been converted to bed-and-breakfast inns. **Stadium High School** at 111 North E Street is in an elaborate château-style structure that was built in 1891 as a luxury hotel for the Northern Pacific Railroad. The building was converted into a high school after a 1906 fire.

⑬ Tacoma Art Museum. Among the highlights of this museum are works by artists of the Northwest and collections of Impressionist and 20th-century European paintings. Also on exhibit are many glass sculptures by Tacoma native Dale Chihuly. ⊠ *12th St. at Pacific Ave.,* ☎ *253/272–4258.* ⊑ *$3.* ⊘ *Tues.–Sat. 10–5, Sun. noon–5.*

⓫ Union Station. This heirloom from the golden age of railroads dates from Tacoma's days as the western terminus of the Northern Pacific Railroad. Built by Reed and Stem, the architects of New York City's Grand Central Station, the copper-domed, Beaux Arts–style depot, which opened in 1911, shows the influence of the Roman Pantheon and 16th-century Italian Baroque building design. The station houses federal district courts; its rotunda (open to the public on weekdays from 10 to 4) contains what's billed as the largest single exhibit of glass sculptures by Dale Chihuly. The area around the station is known as the **Waterfront District.** Many formerly run-down redbrick buildings have been renovated and opened as shops and businesses; the atmosphere here has been getting hipper by the minute. The first section of the Tacoma branch of the **University of Washington** opened in 1997 across from Union Station. ⊠ *1717 Pacific Ave.,* ☎ *253/931–7884.*

⓬ Washington State History Museum. Adjacent to Union Station inside a 1996 building with same opulent architecture and mammoth arches, Washington's official history museum presents interactive exhibits and multimedia installations about the exploration and settlement of the state. Indian, Eskimo, pioneer, and other artifacts are also on display. ⊠ *1911 Pacific Ave.,* ☎ *253/272–3500.* 🎫 *$7.* 🕐 *Tues.–Sat. 10–5, Thurs. 10–8, Sun. 1–5.*

⓰ Wright Park. The chief attraction at this 28-acre park, all of which is on the National Register of Historic Places, is the glass-domed **W. W. Seymour Botanical Conservatory** (⊠ 4th and S. G Sts., ☎ 253/591–5330), a Victorian-style greenhouse with exotic flora. Across the street is the **Karpeles Manuscript Library Museum** (⊠ 407 S. G St., ☎ 253/383–2575), which preserves and exhibits letters and documents by individuals who have shaped history. ⊠ *Between 6th and Division Sts., Yakima and Tacoma Aves.,* ☎ *253/591–5331.* 🎫 *Free.* 🕐 *Park daily dawn–dusk, conservatory daily 8:30–4:20, museum daily 10–4.*

Dining and Lodging

$$–$$$ ✕ **E. R. Rogers Restaurant.** One of the best restaurants in the Tacoma area is 10 mi south of town in Steilacoom, the oldest incorporated town in Washington. Housed in an 1891 mansion with views of the Tacoma Narrows Bridge, the E. R. Rogers is decorated in Victorian style, with lace valances, brass fixtures, and antiques. Salmon dishes and prime rib with Yorkshire pudding are menu highlights. Brunch is served on Sunday. ⊠ *1702 Commercial St., Steilacoom,* ☎ *253/582–0280. MC, V. No lunch.*

$$–$$$ ✕ **Harbor Lights.** This waterfront institution adorned with glass floats, stuffed fish, life preservers, and other nautical furnishings hasn't changed since the '50s. Many of the seafood and other preparations are also classic—the steamed clams (in season) and the fish-and-chips (light and not greasy) are particularly good. The view of Commencement Bay is splendid, so try to snag a window seat. ⊠ *2761 Ruston Way,* ☎ *253/752–8600. AE, DC, MC, V. No lunch Sun.*

$$ ✕ **Lobster Shop.** Of this traditional seafood restaurant's two locations, the older one, on Dash Point, is cozier than its sister on Ruston Way. But both have fine views of Commencement Bay and simply prepared seafood, with salmon the perennial favorite. There's a cocktail lounge on Ruston Way; beer and wine are available on Dash Point. ⊠ *6912 Soundview Dr. NE (off Dash Point Rd.),* ☎ *253/927–1513;* ⊠ *4013 Ruston Way,* ☎ *253/759–2165. AE, DC, MC, V.*

$$ ✕ **Luciano's.** Chef Alfredo Russo and his staff prepare southern Italian cuisine with a Neapolitan influence. The decor takes advantage of the waterfront setting, with three-story-high skylights and black or red exposed beams against forest-green walls. Recommended dishes include the sautéed veal and the charbroiled king salmon topped with horseradish, lemon, dill, and cream sauce. ⊠ *3327 Ruston Way,* ☎ *253/756–5611. MC, V.*

$$ ✕ **Old House Café.** Its location in the heart of the Proctor District shopping area makes this upstairs café an especially convenient place for lunch. The huge warm scallop salad contains sweet peppers, fresh wild greens, vegetables, and perfectly braised scallops. Or try the baked king salmon, with fresh spinach and raspberries wrapped in phyllo dough. The café's interior incorporates many antique fixtures, including a stained-glass window from a Yakima building and light fixtures from a turn-of-the-century Seattle bank. ⊠ *2717 N. Proctor St.,* ☎ *253/759–7336. AE, MC, V. Closed Sun. No dinner Mon.*

$–$$ ✕ **The Swiss.** The former Swiss Hall holds this extremely popular Waterfront District eatery that serves creative fare like sandwiches with artichoke hearts and pesto cream cheese. A high, pressed-tin ceiling covers the main dining and bar area. Rooms in the back have pool tables and a stage where jazz is played on the weekends. ⊠ *1904 S. Jefferson Ave.,* ☎ *253/572–2821. No credit cards.*

$ ✕ **Antique Sandwich Company.** You can get breakfast, lunch, or dinner at this deli-style café that specializes in hearty soups, classic children's food like waffles and peanut butter and jelly sandwiches, and well-prepared espresso drinks. Old posters on the walls, plastic bears for serving honey, and a toy-covered children's play area help set a cheerful mood. On weekends come hear live folk and classical music; Tuesday is open-mike night. ⊠ *5102 N. Pearl St.,* ☎ *253/752–4069. Reservations not accepted. AE, MC, V.*

$$$ ▥ **Chinaberry Hill.** Original fixtures and stained-glass windows are among the grace notes in this B&B in a 1889 Queen Anne–style home in the Stadium Historic District. Former Coloradans Cecil and Yarrow Wayman have furnished each room with an antique feather bed, robes, and fine-quality linens; three rooms have whirlpool tubs. The carriage house in back, which sleeps six, contains memorabilia from its "horse and buggy" days. Room rates include a breakfast of a seasonal fruit cup followed by an enormous hot entrée. ⊠ *302 N. Tacoma Ave., 98403,* ☎ *253/272–1282,* ℻ *253/272–1335. 5 rooms. AE, D, MC, V.*

$$$ ▥ **Sheraton Tacoma Hotel.** The only high-quality alternative to the Victorian B&Bs in the city is adjacent to the convention center. Most rooms in the 26-story hotel are smallish but have tasteful art, unobtrusive corporate decor, and views of Commencement Bay, Mount Rainier, or both. Guests in the executive suites have a concierge and receive a complimentary Continental breakfast. The view from Altezzo, the moderately priced Italian restaurant atop the hotel, provides a good orientation to Tacoma's geography. The well-made entrées include cioppino, meat dishes, and pastas. ⊠ *1320 Broadway Plaza, 98402,* ☎ *253/572–3200 or 800/845–9466,* ℻ *253/591–4105. 319 rooms. 2 restaurants, 3 bars, in-room modem lines, room service, hot tub, sauna, dry cleaning, concierge, business services, meeting rooms, parking (fee). AE, DC, MC, V.*

$$–$$$ ▥ **The Villa.** Friendly hosts Becky and Greg Anglemyer operate this Stadium Historic District B&B. The focal point of the grand entrance to their Mediterranean-style mansion is a curved wooden staircase leading to the guest suites. The Bay View suite has a fireplace and views of Commencement Bay and the Olympic Mountains. You can lounge in several downstairs rooms, one of them a glassed-in sunporch teeming with plants and flowers. The room rates include a full gourmet breakfast. ⊠ *705 N. 5th St., 98403,* ☎ *253/572–1157,* ℻ *253/572–1805. 4 rooms. MC, V. Business services. AE, MC, V.*

\$\$ ☷ **Commencement Bay Bed & Breakfast.** This home in north Tacoma contains three individually decorated rooms. Myrtle's Room has a four-poster queen bed and a view of the bay, the Cascade Range, and Mount Rainier. All rooms have telephones and voice mail, and two have TVs with VCRs. Hosts Sharon and Bill Kaufmann supply a full breakfast (included in the room rates) and plenty of information about the area. ⊠ *3312 N. Union Ave., 98407,* ☎ *253/752–8175,* ᶠᵃˣ *253/759–4025. 3 rooms. Hot tub, business services. MC, V.*

Nightlife and the Arts
BARS AND LOUNGES

Head to **McCabe's** (⊠ 2611 Pacific Ave., ☎ 253/272–5403) for country music and dancing (lessons provided most nights). On weekends, live jazz and blues heighten the Cajun atmosphere at **Roof-n-Doof's New Orleans Cafe** (⊠ 754 Pacific Ave., ☎ 253/572–5113). **The Swiss** (⊠ 1904 S. Jefferson Ave., ☎ 253/572–2821) has microbrews on tap, pool tables, and weekend jazz. The music varies from night to night at the **Vault** (⊠ 1025 Pacific Ave., ☎ 253/572–3145), a dance club.

The theaters of the **Broadway Center for the Performing Arts** (☎ 253/591–5890) present concerts and musicals and other theatrical productions (☞ Sights to See, *above*).

Outdoor Activities and Sports
GOLF

The **Elks-Allenmore Public Golf Course** (⊠ 2125 S. Cedar St., ☎ 253/627–7211) is an 18-hole, par-71 course; the greens fee is \$20, plus \$20 for a cart. **North Shore Golf and Country Club** (⊠ 4101 North Shore Blvd., ☎ 253/927–1375) is an 18-hole, par-71 course; the greens fee is \$20 on weekdays and \$30 on weekends, plus \$20 for a cart. Call seven days in advance to obtain a tee time.

SPECTATOR SPORTS

The **Tacoma Rainiers,** the Class AAA affiliate of the Seattle Mariners baseball team, play at Cheney Stadium (⊠ 2502 S. Tyler St., ☎ 253/752–7707). The **Tacoma Rockets** (☎ 360/627–3653) of the Western Hockey League play their games at the Tacoma Dome (⊠ 2727 E. D St., ☎ 253/272–3663).

Spanaway Speedway (⊠ 16413 22nd Ave. E, Spanaway, ☎ 253/537–7551), 7 mi south of Tacoma, hosts auto racing. Midweek competition features amateurs racing their "street legal" automobiles.

Shopping
Antique Row (⊠ Broadway and St. Helen's St. between 7th and 9th Sts.) contains a few upscale antiques stores and boutiques selling collectibles and 1950s paraphernalia. Several establishments are merely glorified junk shops, though some of them are still fun to poke through. A farmers' market is held here during the summer on Thursday.

Freighthouse Square Public Market, on the corner of 25th and D streets, is a former railroad warehouse that's been converted into several small gift shops, offbeat boutiques, and ethnic food stalls.

The **Proctor District** in Tacoma's north end has several dozen businesses of all types. The district's **Pacific Northwest Shop** (⊠ 2702 N. Proctor St., ☎ 253/752–2242) sells apparel, books, pottery, food, and wine from the region. Neon lights in the shape of little blue mice adorn the marquee of the **Blue Mouse Theater** (⊠ 2611 N. Proctor St., ☎ 253/752–9500) screening room.

Tacoma Mall (⊠ Tacoma Mall Blvd. off I–5, ☏ 253/475–4565), 1½ mi south of the Tacoma Dome, contains department stores, specialty shops, and restaurants.

Tacoma Essentials

Arriving and Departing

BY BOAT

Argosy Cruises (⊠ Pier 55, Seattle, ☏ 206/623–4252) operates daily tour-boat service to Tacoma.

BY BUS

Pierce Transit (☏ 253/581–8000) runs a shuttle between Seattle and Tacoma. **Shuttle Express** (☏ 425/487–7433) provides service between Sea-Tac Airport and Tacoma. Rides can be arranged in advance or upon arrival.

BY CAR

Interstate 5 is the main north–south route into Tacoma.

BY PLANE

Sea-Tac International Airport (☞ Seattle A to Z *in* Chapter 4) is 18 mi from Tacoma.

Getting Around

BY BUS

Pierce Transit (☏ 253/581–8000) provides local bus service.

BY CAR

Pearl Street and Broadway are two of the main north–south streets through downtown Tacoma. Ruston Way winds to the northwest along the Commencement Bay waterfront.

Contacts and Resources

GUIDED TOURS

Tacoma Architectural Foundation (☏ 253/594–7839) conducts Saturday walking tours ($5) of Tacoma that begin at the Washington State History Museum (⊠ 1911 Pacific Ave.).

VISITOR INFORMATION

Tacoma–Pierce County Visitor and Convention Bureau (⊠ Box 1754, Tacoma 98401, ☏ 253/627–2836 or 800/272–2662).

MOUNT RAINIER NATIONAL PARK

Magnificent 14,411-ft-high Mount Rainier—the fifth-highest mountain in the lower 48 states—is the centerpiece of Mount Rainier National Park, about 60 mi southeast of Tacoma. The mountain is so big it creates its own weather system. The local Native Americans called the mountain Tahoma, "the mountain that was God," and dared not ascend its eternally ice-bound summit. In 1792 the first European to visit the region, British explorer George Vancouver, gazed in amazement at its majestic dome and named it after his friend Rear Admiral Peter Rainier.

Mount Rainier National Park encompasses nearly 400 square mi of wilderness. Three hundred miles of hiking trails, from easy to advanced, crisscross the park, which contains lakes, rivers, glaciers, isolated cross-country-skiing spots, and ample camping facilities. Bears, mountain goats, deer, elk, eagles, beavers, and mountain lions live within the park; the abundant flora includes old-growth Douglas fir, hemlock, cedar, ferns, and wildflowers.

Admission is $10 per vehicle, $5 for those who arrive by any other means. It is possible to sample Rainier's main attractions—Longmire, Paradise, the Grove of Patriarchs, and Sunrise—in a single day by car, but you'll need to stay longer to stop more than just briefly elsewhere in the park or hike the forest, meadow, and high-mountain trails. Be forewarned: A narrow and winding paved road links Rainier's main sights; during the peak months of July and August, traffic can be slow and heavy.

Finding a decent meal around Mount Rainier isn't difficult, but lodging can be a problem; book in advance if possible. The park contains five drive-in campgrounds—Cougar Rock, Ipsut Creek, Ohanapecosh, Sunshine Point, and White River—which have almost 700 campsites for tents and RVs. All are first-come, first-served and have parking spaces, drinking water, garbage cans, fire grates, and picnic tables with benches; most have flush or pit toilets, but none have hot water. In the winter, chains are required to reach Paradise.

Ashford

53 mi southeast of Tacoma; from I–5's Exit 127 follow Hwy. 512 east to Rte. 7 south to Hwy. 706 east.

Originally built to service loggers, Ashford now exists to accommodate the 2 million annual visitors to Mount Rainier National Park. Stores, restaurants, and lodgings are along Highway 706.

Dining and Lodging

$ ✕ **Wild Berry Restaurant.** The ski-and-hot-tub crowd stokes up for a long day in the woods at this ramshackle eatery. Salads, pizzas, crepes, sandwiches, and home-baked desserts are served in relaxed surroundings. ⊠ *37720 Hwy. 706 E, 4 mi east of Ashford,* ☏ *360/569–2628. MC, V.*

$$–$$$ ✕⊞ **Alexander's Country Inn.** The gingerbread facade and fairy-book turret of this well-maintained 1912 inn are products of a later renovation. The rooms here sparkle with fresh paint, carpeting, antiques, and marble-top pine bedside tables, but the walls in the main house are thin. Of the two adjacent ranch houses, the Chalet has more of the country-quaint qualities of the inn. The decor of the Forest House has little to recommend it, but moss covers its private backyard. A large hot tub outside the main house overlooks a trout pond, and a second-floor sitting room has a fireplace and stained-glass doors. Room rates include a hearty breakfast and evening wine. The inn's cozy restaurant (closed on weekdays in winter), the best place in town for lunch or dinner, serves fresh fish and pasta dishes; the bread and the desserts are baked on the premises. ⊠ *37515 Hwy. 706 E (4 mi east of Ashford), Ashford 98304,* ☏ *360/569–2300 or 800/654–7615,* ℻ *360/569–2323. 12 rooms, 2 3-bedroom houses. MC, V. Restaurant, hot tub.*

$$–$$$ ⊞ **Wellspring.** The nine log cabins at this spalike facility take advantage of the views of the surrounding woodlands. The romantic Nest room contains a hanging bed and a pillow-strewn floor. The Tatoosh, which has a huge stone fireplace and a whirlpool tub, can accommodate up to 10 people. Two huts in the compound shelter outdoor hot tubs, saunas, and massage rooms. The fee structure varies depending on how many of the spa amenities you use. A breakfast basket is delivered to the cabins in the morning. ⊠ *54922 Kernehan Rd., off Hwy. 706 E, 98304,* ☏ *360/569–2514,* ℻ *360/569–2285. 9 cabins. Hot tubs, saunas, spa. AE, DC, MC, V.*

Mount Rainier National Park

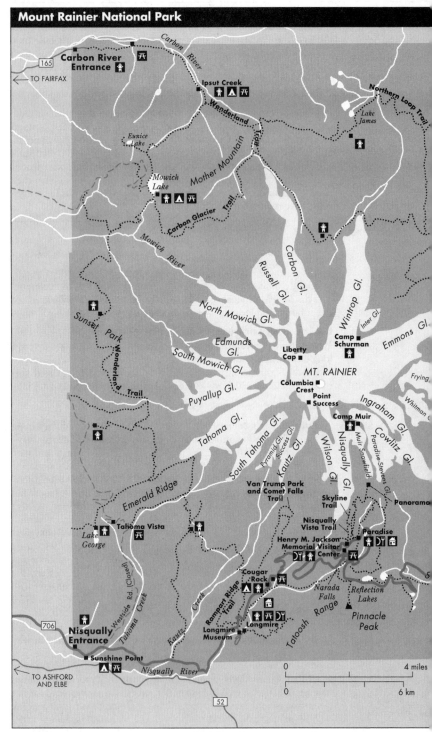

Carbon River Entrance

TO FAIRFAX

165

Ipsut Creek

Carbon River

Wonderland Trail

Northern Loop Trail

Lake James

Eunice Lake

Mowich Lake

Mother Mountain Trail

Carbon Glacier Trail

Carbon Gl.

Russell Gl.

Wintrop Gl.

Inter Gl.

Emmons Gl.

Frying

Whitman

Mowich River

Sunset Park

North Mowich Gl.

Edmunds Gl.

South Mowich Gl.

Camp Schurman

Liberty Cap

MT. RAINIER

Wonderland Trail

Puyallup Gl.

Columbia Crest

Point Success

Camp Muir

Ingraham Gl.

Cowlitz Gl.

Tahoma Gl.

South Tahoma Gl.

Pyramid Gl.

Success Gl.

Kautz Gl.

Wilson Gl.

Nisqually Gl.

Muir Snowfield

Paradise-Stevens Gl.

Emerald Ridge

Van Trump Park and Comet Falls Trail

Skyline Trail

Panorama

Nisqually Vista Trail

Lake George

Tahoma Vista

Henry M. Jackson Memorial Visitor Center

Paradise

Westside Rd. (Closed)

Cougar Rock

Narada Falls

Reflection Lakes

Tatoosh Range

Pinnacle Peak

Rampart Ridge Trail

Longmire Museum

Longmire

706

Nisqually Entrance

Tahoma Creek

Kautz Creek

Sunshine Point

TO ASHFORD AND ELBE

Nisqually River

52

| 0 | | | 4 miles |
| 0 | | | 6 km |

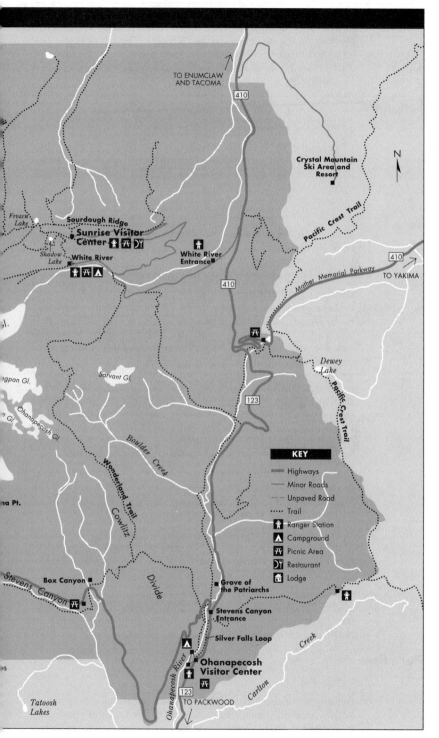

$-$$ ☎ **The Bunkhouse.** "The place to stop on the way to the top" was built in 1908 to house loggers and was originally located a few miles down the road, in the long-gone town of National. The rooms at this old-style motel range from inexpensive single bunks to private suites. ⊠ *30205 Hwy. 706 E, 98304,* ☎ *360/569–2439,* FAX *360/569–2436. Hot tub. MC, V.*

Longmire

12 mi east of Ashford on Hwy. 706.

Glass cases at the **Longmire Museum** contain a few preserved plants and animals from Mount Rainier National Park, including a friendly-looking stuffed cougar. Photos and geographical displays provide an overview of the park's history. ⊠ *Hwy. 706, 6 mi east of Nisqually entrance,* ☎ *360/569–2211, ext. 3314.* ☉ *July–Labor Day, daily 9–5; Labor Day–June, daily 9–4:15.*

The ½-mi **Trail of Shadows,** which begins just across the road from the National Park Inn, passes colorful soda springs, James Longmire's old homestead cabin, and the foundation of the old Longmire Springs Hotel, which was destroyed around the turn of the century.

Dining and Lodging

$$-$$$ ✕☎ **National Park Inn.** An early 1990s renovation robbed the only year-round lodging in the park of much of its charm—the old stone fireplaces are still here, but the public areas have a generic country-inn feel. The small rooms mix budget-motel functionality (though without TVs and telephones) with wistful backwoods touches such as wrought-iron lamps and antique bentwood headboards. The fare at the large restaurant sounds more exotic than it tastes: maple-coated chicken, a stir-fry with vegetables and tenderloin steak, and pan-fried snapper with lemon butter and wine. For breakfast, try the home-baked cinnamon rolls with cream-cheese frosting. ⊠ *Hwy. 706, 6 mi east of Nisqually entrance, 98304,* ☎ *360/569–2275. 25 rooms, 18 with bath. Restaurant, shop. MC, V.*

Outdoor Activities and Sports

The Longmire Ski Touring Center (☎ 360/569–2411), adjacent to the National Park Inn, rents cross-country ski equipment and provides lessons from mid-December to early April.

Mount Rainier Guest Services (⊠ National Park Inn, Hwy. 706, ☎ 360/569–2411) rents cross-country ski equipment, snowshoes, and hiking gear from mid-December to early April. Ed Strauss (☎ 360/569–2271), a ski instructor, is also a tour guide.

En Route   From Longmire, Highway 706 climbs northeast into the mountains toward Paradise. Both the gorgeous **Christine Falls,** north of the highway 1½ mi past Cougar Rock Campground, and Narada Falls, 3 mi farther on, are spanned by graceful stone footbridges.

Paradise

9 mi east of Longmire on Hwy. 706.

Fantastic mountain views, alpine meadows crosshatched with nature trails, a welcoming lodge and restaurant, and an excellent visitor center combine to make Paradise the primary goal of most visitors to Mount Rainier National Park.

Exhibits at the **Henry M. Jackson Visitor Center** focus on geology, mountaineering, glaciology, winter storms, and alpine ecology. Two worthwhile 20-minute multimedia programs repeat at half-hour intervals. ⊠ *Hwy. 706, 20 mi east of Nisqually entrance,* ☎ *360/569–2211.* ⊙ *Early May–mid-Oct., daily 9–6; mid-Oct.–Apr., weekends and holidays 10–5.*

Hiking trails to various points begin at the Henry M. Jackson Visitor Center. One outstanding, if grueling, way to explore the high country is to hike the 5-mi Skyline Trail to Panorama Point, which has stunning 360° views.

Dining and Lodging

$$–$$$ ✕⊡ **Paradise Inn.** With its hand-carved cedar logs, burnished parquet floors, stone fireplaces, Indian rugs, and glorious mountain views, this 75-year-old inn is loaded with atmosphere. Its smallish, sparsely furnished rooms, however, are not equipped with TVs or telephones and have thin walls and showers that tend to run cold during periods of peak use. The attraction here is the alpine setting. The full-service dining room serves leisurely Sunday brunches in summer; the lodge also has a small snack bar and a snug lounge. ⊠ *Hwy. 706 (mailing address: c/o Mount Rainier Guest Services, Box 108, Star Rte., Ashford 98304),* ☎ *360/569–2275,* ℻ *360/569–2770. 127 rooms, 96 with bath. MC, V. Closed Nov.–mid-May.*

Outdoor Activities and Sports

MOUNTAIN CLIMBING

The highly regarded concessionaire **Rainier Mountaineering** (⊠ Paradise 98398, ☎ 360/627–6242 in winter, 360/569–2227 in summer) teaches the fundamentals of mountaineering at one-day classes held during the climbing season, which lasts from late May through early September. Participants are evaluated for their fitness for the climb; they must be able to withstand a 16-mi round trip with a 9,000-ft gain in elevation. Those who meet the fitness requirement may choose between guided two- and four-day summit climbs, the latter via the more demanding Emmons Glacier. Experienced climbers can fill out a climbing card at the Paradise, White River, or Carbon River ranger station and lead their own groups of two or more.

SKIING

Mount Rainier is a major cross-country ski center. The ungroomed trails around Paradise are particularly popular.

SNOWSHOEING

Snowshoe rentals are available at the **Longmire Ski Touring Center** (☞ *above*). From December through April, park rangers lead free twice-daily snowshoe walks that start at the visitor center at Paradise and cover 1¼ mi in about two hours.

Eastern Side of Mount Rainier National Park

21 mi east of Paradise on Hwy. 706.

★ The **Grove of the Patriarchs,** a small island of 1,000-year-old trees protected from the fires that afflicted surrounding areas, is one of Mount Rainier National Park's most stunning features. A 2-mi loop trail that begins just west of the Stevens Canyon entrance heads over a small bridge through lush old-growth forest of Douglas fir, cedar, and hemlock.

As you head north from the Grove of the Patriarchs are the White River and the **Sunrise Visitor Center,** from which you can watch the alpenglow fade from Mount Rainier's domed summit. The visitor center has exhibits on this region's alpine and subalpine ecology. ⊠ *70002 S.R. 410 E, Enumclaw,* ☎ *360/569–2211, ext. 2357.* ⊙ *July 4–Oct. 1, daily 9–6.*

Outdoor Activities and Sports

SKIING

If you want to cross-country ski with fewer people, try the trails in and around the Ohanapecosh/Stevens Canyon area, which are just as beautiful as those at Paradise. Never ski on the plowed main roads—the snowplow operator can't see you.

SNOWMOBILING AND SNOWSHOEING

Snowmobiling is allowed on the east side of the park on sections of Highway 123 and Stevens Canyon Road—between the ranger station at Ohanapecosh Visitor Center and Box Canyon—and on Highway 410, which is accessible from the north entrance. Highway 410 is unplowed after its junction with the road to the Crystal Mountain Ski Area. A State of Washington Sno-Park permit, available at stores and gas stations throughout the area, is required to park in the area near the north park entrance arch. Highways 123 and 410 are good places to snowshoe.

Mount Rainier National Park Essentials

Getting Around

BY BUS

Gray Line of Seattle (☎ 206/624–5813) operates daily tours to Longmire and Paradise in the summer.

BY CAR

Most visitors arrive at the park's Nisqually entrance, the closest entrance to I–5, via **Highway 706. Highway 410** enters the park from the east. **Highway 123** enters from the southeast. Highways 410 and 123 are usually closed in winter. **Highway 165** leads to Ipsut Creek Campground through the Carbon River entrance to Mowich Lake, in the park's northwest corner.

Visitor Information

Superintendent, Mount Rainier National Park (✉ Tahoma Woods, Star Rte., Ashford 98304, ☎ 360/569–2211).

THE OLYMPIC PENINSULA

The rugged Olympic Peninsula is the most northwestern corner of the lower 48 United States. Much of it is wilderness, with the magnificent Olympic National Park and Olympic National Forest at its heart. The peninsula has tremendous variety: the wild Pacific shore, the sheltered waters along the Hood Canal and the Strait of Juan de Fuca, the rivers of the Olympic Rain Forest, and the towering Olympic Mountains.

Although the region's economy—primarily lumber and fishing—assures some ties to the outside world, the peninsula is in many ways isolated and largely self-sufficient. Its inaccessible terrain and the unique climates caused by the Olympic Mountains add to this feeling of separateness: The mountains trap incoming clouds, creating a rain forest to the west and a dry "rain shadow" area on the east. As a result, the peninsula has the wettest and the driest climates in the coastal Pacific Northwest.

A benefit of this ambiguous environment is that wildlife flourishes. Visitors in search of the great outdoors, however, should be aware that much of the Olympic Peninsula is stringently protected. Within the national park, all hunting, firearms, and off-road vehicles are prohibited, as is any disturbance to plants or wildlife. Although hunting and fishing are permitted in portions of the national forest, many areas are maintained as complete wilderness. Furthermore, Native American tribal regulations restrict access to, and activity within, certain parts of reservations; check with local authorities for details.

Because of the rugged terrain and some difficult roads, much of the peninsula is accessible only to backpackers, but the 300-mi loop made by U.S. 101 (called Highway 101 by most locals) provides glimpses of some of its most interesting features. The various side roads off 101, meanwhile, offer excellent (if sometimes unpaved) opportunities for exploration of more remote towns, beaches, and mountains. This section describes a journey clockwise, primarily around U.S. 101 (although jaunts from the main drag are suggested), beginning and ending in Olympia.

Trout and salmon are particularly abundant in rivers throughout the peninsula. In Aberdeen and Hoquiam, bottomfish and salmon are the primary catches. For more information about fishing in the region, contact the **North Olympic Peninsula Visitor and Convention Bureau** (☞ The Olympic Peninsula Essentials, *below*).

Olympia

⑲ *28 mi south of Tacoma on I–5.*

Olympia, Washington's capital and one of the oldest cities in the state—it was founded in 1850—retains a relaxed air even when the state legislature is in session. When the legislators are away, the mood can be downright somnolent.

The **Capitol Campus** holds Olympia's main attractions. The handsome Neo-Roman–style **Legislative Building** was erected in 1928. Its 287-ft dome closely resembles that of the Capitol Building in Washington, D.C. Visitors' galleries provide glimpses of state senators and representatives in action. The grounds surrounding the Legislative Building contain memorials, monuments, rose gardens (at their best in summer), and Japanese cherry trees (usually in glorious bloom around the end of April). The 1920s **Conservatory** is open year-round on weekdays from 8 to 3 and also on weekends in summer. Directly behind the Legislative Building is the modern **State Library,** which has exhibits devoted to Washington's history. Murals by Washington artists Mark Tobey and Kenneth Callahan hang here. ⊠ *Legislative Bldg., Capitol Way between 10th and 14th Aves.,* ☎ *360/586–8687.* 🖭 *Free.* ⊙ *Tours daily on the hr 10–3.*

The 1920s mansion of a local banker houses the **State Capitol Museum.** Exhibits survey local art, history, and natural history. The permanent collection includes rare local Native American baskets. ⊠ *211 W. 21st St., off Capitol Way, 7 blocks south of the Legislative Bldg.,* ☎ *360/ 753–2580.* 🖭 *Free; donations accepted.* ⊙ *Tues.–Fri. 10–4, weekends noon–4.*

The **Japanese Garden,** a product of the sister-city relationship between Olympia and Yashiro, Japan, opened in 1989. Within the garden are a waterfall, a bamboo grove, a koi pond, and stone lanterns. ⊠ *Union and Plum Sts. east of the Capitol Campus, no phone.* 🖭 *Free.* ⊙ *Daily dawn–dusk.*

OFF THE
BEATEN PATH
    WOLFHAVEN INTERNATIONAL – This 80-acre sanctuary dedicated to wolf conservation is 15 mi south of Olympia. You can take walk-through guided tours year-round. On Friday and Saturday evenings in the summer, the facility opens for a public Howl-in (reservations essential), with tours, musicians performing around a campfire, and howling with the wolves. ⊠ *3111 Offut Lake Rd. (from Olympia, take I–5 south to Exit 99*

Olympic Peninsula

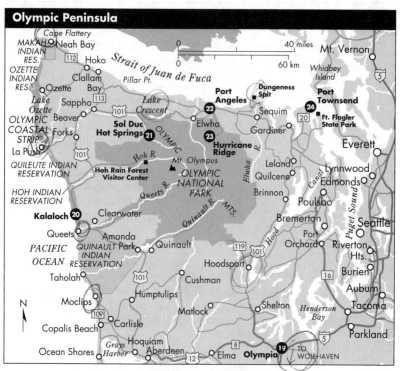

and follow brown-and-white signs east for 7 mi), Tenino, ☎ 800/448–9653. 🎫 *Daily tours $5, Howl-ins $6.* ☺ *Guided walking tours May–Sept., Wed.–Mon. 10–4; Oct.–Apr., Wed.–Mon. 10–3. Howl-ins May–Labor Day, Fri.–Sat. 6:30–9:30.*

Dining and Lodging

$$$ ✕ **La Petite Maison.** The chefs at Olympia's premier fine-dining establishment prepare imaginative French food inside a converted 1890s farmhouse. Classical music, unobtrusive service, and crisp linens create a quietly elegant ambience. For dinner try crab cakes and other delicately prepared local seafood or rack of lamb marinated in rosemary, garlic, and Dijon mustard. An eclectic wine list and excellent desserts, among them a Grand Marnier torte, complete the picture. ✉ *101 Division St.,* ☎ *360/943–8812. MC, V. Closed Sun. No lunch Mon. or Sat.*

$$ ✕ **Alice's Restaurant.** A rural farmhouse adjacent to the Johnson Creek
★ Winery in the Skookumchuck Valley, 15 mi southeast of Olympia, holds this restaurant, whose ambience is right out of a Norman Rockwell illustration. The winery's vintages accompany six-course meals that are sophisticated variations on classical American cuisine. Vegetable appetizers, soup, a fish course, and home-baked bread precede robust entrées—anything from wild game to oysters or steak. ✉ *19248 Johnson Creek Rd. E (from Olympia, follow Capitol Blvd. south, head east at Hwy. 507 in Tenino for 5 mi, and turn right onto Johnson Creek Rd. for 5 mi),* ☎ *360/264–2887. Reservations essential. AE, MC, V. Closed Mon.–Tues. No lunch.*

$–$$ ✕ **Capitale Espresso-Grill.** The diverse and uncommon menu at this intimate café includes Pacific Rim dishes like chili-encrusted salmon, but you'll also find inventive pizzas and salads. The café is open for breakfast. ⊠ *609 Capitol Way*, ☎ *360/352–8007. Reservations not accepted. MC, V. Closed Sun.*

$ ✕ **The Spar Cafe-Bar (and Tobacco Merchant).** This family-owned-and-operated business has been an Olympia tradition since 1935. The store's original humidified cabinets hold stacks of imported cigars. The fare for breakfast, lunch, or dinner is mostly diner-oriented. ⊠ *114 E. 4th Ave.*, ☎ *360/357–6444. Reservations not accepted. AE, DC, MC, V.*

$$ ⊡ **The Holiday Inn Select.** Large but friendly, this hotel close to downtown has views of Capitol Lake, the capitol dome, and the surrounding hills. The rooms are spacious and comfortable; those facing the water are especially appealing. The rates include breakfast. ⊠ *2300 Evergreen Park Dr., 98502*, ☎ *360/943–4000*, ℻ *360/357–6604. 177 rooms. 2 restaurants, bar, no-smoking rooms, pool, hot tub. AE, D, MC, V.*

Nightlife
The **Fourth Avenue Tavern** (⊠ 210 E. 4th Ave., ☎ 360/786–1444), a beer-and-wine joint with pool tables and assorted games, serves up 26 brews on tap, homemade pizza, and, on weekends, live rock music.

En Route Highway 8 and U.S. 12 head west from Olympia to Gray's Harbor, where U.S. 12 connects briefly with U.S. 101 near the not particularly scenic seaport towns of **Hoquiam** and **Aberdeen.** Heading west out of Hoquiam on Highway 109, you'll notice twin nuclear reactors and, in spring, the thousands of migratory shorebirds and peregrine falcons that stay in **Bowerman Basin.** Highway 109 becomes a coastal road when it veers north at Ocean City.

Copalis Beach

21 mi from Hoquiam on Hwy. 109.

Copalis Beach consists of a few roadside stores and motels to service visitors who have come to the easily accessible beach and picnic areas.

Lodging
$$ ⊡ **Iron Springs Resort.** The cottages here accommodate from 2 to 10 people. Each has its own fireplace and kitchen; dimly lit older cabins are decorated with a fun hodgepodge of furniture from the 1950s to the 1970s; newer ones (Nos. 22 to 25) are brighter and more comfortable, with wide ocean views. Cottage No. 6 has no view, but all the others have unobstructed beach, river, or forest views. ⊠ *3707 Hwy. 109 (3 mi north of Copalis Beach), 98535*, ☎ *360/276–4230*, ℻ *360/276–4365. 25 units. Pool. AE, MC, V.*

Moclips

8 mi north of Copalis Beach on Hwy. 109.

The homes in unpretentious Moclips are scattered among the woods hugging the main road high above the ocean.

Dining and Lodging
$$ ✕⊡ **Ocean Crest Resort.** Casual and alluringly sea-worn, the Ocean Crest rests high on a bluff above a stunning stretch of the Pacific. The accommodations vary from single studios with no views or fireplaces to large studios with both; there are well-situated family cottages as well. All the rooms have functional furnishings, and the resort has direct access to the beach down a maze of steps. A health club across the street has an indoor pool, a hot tub, and a weight room with aer-

obic machines. Moss-covered woods frame the restaurant's ocean views. The menu is standard for the area—Dungeness crab and other local seafoods served with heavy sauces, as well as pastas, steak, and lamb. Breakfast is served. ⊠ *4651 Hwy. 109, 98562,* ☎ *360/276–4465,* ℻ *360/276–4149. 45 rooms. Restaurant, bar, pool, hot tub, health club. AE, D, MC, V.*

OFF THE
BEATEN PATH

HIGHWAY 109 NORTH FROM MOCLIPS – The beaches along Highway 109 north from Moclips are magnificent, particularly where the highway ends, 8 mi north of Moclips at Taholah. Sea-tossed logs and driftwood piled along the beach make it more difficult to access the water, though the setting is closer to the way nature intended things. Taholah, the central town on the Quinault Indian reservation, has a gas station, but it's not geared toward tourists and its residents aren't especially friendly.

Quinault

38 mi north of Hoquiam on U.S. 101.

U.S. 101 heads north from Hoquiam along the west fork of the Hoquiam River to Quinault Lake. The lake is part of the Olympic National Park. The town of Quinault contains the Lake Quinault Lodge and a general store.

Dining and Lodging

$$$ ✕🏨 **Lake Quinault Lodge.** The lodge is set on a perfect glacial lake amid the Olympic National Forest. Old-growth woodlands are an easy hike away, and there is abundant salmon and trout fishing. The main lodge, built in 1926 of cedar shingles, has antiques-filled public rooms and a large stone fireplace. Most of the sparsely furnished guest rooms have views of landscaped lawns that frame the perfectly serene lake. At the very fine restaurant, try the oyster appetizer, the baked salmon in capers and onions, or the seafood fettuccine with Dungeness crab, lobster, salmon, scallops, and shrimp. The old-fashioned bar is lively and pleasant. Hiking and jogging trails are within easy access. ⊠ *S. Shore Rd. (Box 7), 98575,* ☎ *360/288–2900 or 800/562–6672,* ℻ *360/288–2901. 92 rooms. Restaurant, bar, indoor pool, hot tub, sauna, putting green. MC, V.*

Kalaloch

⑳ *32 mi west of Quinault on U.S. 101.*

Many well-marked trails lead from the coastal highway north of Kalaloch (pronounced *Kway*-lock)—each ¼ mi or less in length—to spectacular Pacific beaches.

Dining and Lodging

$$–$$$ ✕🏨 **Kalaloch Lodge.** Old cabins, new log cabins, an old lodge, and a
★ new hotel make up this facility within the Olympic National Forest. Lodge rooms are unadorned, rustic, and clean; most have ocean views and fireplaces. A few larger cabins have private outdoor picnic areas near the beach. The old cabins can be drafty in winter and have minimal kitchens and other amenities, though they are atmospheric. The informal lodge offers few resort-type amenities but abundant opportunities for beachcombing, hiking, and other activities. Fresh salmon and oysters are menu highlights; the salmon topped with Dungeness crab is especially good. Dinner is also served in the upstairs cocktail lounge, which, like the restaurant, has unobstructed ocean views. ⊠ *157151 U.S. 101 (HC 80, Box 1100), Forks-Kalaloch 98331,* ☎ *360/*

962–2271, ⅨX 360/962–3391. *58 rooms and cabins. Restaurant. AE, MC, V.*

OFF THE
BEATEN PATH

HOH RAIN FOREST – This rich ecosystem of conifers, hardwoods, grasses, mosses, and other flora shelters elk, otters, beavers, salmon, flying squirrels, and other wildlife. The average rainfall here is 150 inches a year. The Hoh Visitor Center, at the campground and ranger center at road's end, has information about the nature trails. The Hall of Mosses trail is a well-maintained ¾-mi path; the 1¼-mi Spruce Trail follows the Hoh River. Naturalist-led campfire programs and walks are conducted daily in July and August. The 18-mi Hoh River Trail follows the Hoh River to the base of Mount Olympus, which rises 7,965 ft above the forest floor. The technical climb requires experience and equipment, but the views from the base are spectacular. ✉ *From U.S. 101 (about 20 mi north of Kalaloch) take Upper Hoh Rd. 18 mi east to Hoh Rain Forest Visitor Center,* ☎ *360/374–6925.* 🎫 *Park $10.* ☉ *Visitor Center year-round but often unstaffed Sept.–May.*

Forks

35 mi north of Kalaloch on U.S. 101.

The little town of Forks is famous throughout the Northwest for its lavish and enjoyable Fourth of July celebrations (☎ 360/374–2531), which last three days. This is classic Americana with a Northwest spin. Giant logging trucks participate in the parade, and the festivities include demolition derbies, marathon runs, arts and crafts, fireworks, a mountain-bike race, a play, and plenty of food.

La Push

15 mi west of Forks on Hwy. 106 (La Push Rd.).

La Push is the tribal center of the Quileute Indians. One theory about the town's name is that it is a variation on the French *la bouche,* "the mouth"; this makes sense, since it's at the mouth of the Quileute River. The coast here is dotted with offshore rock spires known as seastacks, and you may catch a glimpse of bald eagles nesting in the nearby cliffs. During low tide, the tide pools on nearby Second and Third beaches brim with life, and you can walk out to some seastacks. Gray whales play offshore during their annual migrations, and most of the year the waves are great for surfing and kayaking (if you bring a wet suit).

OFF THE
BEATEN PATH

THE NORTHWESTERN COAST – From Forks, U.S. 101 continues north and east through the Soleduck River valley, known for great salmon fishing. At Sappho, Burnt Mountain Road (Highway 113) heads north to Highway 112. If you head west on Highway 112, you'll eventually end up at Neah Bay and Cape Flattery. The Makah Indian Reservation is at Neah Bay; 500-year-old artifacts are carefully preserved and displayed in the Makah Museum. If you head southwest on Hoko-Ozette Road at Hoko, 18 mi east of Neah Bay, you'll end up at beautiful Ozette Lake, where a 3-mi planked trail leads to pristine beaches and campsites (☎ 360/963–2725 to reserve a space). The 57-mi Olympic Coastal Strip between the edge of the Quinault Indian Reservation and Cape Flattery is accessible from here.

En Route U.S. 101 at Sappho leads east through the Olympic National Forest toward Lake Crescent. The Washington State Department of Fisheries operates the **Soleduck Hatchery,** 8 mi east of Sappho. Interpretive displays describe the nuances of fish breeding. ⊠ *1420 Pavel Rd.,* ☎ *360/ 327–3246.* 🎫 *Free.* ☉ *Daily 8–4:30.*

Lake Crescent

28 mi east of Forks on U.S. 101.

The appearance of deep-azure Lake Crescent, a mountain lake in an enormous crescent shape, changes depending on your perspective. In the evening, low bands of clouds often linger over its reflective surface, caught between the surrounding mountains. Along the lake's 12-mi perimeter are campgrounds, resorts, trails, and places to canoe and fish. Among Lake Crescent's famous guests was Franklin D. Roosevelt, whose negotiations with U.S. senators and Park Department officials at the Lake Crescent Lodge in 1937 led to the creation of the Olympic National Forest. The original lodge buildings of 1915 are still in use, well worn but still comfortable.

Dining and Lodging

$$–$$$ ✕🏨 **Lake Crescent Lodge.** The big main lodge and small cabins at this facility 20 mi west of downtown Port Angeles overlook Lake Crescent. Units in the lodge are minimal—bathrooms down the hall, dimly lit rooms. Standard motel-style units are available with private baths and lake views but no TVs or phones. Trout fishing, hiking, evening nature programs, and boating are among the daily activities. The food in the restaurant is nothing special, but the service is cheerful and efficient. ⊠ *416 Lake Crescent Rd., Port Angeles 98363,* ☎ *360/928– 3211. 52 units. Restaurant, boating, fishing. AE, DC, MC, V. Closed Nov.–Apr.*

Sol Duc Hot Springs

㉑ *12 mi from Lake Crescent on Soleduck Rd., south from U.S. 101 at Fairholm.*

Native Americans have known about the soothing waters of Sol Duc Hot Springs for generations, and since the first resort opened here, tourists have learned about it as well. There are three hot sulfur pools, ranging in temperature from 98°F to 104°F. The **Sol Duc Hot Springs Resort** (☞ *below*), which dates from 1910, has cabins, a restaurant, and a hamburger stand. It is not necessary to stay at the resort to use the hot springs. ⊠ *Soleduck Rd.,* ☎ *360/327–3583.* 🎫 *Springs $6 per day.* ☉ *Mid-May–Sept., daily 9–9; Apr.–mid-May and Oct., daily 9–5.*

Dining and Lodging

$$ ✕🏨 **Sol Duc Hot Springs Resort.** The 32 cheery if minimally outfitted cabins at this century-old resort all have separate bathrooms, and some have kitchens. The attractive dining room serves unpretentious meals (breakfast, lunch, and dinner) drawing on the best of the Northwest: salmon, crab, fresh vegetables, and fruit. ⊠ *Soleduck Rd. (Box 2168), 98362,* ☎ *360/327–3583,* 📠 *360/327–3398. 32 units and camping and RV facilities. Restaurant, pool, hot springs. MC, V. Closed mid-Oct.–mid-May.*

Port Angeles

㉒ *27 mi east of Lake Crescent on U.S. 101.*

Port Angeles is a commercial fishing port directly across the Strait of Juan de Fuca from Victoria, British Columbia. You enter Port Angeles after passing miles of billboards advertising chain restaurants, cheap lodging, and auto repair shops, but the town does have a few natural and historical points of interest.

The **Ediz Hook,** at the western end of Port Angeles, is one of two natural sand spits (fingers of land formed when a repetitive tidal pattern pushes sand in a particular direction over a long period of time) on the Olympic Peninsula. Protecting ships from storms and waves, the Hook is what makes Port Angeles an excellent port. It's also a fine place to take a walk by the water and check out the marine life. From downtown, take Front Street west and follow it as it meanders past the lumber mill.

The **Clallam County Historical Museum** is a handsome 1914 Georgian Revival building that was a courthouse. You can explore the original courtroom, which is still intact, and sit in the judge's chair. An engaging exhibition details the lifestyles and history of Port Angeles's Native American and Caucasian communities. The museum is scheduled to relocate to the nearby Lincoln School at 8th and C streets in late 1998. ⊠ *223 E. 4th St.,* ☎ *360/417–2364.* ☞ *Free; donations accepted.* ☺ *June–Aug., Mon.–Sat. 10–4; Sept.–May, weekdays 10–4.*

The **Port Angeles Fine Arts Center,** a small but surprisingly sophisticated museum, is inside the former home of artist and publisher Esther Barrows Webster, one of Port Angeles's most energetic and cultured citizens. Outdoor sculpture and trees surround the center, which has panoramic views of the city and the harbor. Exhibitions emphasize the works of emerging and well-established Pacific Northwest artists in various media. ⊠ *1203 W. Lauridsen Blvd.,* ☎ *360/457–3532.* ☞ *Free.* ☺ *Thurs.–Sun. 11–5, and by appointment.*

The city of Port Angeles and Peninsula College operate the modest **aquarium** of the Arthur D. Feiro Marine Laboratory. Many kinds of local sea life, including octopuses, scallops, rockfish, and anemones, are on display, and there are a few touch tanks. The tour is self-guided, but volunteers are on hand to answer questions. ⊠ *Port Angeles City Pier,* ☎ *360/452–9277, ext. 264.* ☞ *$3.* ☺ *June–Aug., daily 10–8; Sept.–May, weekends noon–4.*

★ ㉓ The view from 5,200-ft-high **Hurricane Ridge,** 17 mi south of Port Angeles, includes the Olympics, the Strait of Juan de Fuca, and Vancouver Island. The road leading to the ridge is easily negotiated by car. In the summer, rangers lead hikes and give talks about local geology and flora and fauna. Paved walkways that are accessible to users of wheelchairs and trails for advanced climbers provide an opportunity to see wildflowers like glacier lilies and lupine, as well as deer, marmots, and other animals. In winter, when accessible, the area has miles of cross-country ski routes and a modest downhill ski operation. ⊠ *National Park Visitor Center, 600 E. Park Ave., Port Angeles 98362,* ☎ *360/452–0330.* ☺ *Daily 9–4.*

Dining and Lodging

$$$–$$$$ ✕ **C'est Si Bon.** The atmosphere at the most elegant restaurant on the
★ decidedly informal Olympic Peninsula has a playful ambience. Ornate lighting fixtures illuminate large European oil paintings hanging against bold red walls. The food prepared by French expatriates Norbert and Michele Juhasz is outstanding—escargots cooked in Pernod, seafood gratinée, and a hearty onion soup are typical appetizers; entrées include filet mignon with Dungeness crab, sturgeon baked in phyllo, and lamb tenderloins. The wine list is superb, as are the desserts (especially the chocolate mousse). ⊠ *2300 Hwy. 101E (4 mi east of Port Angeles),* ☎ *360/452–8888. Reservations essential. AE, DC, MC, V. Closed Mon. No lunch.*

$ ✕ **First Street Haven.** Small and informal, this storefront restaurant serves high-quality breakfasts and lunches, plus good espresso drinks and desserts. Breakfast (served all day on Sunday) includes omelets, various renditions of scrambled eggs, and Belgian waffles with fresh fruit. Fresh salads, thick sandwiches, well-prepared fajitas and chili, and homemade quiche are available at lunch. All the muffins, coffee cakes, and scones are baked on the premises. ⊠ *107 E. 1st St., ☎ 360/457–0352. Reservations not accepted. No credit cards. No dinner.*

$$$–$$$$ 🏠 **Domaine Madeleine.** The owners of this luxury B&B on a bluff above
   ★   the Strait of Juan de Fuca love to pamper their guests. Each of the four rooms, decorated with either Impressionist or Asian accents, has a view of the water set against impeccably landscaped grounds. Gas fireplaces, whirlpool tubs, VCRs (you can borrow videos from an extensive collection), and CD/tape players are other pluses. The living room has a 14-ft basalt fireplace, antique Asian furnishings, and a harpsichord. For breakfast (included in the room rates) expect a five-course gourmet affair with fresh baguettes and entrées like chicken crepes and seafood omelets. ⊠ *146 Wildflower La., 8 mi east of Port Angeles, ☎ 360/457–4174, FAX 360/457–3037. 4 rooms. AE, D, DC, MC, V.*

$$–$$$ 🏠 **Tudor Inn.** This B&B in a 1910 Tudor-style house in a residential neighborhood is about 12 blocks from the dock for the Victoria-bound ferry. The largest room has a private balcony, a fireplace, and an English garden painted on the wall; the smaller rooms have just enough space for the bed and a dresser. The cheerful and efficient owners, Jane and Jerry Glass, serve a breakfast of eggs, bacon, and muffins; afternoon tea includes fresh scones and other goodies. All are included in the room rates. No smoking is permitted at the inn. ⊠ *1108 S. Oak St., 98362, ☎ 360/452–3138. 5 rooms. MC, V.*

$ 🏠 **Flagstone Motel.** Many of the small but immaculate rooms here have views of the harbor or Mount Olympus. Even better, you can melt yourself down in the heated pool and sauna, knowing that fresh coffee and sweet rolls will get you started again in the morning. ⊠ *415 E. 1st St., 98362, ☎ 360/457–9494, FAX 360/457–9494. 45 rooms. Pool, sauna. AE, D, DC, MC, V.*

Outdoor Activities and Sports

Hurricane Ridge (☞ *above*) has a modest downhill skiing operation, with two rope tows and a lift, as well as miles of cross-country ski trails.

Sequim

17 mi east of Port Angeles on U.S. 101.

As seen from U.S. 101, Sequim appears to be nothing more than a series of strip malls and slow-moving RVs. But just a few miles north is the beautiful and fertile Dungeness region. This flat area, framed to the south by the majestic Olympic Mountains, remains comparatively dry year-round. At its northern tip is the **Dungeness Spit,** a natural finger of sand that shelters the bay from the crashing surf. The 8-mi spit (one of the longest in the world) extends to the Dungeness Lighthouse, in operation since 1867. A temporary home to at least 30,000 migratory waterfowl each year (spring and fall are the best viewing times, but many species live here in summer), the entire spit has been protected within the Dungeness National Wildlife Refuge since 1915. ⊠ *Kitchen Rd., 3 mi north from U.S. 101, 4 mi west of Sequim, ☎ 360/457–8451 for Wildlife Refuge, 360/683–5847 for campground.* 🎫 *Refuge $2 per family, campsites $10.* ☺ *Wildlife Refuge daily dawn–dusk, campground Feb.–Sept.*

The **Olympic Game Farm**—part petting zoo, part safari—is unique among exotic-animal habitats. For years the farm's exclusive client was Walt Disney Studios, and many of the bears and tigers here are former movie stars. The more than 200 acres include a studio barn with movie sets, a snack bar, and a gift shop. Guided lecture tours take place at 2 PM in the summer. ⌧ *1423 Ward Rd.,* ☎ *360/683–4295 or 800/778–4295.* ⌧ *$6.* ☉ *Weekdays 9–5, weekends 9–6.*

In 1977, 12,000-year-old mastodon remains were discovered near Sequim. You can view these Ice Age creatures at the **Sequim-Dungeness Museum,** along with exhibits about Captain Vancouver, the early Klallam Indians, and the area's pioneer towns. ⌧ *175 W. Cedar St.,* ☎ *360/683–8110.* ⌧ *Free.* ☉ *May–Sept., Wed.–Sun. noon–4; Oct.–Nov. and mid-Feb.–Apr., weekends noon–4.*

Dining and Lodging

$$–$$$ ✕ **The Three Crabs.** This large crab shack on the beach specializes in Dungeness's famed specialty. Crabs are served in a number of ways, but try them chilled to fully appreciate the meat's sweetness, some of which is lost with steaming. Meat and other dishes are also on the large menu, along with children's plates. ⌧ *11 Three Crabs Rd.,* ☎ *360/683–4264. MC, V.*

$$–$$$ 🏠 **Greywolf Inn.** Peggy and Bill Melang, from North Carolina and still brimming with southern hospitality, had fun turning their family home into a B&B. Each room is individually decorated; one looks imported from China, with a black-lacquer four-poster bed and wardrobe, and another is done in a Bavarian theme, with a feather bed under a pine canopy. The glass-enclosed dining room and deck overlook a meadow, and a woodland trail winds through the property's 5 acres. ⌧ *395 Keeler Rd., 98392,* ☎ *360/683–5889 or 800/914–9055,* FAX *360/683–1487. 5 rooms. Outdoor hot tub, business services. AE, D, MC, V.*

Nightlife and the Arts

The Jamestown Sk'lallam tribe's enormous yet oddly subdued **7 Cedars Casino** (⌧ 270756 Hwy. 101., east of Sequim, ☎ 360/683–7777) has blackjack, roulette, and slots. One end of the casino is devoted to bingo.

Port Townsend

㉔ *31 mi from Sequim, 18 east on U.S. 101 and north on Hwy. 20.*

Many writers, musicians, painters, and other artists live in Port Townsend, the largest city on the northern tip of the Olympic Peninsula. Handsome restored 1870s brick buildings with shops and restaurants inside line its waterfront; the many impressive yachts docked here attest to the area's status as one of greater Seattle's premier sailing spots.

The "Genuine Bull Durham Smoking Tobacco" ad on the **Lewis Building** (⌧ Madison and Water Sts.) is among the many relics of Port Townsend's glory days as a maritime center. The **bell tower** on Jefferson Street, at the top of the Tyler Street stairs, is the last of its kind in the country. Built in 1890, it was used to call volunteer firemen to duty; it houses artifacts from the city museum, including a 19th-century horse-drawn hearse that you can peek at through the windows.

The 1892 City Hall building—Jack London languished briefly in the jail here on his way to the Klondike—contains the **Jefferson County Historical Museum,** four floors of Native American artifacts, photos of the Olympic Peninsula, and exhibits chronicling Port Townsend's past. ⌧ *210 Madison St.,* ☎ *360/385–1003.* ⌧ *$2 suggested donation.* ☉ *Mon.–Sat. 11–4, Sun. 1–4.*

The neatly manicured grounds of 443-acre **Fort Worden State Park** include a row of restored Victorian officers' houses, a World War II balloon hangar, and a sandy beach that leads to the **Point Wilson Lighthouse.** The fort, which was built on Point Wilson in 1896, 17 years after the lighthouse, hosts art events sponsored by Centrum (☞ Nightlife and the Arts, *below*). The **Marine Science Center** has aquariums and touch tanks where you can reach in and feel slimy sea creatures like crabs and anemones. ⊠ *200 Battery Way,* ☎ *360/385–4730.* ⌦ *Park day use free, Marine Science Center $2.* ☉ *Park daily dawn–dusk, Marine Science Center Tues.–Sun. noon–6.*

A 15- to 20-minute drive south of town leads to the tip of Marrowstone Island and **Fort Flagler State Park.** The century-old gun placements and bunkers are interesting, but the main attractions are the beaches, campgrounds, and 7 mi of wooded and oceanfront hiking trails—the nameless remnants of old army roads that radiated from a perimeter road. The inlets of the island are great for paddling around, and you can rent canoes, kayaks, and pedal boats from the **Nordland General Store** (☎ 360/385–0777), near the park entrance. ⊠ *10341 Flagler Rd. (from Port Townsend take Hwy. 20 and Hwy. 19 south to Hwy. 116 east), Nordland,* ☎ *360/385–1259.* ⌦ *Day use free, campground $10–$16.* ☉ *Daily dawn–dusk.*

Guided Historical Tours (⊠ 820 Tyler St., ☎ 360/385–1967) conducts several tours of Port Townsend, the most popular of which is a one-hour walking tour of the waterfront and downtown, focusing on the town's architecture, history, and humor.

Dining and Lodging

$$$ ✕ **Lonny's.** Chef-owner Lonny Ritter aims to provide a sensual dining experience. The handsome wooden furnishings and the texture of the ocher-color walls at his restaurant are as carefully selected as the professional staff and the extensive wine collection. Entrées on the seasonally changing menu might include a char-grilled Peking duck breast with Italian sausage stuffing or Lonny's signature Dungeness crab dish, prepared with basil butter, heavy cream, and sweet Gorgonzola cheese. The vegetarian entrées here are thoughtfully conceived. ⊠ *2330 Washington St.,* ☎ *360/385–0700. MC, V. Closed Tues. in winter.*

$$ ✕ **Fountain Café.** The new owners of this funky, art- and knickknack-filled café retained favorite dishes such as Oysters Dorado but added creative grilled sandwiches for lunch and new entrées for dinner. Count on seafood and pastas with imaginative twists—smoked salmon in a light cream sauce with a hint of Scotch, for example. Expect the occasional wait (call ahead to get your name on the list for tables) at this local hot spot. ⊠ *920 Washington St.,* ☎ *360/385–1364. Reservations not accepted. MC, V. Closed Tues. in winter.*

$–$$ ✕ **Salal Café.** Informal and bright, this restaurant prepares healthful cuisine and is especially beloved for its ample, all-day Sunday breakfasts (you can also get breakfast the rest of the week). The lunch menu mixes standard American fare with vegetarian options. Dinners are more exotic, with entrées such as tofu Stroganoff, mushroom risotto with oysters, and pan-seared sea scallops. Try to get a table in the glassed-in back room, which faces a plant-filled courtyard. ⊠ *634 Water St.,* ☎ *360/385–6532. Reservations not accepted. No credit cards. No dinner Tues.–Wed.*

$$–$$$ ⚏ **James House.** This antiques-filled Victorian-era inn rests proudly on the bluff overlooking downtown Port Townsend and the waterfront. Some guest rooms are spacious and have waterfront views, whereas

others are small and share baths. The hardwood floors, though exquisite, are creaky, and the sounds of footsteps and conversations drift into the rooms. Gourmet breakfasts are served in the formal dining room, as is complimentary sherry in the evening. The gardener's cottage next door has a wood-burning fireplace, a whirlpool tub, and other modern amenities. ⊠ *1238 Washington St., 98368,* ☎ *360/385–1238 or 800/385–1238,* 𝔽𝔸𝕏 *360/379–5551. 12 rooms, 10 with bath. Dining room. MC, V.*

$$ 🏨 **Palace Hotel.** The decor of this spacious hotel reflects the building's history as a bordello: One can easily imagine the exposed brick lobby filled with music and men waiting for the ladies whose names now grace hallway plaques. The large rooms have 14-ft ceilings and worn antiques. The outstanding corner suite—Miss Marie's—has full views of the bay and the original working fireplace from Marie's days as a madam. ⊠ *1004 Water St., 98368,* ☎ *360/385–0773 or 800/962–0741,* 𝔽𝔸𝕏 *360/946–5287. 15 rooms, 12 with bath. AE, D, MC, V.*

$$ 🏨 **Tides Inn.** You might recognize this place from the movie *An Officer and a Gentleman,* which was filmed around Port Townsend and Fort Worden: The waterfront inn was the setting for those steamy love scenes between Richard Gere and Debra Winger. Comfortable and unfancy, the Tides has a briny smell and a seaside-motel atmosphere. Some rooms have small private decks that extend over the water's edge. All the rooms have TVs and phones; some have kitchens, decks, hot tubs, or all three. A Continental breakfast (muffins and juice) is served each morning. ⊠ *1807 Water St., 98368,* ☎ *360/385–0595 or 800/822–8696,* 𝔽𝔸𝕏 *360/385–7370. 21 rooms. AE, D, DC, MC, V.*

Nightlife and the Arts

NIGHTLIFE

Back Alley (⊠ 923 Washington St., ☎ 360/385–2914), a favorite with locals, hosts rock-and-roll musicians on weekends. Secluded **Sirens** (⊠ 832 Water St., 3rd floor, ☎ 360/379–0776) overlooks the water and books a variety of musical acts on weekends. The large old **Town Tavern** (⊠ 639 Water St., ☎ 360/385–4706) has live music—from jazz to blues to rock—on weekends.

THE ARTS

Centrum (⊠ Box 1158, 98368, ☎ 800/733–3608), Port Townsend's well-respected performing-arts organization, presents performances, workshops, and conferences throughout the year at Fort Worden State Park. The **Centrum Summer Arts Festival** runs from June to September.

Outdoor Activities and Sports

BICYCLING

P. T. Cyclery (⊠ 100 Tyler St., south of Water St., ☎ 360/385–6470) rents mountain bikes year-round. The nearest place to go riding is Fort Worden, but you can range as far afield as Fort Flagler, the lower Dungeness trails (no bikes are allowed on the spit itself), or across the water to Whidbey Island.

BOAT CRUISE

P. S. Express (⊠ 431 Water St., ☎ 360/385–5288) operates narrated passenger tours to San Juan Island from April to October for $49 round-trip.

KAYAK TOURS

Kayak Port Townsend (⊠ 435 Water St., ☎ 360/385–6240) conducts guided kayak tours from April to September ($40 for about three hours or $70 for a full day with lunch).

Shopping

The best shopping in Port Townsend can be found along the waterfront; many of the boutiques and stores here carry Northwest arts and crafts. **North by Northwest Gallery** (⊠ 18 Water St., ☎ 360/385–0955) specializes in Eskimo and Native American art, artifacts, jewelry, and clothing. **Russell Jaqua Gallery** (⊠ 21 Taylor St., ☎ 360/385–5262) exhibits blacksmith and other iron-work creations. **William James Bookseller** (⊠ 829 Water St., ☎ 360/385–7313) stocks used and out-of-print books in all fields, with an emphasis on nautical, regional history, and theology titles.

Three dozen dealers at the two-story **Port Townsend Antique Mall** (⊠ 802 Washington St., 360/385–2590) flea market sell merchandise ranging from pricey Victorian collectors' items to cheap, funky junk.

More shops are uptown on **Lawrence Street** near an enclave of Victorian houses.

En Route U.S. 101 travels south along the west side of Hood Canal past oyster-picking and clam-digging areas. The retail store of the **Hamma Hamma Oyster Company** (⊠ N. 35959 Hwy. 101, ☎ 360/877–5811), south of the town of Eldon, sells fresh salmon, mussels, crab, shrimp, and other seafood; you purchase these plus pickled and smoked items and then dine on the picnic tables outside. The store is open daily from 9:30 to 5:30, but it's closed on Wednesday in winter.

Hoodsport

66 mi south of Port Townsend, Hwy. 20 to U.S. 101.

Near the southern bend of Hood Canal and the town of Hoodsport is the **Hoodsport Winery,** whose wines include chardonnays, Rieslings, and even gooseberry and rhubarb. The staff gives tours and tastings on an informal basis as requested. ⊠ N. 23501 Hwy. 101, ☎ 360/877–9894. ⌷ Free. ☉ Daily 10–6.

OFF THE   **LAKE CUSHMAN –** An important source of water for Tacoma's power-
BEATEN PATH   house on Hood Canal, the lake is the trailhead to numerous hiking
                 paths, including one to the awe-inspiring Staircase Rapids on the
                 Skokomish River. Here the steep country gives rise to rushing cataracts
                 and boulder-strewn rapids, broken up by deep pools where Dolly Var-
                 den trout rest. ⊠ *11 mi west of Hoodsport on Staircase Rd. (Rte. 119).*

En Route If you continue south on U.S. 101, you'll pass the sawmill town of **Shelton** before arriving back in Olympia.

The Olympic Peninsula Essentials

Arriving and Departing

BY BUS

Jefferson Transit (☎ 800/436–3950) services Port Angeles from Seattle and Olympia. **Olympic Bus Lines** (☎ 800/550–3858) offers service twice daily to Port Angeles from downtown Seattle and Sea-Tac Airport. Reservations are recommended.

BY CAR

Interstate 5 skirts the southeastern edge of the Olympic Peninsula.

BY FERRY

Washington State Ferries (☎ 206/464–6400) travel from Seattle to Bainbridge Island; from the ferry terminal, drive west on Highway 305, north on Route 3, and west on Highway 104 over the Hood Canal bridge to Discovery Bay, until you reach U.S. 101.

BY PLANE

Fairchild International Airport (⊠ 1404 Fairchild International Airport Rd., ☎ 360/457–1138) is west of Port Angeles off U.S. 101 (take Airport Road north from 101). **Jefferson County International Airport** (⊠ 310 Airport Rd., ☎ 360/385–0656) is south of Port Townsend off Highway 19. **Port Townsend Airways** (☎ 800/385-6554) flies charter planes between Sea-Tac Airport and Port Townsend.

Harbor Air has scheduled service to Port Angeles from Seattle, the San Juan Islands, and elsewhere. **Horizon Air** has scheduled service between Seattle and Port Angeles. *See* Air Travel *in* the Gold Guide for airline phone numbers.

Getting Around
BY BUS

Traveling by bus is slow going on the Olympic Peninsula. **Clallam Transit** (☎ 360/452–4511 or 800/858–3747), **Jefferson Transit** (☎ 800/436–3950), and **West Jefferson Transit** (☎ 360/452–1397 or 800/436–3950) service the area.

BY CAR

U.S. 101 loops around the Olympic Peninsula. **Highway 112** heads west from U.S. 101 at Port Angeles to Neah Bay. **Highway 113** winds north from U.S. 101 at Sappho to Highway 112. **Highway 110** travels west from U.S. 101 at Forks to La Push. **Highway 109** leads west from U.S. 101 at Hoquiam to Copalis Beach, Moclips, and Taholah. **Highway 8** heads west from U.S. 101 at Olympia. At Elmo, Highway 8 connects with **U.S. 12,** which travels west to Hoquiam and Aberdeen.

Guided Tours
Olympic Raft and Guide (☎ 360/452–1443) conducts white-water and scenic float trips on the Hoh and Elwha rivers. **Peak Six Tours** (⊠ 4883 Upper Hoh Rd., Forks, ☎ 360/374–5254) provides gear and information for hiking, biking, camping, climbing, and sightseeing on the Olympic Peninsula.

Visitor Information
North Olympic Peninsula Visitor and Convention Bureau (⊠ Box 670, Port Angeles 98362, ☎ 360/452–8552 or 800/942–4042). **Olympic National Forest** (⊠ 1835 Blacklake Blvd., Olympia 98512, ☎ 360/956–2400). **Olympic National Park** (⊠ 1835 Blacklake Blvd., Olympia 98512, ☎ 360/956–4501). **Port Angeles Chamber of Commerce** (⊠ 121 E. Railroad Ave., 98362, ☎ 360/452–2363). **Port Townsend Chamber of Commerce** (⊠ 2437 E. Sims Way, 98368, ☎ 360/385–2722). **Sequim-Dungeness Valley Chamber of Commerce** (⊠ Box 907, Sequim 98382, ☎ 360/683–6197 or 800/737–8462).

LONG BEACH PENINSULA

If the waters of the Pacific Ocean and the mighty Columbia River had met in a less turbulent manner, a huge seaport might sit at the river's mouth. Instead, you'll find a long, undeveloped beach—bounded to the west by the Pacific and the east by Willapa Bay—known as the Long Beach Peninsula. Fishing villages and cranberry bogs dot this region just north of the Oregon border, about a two-hour drive from Portland.

Great for hiking, biking, bird-watching, and beachcombing, the peninsula is also the perfect place for holing up in front of a crackling fire and reading a good book, or venturing out to witness a winter storm, of which there are plenty. Be careful if you swim here, though. Shifting sands underfoot and tremendous undertows account for several drownings each year.

Within the Long Beach Peninsula is North America's longest uninterrupted stretch (28 mi) of sandy beach. Unfortunately, the locals drive cars, trucks, recreational vehicles, and motorcycles up and down this pristine belt of sand, despite the trauma this practice may wreak on the clamming beds or the psyche of beachgoers. (From April to Labor Day, 40% of the beach is off-limits to motor vehicles, so it is possible to find quiet.) Inland, the peninsula-area marshes host migrating birds, among them trumpeter swans. A stand of old-growth red cedar trees can be found on Long Island in a natural preserve, accessible only by private boat, that is home to the spotted owl, the marbled murelet, elk, and black bears.

Chinook

118 mi from Olympia, west on U.S. 101 and Hwy. 8, southwest on Hwy. 107, south on U.S. 101 and Hwy. 4, and west on Hwy. 401.

Chinook was named for a Native American tribe that helped William Clark and Meriwether Lewis during their stay on the Pacific coast. The community has been in an economic recession for some years, and though it's drab in places there are points of interest.

The **Sea Resources Hatchery Complex** (⊠ Houtchen Rd., ☎ 360/777–8229) conducts free tours of its hatchery and fish-rearing ponds. Phone ahead to arrange a tour.

㉕ The construction of the fort for which the **Fort Columbia State Park and Interpretive Center** is named was supposed to begin in 1864, to coincide with the building of Forts Canby and Stevens. Fort Columbia was not built until 1902; electricity, plumbing, and steam, which weren't in the original plans, were provided. The interpretive center illustrates barracks life and has displays of Chinook Indian culture. A hike behind the fort up Scarborough Hill yields a breathtaking view of the peninsula and the Columbia River. ⊠ *U.S. 101, 2 mi east of Chinook,* ☎ *360/777–8221.* ▨ *Free.* ☺ *Memorial Day–Sept., Wed.–Sun. 10–5.*

Dining

$$–$$$ ✕ **The Sanctuary.** The soft lighting, stained-glass windows, and fine Pacific Rim cuisine at the Sanctuary may come as a bit of a surprise given the run-down condition of the century-old church building that houses the restaurant. The ever-evolving menu highlights fresh local seafood—possible entrées include fresh halibut with roasted red pepper or rice and vegetables wrapped in seaweed. The homemade desserts are delicious. Local labels and a few foreign vintages are represented on the wine list. ⊠ *U.S. 101 and Hazel St.,* ☎ *360/777–8380. Reservations essential. AE, D, MC, V. Closed Mon.–Tues. No lunch.*

Ilwaco

13 mi west of Chinook on Hwy. 401.

From 1884 to 1910, gill-net and trap fishermen around Ilwaco fought one another with knives, rifles, and threats of lynchings over access to and ownership of the fishing grounds. Today, the port community of 600 is home to salmon, crab, tuna, charter, and other commercial boat-

Long Beach Peninsula

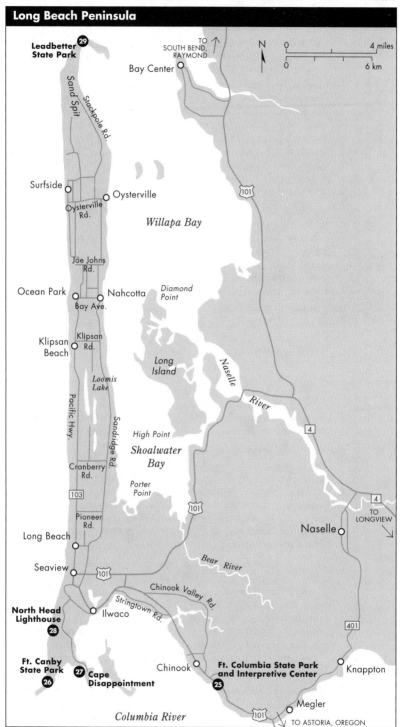

Leadbetter State Park 29

Bay Center

TO SOUTH BEND, RAYMOND

N

0   4 miles
0   6 km

Sand Spit

Stackpole Rd.

101

Surfside

Oysterville

Oysterville Rd.

Willapa Bay

Joe Johns Rd.

Diamond Point

Ocean Park

Nahcotta

Bay Ave.

Klipsan Beach

Klipsan Rd.

Long Island

Naselle

Loomis Lake

Pacific Hwy.

Sandridge Rd.

River

4

High Point

Shoalwater Bay

Cranberry Rd.

103

Porter Point

101

4

TO LONGVIEW

Pioneer Rd.

Long Beach

Naselle

Seaview

101

Bear River

Chinook Valley Rd.

North Head Lighthouse 28

Ilwaco

Stringtown Rd.

Ft. Canby State Park 26

27 **Cape Disappointment**

Chinook

401

Ft. Columbia State Park and Interpretive Center 25

Knappton

Megler

101

TO ASTORIA, OREGON

Columbia River

ing operations. A 3-mi scenic loop winds past Fort Canby State Park to North Head Lighthouse and through the town of Ilwaco.

The dioramas and miniatures of Long Beach towns at the **Ilwaco Heritage Museum** illustrate the history of southwestern Washington, beginning with the Native Americans; moving on to the influx of traders, missionaries, and pioneers; and concluding with the contemporary workers and owners of the fishing, agriculture, and forest industries. The museum also houses a model of the peninsula's "clamshell railroad," a narrow-gauge train that transported passengers and mail along the beach. Ground-up clam and oyster shells formed the rail bed on which the tracks were laid. ⊠ *115 S.E. Lake St., off U.S. 101 N,* ☎ *360/642–3446.* 🖾 *$3.* ☉ *May–Aug., Mon.–Sat. 9–5, Sun. noon–4; Sept.–Apr., Mon.–Sat. 10–4.*

26 The 1,700-acre **Fort Canby State Park** was an active military installation until 1957, when it was turned over to the Washington State Parks and Recreation Commission. Many bunkers that guarded the mouth of the Columbia remain today. The park attracts beachcombers, hikers, ornithologists, and fishermen; during winter storms it's fun to watch the huge waves crash against the Columbia River bar. All the park's 250 campsites have stoves and tables; some sites have water and sewer and electric hook-ups.

Exhibits at the **Lewis & Clark Interpretive Center** (☎ 360/642–3029 or 360/642–3078) describe the 8,000-mi round-trip journey of the Corps of Volunteers for Northwest Discovery, which left Wood River, Illinois, in 1803 and arrived at Cape Disappointment in 1805 (they got back to Illinois in 1807). Artworks, photographs, and the journal entries of volunteers are arranged along ramps that lead to a view of the spot where the Columbia empties into the Pacific. ⊠ *Robert Gray Dr., 2½ mi southwest of Ilwaco off U.S. 101,* ☎ *360/642–3078.* 🖾 *Park and interpretive center free, campsites $11–$16.* ☉ *Park daily dawn–dusk, interpretive center daily 10–5.*

27 **Cape Disappointment** was named in 1788 by Captain John Meares, an English fur trader who had been unable to find the Northwest Passage. This harbor—known as "the graveyard of the Pacific"—has been the scourge of sailors since the 1700s: More than 250 ships have sunk after running aground on its treacherous sandbars. A ½-mi path from the Lewis & Clark Interpretive Center leads to the **Cape Disappointment Lighthouse.** Built in 1856, it's the oldest lighthouse on the West Coast still in use.

The **U.S. Coast Guard Station Cape Disappointment** (☎ 360/642–2384) is the largest search-and-rescue station on the Northwest coast. The rough conditions of the Columbia River bar provide plenty of lessons for the students of the on-site **National Motor Life Boat School.** The only institution of its kind, the school teaches elite rescue crews from around the world advanced skills in navigation, mechanics, fire fighting, and lifesaving. The observation platform on the North Jetty at Fort Canby State Park is a good viewing spot for watching the motor lifeboats. Informal tours are possible if you call ahead.

28 **North Head Lighthouse** was built in 1899 to help skippers sailing from the north who could not see the Cape Disappointment Lighthouse. High on a bluff over pounding surf, North Head presides over a strikingly different terrain than Cape Disappointment. Stand amid the windswept trees here and you'll get superb views of the Long Beach Peninsula. ⊠ *From Cape Disappointment follow the Spur 100 road for 2 mi,* ☎ *360/642–3078.* 🖾 *$1.* ☉ *Apr.–Sept., daily 10–5; Oct.–Mar., weekends only, hrs subject to volunteer availability.*

Lodging

$$–$$$ ⊞ **Chick-a-dee Inn.** This B&B inside a 1928 New England–style church sits on a knoll overlooking the port of Ilwaco. All but two of the guest rooms are upstairs in the old Sunday-school rooms, and all are cozily furnished with antiques, armoires, and eyelet or printed chintz curtains and coverlets. A full American breakfast, included in the room rate, is served on the altar stage in the sanctuary. ⊠ *120 Williams St. NE, 98624,* ☎ *360/642–8686,* FAX *360/642–8686. 10 rooms, 7 with bath. MC, V.*

Outdoor Activities and Sports

FISHING

The fish that swim in the waters near Ilwaco include salmon, rock cod, lingcod, flounder, perch, sea bass, and sturgeon. A free fishing guide is available from the **Port of Ilwaco** (⊠ Box 307, 98624, ☎ 360/642–3145).

WHALE-WATCHING

Gray whales pass by the Long Beach Peninsula twice a year: December through February, on their migration from the Arctic to their winter breeding grounds in Californian and Mexican waters; and March through May, on the return trip north. The view from the North Head Lighthouse (☞ *above*) is particularly spectacular. The best conditions exist in the mornings, when the water is calm and overcast conditions reduce the glare. Look on the horizon for a whale blow—the vapor, water, or condensation that spouts into the air when the whale exhales. If you spot one blow, you're likely to see others: Whales often make several shorter, shallow dives before a longer dive that can last as long as 10 minutes.

Seaview

2 mi north of Cape Disappointment on Hwy. 103.

Seaview, an unincorporated town, contains several homes dating from the 1800s. The **Shelburne Inn,** built in 1896, is on the National Register of Historic Places. In 1892 U.S. Senator Henry Winslow Corbett built what's now the **Sou'wester Lodge.**

Dining and Lodging

$$–$$$ ✕ **Shoalwater Restaurant.** The Shoalwater Restaurant at the Shelburne Inn, acclaimed by *Gourmet, Bon Appétit,* and *Travel & Leisure,* has a dark wooden interior and a comforting atmosphere. Seafood, brought from the fishing boats to the restaurant's back door, is as fresh as it can be; local mushrooms and salad greens are gathered from the peninsula's woods and gardens. Try the panfried Asian-style crab and shrimp cakes. Ann Kischner, a master pastry chef, creates some exquisite desserts. Lunch is served daily in the Heron & Beaver Pub; the restaurant offers a Sunday brunch during summer. ⊠ *Pacific Hwy. and N. 45th St.,* ☎ *360/642–4142. AE, D, DC, MC, V. No lunch in restaurant.*

$$ ✕ **42nd Street Cafe.** Chef Cheri Walker spent more than a decade honing her skills at the peninsula's finest eateries before opening her own place. Her fare is inspired, original, and reasonably priced—pastas, meats, and seafood dishes such as grilled Willapa Bay oysters, grilled chinook salmon with shaved almonds, and halibut stew. All meals include salad, homemade bread, and dessert. ⊠ *Hwy. 103 and 42nd Pl.,* ☎ *360/642–2323. No lunch Mon.–Tues.*

$$–$$$ ⊞ **Shelburne Inn.** Sitting along the peninsula's main thoroughfare, be-
★ hind a white picket fence enclosing rose and other gardens, is a wood-frame Craftsman-style building that is the oldest continuously run

hotel in Washington. Fresh flowers, original works of art, antiques, and fine-art prints adorn the guest rooms, most of which have decks or balconies. Beds have either handmade quilts or hand-crocheted bedspreads. The complimentary gourmet breakfast is unforgettable—you can choose from among five or six entrées, which might include an asparagus omelet or grilled oysters with salsa. You needn't stray far for lunch or dinner: The on-site Shoalwater Restaurant (☞ *above*) is superb. The Shelburne's only drawback is that it is right on the highway; if you need quiet, ask for a room on the west side. ⊠ *Hwy. 103 and N. 45th St., 98644,* ☎ *360/642–2442,* 𝔽𝔸𝕏 *360/642–8904. 15 rooms. Restaurant, pub. AE, MC, V.*

$–$$ 🏨 **Sou'wester Lodge.** A stay at the Sou'wester is a bohemian experience. Proprietors Len and Miriam Atkins came to Seaview from South Africa, by way of Israel and Chicago, where they worked with the late psychologist Bruno Bettelheim, and they are always up for a stimulating conversation. The lodge was built in 1892 as the summer retreat for Henry Winslow Corbett, a Portland banker, timber baron, shipping and railroad magnate, and U.S. senator. Rooms and apartments are not "decorated"—instead they are the repository of things carefully collected over the years, including handmade quilts and original paintings and drawings. Soirees and chamber-music concerts sometimes occur in the parlor. Beach cottages and the classic mobile-home units just behind the beach have cooking facilities; guests are also welcome to make breakfast in the Atkinses' homey kitchen. ⊠ *Beach Access Rd. (Box 102), 98644,* ☎ *360/642–2542. 3 rooms share 1 bath; 6 suites; 4 cottages; 10 trailers. Beach. D, MC, V.*

Long Beach

½ mi north of Seaview on Hwy. 103.

Tourist-oriented Long Beach bears a striking resemblance to Coney Island in the 1950s. Along its boardwalk, which stretches southwest from 10th Street to Bolstadt Street, you'll find everything from cotton candy and hot dogs to go-carts and bumper cars. Each August the community of 1,400 hosts the **Washington State International Kite Festival** (☎ 800/451–2542), which bills itself as the largest and most popular event of its kind in the Western Hemisphere.

At the interesting **World Kite Museum and Hall of Fame,** you can view an array of kites and learn about kite making, kite history, and international kiting celebrities. ⊠ *N. Pacific Hwy. (Hwy. 103) at 3rd St. N,* ☎ *360/642–4020.* 🎟 *$1.50.* ☉ *June–Aug., daily 11–5; May and Sept.–Oct., Fri.–Mon. 11–5; Nov.–Apr., weekends 11–5.*

Dining and Lodging

$$–$$$ ✕ **Columbia Lightship.** The restaurant on the beach side of the Edgewater Inn has great views. Don't be surprised to see kites or a large wind sock floating in the air as you gaze out from the open-air bar, which serves Washington wines and local microbrews. For lunch there's fish-and-chips, fresh salads, quiche, pasta, and sandwiches. Dinner entrées include pastas, prime rib, grilled salmon, steamed Willapa Bay clams, and Cajun-style or panfried Willapa Bay oysters. A complete breakfast buffet is prepared in summer only. ⊠ *409 10th St. SW,* ☎ *360/642–3252. MC, V.*

$$ ✕ **Doogers.** Locals will urge you to eat here—listen to them. Doogers serves seafood all day long: The ample portions come with potatoes and shrimp-topped garlic toast. ⊠ *900 S. Pacific Hwy. (Hwy. 103),* ☎ *360/642–4224. AE, D, MC, V.*

$ ✕ **My Mom's Pie Kitchen.** Small and frilly, this lunch spot serves an unusual, albeit limited, selection of comfort food—homemade meat loaf sandwiches, crab cakes, and the like. It's worth dropping by just for the pies—banana whipped cream, chocolate almond, pecan, sour-cream raisin, fresh raspberry, and more. ⊠ *4316 S. Pacific Hwy. (Hwy. 103),* ☎ *360/642–2342. Reservations not accepted. MC, V. Closed Sun.– Tues. No dinner.*

$$ 🏨 **Edgewater Inn Motel.** The Edgewater's two boxy buildings sit behind the sand dunes at the main entrance to the public beach. The motel-style rooms have heavy nylon curtains that peel back to expose an expansive parking lot and, beyond that, the beach. ⊠ *409 10th St. SW, 98631,* ☎ *360/642–2311 or 800/561–2456,* FAX *360/642–8018. 84 rooms. Restaurant, bar. AE, D, DC, MC, V.*

$–$$$ 🏨 **Breakers Motel and Condominiums.** Four identical buildings on the beach hold contemporary one- and two-bedroom condominiums. The decor varies, but most are comfortable, "beachy," and clean. Many have wood-burning fireplaces, TVs, VCRs, and private balconies with exceptional views of the dunes and the surf. Some units have kitchenettes. ⊠ *26th St. and Hwy. 103, 98631,* ☎ *360/642–4414 or 800/ 288–8890,* FAX *360/642–8772. 114 rooms. Indoor pool, spa, playground. AE, D, DC, MC, V.*

Outdoor Activities and Sports

BICYCLING

Long Beach Bike Shop (⊠ 1st Place Shopping Center, 811 S. Pacific Hwy., ☎ 360/642–7000) rents bikes.

GOLF

The **Peninsula Golf Course** (⊠ 9604 Pacific Hwy., ☎ 360/642–2828), a nine-hole, par-33 course, is on the northern edge of Long Beach. The greens fee is $9; an optional cart costs $9.

HORSEBACK RIDING

Back Country Horse Rides (⊠ 10th St. next to Edgewater Inn, ☎ 360/ 642–2576) rents horses. Horses are also available for rent at **Skippers** (⊠ S. 10th St. and Beach Access Rd., ☎ 360/642–3676).

Shopping

Gray Whale Gallery & Gifts (⊠ 105 N. Pacific Hwy., ☎ 360/642–2889) carries Northwest art, cards, jewelry, and cranberry products. **Long Beach Kites** (⊠ 104 N. Pacific Hwy., ☎ 360/642–2202) stocks box, dragon, and many other kites. **North Head Gallery** (⊠ 600 S. Pacific Hwy., ☎ 360/642–8884) sells the works of Elton Bennett and other Northwest artists.

Ocean Park

9 mi north of Long Beach on Hwy. 103.

Ocean Park is the commercial center of the peninsula's quieter north end. It was founded as a camp for the Methodist Episcopal Church of Portland in 1883, but the law that prohibited the establishment of saloons and gambling houses no longer exists. The **Taylor Hotel,** built in 1892 on Bay Avenue and N Place, houses retail businesses and is the only structure from the early days that is open to the public.

Lodging

$$–$$$ 🏨 **Caswell's on the Bay B&B.** From the outside, this B&B with a wraparound porch looks like an old Victorian house. But inside it's clearly a modern creation (Caswell's was built in 1995), with high ceilings and enormous windows looking onto Willapa Bay and the iso-

lated Long Island wildlife sanctuary. From afternoon tea to Ralph
Lauren sheets, the innkeepers go to great lengths to indulge their
guests. The rooms, outfitted antique bedroom sets, have sitting areas
and waterside or garden views. The rates include a full breakfast. ✉
25204 Sandridge Rd., 98640, ☎ *360/665–6535,* FAX *360/665–6500.
5 rooms. MC, V.*

Outdoor Activities and Sports
The **Surfside Golf and Country Club** (✉ 31508 Jay Pl., behind the Surfside Inn, ☎ 360/665–4148), 2 mi north of Ocean Park, is a nine-hole,
par-36 course. The greens fee is $12; an optional cart costs $12.

Nahcotta

3 mi from Ocean Park, east on Bay Ave. to Hwy. 103 (Sandridge Rd.).

Nahcotta, on the bay side of the Long Beach Peninsula, supports an
active oyster industry—oysters are shucked and canned on the docks
on Willapa Bay. Named for a Native American chief, Nahcotta was
the northernmost point on the peninsula's defunct narrow-gauge railway; the schedule is still posted in the Nahcotta Post Office. The
town's port is a good place from which to view Long Island, home of
an old-growth cedar forest that can be reached only by private boat.

Dining
$$$ ✕ **The Ark.** This rambling nautical shack, the creation of Jamella Lucas
★   and Nanci Main, was a favorite of the late James Beard. Seafood
reigns supreme—the house specialty is oysters, which are raised in beds
behind the restaurant. The menu includes unusual entrées like Scotch
salmon and sturgeon with ginger, garlic, and a sake glaze. The bakery
here produces breads, muffins, and desserts. Less-expensive lighter
fare, including soup and sandwiches, is available at the bar. ✉ *273
Sandridge Rd.,* ☎ *360/665–4133. AE, MC, V. Closed Mon.*

Outdoor Activities and Sports
Clamming is a popular pastime here; the season varies depending on
the supply. For details, call 360/665–4166 or 360/902–2250.

Oysterville

6 mi north of Nahcotta on Hwy. 103 (Sandridge Rd.).

Oysterville bears an unsettling resemblance to the set of *Little House
on the Prairie.* Signs posted on the fence of each building tell when the
home or business was built and who lived in it. You can tour the re-
stored **Oysterville Church** (pick up a free historical map of Oysterville
here), the schoolhouse, the late-19th-century tannery, and the home
of the mayor. The town, established in 1854, did not survive the oys-
ter industry's decline in the late 1800s. The native shellfish were har-
vested to extinction and, although they were replaced with a Japanese
oyster, the industry never made a comeback.

Leadbetter State Park

⓴ *3 mi north of Oysterville; take Sandridge Rd. to the left and follow
the signs.*

Leadbetter State Park, at the northernmost tip of Long Beach Penin-
sula, is a wildlife refuge and a good spot for bird-watching. The dune
area at the very tip of the point is closed from April to August to pro-
tect the nesting snowy plover. Black brants, sandpipers, turnstones, yel-
lowlegs, sanderlings, knots, and plovers are among the 100 species
biologists have recorded at the point. From the parking lot, a ½-mi paved

wheelchair-accessible path leads to the ocean and a 2½-mi loop trail winds through the dunes along the ocean and Willapa Bay. Several trails along the loop lead to isolated patches of coast. ⊠ *Off Stackpole Rd.,* ☎ *360/642–3078.* ⚑ *Free.* ☾ *Apr.–mid-Oct., daily 6:30* AM*–dusk; mid-Oct.–Mar., daily 8* AM*–dusk.*

Long Beach Peninsula Essentials

Arriving and Departing

BY CAR

From I–5 near the Oregon border, take **Highway 4** west from Kelso to **Highway 401** (if you're going to Chinook, Ilwaco, or Seaview) or **U.S. 101** (if you're going to Long Beach and points north). From Olympia, take **U.S. 101** west and continue west as the road becomes **Highway 8** and **U.S. 12.** At Montesano pick up **Highway 107** and continue south on U.S. 101 when the roads merge.

Getting Around

U.S. 101 curves around the southern part of the peninsula. **Highway 103** travels north through the peninsula.

Visitor Information

Long Beach Peninsula Visitors Bureau (⊠ U.S. 101 and Hwy. 103, Box 562, 98631, ☎ 360/642–2400 or 800/451–2542).

MOUNT ST. HELENS

Since its eruption in 1980, Mount St. Helens has become a popular destination. The 8,365-ft-high mountain, formerly 9,665 ft high, is part of the string of volcanic peaks in the Cascade Range that includes Mount Rainier and Mount Baker to the north and Mount Hood (in Oregon) to the south. The mountain is most easily accessed by driving along the Spirit Lake Memorial Highway (Highway 504), whose predecessor was destroyed in a matter of minutes on May 18, 1980. The highway has unparalleled views of the mountain and the surrounding Toutle River valley.

The Eruption of Mount St. Helens, a 30-minute giant-screen film, plays every 45 minutes from 9 AM to 6 PM at the Cinedome theater (⊠ I–5's Castle Rock Exit 49, ☎ 360/274–9844). Admission is $5.

Mount St. Helens National Volcanic Monument

151 mi from Seattle, south on I–5 and east on Hwy. 504.

The U.S. Forest Service operates the Mount St. Helens National Volcanic Monument. The $8-per-person user fee (children under 15 are admitted free) is good for three days.

The three visitor centers along Highway 504 on the west side of the forest are open daily from 9 to 6. The **Mount St. Helens Visitor Center** (⊠ Hwy. 504, 5 mi east of I–5, Silver Lake, ☎ 360/274–2100) does not have great views of the mountain, but it has exhibits documenting the eruption and a walk-through volcano. Exhibits at the **Coldwater Ridge Visitor Center** (⊠ Hwy. 504, 43 mi east of I–5, ☎ 360/274–2131), a multimillion-dollar facility, document the great blast and its effects on the surrounding 150,000 acres—which were devastated but are in the process of a remarkable recovery. A ¼-mi trail leads from the visitor center to Coldwater Lake, which has a recreation area. The **Johnston Ridge Observatory** (⊠ Hwy. 504, 53 mi east of I–5, ☎ 360/274–2140) has the most spectacular views of the crater and lava dome.

Exhibits here interpret the geology of the mountain and explain how scientists monitor an active volcano.

On the east side of the mountain are two bare-bones visitor centers, **Windy Ridge** and **Ape Cave.** On the south side of the mountain there's a center at **Lava Canyon.**

The dining options at Mount St. Helens are limited. **Coldwater Ridge Visitor Center** (✉ Hwy. 504, 43 mi east of I–5, ☎ 360/274–2131) has a small concession area. **Weyerhauser/Hoffstadt Bluff Visitor Center** (✉ Hwy. 504, 27 mi east of I–5, ☎ 360/274–7750), run by Cowlitz County, contains the only full-service restaurant along Highway 504.

Climbing
Climbing is restricted to the south side of the mountain. Permits (☎ 360/247–3900 or 360/247–3961) are required; the fee is $15 per person.

Mount St. Helens Essentials

Arriving and Departing
BY CAR

The Castle Rock exit (No. 49) of **I–5** is just outside the western entrance to the monument. Follow **Highway 504** into the park. You can access the park from the north by taking **Forest Service Road 25** south from U.S. 12 at the town of Randle. Forest Service Road 25 connects with **Forest Service Road 90,** which heads north from the town of Cougar. The two forest-service roads are closed in winter.

Getting Around
BY CAR

Highway 504 is the main road through the monument.

Visitor Information
Mount St. Helens National Volcanic Monument (☎ 360/247–3900).

CROSSING THE CASCADES

Interstate 90 heading east from Seattle winds through bucolic farmland with snowcapped mountains in the background. Nestled in the foothills is Snoqualmie Falls, one of the area's most popular attractions. Small mining towns dot the mountains, and to the north of I–90 is Leavenworth, an alpine-style village with excellent sporting opportunities. Crossing over the mountains, you'll emerge in eastern Washington— seemingly a different state in both attitude and climate. Ellensburg, a pleasant college town, is an excellent stop on the way to the wineries of the Yakima Valley.

Snoqualmie

③⓪   *28 mi east of Seattle on I–90.*

★   Spring and summer snowmelt turns the Snoqualmie River into the thundering torrent known as **Snoqualmie Falls** as the river cascades through a 268-ft rock gorge (100 ft higher than Niagara Falls) to a 65-ft-deep pool below. The falls, which were considered sacred by the native people who lived along the river bank, are Snoqualmie's biggest attraction (though some visitors come to see locations David Lynch used in his TV series *Twin Peaks*). A 2-acre park, including an observation platform 300 ft above the Snoqualmie River, offers a view of Snoqualmie Falls and the surrounding area. You can hike the **River Trail,** a 3-mi round-trip route through trees and open slopes that ends at the base of the falls. Be prepared for an uphill workout on the return to the trailhead.

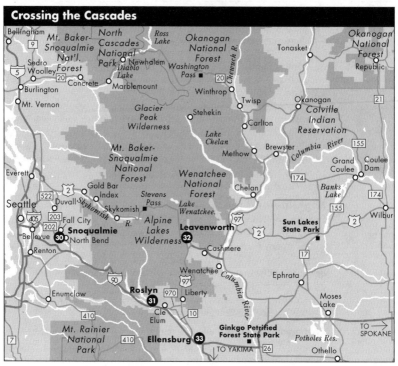

Crossing the Cascades

The vintage cars of the **Snoqualmie Valley Railroad,** built in the mid-1910s for the Spokane, Portland, and Seattle Railroad, travel between the landmark **Snoqualmie Depot** and a depot in North Bend. The 50-minute (round-trip) excursion passes through woods and farmland. The **Northwest Railway Museum** within Snoqualmie's depot displays memorabilia and has a bookstore. ⊠ *Snoqualmie Depot: 38625 S.E. King St., at Hwy. 202,* ☎ *206/746–4025 (Seattle) or 425/888–0373 (Snoqualmie).* ⊠ *$6.* ⊙ *Trains May–Sept., weekends and holidays; Oct., Sun. only; on the hr 11–4 from Snoqualmie and on the ½ hr 11:30–3:30 from North Bend. Museum, depot, and bookstore Thurs.–Mon. 10–5.*

Winding north through heavy forest from Snoqualmie, Highway 203 becomes plain old Main Street when it reaches the unassuming town of **Duvall,** a good place to stop for a little antiquing or bookshop browsing, a glimpse of the Snoqualmie River, or a mid-afternoon latte. To return to Seattle you can backtrack to Snoqualmie or head west on the Woodinville–Duvall Road.

Dining and Lodging

$$$$ ✕ **The Herbfarm.** If there is such a thing as Northwest cuisine, then
★ this intimate restaurant must rank as its temple. A nine-course meal served at two to three seatings a night includes five glasses of Northwest wine and takes between four and five hours. Try such delicacies as goat's-milk-cheese and parsley biscuits, green pickled walnuts in the husk, salmon with a sauce of fresh garden herbs, and sorbet of rose geranium and lemon verbena. The Herbfarm is often booked up months in advance. A devastating fire swept through the restaurant in early 1997, but renovations should be complete by the time you read this. ⊠ *32804 Issaquah–Fall City Rd. (from I–90 Exit 22 head left, then take 1st right onto Preston–Fall City Rd.; follow this 3 mi to Y in road,*

then go left over the bridge and another ½ mi), Fall City, ☎ 206/784–2222. Reservations essential. MC, V. No lunch. Closed on most weekdays and for a few wks mid-Feb.–Mar.

$$$$ ✕🏠 **Salish Lodge.** Eight of the 91 rooms at this lodge look out over
★   Snoqualmie Falls, and others have a view upriver. All have an airy feeling, wood furniture, whirlpool baths, and window seats or balconies. The restaurant's elaborate Saturday and Sunday brunches include eggs, bacon, fish, fresh fruit, pancakes, and the Salish's renowned oatmeal. Jacket and tie are required for dinner; reservations are essential. Breakfast is served on weekdays. ⊠ *6501 Railroad Ave. SE, 98065,* ☎ *425/888–2556 or 800/826–6124,* 𝔽𝔸𝕏 *425/888–2420. 91 rooms. 2 restaurants, bar, spa, health club, laundry service, concierge, business services, meeting rooms. AE, D, DC, MC, V.*

Nightlife and the Arts

Snoqualmie Falls Forest Theater (☎ 425/222–7044) presents two or three plays, usually melodramas performed by acting students and community performers, in a 250-seat outdoor amphitheater near Fall City—from I–90 take Exit 22 and go 4 mi; take a right on David Powell Road, follow signs, and continue through the gate to the parking area. Tickets are $13. For another $12, you can enjoy a salmon or steak barbecue after the matinee or before the evening performance. Reservations are required for dinner.

Outdoor Activities and Sports

Snoqualmie Pass has three downhill and cross-country ski areas—**Alpental, Ski Acres,** and **Snoqualmie Summit** (⊠ Mailing address for all three: 3010 77th St. SE, Mercer Island 98040, ☎ 206/232–8182). Each area rents equipment and has a full restaurant and lodge facilities.

Roslyn

③① *58 mi from Snoqualmie; 83 mi from Seattle, east on I–90 and north on Hwy. 903.*

Roslyn, a former coal-mining town, gained notoriety as the real-life stand-in for the Alaskan town of Cicely on the TV program *Northern Exposure.* The **Brick Tavern** (⊠ 1 Pennsylvania Ave., ☎ 509/649–2643), which opened in 1889, is the oldest operating bar in Washington. Roslyn is also notable for its two dozen ethnic cemeteries, established by communities of miners in the late 1800s and early 1900s.

Dining

$–$$ ✕ **Roslyn Café.** High ceilings and neon in the window add a touch of nostalgia to this funky café, whose exterior appeared on *Northern Exposure.* The hamburgers are delicious (try the one with spinach and onions), but entrées also include fresh halibut in dill sauce. Save room for the decadent desserts. ⊠ *28 Pennsylvania Ave., ☎ 509/649–2763. Reservations not accepted. MC, V. Dinner days and hrs vary; call ahead.*

Cle Elum

3 mi east of Roslyn, 86 mi east of Seattle on I–90.

Cle Elum (pronounced klee *ell*-um), another former coal-mining town, doesn't have many sights, but because it's right off I–90 it's a convenient stop for lunch or gas.

Dining and Lodging

$$ ✕⌂ **Mama Vallone's Steakhouse and Inn.** The pasta dishes, the pasta and *fagioli* soup (a tomato-based soup with vegetables and beans), and the *bagna calda* (a bath of olive oil, garlic, anchovies, and butter for dredging vegetables and meat) are worthy favorites at this cozy and informal restaurant (closed on Monday; no lunch). For Sunday brunch, you might find ravioli or tortellini along with a standard eggs-and-ham buffet. The inn upstairs was built in 1906 as a boardinghouse for unmarried miners; today there are three moderately priced rooms with antique-style furnishings. ⊠ *302 W. 1st St., 98922,* ☎ *509/674–5174. 3 rooms. Restaurant. AE, DC, MC, V.*

Leavenworth

★ **㉜**   *42 mi from Cle Elum, south on Hwy. 10, east (at Teanaway) on Hwy. 970, and north on U.S. 97; 128 mi from Seattle, I–5 north to U.S. 2 east.*

Participants in a 1997 poll conducted by *Seattle* magazine voted Leavenworth one of their favorite weekend getaways. And it's easy to see why: The charming (if occasionally *too* cute) Bavarian-style village, home to creative restaurants and attractive lodgings, is a hub for some of the Northwest's best skiing, hiking, rock climbing, rafting, canoeing, and snowshoeing.

Leavenworth was a railroad and mining center for many years, but by the 1960s it had fallen on hard times. Civic leaders, looking for ways to capitalize on the town's setting in the heart of the Central Cascade Range, convinced shopkeepers and other businesspeople to maintain a gingerbread Tyrolean style—even the Safeway supermarket and the Chevron gas station carry out the theme. Restaurants prepare Bavarian-influenced dishes, candy shops sell gourmet Swiss-style chocolates, and stores and boutiques stock music boxes, dollhouses, and other Bavarian items. Events held throughout the year, modeled after those in a typical Bavarian village, foster a European spirit of simple elegance in a setting that is never short of spectacular.

The **Marlin Handbell Ringers** keep alive an 18th-century English tradition that evolved into a musical form. Twelve ringers play 107 bells covering 5½ chromatic octaves. The bells are rung as part of the town's Christmas festivities and also in early May. Also noteworthy is the **Nutcracker Museum** (⊠ 735 Front St., ☎ 509/548–4708), which contains more than 2,500 different kinds of antique and present-day nutcrackers. The museum is open from May to October, daily from 2 to 5.

Dining and Lodging

$$$ ✕ **Lorraine's Edel House.** The candlelit rooms at this modest restau
★   rant, a rare Leavenworth eatery that doesn't focus on German food, are quiet and cozy. From the appetizer of mussels sautéed in an orange cream sauce to exotic dessert wines and a homespun white- and dark-chocolate creation, you'll savor imaginatively mouthwatering combinations. The entrées include Asian-accented pastas, game and fish, and more obscure offerings like grilled wild boar or braised oxtail with caramelized purple onions, celery, and baby carrots. ⊠ *320 9th St.,* ☎ *509/548–4412. D, DC, MC, V.*

$$–$$$ ✕ **Restaurant Osterreich.** Chef Leopold Haas, who hails from Austria, prepares haute German cuisine—authentic Austrian and European dishes like the appetizer of marinated duck breast in a dumpling coating, or the elk stew entrée. The menu changes daily. The atmosphere is infinitely more casual than the food. ✉ *Tyrolean Ritz Hotel, 633A Front St.,* ☎ *509/548–4031. MC, V. Closed Mon.*

$$ ✕ **Cougar Inn.** This family restaurant, established in 1890, is on the shores of Lake Wenatchee, about 25 mi from Leavenworth. Locals often come by boat and tie up at the restaurant's dock. Great views of the lake can be had, especially in summer from the big outdoor deck. Breakfast, lunch, and dinner are served daily; the hearty American-style Sunday brunch is especially popular. The dinner menu includes a sirloin steak for two, fried and baked fish, burgers, and standard pastas. ✉ *23379 Hwy. 207, Lake Wenatchee,* ☎ *509/763–3354. AE, MC, V.*

$$ ✕ **Pewter Pot.** This intimate restaurant with lace curtains and fresh flowers is worth the 10-mi drive from Leavenworth to the town of Cashmere. Start with one of the great soups and follow it up with an entrée of stuffed breast of chicken with an apple-cider sauce; turkey and dressing; or sour-cream beef potpie. The deep-dish marionberry pie is memorable. ✉ *124½ Cottage Ave., Cashmere,* ☎ *509/782–2036. Reservations essential. MC, V. Closed Sun.–Mon.*

$ ✕ **Baren Haus.** The cuisine at this spacious, noisy, and often crowded beer-hall-style room may not be haute, or even particularly interesting, but the generous servings and low prices will appeal to those traveling on a budget. House specialties include German-style sandwiches and pizzas. ✉ *208 9th St.,* ☎ *509/548–4535. MC, V.*

$ ✕ **Danish Bakery.** Come to this small shop for tasty homemade pastries, strong espresso drinks, and friendly service. ✉ *731 Front St.,* ☎ *509/548–7514. Reservations not accepted. No credit cards.*

$ ✕ **Leavenworth Brewery.** The only brewery in Leavenworth pours 8 to 10 fresh brews—the selection changes every two to three weeks. The highly trained brew masters provide detailed descriptions of their beers (daily brewery tours are given at 2 PM). Sandwiches and bar food are available. ✉ *636 Front St.,* ☎ *509/548–4545. Reservations not accepted. MC, V.*

$$–$$$ 🏨 **Pension Anna.** Rooms and suites at this family-run Austrian-style pension in the heart of the village are decorated with sturdy antique pine furniture; added touches include fresh flowers and comforters on the beds. Two of the suites have whirlpool baths. A hearty European-style breakfast (cold cuts, meats, cheeses, soft-boiled eggs), included in the lodging rate, is served in a room decorated in traditional European style with crisp linens, pine decor, dark-green curtains, and a cuckoo clock. ✉ *926 Commercial St., 98826,* ☎ *509/548–6273 or 800/509–2662, ℻ 509/548–4656. 12 rooms, 3 suites. AE, D, MC, V.*

$$–$$$ 🏨 **Pine River Ranch.** Mountains completely surround this B&B on 32 acres, 16 mi outside Leavenworth. Two extremely private suites have kitchens, gas fireplaces, whirlpool tubs, stereos, televisions with VCRs, and decks. Four rooms in the farmhouse in front are significantly less spacious and private but still quite nice. A full breakfast is served in the dining room, but guests staying in the suites can have it delivered to them. ✉ *19668 Hwy. 207, 98826,* ☎ *509/763–3959, ℻ 509/763–2073. 6 rooms. AE, D, MC, V.*

$$–$$$ 🏨 **Run of the River.** Pierre Cardin bathrobes, toothpaste and toothbrushes, and private whirlpool tubs are among the amenities at this luxury accommodation. Each room is decorated with handmade willow furnishings and plush carpeting and is equipped with a TV. Innkeepers Monty and Karen Turner live in the house next door and are readily at hand to meet your needs. Breakfast is served in an enormous dining room on the main floor. ✉ *9308 E. Leavenworth Rd., 98826,* ☎ *509/548–7171 or 800/288–6491, ℻ 509/548–7547. 6 rooms. Dining room, refrigerators. AE, D, MC, V.*

$$ ⊞ **Evergreen Motel.** Popular with hikers and skiers, the Evergreen was built in the 1930s. The property still has much of the charm of the roadside inn it once was. Some of its two-bedroom suites have fireplaces or kitchens (though no utensils); others have multiple beds and can sleep up to six comfortably. The room rates include a Continental breakfast served by the very friendly staff. ⊠ *1117 Front St., 98826,* ☎ *509/548–5515 or 800/327–7212,* ℻ *509/548–6556. 39 rooms. AE, D, DC, MC, V.*

$$ ⊞ **Haus Rohrbach.** This alpine-style B&B sits on the side of a hill with an unobstructed view of the village and the entire surrounding valley. The center of activity is a large lodgelike room with a wood stove, a kitchen area, and tables for dining, playing games, socializing, or taking in the scenery. Guest rooms have double or queen-size beds (some have a sofa bed or daybed as well), down comforters, and pine furniture. The suites have king-size beds, whirlpool tubs, gas fireplaces, easy chairs, and small but fully equipped kitchens. The full breakfast served here typically includes Dutch babies or sourdough pancakes and sausage. ⊠ *12882 Ranger Rd., 98826,* ☎ *509/548–7024 or 800/548–4477,* ℻ *509/548–5038. 7 rooms, 5 with bath; 3 suites. Pool, hot tub. AE, D, DC, MC, V.*

$$ ⊞ **Linderhoff Motor Inn.** This non-Bavarian-style motel at the west end of Leavenworth is one of the nicest in town for the money. Rooms have contemporary decor, locally crafted pine furnishings, and TVs and phones. Options include standard rooms, honeymoon suites with whirlpool tubs and fireplaces, and town-house units that sleep up to eight and have fully equipped kitchens and two bathrooms. You can have your complimentary Continental breakfast—fresh fruit juice, muffins, and Danish pastries—in your room or outside on the inn's balcony. ⊠ *690 Hwy. 2, 98826,* ☎ *509/548–5283 or 800/828–5680,* ℻ *509/548–6705. 34 rooms. Pool, hot tub. AE, D, DC, MC, V.*

$ ⊞ **Edelweiss Hotel.** The hotel above the restaurant of the same name has small, plainly furnished rooms. It's not the place to go for a romantic weekend, but if you're on a budget and simply need a place to lay your head, the price ($19.45 for a single room; no windows or TV) is hard to beat. The service is genial if occasionally harried. ⊠ *843 Front St., 98826,* ☎ *509/548–7015,* ℻ *509/548–2104. 14 rooms, 5 with bath. MC, V.*

Outdoor Activities and Sports

FISHING

Trout and salmon are plentiful in many streams and lakes around Lake Wenatchee. **Leavenworth Ranger Station** (☎ 509/782–1413) issues permits for the Enchantment Lakes and Alpine Lake Wilderness area.

GOLF

Leavenworth Golf Club (⊠ 9101 Icicle Rd., ☎ 509/548–7267) has an 18-hole, par-71 course. The greens fee is $20, plus $20 for an optional cart.

HIKING

The Leavenworth Ranger District contains more than 320 mi of scenic trails, among them Hatchery Creek, Icicle Ridge, the Enchantments, Tumwater Canyon, Fourth of July Creek, Snow Lake, Stuart Lake, and Chatter Creek. Contact the **Leavenworth Ranger District** (⊠ 600 Sherburne St., 98826, ☎ 509/782–1413) or the **Lake Wenatchee Ranger Station** (⊠ 22976 Hwy. 207, ☎ 509/763–3101) for more information.

HORSEBACK RIDING

Hourly and daily horseback rides and pack trips are available at **Eagle Creek Ranch** (⊠ 7951 Eagle Creek Rd., ☎ 509/548–7798).

SKIING

More than 20 mi of cross-country ski trails lace the Leavenworth area. **Mission Ridge** (☏ 800/374–1693) has 35 major downhill runs and night skiing from late December to early March. **Stevens Pass** (☏ 360/973–2441 or 360/634–1645) has 36 major downhill runs and slopes and lifts for skiers of every level. Several shops in Leavenworth rent and sell ski equipment. For more information, contact the **Leavenworth Winter Sports Club** (☏ 509/548–5115).

WHITE-WATER RAFTING

Rafting is a popular sport from March to July; the prime high-country runoff occurs in May and June. The Wenatchee River, which runs through Leavenworth, is generally considered the best white-water river in the state—a Class 3 on the International Canoeing Association scale. Depending on the season and location, anything from a relatively calm scenic float to an invigorating white-water shoot is possible on the Wenatchee or on one of several other nearby rivers.

Rafting outfitters and guides in the area include **All Rivers Adventures/Wenatchee Whitewater** (☏ 509/782–2254 or 800/743–5628), **Alpine Adventures** (☏ 800/926–7238 or 509/548–4159), **Leavenworth Outfitters** (☏ 509/763–3733 or 800/347–7934), and **Northern Wilderness River Riders** (☏ 509/548–4583).

Ellensburg

33 *50 mi south of Leavenworth on U.S. 97, 110 mi east of Seattle on I–90.*

The discovery of coal and iron ore near Ellensburg in the late 19th century gave the city hope of becoming the Pittsburgh of the West, an aspiration that went up in smoke when a Fourth of July fire engulfed the city in 1889. Shortly after the blaze, the mid-19th-century architecture was replaced by Victorian brick buildings, many of which remain to this day. Stroll through Ellensburg's historic downtown district and you'll pass art galleries, used-book stores, an old-time hardware store, and one antiques shop after another.

Ellensburg is home to the 7,000-student Central Washington University. Every weekend the university hosts hour-long **Chimposiums,** at which you can see chimpanzees using sign language. ✉ *D St. and Nicholson Blvd.,* ☏ *509/963–2244.* 🎫 *$10.* ⏲ *Sat. 9:15 AM and 10:45 AM, Sun. 12:15 PM and 2 PM.*

The promoters of the **Ellensburg Rodeo** (☏ 800/637–2444) tout the four-day event during Labor Day weekend as "the greatest show on dirt."

OFF THE BEATEN PATH

DICK AND JANE'S SPOT – Hidden in suburbia near downtown Ellensburg is the area's most captivating attraction. The home of artists Dick Elliott and Jane Orleman is a continuously growing whimsical sculpture. Drive by and you'll see a collage of 20,000 bottle caps, 1,500 bicycle reflectors, bicycle pinwheels, and bizarre statues, all thrown together haphazardly on the outside of the house. Their masterpiece stands on private property, so don't cross the fence, but try to view the recycled creation from all angles. ✉ *101 N. Pearl St.,* ☏ *509/925–3224.*

Dining

$–$$ ✕ **Valley Cafe.** Lunch at this art deco eatery in a late-1930s structure includes a chicken Dijon sandwich, Mediterranean tortellini salad, and the café plate—a cup of soup with an open-face sandwich. Lamb, salmon, chicken tortellini, and pasta primavera are among the dinner highlights. ⊠ *105 W. 3rd Ave.,* ☎ *509/925–3050. AE, D, DC, MC, V.*

Crossing the Cascades Essentials
Arriving and Departing
BY BUS

Metro Bus 210 originates in downtown Seattle (☞ Seattle A to Z *in* Chapter 4) and travels to Snoqualmie and North Bend. **Greyhound Lines** (☎ 800/231–2222) or its affiliate, Northwest Trailways, travels from Seattle to Snoqualmie, Leavenworth, Cle Elum, and Ellensburg.

BY CAR

Interstate 90 east of Seattle is not an easy road to drive. To reach the towns east of the Cascades, you must go over Snoqualmie Pass—a 3,000-ft-high, treacherous stretch of road. Chains are often required in winter; call 888/866–4636 for pass conditions. Getting to Leavenworth via U.S. 2 over Stevens Pass can also be difficult in winter. The drive to Leavenworth from Seattle (I–5 north to U.S. 2 east) usually takes a little more than two hours in good weather.

BY TRAIN

Amtrak (☎ 800/872–7245) travels from Seattle to Wenatchee, which is 20 minutes from Leavenworth; a free county bus travels between Wenatchee and Leavenworth.

Getting Around
BY CAR

Interstate 90 skirts the southern portion of the Central Cascades. **U.S. 2** runs parallel to I–90, 25 to 65 mi to the north. **Highway 203** north from I–90 at North Bend passes through Snoqualmie and Duvall before it connects with U.S. 2 at Monroe. **U.S. 97** heads north from I–90 at Ellensburg and connects with U.S. 2 east of Leavenworth.

Visitor Information
Ellensburg Chamber of Commerce and Forest Service Office (⊠ 436 N. Sprague St., 98926, ☎ 509/925–3137). **Leavenworth Chamber of Commerce** (⊠ 894 U.S. 2, Box 327, 98826, ☎ 509/548–5807). **Upper Snoqualmie Valley Chamber of Commerce** (⊠ Box 356, North Bend 98045, ☎ 425/888–4440).

YAKIMA VALLEY WINE COUNTRY

America's second-largest producer of wines, Washington has been blessed with just the right soil, growing season, and climate for premium grape and wine production. Its vineyards share the same latitude (46°) and growth cycle of the great French wine-producing regions of Bordeaux and Burgundy. The Columbia and Yakima valleys have a low average rainfall, and irrigation allows for moisture control during critical growth phases. Warm, sunny days build heavy sugars, and cool nights help to retain high acid levels in the grapes. The results are balanced wines of superior flavor and quality.

The grapes grown in eastern Washington include cabernet sauvignon, Johannisberg Riesling, chardonnay, sauvignon blanc, chenin blanc, grenache, merlot, semillon, muscat, and gewürztraminer. The Yakima Valley, the viticultural center of the state, is home to the largest group of wineries. Wine operations vary from small wineries on the back of residential property to large commercial operations. Barrels are tapped and wine tasting begins about the last week of April. The **Yakima Valley Wine Grower Association** (⊠ Box 39, Grandview 98930) publishes a map-brochure that lists local wineries with tasting-room tours. Most

Yakima Valley

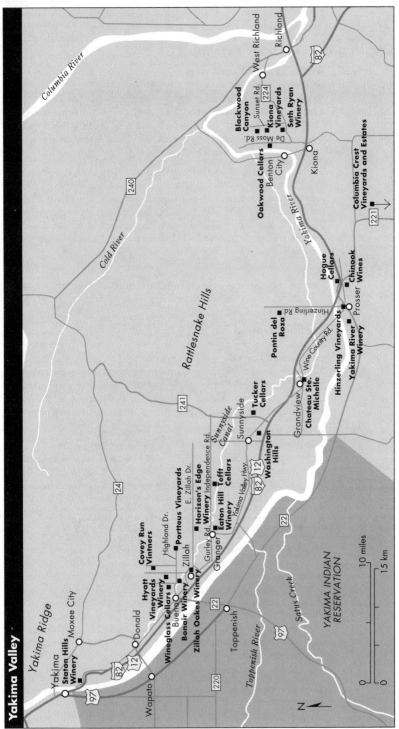

Columbia River

Richland

West Richland

82

Blackwood
Canyon

Sunset Rd.

224

**Kiona
Vineyards**

**Seth Ryan
Winery**

De Moss Rd.

240

Oakwood Cellars

Benton
City

Kiona

221

**Columbia Crest
Vineyards and Estates**

Cold River

Yakima River

**Hogue
Cellars**

**Chinook
Wines**

Rattlesnake Hills

Hinzerling Rd.

**Pontin del
Roza**

Prosser

Wine County Rd.

Hinzerling Vineyards

Chateau Ste.
Michelle

**Yakima River
Winery**

241

Sunnyside
Canal

**Tucker
Cellars**

Grandview

Sunnyside

Washington
Hills

Porteus Vineyards

E. Zillah Dr.

Horizon's Edge

Independence Rd.

**Tefft
Cellars**

Highland Dr.

Yakima Valley Hwy.

12

82

22

**Covey Run
Vintners**

Gurley Rd.

**Eaton Hill
Winery**

Granger

24

**Hyatt
Vineyards
Winery**

Buena

Zillah

Wineglass Cellars

Bonair Winery

Zillah Oakes Winery

22

Moxee City

Donald

Wapato

Toppenish

97

Toppenish River

Satus Creek

**YAKIMA INDIAN
RESERVATION**

Yakima Ridge

Yakima

**Staton Hills
Winery**

82

12

97

220

N

10 miles

15 km

wineries are easily accessed from I–82 or U.S. 97. Some wineries close their tasting rooms without notice in winter. If you're visiting in January or February, it's wise to call ahead to be sure an establishment is open.

With more than 300 days of sunshine each year, Yakima is one of the most diverse agricultural valleys in the country. Harvests begin in April with asparagus and cherries. The soft fruits—apricots, peaches, and the like—begin to ripen by late spring or early summer. The hops are ready for harvesting by late August. Yakima's famous apples are picked in October. Often likened to northern California's Napa Valley 40 years ago, the Yakima Valley retains a welcoming informality; wineries are managed by unpretentious connoisseurs, and their cellar masters are often on hand to answer questions.

Yakima

38 mi southeast of Ellensburg on U.S. 97/I–82.

The city of Yakima, a crossroads of agricultural production and county bureaucracy, has had a few setbacks over the years. The town's original settlement, founded in the early 1880s, was several miles to the south, where city fathers had greedily bought up land in anticipation of the coming railroad; upon learning this, Northern Pacific nimbly moved its train terminal 5 mi north, leaving the local sharks in the dust.

By the 1980s, Yakima was gaining prominence as an agricultural and convention center, but Mount St. Helens, which had other plans for the city, dumped 800,000 tons of ash on it in 1980, making more than a physical mess of things. The crops are thriving again, but the city is struggling with urban growth: Though Yakima is considered by various polls to be among the most livable cities in the nation, it's cluttered with chain stores and outlet malls. There is a small downtown historic district, but little else suggests Yakima's former glory as an Old West outpost. The town is, however, a useful base for exploring the diverse wine-producing region.

The **Yakima Valley Museum and Historical Association** (⊠ 2105 Tieton Dr., ☎ 509/248–0747) has a comprehensive collection of horse-drawn vehicles, and a model of Yakima native and Supreme Court Justice William O. Douglas's office in Washington, D.C. The **Yakima Electronic Railway Museum** (⊠ 3rd Ave. and W. Pine St., ☎ 509/575–1700) is a good option for railroad buffs.

Dining and Lodging

$ ✕ **Grant's Brewery Pub.** America's oldest brew pub is a Yakima institution. The usual pub grub—burgers, salads, sandwiches—complements the suds daily and there's live jazz on weekends. ⊠ *32 N. Front St.,* ☎ *509/575–2922. MC, V.*

$$–$$$ ✕⌂ **Birchfield Manor.** The only true luxury accommodation in the val-
★ ley sits on a perfectly flat plateau in Moxee City, 2 mi outside Yakima, surrounded by fields and grazing cattle. The Old Manor House contains an award-winning restaurant and four upstairs rooms. A recently constructed cottage house maintains the country ambience while providing every modern convenience; its rooms, each with a whirlpool tub, a steam-sauna shower, a TV with VCR, and a gas fireplace, have been designed for maximum privacy. Owner Will Masset, a European-trained chef, oversees the restaurant (reservations essential), whose menu changes seasonally. All entrées include an appetizer, the exotic homemade bread of the day, and a salad. The downstairs wine cellar is filled with local and imported vintages. ⊠ *2018 Birchfield Rd.,*

98901, ☎ 509/452–1960, ᶠᴬˣ 509/452–2334. 11 rooms. AE, DC, MC, V.

Outdoor Activities and Sports

The popular **Apple Tree Golf Course** (⊠ 8804 Occidental Ave., ☎ 509/966–5877) is an 18-hole, par-72 course. The greens fee ranges from $35 to $50; an optional cart costs $24.

Wapato

7 mi east of Yakima, I–82 to Exit 40.

If you're only going to make one stop in the wine country, **Staton Hills Winery,** which produces sparkling wines and cabernet sauvignon, merlot, pinot noir, and chardonnay wines, would be a good choice. The main building has a huge stone fireplace and a commanding view of the valley. ⊠ 71 Gangl Rd., off Thorpe–Parker Rd., ☎ 509/877–2112. ☉ Mar.–Oct., daily 11–5:30; Nov.–Feb., daily noon–5.

Toppenish

9 mi southeast of Wapato on U.S. 97.

The Toppenish Mural Association began commissioning murals in 1989 to draw commerce to the small town. The resulting 40-plus colorful paintings, in a variety of styles by artists from around the region, commemorate the town's history and western spirit. You can wander through shops that sell crafts and antiques, or stop by the **Hops Museum** (⊠ 22 S. B St., ☎ 509/865–4677) or the **Yakima Nation Cultural Center** (⊠ U.S. 97, ☎ 509/865–2800).

Zillah

10 mi east of Wapato, 17 mi east of Yakima on I–82.

Zillah, a town named after the daughter of a railroad manager, contains seven wineries.

The grapes at **Zillah Oakes Winery,** grown at vineyards on the southern slopes of the Rattlesnake Mountains, are used to produce muscat, chardonnay, Riesling, and other wines. ⊠ Vintage Valley Pkwy. off I–82, ☎ 509/829–6990. ☉ Apr.–Nov., daily 10–5; Dec.–Mar., daily 11–4:40.

Bonair Winery specializes in chardonnay, cabernet, and Riesling wines. It's run by the Puryear family, who after years of amateur wine making in California began commercial production in their native Yakima Valley. ⊠ 500 S. Bonair Rd. (head north from I–82's Exit 52 on Cheyne Rd., turn left on Highland Dr. and left on Bonair), ☎ 509/829–6027. ☉ Apr.–Nov., daily 10–5; Dec.–Mar., weekends and most weekdays 10–4:30.

You'll find an unusual collection of wine glasses at **Wineglass Cellars,** which produces merlot, cabernet sauvignon, pinot noir, and chardonnay wines. ⊠ 206 N. Bonair Rd. (head north from I–82's Exit 52), ☎ 509/829–3011, ☉ Presidents' Day–Nov., Fri.–Sun. 10:30–5.

Hyatt Vineyards Winery specializes in barrel-fermented chardonnay, merlot, sauvignon blanc, late-harvest Riesling, and premium dessert wines. ⊠ 2020 Gilbert Rd., off Bonair Rd., ☎ 509/829–6333. ☉ Apr.–Nov., daily 11–5; Dec. and Feb.–Mar., daily 11–4:30.

Covey Run Vintners, one of the valley's largest wineries, has expansive decks and grounds with commanding views of the surrounding vineyards and orchards. Through large windows off the tasting room you can watch the wine—cabernet sauvignon, chardonnay, Riesling, merlot, and chenin blanc—being made. ⊠ *1500 Vintage Rd. (head north from I–82's Exit 52, turn east on Highland Dr., and north on Vintage),* ☎ *509/829–6235.* ⏱ *Apr.–Oct., daily 10–5; Nov.–Mar., daily 11–4:30.*

Portteus Vineyards, a favorite among Washington residents, limits its production mainly to cabernet sauvignon and chardonnay wines from grapes grown at a 1,440-ft elevation on 47 acres above Zillah. ⊠ *5201 Highland Dr. (head north from I–82's Exit 52),* ☎ *509/829–6970.* ⏱ *Mid-Feb.–Nov., daily noon–5; Dec.–mid-Feb. by appointment.*

Horizon's Edge Winery takes its name from its tasting room's view of the Yakima Valley, Mount Adams, and Mount Rainier. The label produces sparkling wines, barrel-fermented chardonnays, and pinot noir, cabernet sauvignon, and muscat canelli wines. ⊠ *4530 E. Zillah Dr., east of Yakima Valley Hwy.,* ☎ *509/829–6401.* ⏱ *May–Nov., weekdays 11–5, weekends 10–5; Dec.–Feb. by appointment.; Mar.–Apr., weekends 11–5.*

Dining

$$ ✕ **Squeeze Inn Restaurant.** A family-operated establishment (since 1932), the Squeeze Inn looks as time-worn as the surrounding structures on Zillah's main street. Prime rib and choice-cut steaks are the big draws, but you'll also find seafood on the menu. Come here for hearty breakfasts, too. ⊠ *611 E. 1st Ave.,* ☎ *509/829–6226. MC, V. Closed Sun.*

$ ✕ **El Ranchito.** The food—for breakfast, lunch, or dinner—is tasty and inexpensive at this large, authentic, cafeteria-style Mexican restaurant and tortilla factory. ⊠ *1319 E. 1st Ave.,* ☎ *509/829–5880. Reservations not accepted. No credit cards.*

Granger

6 mi east of Zillah on I–82.

Eaton Hill Winery, in the restored Rinehold Cannery building, produces Riesling and semillon wines. ⊠ *530 Gurley Rd., off Yakima Valley Hwy.,* ☎ *509/854–2220.* ⏱ *Apr.–Nov., Fri.–Wed. 10–5; Dec.–Mar., usually Fri.–Wed. noon–4.*

Tefft Cellars sells limited editions of its wines. The tasting room is behind the home of owners Joe and Pam Tefft. ⊠ *1320 Independence Rd. (take Gurley Rd. east from Yakima Valley Hwy.; it becomes Independence), Outlook,* ☎ *509/837–7651.* ⏱ *Apr.–Nov., daily noon–5 or by appointment.*

Sunnyside

7 mi east of Granger on I–82.

Washington Hills produces Washington Hills, Apex, and W. B. Bridgman wines—several whites, a red, and a blush. You can picnic in the winery's English gardens. ⊠ *111 E. Lincoln Ave., off Yakima Valley Hwy.,* ☎ *509/839–9463.* ⏱ *Daily 11–5:30.*

Tucker Cellars produces 20,000 gallons of wine—cabernet sauvignon, chardonnay, Riesling, gewürztraminer, and muscat canelli—each year. The Tucker family market, east of Sunnyside on U.S. 12, sells homegrown fruits and vegetables in addition to wine. ⊠ *70 Ray Rd., off Yakima Valley Hwy.,* ☎ *509/837–8701.* ⏱ *Apr.–Oct., daily 9–5; Nov.–Mar., daily 9–4.*

Dining and Lodging

$ ✕ **El Conquistador.** The broad menu at this Mexican restaurant includes everything from burritos and fajitas to shrimp sautéed with green peppers and onions and served with a tangy salsa. ⊠ *612 E. Edison Ave.,* ☎ *509/839–2880. MC, V. No lunch.*

$–$$ ⌂ **Sunnyside Inn Bed & Breakfast.** Each clean and comfortable room in this 1910 house on the main road in Sunnyside comes with cable TV and a private phone line. Seven rooms have whirlpool baths. The rates include a breakfast of breads, pastries, meats, and a griddle entrée. Families are welcome. ⊠ *800 E. Edison Ave., 98944,* ☎ *509/839–5557 or 800/221–4195,* ⨳ *509/839–5350. 8 rooms. AE, MC, V.*

Grandview

7 mi east of Sunnyside on I–82.

The state's oldest winery is **Chateau Ste. Michelle,** where many of the company's merlot and cabernet sauvignon wines (under the Columbia Crest label) are made in a building dating from the 1930s. In view are European-style open-top fermentors and a collection of wood aging tanks. ⊠ *W. 5th St. and Ave. B off Wine Country Rd.,* ☎ *509/882–3928.* ☉ *Daily 10–4:30.*

Prosser

7 mi east of Grandview on I–82.

The **Yakima River Winery,** specializing in barrel-aged red wines and dessert wines, is southwest of town. ⊠ *143302 N. River Rd., off Wine Country Rd.,* ☎ *509/786–2805.* ☉ *Mar.–Nov., daily 10–5; Dec.–Feb., generally noon–4 (call ahead).*

Pontin del Roza is named for its owners, the Pontin family, and the grape-friendly southern slopes of the Yakima Valley, known as the Roza. The winery produces Rieslings (some say their best wines), chenin blancs, chardonnays, sauvignon blancs, and cabernet sauvignons. ⊠ *Rte. 4, off Hinzerling Rd.,* ☎ *509/786–4449.* ☉ *Daily 10–5.*

Hinzerling Vineyards specializes in estate-grown cabernet and late-harvest gewürztraminer and Riesling wines. ⊠ *1520 Sheridan Rd., off Wine Country Rd.,* ☎ *509/786–2163.* ☉ *Mar.–Dec. 24, Mon.–Sat. 11–5, Sun. 11–4.*

East of Prosser is **Chinook Wines,** operated by Kay Siman and Clay Mackey, vintners known for dry chardonnay and sauvignon blanc wines. ⊠ *Wine Country Rd. east of I–82,* ☎ *509/786–2725.* ☉ *Presidents' Day–Dec. 24, Fri.–Sun. noon–5.*

Hogue Cellars, which has won numerous awards, is housed at the Prosser Industrial Park, east of Chinook Wines. There's a tasting room here and a gift shop that carries Hogue Farm's foods and wines—cabernet sauvignon, merlot, and fumé blanc among them—and other locally made products. ⊠ *Wine Country Rd. at I–82's Exit 82,* ☎ *509/786–4557.* ☉ *Daily 10–5.*

Dining

$–$$ ✕ **Wine Country Inn.** This restaurant alongside the Yakima River serves steaks, fish, pastas, and regional dishes like a breast of duck in a blueberry ginger sauce. For Sunday brunch there are homemade pastries, apple sausages, and egg dishes. In warm weather you can dine on an old-fashioned porch that overlooks the river. The inn, a B&B, has four rooms available. ⊠ *1106 Wine Country Rd.,* ☎ *509/786–2855. AE, MC, V. No dinner Mon.–Tues.*

Benton City

16 mi east of Prosser on I–82.

Seth Ryan Winery, operated by the Brodzinski and Olsen families, produces German-style gewürztraminer and Riesling wines, plus cabernet sauvignons, cabernet francs, and merlots. ⊠ *Sunset Rd. (Rte. 2) off Hwy. 224,* ☎ *509/588–6780.* ☉ *Weekends 11–6 (noon–5 in winter).*

Almost all the work is done by hand at **Oakwood Cellars,** a boutique winery in the foothills of the Red Mountains that produces award-winning lembergers, merlots, cabernet sauvignons, and semillons. ⊠ *40504 N. Demoss Rd., off Hwy. 224,* ☎ *509/588–5332.* ☉ *Mar.–Nov., weekends noon–6; Dec.–Feb., call ahead.*

Kiona Vineyards, the producers of the first commercial lemberger wine released in this country, also make Riesling, chenin blanc, cabernet sauvignon, merlot, and barrel-fermented chardonnay wines. ⊠ *Sunset Rd. (Rte. 2) off Hwy. 224,* ☎ *509/588–6716.* ☉ *Daily noon–5.*

The workers at **Blackwood Canyon** employ Old World wine-making techniques. The winery specializes in chardonnays, semillons, merlots, cabernets, and late-harvest wines. ⊠ *Red Mountain Rd. off Sunset Rd. north of Hwy. 224,* ☎ *509/588–6249.* ☉ *Daily 10–6.*

Paterson

26 mi south of Prosser on Hwy. 221.

The imposing 16-acre grounds of **Columbia Crest Vineyards and Estates** lie in the hills above the Columbia River near the Washington-Oregon border. The winery itself is in a building that covers more than 9 acres. Merlots, cabernets, chardonnays, and sauvignon blancs are among the wines produced here. ⊠ *Columbia Crest Dr. (Hwy. 221),* ☎ *509/875–2061.* ☉ *Daily 10–4:30.*

Yakima Valley Wine Country Essentials

Arriving and Departing

BY BUS

Greyhound (⊠ Depot: 801 Okanogan St., ☎ 509/925–1177 or 800/231–2222) has daily bus service from Seattle (2½ hours) and elsewhere).

BY CAR

Interstate 82 and U.S. 12 are the main routes to and through the Yakima Valley.

BY PLANE

Horizon Air and United Express serve the **Yakima Air Terminal** (⊠ W. Washington Ave., ☎ 509/575–6149). See Air Travel *in* the Gold Guide for airline phone numbers.

Getting Around

BY CAR

The **Yakima Valley Highway** winds through the northern part of the valley. Many of the wineries in the southern and eastern portions of the valley are on or off of **Wine Country Road.**

Guided Tours

Accent! Tours & Charters (⊠ 3701 River Rd., Yakima, ☎ 509/575–3949) operates informative tours of Yakima-area wineries. **Moonlit Rides** (⊠ 3908 River Rd., Yakima, ☎ 509/575–6846) also conducts tours of the Yakima area.

Visitor Information

Yakima Valley Visitors & Convention Bureau (⊠ 10 N. 8th St., Yakima 98901, ☎ 509/575–3010 or 800/221-0751).

EASTERN WASHINGTON

Revised by
Stephen Sadis

Spokane (pronounced Spo-*can*) bills itself as the "Capital of the Inland Empire." Wedged against the Idaho border, the city of 400,000 is separated from Seattle by nearly 300 mi and the formidable Cascade Range. Spokane combines the modernity of Seattle with the idealism and friendly charm of a small town.

The Spokane River has been the lifeblood of this area for centuries. The bank of the river on the northern edge of what is now downtown was a favorite campsite and source of salmon for Native Americans. It was here that white settlers built their first sawmill and traded with the Spokane and Coeur d'Alene tribes. Most of the city's major civic and cultural facilities sit along the river's banks.

Follow the Spokane River west about 100 mi and you'll reach the Grand Coulee Dam, the Eighth Wonder of the World. The aptly named Electric City near the dam and Coulee City to the south serve as launching points for recreational activities on and around the 151-mi-long Lake Roosevelt. On the spillover side of the dam, the 30-mi drive along Banks Lake is one of the most beautiful Washington has to offer.

Spokane

282 mi east of Seattle on I–90; 200 mi from Yakima, north on I–82 and east on I–90.

Spokane is the largest city between Seattle and Minneapolis, but the feel is more family-oriented than cosmopolitan. Dry, hot summers make it easy to plan golf, fishing, and hiking excursions, and long, snowy winters provide nearly six months to enjoy skiing, snowboarding, and sledding.

A Good Tour

Numbers in the margin correspond to points of interest on the Spokane map.

Begin your tour of Spokane west of downtown (about 1 mi east of the airport) at the **Finch Arboretum,** which is on Woodland Boulevard off Sunset Boulevard. From the arboretum, head east on Sunset Boulevard, north (left) on Chestnut Street, and west (left) on 1st Avenue to get to the **Cheney Cowles Memorial Museum** ㉞. Riverside Avenue, a block north of 1st Avenue, leads east to **Riverfront Park** ㉟. Two miles south of Riverfront Park on Grand Boulevard is pleasant **Manito Park** ㊱. To get to the **Arbor Crest Cliff House,** take I–90 east 6 mi to Exit 287. Head north on Argonne Road across the Spokane River, east on Upriver Drive, and north on Fruithill Road.

TIMING

You could easily drive this route in an hour. Plan to spend a half day at Riverfront Park, with half- to one-hour stops at the other sights.

Sights to See

Arbor Crest Cliff House. The eclectic mansion of Royal Riblet, the inventor of a square-wheel tractor and the poles that hold up ski lifts, was built in 1924. Sample complimentary Arbor Crest wines, enjoy the striking view of the Spokane River below, or meander through the impeccably kept grounds (the house is not open for touring). ⊠ *4705 N. Fruithill Rd.,* ☎ *509/927–9894.* ⚏ *Free.* ☉ *Daily noon–5.*

㉞ Cheney Cowles Memorial Museum. An audiovisual display and the artifacts at this museum trace Spokane's history; works by area artists are also on exhibit. The museum's Native American collection includes baskets and beadwork of the Plateau Indians. The adjacent **Campbell House** surveys Spokane's mining-era past. Guided tours of the three-story Victorian begin every 45 minutes. ⊠ *2316 W. 1st Ave., between Hemlock and Coeur d'Alene Sts.,* ☎ *509/456–3931.* ⚏ *$4; ½ price Wed. 10–5.* ☉ *Tues. and Thurs.–Sat. 10–5, Wed. 10–9, Sun. 1–5.*

Finch Arboretum. This mile-long patch of green along Garden Springs Creek has an extensive botanical garden with 2,000 labeled trees, shrubs, and flowers. You can stroll beside the creek on the well-manicured paths outlined in the walking tour (the map is available in the brown box at the parking lot), or follow your whim—depending on the season—through flowering rhododendrons, hibiscus, magnolias, dogwoods, hydrangeas, and more. ⊠ *3404 W. Woodland Blvd., off Sunset Blvd. (from downtown, head west on 2nd Ave. and Sunset),* ☎ *509/625–6657.* ⚏ *Free.* ☉ *Daily dawn–dusk.*

㊱ Manito Park and Gardens. The 90-acre tract, a pleasant place to stroll in summer, holds a formal Renaissance-style garden, a conservatory, rose and perennial gardens, a Japanese garden (complete with koi-stocked pools), and a duck pond. ⊠ *S. Grand Blvd. between 17th and 25th Aves.,* ☎ *509/625–6622.* ⚏ *Free.* ☉ *Daily 8–7.*

㉟ Riverfront Park. The 100-acre park built for the Expo '74 world's fair is Spokane's main attraction. Sprawling across several islands in the Spokane River, one of which contains a spectacular waterfall, the park was developed from old downtown railroad yards. One of the modernist buildings from Expo '74 houses an Imax theater, a skating rink, and an exhibition space. The stone clock tower of the former **Great Northern Railroad Station** (⊠ 516 N. Tower Rd.), which was built in 1902, stands in sharp architectural contrast to the Expo '74 building.

A children's train chugs around the park in the summertime. At the south edge of the park, a 1909 **carousel,** hand-carved by master builder Charles I. D. Looff, is a local landmark. Another icon here is the giant red sled shaped like a Radio Flyer wagon. A small farmers' market takes place from Wednesday to Sunday. ⊠ *Riverfront Park, 507 N. Howard St.,* ☎ *509/625–6600.* ⚏ *Park free, summer day pass good for most attractions $9.95.* ☉ *Park 4 AM–midnight, rides Apr.–Oct. (hrs vary by month or day of wk but at least 11–5 daily and until as late as 10 during summer), skating rink Oct.–Mar. (days and hrs vary).*

Dining and Lodging

$$$ ✕ Paprika. Stuffed ahi tuna and stuffed poblano chilies are among the eclectic dishes served at this formal, intimate restaurant in the South Hill neighborhood. ⊠ *1228 S. Grand Blvd.,* ☎ *509/455–7545. AE, D, DC, MC, V.*

$$$ ✕ Patsy Clark's. The chefs at the restaurant inside one of Spokane's finest mansions prepare everything from Moroccan lamb kabobs to Jamaican jerk pork to a three-mushroom moussaka. The lunchtime menu

Spokane

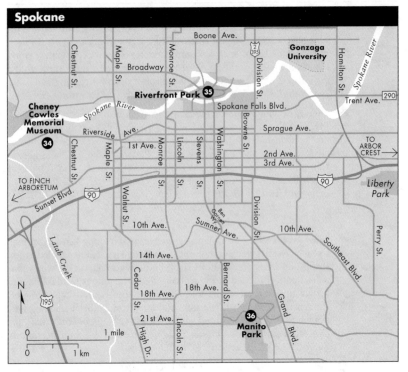

includes an ahi tuna stir-fry, a seven-vegetable black-bean burger, and more-traditional salads and sandwiches. A Tiffany stained-glass window is one of many opulent appointments. ⊠ *2208 W. 2nd Ave.,* ☎ *509/838–8300. AE, D, DC, MC, V. No lunch Sat.*

$$ ✕ **Clinkerdagger's.** A former flour mill with great views of the Spokane River houses Clink's (as this fine restaurant is known locally), which specializes in seasonal fresh seafood and rock-salt-roasted prime rib. For an American culinary tour, try the grilled Alaskan scallop appetizer, the aged New York steak, and the house-made key lime pie. Salads, pastas, and sandwiches are served for lunch. ⊠ *621 W. Mallon Ave.,* ☎ *509/328–5965. AE, D, DC, MC, V. No lunch Sun.*

$$ ✕ **Fugazzi Bakery and Cafe.** The aroma of potato-rosemary, Kalamata-olive, and other freshly baked breads fills Fugazzi's wrought-iron and glass-brick interior. Braised duck quesadillas and salmon egg rolls are among the appetizers; for an entrée try Thai ginger-chicken sausage over fettuccine, grilled sirloin, or roasted spring leg of lamb. Sandwiches, pastas, and some vegetarian dishes are on the lunch menu. ⊠ *1 N. Post St.,* ☎ *509/624–1133. AE, MC, V. Closed Sun.–Mon.*

$$ ✕ **Luna.** You'll find pasta, seafood, and gourmet pizza baked in wood-fired ovens at this neighborhood Italian restaurant with more than 400 vintages on its wine list. ⊠ *5620 S. Perry St.,* ☎ *509/448–2383. AE, DC, MC, V.*

$ ✕ **Elk Café.** East of downtown in the laid-back Brown's Addition is the self-proclaimed home of the oldest soda fountain in Spokane. Breakfast is served daily—don't miss the potatoes. Sandwiches and pesto pizzas are the favorites for lunch and dinner. Singers often serenade patio guests. ⊠ *1931 W. Pacific Ave.,* ☎ *509/456–0454. D, MC, V.*

$ ✕ **Rock City Grill.** Upbeat and close to Riverfront Park, the Grill prepares excellent pastas and gourmet pizzas baked in wood-fired ovens. ⊠ *505 W. Riverside Ave.,* ☎ *509/455–4400. AE, D, DC, MC, V.*

$$–$$$ 🏨 **Cavanaugh's Inn at the Park.** This hotel's greatest asset is its location, adjacent to Riverfront Park and a two-block walk from the downtown shopping district. Popular with business travelers, the inn contains multiroom corporate suites with work areas and large tables. All five stories in the main building open onto an atrium lobby; more guest rooms are in two newer wings. ⊠ *303 W. North River Dr., 99201,* ☎ *509/326–8000 or 800/843–4667,* 𝔽𝔸𝕏 *509/325–7329. 402 rooms. Restaurant, bar. AE, D, DC, MC, V.*

$$–$$$ 🏨 **Doubletree Hotel Spokane City Center.** Convenient to downtown cultural facilities, this hotel on the Spokane River has rooms with cherry and mahogany armoires and desks, coffeemakers, irons, and two phones. The hotel's messaging system allows guests to leave personalized greetings for callers. ⊠ *322 N. Spokane Falls Ct., 99201,* ☎ *509/ 455–9600 or 800/848–9600,* 𝔽𝔸𝕏 *509/455–6285. 379 rooms. 2 restaurants, bar, indoor pool, sauna, exercise room. AE, D, DC, MC, V.*

$$–$$$ 🏨 **Ridpath Hotel.** Business and leisure travelers like the downtown Ridpath. The newly remodeled rooms at this WestCoast property contain reproduction antique furnishings and dark green and cherry-wood interiors; some suites have private whirlpool tubs. All guests have access to a nearby full-service health club. Ankeny's Restaurant atop the hotel has a panoramic view of the city. ⊠ *515 W. Sprague Ave., 99201,* ☎ *509/838–2711 or 800/426–0670,* 𝔽𝔸𝕏 *509/747–6970. 350 rooms. 2 restaurants, 2 bars, pool, exercise room. AE, D, DC, MC, V.*

$$ 🏨 **Mariana Stolz House.** Jim and Phyllis Maguire's B&B across from Gonzaga University has something of a split personality: Leaded glass china cabinets, Renaissance Revival armchairs, and the original dark-fir woodwork compete with run-of-the-mill lamps and fake-flower arrangements you might expect at a chain motel. But there's nothing awkward about their hospitality: In the evening, enjoy the Maguires' homemade liqueurs before retiring under antique quilts. ⊠ *427 E. Indiana Ave.,* ☎ *509/483–4316 or 800/978–6587,* 𝔽𝔸𝕏 *509/483–6773. 4 rooms, 2 with bath. AE, D, DC, MC, V.*

$$ 🏨 **Sun Tree 8 Inn.** The newer Sun Tree at Division Street is more expensive than the smaller, older location a few blocks away on Post Street: Doubles start at $50 at Post Street, $59 at Division Street. At both you get clean rooms, cable TV, and a complimentary Continental breakfast. ⊠ *123 S. Post St.,* ☎ *509/838–8504. 45 rooms.* ⊠ *211 S. Division St.,* ☎ *509/838–6630 or 800/888–6630. 80 rooms. AE, D, DC, MC, V.*

$$ 🏨 **Waverly Place.** Mother-and-daughter team Marge and Tammy Arndt have created a bed-and-breakfast inn whose distinctive late-Victorian furnishings seem truly at home amid the graceful architecture of their turreted Queen Anne home. The rooms are airy and comfortable, with queen-size reproduction beds and braided and dhurrie rugs over shiny hardwood floors. Menus for breakfast (included in the room rates) and dinner reflect the innkeepers' Swedish heritage. ⊠ *709 W. Waverly Pl., 99205,* ☎ *509/328–1856. 4 rooms, 1 with bath. Pool. AE, D, MC, V.*

Nightlife and the Arts

NIGHTLIFE

The downtown area, especially along Division Street near Riverside Avenue, abounds with small local taverns. **Fort Spokane Brewery** (⊠ 401 W. Spokane Falls Blvd., ☎ 509/838–3809) is an upscale bar across from Riverfront Park. The atmosphere is friendly and the microbrews are excellent—the Border Run, a sweet, smooth ale, is not to be missed. Musicians perform on Friday and Saturday night. You can tour the brewery on weekdays from 11 to 5.

Dempsey's Brass Rail (✉ 909 W. 1st St., ☎ 509/747–5362) is actually two establishments in one: Downstairs it's Spokane's most popular gay bar and restaurant; upstairs it's a dance club popular with the local college crowd, gay and straight. On Friday and Saturday, there's a cover charge.

THE ARTS

Interplayers Ensemble (✉ 174 S. Howard St., ☎ 509/455–7529) is a professional theater company whose season runs from October through June. The 200-seat **Spokane Civic Theatre** (✉ 1020 N. Howard St., ☎ 509/325–2507) presents musicals and dramas. The **Spokane Symphony** plays a season of classical and pops concerts from September to May in the Opera House (✉ 601 W. Riverside Ave., ☎ 509/624–1200). The **Theatre Ballet of Spokane** and various entertainers perform in the Metropolitan Performing Arts Center (✉ 901 W. Sprague St., ☎ 509/455–6500), a restored neoclassical structure built in 1915.

Outdoor Activities and Sports

BASEBALL

The **Spokane Indians** baseball team, the Northwest League's Class A affiliate of the Kansas City Royals, plays at Seafirst Stadium (✉ 602 N. Havana St., ☎ 509/535–2922).

BICYCLING

Rent a bike at **Quinn's** (✉ Riverfront Park, on the Howard Street Bridge, ☎ 509/456–6545) for as little as $4 per hour and get out on the miles of trails along the Spokane River. The shop is open daily from June to September and on weekends the rest of the year.

CLIMBING

You can get a taste of rock climbing on the indoor wall at **Mountain Gear** (✉ 2002 N. Division St., ☎ 509/325–9000 or 800/829–2009). A three-hour class costs $20. Climbing shoes cost $6 a day.

GOLF

Hangman Valley Golf Course (✉ 2210 E. Hangman Valley Rd., ☎ 509/448–1212), an 18-hole, par-72 course, has a greens fee of $14.50; a cart (optional) costs $22.

HIKING

The hills around Spokane are laced with trails, almost all of which connect with the 41-mi **Centennial Trail,** which winds along the Spokane River. The well-marked trail begins in Nine Mile Falls, northwest of Spokane, and ends in Idaho; maps are available at the visitor center at 201 West Main Avenue. Northwest of downtown at **Riverside State Park** (✉ Hwy. 291; from downtown head north on Division St. and west on Mission Rd., ☎ 509/456–3964), a paved trail leads through a 17-million-year-old fossil forest in Deep Creek Canyon. From here it's easy to get to the western end of the Centennial Trail by crossing the suspension bridge at the day-use parking lot; trails heading both left and right will lead to the Centennial.

HOCKEY

The **Spokane Chiefs** of the Western Hockey League play at Veterans Memorial Arena (✉ 720 W. Mallon Ave., ☎ 509/328–0450).

SKIING

49° North (✉ U.S. 395, ☎ 509/935–6649), an hour north of Spokane in the Kaniksu National Forest, is an 800-acre family-oriented resort. Lift tickets and snowboards cost about $25, ski rentals $16. **Mount Spokane** (✉ Hwy. 206, ☎ 509/238–6281), 31 mi northeast of Spokane, is a modest downhill resort with 10 mi of groomed cross-country ski trails. A state Sno-Park permit, available at the resort, is required here.

Coulee Dam National Recreation Area

87 mi from Spokane, west on U.S. 2 and northwest on Hwy. 174.

The Grand Coulee Dam, the largest concrete structure in the world—it's almost a mile long—is an engineering marvel that has justly earned its status as the Eighth Wonder of the World. Beginning in 1932, 9,000 men excavated 45 million cubic yards of rock and soil and dammed the Grand Coulee, a gorge created by the Columbia River, with 12 million cubic yards of concrete—enough to build a sidewalk the length of the equator. By the time the dam was completed in 1941, 77 men had perished, and 11 towns were submerged under the newly formed Roosevelt Lake. The dam turned eastern Washington's arid soil into fertile farming land, but not without consequence: Fishing areas that were a source of food and spiritual identity for Native Americans were destroyed. Half the dam was built on the Colville Indian Reservation; the Colville tribes later received restitution in excess of $75 million from the U.S. Government.

In 1946 most of Roosevelt Lake and the arid hills surrounding it were designated the Coulee Dam National Recreation Area. **Crown Point Vista,** about 5 mi west of Grand Coulee on Highway 174, may have the best vantage for photographs of the dam, Roosevelt Lake, Rufus Woods Lake (below the dam), and the town of Coulee Dam.

After nightfall from Memorial Day through September, the dam is transformed into an unlikely entertainment complex by an extravagant **laser light show.** With 300-ft eagles flying across the white water that flows over the dam, the show is spectacular, if sometimes hokey. The audio portion is broadcast on KEYG 1490 AM and 98.5 FM. Show up early to get a good seat.

The **Visitor's Arrival Center** has colorful displays about the dam, a 13-minute film on the site's geology and the dam's construction, and information about the laser light show. The U.S. Bureau of Reclamation, which oversees operation and maintenance of the dam, conducts tours year-round, weather and maintenance schedules permitting. ✉ *U.S. 155 north of Grand Coulee,* ☎ *509/633–9265,* ☉ *Late May–July, daily 8:30 AM–11 PM; Aug., daily 8:30 AM–10:30 PM; Sept., daily 8:30 AM–9:30 PM; Oct.–late May, weekdays 9–5.*

Highway 155 passes through the **Colville Indian Reservation,** one of the largest reservations in Washington, with about 7,700 enrolled members in the Colville Confederated Tribes. This was the final home for Chief Joseph and the Nez Percé, who fought a series of fierce battles with the U.S. Army in the 1870s after the U.S. Government enforced a treaty that many present-day historians agree was fraudulent. The Nez Percé intended to leave their lands peacefully, but a U.S. general, told they were planning to fight, attacked. Led by Chief Joseph, the tribe won many skirmishes and was making a run for the Canadian border, only to be stopped by soldiers 30 mi shy of it. "I will fight no more forever," Chief Joseph declared in defeat; after a stay in prison, he lived on the Colville reservation until his death in 1904. There's a memorial to him off Highway 155 east of the town of Nespelem, 17 mi north of the dam; four blocks away (two east and two north) is his grave. You can drive through the reservation's undeveloped landscape, and except for a few highway signs you'll feel like you've time traveled to pioneer days. For a better understanding of frontier history, visit the **Colville Confederated Tribes Museum and Gift Shop** (✉ 512 Mead Way, ☎ 509/633–0751), ½ mi north of Grand Coulee Dam via Highway 155.

Sun Lakes State Park, about 30 mi south of the Grand Coulee Dam on Highway 17, is a surreal reminder of the colossal power of nature. During the last ice age, a lake in Montana—or rather, a lake *covering* most of Montana—burst through the ice dam holding it; the flood raged toward the sea with 10 times the combined flow of all the world's rivers, altering the landscape so drastically that its ripple marks are visible from outer space. Presentations at the park's Interpretive Center survey the area's geology, and an excellent film describes the great floods. ⊠ *From Grand Coulee Dam take Hwy. 155 south, U.S. 2 east, and Hwy. 17 south,* ☎ *509/632–5214.* 🎫 *Free.* ☉ *May–Sept., daily 10–6.*

Dining and Lodging

$ ✕ **Flo's Place.** One mile south of the dam, this diner dishes up heaps of local color along with loggers' food: biscuits and gravy, corned-beef hash, hamburgers, chicken-fried steak, and chef's salads. Flo's closes at 2 PM daily. ⊠ *316 Spokane Way, Grand Coulee,* ☎ *509/633–3216. No credit cards. No dinner.*

$ ✕ **Melody Restaurant.** This casual family-friendly spot with excellent views of Grand Coulee Dam prepares sandwiches, steaks, seafood, and pasta and is open for breakfast. ⊠ *512 River Dr., Coulee Dam,* ☎ *509/ 633–1151. AE, D, MC, V.*

$ ✕ **Siam Palace.** Locals love this informal restaurant that serves delicious and moderately priced Chinese, Thai, and American food. ⊠ *213 Main St., Grand Coulee,* ☎ *509/633–2921. D, MC, V.*

$–$$ 🏠 **Coulee House Motel.** This motel with "the best dam view in town" (someone had to say it) has modern rooms decorated in earth tones. Some rooms have kitchenettes. ⊠ *110 Roosevelt Way, Coulee Dam, 99116,* ☎ *509/633–1101 or 800/715–7767,* 📠 *509/633–1416. Pool, 2 hot tubs, coin laundry. AE, D, DC, MC, V.*

$–$$ 🏠 **Ponderosa Motel.** Sunny rooms with oak armoires, floral-print comforters, and views of the dam and the summertime laser light show are among the Ponderosa's assets. Some rooms have microwaves and refrigerators. ⊠ *10 Lincoln St., Coulee Dam 99116,* ☎ *509/633– 2100 or 800/633–6421,* 📠 *509/633–2633. 34 rooms. Pool, hot tub. AE, D, MC, V.*

$ 🏠 **The Gold House Inn.** Some of the rooms at this contemporary B&B have breathtaking views of Grand Coulee Dam. ⊠ *411 Partello Park, Grand Coulee 99133,* ☎ *509/633–3276 or 800/835–9369,* 📠 *509/ 633–1298. 7 rooms. AE, D, MC, V.*

Camping

🏕 **Spring Canyon.** The National Park Service runs the closest public campground to the dam. It's a good place to set your tent if you plan to catch the laser show. For $10 you get a site with a view of the lake but no privacy. On the grounds are rest rooms, swimming areas, and a playground. ⊠ *Hwy. 174, 13 mi west of Grand Coulee,* ☎ *509/725– 2715. 87 sites. No credit cards.*

Outdoor Activities and Sports

There is year-round fishing in Banks Lake, Roosevelt Lake, and Rufus Woods Lake. Roosevelt Lake, a haven for bald eagles, is a popular spot to rent or launch motorboats and houseboats or engage in swimming, waterskiing, and other water sports.

The Palouse

158 mi from Spokane to Walla Walla south on U.S. 195, west on Hwy. 26, and south on Hwy. 127 and U.S. 12; 62 mi from Spokane to Colfax and 76 mi to Pullman, south on U.S. 195.

Those interested in Northwest history will find the Palouse, south of Spokane near the Idaho border, particularly rich. The Lewis and Clark expedition passed through in 1805, and the U.S. Cavalry lost an important battle to the Indians on the site of the **Steptoe Battlefield.** The battlefield is north of **Pullman** on U.S. 195 near Rosalia.

On U.S. 12 between Colfax and Walla Walla, **Dayton** is worth a stop just to see the 88 Victorian buildings listed on the National Register of Historic Places. A brochure with two self-guided walking tours of Dayton is available from the **Dayton Chamber of Commerce** (⊠ 166 E. Main St., ☎ 509/382–4825).

In 1836 missionary Marcus Whitman built a medical mission 7 mi west of present-day **Walla Walla.** A band of Cayuse Indians massacred Whitman and more than a dozen other settlers in 1847; a **visitor center** (⊠ Off U.S. 12, 7 mi west of Walla Walla, ☎ 509/529–2761) marks the site. Nearby **Fort Walla Walla Park** (⊠ 755 Myra Rd., ☎ 509/525–7703) has 14 historic buildings and a pioneer museum.

History buffs can take a walking or bicycle tour of Walla Walla, one of the earliest settlements in the Inland Northwest. Maps are available from the Chamber of Commerce (☞ Visitor Information, *below*). **Pioneer Park** (⊠ E. Alder St.), which has a fine aviary, was landscaped by sons of Frederick Law Olmsted, who designed New York City's Central Park.

Just north of its confluence with the Snake River, the Palouse River gushes over a basalt cliff higher than Niagara Falls and drops 198 ft into a steep-walled basin. Those who are sure-footed can hike to an overlook above the falls, part of **Palouse Falls State Park,** which are at their fastest during spring runoff in March. Just downstream from the falls is the **Marmes Rock Shelter,** where remains of the earliest-known inhabitants of North America, dating back 10,000 years, were discovered by archaeologists. The park's has 10 primitive campsites. ⊠ *Hwy. 261, 65 mi north of Walla Walla (U.S. 12 north to Hwy. 261 west),* ☎ *509/ 646–3252.* ☞ *$5 per vehicle, $7 for campsites.* ☉ *Park daily dawn– dusk, campsites mid-Mar.–Sept.*

Eastern Washington Essentials

Arriving and Departing

BY BUS

Greyhound Lines (⊠ W. 221 1st Ave., in the Amtrak station, ☎ 509/ 624–5251) runs daily buses to Spokane from Seattle (5–6½ hrs) and Portland (8–13 hrs). Greyhound buses stop in Pullman and Walla Walla.

BY CAR

Spokane can be reached by **I–90** from the east or west. **U.S. 195** passes north–south through the city. The Grand Coulee Dam is 20 mi north of **U.S. 2** on **Highway 174.** To get to the Palouse from Spokane, drive south on **U.S. 195** to Pullman. Or, when U.S. 195 reaches Colfax, take **Highways 26 and 127,** and then **U.S. 12** to Walla Walla.

BY PLANE

Spokane Airport (⊠ 9000 W. Airport Dr., ☎ 509/455–6455) is served by Horizon, Northwest, and United. *See* Air Travel *in* the Gold Guide for airline numbers. Pullman has a small airport that it shares with Moscow, Idaho, 8 mi to the east.

Amtrak (⊠ W. 221 1st Ave., ☎ 509/624–5144 or 800/872–7245) serves Spokane from Seattle and Portland four times a week. There is no train service to the Palouse.

Getting Around
Spokane has an extensive local bus system. The fare is 75¢; exact change or a token is required. You can pick up schedules, route maps, and tokens at the **bus depot** (⊠ 1229 W. Boone Ave., ☎ 509/328–7433) or the **Plaza** (⊠ 510 W. Riverside Ave., between Wall and Post Sts.), the major downtown transfer point.

Downtown Spokane is laid out along a true grid: Streets run north–south, avenues east–west, and many of them are one-way. A good way to explore the city is to follow the **City Loop Drive,** which takes you out of the city and into the residential hills of greater Spokane; start at Stevens and Riverside streets and follow the arrowhead signs. **Yellow Cab** (☎ 509/624–4321) serves the greater Spokane area. The north–south-running **Highway 155** is the main road through the Grand Coulee Dam area.

Contacts and Resources
Grand Coulee Chamber of Commerce (⊠ Box 760, 99133, ☎ 509/633–3074). **Pullman Chamber of Commerce** (⊠ 415 N. Grande Ave., 99163, ☎ 509/334–3565). **Spokane Area Visitors Information** (⊠ 201 W. Main Ave., 99202, ☎ 509/747–3230 or 800/248–3230). **Walla Walla Chamber of Commerce** (⊠ 29 E. Sumach St., 99362, ☎ 509/525–0850).

WASHINGTON A TO Z

Arriving and Departing

By Bus
Greyhound Lines (☎ 800/231–2222) connects Washington with adjoining states and Canada.

By Car
Interstate 5 is the main north–south route through the state. **Interstate 90** enters Washington from the east and runs across the Cascades to Seattle.

By Ferry
A number of ferries service destinations in Washington and Canada. In Anacortes, about 90 minutes north of Seattle, the **Washington State Ferries** (☎ 206/464–6400) depart for Vancouver Island, British Columbia. Bellingham is the southern terminus of the **Alaska Marine Highway System** (☎ 800/642–0066), providing transportation between Bellingham and Alaska's Inside Passage. **Victoria San Juan Cruises** (☎ 800/443–4552) operates passenger-only service between Bellingham and Victoria, British Columbia, in the summer.

By Plane
Seattle-Tacoma International Airport (☞ Seattle A to Z *in* Chapter 4) is served by most major airlines. See Air Travel *in* the Gold Guide for airline numbers.

By Train
Amtrak (☎ 800/872–7245) serves major cities and towns throughout the state.

Contacts and Resources

Emergencies

Throughout Washington State, except on Orcas Island and Long Beach Peninsula, dial 911 for **police, ambulance,** or other emergencies. On Orcas dial "0" or 360/468–3663; on Long Beach dial 360/642–2911 for police and 360/642–4200 for fire.

Guided Tours

CRUISES AND WHALE-WATCHING

San Juan Islands Shuttle Express (⊠ Alaska Ferry Terminal, 355 Harris Ave., Bellingham, ☎ 360/671–1137) operates whale-watching trips. **Victoria San Juan Cruises** (⊠ Alaska Ferry Terminal, 355 Harris Ave., Bellingham, ☎ 800/443–4552) operates all-day nature cruises through the San Juan Islands to Victoria. **Western Prince Cruises** (⊠ Friday Harbor, San Juan Island, ☎ 360/378–5315) charters boats for half-day whale-watching cruises during the summer; in the spring and fall, bird-watching and scuba-diving tours are offered.

ORIENTATION

Hesselerave International (⊠ 1268 Mount Baker Hwy., Bellingham, ☎ 360/734–3570) operates a variety of tours and trips in the Northwest. **Sunshine Ventures** (⊠ 909 Alder St., Sumner, ☎ 800/377–4970) operates walking and general tours of Tacoma and the entire Northwest region.

Outdoor Activities and Sports

FISHING LICENSES

You can pick up a fishing license at any sporting-goods store in the state. A three-day license costs about $5 for nonresidents. For more information, call the **Department of Fish and Wildlife** (☎ 360/902–2700).

SKIING

Skiers with motor vehicles are required to purchase Sno-Park permits ($7 for a one-day pass or $20 for a season pass); you can pick them up at ski resorts and sporting-goods stores. For more information, call the state parks department's **Office of Winter Recreation** (☎ 360/902–8552). For information about snow conditions, call 888/766–4636.

Visitor Information

National Park Service (☎ 206/470–4060). **Washington State Parks Department** (☎ 800/233–0321 for campsite and other park information). **Washington State Tourism** (⊠ 101 General Administration Bldg., Olympia 98504, ☎ 800/544–1800).

6 Vancouver

The spectacular setting of cosmopolitan Vancouver has drawn people from around the world to settle here. The ocean and mountains form a dramatic backdrop to downtown's gleaming towers of commerce and make it easy to pursue all kinds of outdoor pleasures. You can trace the city's history in Gastown and Chinatown, savor the wilderness only blocks from the city center in Stanley Park, or dine on superb ethnic or Pacific Northwest cuisine before you sample the city's vibrant nightlife.

VANCOUVER IS A YOUNG CITY, even by North American standards. It was not yet a town when British Columbia became part of the Canadian confederation in 1870. The city's history, such as it is, remains visible to the naked eye: Eras are stacked east to west along the waterfront, from cobblestone late-Victorian Gastown to shiny postmodern glass cathedrals of commerce.

Updated by
Melissa Rivers

The Chinese were among the first to recognize the possibilities of Vancouver's setting. They came to British Columbia during the 1850s seeking the gold that inspired them to name the province Gum-shan, or Gold Mountain. As laborers they built the Canadian Pacific Railway, giving Vancouver a purpose—one beyond the natural splendor that Royal Navy captain George Vancouver admired during his lunchtime cruise around its harbor on June 13, 1792. The transcontinental railway, along with the city's Great White Fleet of clipper ships, gave Vancouver a full week's edge over the California ports in shipping tea and silk to New York at the dawn of the 20th century.

Vancouver's natural charms are less scattered than those in many other cities. On clear days, the mountains appear close enough to touch. Two 1,000-acre wilderness parks lie within the city limits. The salt water of the Pacific and fresh water direct from the Rocky Mountain Trench form the city's northern and southern boundaries.

Bring a healthy sense of reverence when you visit: Vancouver is a spiritual place. For its original inhabitants, the Coast Salish peoples, it was the sacred spot where the mythical Thunderbird and Killer Whale flung wind and rain all about the heavens during their epic battles—how else to explain the coast's fits of meteorological temper? Devotees of a later religious tradition might worship in the sepulchre of Stanley Park or in the rough-hewn interior of Christ Church Cathedral, the city's oldest church.

Vancouver, with a metropolitan area population of 1.7 million people, is booming. A tremendous number of Asians have migrated here, including many from Hong Kong who are drawn to the city because of its supportive business environment and protective banking regulations. The mild climate, exquisite natural scenery, and thriving cultural scene also bring new residents to British Columbia's business center. The number of visitors is increasing because of the city's scenic attractions and its proximity to outdoor activities. Many people get their first glimpse of Vancouver when catching an Alaskan cruise, and many return at some point to spend more time here.

Pleasures and Pastimes

Dining

The gastronomical experience here is satisfyingly diverse; restaurants—from the bustling downtown area to trendy beachside neighborhoods—have enticing locales in addition to succulent cuisine. The wave of Asian immigration and tourism has brought a proliferation of upscale Chinese, Japanese, Korean, Thai, and Vietnamese restaurants. Cutting-edge establishments perfecting and defining Pacific Northwest fare—including homegrown regional favorites such as salmon and oysters, accompanied by British Columbia and Washington State wines—have become some of the city's leading attractions.

The Great Outdoors

Nature has truly blessed this city, surrounding it by verdant forests, towering mountains, coves, inlets, rivers, and the wide sea. Biking, hiking, skiing and snowboarding, rafting, and sailing are among the many outdoor activities available throughout the city. Whether you prefer to relax on a beach by yourself or join a kayaking tour with an outfitter, Vancouver has plenty to offer.

Nightlife and the Arts

Vancouverites support the arts enthusiastically. Touring musicals, serious dramas, and experimental theatrical pieces are presented year-round, as are film, performing-arts, and other cultural festivals. The city's opera, ballet, and symphonic companies are thriving. And there's a complete range of live music, from jazz and blues to heavy metal.

EXPLORING VANCOUVER

Vancouver may be small when compared to New York or even San Francisco, but it still takes time to explore. You can see a lot of the city in two days, but a day or two more will give you time to explore sights in the larger Vancouver area and the surrounding countryside.

Many sights of interest are concentrated in the hemmed-in peninsula of downtown Vancouver. The heart of Vancouver—which includes the downtown area, Stanley Park, and the West End high-rise residential neighborhood—sits on this peninsula bordered by English Bay and the Pacific Ocean to the west; by False Creek, the inlet home to Granville Island, to the south; and by Burrard Inlet, the working port of the city, to the north, past which loom the North Shore mountains. The oldest part of the city—Gastown and Chinatown—lies at the edge of Burrard Inlet, around Main Street, which runs north–south and is roughly the dividing line between the east side and the west side. All the avenues, which are numbered, have east and west designations. One note about printed Vancouver street addresses: Suite numbers often appear *before* the street number, followed by a hyphen.

Great Itineraries

IF YOU HAVE 1–2 DAYS

If you have only one day in Vancouver, start with an early morning drive through Stanley Park to see the Vancouver Aquarium and other sights such as Second Beach on English Bay. Head northeast from the park on Denman Street to Robson Street to lunch and meander on foot through the trendy shops lining the street between Denman and Burrard, and then walk northeast on Burrard Street to view the many buildings of architectural interest. Stop along the way at the Vancouver Art Gallery, the Canadian Craft Museum, and the tiny Sri Lankan Gem Museum.

On day two take a more leisurely paced walking tour of the shops, eateries, and cobblestone streets of Gastown and Chinatown. There are plenty of places to eat and shop in both districts.

IF YOU HAVE 3–4 DAYS

If you have another day to tour Vancouver following your exploration of Stanley Park, Robson Street, Gastown, and Chinatown, head to the south side of False Creek and English Bay on day three to delve into the many boutiques, dining outlets, theaters, and lively public markets of Granville Island. Buses and ferries provide easy transit. Parking is plentiful should you prefer to drive, but touring Granville Island is best accomplished on foot.

On day four, you'll need a car to tour the far-flung sights south of downtown Vancouver. Museum and history buffs will want to tour the Museum of Anthropology on the campus of the University of British Columbia, the Vancouver Museum, the high-tech Pacific Space Centre, and the Vancouver Maritime Museum, all just south of downtown in the Kitsilano area.

IF YOU HAVE 5–7 DAYS

If you have another two days to explore and you've already seen Stanley Park, Robson Street, Gastown, Chinatown, Granville Island, and the museums and gardens of Vancouver and parks on the North Shore, don't miss a side trip to beautiful Whistler (☞ Chapter 5) in the mountains north of the city. Although it's ranked one of the top ski destinations in the world, this growing resort has an ever-expanding array of outdoor activities and festivals that make it worth a visit any time of year.

Robson to the Waterfront

Numbers in the text correspond to numbers in the margin and on the Downtown Vancouver map.

A Good Walk

Begin your tour of Vancouver on **Robson Street** ①, also referred to as Vancouver's Rodeo Drive because of the sheer number of see-and-be-seen sidewalk cafés and high-end boutiques, and as Robson Strasse because of its European flavor. Start at the northwest end near the cross street of Bute or Thurlow and follow Robson southeast to Hornby to reach landscaped **Robson Square** ② and the outstanding **Vancouver Art Gallery** ③. On the north side of the gallery across Hornby Street sits the **Hotel Vancouver** ④, one of the city's best-known landmarks. Cathedral Place, a spectacular office tower, stands across the street on the corner of Hornby and Georgia. Three large sculptures of nurses at the corners of the building are replicas of the statues that ornamented the art deco Georgia Medical-Dental Building, the site's previous structure. To the left of Cathedral Place is the Gothic-style **Christ Church Cathedral** ⑤, the oldest church in Vancouver. Head east up Burrard and you'll see on your right a restored terra-cotta arch—formerly the front entrance to the medical building—and frieze panels showing scenes of individuals administering care; these decorate the **Canadian Craft Museum** ⑥, one of the first national cultural facilities dedicated to crafts. Farther still up Burrard, on the opposite side of the street, is the **Marine Building** ⑦, its terra-cotta bas-reliefs making it one of Canada's best examples of art deco architecture.

Across the street (due east, on the corner of Burrard and Hastings) is the elaborate **Vancouver Club** ⑧, the private haunt of the city's top business movers and shakers. This marks the start of the old financial district, which runs southeast along Hastings, where temple-style banks, investment houses, and businesspeople's clubs survive as evidence of the city's sophisticated architectural advances prior to World War I. Until the period between 1966 and 1972, when the first of the bank towers and underground malls on West Georgia Street were developed, this was Canada's westernmost business terminus. **Sinclair Centre** ⑨, at Hastings and Howe streets, is a magnificently restored complex of government buildings that now houses offices and retail shops. Near Granville Street you'll find the former headquarters of the **Canadian Imperial Bank of Commerce (CIBC)** ⑩. The more Gothic **Royal Bank** ⑪ stands directly across the street.

Head northeast up Seymour toward Burrard Inlet to the **Waterfront Station** ⑫. From here, you can either meander through the station and the courtyards to its left or turn north up Cordova, take a right on Howe, and you'll face the soaring canopies of **Canada Place** ⑬, site of Van-

Greater Vancouver *(Boxes Refer to Detail Maps)*

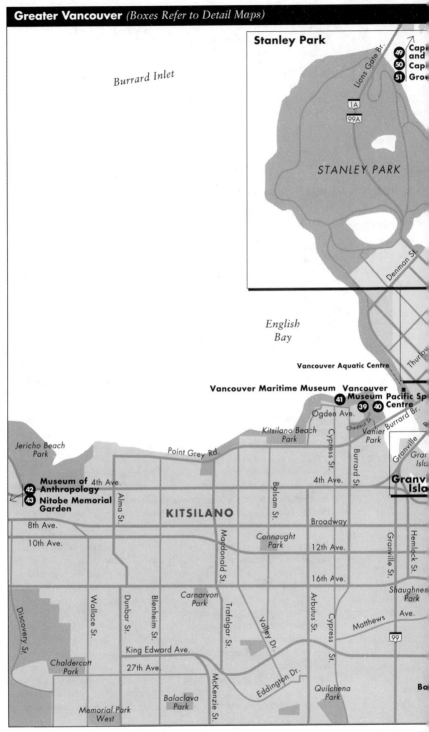

Stanley Park

49 Cap
and
50 Cap
51 Gro

Lions Gate Br.

1A
99A

STANLEY PARK

Denman St.

Burrard Inlet

English Bay

Vancouver Aquatic Centre

Thurlow

Vancouver Maritime Museum   Vancouver
41   Museum Pacific Sp
39 40 Centre

Ogden Ave.   Chestnut St.   Burrard Br.

Kitsilano Beach   Cypress St.   Vanier
Park   Park

Jericho Beach
Park   Point Grey Rd.   Granville

Balsam St.   Grar
Isla

Museum of 4th Ave.   4th Ave.   Granvi
42 Anthropology   Isla
43 Nitobe Memorial   Alma St.
   Garden

KITSILANO   Broadway

8th Ave.   Macdonald St.   Connaught
                                        Park   12th Ave.   Granville St.
10th Ave.   Hemlock St.

                                                    16th Ave.

Carnarvon   Arbutus St.   Shaughnes
Park   Park
Discovery St.   Wallace St.   Dunbar St.   Blenheim St.   Trafalgar St.   Valley Dr.   Cypress
                                                                                    Matthews St. Ave.

King Edward Ave.   99

Chaldercott
Park   27th Ave.
                                                              Eddington Dr.   Quilchena
                                                                              Park   Bo

Memorial Park   Balaclava
West   Park   McKenzie St.

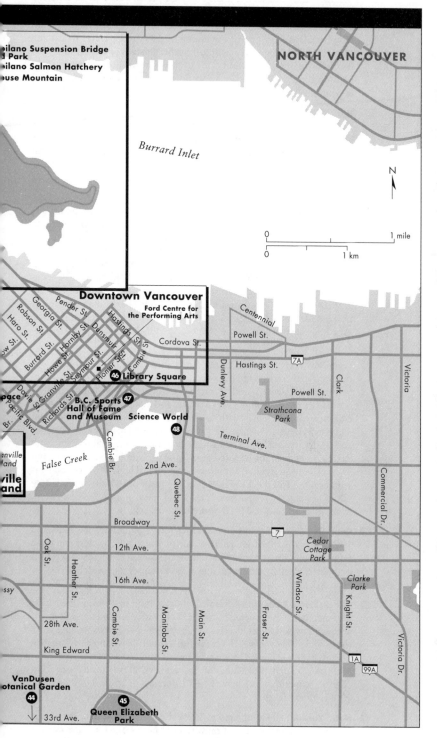

Capilano Suspension Bridge
and Park
Capilano Salmon Hatchery
Grouse Mountain

NORTH VANCOUVER

Burrard Inlet

N

0 .... 1 mile
0 .... 1 km

Downtown Vancouver
Ford Centre for
the Performing Arts

Centennial

Georgia St.
Pender St.
Robson St.
Haro St.
Hastings St.
Dunsmuir St.
Cordova St.
Powell St.

Burrard St.
Hornby St.
Howe St.
Seymour St.
Homer St.
Cambie St.

Hastings St.

7A

Library Square **46**

Powell St.

B.C. Sports **47**
Hall of Fame
and Museum   Science World

Dunlevy Ave.

Clark

Victoria

Strathcona
Park

Pacific Blvd.
Richards St.
Granville St.
Davie St.

48

Terminal Ave.

Granville
Island

False Creek

Cambie Br.

2nd Ave.

Quebec St.

Broadway

7

Cedar
Cottage
Park

Commercial Dr.

Oak St.

Heather St.

12th Ave.

16th Ave.

Cambie St.

Manitoba St.

Main St.

Fraser St.

Windsor St.

Clarke
Park

Knight St.

28th Ave.

King Edward

1A

99A

Victoria Dr.

**VanDusen
Botanical Garden**
44

33rd Ave.

45
**Queen Elizabeth
Park**

couver's primary cruise-ship pier, the Trade and Convention Center, and the luxurious Pan Pacific Hotel (☞ Lodging, *below*). Here you can stop for a snack in one of the dining outlets on the water or catch a film at the IMAX theater. Stop off at the **Vancouver Tourist Info Centre** ⑭ across the street (next door to the Waterfront Centre Hotel) to pick up brochures on other Vancouver attractions and events before leaving the area.

TIMING

This walking tour, with time to take in the intriguing architecture along the route, will take approximately two to three hours if you're not drawn into all the shops along the way. Allow about an hour at the Canadian Craft Museum, and another two to three to see the collections at the Vancouver Art Gallery.

Sights to See

🔞 **Canada Place.** Originally built on an old cargo pier to be the off-site Canadian pavilion in Expo '86, Canada Place was later converted into Vancouver's trade and convention center. The shore end is dominated by the luxurious **Pan Pacific Hotel** (☞ Lodging, *below*), which has a three-story lobby and waterfall. The fabric roof shaped like 10 sails that covers the convention space has become a landmark of Vancouver's skyline. Below is a cruise-ship facility, and at the north end are an IMAX theater, a restaurant, and an outdoor performance space. A promenade runs along the pier's west side, affording views of the Burrard Inlet harbor and Stanley Park. ⊠ *999 Canada Pl.,* ☎ *604/775–8687.*

🄍 **Canadian Craft Museum.** Opened in 1992, the museum is one of the first national cultural facilities dedicated to crafts—historical and contemporary, functional and decorative. Craft embodies the human need for artistic expression in everyday life, and examples here range from elegantly carved utensils with decorative handles to colorful hand-spun and handwoven garments. The two-level museum has exhibits, lectures, and the Museum Shop. The structure was once a medical building, still evident outside in the restored terra-cotta arch and frieze panels showing scenes of individuals administering care. The restful courtyard is a quiet place to take a break. ⊠ *639 Hornby St.,* ☎ *604/687–8266.* ☜ *$5.* ☉ *Apr.–Oct., Mon.–Sat. 10–5, Sun. noon–5; Nov.–Mar., Mon. and Wed.–Sat. 10–5, Sun. noon–5.*

🄍 **Canadian Imperial Bank of Commerce (CIBC).** Built between 1906 and 1908, the former headquarters of one of Vancouver's oldest and most powerful chartered banks has columns, arches, and details that reflect a typically Roman influence. It now houses a jewelry store. ⊠ *698 W. Hastings St.*

🄍 **Christ Church Cathedral.** This tiny church, built in 1895, is the oldest in Vancouver. Constructed in Gothic style with buttresses and pointed-arch windows, it looks like the parish church of an English village from the outside. By contrast, the cathedral's rough-hewn interior is that of a frontier town, with Douglas-fir beams and ornate woodwork that provide excellent acoustics for the vespers, carols, and Gregorian chants frequently sung here. ⊠ *690 Burrard St.,* ☎ *604/682–3848.* ☉ *Weekdays 10–4.*

🄍 **Hotel Vancouver.** Completed in 1939, the Hotel Vancouver (☞ Lodging, *below*) is one of the last railway-built hotels (the final one was the Chateau Whistler, in 1989). Its château style, with details reminiscent of a medieval French castle, has been incorporated into hotels in almost every major Canadian city. The depression slowed construction, which began in 1937, and the hotel was finished only in time for the

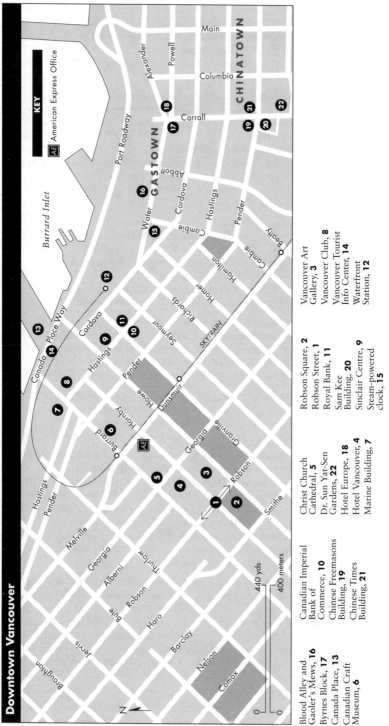

Downtown Vancouver

KEY

AE American Express Office

Burrard Inlet

GASTOWN

CHINATOWN

Main
Powell
Alexander
Columbia
Carrall
Port Roadway
Abbott
Water
Cordova
Hastings
Pender
Cambie
Canada Place Way
Beatty
SKYTRAIN
Hamilton
Homer
Richards
Seymour
Dunsmuir
Howe
Hornby
Burrard
Granville
Georgia
Robson
Smithe
Melville
Thurlow
Bute
Haro
Barclay
Nelson
Comox
Jervis
Broughton
Alberni

N

440 yds
0
400 meters
0

Blood Alley and
Gaoler's Mews, **16**
Byrnes Block, **17**
Canada Place, **13**
Canadian Craft
Museum, **6**

Canadian Imperial
Bank of
Commerce, **10**
Chinese Freemasons
Building, **19**
Chinese Times
Building, **21**

Christ Church
Cathedral, **5**
Dr. Sun Yat-Sen
Gardens, **22**
Hotel Europe, **18**
Hotel Vancouver, **4**
Marine Building, **7**

Robson Square, **2**
Robson Street, **1**
Royal Bank, **11**
Sam Kee
Building, **20**
Sinclair Centre, **9**
Steam-powered
clock, **15**

Vancouver Art
Gallery, **3**
Vancouver Club, **8**
Vancouver Tourist
Info Center, **14**
Waterfront
Station, **12**

visit of King George VI in 1939. It has been renovated three times, most recently in 1996. The exterior of the building, one of the most recognizable on Vancouver's skyline, has carvings of malevolent-looking gargoyles at the corners, an ornate chimney, native chiefs on the Hornby Street side, and an assortment of grotesque mythological figures. ⊠ *900 W. Georgia St., ☎ 604/684–3131.*

❼ Marine Building. This art deco building erected in 1931 is ornamented with terra-cotta bas-reliefs depicting the history of transportation: airships, steamships, locomotives, and submarines. Because most buildings were still using classical or Gothic ornamentation, these motifs were once considered radical and modernistic. From the east, the Marine Building is reflected in bronze by 999 West Hastings, and from the southeast it is mirrored in silver by the Canadian Imperial Bank of Commerce. Stand on the corner of Hastings and Hornby streets for the best view of the building. ⊠ *355 Burrard St.*

❷ Robson Square. Built in 1975 and designed by architect Arthur Erickson to be *the* gathering place of downtown Vancouver, Robson Square functions from the outside as a park. Here you'll find the **Vancouver Art Gallery** (☞ *below*), government offices, and law courts woven together by landscaped walkways, as well as a block-long glass canopy over one of the walkways and a waterfall. An ice-skating rink and restaurants occupy the below-street level. ⊠ *800 Robson St.*

❶ Robson Street. If you're up for a day of shopping, amble down this street (☞ Shopping, *below*), whose stores carry everything from souvenirs to high fashions. There are plenty of places to stop for tea, espresso, or lunch. Europeans of diverse backgrounds settled west of Burrard Street in the 1950s and 1960s, and their influence can still be felt.

⓫ Royal Bank. Gothic in style, this building was intended to be half of a symmetrical building that because of the depression was never completed. Striking, though, is the magnificent hall, reminiscent of a European cathedral. The building is still a bank. ⊠ *685 W. Hastings St.*

❾ Sinclair Centre. Outstanding Vancouver architect Richard Henriquez knitted four government office buildings into Sinclair Centre, an office-retail complex. The two Hastings Street buildings—a 1905 **Post Office** with an elegant clock tower and the 1913 **Winch Building**—are linked with the **Post Office Extension** and **Customs Examining Warehouse** to the north. Painstaking and costly restoration involved finding master masons—the original terrazzo suppliers in Europe—and uncovering and refurbishing the pressed-metal ceilings. ⊠ *757 W. Hastings St., ☎ 604/666–4438.*

❸ Vancouver Art Gallery. The city's best art museum has sculpture and modern art, as well as some native works, but paintings by artist Emily Carr of British Columbia make up the most popular permanent collection. This museum was a classical-style 1912 courthouse until architect Arthur Erickson converted it to a spacious gallery in 1980. The lions that guard the majestic front steps and the use of columns and domes are some of the features borrowed from ancient Roman architecture. ⊠ *750 Hornby St., ☎ 604/662–4719.* ▨ *$9.50.* ☉ *Mon.– Wed. and Fri. 10–6, Thurs. 10–9, Sat. 10–5, Sun. noon–5.*

❽ Vancouver Club. The architecture of this gathering place for the city's elite evokes that of private clubs in England inspired by Italian Renaissance palaces. The Vancouver Club, built between 1912 and 1914, is still the private haunt of city businesspeople. ⊠ *915 W. Hastings St., ☎ 604/685–9321.*

⑭ **Vancouver Tourist Info Centre.** Here you'll find brochures and personnel to answer questions, as well as an attractive Northwest Coast native art collection. ✉ *200 Burrard St.,* ☏ *604/683–2000.* ☺ *Sept.–June, weekdays 8:30–5, Sat. 9–5; July–Aug., daily 8–6.*

⑫ **Waterfront Station.** The third and most imposing of three Canadian Pacific Railway passenger terminals in Vancouver was constructed from 1912 to 1914. It replaced the other two as the western terminus for Canada's transcontinental railway. After Canada's railways merged, the station became obsolete until a 1978 renovation turned it into an office-retail complex and SeaBus terminal. Murals in the waiting rooms (now used by Skytrain, SeaBus, West Coast Express, and B.C. Transit passengers) show the scenery travelers once saw on journeys across Canada. ✉ *601 W. Cordova St.,* ☏ *604/521–0400 for B.C. Transit.*

Chinatown and Gastown

Gastown is where Vancouver originated after smooth talker "Gassy" Jack Deighton arrived at Burrard Inlet in 1867 with his wife, some whiskey, and few amenities, and managed to con local loggers and trappers into building him a saloon for a barrel of whiskey. When the transcontinental train arrived in 1887, Gastown became the transfer point for trade with the Far East and was soon crowded with hotels and warehouses. The Klondike gold rush encouraged further development until 1912, when the "Golden Years" ended. From the 1930s to the 1950s hotels were converted into rooming houses, and the warehouse district shifted elsewhere. The neglected area gradually became run down. However, both Gastown and Chinatown were declared historic districts in the late 1970s and have been revitalized. Gastown is now chockablock with boutiques, cafés, loft apartments, and souvenir shops.

The Chinese were among the first inhabitants of Vancouver. There was already a sizable Chinese community in British Columbia because of the 1858 Cariboo gold rush in central British Columbia, but the greatest influx from China came in the 1880s, during construction of the Canadian Pacific Railway, when 15,000 laborers were imported. Even while doing the hazardous work of blasting the rail bed through the Rocky Mountains, however, the Chinese were discriminated against. The Anti-Asiatic Riots of 1907 stopped growth in Chinatown for 50 years, and immigration from China was discouraged by more and more restrictive policies, climaxing in a $500 head tax during the 1920s. In the 1960s the city council planned bulldozer urban renewal for Strathcona, the residential part of Chinatown, as well as freeway connections through the most historic blocks of the district. Fortunately, the project was halted, and today Chinatown is an expanding, vital neighborhood fueled by investment from Vancouver's most notable newcomers—immigrants from Hong Kong. The best way to view the buildings in Chinatown is from the south side of Pender Street, where the Chinese Cultural Center stands. From here you'll see the important details that adorn the upper stories. The style of architecture in Vancouver's Chinatown is patterned on that of Canton.

Numbers in the text correspond to numbers in the margin and on the Downtown Vancouver map.

A Good Walk

Pick up Water Street at Richards Street and head east into Gastown. At the corner of Water and Cambie streets, you can see and hear the world's first **steam-powered clock** ⑮ (it chimes on the quarter hour). Along the way you'll pass **Blood Alley and Gaoler's Mews** ⑯, which are tucked behind 12 Water Street. Two buildings of historical and architectural note are the **Byrnes Block** ⑰ on the corner of Water and Carrall streets and the **Hotel Europe** ⑱ (1908–09) at Powell and Alexander streets. A statue of Gassy Jack stands on the west side of Maple Tree Square, at the intersection of Water, Powell, Alexander, and Carrall streets, where he built his first saloon.

From Maple Tree Square it's only three blocks south on Carrall Street to Pender Street, where Chinatown begins. This route passes through a rough part of town, so it's far safer to backtrack two blocks on Water Street through Gastown to Cambie Street, then head south to Pender and east to Carrall. The corner of Carrall and Pender streets, now the western boundary of Chinatown, is one of the neighborhood's most historic and photogenic spots. It's here that you'll find the **Chinese Freemasons Building** ⑲ (circa 1901) and the **Sam Kee Building** ⑳ (circa 1913), and, directly across Carrall Street, the **Chinese Times Building** ㉑ (circa 1902). Across Pender are the first living classical Chinese gardens built outside China, the **Dr. Sun Yat-Sen Gardens** ㉒, tucked behind the Chinese Cultural Center, which houses exhibition space, classrooms, and the occasional mah-jongg tournament. Finish up by poking around in the open-front markets and import shops that line several blocks of Pender running east.

TIMING

The walk itself will take from two to three hours depending on your pace; allow extra time for the guided tour of the garden in Chinatown. Daylight hours are best, although shops and restaurants are open into the night in both areas. There are few traffic signals for safe crossings in Gastown, so avoid commuter rush hours.

Sights to See

★ ⑯ **Blood Alley and Gaoler's Mews.** Once the site of the city's first civic buildings—the constable's cabin and customs house, and a two-cell log jail—today the cobblestone street with antique lighting is home to architectural offices. ⊠ *Behind 12 Water St.*

⑰ **Byrnes Block.** This building was constructed on the site of Gassy Jack's second saloon after the 1886 Great Fire. The date is just visible at the top of the building above the door where it says "Herman Block," which was its name for a short time. ⊠ *Water and Carrall Sts.*

⑲ **Chinese Freemasons Building.** Two completely different facades distinguish a fascinating structure on the northwest corner of Pender and Carrall streets: The side facing Pender presents a fine example of Cantonese-imported recessed balconies; the Carrall Street side displays the standard Victorian style common throughout the British Empire. Dr. Sun Yat-Sen hid for months in this building from agents of the Manchu dynasty while he raised funds for its overthrow, which he accomplished in 1911. ⊠ *W. Pender St.*

㉑ **Chinese Times Building.** This building, on the north side of Pender Street just east of Carrall, dates from 1902. Police officers could hear the clicking sounds of clandestine mah-jongg games played after sunset on the building's hidden mezzanine floor. But attempts by vice squads to enforce restrictive policies against the Chinese gamblers proved fruitless, because police were unable to find the players. Meandering down Pender Street, you can still hear mah-jongg games going on behind the colorful facades of other buildings in Chinatown. ⊠ *1 E. Pender St.*

★ ㉒ **Dr. Sun Yat-Sen Gardens.** Fifty-two artisans from Suzhou, China, using no power tools, screws, or nails, constructed these gardens in the 1980s. Their design incorporates elements and traditional materials from several of Suzhou's centuries-old private gardens. Free guided tours are conducted throughout the day; telephone for times. ⊠ *578 Carrall St.,* ☎ *604/689–7133.* ⊒ *$5.50.* ⊙ *Daily 10–7:30.*

⑱ **Hotel Europe.** Once billed as the best hotel in the city, this circa 1908–1909 flatiron building was Vancouver's first reinforced concrete structure. Designed as a functional commercial building, the hotel lacks ornamentation and fine detail, its style unusually utilitarian for the time. ⊠ *Alexander and Powell Sts.*

⑳ **Sam Kee Building.** *Ripley's Believe It or Not!* recognizes this 6-ft-wide structure as the narrowest building in the world. Its bay windows overhang the street, and the basement burrows under the sidewalk. ⊠ *8 W. Pender St.*

★ **⑮** **Steam-powered clock.** An underground steam system powers the world's first steam clock. Every quarter hour the whistle blows, and on the hour a huge cloud of steam spews from the clock. It was built by Ray Saunders of Landmark Clocks (⊠ *123 Cambie St.,* ☎ *604/669–3525*). ⊠ *Water and Cambie Sts.*

Stanley Park

A 1,000-acre wilderness park just blocks from the downtown section of a major city is both a rarity and a treasure. In the 1860s, because of a threat of American invasion, the area that is now Stanley Park was designated a military reserve (though it was never needed). When the city of Vancouver was incorporated in 1886, the council's first act was to request that the land be set aside for a park. In 1888 permission was granted and the grounds were named Stanley Park after Lord Stanley, then governor general of Canada.

Spend a morning or afternoon in Stanley Park and you'll get a capsule tour of Vancouver that includes beaches, the ocean, the harbor, Douglas fir and cedar forests, and a good look at the North Shore mountains. The park sits on a peninsula, and along the shore is a pathway 9 km (5½ mi) long called the seawall. You can drive or bicycle the mostly flat route all the way around. Bicycles are for rent at the foot of Georgia Street near the park entrance. Cyclists must ride in a counterclockwise direction and stay on their side of the path.

Numbers in the text correspond to numbers in the margin and on the Stanley Park map.

A Good Biking or Driving Tour

A good place to start is at the foot of Alberni Street beside Lost Lagoon. Go through the underpass and veer right to the seawall past **Malkin Bowl** ㉓, an open amphitheater. Just past the amphitheater is a cutoff to the left that leads to the renowned **Vancouver Aquarium** ㉔; the main road continues on to the rest of the park's sights. The old wood structure that you pass next is the Vancouver Rowing Club, a private athletic club established in 1903; a bit farther along is the Royal Vancouver Yacht Club. About ½ km (⅓ mi) away is the causeway to **Deadman's Island** ㉕.

If you continue straight past the causeway, ahead at the water's edge is the **Nine O'Clock Gun** ㉖. To the north is Brockton Point and its small but functional lighthouse and foghorn. The **totem poles** ㉗, which are a bit farther down the road and slightly inland on your left, are a popular photo stop. Continue on and you'll pass the miniature steam train, five minutes northwest of the aquarium; it's a big hit with children. The children's water park across the road is also popular throughout the summer.

At km 3 (mi 2) is **Lumberman's Arch** , a huge log archway. About 2 km (1 mi) farther is the Lions Gate Bridge—the halfway point of the seawall. Just past the bridge is **Prospect Point** ㉙, where cormorants build nests. Continuing around the seawall, you'll come to the English Bay side and the beginning of sandy beaches. The imposing rock just off-shore is **Siwash Rock** ㉚, the focus of a native legend.

The next attraction along the seawall is the large saltwater pool at **Second Beach** ㉛. You can take a shortcut from here back to Lost Lagoon by walking along the perpendicular road behind the pool, which cuts into the park. The wood footbridge that's ahead will lead you to a path along the south side of the lagoon to your starting point at the foot of Alberni or Georgia Street. If you continue along the seawall, you will emerge from the park into a high-rise residential neighborhood, the West End. You can walk back to Alberni Street along Denman Street, where there are places to stop for coffee, ice cream, or a drink.

TIMING

You'll find parking near most of the sights in the park; expect a driving tour to take about an hour. Your biking time will depend on your speed, but with stops to see the sights, expect it to take several hours. Add at least two hours to see the aquarium thoroughly, and you've filled a half- to full-day tour. Stanley Park becomes crowded on weekends; on weekday afternoons the local jogging and biking traffic is at its lowest.

Sights to See

㉕ **Deadman's Island.** A former burial ground for the local Salish people and the early settlers is now a small naval training base called H.M.C.S. *Discovery* and is not open to the public.

㉘ **Lumberman's Arch.** Made of logs, this large archway is dedicated to the workers in Vancouver's first industry. Beside the arch is an asphalt path that leads back to Lost Lagoon and the Vancouver Aquarium.

㉓ **Malkin Bowl.** An open amphitheater becomes a theater under the stars during the summer. ⊠ *1st right off Pipeline Rd. past park entrance,* ☏ *604/687–0174.*

㉖ **Nine O'Clock Gun.** This cannonlike apparatus by the water was originally used to alert fishermen to a curfew ending weekend fishing; now it signals 9 o'clock every night.

㉙ **Prospect Point.** Here cormorants build their seaweed nests along the cliff's ledges. The large black diving birds are distinguished by their long necks and beaks; when not nesting, they often perch atop floating logs or boulders. Another remarkable bird found along the park's shore is the beautiful great blue heron, which reaches up to 4 ft tall and has a wing span of 6 ft. Herons prey on passing fish in the waters here; the oldest heron rookery in British Columbia is in the trees near the aquarium.

㉛ **Second Beach.** In summer a draw is the big saltwater children's pool with lifeguards, but in winter, when the pool is drained, skateboarders perform stunts here.

㉚ **Siwash Rock.** Legend tells of a young Native American who, about to become a father, bathed persistently to wash his sins away so that his son could be born pure. For his devotion he was blessed by the gods and immortalized in the shape of Siwash Rock, just offshore. Two small rocks, said to be his wife and child, are on the cliff above the site.

㉗ **Totem poles.** Totem poles were not made in the Vancouver area; these, carved of cedar by the Kwakiutl and Haida peoples late in the last cen-

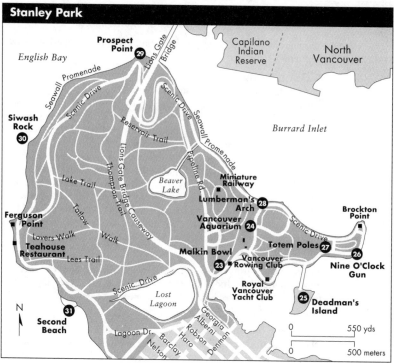

tury, were brought to the park from the north coast of British Columbia. The carved animals, fish, birds, and mythological creatures are like family coats-of-arms or crests.

★ ☾ ㉔ **Vancouver Aquarium.** The humid Amazon rain-forest gallery has piranhas, giant cockroaches, alligators, tropical birds, and jungle vegetation. Other displays show the underwater life of coastal British Columbia, the Canadian arctic, and other areas of the world. Huge tanks (populated with orca and beluga whales and playful sea otters) have large windows for underwater viewing. ☎ 604/682–1118. ✉ $12. ☺ July–Labor Day, daily 9:30–8; Labor Day–June, daily 10–5:30.

Granville Island

Granville Island was just a sandbar until World War I, when the federal government dredged False Creek for access to the sawmills that lined the shore. The sludge from the creek was heaped up onto the sandbar to create the island and to house much-needed industrial- and logging-equipment plants. By the late 1960s, however, many of the businesses that had once flourished on Granville Island had deteriorated. Buildings were rotted, rat-infested, and dangerous. In 1971 the federal government bought up leases from businesses that wanted to leave and proposed an imaginative plan to refurbish the island with a public market, marine activities, and artisans' studios. The opposite shore of False Creek was the site of Expo '86 and is now part of the largest urban redevelopment plan in North America.

The small island has no residents except for a houseboat community. Most of the former industrial buildings and tin sheds have been retained but are painted in upbeat reds, yellows, and blues. Through a committee of community representatives, the government regulates the types of businesses on Granville Island; most of the businesses permitted involve food, crafts, marine activities, and the arts.

Numbers in the text correspond to numbers in the margin and on the Granville Island map.

A Good Walk

To reach Granville Island on foot, make the 15-minute walk from downtown Vancouver to the south end of Hornby Street. Aquabuses (☎ 604/689–5858) depart here and deliver passengers across False Creek to Granville Island Public Market. The Granville Island Ferries (☎ 604/684–7781), which leave every five minutes from a dock behind the Vancouver Aquatic Centre, are another option. Still another way to reach the island is to take a 20-minute ride on a B.C. Transit (☎ 604/521–0400) bus; to do this take a University of British Columbia (U.B.C.), Granville, Arbutus, Cambie, or Oak bus from downtown to Granville and Broadway, and transfer to Granville Island Bus 51 or False Creek Bus 50 from Gastown or stops on Granville Street. Parking is free for up to three hours; paid parking is available in garages on the island.

The ferry will drop you off at the **Granville Island Public Market** ㉜, which contains fast-food outlets and produce, meat, coffee, liquor, and flower stalls. The **Granville Island Information Centre** ㉝ is catercorner to the market.

Walk south on Johnston Street to begin a clockwise loop tour of the island. Ocean Cement is one of the last of the island's former industries; its lease does not expire until the year 2004. Next door is the **Emily Carr Institute of Art and Design** ㉞. Past the art school, on the left, is Sea Village, one of the only houseboat communities in Vancouver. Take the boardwalk that starts at the houseboats and continues partway around the island.

As you circle around to Cartwright Street, stop in Kakali at Number 1249, where you can watch the fabrication of fine handmade paper from such materials as blue jeans, herbs, and sequins. Another unusual artisan on the island is the glassblower at the New-Small Sterling Glass Studio (✉ 1404 Old Bridge St.), around the corner. The next two attractions will make any child's visit to Granville Island a thrill. First, on Cartwright Street, is the **Granville Island Water Park** ㉟. A bit farther down the street, beside Isadora's restaurant, is the **Kids Only Market** ㊱, selling anything and everything a child could desire. Cross Anderson Street and walk down Duranleau Street. On your left are the seafaring stores of the **Maritime Market** ㊲. The last place to explore on Granville Island is the **Net Loft** ㊳, a collection of small, high-quality stores. Once you have come full circle, you can either take the ferry back to downtown Vancouver or stay for dinner and catch a play at the Arts Club (☎ 604/687–1644) or the Waterfront Theater (☎ 604/685–6217).

TIMING

If your schedule is tight, you can tour Granville Island in three to four hours; if you're a shopping fanatic, plan for a full day here.

Sights to See

㉞ **Emily Carr Institute of Art and Design.** The institute's three main buildings—wooden structures formerly used for industrial purposes—were renovated in the 1970s. The **Charles H. Scott Gallery,** just inside the front door to your right, hosts contemporary exhibitions in various media. ✉ *1399 Johnston St.,* ☎ *604/687–3800.* ☞ *Free.* ⊙ *Daily noon–5.*

Granville Island

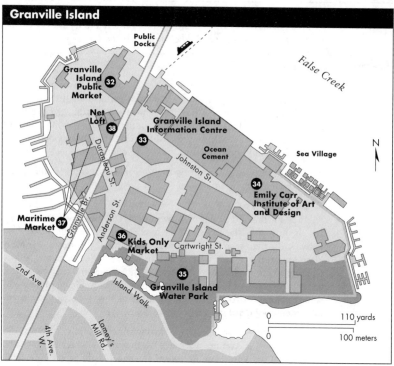

33 Granville Island Information Centre. Maps are available here, and a slide show depicts the evolution of Granville Island. Ask about special-events days; boat shows, outdoor concerts, and dance performances often occur on the island. ⊠ *1592 Johnston St.,* ☎ *604/666–5784.* ☺ *Daily 8–6.*

★ **32 Granville Island Public Market.** Because no chain stores are allowed in this 50,000-square-ft building, each outlet is unique; most sell high-quality merchandise. You can pick up a snack, espresso, or fixings for lunch on the wharf here, and year-round you'll see mounds of raspberries, strawberries, blueberries, and more exotic fruits like persimmons. There's plenty of outdoor seating on the water side of the market. ⊠ *1669 Johnston St., under Granville St. bridge, 2nd floor,* ☎ *604/666–6477.* ☺ *Memorial Day–Labor Day, daily 9–6; Labor Day–Memorial Day, Tues.–Sun. 9–6.*

35 Granville Island Water Park. This kids' paradise has a wading pool, sprinklers, and a fire hydrant made for children to shower one another. ⊠ *1318 Cartwright St.,* ☎ *604/257–8195.* 🎫 *Free.* ☺ *Late May–early Sept., daily 10–6.*

36 Kids Only Market. Yet another slice of kids' heaven on Granville Island, the Kids Only Market has two floors of small shops selling toys, arts-and-crafts materials, dolls, records and tapes, chemistry sets, and other good kid stuff. ⊠ *1496 Cartwright St.,* ☎ *604/689–8447.* ☺ *Daily 10–6.*

37 Maritime Market. These businesses are all geared to the sea. The first walkway to the left, Maritime Mews, leads to marinas and dry docks. ⊠ *1650 Duranleau St.,* ☎ *604/687–1556.*

38 Net Loft. In this blue building is a collection of small, high-quality stores, including a bookstore, a crafts store-gallery, a kitchenware shop, a postcard shop, a custom-made hat shop, a handmade paper store, a British Columbian native art gallery, and a do-it-yourself jewelry store. ⊠ *1666 Johnston St., across from Public Market,* ☎ *604/876–6637.*

Greater Vancouver

The metropolis of Vancouver includes North Vancouver across Burrard Inlet and the larger, more residential peninsula south of downtown bordered by English Bay to the north, the Strait of Georgia to the west, and the Fraser River to the south. There are wonderful museums, gardens, and natural sights sprinkled throughout Greater Vancouver, but you'll need a car to maximize your time.

Numbers in the text correspond to numbers in the margin and on the Greater Vancouver map.

A Good Drive

South of the Burrard Bridge in Vanier Park is the **Vancouver Museum** ㉟, which showcases the city's history in cheerful, life-size displays. Also here are the high-tech **Pacific Space Centre** ㊵ and the **Vancouver Maritime Museum** ㊶. After visiting one or more of the museums, follow Cypress Street south out of the park to 4th Avenue, and then head west to the University of British Columbia to visit the amazing **Museum of Anthropology** ㊷. You can pause for a moment of reflection at the **Nitobe Memorial Garden** ㊸, also on campus.

Follow Southwest Marine Drive through the university campus and turn left on 41st Avenue. Turn left again on Oak Street to reach the entrance of the **VanDusen Botanical Garden** ㊹ (it'll be on your left). Return to 41st Avenue, continue farther east, and then turn left on Cambie Street to reach **Queen Elizabeth Park** ㊺, which overlooks the city.

Head back downtown across the Cambie Bridge (stay in the right lane), which flows onto Smithe Street. Turn right onto Homer Street and look for parking in the next few blocks so that you can stop to see **Library Square** ㊻, the city's multimillion-dollar central library project that resembles Rome's Colosseum. From there it's only three more blocks to B.C. Place, where you'll find the **B.C. Sports Hall of Fame and Museum** ㊼. Turn south on Cambie and follow it to Pacific Boulevard (don't cross the Cambie Bridge), which winds east around False Creek and turns into Quebec Street at the head of the creek. Turn right here, and right again into the parking lot of **Science World** ㊽.

From Science World head straight across Quebec to Main Street, turn left, and make a second left at the Georgia Viaduct, which leads onto Dunsmuir. Follow it for eight or so blocks. Turn left onto Howe Street and then right onto Georgia, which winds through town and Stanley Park and across the Lions Gate Bridge to North Vancouver. Follow the signs into the mountains of the North Shore to see the **Capilano Suspension Bridge and Park** ㊾, where a cedar-plank footbridge swings high above the Capilano River. Nearby in the Capilano Regional Park, the **Capilano Salmon Hatchery** ㊿ is another good spot to visit. Up the hill a bit farther, at the end of Nancy Greene Way, is **Grouse Mountain** ⑤①, where a funicular gives you great city views.

TIMING

To cover all the sights of Greater Vancouver, taking sufficient time at each of the museums and gardens, could easily take two days. Either pick and choose those you really want to see, or limit yourself to the sights south of the city one day and save the remaining sights downtown and on the North Shore for another day.

Sights to See

47 **B.C. Sports Hall of Fame and Museum.** Part of the B.C. Place Stadium complex, this museum celebrating the province's sports achievers shows video documentaries and has photographs, costumes, and sporting equipment on display. Bring tennis shoes to wear in the high-tech, hands-on participation gallery. ⊠ *B.C. Pl., 777 Pacific Blvd. S, Gate A,* ☎ *604/687–5525.* ☞ *$6.* ☉ *Daily 10–5.*

50 **Capilano Salmon Hatchery.** In the Capilano Regional Park, the hatchery has viewing areas and exhibits about the life cycle of the salmon. ⊠ *4500 Capilano Park Rd., North Vancouver,* ☎ *604/666–1790.* ☞ *Free.* ☉ *Call for seasonal hrs.*

49 **Capilano Suspension Bridge and Park.** At this, Vancouver's oldest tourist attraction (the original bridge was built in 1889), you can get a taste of the mountains and test your mettle on the swaying, 450-ft cedar plank suspension bridge that hangs 230 ft above the rushing Capilano River. The amusement park also has viewing decks, nature trails amid tall firs and cedars, a gift shop, a totem-carving shed, and displays for the kids. ⊠ *3735 Capilano Rd., North Vancouver,* ☎ *604/ 987–7474.* ☞ *Call for admission fees.* ☉ *Summer, daily 8–dusk; winter, daily 9–5; call for exact hrs.*

51 **Grouse Mountain.** The Skyride to the top is a great way to take in stunning city, sea, and mountain vistas. In the theater at the peak you can catch a film on Vancouver's transformation from a string of scattered native, trapper, and logger settlements to a bustling modern metropolis. ⊠ *6400 Nancy Greene Way, North Vancouver,* ☎ *604/984–0661.* ☞ *Ride and theater $15.* ☉ *Call for seasonal hrs.*

46 **Library Square.** Built to evoke images of the Colosseum in Rome, the spiraling library building, open plazas, frescoed waterfall, and shaded atriums of the new Library Square were completed in 1995. This architectural stunner is a favorite backdrop for movie productions. The book collection is moved about on motorized shelving systems in the ultra-high-tech library that fills the core of the structure; the outer edge of the spiral houses trendy boutiques, coffee shops, and a fine book and gift shop. ⊠ *350 W. Georgia St.,* ☎ *604/331–3600.* ☉ *Mon.– Tues. 10–9, Thurs.–Sat. 10–6; also Oct.–Apr., Sun. 1–5.*

★ **42** **Museum of Anthropology.** The MOA is Vancouver's most spectacular museum, focusing on the arts of the Pacific Northwest natives and aboriginals from around the world, including the works of Bill Reid, Canada's most respected Haida carver. Reid's *The Raven and the First Men,* which took five carvers more than three years to complete, is its centerpiece. Arthur Erickson designed the award-winning structure that houses the museum. In the Great Hall are large and dramatic totem poles, ceremonial archways, and dugout canoes—all adorned with carvings of frogs, eagles, ravens, bears, and salmon. You'll also find exquisite carvings of gold, silver, and argillite (a black stone found in the Queen Charlotte Islands), as well as masks, tools, and costumes from many other cultures. The museum's ceramics wing contains several hundred pieces from 15th- to 19th-century Europe. ⊠ *University of British Columbia, 6393 N.W. Marine Dr.,* ☎ *604/822–5087.* ☞ *$5, free Tues.* ☉ *Tues. 11–9, Wed.–Sun. 11–5.*

43 **Nitobe Memorial Garden.** This 2½-acre garden is considered the most authentic Japanese garden outside Japan. The circular path around the park symbolizes the cycle of life and provides a tranquil view from every direction. In April and May cherry blossoms are the highlight, and in June the irises are magnificent. ⊠ *University of British Columbia,*

1903 West Mall, ☎ *604/822–6038.* ▭ *$3.* ☉ *Summer, daily 10–6; winter, weekdays 10–3.*

Ⓒ ④⓪ **Pacific Space Centre.** A virtual-reality Cyberwalk and a kinetic space-ride simulator are among the interactive exhibits and high-tech learning systems at this fascinating facility that's so advanced it was granted status as a NASA Teacher Resource Center. Films screening at the on-site theater highlight Canada's achievements in space, and astronomy shows take place at the **H. R. MacMillan Planetarium.** If the sky is clear, the half-meter telescope at the **Gordon MacMillan Southam Observatory** is focused on whatever stars or planets are worth watching that night. ✉ *Vanier Park, 1100 Chestnut St.,* ☎ *604/738–7827; 604/738–2855 special-events schedule.* ▭ *Observatory free, planetarium fee varies.* ☉ *Observatory daily 7 PM–11 PM; planetarium shows daily June–Aug. (times vary), Sept.–May, Tues.–Sun.*

④⑤ **Queen Elizabeth Park.** Besides views of downtown, the park has lavish gardens brimming with roses and other flowers, an abundance of grassy picnicking spots, and illuminated fountains. In the **Bloedel Conservatory,** you can see tropical and desert plants and 35 species of free-flying tropical birds. Other park facilities include 20 tennis courts, a pitch-and-putt golf course, and a restaurant. ✉ *Cambie St. and 33rd Ave.,* ☎ *604/872–5513.* ▭ *Conservatory $3.* ☉ *Apr.–Sept., weekdays 9–8, weekends 10–9; Oct.–Mar., daily 10–5.*

Ⓒ ④⑧ **Science World.** In a gigantic shiny dome built over an Omnimax Theater for Expo '86, this hands-on museum encourages visitors to touch and participate in the theme exhibits. The special Search Gallery is aimed at younger children, as are the fun-filled demonstrations given in Center Stage. ✉ *1455 Quebec St.,* ☎ *604/268–6363.* ▭ *Science World $9, Omnimax $9, combination ticket $12.* ☉ *Weekdays 10–5, weekends 10–6.*

Ⓒ ④① **Vancouver Maritime Museum.** This museum on English Bay traces the history of marine activities on the West Coast. Permanent exhibits depict the port of Vancouver, the fishing industry, and early explorers; the model ships on display are a delight. Traveling exhibits vary but always have a maritime theme. Guided tours are led through the double-masted schooner *St. Roch,* the first ship to sail in both directions through the treacherous Northwest Passage. Restored heritage boats from different cultures are moored behind the museum, and a huge Kwakiutl totem pole stands out front. ✉ *1905 Ogden Ave., north end of Cypress St., also accessible via Granville Island Ferry,* ☎ *604/257–8300.* ▭ *$5.* ☉ *May–Aug., daily 10–5; Sept.–Apr., Tues.–Sun. 10–5.*

Ⓒ ③⑨ **Vancouver Museum.** Life-size replicas of a trading post, a Victorian parlor, and an 1897 Canadian Pacific Railway passenger car, as well as a real dugout canoe, are the highlights at this museum whose exhibits focus on the city's early history and native art and culture. ✉ *1100 Chestnut St., Vanier Park,* ☎ *604/736–4431.* ▭ *$5, extra charge for special exhibitions.* ☉ *Summer, daily 10–5; winter, Tues.–Sun. 10–5.*

④④ **VanDusen Botanical Garden.** On what was once a 55-acre golf course grows one of the largest collections of ornamental plants in Canada. Native and exotic plant displays include a shrubbery maze and herb gardens; rhododendrons bloom in May and June. For a bite to eat, stop in Sprinklers Restaurant (☎ *604/261–0011*), on the grounds. ✉ *5251 Oak St., at 37th Ave.,* ☎ *604/878–9274.* ▭ *$5, ½ price Oct.–May.* ☉ *July–Aug., daily 10–9; Oct.–Apr., daily 10–4; May–June and Sept., daily 10–6.*

DINING

Vancouver dining is usually fairly informal; casual but neat dress is appropriate everywhere except a few expensive restaurants that require jacket and tie (indicated in the text). *See* the Downtown Vancouver Dining map to locate downtown restaurants and the Greater Vancouver Dining map to locate restaurants in Kitsilano, Granville Island, and other neighborhoods away from downtown.

CATEGORY	COST*
$$$$	over C$40
$$$	C$30–C$40
$$	C$20–C$30
$	under C$20

per person for a three-course meal, excluding drinks, service, and sales tax

Downtown

American

$$ ✕ **Griffin's.** Sunday brunch here is cheerful, energetic, and kid-oriented: A special buffet is chockablock with favorite foods for the younger set. The rest of the week the emphasis is on the adult crowd. This brasserie uniquely blends the charm of old Italy with sophisticated design. Squash-yellow walls, bold black-and-white tiles, and splashy food art keep it lively. The open kitchen prepares inspired cuisine from fresh, regional ingredients, including buffet selections such as convict bread (a round loaf stuffed with goat cheese, olives, tomatoes, and peppers in olive oil), smoked salmon, chicken pasta al pesto, and baked Pacific cod. ✉ *900 W. Georgia St.,* ☎ *604/662–1900. Reservations essential. AE, D, DC, MC, V.*

California

$$ ✕ **Delilah's.** Cherubs dance on the ceiling, candles flicker on the ta-
★ bles, and martini glasses clink in toasts at this incredibly popular restaurant. Under the direction of chef Peg Montgomery, the nouvelle California cuisine is delicious, innovative, and beautifully presented. The menu, which changes seasonally, lets you choose two- or five-course prix-fixe dinners. Try the pancetta, pine nut, Asiago, and mozzarella fritters with sun-dried tomato aioli and the grilled swordfish with blueberry-lemon compote if they're available. Patrons have been known to line up before Delilah's opens for dinner. ✉ *1739 Comox St.,* ☎ *604/687–3424. Reservations not accepted. DC, MC, V. No lunch.*

Chinese

$$–$$$ ✕ **Imperial Chinese Seafood.** This elegant Cantonese restaurant in the
★ art deco Marine Building has two-story floor-to-ceiling windows with stupendous views of Stanley Park and the North Shore mountains across Coal Harbour. Any dish featuring lobster, crab, or shrimp from the live tanks is recommended, as is the dim sum served every day from 11 to 2:30. Portions tend to be small and pricey (especially the abalone, shark's fin, and bird's nest delicacies) but never fail to please. ✉ *355 Burrard St.,* ☎ *604/688–8191. Reservations essential. AE, MC, V.*

$$ ✕ **Kirin Mandarin Restaurant.** Fish swim in tanks set into the slate-green walls, part of the lavish decorations of this restaurant serving a smattering of northern Chinese cuisines. Dishes include Shanghai-style smoked eel, Peking duck, and Szechuan hot-and-spicy scallops. Kirin is just two blocks from most of the major downtown hotels. A second location at Cambie focuses on milder Cantonese seafood creations. ✉ *102–1166 Alberni St.,* ☎ *604/682–8833;* ✉ *555 W. 12th Ave., 2nd floor,* ☎ *604/879–8038. Reservations essential. AE, DC, MC, V.*

Downtown Vancouver Dining

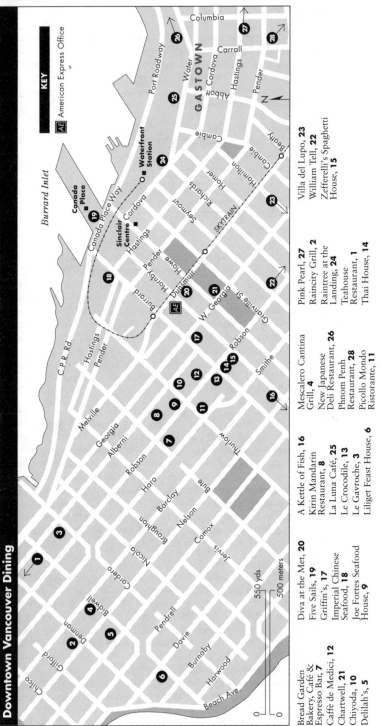

KEY

AE American Express Office

Burrard Inlet

Canada Place

Sinclair Centre

Waterfront Station

GASTOWN

Bread Garden
Bakery, Café &
Espresso Bar, **7**
Caffè de Medici, **12**
Chartwell, **21**
Chiyoda, **10**
Delilah's, **5**

Diva at the Met, **20**
Five Sails, **19**
Griffin's, **17**
Imperial Chinese
Seafood, **18**
Joe Fortes Seafood
House, **9**

A Kettle of Fish, **16**
Kirin Mandarin
Restaurant, **8**
La Luna Café, **25**
Le Crocodile, **13**
Le Gavroche, **3**
Liliget Feast House, **6**

Mescalero Cantina
Grill, **4**
New Japanese
Deli Restaurant, **26**
Phnom Penh
Restaurant, **28**
Picollo Mondo
Ristorante, **11**

Pink Pearl, **27**
Raincity Grill, **2**
Raintree at the
Landing, **24**
Teahouse
Restaurant, **1**
Thai House, **14**

Villa del Lupo, **23**
William Tell, **22**
Zefferelli's Spaghetti
House, **15**

$$ ✕ **Pink Pearl.** This noisy, 680-seat Cantonese restaurant has tanks of live seafood—crab, shrimp, geoduck, oysters, abalone, rock cod, lobsters, and scallops. Menu highlights include clams in black-bean sauce, crab sautéed with five spices (a spicy dish sometimes translated as crab with peppery salt), and Pink Pearl's version of crisp-skinned chicken. Arrive early for dim sum on the weekend if you don't want to wait in a long line. ⊠ *1132 E. Hastings St.,* ☎ *604/253–4316. Reservations essential. AE, DC, MC, V.*

Continental

$$$–$$$$ ✕ **Chartwell.** Named after Sir Winston Churchill's country home (a
★ painting of which hangs over the green marble fireplace), the flagship dining room at the Four Seasons hotel (☞ Lodging, *below*) looks like an upper-class British club. Floor-to-ceiling dark wood paneling, deep leather chairs, and a quiet setting make this the city's top spot for a power lunch. The chefs cook robust, inventive Continental food as well as lighter offerings and low-calorie, low-fat entrées. Favorites include tomato basil soup with gin, rack of lamb, and a number of salmon offerings. ⊠ *791 W. Georgia St.,* ☎ *604/844–6715. Reservations essential. Jacket and tie. AE, DC, MC, V.*

$$$–$$$$ ✕ **William Tell.** Silver service plates, embossed linen napkins, and a silver vase on each table set the tone of Swiss luxury in this establishment in the Georgian Court Hotel. Chef Christian Lindner offers excellent sautéed veal sweetbreads with red-onion marmalade and marsala sauce and Swiss specialties such as cheese fondue, pickled herring with apples, and thinly sliced veal with mushrooms in a light white wine sauce. A bar and bistro area caters to a more casual crowd. Reserve in advance for the all-you-can-eat Swiss Farmer's Buffet on Sunday night. ⊠ *765 Beatty St.,* ☎ *604/688–3504. Reservations essential. Jacket and tie. AE, DC, MC, V.*

$$$ ✕ **Teahouse Restaurant.** The best of the Stanley Park restaurants is perfectly poised for watching sunsets over the water, especially from a glassed-in wing that resembles a conservatory. The country French and seafood menu includes cream of carrot soup, lamb with herb crust, and the perfectly grilled fish. ⊠ *7501 Stanley Park Dr., Ferguson Point, Stanley Park,* ☎ *604/669–3281. Reservations essential. AE, MC, V.*

Deli

$ ✕ **La Luna Café.** This unpretentious bilevel deli in the heart of Gastown serves fragrant coffees and teas and soup-and-salad lunches, but the luscious sourdough cinnamon rolls steal the show. Have one heated and slathered with butter if you plan to eat in at one of the small tables, or get one to go: These rolls are not to be missed! ⊠ *117 Water St.,* ☎ *604/687–5862. AE, MC, V.*

Eclectic

$$ ✕ **Diva at the Met.** The multitiered restaurant at the Metropolitan Hotel (☞ Lodging, *below*) is quickly becoming a local favorite. The innovative nouvelle cuisine served here is as appealing as the Impressionist art adorning the walls. Top creations from the glass-walled kitchen include charred ahi tuna on a warm bean salad with grilled asparagus and red pepper aioli, and veal London broil with foie gras, mushroom risotto, and balsamic reduction. The after-theater crowd heads here for dessert: Fresh sorbets, chocolate anise crème brûlée, and Stilton cream cheesecake draw rave reviews. ⊠ *645 Howe St.,* ☎ *604/687–7788. AE, DC, MC, V.*

French

$$$ ✕ **Le Gavroche.** At this century-old house, a woman dining with a man will be offered a menu without prices. The classic French cooking, lightened—but by no means reduced—to nouvelle cuisine, includes simple dishes such as smoked salmon with blini and sour cream and more complex offerings like grilled veal tenderloin with chanterelles and lobster sauce. The excellent wine list stresses Bordeaux. Tables by the front window have mountain and water views. ⊠ *1616 Alberni St.,* ☎ *604/ 685–3924. Reservations essential. AE, DC, MC, V. No lunch weekends.*

$$ ✕ **Le Crocodile.** In a roomy location off Burrard Street, chef Michael Jacob serves simple food at reasonable prices—innards, a caramel-sweet onion tart, and old standards like duck à l'orange. ⊠ *100–909 Burrard St.,* ☎ *604/669–4298. Reservations essential. AE, DC, MC, V. Closed Sun. No lunch Sat.*

Italian

$$$ ✕ **Caffè de Medici.** This somewhat formal restaurant has ornate molded ceilings, green-velvet curtains and chair coverings, portraits of the Medici family, and a courtly, peaceful atmosphere. Although an enticing antipasto table sits in the center of the room, consider the *bresaola* (air-dried beef marinated in olive oil, lemon, and pepper) as an appetizer, followed by the rack of lamb entrée in a mint, mustard, and vermouth sauce. ⊠ *1025 Robson St.,* ☎ *604/669–9322. Reservations essential. AE, D, DC, MC, V. No lunch weekends.*

$$$ ✕ **Villa del Lupo.** Ask the top chefs in town where they head for Ital-
★ ian, and Villa del Lupo is the answer more often than not. Country-house decor sets a romantic tone, but come prepared to roll up your sleeves and mop up the sauce with a chunk of crusty bread. Pasta stuffed with roasted duck, veggies, and ricotta cheese; rabbit loin with mushrooms, black olives, and thyme; and braised lamb osso buco in a sauce of tomatoes, red wine, cinnamon, and lemon are favorites here. ⊠ *869 Hamilton St.,* ☎ *604/688–7436. Reservations essential. AE, MC, V. No lunch weekends.*

$$ ✕ **Picollo Mondo Ristorante.** Soft candlelight, bountiful flower arrangements, and fine European antiques create a romantic mood at this intimate northern Italian restaurant on a quiet street one block off Robson. Start with the seafood puff pastry with chive-vermouth cream sauce and follow up with the classic osso buco or the linguine tossed with smoked Alaskan cod, capers, and red onions. The award-winning wine cellar stocks more than 3,000 bottles. ⊠ *850 Thurlow St.,* ☎ *604/ 688–1633. Reservations essential. AE, DC, MC, V. Closed Sun. No lunch Sat.*

$$ ✕ **Zefferelli's Spaghetti House.** As you might guess from the name, spaghetti, penne, fusilli, tortellini, and fettuccine dressed in creative but subtle sauces—from roasted garlic, broccoli, feta cheese, and tomato sauce to traditional meat sauce—play first string at Zefferelli's, but grilled prawns and chicken saltimbocca (with prosciutto and sage in marsala wine) are strong competition. Done up in forest green, mustard, and persimmon, the trendy dining room has an open kitchen at one end and a wall of windows overlooking busy Robson Street at the other. ⊠ *1136 Robson St.,* ☎ *604/687–0655. Reservations essential. AE, DC, MC, V. No lunch weekends.*

Japanese

$$ ✕ **Chiyoda.** The *robata* (grill) bar curves through Chiyoda's main room: On one side are the customers and an array of flat baskets full of the day's offerings; on the other side are the chefs and grills. There are 35 choices of things to grill, from squid, snapper, and oysters to eggplant, mushrooms, onions, and potatoes. The finished dishes, dressed with sake, soy sauce, or *ponzu* (vinegar and soy sauce), are dramatically passed over on the end of a long wooden paddle. ⊠ *200– 1050 Alberni St.,* ☎ *604/688–5050. Reservations essential. AE, DC, MC, V. Closed Sun. No lunch Sat.*

$ ✕ **New Japanese Deli Restaurant.** The least expensive sushi in town is served in the high-ceilinged main-floor room of a turn-of-the-century building on Powell Street, once the heart of Vancouver's Japantown. The food is especially fresh and good if you can make it an early lunch: Sushi rectangles and rolls are made at 11 AM for the 11:30 opening, and there are all-you-can-eat sushi and tempura lunch specials on weekdays. ✉ *381 Powell St.,* ☎ *604/662–8755. No credit cards. Closed Sun.*

Mexican/Spanish

$$–$$$ ✕ **Mescalero Cantina Grill.** The look and feel here is of Santa Fe, from
★   stucco walls and leather chairs inside to a charming greenery-draped patio for open-air dining. Tapas are the main draw—Cajun beef and black bean tostada; panfried blue cornmeal-crusted oysters; roast chicken and chorizo chimichangas; and grilled salmon, asparagus, and goat-cheese burritos—but dinner selections such as blackened red snapper with avocado, corn, black-bean, and vodka salsa with crème fraîche are equally good. The Bandito Brunch on weekends draws a crowd. ✉ *1215 Bidwell St.,* ☎ *604/669–2399. Reservations essential. AE, MC, V.*

Pacific Northwest

$$ ✕ **Liliget Feast House.** Only a few blocks from English Bay, this downstairs "longhouse" serves the original Northwest Coast cuisine: Bannock bread, baked sweet potato with hazelnuts, alder-grilled salmon, toasted seaweed with rice, steamed fern shoots, barbecued venison, and soapberries for dessert. Try the authentic but odd dish—"oolichan grease"—that's prepared from candlefish. Native music is piped in, and Northwest Coast native masks (for sale) peer from the walls. ✉ *1724 Davie St.,* ☎ *604/681–7044. Reservations essential. AE, MC, V. No lunch.*

$$ ✕ **Raincity Grill.** This West End hot spot across the street from English Bay is a neighborhood favorite. The setting, with candlelit tables, balloon-back chairs, cushioned banquettes, and enormous flower arrangements, is very sophisticated. All the same, it plays second fiddle to a creative weekly menu that highlights the best regional seafood, meats, and produce. Grilled romaine spears are used in the Caesar salad, giving it a delightful smoky flavor. Varying preparations of salmon and duck are usually available, as is at least one vegetarian selection. ✉ *1193 Denman St.,* ☎ *604/685–7337. Reservations essential. AE, DC, MC, V.*

$$ ✕ **Raintree at the Landing.** In a beautifully renovated heritage building in busy Gastown, this spacious restaurant has waterfront views, a local menu, and a wine list with Pacific Northwest vintages. The kitchen, focusing on healthy cuisine, teeters between willfully eccentric and exceedingly simple; it bakes its own bread and makes luxurious soups. Main courses, which change daily, may include salmon and crab gnocchi, smoked Fraser Valley duck breast, and grilled marlin with basil risotto cakes. ✉ *375 Water St.,* ☎ *604/688–5570. Reservations essential. AE, DC, MC, V. No lunch weekends.*

Pacific Rim

$$$$ ✕ **Five Sails.** On the fourth floor of the Pan Pacific Hotel, this special-occasion restaurant has a stunning panoramic view of Canada Place, Lions Gate Bridge, and the lights of the north shore across the bay. Austrian chef Ernst Dorfler has a special flair for presentation, from the swan-shape butter served with breads early in the meal to the chocolate ice-cream bonbon served at the end. The broad-reaching, seasonally changing Pacific Rim menu often includes caramelized swordfish, ahi in red Thai curry vinaigrette, terrine of duck, and old favorites like medallions of British Columbia salmon or lamb from Salt Spring Island. ✉ *Pan Pacific Hotel, 300–999 Canada Pl., ☎ 604/662–8211. Reservations essential. AE, DC, MC, V. No lunch.*

Seafood

$$ ✕ **Joe Fortes Seafood House.** Reserve a table on the second-floor bal-
★   cony at this Vancouver seafood hot spot to take in the view of the broad wall murals, the mounted blue marlins, and, most especially, the boy-meets-girl scene at the noisy bar downstairs. The signature panfried Cajun oysters, clam and corn fritters, salmon with smoked apple and cider chutney, and seared sea scallops in a sesame and oyster glaze are tasty and filling but are often overlooked in favor of the reasonably priced blue-plate special. ✉ *777 Thurlow St., ☎ 604/669–1940. Reservations essential. AE, D, DC, MC, V.*

$$ ✕ **A Kettle of Fish.** Since opening in 1979, this family-run restaurant at the northeast end of Burrard Bridge has attracted a strong local following; count on getting top-quality seafood here. The menu varies daily according to market availability, but there are generally 15 kinds of fresh seafood that are either grilled, sautéed, poached, barbecued, or blackened Cajun-style. The British Columbia salmon and the seafood combo plate are always good choices. ✉ *900 Pacific Blvd., ☎ 604/682–6661. AE, DC, MC, V. No lunch weekends.*

Southeast Asian

$ ✕ **Phnom Penh Restaurant.** Part of a small cluster of Southeast Asian
★   shops on the fringes of Chinatown, this eatery has potted plants and framed views of Angkor Wat. The hospitable staff serves unusually robust Vietnamese and Cambodian fare, including crisp, peppery garlic prawns fried in the shell and a salad with sliced warm beef crusted with ground salt and pepper. ✉ *244 E. Georgia St., ☎ 604/253–8899; ✉ 955 W. Broadway, ☎ 604/734–8988. AE, MC, V. Closed Tues.*

$ ✕ **Thai House.** This sun-filled second-floor diner overlooking Robson Street offers a great lunch deal from 11 to 3: For less than $8, patrons feast on a spring roll, soup, salad, rice, and a choice of 18 typical Thai dishes for the main course. The mild, smoky flavor of *kai pad khing* (boneless chicken with ginger, mushroom, and onions) is satisfying, but the tangy Thai garlic chicken is even better. ✉ *1116 Robson St., ☎ 604/683–3383. AE, MC, V.*

Greater Vancouver

American

$ ✕ **Isadora's.** Not only does Isadora's offer good coffee and a "West Coast–fresh" menu that ranges from lox and bagels to vegetarian pastas and seafood platters, but it also has children's specials (the pizzas come with faces here) and an inside play area packed with toys. In summer the restaurant opens onto Granville Island's water park. Service can be slow, but the staff is friendly. The restaurant is no-smoking. Vegan dishes (prepared without animal products) are available on request. ✉ *1540 Old Bridge St., Granville Island, ☎ 604/681–8816. DC, MC, V. No dinner Mon. Sept.–May.*

$ ✕ **Nazarre BBQ Chicken.** The best barbecued chicken in town comes from this funky storefront on Commercial Avenue in the Little Italy neighborhood. Owner Gerry Moutal massages his chickens for tenderness before he puts them on the rotisserie and bastes them with a mixture of rum and spices. Chicken comes with roasted potatoes and a choice of mild, hot, or extra spicy garlic sauce. You can eat in, at one of four rickety tables, but the service can be surly at times; we recommend takeout. ✉ *1859 Commercial Dr., ☎ 604/251–1844. Reservations not accepted. No credit cards.*

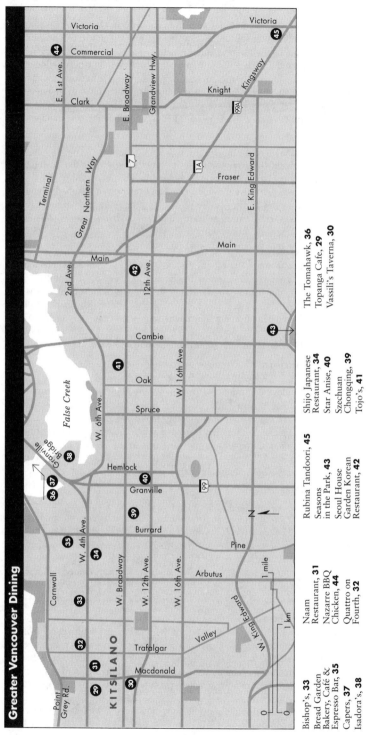

Greater Vancouver Dining

Bishop's, 33

Bread Garden
Bakery, Café &
Espresso Bar, **35**

Capers, 37

Isadora's, 38

Naam
Restaurant, **31**

Nazarre BBQ
Chicken, **44**

Quattro on
Fourth, **32**

Rubina Tandoori, **45**

Seasons
in the Park, **43**

Seoul House
Garden Korean
Restaurant, **42**

Shijo Japanese
Restaurant, **34**

Star Anise, **40**

Szechuan
Chongqing, **39**

Tojo's, **41**

The Tomahawk, **36**

Topanga Cafe, **29**

Vassili's Taverna, **30**

Bakery

$ ✕ **Bread Garden Bakery, Café & Espresso Bar.** Once a croissant bakery, this is now the ultimate Kitsilano 24-hour hangout. Salads, quiches, elaborate cakes and pies, giant muffins, and cappuccino draw a steady stream of the young and fashionable. The wait in line may be long here or at any of its other locations. Reports indicate that quality has suffered with the rapid expansion, but the Garden's following is still strong. ⊠ *1880 W. 1st Ave., Kitsilano,* ☎ *604/738–6684;* ⊠ *2996 Granville St.,* ☎ *604/736–6465;* ⊠ *812 Bute St.,* ☎ *604/688–3213. AE, MC, V.*

Chinese

$ ✕ **Szechuan Chongqing.** At this unpretentious, white-tablecloth restaurant, try the Szechuan-style crunchy green beans tossed with garlic or the Chongqing chicken—a boneless chicken served on a bed of spinach cooked in dry heat until crisp, giving it the texture of dried seaweed and a salty, rich, and nutty taste. ⊠ *1668 W. Broadway,* ☎ *604/734–1668. Reservations essential. AE, MC, V.*

Continental

$$$ ✕ **Seasons in the Park.** Seasons, in Queen Elizabeth Park, has a commanding view over gardens to the city lights and the mountains beyond. A comfortable room with light wood and white tablecloths sets the mood for conservative Continental standards like grilled salmon with fresh mint and roast duck with sun-dried cranberry sauce. Weekend brunch is popular. ⊠ *Queen Elizabeth Park, 33rd and Cambie St.,* ☎ *604/874–8008. Reservations essential. AE, MC, V.*

East Indian

$$ ✕ **Rubina Tandoori.** For the best East Indian food in the city, try Rubina Tandoori, 20 minutes from downtown. The large menu spans most ★ of the subcontinent's cuisines, and the especially popular *chevda* (an East Indian salty snack) is shipped to fans all over North America. Nonsmokers sit in the smaller, funkier back room with paintings of coupling gods and goddesses; smokers dine in the slightly more subdued front room. ⊠ *1962 Kingsway,* ☎ *604/874–3621. Reservations essential. DC, MC, V. Closed Sun.*

Greek

$$ ✕ **Vassili's Taverna.** The menu in this family-run restaurant in the heart of the city's small Greek community is almost as conventional as the decor: checked tablecloths and mandatory paintings of fishing villages and the blue Aegean Sea. At Vassili's, though, even standards become memorable because of the flawless preparation. The house specialty is a deceptively simple *kotopoulo* (a half chicken, pounded flat, herbed, and charbroiled). ⊠ *2884 W. Broadway,* ☎ *604/733–3231. Reservations essential. AE, DC, MC, V. Closed Mon. No lunch weekends.*

Health Food

$ ✕ **Capers.** Hidden in the back of the most lavish health food store in ★ the Lower Mainland, Capers drips with earth-mother chic: wood tables, potted plants, and heady aromas from the store's bakery. Breakfast starts at 8 o'clock: bacon (with no additives) and eggs (from free-range chickens), or featherlight blueberry pancakes. Top choices from the lunch and dinner menu include roasted squash soup and local mushrooms with capellini. The newer 4th Avenue location, with its dining room above the store, is by far the nicer of the two; the West Vancouver store is somewhat old and dingy. ⊠ *2496 Marine Dr., West Vancouver,* ☎ *604/925–3374;* ⊠ *2285 W. 4th Ave.,* ☎ *604/739–6685. MC, V. No dinner Sun. at Marine Dr.*

$ ✗ **Naam Restaurant.** Vancouver's oldest organic eatery is open 24 hours, so if you need to satisfy a late-night tofu-burger craving, rest easy. The Naam also serves wine, beer, cappuccino, fresh juices, and wicked chocolate desserts, along with vegetarian stir-fries. Wood tables and kitchen chairs help create a homey atmosphere. On warm summer evenings, try the outdoor courtyard at the back of the restaurant. ⊠ *2724 W. 4th Ave.,* ☎ *604/738–7151. MC, V.*

Italian

$$ ✗ **Quattro on Fourth.** This northern Italian restaurant in Kitsilano shot to stardom quickly. A mosaic floor, mustard-color walls with stark-green-and-mauve-stenciled borders, cherry-stained tables, and a wraparound covered porch for alfresco dining enhance the Mediterranean atmosphere. Mushroom lovers usually jump at the truffle fettuccine, but if you can't make up your mind, there's the antipasto platter and *combinazione* (a plate for two with the five most popular pastas and sauces). The gelato trio is a perfect topper. ⊠ *2611 W. 4th Ave.,* ☎ *604/734–4444. Reservations essential. AE, DC, MC, V. No lunch.*

Japanese

$$$ ✗ **Tojo's.** Hidekazu Tojo is a sushi-making legend here, with more than
★ 2,000 preparations tucked away in his creative mind. His handsome blond-wood tatami rooms, on the second floor of a modern green-glass tower on West Broadway, provide the proper ambience for intimate dining, but Tojo's 10-seat sushi bar stands as the centerpiece. With Tojo presiding, it offers a convivial ringside seat for watching the creation of edible art. Although tempura and teriyaki dinners will satisfy, the seasonal menu is more exciting. In fall, ask for *dobin mushi,* a soup made from pine mushrooms. In spring, try salad made from scallops and pink cherry blossoms. ⊠ *202–777 W. Broadway,* ☎ *604/872–8050. Reservations essential. AE, DC, MC, V. Closed Sun. No lunch.*

$$ ✗ **Shijo Japanese Restaurant.** Shijo has an excellent and very large sushi bar, a smaller robata bar, tatami rooms, and a row of tables overlooking 4th Avenue. The epitome of modern urban Japanese chic is conveyed through the jazz music, handsome lamps with a bronze finish, and lots of black wood. Count on creatively prepared sushi in generous proportions, eggplant *dengaku* (topped with light and dark miso paste and broiled), and shiitake foil *yaki* (fresh shiitake mushrooms cooked in foil with lemony ponzu sauce). ⊠ *1926 W. 4th Ave.,* ☎ *604/732–4676. Reservations essential. AE, DC, MC, V. No lunch weekends.*

Korean

$ ✗ **Seoul House Garden Korean Restaurant.** This bright restaurant, decorated in Japanese style, serves a full menu of Japanese and Korean food, including sushi. The best bet is the Korean barbecue, which you cook at your table; the dinner of marinated beef, pork, chicken, or fish comes complete with a half dozen side dishes—kimchi, salads, stir-fried rice, and pickled vegetables—as well as soup and rice. Service can be chaotic. ⊠ *36 E. Broadway,* ☎ *604/874–4131. Reservations essential. MC, V. No lunch Sun.*

Mexican

$ ✗ **Topanga Cafe.** Arrive before 6:30 or after 8 PM to avoid waiting in line for this 40-seat Kitsilano classic. The Tex-Mex food hasn't changed much since 1978, when the Topanga started dishing up fresh salsa and homemade tortilla chips. Quantities are still huge and prices low. Kids can color blank menu covers while waiting for food; one hundred of their best efforts are framed on the walls. ⊠ *2904 W. 4th Ave.,* ☎ *604/733–3713. Reservations not accepted. MC, V. Closed Sun.*

Pacific Northwest

$$$–$$$$ ✕ **Bishop's.** John Bishop established this restaurant as a favorite in 1985 by serving West Coast Continental cuisine with an emphasis on British Columbia seafood. The seasonal menu might include medallions of venison, smoked Alaskan black cod, seared lamb loin, roast rabbit leg, or linguine tossed with fresh acorn squash. The small white rooms—their only ornament some splashy expressionistic paintings—are favored by Pierre Trudeau, Robert De Niro, and other celebrity patrons. ✉ *2183 W. 4th Ave.,* ☎ *604/738–2025. Reservations essential. AE, DC, MC, V. Closed 1st wk in Jan. No lunch.*

$ ✕ **The Tomahawk.** North Vancouver was mostly trees in 1926, when the Tomahawk first opened. Over the years, the original hamburger stand grew and mutated into part Northwest Coast native kitsch museum, part gift shop, and part restaurant. Renowned for its Yukon breakfast—five slices of back bacon, two eggs, hash browns, and toast—the Tomahawk also serves gigantic muffins, excellent French toast, and pancakes. At lunch and dinner, the menu switches to oysters, trout, and burgers named for native chiefs. ✉ *1550 Philip Ave.,* ☎ *604/988–2612. AE, MC, V.*

Pacific Rim

$$$ ✕ **Star Anise.** When Sammy Lalji left the highly regarded Bishop's (☞
★ *above*) to open his own restaurant, he built a faithful following in record time. His superior skills in attentive service, imaginative presentation, and excellent preparation of Pacific Rim cuisine with French flair shine in this intimate, no-smoking location just off Granville. Don't miss the crab and shrimp sausage on wilted spinach salad or the grilled enoki mushrooms with tomato risotto; the juniper-marinated venison with raspberry vinegar and crème fraîche is another fine choice. ✉ *1485 W. 12th Ave.,* ☎ *604/737–1485. Reservations essential. AE, D, DC, MC, V. No lunch weekends.*

LODGING

Vancouver hotels, especially the more expensive properties downtown, are fairly comparable in facilities. Unless otherwise noted, expect to find the following amenities: minibars, in-room movies, no-smoking rooms/floors, room service, massage, exercise room, baby-sitting, laundry service and dry cleaning, concierge, business services, meeting rooms, and parking (for which there is usually an additional fee). Lodgings in the moderate to inexpensive categories do not generally offer much in the way of amenities (no in-room minibar, restaurant, room service, pool, exercise room, and so on).

CATEGORY	COST*
$$$$	over C$300
$$$	C$200–C$300
$$	C$125–C$200
$	under C$125

All prices are for a standard double room for two, excluding 10% provincial accommodation tax, 15% service charge, and 7% GST.

$$$$ 🏨 **Four Seasons.** This 28-story hotel adjacent to the Vancouver Stock Exchange is attached to the Pacific Centre shopping mall. Standard rooms are average in size and comforts; roomier corner rooms are recommended. Service at this luxury property is top notch, and the attention to detail is outstanding. The formal dining room, Chartwell (☞ Dining, *above*), is one of the best in the city. Even pets receive red-carpet treatment here—they're served Evian and pet treats in silver bowls. ✉ *791 W. Georgia St., V6C 2T4,* ☎ *604/689–9333, 800/268–6282 in Canada, 800/332–3442 in the U.S.;* 📠 *604/844–6744. 274 rooms,*

Vancouver Lodging

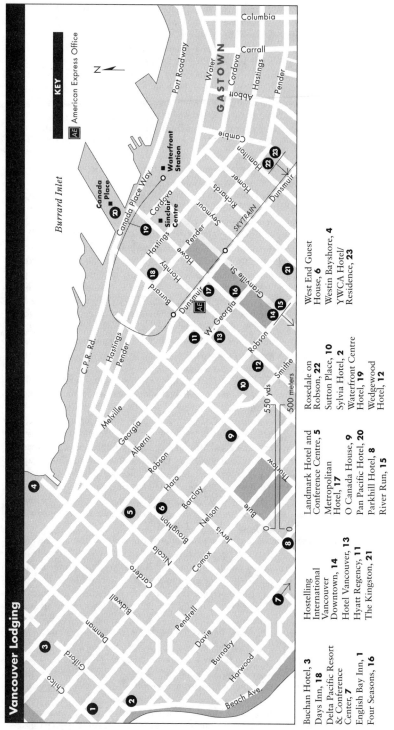

KEY

AE American Express Office

Burrard Inlet

Canada Place

Waterfront Station

Sinclair Centre

GASTOWN

SKYTRAIN

Buchan Hotel, **3**
Days Inn, **18**
Delta Pacific Resort & Conference Center, **7**
English Bay Inn, **1**
Four Seasons, **16**

Hostelling International Vancouver Downtown, **14**
Hotel Vancouver, **13**
Hyatt Regency, **11**
The Kingston, **21**

Landmark Hotel and Conference Centre, **5**
Metropolitan Hotel, **17**
O Canada House, **9**
Pan Pacific Hotel, **20**
Parkhill Hotel, **8**
River Run, **15**

Rosedale on Robson, **22**
Sutton Place, **10**
Sylvia Hotel, **2**
Waterfront Centre Hotel, **19**
Wedgewood Hotel, **12**

West End Guest House, **6**
Westin Bayshore, **4**
YWCA Hotel/ Residence, **23**

111 suites. 2 dining rooms, bar, lobby lounge, indoor-outdoor pool, hot tub, sauna, aerobics, shops, piano. AE, DC, MC, V.

$$$$ ☎ **Hyatt Regency.** The standard rooms of this 34-story hotel are spacious and decorated in deep, dramatic colors and dark wood; all are equipped with irons and boards, coffeemakers, bathrobes, and voice mail. Ask for a corner room with a balcony on the north or west side for the best view. Automated check-in service (via a kiosk) is available in the bustling lobby. For a small fee, the Regency Club gives you the exclusivity of a floor accessed by keyed elevators; your own concierge; a private lounge; and complimentary breakfast. ⊠ *655 Burrard St., V6C 2R7,* ☎ *604/683–1234 or 800/233–1234,* ☎ *604/689–3707. 612 rooms, 34 suites. Restaurant, 2 bars, café, in-room modem lines, in-room safes, pool, sauna, shops, children's programs (ages 6–12), travel services, car rental. AE, D, DC, MC, V.*

$$$$ ☎ **Pan Pacific Hotel.** Sprawling Canada Place, on a pier right by the financial district, houses the luxurious Pan Pacific, the Vancouver Trade and Convention Centre, and a cruise-ship terminal. The hotel's three-story atrium lobby has a dramatic totem pole and waterfall, and the lounge, restaurant, and café all have huge expanses of glass with views of the harbor and mountains. Earth tones and varied textures give the rooms an understated elegance. Corner rooms overlooking the harbor are favorites. ⊠ *300–999 Canada Pl., V6C 3B5,* ☎ *604/662–8111, 800/663–1515 in Canada, 800/937–1515 in the U.S.;* ☎ *604/685–8690. 467 rooms, 39 suites. 3 restaurants, coffee shop, lobby lounge, in-room modem lines, in-room safes, in-room VCRs, pool, barbershop, beauty salon, hot tubs, saunas, steam rooms, aerobics, health club, indoor track, paddle tennis, racquetball, squash, shops, convention center, travel services. AE, DC, MC, V.*

$$$$ ☎ **Sutton Place.** The feel here is more exclusive guest house than large
★   hotel: The lobby has sumptuously thick carpets, enormous displays of flowers, and European furniture. The rooms are furnished with rich, dark woods reminiscent of 19th-century France. Despite its size, this hotel maintains a significant level of intimacy and exclusivity. The Fleuri Restaurant serves a great Sunday brunch; Le Club, a fine Continental restaurant, is for special occasions. Le Grande Residence, a luxury apartment hotel suitable for extended stays, adjoins the hotel. ⊠ *845 Burrard St., V6Z 2K6,* ☎ *604/682–5511 or 800/961–7555,* ☎ *604/682–5513. 350 rooms, 47 suites. Restaurant, bar, café, lobby lounge, kitchenettes, indoor pool, beauty salon, sauna, spa, steam room, health club, bicycles, piano. AE, D, DC, MC, V.*

$$$$ ☎ **Waterfront Centre Hotel.** Dramatically elegant, the 23-story glass
★   hotel opened in 1991 across from Canada Place, which can be reached from the hotel by an underground walkway. Views from the caramel-color lobby and 70% of the guest rooms are of Burrard Inlet. The rooms are attractively furnished with contemporary artworks; armoires conceal the TV. Large corner rooms have the best views. A string quartet entertains in the lobby restaurant, Herons, during Sunday brunch. ⊠ *900 Canada Pl. Way, V6C 3L5,* ☎ *604/691–1991 or 800/441–1414,* ☎ *604/691–1999. 460 rooms, 29 suites. Restaurant, pool, steam room, shops, travel services, car rental. AE, D, DC, MC, V.*

$$$–$$$$ ☎ **Wedgewood Hotel.** An owner who cares fervently about her guests
★   runs this small hotel whose intimate lobby is decorated with polished brass, beveled glass, a fireplace, tasteful artworks, and fine antiques. Expect all the extra touches: nightly turndown service, afternoon ice delivery, flowers on the balcony, robes, and a morning newspaper. No tour groups or conventions stop here; the Wedgewood's clients are almost exclusively corporate, except on weekends, when the place turns into a couples' retreat. ⊠ *845 Hornby St., V6Z 1V1,* ☎ *604/689–7777 or 800/663–0666,* ☎ *604/608–5348. 59 rooms, 34 suites. Restaurant,*

bar, in-room safes, sauna, piano, travel services. AE, D, DC, MC, V.

$$$ 🖭 **Delta Pacific Resort & Conference Center.** Its facilities are what make this property on 14 acres a resort: swimming pools (one indoor, with a three-story tubular water slide), tennis courts with a pro, an outdoor fitness circuit, aqua-exercise classes, outdoor volleyball nets, a play center and summer camps for children, and a playground. In spite of the hotel's size, the atmosphere is casual and friendly. Guest rooms are modern, with contemporary decor and a pleasant blue and green color scheme. ⊠ *10251 St. Edwards Dr., Richmond V6X 2M9,* ☎ *604/278–9611, 800/268–1133 in Canada, 800/877–1133 in the U.S.;* ℻ *604/276–1121. 453 rooms, 5 suites. 2 restaurants, lobby lounge, in-room modem lines, indoor pool, 2 outdoor pools, barbershop, beauty salon, hot tub, saunas, putting green, squash, bicycles, children's programs (ages 5–12), convention center, travel services, car rental, free parking. AE, DC, MC, V.*

$$$ 🖭 **Hotel Vancouver.** The copper roof of this grand château-style hotel
★ dominates Vancouver's skyline. Opened in 1939 by the Canadian National Railway, the hotel commands a regal position in the center of town. Even the standard guest rooms have an air of prestige, with mahogany furniture, attractive linens, and the original, deep bathtubs. Suites, with French doors and graceful wing-back chairs, take up two floors and come with extra services and amenities. Afternoon tea in the lobby lounge is a real treat. ⊠ *900 W. Georgia St., V6C 2W6,* ☎ *604/684–3131 or 800/441–1414,* ℻ *604/662–1937. 504 rooms, 46 suites. 3 restaurants, lobby lounge, in-room modem lines, indoor lap pool, hot tub, spa, steam rooms, shops, piano, travel services, car rental. AE, D, DC, MC, V.*

$$$ 🖭 **Metropolitan Hotel.** This 18-story hotel built in 1984 by the Hong Kong Mandarin chain is now a member of the Preferred Hotels group. Although the rates went down, the surroundings were improved during 1996 renovations: The lobby, still restrained and tasteful, now has a view of the hotel's new restaurant, Diva at the Met (☞ Dining, *above*), through an etched-glass wall. A slight Asian theme touches the rich dark-mahogany furnishings. Standard rooms are surprisingly spacious and have narrow balconies, but the even bigger studio suites are only slightly more expensive than a standard room. Rooms on the business floor have in-room faxes, printers, and modem lines. ⊠ *645 Howe St., V6C 2Y9,* ☎ *604/687–1122 or 800/667–2300,* ℻ *604/689–7044. 179 rooms, 18 suites. Restaurant, bar, indoor lap pool, men's steam room, racquetball, squash. AE, DC, MC, V.*

$$$ 🖭 **Westin Bayshore.** The Bayshore, perched right on the best part of the harbor adjacent to Stanley Park, has truly fabulous views. It's the perfect place to stay in summer, especially for a family, because of its huge outdoor pool, sundeck, grassy areas, and extensive recreational facilities. The tower rooms have the best views of the water. ⊠ *1601 W. Georgia St., V6G 2V4,* ☎ *604/682–3377 or 800/228–3000,* ℻ *604/687–3102. 484 rooms, 33 suites. Restaurant, 2 bars, café, indoor pool, outdoor pool, barbershop, beauty salon, steam rooms, boating, fishing, bicycles, billiards, piano, travel services, airport shuttle, car rental. AE, D, DC, MC, V.*

$$–$$$ 🖭 **Parkhill Hotel.** Cool pastel shades echo the colors of the Impressionist prints decorating the surprisingly spacious rooms in this West End hotel just a block from the seawall and sandy Sunset Beach. Large, comfortable sitting areas, half-moon balconies with city or bay views, minirefrigerators, hair dryers, and complimentary downtown shuttle services are part of the package. ⊠ *1160 Davie St., V6E 1N1,* ☎ *604/685–1311 or 800/663–1525,* ℻ *604/681–0208. 191 rooms. 2 restaurants, lounge, in-room safes, pool, sauna, travel services, car rental. AE, D, DC, MC, V.*

\$\$–\$\$\$ ▦ **Rosedale on Robson.** If you plan to be in town a while and want
★ to keep expenses down by doing some of your own cooking, look into
a room at the all-suite Rosedale on Robson. Rooms in shades of peach
and light green are generous in size and have European kitchens,
bleached hemlock furniture, and garden patios or balconies overlooking the city. Rooms on upper floors on the north side have views
of Coal Harbour. You'll find charming gardens with strolling paths on
the second and third floors of the complex. ⊠ *838 Hamilton St., V6B
5W4,* ☎ *604/689–8033 or 800/661–8870,* ℻ *604/689–4426. 275
suites. Restaurant, bar, kitchenettes, refrigerators, room service, indoor
lap pool, hot tub, sauna, steam room, coin laundry. AE, DC, MC, V.*

\$\$ ▦ **English Bay Inn.** This renovated 1930s Tudor house is one block from
★ the ocean and Stanley Park. The guest rooms have wonderful sleigh
beds (in all but one room) with matching armoires and Ralph Lauren
linens. The common areas of this no-smoking inn are furnished with
museum-quality antiques: The sophisticated but cozy parlor has wing-
back chairs, a fireplace, a gilt Louis XIV clock and candelabra, and
French doors overlooking the front garden. Breakfast is served in a rather
formal room with a Gothic dining room suite, a fireplace, and a 17th-
century grandfather clock. ⊠ *1968 Comox St., V6G 1R4,* ☎ *604/683–
8002. 4 rooms, 1 suite. Free parking. AE, MC, V.*

\$\$ ▦ **Landmark Hotel and Conference Center.** The towering Landmark
is still the tallest hotel (42 stories) in downtown Vancouver and contains some of the prettiest guest rooms in town. The bold jewel tones
(emerald, sapphire, and ruby) of paintings by British Columbia's
beloved Emily Carr (whose works hang in every room) are repeated
on walls and furnishings. All rooms enjoy a fine view, but the Cloud
Nine revolving restaurant on the top floor is a great place for an unobstructed view of Vancouver over an early breakfast buffet (in summer only); go elsewhere for dinner. ⊠ *1400 Robson St., V6G 1B9,* ☎
604/687–0511 or 800/325–3535, ℻ *604/687–2801. 351 rooms, 7
suites. Restaurant, café, sports bar, saunas, travel services. AE, DC,
MC, V.*

\$\$ ▦ **O Canada House.** New to the growing list of bed-and-breakfasts in
Vancouver, O Canada House is a beautifully restored 1897 Victorian
oozing with period charm inside and out. Each bedroom is fairly spacious and appointed in late-Victorian antiques; modern touches, including
a TV with VCR, a refrigerator, and a phone, are discreetly tucked out
of sight. Guests often gather in the evening near the fireplace in the
front parlor and assemble again in the morning in the formal dining
room for a gourmet breakfast—though breakfast served on the
wraparound porch is also an option. ⊠ *1114 Barclay St., V6E 1H1,*
☎ *604/688–0555,* ℻ *604/488–0556. 5 rooms. Free parking. AE, MC,
V.*

\$\$ ▦ **West End Guest House.** This Victorian house, built in 1906, is a true
★ "painted lady," from its front parlor, cozy fireplace, and early 1900s
furniture to its green-trimmed pink exterior. Most of the small but handsome rooms have high brass beds, antiques, and gorgeous linens. The
basement suite has a gas fireplace in the sitting area and a side garden
view. The inn's genial host, Evan Penner, adds small touches such as
a pre-dinner glass of sherry, duvets and feather mattress pads, terry
bathrobes, and turndown service. The inn is in a residential neighborhood
two minutes from Robson Street. Room rates at this no-smoking establishment include a full breakfast. ⊠ *1362 Haro St., V6E 1G2,* ☎
604/681–2889, ℻ *604/688–8812. 7 rooms. Bicycles, free parking.
AE, D, MC, V.*

\$–\$\$ ▦ **Days Inn.** Business travelers looking for a bargain will find this lo-
cation convenient. The six-story hotel, which opened as the Abbotsford in 1920, is the only moderately priced hotel in the business core.

Recent renovations of the guest rooms and the lobby have made it even more agreeable. Rooms are bright, clean, and utilitarian; standard units are large, but there is no room service and few amenities. Suites 310, 410, 510, and 610 have a harbor view. ⊠ *921 W. Pender St., V6C 1M2,* ☎ *604/681–4335,* FAX *604/681–7808. 74 rooms, 11 suites. Restaurant, 2 bars, in-room safes, billiards, coin laundry, free off-site parking. AE, D, DC, MC, V.*

$–$$ ☱ **River Run.** This unique bed-and-breakfast inn rests in the serene Fraser River delta in the village of Ladner, 30 minutes' drive south of downtown Vancouver and 10 minutes north of the ferries to Vancouver Island. You can choose among a little gem of a floating house; a room in the owner's larger floating home; a net loft (complete with Japanese soaking tub on the deck and a cozy captain's bed tucked away in the rafters); and a river's-edge cottage with a two-person whirlpool tub, full kitchen, fireplace, and deck. A canoe and a kayak are available to guests. Afternoon refreshments and breakfast are included in the tariff at this no-smoking inn. ⊠ *4551 River Rd. W, Ladner V4K 1R9,* ☎ *604/946–7778,* FAX *604/940–1970. 1 room, 3 suites. Kitchenettes, bicycles, free parking. MC, V.*

$ ☱ **Buchan Hotel.** This three-story 1930s building is conveniently set in a tree-lined residential street a block from Stanley Park. For the budget price, you rent tiny, institutional rooms with very basic furnishings, ceiling fans, and color TV, but no telephone or air-conditioning. There's also a TV lounge, a public telephone, and storage for bikes and skis. The pension-style rooms with shared bath down the hall are perhaps the most affordable accommodations in downtown. This is a no-smoking hotel. ⊠ *1906 Haro St., V6G 1H7,* ☎ *604/685–5354 or 800/668–6654,* FAX *604/685–5367. 60 rooms, 30 with bath. Coin laundry. AE, DC, MC, V.*

$ ☱ **Hostelling International Vancouver Downtown.** Vancouver's newest ★ hostel, conveniently located in the West End, is just blocks from Sunset Beach on English Bay, within walking distance of Stanley Park and a quick ferry ride to Granville Island. The hostel itself is tidy and secure; access to the wings of private rooms and the men's and women's dorms requires a card key. Amenities include a shared kitchen and dining room, a TV room, a garden patio and rooftop garden, a games room, and storage for luggage and bikes. The staff here is extremely friendly and informative, and the low price can't be beat. ⊠ *1114 Burnaby St., V6E 1P1,* ☎ *604/684–4565,* FAX *604/684–4540. 23 rooms, 7 with private bath; 224 dormitory beds. Dining room, no-smoking floors, bicycles, library, coin laundry.*

$ ☱ **The Kingston.** The Kingston is a small budget hotel convenient to shopping. It's an old-style, four-story building, with no elevator—the type of establishment you'd find in Europe. The spartan rooms are small and immaculate and share a bathroom down the hall. All rooms have phones and a few have TVs and private baths. Rooms on the south side are sunnier. The room rate includes a Continental breakfast. ⊠ *757 Richards St., V6B 3A6,* ☎ *604/684–9024,* FAX *604/684–9917. 56 rooms, 8 with bath. Sauna, coin laundry, free overnight parking (fee during day). AE, MC, V.*

$ ☱ **Sylvia Hotel.** To stay at the Sylvia Hotel from June through August you'll need to book six months to a year ahead. This older, ivy-covered hotel is popular because of its low rates and near-perfect location: about 25 ft from the beach on scenic English Bay, 200 ft from Stanley Park, and a 20-minute walk from Robson Street. The unadorned rooms have worn, plain furnishings. Suites are huge, and all have kitchens. ⊠ *1154 Gilford St., V6G 2P6,* ☎ *604/681–9321. 97 rooms, 18 suites. 2 restaurants, lounge, laundry service, dry cleaning. AE, DC, MC, V.*

$ ⚏ **YWCA Hotel/Residence.** A secured 12-story building in the heart of
★ the entertainment district, the YWCA has bright, airy, and very comfortable rooms. All have cheery floral bedspreads, white laminated night-
stands and desks, minirefrigerators, and phones. Some have sinks and
share a bath down the hall, others share adjacent baths, and still others
have private baths. The hotel is open to men and women and offers
discounts for senior citizens, students, and YWCA members. ✉ *733
Beatty St., V6B 2M4,* ☎ *604/895–5830, 800/663–1424 in British
Columbia and Alberta,* ⛶ *604/681–2550. 155 rooms, 30 with private bath. No-smoking floors, refrigerators, coin laundry, meeting
rooms. MC, V.*

NIGHTLIFE AND THE ARTS

For **information on events,** pick up a free copy of the *Georgia Straight*
(available at cafés and bookstores around town), or look in the entertainment section of the *Vancouver Sun* (Thursday's paper has listings in the "What's On" column). Call the **Arts Hotline** (☎ 604/
684–2787) for the latest lineups in entertainment. For tickets, book
through **Ticketmaster** (☎ 604/280–3311).

Nightlife

Bars and Lounges

DOWNTOWN

The **Bacchus Lounge** (✉ Wedgewood Hotel, 845 Hornby St., ☎ 604/
689–7777) is stylish and chic, with a pianist providing soothing background music. The **Garden Lounge** (✉ Four Seasons, 791 W. Georgia
St., ☎ 604/689–9333) is bright and airy with African flora and a waterfall, plus big soft chairs you won't want to get out of; a pianist plays
here on the weekends. The **Gérard Lounge** (✉ Sutton Place Hotel, 845
Burrard St., ☎ 604/682–5511), a major film-industry hangout, is
probably the nicest in the city because of its fireplaces, wing-back
chairs, dark wood, and leather. The sophisticated lobby bar at the **Hotel
Vancouver** (✉ 900 W. Georgia St., ☎ 604/684–3131) is the place to
see and be seen; musicians perform live in the evenings from 4 PM, and
55 wines are available by the glass.

One of the city's hot pool halls is the **Automotive Billiards Club** (✉ 1095
Homer St., ☎ 604/682–0040). For a lively atmosphere, try **Joe Fortes**
(✉ 777 Thurlow St., ☎ 604/669–1940), known in town as the local
meat market. The **Soho Café and Billiards** (✉ 1144 Homer St., ☎ 604/
688–1180) is the place to go to sip and shoot.

GRANVILLE ISLAND

The **Backstage Lounge** (✉ 1585 Johnston St., ☎ 604/687–1354), behind the main stage at the Arts Club Theatre and the hangout for local
and touring musicians and actors, stocks many Scotches. The after-work
crowd heads to **Bridges** (☎ 604/687–4400), near the Public Market
overlooking False Creek. **Pelican Bay** (✉ Granville Island Hotel, ☎
604/683–7373) is a somewhat upscale lounge.

Brew Pubs

The brewmasters at **Steam Works** (✉ 375 Water St., ☎ 604/689–2739)
on the edge of bustling Gastown use an age-old steam process and large
copper kettles (visible through glass walls in the dining room downstairs) to whip up six to nine brews; the espresso ale is interesting. The
Yaletown Brewing Company (✉ 1111 Mainland St., ☎ 604/681–
2739) is based in a huge renovated warehouse with a glassed-in brewery turning out eight tasty microbrews; it also has a darts and billiards
pub and a restaurant with an open-grill kitchen.

Casinos

Vancouver has a few casinos; proceeds go to local charities and arts groups. No alcohol is served. The **Great Canadian Casino** (⊠ Holiday Inn, 2477 Heather St., ☏ 604/872–5543) is in downtown Vancouver. The **Royal Diamond Casino** (⊠ 106B-750 Pacific Blvd. S, ☏ 604/685–2340) is in the Plaza of Nations Expo site downtown.

Comedy Clubs

The cheerful **Punchlines Comedy Theatre** (⊠ 15 Water St., ☏ 604/684–3015) is in Gastown. **Yuk Yuks** (⊠ 750 Pacific Blvd., ☏ 604/687–5233) is good for a few laughs.

Gay and Lesbian Nightlife

Celebrities (⊠ 1022 Davie St., ☏ 604/689–3180) is a multilevel space with dancing, billiards, and Wednesday-night drag shows.
Denman Station (⊠ 860 Denman St., ☏ 604/669–3448), a friendly and low-key pub, is patronized by gay men and lesbians.
Odyssey (⊠ 1251 Howe St., ☏ 604/689–5256) is one of Vancouver's most popular gay discos.

Music

DANCE CLUBS

Graceland (⊠ 1250 Richards St., ☏ 604/688–2648), featuring progressive European, North American, and tribal dance music, attracts a youngish dance crowd. The nitrogen fog screen, automated lighting, and go-go dancers at **Mars** (⊠ 1320 Richards St., ☏ 604/662–7707) get dancers into the swing of things. Dance clubs come and go, but lines still form every weekend at **Richard's on Richards** (⊠ 1036 Richards St., ☏ 604/687–6794) for live and taped dance tunes.

JAZZ

A jazz and blues hot line (☏ 604/682–0706) has information on concerts and clubs. Beatnik poetry readings would seem to fit right in at the **Chameleon Urban Lounge** (⊠ 801 W. Georgia St., ☏ 604/669–0806) in the basement of the Hotel Georgia, but it's the sophisticated mix of jazz, R&B, and Latin tunes that draws the crowds. The **Alma Street Café** (⊠ 2505 Alma St., ☏ 604/222–2244), a restaurant, is a traditional venue with good mainstream jazz; live performances have the spotlight Wednesday through Saturday. The **Glass Slipper** (⊠ 185 E. 11th Ave., ☏ 604/877–0066) presents jazz, from the mainstream to the contemporary, to a hushed crowd there to listen to the music. A Big Band dance sound carries into the night at **Hot Jazz** (⊠ 2120 Main St., ☏ 604/873–4131).

ROCK

The **Commodore Ballroom** (⊠ 870 Granville St., ☏ 604/681–7838), a Vancouver institution restored to its original art deco style, presents live musicians ranging from B.B. King to zydeco bands. Taped classic rock, plenty of music memorabilia, and specialty salads and sandwiches are dished up at Vancouver's edition of the **Hard Rock Cafe** (⊠ 686 W. Hastings St., ☏ 604/687–7625). **The Rage** (⊠ 750 Pacific Blvd. S, ☏ 604/685–5585) nightclub has alternative music and draws a young crowd. The **Town Pump** (⊠ 66 Water St., ☏ 604/683–6695) is the main venue for local and touring rock bands.

The Arts

Dance

Ballet British Columbia (☏ 604/732–5003) mounts productions and hosts out-of-town companies from September to April. Local modern dance companies worth seeing are Karen Jamison, Judith Marcuse, and JumpStart. Most performances by these companies can be seen at the

Queen Elizabeth Theatre (☞ Theater, *below*). Two other top dance venues are the Fireside Arts Centre (⊠ 280 E. Cordova, ☎ 604/689–0926) and the Vancouver East Cultural Centre (☞ Theater, *below*).

Film

For **foreign films and original works,** try the Park Theater (⊠ 3440 Cambie St., ☎ 604/876–2747), the Ridge Theatre (⊠ 3131 Arbutus St., ☎ 604/738–6311), and the Varsity Theater (⊠ 4375 W. 10th Ave., ☎ 604/222–2235). Tickets are half price on Tuesdays at all **Cineplex Odeon** theaters. **Pacific Cinématèque** (⊠ 1131 Howe St., ☎ 604/688–8202) shows esoteric foreign and art films. The **Vancouver International Film Festival** (☎ 604/685–0260) is held during September or October in several theaters around town.

Music

CHAMBER MUSIC AND SMALL ENSEMBLES

The **Early Music Society** (☎ 604/732–1610) performs medieval, Renaissance, and Baroque music throughout the year and hosts the Vancouver Early Music Summer Festival, one of the most important early music festivals in North America. Concerts by the **Friends of Chamber Music** (no phone) are worth watching for. Programs of the **Vancouver Recital Society** (☎ 604/736–6034) are always of excellent quality.

CHORAL GROUPS

Choral groups like the Bach Choir (☎ 604/921–8012), the Vancouver Cantata Singers (☎ 604/921–8588), and the Vancouver Chamber Choir (☎ 604/738–6822) play a major role in Vancouver's classical music scene.

ORCHESTRAS

The **CBC (Canadian Broadcasting Company) Orchestra** (☎ 604/662–6000) performs at the restored Orpheum Theatre. The **Vancouver Symphony Orchestra** (☎ 604/684–9100) is the resident company at the Orpheum.

Opera

Vancouver Opera (☎ 604/682–2871) stages five high-caliber productions a year, usually in October, November, February, March, and June, at the Queen Elizabeth Theatre (⊠ 600 Hamilton St.).

Theater

Arts Club Theatre (⊠ 1585 Johnston St., ☎ 604/687–1644) has two stages on Granville Island and theatrical performances all year.
Back Alley Theatre (⊠ 751 Thurlow St., ☎ 604/738–7013) hosts *Theatresports,* a hilarious improv event.
Bard on the Beach (☎ 604/739–0559) is a summer series of Shakespeare's plays performed under a huge tent on the beach at Vanier Park.
Carousel Theatre (☎ 604/669–3410) performs off-off-Broadway shows at the Waterfront Theatre (⊠ 1405 Anderson St.) on Granville Island.
Ford Centre for the Performing Arts (⊠ 777 Homer St., ☎ 604/844–2808) attracts major productions and top touring companies.
The Fringe (☎ 604/873–3646), Vancouver's annual, live theatrical arts festival, is staged in September at churches, dance studios, and theater halls around town.
Queen Elizabeth Theatre (⊠ 600 Hamilton St., ☎ 604/665–3050) is a major venue in Vancouver for traveling Broadway musicals as well as opera and other events.
Vancouver East Cultural Centre (⊠ 1895 Venables St., ☎ 604/254–9578) is a multipurpose performance space.
Vancouver Playhouse (⊠ 160 W. 1st St., ☎ 604/872–6622) is the leading venue in Vancouver for mainstream theatrical shows.

30%*
more
charming.

*(*depending on the exchange rate)*

Air Canada can't take credit for the very generous exchange rate on American currency. But, in all modesty, we do pride ourselves on getting a lot of other things right. *Like more nonstops* between the USA and Canada than any other airline. Not to mention convenient connections to our vast global network. We even offer you your choice of Mileage Plus®[1], OnePass®[2] or our own Aeroplan®[3] miles.

So to say that we are eager to please would be a remarkable understatement. However, this may help to explain why Americans polled by Business Traveler International Magazine declared Air Canada *The Best Airline to Canada.* For the fifth year in a row (wow, thanks guys). And why more people fly Air Canada from the USA to Canada than any other airline. Air Canada. We're like a regular airline, only nicer.

For more details, please call your travel agent or Air Canada at 1-800-776-3000. For great holiday packages, call **Air Canada's Canada at 1-800-774-8993 (ext. 8045).** And feel free to visit us on our Internet site at this address: http://www.aircanada.ca

[1]Mileage Plus is a registered trademark of United Airlines. [2]OnePass is a registered trademark of Continental Airlines. [3]Aeroplan is a registered trademark of Air Canada.

*The **nicer** way to fly.*

Pick up the phone.

Pick up the miles.

1-800-FLY-FREE

Is this a great time, or what? :-)

Now when you sign up with MCI you can receive up to 8,000 bonus frequent flyer miles on one of seven major airlines.

Then earn another 5 miles for every dollar you spend on a variety of MCI services, including MCI Card® calls from virtually anywhere in the world.*

You're going to use these services anyway. Why not rack up the miles while you're doing it?

OUTDOOR ACTIVITIES AND SPORTS

Beaches

An almost continuous string of beaches runs from Stanley Park to the University of British Columbia. The water is cool, but the beaches are sandy, edged by grass. Liquor is prohibited in parks and on beaches. For information, call the **Vancouver Board of Parks and Recreation** (☎ 604/257–8400).

Kitsilano Beach, over the Burrard Bridge from downtown, has a lifeguard and is the city's busiest—portable radios, volleyball games, and sleek young people are ever present. The part of the beach nearest the Maritime Museum is the quietest. Facilities include a playground, tennis courts, a heated saltwater pool, concession stands, and nearby restaurants and cafés.

The **Point Grey beaches** give you a number of different options. Jericho, Locarno, and Spanish Banks, which begin at the end of Point Grey Road, offer a huge expanse of sand, especially in summer and at low tide. The shallow water here, warmed slightly by sun and sand, is best for swimming. Farther out, toward Spanish Banks, you'll find the beach less crowded, but the last concession stand and rest rooms are at Locarno. If you keep walking along the beach just past Point Grey, you'll hit Wreck Beach, Vancouver's nude beach.

Among the **West End beaches,** Second Beach and Third Beach, along Beach Drive in Stanley Park, draw families. Second Beach has a guarded saltwater pool. Both have concession stands and rest rooms. The liveliest of the West End beaches is English Bay Beach, at the foot of Denman Street. A water slide, live music, a windsurfing outlet, and other concessions here stay jumping all summer long. Farther along Beach Drive, Sunset Beach, surprisingly quiet considering the location, has a lifeguard but no facilities.

Participant Sports

Biking

Stanley Park (☞ Stanley Park *in* Exploring Vancouver, *above*) is the most popular spot for family cycling. Rentals are available here from **Bayshore Bicycles** (⊠ 745 Denman St., ☎ 604/688–2453) or **Spokes Bicycle Rentals & Espresso Bar** (⊠ 1798 W. Georgia St., ☎ 604/688–5141).

A good summer biking route is along the North or South Shore of **False Creek.** For bikes, try **Granville Island Bike Rentals** (⊠ 1496 Cartwright, ☎ 604/669–2453) or **Granville Island Water Sports** (⊠ Charter Boat Dock, ☎ 604/662–7245).

Cycling British Columbia (⊠ 1367 W. Broadway, Suite 332, ☎ 604/737–3034) is the best source for bike route maps and biking guidebooks.

Boating

Several charter companies offer a cruise-and-learn vacation, usually to the Gulf Islands. **Sea Wing Sailing Group, Ltd.** (⊠ Granville Island, ☎ 604/669–0840) offers a five-day trip teaching the ins and outs of sailing. If you'd rather rent a speedboat to zip around the bay for a day, contact **Granville Island Boat Rentals** (☎ 604/682–6287).

Fishing

You can fish for salmon all year in coastal British Columbia. **Sewell's Marina Horseshoe Bay** (⊠ 6695 Nelson St., Horseshoe Bay, ☎ 604/

921–3474) organizes a daily four-hour trip on Howe Sound and has hourly rates on U-drives. **Bayshore Yacht Charters** (⊠ 1601 W. Georgia St., ☎ 604/691–6936) has fishing charters.

Golf

Lower Mainland golf courses are open all year. Spacious **Fraserview Golf Course** (⊠ 7800 Vivian St., ☎ 604/280–1818), an 18-hole municipal course, is under renovation until July 1998. Call for updated course information and fees. The 18-hole, par-72 course at **Furry Creek Golf and Country Club** (⊠ Hwy. 99, Furry Creek, ☎ 604/896–2224), north of Vancouver overlooking scenic Howe Sound, is challenging but forgiving. The greens fee ranges from $45 to $85 and includes a mandatory cart.

Northview Golf and Country Club (⊠ 6857 168th St., Surrey, ☎ 604/574–0324), easily accessible from Vancouver, has two Arnold Palmer–designed 18-hole courses (both par 72) and is the home of the Greater Vancouver Open. The greens fee for the Ridge course, where the PGA tour plays, ranges from $40 to $75, the fee for the Canal course from $30 to $55; an optional cart at either costs $28.50. **Peace Portal Golf Course** (⊠ 6900 4th Ave., South Surrey, ☎ 604/538–4818), near White Rock, a 45-minute drive from downtown, is a fine 18-hole, par-72 course. The greens fee ranges from $25 to $45; an optional cart costs $27. The 18-hole, par-72 course at **Westwood Golf and Country Club** in nearby Coquitlam (⊠ 3251 Plateau Blvd., ☎ 604/552–0777) was a runner-up in the "Best New Course in Canada" category in *Golf Digest*. The greens fee ranges from $60 to $100 and includes a cart. The course is closed in November.

Health and Fitness Clubs

The **YMCA** (⊠ 955 Burrard St., ☎ 604/681–0221) downtown has daily rates; facilities include pools and weight rooms, as well as racquetball, squash, and handball courts. The **YWCA** (⊠ 580 Burrard St., ☎ 604/662–8188) has drop-in rates that let you participate in all activities for the day; the facility has pools, weight rooms, and fitness classes. The **Bentall Centre Athletic Club** (⊠ 1055 Dunsmuir St., lower level, ☎ 604/689–4424) has racquetball and squash courts, weight rooms, and aerobics.

Hiking

Pacific Spirit Park (⊠ 4915 W. 16th Ave., ☎ 604/224–5739), more rugged than Stanley Park, has 61 km (38 mi) of trails, a few rest rooms, and a couple of signboard maps. Go for a wonderful walk in the West Coast arbutus and evergreen woods only 15 minutes from downtown Vancouver. The **Capilano Suspension Bridge and Park** (☞ Greater Vancouver *in* Exploring Vancouver, *above*), on the North Shore, provides a scenic hike.

Jogging

The seawall around **Stanley Park** (☞ Stanley Park *in* Exploring Vancouver, *above*) is 9 km (5½ mi) long and gives an excellent minitour of the city. You can take a shorter run of 4 km (2½ mi) in the park around Lost Lagoon. The **Running Room** (⊠ 1519 Robson St., ☎ 604/684–9771) is a good source for information on fun runs in the area.

Tennis

There are 180 free public courts around town; contact the **Vancouver Board of Parks and Recreation** (☎ 604/257–8400) for locations. **Stanley Park** has 15 well-surfaced outdoor courts near English Bay Beach; many of the other city parks have public courts as well.

Water Sports

KAYAKING

Rent a kayak from **Ecomarine Ocean Kayak Center** (⊠ 1668 Duran-leau St., ☎ 604/689–7575) on Granville Island to explore the waters of False Creek and the shoreline of English Bay.

WINDSURFING

Sailboards and lessons are available at **Windsure Windsurfing School** (⊠ Jericho Beach, ☎ 604/224–0615) and **Windmaster** (⊠ English Bay Beach, ☎ 604/685–7245). The winds aren't very heavy on English Bay, making it a perfect locale for learning the sport. You'll have to travel north to Squamish for more challenging high-wind conditions.

Spectator Sports

Vancouver's in-line roller-hockey team and professional basketball and hockey teams play at **General Motors Place** (⊠ 800 Griffith Way, ☎ 604/899–7400). **Ticketmaster** (☎ 604/280–4400) sells tickets to many local sports events.

Baseball

The **Canadians** (☎ 604/872–5232) of the AAA Pacific Coast League play in old-time Nat Bailey Stadium (⊠ 4601 Ontario St.), which has one of the few remaining manual scoreboards in Canada.

Basketball

The **Vancouver Grizzlies** (☎ 604/899–4666) of the National Basket-ball Association play at General Motors Place.

Football

The **B.C. Lions** (☎ 604/583–7747) of the Canadian Football League play at B.C. Place Stadium (⊠ 777 Pacific Blvd., ☎ 604/669–2300).

Hockey

The **Vancouver Canucks** (☎ 604/899–4600) of the National Hockey League play at General Motors Place.

In-Line Roller Hockey

New to Vancouver is an in-line roller hockey team, the **Vancouver Voodoo** (☎ 604/899–7400); they scrimmage June to August at General Mo-tors Place.

Soccer

The **Vancouver Eighty-Sixers** (☎ 604/273–0086) play soccer in Swan-gard Stadium (⊠ Central Park, Kingsway and Boundary St., Burnaby, ☎ 604/435–7121).

SHOPPING

Unlike many cities where suburban malls have taken over, Vancouver is full of individual boutiques and specialty shops. Antiques stores, eth-nic markets, art galleries, high-fashion outlets, and fine department stores dot the city. Store hours are generally from 9:30 to 6 on Monday, Tues-day, Wednesday, and Saturday, from 9:30 to 9 on Thursday and Fri-day, and from noon to 5 on Sunday.

Shopping Districts and Malls

Fourth Avenue, from Burrard to Balsam streets, has an eclectic mix of stores selling everything from sophisticated women's clothing to surf-boards. **Oakridge Shopping Centre** (⊠ 650 W. 41st Ave., at Cambie St., ☎ 604/261–2511) has chic, expensive stores that are fun to browse through. The immense **Pacific Centre Mall** (⊠ 550–750 W. Georgia St., ☎ 604/688–7236), on two levels and mostly underground, in the heart of downtown, connects the Eaton's and Bay department stores, which stand at opposite corners of Georgia and Granville streets. Stores around **Sinclair Centre** (⊠ 757 W. Hastings St., ☎ 604/666–4483) cater to sophisticated and upscale tastes. **Robson Street,** stretching from Burrard to Bute streets, is chockablock with small boutiques and cafés. Vancouver's liveliest street is not only for the fashion-conscious; it also provides many excellent corners for people-watching and attracts an array of street performers.

The huge **Vancouver Flea Market** (⊠ 703 Terminal Ave., ☎ 604/685–0666), with more than 360 stalls, is held weekends and holidays from 9 to 5. It is easily accessible from downtown on the SkyTrain, if you exit at the Main Street station.

Ethnic Districts
Chinatown—centered on Pender and Main streets—is an exciting, bustling place for restaurants, exotic foods, and distinctive architecture (☞ Chinatown and Gastown *in* Exploring Vancouver, *above*). Commercial Drive (around East 1st Avenue) is the heart of the Italian community, here called **Little Italy.** You can sip cappuccino in coffee bars where you may be the only one speaking English, or buy sun-dried tomatoes, real Parmesan, or an espresso machine. **Little India** is on Main Street around 50th Avenue. Curry houses, sweetshops, grocery stores, discount jewelry, and silk shops abound. A small **Japantown** on Powell Street at Dunlevy Street contains grocery stores, fish stores, and a few restaurants.

Department Stores

Among Vancouver's top department stores is Canadian-owned **Eaton's** (⊠ 701 Granville St., ☎ 604/685–7112), which carries everything: clothing, appliances, furniture, jewelry, accessories, and souvenirs. Many malls have branches. **Holt Renfrew** (⊠ 633 Granville St., ☎ 604/681–3121) is smaller, focusing on high fashion for men and women. You'll find this Canadian store in most malls as well.

Auction Houses

On Wednesday at noon and 7 PM, art and antiques auctions are held at **Love's** (⊠ 1635 W. Broadway, ☎ 604/733–1157). **Maynard's** (⊠ 415 W. 2nd Ave., ☎ 604/876–6787) auctions home furnishings on Wednesday at 7 PM.

Specialty Stores

Antiques
A stretch of antiques stores runs along Main Street from 19th to 35th avenues. **Folkart Interiors** (⊠ 3715 W. 10th Ave., ☎ 604/228–1011) specializes in whimsical British Columbia folk art and Western Canadian antiques. The **Vancouver Antique Center** (⊠ 422 Richards St., ☎ 604/681–3248) has two floors of antiques and collectibles dealers under one roof. For Oriental rugs, go to **Granville Street** between 7th and 14th avenues.

Art Galleries
There are many private galleries throughout Vancouver. **Buschlen/Mowatt** (⊠ 1445 W. Georgia St., No. 111, ☎ 604/682–1234), among the best in the city, is a showcase for Canadian and international artists. **Diane Farris** (⊠ 1565 W. 7th Ave., ☎ 604/737–2629; call first) often spotlights hot new artists. The **Inuit Gallery of Vancouver** (345 Water St., ☎ 604/688–7323) features an array of coastal native art.

Books

Bollum's Books (⊠ 710 Granville St., ☎ 604/689–1802) carries 250,000 books and CD-ROM titles, all nicely displayed and well lit, with several comfortable sitting areas, including a little café, for browsers. **Duthie's** (⊠ 919 Robson St., ☎ 604/684–4496; ⊠ Library Square, 205–345 Robson St., ☎ 604/602–0610), downtown and near the university, is a book lovers' favorite in Vancouver. **World Wide Books and Maps** (⊠ 736A Granville St., downstairs, ☎ 604/687–3320), one of several specialty bookstores in town, sells travel books and maps that cover the world.

Clothes

For unique women's clothing, try **Dorothy Grant** (⊠ 757 W. Hastings St., ☎ 604/681–0201), where traditional Haida native designs meld with modern fashion in a boutique that looks more like an art gallery than a store. Handmade Italian suits, cashmere, and leather for men are sold at stylish **E. A. Lee** (⊠ 466 Howe St., ☎ 604/683–2457); there are also a few women's items to browse through. **George Straith** (⊠ Hotel Vancouver, 900 W. Georgia St., ☎ 604/685–3301) carries traditional tailored designer fashions for men and women.

Ultrachic **Leone** (⊠ 757 W. Hastings St., ☎ 604/683–1133) carries designer collections. Trendy men's and women's casual wear by Ralph Lauren is available at the **Polo Store** (⊠ 375 Water St., ☎ 604/682–7656). At the architecturally stunning **Versus** (⊠ 1008 W. Georgia St., ☎ 604/688–8938) boutique, ladies and gents sip cappuccino as they browse through the designs of the late Gianni Versace. Buttoned-down businesswomen shop at **Wear Else?** (⊠ 789 W. Pender St., ☎ 604/662–7890).

Gifts

One of the best places in Vancouver for good-quality souvenirs (West Coast native art, books, music, jewelry, and so on) is the **Clamshell Gift Shop** (⊠ Vancouver Aquarium, ☎ 604/685–5911) in Stanley Park. **Hill's Indian Crafts** (⊠ 165 Water St., ☎ 604/685–4249), in Gastown, sells Haida, Inuit, and Salish native art. **Leona Lattimer's** (⊠ 1590 W. 2nd Ave., ☎ 604/732–4556) shop, near Granville Island and built like a longhouse, is full of native arts and crafts ranging from cheap to priceless. At the **Salmon Shop** (☎ 604/666–6477) in the Granville Island Public Market you can pick up smoked salmon wrapped for travel.

VANCOUVER A TO Z

Arriving and Departing

By Bus

Greyhound Lines (☎ 604/662–3222; 800/661–8747 in Canada; 800/231–2222 in the U.S.) is the largest bus line serving Vancouver. The Pacific Central Station (⊠ 1150 Station St.) is the depot. **Quick Shuttle** (☎ 604/244–3744; 800/665–2122 in the U.S.) bus service runs between Vancouver and Seattle five times a day in winter and up to eight times a day in summer. The depot is at 180 West Georgia Street.

By Car

Interstate 5 becomes **Highway 99** at the U.S.–Canada border. Vancouver is a three-hour drive (226 km/140 mi) from Seattle. It's best to avoid border crossings during peak times such as holidays and weekends. Highway 1, the **Trans-Canada Highway,** enters Vancouver from the east. To avoid traffic, arrive after rush hour (8:30 AM).

By Ferry

B.C. Ferries (☎ 250/386–3431; 888/223–3779 in British Columbia only) serves Vancouver, Victoria, and other cities in British Columbia. For more information about the system and other ferries that serve the area, *see* Ferry Travel *in* the Gold Guide.

By Plane

Vancouver International Airport (✉ Grant McConachie Way, ☎ 604/276–6101) is on Sea Island, about 14 km (9 mi) south of downtown on Highway 99. An airport improvement fee is assessed on all flight departures: $5 for flights within British Columbia, $10 for flights within Canada, and $15 for international flights. American, Continental, Delta, Horizon Air, Northwest, Reno, and United serve the airport. The two major domestic carriers are Air Canada and Canadian. *See* Air Travel *in* the Gold Guide for airline numbers.

Air B.C. (☎ 604/688–5515 or 800/776–3000) operates 30-minute harbor-to-harbor service (downtown Vancouver to downtown Victoria) several times a day. Planes leave from near the Westin Bayshore Hotel (✉ 1601 W. Georgia St.). **Helijet Airways** (☎ 604/682–1468) has helicopter service from downtown Vancouver to downtown Victoria. The heliport is near Vancouver's Pan Pacific Hotel (✉ 300–999 Canada Pl.).

BETWEEN THE AIRPORT AND DOWNTOWN

The drive from the airport to downtown takes 20 to 45 minutes, depending on the time of day. Airport hotels offer free shuttle service to and from the airport.

The **Vancouver Airporter Service** (☎ 604/244–9888) bus leaves the international and domestic arrivals levels of the terminal building approximately every half hour, stopping at major downtown hotels. It operates from 6 AM until midnight. The fare is $9 one-way and $15 round-trip.

Taxi stands are in front of the terminal building on domestic and international arrivals levels. The taxi fare to downtown is about $22. Area cab companies are **Yellow** (☎ 604/681–1111) and **Black Top** (☎ 604/681–2181).

Limousine service from **Airlimo** (☎ 604/273–1331) costs a bit more than the taxi fare to downtown: The current rate is about $30.

By Train

The **Pacific Central Station** (✉ 1150 Station St.) is the hub for rail, bus, and SkyTrain service. The **VIA Rail** (☎ 800/561–8630) station is at Main Street and Terminal Avenue. VIA provides transcontinental service through Jasper to Toronto three times a week. Passenger trains leave the **B.C. Rail** (☎ 604/631–3500) station in North Vancouver for Whistler and the interior of British Columbia. **Amtrak** (☎ 800/835–8725 in the U.S. or 800/872–7245 in B.C.) has one round-trip per day between Seattle and Vancouver.

Getting Around

By Bus

Exact change is needed to ride **B.C. Transit** (☎ 604/521–0400) buses: $1.50. Books of 25 tickets are sold at convenience stores and newsstands; look for a red, white, and blue "Fare Dealer" sign. Day passes, good for unlimited travel after 9:30 AM, cost $4.50 for adults. They are available from fare dealers and any SeaBus or SkyTrain station. Transfers are valid for 90 minutes and allow travel in both directions. Because of traffic and overcrowding, this mode can be time-consuming and uncomfortable; however, you can get just about anywhere you need to go in the city by bus.

By Car

Because no freeways cross Vancouver, rush-hour traffic still tends to be horrendous. The worst bottlenecks outside the city center are the North Shore bridges, the George Massey Tunnel on Highway 99 south of Vancouver, and Highway 1 through Coquitlam and Surrey. Parking downtown is expensive and tricky to find. Right turns are allowed on most red lights after you've come to a full stop.

By Ferry

The **SeaBus** is a 400-passenger commuter ferry that crosses Burrard Inlet from the foot of Lonsdale (North Vancouver) to downtown. The ride takes 13 minutes and costs the same as the transit bus (and it's much faster). With a transfer, connection can be made to any B.C. Transit bus or SkyTrain. **Aquabus Ferries** (☎ 604/689–5858) connect several stations on False Creek, including Science Center, Granville Island, Stamp's Landing, and the Hornby Street dock.

By Rapid Transit

Vancouver has a one-line, 25-km (16-mi) rapid transit system called **SkyTrain,** which travels underground downtown and is elevated for the rest of its route to New Westminster and Surrey. Trains leave about every five minutes. Tickets, sold at each station from machines (correct change is not necessary), must be carried with you as proof of payment. You may use transfers from SkyTrain to SeaBus (☞ *above*) and B.C. Transit buses and vice versa. The SkyTrain is convenient for transit between Gastown and Science World, but that's about it for points of interest.

By Taxi

It is difficult to hail a cab in Vancouver; unless you're near a hotel, you'd have better luck calling a taxi service. Try **Yellow** (☎ 604/681–1111) or **Black Top** (☎ 604/683–4567).

Contacts and Resources

B&B Reservation Agencies

A Home Away From Home (⊠ 1441 Howard Ave., V5B 3S2, ☎ 604/294–1760, ℻ 604/294–0799). **Best Canadian Bed and Breakfast Network** (⊠ 1090 W. King Edward Ave., V6H 1Z4, ☎ 604/738–7207). **Town & Country Bed and Breakfast** (⊠ 2803 W. 4th Ave., V6K 1K2, ☎ 604/731–5942).

Car Rental

Avis (☎ 604/606–2847 or 800/331–1212). **Budget** (☎ 604/668–7000; 800/527–0700 in the U.S.). **Thrifty Car Rental** (☎ 604/606–1666 or 800/367–2277).

Consulates

United States (⊠ 1075 W. Pender St., ☎ 604/685–4311). **United Kingdom** (⊠ 800–1111 Melville St., ☎ 604/683–4421).

Emergencies

Ambulance (☎ 911). **Fire** (☎ 911). **Police** (☎ 911).

Doctors are on call through the emergency ward at **St. Paul's Hospital** (⊠ 1081 Burrard St., ☎ 604/682–2344), a downtown facility open around the clock. **Medicentre** (⊠ 1055 Dunsmuir St., lower level, ☎ 604/683–8138), a drop-in clinic in the Bentall Centre, is open weekdays. Dentists are on call at **Dentacentre** (⊠ 1055 Dunsmuir St., lower level, ☎ 604/669–6700), which is next door and is also open weekdays.

Guided Tours

Tour prices fluctuate, so inquire about current rates when booking tours. Kids are generally charged half the adult fare.

AIR

Tour the mountains and fjords of the North Shore by helicopter for around $200 per person (minimum of three people) for 50 minutes: **Vancouver Helicopters** (☎ 604/270–1484) flies from the Harbour Heliport downtown. You can see Vancouver from the air for $70 for 30 minutes: **Harbour Air**'s (☎ 604/688–1277) seaplanes leave from beside the Westin Bayshore Hotel.

BOAT

Aquabus Ferries (✉ 1656 Duranleau St., ☎ 604/689–5858) runs a 25-minute City Skyline cruise departing from Hornby dock or Granville Island for $6. Their English Bay Cruise runs 50 minutes from Granville Island out into the bay, passing Siwash Rock and Stanley Park, and returning along the Kitsilano shoreline; the fare is $15.

Fraser River Connection (✉ 810 Quayside Dr., in the Information Centre at Westminster Quay, ☎ 604/525–4465) will take you on a seven-hour tour of a fascinating working river—past log booms, tugs, and houseboats. Between May and October ride from New Westminster to Fort Langley aboard a convincing replica of an 1800s-era paddle wheeler for less than $50.

Harbour Ferries (✉ 1 N. Denman St., ☎ 604/688–7246) has several worthwhile excursions, including one on the Royal Hudson, Canada's only functioning steam train, which heads along the mountainous coast up Howe Sound to the logging town of Squamish. After a break here, you sail back to Vancouver on the M.V. *Britannia*. The trip costs about $75 and takes 6½ hours; reservations are advised.

Harbour Ferries also operates a 1½-hour narrated tour of Burrard Inlet aboard the paddle wheeler M.V. *Constitution*; the tour operates from Wednesday to Sunday and costs less than $20. Sunset cruises are also available.

ECOLOGY

English Bay Sea Kayaking Company (☎ 604/898–4979) has guided half-day ($75) and sunset ($45) sea kayaking tours for a closer look at the inlets and bays of Vancouver's waterfront. **Lotus Land Tours** (☎ 604/684–4922) runs a six-hour sea-canoe (similar to but wider than a kayak) trip that visits Twin Island (an uninhabited provincial marine park) to explore the marine life that populates the area's intertidal zone; cost is $120 and includes a salmon barbecue lunch. A good operator with a number of interpretative day hikes around Vancouver is **Path of Logic Wilderness Adventures** (☎ 604/802–2082). Guided hikes (for $35 and up) through the rain forests and canyons surrounding Vancouver are available through **Rockwood Adventures** (☎ 604/926–7705). A unique way to see the heights of the city with an environmental focus is the Grouse Mountain downhill mountain biking trip offered by **Velo-City Cycle Tours** (☎ 604/924–0288).

Bluewater Adventures (☎ 604/980–3800) has a multiday natural history cruise to the Gulf Islands and Queen Charlotte Islands, including an Orca and Totems trip that visits long-abandoned Haida native villages to see the fallen totem poles slowly being reclaimed by the landscape. Call for pricing. **Nunatak Expeditions** (☎ 604/987–6727) offers three- to six-day guided sea kayaking trips to the islands and sounds in Canada's Inside Passage, including a fantastic six-day trip in Johnstone Strait in search of orca (killer whale) encounters. The fees range from $350 to $850. **Wild West Adventures** (☎ 604/688–2008) has a weekend camping tour to Mayne Island that incorporates interpretative hikes, sea kayaking around the island, and wildlife watching (seals, otters, eagles, and more); the cost is $200. The company also schedules whale-watching trips to Tofino, using Zodiac boats to explore Clayquote Sound and seek out migrating gray whales each spring; the cost is $210.

ORIENTATION

Gray Line (☎ 604/879–3363) conducts a 3½-hour Grand City bus tour year-round. Departing from the Sandman Inn in winter and the Plaza of Nations in summer, the tour includes Stanley Park, Chinatown, Gastown, English Bay, and Queen Elizabeth Park and costs about $31. Between June and September, Gray Line has a narrated city tour aboard double-decker buses; passengers can get on and off as they choose and are allowed to ride free the following day if they haven't had their fill. The adult fare is about $20. Using minibuses departing from downtown hotels and transit stations, **Vance Tours** (☎ 604/941–5660) has a highlights tour (3½ hours, $33) that includes a visit to the University of British Columbia and a shorter city tour (2½ hours, $30, hotel pickup included).

The **Vancouver Trolley Company** (☎ 604/451–5581) runs turn-of-the-century-style trolleys through Vancouver from April through October on a two-hour narrated tour of Stanley Park, Gastown, English Bay, Granville Island, and Chinatown, among other sights. A day pass allows you to complete one full circuit, getting off and on as often as you like. Start the trip at any of the sights and buy a ticket on board. The adult fare is less than $20. During the rest of the year, the trolley runs the same circuit on a 2½-hour trip, but no on-off option is available. During spring, summer, and fall, **Westcoast City and Nature Sightseeing** (☎ 604/451–1600) accommodates up to 31 people in vans that run a 3½-hour city-highlights tour for about $30 (pickup available from all major hotels downtown).

North Shore tours usually include any or several of the following: a gondola ride up Grouse Mountain, a walk across the Capilano Suspension Bridge, a stop at a salmon hatchery, a visit to the Lonsdale Quay Market, and a ride back to town on the SeaBus. Half-day tours cost between $45 and $55 and are offered by Landsea Tours (☎ 604/255–7272), Harbour Ferries (☎ 604/688–7246), Gray Line (☎ 604/879–3363), and Pacific Coach Lines (☎ 604/662–7575).

PERSONAL GUIDES

Early Motion Tours (☎ 604/687–5088) will pick you up at your hotel for a tour of Vancouver in a Model-A Ford convertible. For about $70 or $80, up to four people can take an hour-long trip around downtown, Chinatown, and Stanley Park; longer tours can also be arranged. **AAA Horse & Carriage** (☎ 604/681–5115) has a one-hour tour of Stanley Park, along the waterfront and through a cedar forest and a rose garden. The cost is $10 per person ($30 for a family of four); the tour departs from the information booth near the zoo. Individualized tours are available from **VIP Tourguide Services,** run by Marcel Jonker (☎ 604/214–4677).

WALKING

The **Gastown Business Improvement Society** (✉ 12 Water St., ☎ 604/683–5650) sponsors free 90-minute historical and architectural walking tours daily from June to August. Meet the guide at 2 PM at the statue of Gassy Jack in Maple Tree Square.

Late-Night Pharmacy
Shopper's Drug Mart (⊠ 1125 Davie St., ☎ 604/669–2424) is open around the clock.

Road Emergencies
BCAA (☎ 604/293–2222) has 24-hour emergency road service for members of AAA or CAA.

Travel Agencies
American Express Travel Service (⊠ 666 Burrard St., ☎ 604/669–2813). **Mirage Holidays** (⊠ 14–200 Burrard St., ☎ 604/685–4008). **P. Lawson Travel** (⊠ 409 Granville St., Suite 150, ☎ 604/682–4272).

Visitor Information
Super, Natural B.C. (☎ 800/663–6000). **Vancouver Tourist Info Centre** (⊠ 200 Burrard St., V6C 3L6, ☎ 604/683–2000, FAX 604/682–6839).

7 British Columbia

Lush inland valleys and Pacific beaches, rugged mountains and forested islands: In this western province you'll find an abundance of outdoor beauty and action. There are plenty of opportunities for whale- and nature-watching, as well as year-round skiing and superb fishing and kayaking. And whether your visit takes you to the Anglophile city of Victoria, small coastal and island towns, or the re-created native village of 'Ksan, you'll encounter the diversity of the area's residents.

Updated by
Melissa Rivers

BRITISH COLUMBIA, CANADA'S WESTERNMOST province, occupies almost 10% of Canada's total surface area, stretching from the Pacific Ocean eastward to the province of Alberta, and from the U.S. border north to the Yukon and Northwest Territories. It spans more than 360,000 square mi, making it larger than every American state except Alaska.

British Columbia's appeal as a vacation destination stems from its status as the most spectacular part of the nation, with salmon-rich waters, coastal scenery, and stretches of snowcapped peaks. The region's natural splendor has ironically become the source of conflict. For more than a century, logging companies have depended on the abundant supply of British Columbia timber, and whole towns are still centered on the industry. Environmentalists and many residents now see the logging industry as a threat to the natural surroundings. Compromises have been achieved in recent years, but the issue is far from resolved.

The province used to be very British and predictable, reflecting its colonial heritage; but no longer. Vancouver (☞ Chapter 6) is an international city whose relaxed lifestyle is spiced by a rich and varied cultural scene embracing large Chinese, Japanese, Italian, and Greek communities. Even Vancouver Island's Victoria, which clings with restrained passion to British traditions and lifestyles, has undergone an international metamorphosis in recent years.

But no matter how modern the province may appear, evidence remains of the earliest settlers: Pacific Coast natives (Haida, Kwakiutl, Nootka, Salish, and others) who occupied the land for more than 12,000 years before the first Europeans arrived en masse in the late 19th century. Today's native residents often face social barriers that have kept them from the mainstream of British Columbia's economy. Although some have gained university educations and have fashioned careers, many are just beginning to make demands on the nonnative population. In dispute are thousands of square miles of land claimed as aboriginal territory, some of which is within such major cities as Vancouver, Prince George, and Prince Rupert. Although the issue of ownership remains undecided, British Columbia's native roots show throughout the province in the wood-carved objects and etched-silver jewelry found in small-town boutiques and in the traditional culinary delights served by big-city dining establishments.

Pleasures and Pastimes

Dining
As is true elsewhere in the Pacific Northwest, you'll find a range of cuisines based on local seafood, herbs, produce, and wild game. Restaurants are generally casual in the region.

CATEGORY	COST*
$$$$	over C$35
$$$	C$25–C$35
$$	C$15–C$25
$	under C$15

per person for a three-course meal, excluding drinks, service, and 7% Goods & Services Tax (GST)

Lodging
Accommodations across the province range from bed-and-breakfasts and rustic cabins to deluxe chain hotels. In the cities you'll find an abun-

dance of lodgings, but once you get off the beaten path, guest rooms are often a rare commodity and usually require advance booking.

CATEGORY	COST*
$$$$	over C$180
$$$	C$110–C$180
$$	C$70–C$110
$	under C$70

All prices are for a standard double room, excluding 10% provincial accommodation tax, service charge, and 7% GST.

Outdoor Activities and Sports

CANOEING AND KAYAKING

The Inside Passage, Queen Charlotte Strait, the Strait of Georgia, and the other island-dotted straits and sounds that border the mainland provide fairly protected transit from Washington State to the Alaskan border, with numerous marine parks to explore along the way. Another favorite among paddlers is the Powell Forest Canoe Route, a 60-km (37-mi) circuit of 12 lakes connected by streams, rivers, and well-maintained portage trails along the Powell River.

FISHING

Miles of coastline and thousands of lakes, rivers, and streams bring more than 750,000 fishermen to British Columbia each year. The waters of the province hold 74 species of fish, including Chinook salmon and rainbow trout.

HIKING

Virtually all of British Columbia's provincial parks have fine hiking-trail networks. Heli-hiking is popular here; helicopters deliver hikers to high alpine meadows and untouched mountaintops.

SKIING

British Columbia has hundreds of kilometers of groomed cross-country (Nordic) ski trails in the provincial parks and more than 40 cross-country resorts. Most downhill destinations have carved out cross-country routes along the valleys, and there are thousands more trails in unmanaged areas of British Columbia.

WHALE-WATCHING

Three resident and several transient pods of orca whales travel in the waters around Vancouver Island and are the primary focus of charter boat tours that depart from Victoria between May and October. June and July are the best months to see the whales—harbor seal, sea lion, porpoise, and marine bird sightings are likely anytime.

Exploring British Columbia

When you travel by car, keep in mind that more than three quarters of British Columbia is mountainous terrain. Trips that appear relatively short on a map may take longer, especially in the northern regions and along the coast, where roads are often narrow and winding. In certain areas—most of the uninhabited west coast of Vancouver Island, for example—roads do not exist.

Vancouver Island, surrounded by Pacific waters, has relatively mild winters and summers (usually above 32°F winter, below 80°F summer), although winter brings frequent rains. Likewise, the northern coast around Prince Rupert and the Queen Charlotte Islands has wet winter months and few extremes in temperature. As you move inland, especially toward the Peace River region in the north, the climate becomes much colder. In the southern interior, the Okanagan Valley is arid, with temperatures dropping below freezing in winter and sometimes reaching 90°F in summer.

Numbers in the text correspond to numbers in the margin and on the Southern British Columbia, Downtown Victoria, and Vancouver Island maps.

Great Itineraries

IF YOU HAVE 3-4 DAYS

Begin in ⚏ **Victoria** ①–⑬. Spend one day downtown and another exploring Butchart Gardens and other outlying attractions. On day three, head out to ⚏ **Sooke** ⑭ or one of the Gulf Islands— ⚏ **Galiano** ㉜, ⚏ **Mayne** ㉝, or ⚏ **Saltspring** ㉞—to stay at a romantic country inn for a night.

Another three-day option would be to fly to ⚏ **Prince Rupert** ㊱ to tour the region north of Vancouver Island, including the abandoned Haida villages of the ⚏ **Queen Charlotte Islands** ㊲ for a day or so before spending a day aboard a ferry cruising the breathtaking **Inside Passage** ㉟ on the way to **Port Hardy** ㉚ on Vancouver Island, and taking a plane home from there.

IF YOU HAVE 7-10 DAYS

Begin in ⚏ **Victoria** ①–⑬. Spend one day downtown and another exploring Butchart Gardens and other outlying attractions. On day three, head out to ⚏ **Sooke** ⑭. On day four, visit the Native Heritage Centre in **Duncan** ⑮, the murals of **Chemainus** ⑯, and the petroglyphs in ⚏ **Nanaimo** ⑰. On day five, head west to ⚏ **Tofino** ㉒ and ⚏ **Ucluelet** ㉑ and spend some time whale-watching or hiking around **Pacific Rim National Park** ㉓. Stay overnight in Tofino or Ucluelet. Spend day six backtracking to **Victoria** or making your way to **Nanaimo** to catch the ferry to ⚏ **Vancouver** and the mainland. On day seven, drive through the rolling lowlands of southwestern British Columbia to ⚏ **Harrison Hot Springs** ㊹ for some deep relaxation in the natural springs. Points of interest in the vicinity include Hell's Gate on the Fraser River, Minter Gardens, and the Kilby Historic Store and Farm. Days eight through ten are best spent making the loop through the Okanagan Valley, the fruit-growing capital of the province. You can make stops in ⚏ **Penticton** ㊸ to see the Kettle Valley Steam Railway and Cathedral Provincial Park, ⚏ **Kelowna** ㊷ to tour the vineyards, ⚏ **Vernon** ㊶ for the O'Keefe Historic Ranch, and ⚏ **Kamloops** ㊵ to fish in one of the many lakes or visit the wildlife preserves. Stop for the night in any of these towns.

When to Tour British Columbia

Victoria is at its peak each year from late spring to early fall; book rooms well in advance if you plan to visit from June through August. Summer and fall are the best seasons to tour the islands of the province. Vancouver Island is busy during summer and fall. High Country and the Okanagan Valley have year-round appeal: Winter brings snow for downhill and cross-country skiing, spring is filled with blossoms on fruit trees, and summer has warm, dry temperatures conducive to all the outdoor activities. In fall, pears, apples, and other produce are readily available, harvest festivals are frequent, and the turning leaves add their color.

VICTORIA

Victoria was the first European settlement on Vancouver Island. Originally known as Fort Victoria, it's the oldest city on Canada's west coast. James Douglas chose it in 1843 to be the Hudson's Bay Company's westernmost outpost; it became the capital of British Columbia in

1868. The city is 71 km (44 mi) south of Vancouver and a 2½-hour ferry ride from Seattle.

Exploring Victoria

Numbers in the text correspond to numbers in the margin and on the Downtown Victoria map.

A Good Walk

Begin on the waterfront at the **Visitors Information Centre** ①. Across the way on Government Street is the majestic **Empress Hotel** ②. A short walk south on Government Street will bring you to the **Parliament Buildings** ③ complex on Belleville Street. Follow Belleville one block east to reach the **Royal British Columbia Museum** ④, where you can explore thousands of years of history. Behind the museum and bordering Douglas Street is Thunderbird Park, where totem poles and a ceremonial longhouse stand in one corner of the garden of the **Helmcken House** ⑤. A walk east on Superior Street to Douglas Street leads to **Beacon Hill Park** ⑥. From the park, go north on Douglas Street and stop at the glass-roof **Crystal Gardens Conservatory** ⑦.

From Crystal Gardens, continue north on Douglas Street to View Street, then west to **Bastion Square** ⑧, with its gas lamps, restaurants, cobblestone streets, and small shops. While you're here, you can stop in at the **Maritime Museum of British Columbia** ⑨ and learn about an important part of the province's history. West of Government Street, between Pandora Avenue and Johnson Street, is the **Market Square** ⑩ shopping district. Around the corner from Market Square is Fisgard Street, the heart of **Chinatown** ⑪. A 15-minute walk or a short drive east on Fort Street will take you to Joan Crescent and lavish **Craigdarroch Castle** ⑫ and the **Art Gallery of Greater Victoria** ⑬.

TIMING

Many of the sights are within easy walking distance of one another and could be covered in half a day, but there's so much to see at the Royal British Columbia Museum and the other museums that you should plan on a full day downtown. This will allow time for some shopping and a visit to Craigdarroch Castle.

Sights to See

C **Anne Hathaway's Cottage.** A full-size replica of Shakespeare's wife's thatched home in Stratford-upon-Avon, England, is part of the English Village, a complex with re-created period buildings. The 16th-century antiques inside are typical of Shakespeare's era. The Olde England Inn here is a pleasant spot for tea or an English-style meal, and you can also stay in one of the 50 antiques-furnished rooms. Guided tours leave from the inn in winter and the cottage in summer. The village is touristy but appeals to many people. From downtown Victoria, you can take the Munro bus to the cottage. ⊠ *429 Lampson St.,* ☎ *250/388–4353.* ⊡ *$6.50.* ⊗ *June–Sept., daily 9–8; Oct.–May, daily 10–4.*

⑬ **Art Gallery of Greater Victoria.** This fine museum houses large collections of Chinese and Japanese ceramics and contains the only authentic Shinto shrine in North America. A permanent exhibit of British Columbia native Emily Carr's work is on display. The gallery is a few blocks west of Craigdarroch Castle, off Fort Street. ⊠ *1040 Moss St.,* ☎ *250/384–4101.* ⊡ *$5; Mon. by donation.* ⊗ *Mon.–Wed. and Fri.–Sat. 10–5, Thurs. 10–9, Sun. 1–5.*

⑧ **Bastion Square.** James Douglas chose this spot for the original Fort Victoria and Hudson's Bay Company trading post. Fashion boutiques and restaurants occupy the old buildings, and the cobblestone streets

Southern British Columbia

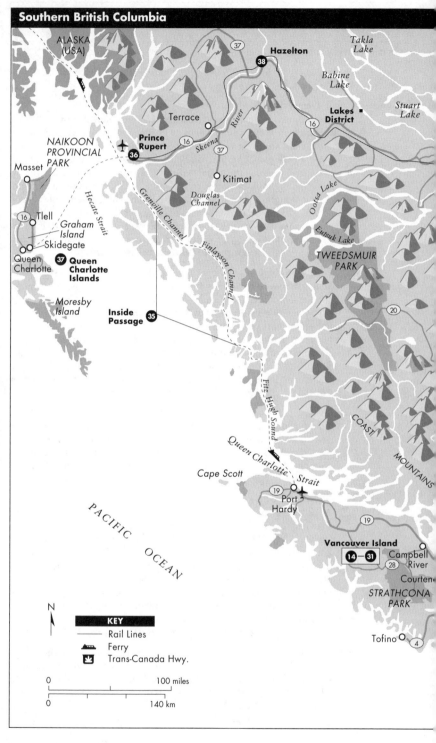

ALASKA
(USA)

37

Hazelton

38

Takla Lake

Babine Lake

Terrace

River

Lakes District ▪

Stuart Lake

NAIKOON PROVINCIAL PARK

Prince Rupert

36

Skeena

16

37

16

Masset

Heçate Strait

Grenville Channel

Douglas Channel

Kitimat

Oosta Lake

16

Tlell

Graham Island

Skidegate

Queen Charlotte

37

Queen Charlotte Islands

Eutsuk Lake

Finlayson Channel

TWEEDSMUIR PARK

Moresby Island

Inside Passage

35

20

Fitz Hugh Sound

Queen Charlotte

Cape Scott

Strait

19

Port Hardy

COAST

MOUNTAINS

PACIFIC OCEAN

19

Vancouver Island

14 — 31

Campbell River

28

Courtene

STRATHCONA PARK

Tofino

4

N

KEY
—— Rail Lines
⚓ Ferry
Trans-Canada Hwy.

0   100 miles

0   140 km

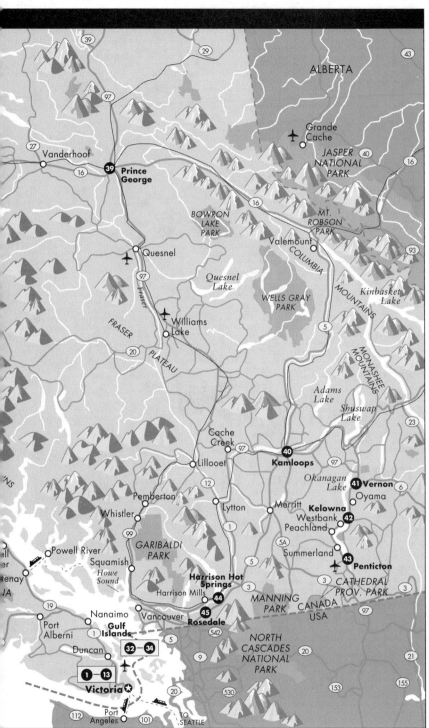

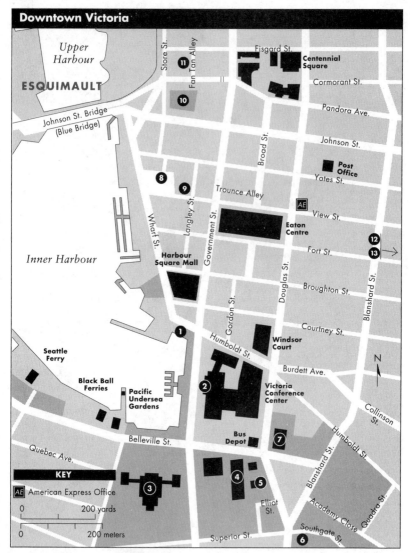

Downtown Victoria

Upper Harbour

ESQUIMAULT

Johnson St. Bridge
(Blue Bridge)

Store St.

Fan Tan Alley

Fisgard St.

Centennial Square

Cormorant St.

Pandora Ave.

Johnson St.

Broad St.

Post Office

Yates St.

Trounce Alley

View St.

Langley St.

Wharf St.

Harbour Square Mall

Government St.

Eaton Centre

Fort St.

Inner Harbour

Gordon St.

Douglas St.

Broughton St.

Blanshard St.

Humboldt St.

Courtney St.

Windsor Court

Burdett Ave.

Seattle Ferry

Black Ball Ferries

Pacific Undersea Gardens

Victoria Conference Center

N

Collinson St.

Belleville St.

Bus Depot

Humboldt St.

Quebec Ave.

KEY

AE American Express Office

0   200 yards

0   200 meters

Blanshard St.

Academy Close

Quadra St.

Elliot St.

Southgate St.

Superior St.

Art Gallery of Greater Victoria, **13**

Bastion Square, **8**

Beacon Hill Park, **6**

Chinatown, **11**

Craigdarroch Castle, **12**

Crystal Gardens Conservatory, **7**

Empress Hotel, **2**

Helmcken House, **5**

Maritime Museum of British Columbia, **9**

Market Square, **10**

Parliament Buildings, **3**

Royal British Columbia Museum, **4**

Visitors Information Centre, **1**

are lighted by gas lamps. ⊠ *Bordered by Yates, Wharf, Government, and Fort Sts.*

❻ Beacon Hill Park. The southern lawns of this spacious park have great views of the Olympic Mountains and the Strait of Juan de Fuca. Also here are lakes, jogging and walking paths, abundant flowers and gardens, a wading pool, a petting zoo, and an outdoor amphitheater for Sunday afternoon concerts. ⊠ *East of Douglas St.*

OFF THE
BEATEN PATH

BUTCHART GARDENS – More than 700 varieties of flowers grow in this impressive site that contains Italian, Japanese, and English rose gardens. In summer, many of the exhibits are illuminated at night, and fireworks light the sky over the gardens on Saturday night. Also on the premises are a teahouse and restaurants. ⊠ *800 Benvenuto Ave., 21 km (13 mi) north of downtown Victoria (take Hwy. 17A from downtown), Brentwood Bay,* ☎ *250/652–5256 or 250/652–4422.* 🎟 *$14.50, discounts in winter.* ☺ *Call for seasonal hrs.*

⓫ Chinatown. The Chinese were responsible for building much of the Canadian Pacific Railway in the 19th century, and their influence still marks the region. If you enter Chinatown (one of the oldest in Canada) from Government Street, you'll walk under the elaborate **Gate of Harmonious Interest,** made from Taiwanese ceramic tiles and decorative panels. Along the street, merchants display paper lanterns, embroidered silks, imported fruits, and vegetables. Narrow **Fan Tan Alley,** off Fisgard Street, was the gambling and opium center of Chinatown.

★ **⓬ Craigdarroch Castle.** This lavish mansion was built as the home of British Columbia's first millionaire, Robert Dunsmuir, who oversaw coal mining for the Hudson's Bay Company. He died in 1889, just a few months before the castle's completion. Converted into a museum depicting turn-of-the-century life, the castle has elaborately framed landscape paintings, stained-glass windows, carved woodwork—precut in Chicago for Dunsmuir and sent by rail—and rooms for billiards and smoking. There's a wonderful view of downtown Victoria from the fourth-floor tower. ⊠ *1050 Joan Crescent, off Fort St.,* ☎ *250/592–5323.* 🎟 *$6.50.* ☺ *Mid-June–mid-Sept., daily 9–7:30; mid-Sept.–mid-June, daily 10–4:30.*

❼ Crystal Gardens Conservatory. Opened in 1925 as the largest saltwater swimming pool in the British Empire, this glass-roof building—owned by the provincial government—houses flamingos, macaws, 75 varieties of other tropical birds, monkeys, and hundreds of blooming flowers. At street level there are several boutiques and the popular Rattenbury's Restaurant. ⊠ *713 Douglas St.,* ☎ *250/381–1213.* 🎟 *$7.* ☺ *Dec.–Apr., daily 10–4:30; May–Aug., daily 8–8; Sept.–Nov., daily 9–6.*

❷ Empress Hotel. The Empress (☞ Lodging, *below*) is a symbol of both the city and the Canadian Pacific Railway. Designed by Francis Rattenbury, whose works dot Victoria, the 1908 property is another of the great châteaus built by Canadian Pacific, still the owners. Stop in for high tea, served at hour-and-a-half intervals during the afternoon (no jeans, shorts, or T-shirts are permitted in the tea lobby). ⊠ *721 Government St.,* ☎ *250/384–8111.*

★ **❺ Helmcken House.** The oldest house in British Columbia was built in 1852 by pioneer doctor and statesman John Sebastian Helmcken. The holdings here include early Victorian furnishings and an intriguing collection of 19th-century medical tools. Audio tours last 20 minutes. **Thunderbird Park,** with totem poles and a ceremonial longhouse constructed by Kwakiutl chief Mungo Martin, occupies one corner of the house's garden. ⊠ *10 Elliot St.,* ☎ *250/361–0021.* 🎫 *$4.* ☉ *May–Sept., daily 10–5; call for winter hrs.*

❾ Maritime Museum of British Columbia. The dugout canoes, model ships, Royal Navy charts, photographs, uniforms, and ship's bells at this museum inside Victoria's original courthouse chronicle the city's seafaring history. A seldom-used 100-year-old cage lift, believed to be the oldest in North America, ascends to the third floor. ⊠ *28 Bastion Sq.,* ☎ *250/385–4222.* 🎫 *$5.* ☉ *Daily 9:30–4:30.*

❿ Market Square. The many specialty shops and boutiques here are enhanced by the historic setting. At the end of the 19th century this area, once part of Chinatown, provided everything a visitor desired: food, lodging, entertainment. ⊠ *West of Government St., between Pandora Ave. and Johnson St.*

★ **❸ Parliament Buildings.** These massive stone structures, completed in 1897, dominate the Inner Harbour. Two statues flank them, one of Sir James Douglas, who chose the site where Victoria was built, the other of Sir Matthew Baille Begbie, the man in charge of law and order during the gold-rush era. Atop the central dome is a gilded statue of Captain George Vancouver, the first European to sail around Vancouver Island. A statue of Queen Victoria reigns over the front of the complex; more than 3,000 lights outline the buildings at night. Another of Francis Rattenbury's creations, the Parliament Buildings typify the rigid symmetry and European elegance of much of the city's architecture. ⊠ *501 Belleville St.,* ☎ *250/387–3046.* 🎫 *Free.* ☉ *Sept.–May, weekdays 8:30–5; June–Aug., daily 9–5.*

★ ☙ **❹ Royal British Columbia Museum.** At what is easily the best attraction in Victoria, you can spend hours wandering through the centuries, back 12,000 years. In the prehistoric exhibit, you can actually smell the pines and hear the calls of mammoths and other ancient wildlife. Or you can explore a turn-of-the-century town, with trains rumbling past. The smell of cedar envelops the Kwakiutl longhouse, while piped-in potlatch songs relate the origins of the genuine ceremonial house before you. The museum also has fine interpretative displays of native artifacts, including an impressive collection of masks. ⊠ *675 Belleville St.,* ☎ *250/387–3014.* 🎫 *$7.* ☉ *Sept.–June, daily 10–5:30; July–Aug., daily 9:30–7.*

❶ Visitors Information Centre. A convenient waterfront location adds to the center's appeal. The bridge immediately to the south has a grand view of the Inner Harbour and, across the water on Songhees Point, the 182½-ft **Welcome Totem,** which was erected in 1994 for the Commonwealth Games. ⊠ *812 Wharf St.,* ☎ *250/953–2033.* ☉ *July–Aug., Mon.–Sat. 9–9, Sun. 9–7; May–June and Sept., daily 9–7; Oct.–Apr., daily 9–5.*

Dining

$$ ✕ **Don Mee's.** A large neon sign invites you inside this traditional Chinese restaurant. Szechuan and Cantonese entrées include sweet-and-sour chicken, almond duck, and bean curd with broccoli. Dim sum is served daily during lunch hours. ⊠ *538 Fisgard St.,* ☎ *250/383–1032. AE, DC, MC, V.*

$$$ ✕ **Chez Daniel.** One of Victoria's old standbys, Chez Daniel serves rich French dishes, though the nouvelle influence has found its way into some creations. The award-winning wine list is varied, and the menu has a wide selection of basic dishes, including rabbit, salmon, duck, and steak. The romantic atmosphere here encourages you to linger. ⊠ *2524 Estevan Ave.,* ☎ *250/592–7424. Reservations essential. AE, MC, V. Closed Sun.–Mon. No lunch.*

GREEK

$ ✕ **Periklis.** You can order standard Greek cuisine in this warm, taverna-style restaurant, but steaks and ribs are also on the menu. The dolmas and baklava are especially good. At night there's Greek dancing and belly dancing. ⊠ *531 Yates St.,* ☎ *250/386–3313. Reservations essential. AE, MC, V. No lunch weekends.*

ITALIAN

$$ ✕ **Il Terrazzo.** The locals' choice for romantic alfresco dining prepares
★ baked garlic served with warm *cambozola* cheese and focaccia; scallops dipped in roasted pistachios and garnished with arugula, Belgian endive, and mango salsa; grilled lamb chops on angel-hair pasta with tomatoes, garlic, mint, and black pepper; and other hearty northern Italian dishes, all piping hot from the restaurant's authentic wood oven. ⊠ *555 Johnson St., off Waddington Alley (call for directions),* ☎ *250/361–0028. Reservations essential. AE, MC, V.*

$$ ✕ **Pagliacci's.** Quiches, veal, and chicken in marsala sauce with fettuccine are among the standout dishes served at this fine trattoria where the pastas are all made in-house. You'll dine surrounded by orange walls covered with photos of Hollywood movie stars. Save room for the cheesecake. ⊠ *1011 Broad St.,* ☎ *250/386–1662. Reservations not accepted. AE, MC, V.*

JAPANESE

$$ ✕ **Tomoe.** A long sushi bar, a few tatami rooms, and tables set comfortably apart are the elements of this low-key restaurant. Choose from satisfying seafood dishes (watch for the occasional exotic offering flown in from Japan) as well as standards such as tempura and teriyaki. ⊠ *726 Johnson St.,* ☎ *250/381–0223. AE, MC, V. Closed Sun.*

MEXICAN

$ ✕ **Cafe Mexico.** Hearty portions of Mexican food, such as *pollo chipotle* (grilled chicken with melted cheddar and spicy sauce on a bed of rice), are served at a redbrick dining establishment just off the waterfront. ⊠ *1425 Store St.,* ☎ *250/386–5454. AE, DC, MC, V.*

PACIFIC NORTHWEST

$$$–$$$$ ✕ **Empress Room.** For a special-occasion dinner, reserve a fireside table here. Beautifully presented Pacific Northwest cuisine vies for attention with the setting when candlelight dances on the tapestried walls beneath an intricately carved mahogany ceiling. Fresh local ingredients go into seasonal dishes such as house-cured Pacific salmon with wild blackberry-ginger butter, pan-roasted Arctic char with wild-rice polenta and gooseberry chutney, or peppered Vancouver Island venison with a black-currant sauce. ⊠ *Empress Hotel, 721 Government St.,* ☎ *250/381–8111. Reservations essential. AE, D, DC, MC, V. No lunch.*

$$ ✕ **Camille's.** Smoked Gruyère cheese and carrot cake (an appetizer), roast loin of venison with wild mushroom polenta, and grainy Dijon-and-mint-crusted lamb with a blackberry port reduction are among the specialties of this intimate restaurant. Camille's has an extensive wine cellar; wine tasting dinners are offered once each week. ⊠ *45 Bastion Sq.,* ☎ *250/381–3433. Reservations essential. AE, MC, V. No lunch.*

SEAFOOD

$$-$$$ ✕ **Marina Restaurant.** This round restaurant overlooking the Oak Bay
   ★   Marina is so popular with locals that it's always crowded and a bit
        noisy. The best bets on the imaginative menu are warm salmon salad,
        grilled marlin in a citrus-sesame vinaigrette, rack of lamb in a port glaze,
        and crab served with drawn butter and Indonesian hot-and-sour sauce.
        The Café Deli downstairs sells Mediterranean picnic foods prepared
        by the chefs upstairs. ✉ *1327 Beach Dr.,* ☎ *250/598–8555. Reserva-
        tions essential. AE, DC, MC, V.*

$$-$$$ ✕ **Pescatore's Fish House and Oyster Bar.** Upbeat Pescatore's special-
        izes in fresh seafood (grilled wild Coho salmon, fresh spinach, and
        smoked Gruyère on Italian flat bread) and Pacific Northwest prepa-
        rations like rosemary-and-garlic-marinated lamb and oyster mush-
        rooms on angel-hair pasta. Daily blue-plate specials tend to be reasonably
        priced and creative—for example, pan-seared chicken breast in
        chanterelle sauce with crushed potatoes and vegetables. ✉ *614 Hum-
        boldt St.,* ☎ *250/385–4512. Reservations essential. AE, MC, V.*

$ ✕ **Barb's Place.** This funky take-out shack, a Victoria institution, is
        on Fisherman's Wharf, on the south side of Victoria Harbour, just off
        Marine Drive. Locals consider the authentic fish-and-chips (with hal-
        ibut) to be the city's best: Pick up an order before taking a quick ride
        on the little harbor ferry across the bay to Songhees Point for a pic-
        nic. ✉ *310 Lawrence St.,* ☎ *250/384–6515. No credit cards. Closed
        Nov.–Mar.*

THAI

$ ✕ **Siam.** The Thai chefs at Siam work wonders with hot and mild dishes.
        The *phad Thai goong* (fried rice noodles with prawns, tofu, peanuts,
        eggs, bean sprouts, and green onions), *panang* (choice of meat in curry
        and coconut milk), and *satay* (grilled, marinated cubes of meat served
        with a spicy peanut sauce) are particularly good options. ✉ *512 Fort
        St.,* ☎ *250/383–9911. Reservations essential. MC, V. No lunch Sun.*

VIETNAMESE

$-$$ ✕ **Le Petit Saigon.** The fare is Vietnamese with French influences at
        this intimate restaurant. The crab, asparagus, and egg swirl soup is a
        house specialty, and combination meals are cheap and tasty. ✉ *1010
        Langley St.,* ☎ *250/386–1412. AE, MC, V.*

Lodging

$$$$ ▥ **The Aerie.** The million-dollar view of Finlayson Arm and the Gulf
   ★   Islands persuaded Leo and Maria Schuster to build their small luxury
        resort here, 30 km (19 mi) north of Victoria. Some of the plush rooms
        in the Mediterranean-style villa have a patio; others have fireplaces and
        whirlpool tubs tucked into window nooks. The dining room (no lunch)
        is open to the public for stunning views and outstanding cuisine. The
        maple-smoked salmon, pheasant consommé, and medallions of veni-
        son in morel sauce are more than worth the drive from Victoria. A full
        gourmet breakfast is included in the tariff. ✉ *600 Ebedora La., Mala-
        hat V0R 2L0,* ☎ *250/743–7115,* FAX *250/743–4766. 11 rooms, 11 suites.
        Dining room, no-smoking rooms, indoor pool, indoor and outdoor hot
        tubs, sauna, spa, tennis court, exercise room, library, meeting room,
        helipad. AE, MC, V.*

$$$$ ▥ **Beaconsfield Inn.** Built in 1905 and restored in 1984, the Beacons-
        field has retained its Old World charm. Dark mahogany wood appears
        throughout the house; down comforters and some canopy beds adorn
        the rooms, reinforcing the Edwardian style. Some rooms in this no-
        smoking inn have fireplaces and whirlpool bathtubs. The room rates
        include a full breakfast with homemade croissants or scones, afternoon

tea, and evening sherry. ⊠ *998 Humboldt St., V8V 2Z8,* ☎ *250/384–4044,* ℻ *250/721–2442. 5 rooms, 4 suites. Breakfast room, no-smoking rooms, library. MC, V.*

$$$$ 🏨 **Clarion Hotel Grand Pacific.** One of Victoria's newest and finest hotels has mahogany woodwork and an elegant ambience. Overlooking the harbor and adjacent to the legislative buildings, the hotel accommodates business travelers and vacationers looking for comfort, convenience, and great scenery; all rooms have terraces, with views of either the harbor or the Olympic Mountains. ⊠ *450 Québec St., V8V 1W5,* ☎ *250/386–0450 or 800/663–7550,* ℻ *250/386–8779. 130 rooms, 15 suites. Dining room, lounge, no-smoking rooms, room service, indoor pool, massage, sauna, aerobics, racquetball, squash, bicycles, laundry service and dry cleaning, business services, convention center, meeting rooms, free parking. AE, D, DC, MC, V.*

$$$$ 🏨 **Empress Hotel.** Stained glass, carved archways, and hardwood floors are among the noteworthy design elements of Victoria's dowager queen, which opened in 1908. Newer rooms added in 1989 are more spacious than the original ones. The Empress is the city's primary meeting place for politicians, locals, and tourists. ⊠ *721 Government St., V8W 1W5,* ☎ *250/384–8111 or 800/441–1414,* ℻ *250/381–4334. 466 rooms, 17 suites. Restaurant, café, 2 lounges, no-smoking rooms, room service, indoor pool, sauna, health club, laundry service and dry cleaning, concierge, business services, convention center, parking (fee). AE, D, DC, MC, V.*

$$$–$$$$ 🏨 **Ocean Pointe Resort.** Across the "blue bridge" (Johnson Street
★   Bridge) from downtown Victoria, the Ocean Pointe opened in 1992 on the site of an old shingle mill in an area once claimed by the Songhees natives. From here you have the best possible view of the lights of the Parliament buildings across the Inner Harbour. Public rooms and half the guest rooms have romantic evening views of downtown Victoria. Amenities include the only full European aesthetics spa in western Canada, with all kinds of beauty treatments. ⊠ *45 Songhees Rd., V9A 6T3,* ☎ *250/360–2999 or 800/667–4677,* ℻ *250/360–5856. 213 rooms, 37 suites. 2 restaurants, lounge, kitchenettes, no-smoking rooms, indoor pool, sauna, spa, 2 tennis courts, exercise room, racquetball, squash, laundry service and dry cleaning, business services, meeting rooms, parking (fee). AE, DC, MC, V.*

$$$–$$$$ 🏨 **Victoria Regent Hotel.** Originally an apartment house, this posh hotel has views of the harbor or city. The outside is plain, with a glass facade, but the interior is sumptuously decorated with warm earth tones and modern furnishings; each suite has a living room, a dining room, a deck, a kitchen, and one or two bedrooms with bath (some with hot tubs). It's a good choice for families. ⊠ *1234 Wharf St., V8W 3H9,* ☎ *250/386–2211 or 800/663–7472,* ℻ *250/386–2622. 10 rooms, 34 suites. Restaurant, kitchenettes, no-smoking rooms, refrigerators, coin laundry, meeting room, free parking. AE, D, DC, MC, V.*

$$$ 🏨 **Abigail's Hotel.** The elegant informality in this no-smoking hotel is
★   especially noticeable in the guest library and sitting room, where hors d'oeuvres are served each evening. Breakfast, included in the room rate, is served in the downstairs dining room. ⊠ *906 McClure St., V8V 3E7,* ☎ *250/388–5363 or 800/561–6565,* ℻ *250/361–1905. 16 rooms. Breakfast room, library, concierge, free parking. MC, V.*

$$$ 🏨 **Bedford Regency.** This European-style hotel in the heart of downtown is reminiscent of San Francisco's small hotels, with personalized service and careful attention to details. Rooms are in earth colors, and many have goose-down comforters, fireplaces, and whirlpool bathtubs. Four rooms on the west side have views of the harbor and are much quieter than those facing the traffic on Government Street. ⊠ *1140*

Government St., V8W 1Y2, ☎ 250/384–6835 or 800/665–6500, ☒ 250/386–8930. 40 rooms. Restaurant, pub, no-smoking rooms, laundry service and dry cleaning, business services, free parking. AE, MC, V.

$$$ ⊞ **Haterleigh Heritage Inn.** Leaded- and stained-glass windows, intricate moldings, and ornate plasterwork on 11-ft ceilings transport guests here to a more gracious time. Mounds of pillows and plump down comforters dress the beds. Some rooms have whirlpool tubs. Extras like sherry and chocolates delivered to your room on check-in are nice touches indeed, as are the hearty family-style breakfasts. ☒ *243 Kingston St., V8V 1V5, ☎ 250/384–9995, ☒ 250/384–1935. 5 double rooms, 1 2-bedroom room, 1 suite. MC, V.*

$$$ ⊞ **Oak Bay Beach Hotel.** Beside the ocean in Oak Bay on the southwest side of the Saanich Peninsula, this Tudor-style hotel is just 10 minutes from the bustle of downtown. The hotel overlooks Haro Strait; the antiques and flower prints decorating the rooms echo the dreamy landscaped grounds above the pebble beach. Most of the highly individual rooms have antiques (lots of slipper chairs and high brass or canopy beds), though a 1992 renovation brought contemporary styling, furniture, and fixtures to some. ☒ *1175 Beach Dr., V8S 2N2, ☎ 250/598–4556 or 800/668–7758, ☒ 250/598–6180. 51 rooms. Restaurant, pub, no-smoking rooms, room service, boating, meeting room, free parking. AE, DC, MC, V.*

$$–$$$ ⊞ **Coast Victoria Harbourside.** West of the Inner Harbour in a residential
★ section of the waterfront, the Coast Victoria has marine views but is away from the traffic on Government Street. Serene relaxation in modern comfort is a theme here, from the warm mahogany-paneled lobby and soothing shades in average-size guest rooms to an extensive health club. ☒ *146 Kingston St., V8V 1V4, ☎ 250/360–1211 or 800/663–1144, ☒ 250/360–1418. 118 rooms, 14 suites. Restaurant, lounge, no-smoking rooms, room service, indoor-outdoor pool, hot tub, sauna, health club, business services, meeting rooms, free parking. AE, DC, MC, V.*

$$–$$$ ⊞ **Holland House Inn.** Two blocks from the Inner Harbour, legislative buildings, and ferry terminals, this no-smoking hotel surrounded by a picket fence exudes a casual elegance. Some rooms have fine art created by locals; some have four-poster beds and fireplaces. All but two rooms have balconies. The room rates include a lavish breakfast. ☒ *595 Michigan St., V8V 1S7, ☎ 250/384–6644, ☒ 250/384–6117. 10 rooms. No-smoking rooms. AE, MC, V.*

$$ ⊞ **Mulberry Manor.** The last building designed by Victoria architect Samuel McClure has been restored and decorated to magazine-cover perfection with antiques, sumptuous linens, and tile baths. The Tudor-style mansion sits behind a high stone wall on an acre of carefully manicured grounds. Charming hosts Susan and Tony Temple serve sumptuous breakfasts with homemade jams and great coffee. ☒ *611 Foul Bay Rd., V8S 1H2, ☎ 250/370–1918, ☒ 250/370–1968. 3 rooms, 1 suite. Breakfast room, no-smoking rooms. MC, V.*

$$ ⊞ **Swans.** Extensive renovations have given a 1913 brick warehouse a new look: There's a brewery, bistro, and pub on the first floor; large apartmentlike guest rooms decorated with Pacific Northwest art fill the upper floors. Swans is a good choice for families. ☒ *506 Pandora Ave., V8W 1N6, ☎ 250/361–3310 or 800/668–7926, ☒ 250/361–3491. 29 rooms. Restaurant, pub, no-smoking rooms, coin laundry. AE, DC, MC, V.*

$–$$ ⊞ **Admiral Motel.** On Victoria harbor along the tourist strip, this modern motel is in the center of things but relatively quiet in the evening. The amiable owners take good care of the rooms, and small pets are permitted. Children under 12 stay free in their parents' room. ⊠ *257 Belleville St., V8V 1X1,* ☎ ℻ *250/388–6267. 29 rooms. Kitchenettes, no-smoking rooms, coin laundry, free parking. AE, D, MC, V.*

$ ☎ **Cats Meow.** Dorm space at this youth hostel costs less than $20 a night; a private room costs about $45 for two people. ⊠ *1316 Grant St., V8R 1M3,* ☎ ℻ *250/595–8878. 1 dorm with 6 beds shares bath, 2 private rooms share bath. No credit cards.*

Nightlife and the Arts

Bars and Clubs

Harpo's (⊠ 15 Bastion Sq., ☎ 250/385–5333) hosts rock, blues, and jazz performers. Call the **Jazz Hotline** (☎ 250/658–5255) for jazz updates. In addition to live music, darts, and brewery tours, **Spinnakers Brew Pub** (⊠ 308 Catherine St., ☎ 250/386–2739) pours plenty of British Columbian microbrewery beer. For dancing, head to **Sweetwater's** (⊠ 27-560 Johnson St., ☎ 250/383–7844), where a youngish crowd moves on two dance floors to taped techno and Top 40.

Music

The **Victoria International Music Festival** (☎ 250/736–2119) presents internationally acclaimed musicians each summer from the first week in July to late August. The **Victoria Symphony** plays in the Royal Theatre (⊠ 805 Broughton St., ☎ 250/386–6121) and at the University Centre Auditorium (⊠ Finnerty Rd., ☎ 250/721–8480).

Opera

The **Pacific Opera Victoria** performs three productions a year in the 900-seat McPherson Playhouse (⊠ 3 Centennial Sq., ☎ 250/386–6121), adjoining the Victoria City Hall.

Outdoor Activities and Sports

Golf

The **Cordova Bay Golf Course** (⊠ 5333 Cordova Bay Rd., ☎ 250/658–4444) is an 18-hole, par-72 course set on the shoreline. The greens fee ranges from $30 to $45, plus $27 for an optional cart.

Whale-Watching

To see the pods of orcas that travel in the waters around Vancouver Island, you can take charter boat tours from Victoria from May to October. These three-hour Zodiac (motor-powered inflatable boat) excursions cost about $75 per person: **Great Pacific Adventures** (☎ 250/386–2277), **Ocean Explorations** (☎ 250/383–6722), and **Seacoast Expeditions** (☎ 250/383–2254) are the top operators.

Shopping

Shopping Centers

Eaton Centre (⊠ 1 Victoria Eaton Centre, at Government and Fort Sts., ☎ 250/382–7141), a department store and mall, has about 100 boutiques and restaurants. **Market Square** (⊠ 560 Johnson St., ☎ 250/386–2441) has three stories of specialty shops and offbeat stores. You'll find many specialty stores on Government Street downtown, particularly in the blocks between 800 and 1400.

Victoria Essentials

Arriving and Departing

BY BOAT

B.C. Ferries (☎ 250/386–3431; 888/223–3779 in British Columbia only) operates daily service between Vancouver and Victoria. The Vancouver terminal is in Tsawwassen, 38 km (24 mi) southwest of downtown at the end of Highway 17. In Victoria, ferries arrive at and depart from Swartz Bay Terminal at the end of Pat Bay Highway, 32 km (20 mi) north of downtown Victoria. The tickets cost about $8 per passenger, and $30 per vehicle. Rates fluctuate depending on the season.

There is year-round passenger service between Victoria and Seattle on the **Victoria Clipper** (☎ 250/382–8100 in Victoria; 206/448–5000 in Seattle; 800/888–2535 in the U.S. only).

Washington State Ferries (☎ 250/381–1551; 206/464–6400 in the U.S.; 800/843–3779 in WA only) cross daily, year-round, between Sidney, just north of Victoria, and Anacortes, Washington. **Black Ball Transport** (☎ 250/386–2202; 206/457–4491 in the U.S.) operates between Victoria and Port Angeles, Washington.

Direct passenger and vehicle service between Victoria and Seattle is available from mid-May to mid-September on the *Princess Marguerite III,* operated by **Clipper Navigation** (☎ 250/480–5555 in Victoria; 206/448–5000 in Seattle; 800/888–2535 in the U.S. only). The boat departs from Ogden Point in Victoria each morning at 7:30 AM and arrives at Seattle's Pier 48 at noon. It departs from Seattle at 1 PM, arriving back at Ogden Point at 5:30. Reservations are advised if you're traveling with a vehicle.

BY BUS
Pacific Coach Lines (☎ 800/661–1725) operates daily service between Victoria and Vancouver on B.C. Ferries.

BY CAR
Highway 17 connects the Swartz Bay ferry terminal on the Saanich Peninsula with downtown Victoria. **Island Highway** (Highway 1, also known as the Trans-Canada Highway) runs south from Nanaimo to Victoria. **Highway 14** connects Sooke to Port Renfrew, on the west coast of Vancouver Island, with Victoria.

BY HELICOPTER
Helijet Airways (☎ 604/628–1468 or 250/382–6222) helicopter service is available from downtown Vancouver to downtown Victoria.

BY PLANE
Victoria International Airport (✉ Willingdon Rd. off Hwy. 17, Sidney) is served by Air B.C., Air Canada, Canadian, Horizon, and Westjet. *See* Air Travel *in* the Gold Guide for airline numbers. Air B.C. provides airport-to-airport service from Vancouver to Victoria at least hourly. Flights take about 35 minutes.

BY TRAIN
B.C. Rail (☎ 604/984–5246, 604/631–3500, or 800/663–8238) operates daily service between Victoria and Whistler.

Getting Around
BY BUS
The **B.C. Transit System** (☎ 250/382–6161) serves Victoria and the surrounding areas. An all-day pass costs $5.

BY TAXI
Empress Taxi (☎ 250/381–2222). **Victoria Taxi** (☎ 250/383–7111).

Contacts and Resources
CAR RENTAL
ABC Rent a Car (☎ 250/388–3153, FAX 250/388–0111).

EMERGENCIES
Ambulance (☎ 911). **Police** (☎ 911).

Victoria General Hospital (⊠ 35 Helmcken Rd., ☎ 250/727–4212).

GUIDED TOURS
Gray Line (☎ 250/388–5248) conducts city tours on. See the Inner Harbour by **Harbour Gondola** (☎ 250/480–8841), complete with an authentically garbed gondolier. **Tally-Ho Horsedrawn Tours** (☎ 250/479–1113) operates a tour of downtown Victoria. **Victoria Carriage Tours** (☎ 250/383–2207) conducts horse-drawn tours of the city.

LATE-NIGHT PHARMACY
McGill and Orme Pharmacies (⊠ 649 Fort St., ☎ 250/384–1195).

VISITOR INFORMATION
Tourism Association of Vancouver Island (⊠ 302–45 Bastion Sq., Victoria V8W 1J1, ☎ 250/382–3551). **Tourism Victoria** (⊠ 812 Wharf St., V8W 1T3, ☎ 250/953–2033).

VANCOUVER ISLAND

Vancouver Island stretches 450 km (279 mi) from Victoria to Cape Scott. More than 95% of the island's population of 684,000 live between Victoria and Campbell River (halfway up the island); 50% live in Victoria itself. Mountains crown the island's center, providing opportunities for skiing, climbing, and hiking. Thick conifer forests blanket it down to soft, sandy beaches on the eastern shoreline and rocky, wave-pounded grottoes and inlets along the western shore.

Sooke

⓮ *42 km (26 mi) west of Victoria on Hwy. 14.*

Sooke is a logging, fishing, and farming community. **East Sooke Park,** on the east side of the harbor, has 350 acres of beaches, hiking trails, and wildflower-dotted meadows.

The **Sooke Regional Museum and Travel Infocentre** exhibits Salish and Nootka crafts and artifacts from 19th-century Sooke. In summer, food fests of barbecued salmon and strawberry shortcake are sometimes held on the front lawn. ⊠ *2070 Phillips Rd., Box 774, V0S 1N0, ☎ 250/642–6351, FAX 250/642–7089. ▣ Donations accepted. ⊙ June–Aug., daily 9–6; Sept.–May, Tues.–Sun. 9–5.*

Dining and Lodging

$ ✕ **Seventeen Mile House.** Stop here on the road between Sooke and Victoria for British pub fare, a beer, or fresh local seafood. Built as a hotel, the house is a study in turn-of-the-century island architecture. ⊠ *5121 Sooke Rd., ☎ 250/642–5942. MC, V.*

$$$$ ✕▣ **Sooke Harbour House.** This oceanfront country inn has one of
★ the finest restaurants in British Columbia: The seafood is just-caught fresh, and the herbs are grown on the property. In the romantic guest rooms, natural wood and white finishes add to each unit's unique theme. French doors in the Herb Garden Room, which is decorated in shades of mint, open onto a private patio. Native American furnishings grace the Longhouse Room. The room rates include breakfast and lunch. ⊠ *1528 Whiffen Spit Rd., R.R. 4, V0S 1N0, ☎ 250/642–3421 or 250/642–4944, FAX 250/642–6988. 13 rooms. Restaurant, no-smoking rooms, beach, meeting room. AE, MC, V.*

Vancouver Island

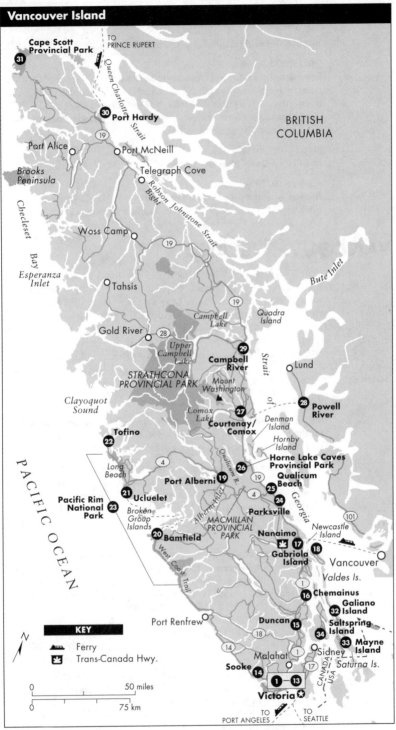

Cape Scott
Provincial Park
31

TO PRINCE RUPERT

Queen Charlotte Strait

30 Port Hardy

(19)

Port Alice

Port McNeill

BRITISH
COLUMBIA

Brooks
Peninsula

Telegraph Cove

Robson Johnstone Strait

Checleset
Bay

Woss Camp

(19)

Esperanza
Inlet

Tahsis

Bute Inlet

(19)

Campbell
Lake

Quadra
Island

Gold River (28)

Upper
Campbell
Lake

STRATHCONA
PROVINCIAL PARK

29
Campbell
River

Strait

Lund

Mount
Washington

Clayoquot
Sound

Comox
Lake

27
Courtenay/
Comox

of

28 Powell
River

Denman
Island

Tofino
22

Hornby
Island

Horne Lake Caves
Provincial Park

Long
Beach

(4)

Qualicum R.

26

Qualicum
Beach

Port Alberni **19**

(19)

Ucluelet
21

Pacific Rim
National
Park **23**

Broken
Group
Islands

(4)

25

24

Parksville

Georgia

(101)

Alberni Inlet

MACMILLAN
PROVINCIAL
PARK

Newcastle
Island

20 Bamfield

Nanaimo
17

Gabriola
Island

18

Vancouver

West Coast Trail

Valdes Is.

(1)

16 Chemainus

Galiano
Island

Port Renfrew

Duncan
15

32
Saltspring
Island

34

33
Mayne
Island

(18)

(14)

Malahat

(1)

Sidney

Saturna Is.

Sooke
14

(17)

1 — **13**

CANADA
USA

Victoria ✪

TO
PORT ANGELES

TO
SEATTLE

KEY

⛴ Ferry
🏵 Trans-Canada Hwy.

PACIFIC OCEAN

N

0   50 miles
0   75 km

$$–$$$ ✕🖭 **Ocean Wilderness.** A large 1940s log cabin sits on 5 forested, beach-front acres, 13 km (8 mi) west of Sooke. Owner Marion Rolston built a rough cedar addition in 1990; she furnishes her home with Victorian antiques she picks up at auction. Romantic canopies and ruffled linens on high beds dominate the spacious guest rooms, which have sitting areas with views of either the Strait of Juan de Fuca or the pretty gardens in the back, as well as private decks or patios. The dining room fare is innovative West Coast treatments of fresh local fish and meats. ⊠ *109 W. Coast Rd., R.R. 2, V0S 1N0,* ☎ FAX *250/646–2116. 9 rooms. Dining room, no-smoking rooms, hot tub, hiking. MC, V.*

Duncan

⑮ *60 km (37 mi) north of Victoria on the Trans-Canada Hwy. (Hwy. 1).*

Duncan is nicknamed City of Totems for the many totem poles that dot the small community. The two carvings behind the City Hall are worth a short trip off the main road.

The **Native Heritage Centre** covers 13 acres on the banks of the Cowichan River. The center includes a native longhouse, a theater, an arts-and-crafts gallery that focuses on carvings and weaving traditions, and native fare served in the Bighouse Restaurant. ⊠ *200 Cowichan Way,* ☎ *250/746–8119,* FAX *250/746–4143.* 🖭 *$8.* ☉ *Mid-May–mid-Oct., daily 9:30–5:30; mid-Oct.–mid-May, daily 10–4:30.*

The **British Columbia Forest Museum,** more a park than a museum, spans 100 acres, combining indoor and outdoor exhibits that focus on the history of forestry in the province. You ride an original steam locomotive around the property and over an old wood trestle bridge. The exhibits show logging and milling equipment. ⊠ *Trans-Canada Hwy.,* ☎ *250/746–1251,* FAX *250/715–1113.* 🖭 *$7.50.* ☉ *May–Sept., daily 9:30–6; Oct.–Apr. by appointment.*

Shopping

Duncan is the home of Cowichan wool sweaters, hand-knitted by the Cowichan people. Sweaters are sold at **Hills Indian Crafts** (☎ 250/746–6731) on the main highway, about 1½ km (1 mi) south of Duncan. **Modeste Wool Carding** (⊠ 2615 Modeste Rd., ☎ 250/748–8983), about 1 km (½ mi) off the highway, also carries handmade knitwear.

Chemainus

⑯ *85 km (53 mi) north of Victoria, 27 km (17 mi) south of Nanaimo.*

Chemainus is known for the bold epic murals that decorate its townscape. Once dependent on the lumber industry, the small community began to revitalize itself in the early 1980s when its mill closed down. Since then, the town has brought in international artists to paint more than 30 murals depicting local historical events around town. Footprints on the sidewalk lead you on a self-guided tour of the murals. Restaurants, shops, tearooms, coffee bars, art galleries, antiques dealers, and the new **Chemainus Theater** (☎ 250/246–9820 or 800/565–7738), which presents live theater (matinees and shows with dinner included), have added to the town's growth.

Lodging

$$$ 🖭 **Little Inn on Willow.** This fairy-tale-looking little cottage is a romantic delight. Built for two, it has a lavishly draped bed, a whirlpool tub, and a fireplace. The cottage is managed by the Pacific Shores Inn next door, which has simpler accommodations with equipped kitchens. ⊠ *Chemainus Rd., Box 958, V0R 1K0,* ☎ *250/246–4987,* FAX *250/246–4785. 1 cottage, 3 rooms (Pacific Shores). MC.*

Nanaimo

⑰ *110 km (68 mi) northwest of Victoria, 115 km (71 mi) southeast of Courtenay; 155 km (96 mi) southeast of Campbell River; 23 km (14 mi) on land plus 38 nautical mi west of Vancouver.*

Petroglyphs (rock carvings) throughout the Nanaimo area represent humans, birds, wolves, lizards, sea monsters, and supernatural creatures. The **Nanaimo District Museum** (⌖ 100 Cameron St., ☎ 250/753–1821) will give you information about local carvings. Eight kilometers (5 miles) south of town at **Petroglyph Provincial Park** (⌖ Hwy. 1, ☎ 250/387–5002), you can follow marked trails that begin at the parking lot to see designs carved thousands of years ago.

Dining and Lodging

$$ ✕ **Mahle House.** This casually elegant place serves innovative North-
★   west cuisine, such as braised rabbit with Dijon mustard and red-wine sauce. Among the items on the regular menu are a succulent carrot and ginger soup and a catch of the day. Attention to detail, an intimate setting, and three country-style rooms make this one of the finest dining experiences in the region. ⌖ *Cedar and Heemer Rds.,* ☎ *250/722–3621. MC, V. Closed Mon.–Tues. No lunch.*

$–$$ ✕ **The Grotto.** A Nanaimo institution that specializes in seafood has a
★   casual waterfront setting. Try oysters on the half shell, the spareribs, garlic prawn pasta, or the seafood platter that's big enough for two. The Kitchen Sink, a heaping bowl of clams, shrimp, and salmon steamed in white wine, herbs, and butter, is a favorite. ⌖ *1511 Stewart Ave.,* ☎ *250/753–3303. AE, MC, V. No lunch.*

$$–$$$ ✕🖭 **Coast Bastion Inn Nanaimo.** This convenient hotel is downtown near the ferry terminal and train and bus stations. Rooms with balconies and modern furnishings have views of the old Hudson's Bay fort and the ocean. There's an Irish deli-pub. ⌖ *11 Bastion St., V9R 2Z9,* ☎ *250/753–6601; 800/663–1144 in the U.S.;* 🖸🖸 *250/753–4155. 179 rooms. Restaurant, lounge, no-smoking rooms, room service, hot tub, sauna, exercise room, laundry service and dry cleaning, meeting rooms. AE, DC, MC, V.*

$$$ 🖭 **Yellow Point Lodge.** Yellow Point is a very popular resort area on
★   a spit of land 24 km (15 mi) south of Nanaimo, 13 km (8 mi) north-east of Ladysmith. Rebuilt in 1986 after a fire destroyed the original, the lodge lost almost nothing of its homey, summer-camp ambience. Nine large lodge rooms and a range of cottages all have private baths; most are available year-round. Perched on a rocky knoll overlooking the Stuart Channel are beach cabins, field cabins, and beach barracks for the hardy; these are closed from mid-October to mid-April, have no running water, and share a central bathhouse. You can stroll the lodge's 178 acres, and there are canoes and kayaks for exploring the shoreline. The room rate includes three full meals and snacks. ⌖ *3700 Yellow Point Rd., R.R. 3, Ladysmith V0R 2E0,* ☎ *250/245–7422,* 🖸🖸 *250/245–7411. 50 rooms. Restaurant (for guests only), no-smoking rooms, saltwater pool, hot tub, sauna, 2 tennis courts, badminton, jogging, volleyball, boating, mountain bikes. MC, V.*

$$–$$$ 🖭 **Best Western Dorchester Hotel.** Upbeat Mediterranean tones of champagne, ocher, and teal brighten the exterior of the Dorchester. Once the Nanaimo Opera House, this hotel in the city center overlooking the harbor has a distinctive character, with gold knockers on each of the doors, winding hallways, and a rooftop patio. The rooms are small but exceptionally comfortable, and most have views of the harbor. ⌖ *70 Church St., V9R 5H4,* ☎ *250/754–6835 or 800/528–1234,* 🖸🖸 *250/*

754–2638. *65 rooms. Restaurant, lounge, no-smoking rooms, room service, library, laundry service and dry cleaning, meeting rooms. AE, D, DC, MC, V.*

Outdoor Activities and Sports

CANOEING AND KAYAKING

Wild Heart Adventures (⊠ Site P, C-5, R.R. 4, V9R 5X9, ☎ 250/722–3683) conducts multiple-day guided sea-kayak expeditions.

Gabriola Island

⑱ *3½ nautical mi (20-min ferry ride) east of Nanaimo.*

A ferry departs from rustic, rural Gabriola Island on a 10-minute ride to **Newcastle Island,** where you can picnic, ride your bicycle, walk on trails leading past old mines and quarries, and catch glimpses of deer, rabbits, and eagles.

Port Alberni

⑲ *80 km (50 mi) west of Nanaimo; 195 km (121 mi) northwest of Victoria.*

Port Alberni is mainly a pulp- and sawmill town and a stopover on the way to Ucluelet and Tofino on the west coast. The salmon-rich waters attract fishermen. From here, you can take a breathtaking trip to towns along the Alberni Inlet and Barkley Sound aboard the **Lady Rose,** a Scottish ship built in 1937. ⊠ *Argyle St. dock,* ☎ *250/723–8313; 800/663–7192 reservations Apr.–Sept.* ⌷ *Bamfield $36, Broken Group Islands $38, Ucluelet $40.* ☉ *Sailings daily 8* AM.

Bamfield

⑳ *100 km (62 mi) southwest of Port Alberni.*

In Bamfield, a remote village of about 200, the seaside boardwalk affords an uninterrupted view of ships heading up the inlet to Port Alberni. The town is well equipped to handle overnight visitors. Bamfield is also a good base for boating trips to the Broken Group Islands and hikes along the West Coast Trail (☞ Pacific Rim National Park, *below*).

Ucluelet

㉑ *100 km (62 mi) west of Port Alberni, 295 km (183 mi) northwest of Victoria.*

Ucluelet, which in the native language means "people with a safe landing place," is totally focused on the sea. Fishing, water tours, and whale-watching are the primary activities. Charter boats (☞ Contacts and Resources *in* British Columbia A to Z, *below*) greet the 20,000 gray whales that pass close to Ucluelet on their migration to the Bering Sea between March and May. Sometimes you can even see the migrating whales from the Ucluelet shore.

Dining and Lodging

$$ ✕ **Whale's Tale.** Prime ribs and local seafood are among the straightforward fare at this rustic, no-frills restaurant. ⊠ *1861 Peninsula Rd.,* ☎ *250/726–4621. MC, V. Closed Nov.–Jan. No lunch.*

$$ ✕ **Wickaninnish Restaurant.** Before the Canadian government ac-
★ quired this wood building for an interpretive center for Pacific Rim National Park, it was an inn. The beach setting, combined with the building's glass exterior and stone-and-beam interior, gives the Wickaninnish an ambience that cannot be matched anywhere else in the area.

Seafood is the primary choice here, especially the West Coast chowder, but if you order the vegetable or vegetable-seafood stir-fry, you won't be disappointed. ⊠ *Long Beach, 16 km (10 mi) north of Ucluelet,* ☎ *250/726–7706. AE, MC, V. Closed mid-Oct.–mid-Feb.*

$$–$$$ ⌂ **Canadian Princess Fishing Resort.** This converted 230-ft steam-powered survey ship holds 36 comfortable, but hardly opulent, staterooms. Each has one to four berths, and all share washrooms. Roomier than the ship cabins, the resort's deluxe shoreside rooms come with more contemporary furnishings; a few have fireplaces. This resort provides the bare necessities—mostly to nature enthusiasts and fishermen. ⊠ *Boat Basin, Box 939, V0R 3A0,* ☎ *250/726–7771 or 800/663–7090,* FAX *250/726–7121. 46 shoreside and 30 shipboard sleeping units. 2 bars, dining room, no-smoking rooms, boating, fishing. AE, DC, MC, V.*

Whale-Watching
Subtidal Adventures (☎ 250/726–7336) runs trips in the area.

Tofino

②②   *42 km (26 mi) northwest of Ucluelet; 337 km (209 mi) northwest of Victoria; 130 km (81 mi) west of Port Alberni.*

The town of Tofino is commercial, with beachfront resorts, motels, and several B&Bs. The surrounding area remains natural; you can walk along the beach discovering caves, cruise around the ancient forests of Meares Island, or take an hour-long water taxi ride to the hot springs north of town.

Dining and Lodging

$$$$ ✕⌂ **The Wickaninnish Inn.** Water surrounds this country inn on three sides, with old-growth forest as a backdrop. The rooms have ocean views, balconies, fireplaces, and soaker tubs. Chef Rodney Butters serves up coastal food at the inn's Pointe Restaurant. An exclusively West Coast wine list complements mussels, clams, and scallops in Rainforest Ale broth; wild mushroom terrine; steamed Dungeness crab; or savory crusted wild boar. ⊠ *Osprey La. at Chesterman Beach, Box 250, V0R 2Z0,* ☎ *250/725–3100 or 800/333–4604,* FAX *250/ 725–3110. 46 rooms, 1 suite. Restaurant, minibars, no-smoking rooms, beach. AE, DC, MC, V.*

$$$–$$$$ ⌂ **Pacific Sands Beach Resort.** A mile north of Pacific Rim National Park, this beachside resort has motel suites and individual two-bedroom cottages, each with a beautiful bay view. The motel rooms have modern furnishings, and fireplaces make them seem cozy. Some of the specialty suites in the three-story addition have hot tubs outside on the deck. ⊠ *1421 Pacific Rim Hwy., Box 237, V0R 2Z0,* ☎ *250/725–3322 or 800/565–2322,* FAX *250/725–3155. 54 rooms, 10 cottages. Kitchenettes, no-smoking rooms, beach, coin laundry. AE, MC, V.*

$$–$$$ ⌂ **Chesterman Beach Bed and Breakfast.** This small, romantic bed-
★   and-breakfast on the beach has rolling ocean surf for a front yard. You can walk the beach, search the tidal pools, or—from March to October—watch whales migrate. The suite in the main house (complete with sauna and full kitchen) and the separate Lookout Suite are romantic and cozy; both have fireplaces and views of the beach. A one-bedroom garden cottage has no ocean view but accommodates up to four. ⊠ *1345 Chesterman Beach Rd., V0R 2Z0,* ☎ FAX *250/725–3726. 4 rooms, 1 cottage. Kitchenettes, no-smoking rooms, refrigerators, beach. MC, V.*

Outdoor Activities and Sports

CANOEING AND KAYAKING

You can rent canoes and kayaks from **Tofino Sea-Kayaking Company** (⊠ Box 620, V0N 3J0, ☎ 250/928–3117 or 250/725–4222).

WHALE-WATCHING

Chinook Charters (☎ 250/725–3431). **Remote Passage Whale Watching** (☎ 250/725–3330). **Sea Trek Tours & Expeditions** (☎ 250/725–4412). **Weigh West Marine Resort** (☎ 250/725–3277).

Pacific Rim National Park

★ ㉓ *85 km (53 mi) west of Port Alberni.*

The first national marine park in Canada, Pacific Rim National Park comprises three separate areas—Long Beach, the Broken Group Islands, and the West Coast Trail—for a combined area of 20,243 acres. ⊠ *Box 280, Ucluelet V0R 3A0,* ☎ *250/726–7721.* ⌦ *Mar. 15–Oct. 15, $8 per vehicle; free rest of yr.* ⊙ *Park daily 8 AM–11 PM; information center Mar. 15–Oct. 15, daily 9:30–5.*

The **Long Beach** unit gets its name from an 11-km (7-mi) strip of hard-packed white sand strewn with driftwood, shells, and the occasional Japanese glass fishing float. It is a favorite spot in summer, and you often have to fight heavy traffic along the twisting Highway 4 from Port Alberni.

The 100 **Broken Group Islands** can be reached only by boat. Many commercial charter tours are available from Ucluelet, at the southern end of Long Beach, and from Bamfield and Port Alberni. The islands and their waters are alive with sea lions, seals, and whales. The sheltered lagoons of Gibraltar, Jacques, and Hand islands offer protection and good boating conditions, but go with a guide.

The **West Coast Trail** stretches along the coast from Bamfield to Port Renfrew. The rewards of a hike here are the panoramic views of the sea, the dense rain forest, sandstone cliffs with waterfalls, and wildlife that includes gray whales and seals. The extremely rugged 77-km (48-mi) trail is for experienced hikers. It can be traveled only on foot, takes an average of six days to complete, and is open from May to late September. A permit is necessary to hike this trail; reservations by phone (☎ 800/663–6000) are available from March to September.

En Route   Heading back to the east coast from Port Alberni, stop off at **Cathedral Grove** in MacMillan Provincial Park on Highway 4. Walking trails lead past Douglas fir trees and western red cedars, some of them 800 years old. Another stop along the way is **Butterfly World** (⊠ Hwy. 4, ☎ 250/248–7026) in Coombs, an enclosed tropical garden housing an amazing collection of exotic, free-flying tropical butterflies.

Parksville

㉔ *38 km (24 mi) northwest of Nanaimo; 47 km (29 mi) east of Port Alberni; 72 km (45 mi) southeast of Courtenay; 154 km (95 mi) north of Victoria.*

Parksville is one of the east island's primary resort areas, where lodges and waterfront motels cater to families, campers, and boaters. In **Rathtrevor Provincial Park** (⊠ Off Hwy. 19, ☎ 250/248–9449), 1½ km (1 mi) south of Parksville, high tide brings ashore the warmest ocean water in British Columbia.

North Island Wildlife Recovery Association's Museum of Nature (1240 Leffler Rd., Errington, ☎ 250/248–8534) surveys the wildlife typical of Vancouver Island. The recovery center houses injured, ill, or orphaned wildlife (primarily birds such as owls, hawks, and eagles) and the largest flight cage in Canada (bald eagles are readied for release here). Errington is a short drive east of Parksville and about a 10-minute drive west of Nanoose Bay.

Lodging

$$–$$$ 🏨 **EcoMed.** Dr. Stefan Kuprowsky ran a successful naturopathic clinic
★   in Vancouver for 10 years before he opened this spa in Nanoose Bay, a few miles southeast of Parksville. EcoMed is in a beautiful spot overlooking Craig Bay (one of the island's warmest swimming bays), adjacent to a bird sanctuary and a nature reserve. You can choose the "bed and healthy breakfast" or select from the extensive spa and natural healing treatments. The suite is an apartment with kitchen, two fireplaces, and a whirlpool bath; the other two rooms are more standard hotel style. Creative vegetarian meals are a feast for the eyes and the palate. ⊠ *Pacific Shores Nature Resort No. 515, 1655 Strougler, R.R. 1, Box 50, Nanoose Bay V0R 2R0,* ☎ *250/468–7133,* ℻ *250/468–7135. 3 units. Indoor pool, hot tub, sauna, spa, boating, mountain bikes. MC, V.*

$$ 🏨 **Holiday Inn Express.** Kids under 19 stay free with their parents at this hotel about a block from the beach. Most of the motel-modern rooms have two queen-size beds. Some rooms have whirlpool tubs. ⊠ *424 W. Island Hwy., V9P 1K8,* ☎ *250/248–2232 or 800/661–3110,* ℻ *250/248–3273. 87 rooms, 3 suites. No-smoking rooms, indoor pool, hot tub, exercise room. AE, DC, MC, V.*

$ 🏨 **Roadhouse Inn.** This small Swiss-style chalet is central to four golf courses. The rooms, on the second floor, are comfortable, with basic furnishings. ⊠ *1223 Smithers Rd., V9P 2C1,* ☎ *250/248–2912. 6 rooms. Restaurant. MC, V.*

Golf

Morningstar Golf Course (⊠ 525 Lowry's Rd., ☎ 250/248–8161) has an 18-hole, par-72 course. The greens fee ranges from $11 to $43; an optional cart costs $34.

Qualicum Beach

㉕ *10 km (6 mi) north of Parksville.*

Qualicum Beach is known largely for its salmon fishing and opportunities for beachcombing. The **Old School House Gallery and Art Centre** (⊠ 122 Fern Rd. W, ☎ 250/752–6133) shows and sells the work of local artists and artisans.

Horne Lake Caves Provincial Park

㉖ *25 km (16 mi) north of Parksville, then 15 km (9 mi) west off Hwy. 19.*

Three of the six caves at Horne Lake Caves Provincial Park are open at all times. If you decide to venture in, bring along a flashlight, warm clothes, and a hard hat, and be prepared to bend and even crawl. Riverbend Cave, 1,260 ft long, requires ladders and ropes in some parts and can be explored only with a guided tour. Spelunking lessons and tours are conducted for all levels, from beginner to advanced. Make reservations for tours. ⊠ *Off Hwy. 19,* ☎ *250/248–7829.* 📷 *Tour fee varies.*

En Route   Between the Horne Lake turnoff and the twin cities of Courtenay and Comox is tiny Buckley Bay, where ferries leave for Denman Island, with connecting service to Hornby Island. Denman contains old-growth forests and long sandy beaches. Hornby's spectacular beaches have earned it the nickname Undiscovered Hawaii of British Columbia.

Courtenay and Comox

㉗ *Courtenay is 220 km (136 mi) northwest of Victoria, 17 nautical mi west of Powell River, and 46 km (29 mi) southeast of Campbell River; Comox is 6 km (4 mi) east of Courtenay.*

Courtenay and Comox are commercial towns that also provide a base for Mount Washington and Forbidden Plateau skiers; Courtenay is the larger of the two. You can also hike along the beach north of here.

Dining and Lodging

$$ ✕ **Old House Restaurant.** The dining is casual at this bi-level restau-
★ rant in a restored 1938 house with large cedar beams and a stone fire-place. The West Coast home-style cuisine—pastas, salads, and sandwiches, along with fancier, more innovative dishes (rack of lamb, panfried flounder, California cioppino)—changes daily. ⊠ *1760 Riverside La., Courtenay,* ☎ *250/338–5406. AE, DC, MC, V.*

$$ 🏨 **Kingfisher Oceanside Inn.** Ten minutes south of Courtenay, this Quality Inn hotel stands among trees and overlooks the Strait of Georgia. Solid furnishings, white stucco walls, a bright lobby with lots of greenery, and rooms with mountain and ocean views make this place special. There's also an RV park. ⊠ *4330 S. Island Hwy., Site 672, R.R. 6, Courtenay V9N 8H9,* ☎ *250/338–1323,* FAX *250/338–0058. 30 units. Restaurant, lounge, pool, tennis court. AE, D, DC, MC, V.*

$ 🏨 **Greystone Manor.** A 1918 house with period furnishings, this B&B looks out on Comox Harbor, where a colony of seals is often visible. The antiques, woodstove, and wood paneling add to the hospitable, cozy feel. The rates include a breakfast—fresh fruit, muffins, and fruit pancakes—that will keep you filled most of the day. You can walk in the English garden and on trails nearby. Smoking is not permitted here. ⊠ *4014 Haas Rd., Site 684–C2, R.R. 6, Courtenay V9N 8H9,* ☎ *250/ 338–1422. 3 rooms. Breakfast room, hiking. MC, V.*

Outdoor Activities and Sports

Mount Washington Ski Resort Ltd. (⊠ Box 3069, Courtenay V9N 5N3, ☎ 250/338–1386), with nearly 22 downhill runs and an elevation of 5,200 ft, is the largest ski area on the island. The resort also has 29 km (18 mi) of cross-country trails. It's a modern, well-organized mountain with snowpack averaging 472 inches a year. **Forbidden Plateau** (⊠ Box 3268, Courtenay V9N 5N4, ☎ 250/334–4744), near Mount Washington, has 15 runs and a vertical drop of 1,150 ft.

Powell River

㉘ *17 nautical mi (75-min ferry ride) east across the Strait of Georgia from Comox; 121 km (75 mi) plus 12½ nautical mi northwest of Vancouver.*

Powell River was established around the MacMillan pulp-and-paper mill, which opened in 1912. The forestry industry continues to have a strong presence in this area. Renowned as a year-round salmon-fishing destination, the mainland Sunshine Coast town has 30 regional lakes that offer exceptional trout fishing. The town has a few B&Bs and restaurants and a park with oceanfront camping. A 60-km (37-mi) canoeing circuit, the **Powell Forest Canoe Route,** can be accessed here. For information, contact the **Powell River Visitor Information Centre** (⊠ 4690 Marine Ave., ☎ 250/485–4701).

Campbell River

㉙ *155 km (96 mi) northwest of Nanaimo; 270 km (167 mi) northwest of Victoria.*

Campbell River draws people who want to fish; some of the biggest salmon ever caught on a line have been landed just off the coast here. You can try for membership in the Tyee Club, which would allow you to fish in a specific area and possibly land a giant chinook. Requirements include landing and registering a tyee (a spring salmon weighing 30 pounds or more). Coho salmon and cutthroat trout are also plentiful in the river.

There are other recreational activities here. The primary access to Strathcona Provincial Park (☞ *below*) is on Highway 28 west from town. You can also arrange to dive in Discovery Passage, kayak, or take a summer whale-watching tour. For information, contact **Campbell River Visitor Information Centre** (⊠ 1235 Shoppers Row, Box 482, V9W 5B6, ☎ 250/287–4636).

Dining and Lodging

$–$$ ✕ **Royal Coachman Inn.** Informal, blackboard-menu restaurants like
★   this one dot the island. The menu, which changes daily, is daring for what is essentially a high-end pub, and the inn draws crowds nightly, especially on Tuesday and Saturday (prime rib nights). Come early for lunch and dinner to avoid a wait. ⊠ *84 Dogwood St.*, ☎ *250/286–0231. AE, MC, V.*

$$–$$$ ✕🏨 **April Point Lodge and Fishing Resort.** This popular 1944 cedar lodge
★   is surrounded by refurbished fishermen's cabins and guest houses that spread across a point of Quadra Island and stretch into Discovery Passage across from Campbell River. Most of the comfortable accommodations are tidy and have kitchen facilities, fireplaces, and sundecks. Kwakiutl and Haida art adorns the lounge and dining room, where fine regional cuisine is served. In summer you can dine on spitted salmon roasted over an open fire. Some units are closed from November to March. ⊠ *1000 April Point Rd., Box 1, V9W 4Z9,* ☎ *250/285–2222,* FAX *250/285–2411. 39 units. 2 restaurants, 2 bars, no-smoking rooms, hiking, scuba diving, dock, snorkeling, fishing, bicycles, piano, baby-sitting, coin laundry, laundry service, business services, meeting rooms, airport shuttle, helipad. AE, D, DC, MC, V.*

$$–$$$ 🏨 **Tsa-Kwa-Luten Lodge.** Operated by members of the Kwakiutl tribe, this resort offers authentic Pacific coast native food and cultural activities. It stands on a high bluff amid 1,100 acres of forest on Quadra Island, a 10-minute ferry ride from Campbell River. Each room in the main lodge has a sea view; many have a fireplace and loft. Four beachfront cabins have fireplaces, whirlpool tubs, kitchen facilities, private verandas, and two to four bedrooms. You can take part in traditional dances in the lounge, which resembles a longhouse, and visit nearby petroglyphs. ⊠ *Lighthouse Rd., Box 460, Quathiaski Cove V0P 1N0,* ☎ *250/285–2042 or 800/665–7745,* FAX *250/285–2532. 36 units. Dining room, lounge, no-smoking rooms, room service, hot tub, sauna, exercise room, fishing, mountain bikes, laundry service, business services, meeting rooms. AE, DC, MC, V.*

Outdoor Activities and Sports

CANOEING AND KAYAKING

Island Sauvage (⊠ R.R. 1, Sayward V0P 1R0, ☎ 250/282–3644 or 800/667–4354) specializes in guided sea kayaking and rents canoes and kayaks.

GOLF

Storey Creek Golf Club (⊠ McGimasey Rd., Campbell River, ☎ 250/923–3673) has an 18-hole, par-72 course. The greens fee runs from $22 to $36; an optional cart costs $23.

HIKING

Island Sauvage (⊠ R.R. 1, Sayward V0P 1R0, ☎ 250/282–3644 or 800/667–4354) can arrange heli-hiking.

Strathcona Provincial Park

40 km (25 mi) west of Campbell River.

Strathcona Provincial Park (☎ 250/387–5002), the largest provincial park on Vancouver Island, encompasses **Mount Golden Hinde,** at 7,220 ft the island's highest mountain; and **Della Falls,** Canada's highest waterfall, reaching 1,440 ft. This wilderness park's multitude of lakes and 161 campsites attracts summer hikers, fishermen, and campers. The main access is by Highway 28 from Campbell River; Mount Washington and Forbidden Plateau can be reached by roads out of Courtenay.

The **Strathcona Park Lodge and Outdoor Education Center,** well known for its wilderness-skills programs, has information on the park's facilities. It also has a variety of accommodations. ⊠ *Education Center, Hwy. 28, Upper Campbell Lake, about 45 km (28 mi) west of Hwy. 19, Box 2160, Campbell River V9W 5C9,* ☎ *250/286–3122.* ⊙ *Call for hrs.*

Johnstone Strait

East side of Vancouver Island, between Campbell River and Telegraph Cove.

Pods of resident orcas live year-round in Johnstone Strait; in **Robson Bight** they like rubbing against the beaches. Because of their presence, Robson Bight has been made into an ecological preserve: Whales there must not be disturbed by human observers. Some of the area's best whale-watching tours are conducted nearby, out of **Telegraph Cove,** a village built on pilings over water.

Whale-Watching

In Telegraph Cove, you can rent canoes and kayaks from **North Island Boat, Canoe, and Kayak** (☎ 250/949–7707). Half-day whale-watching expeditions are available through **Stubbs Island Whale Watching** (☎ 250/928–3185) on the west coast of Johnstone Strait. **Seasmoke Tours** (☎ 250/974–5225), in Alert Bay on the east coast, has half-day tours.

Island Sauvage (⊠ R.R. 1, Sayward V0P 1R0, ☎ 250/282–3644 or 800/667–4354) and the **Canadian Outback Adventure Company** (⊠ 206–1110 Hamilton St., Vancouver, ☎ 250/688–7206) conduct week-long sea-kayaking trips among the orcas in the strait.

Port Hardy

❸⓿ *238 km (148 mi) northwest of Campbell River; 499 km (309 mi) northwest of Victoria; 274 nautical mi southeast of Prince Rupert.*

Port Hardy is the departure and arrival point for B.C. Ferries (☞ Getting Around *in* British Columbia A to Z, *below*) going through the scenic Inside Passage to and from Prince Rupert, the coastal port serving the Queen Charlotte Islands. B.C. Ferries has also added a "Discovery Coast Passage" route out of Port Hardy that travels to Bella Coola and other small communities along the scenic mid-coast. In summer the town can be crowded, so book your accommodations early. Ferry reservations for the trip between Port Hardy and Prince Rupert and Port Hardy and Bella Coola should also be made well in advance.

Lodging

$ 🖭 **Glen Lyon Inn.** The rooms have a full ocean view of Hardy Bay and, like most other area motels, have clean, modern amenities. Eagles can often be spotted eyeing the water for fish to prey on. The inn is a short ride from the ferry terminal. You can arrange fishing charters here. ⌧ *6435 Hardy Bay Rd., Box 103, V0N 2P0,* ☎ *250/949–7115,* 𝔽𝔸𝕏 *250/ 949–7415. 29 rooms. Restaurant, lounge, no-smoking rooms. AE, D, DC, MC, V.*

Cape Scott

60 km (37 mi) northwest of Port Hardy on logging roads.

㉛ The northernmost part of Vancouver Island is Cape Scott. **Cape Scott Provincial Park** (☎ 250/954–4600 or 250/387–5002), a wilderness camping region, is designed for well-equipped and experienced hikers. At Sand Neck, a strip of land that joins the cape to the mainland of the island, you can see both the eastern and the western shores at once.

Vancouver Island Essentials

BY BOAT

B.C. Ferries (☎ 250/386–3431; 888/223–3779 in British Columbia only) provides service from outside Vancouver and Victoria to Nanaimo.

BY BUS

Island Coach Lines (☎ 250/385–4411) serves the Vancouver Island area. **Laidlaw Coach Lines** (☎ 250/385–4411) covers the east side of Vancouver Island from Victoria to Port Hardy and also services Tofino and Port Alberni on the west side of the island. **Maverick Coach Lines** (☎ 604/662–8051) operates between Vancouver and Nanaimo. **West Coast Trail Connector** (☎ 250/475–2010) provides service on the western side of Vancouver Island, traveling to Sooke and Port Renfrew.

BY CAR

Island Highway (Highway 1) heads north from Victoria to the eastern side of Vancouver Island. **Highway 14** heads west from Victoria to Sooke.

BY TRAIN

VIA Rail (☎ 800/835–3037) provides service between Victoria and Nanaimo.

Getting Around

BY CAR

Island Highway (Highway 1) runs north from Victoria to Nanaimo. **Highway 19** continues north up the eastern side of the island. **Highway 14** connects Sooke to Port Renfrew, on the west coast of Vancouver Island, with Victoria.

Contacts and Resources

EMERGENCIES

Dial 0 for an ambulance or the police.

VISITOR INFORMATION

Tourism Association of Vancouver Island (⌧ 302–45 Bastion Sq., Victoria V8W 1J1, ☎ 250/382–3551).

THE GULF ISLANDS

Traveling up the northeastern coastline of Vancouver Island in the late 1790s, Captain George Vancouver dubbed the expansive body of water on which he sailed the Gulf of Georgia, thinking that it led to open sea. The name of the waterway was later changed to the Strait of Georgia when further exploration revealed that the British Columbia mainland lay to the east, but the islands dotting the strait continue to be known as the Gulf Islands.

A temperate climate, scenic beaches, towering promontories, rolling pasturelands, and virgin forests are common to many of the Gulf Islands—Galiano, Mayne, and Saltspring are among the most popular. Marine birds are numerous, and unusual vegetation such as arbutus trees (also known as madrones, a leafy evergreen with red peeling bark) and Garry oaks differentiate the islands from other areas around Vancouver.

Galiano Island

32 *20 nautical mi (almost 2 hrs by ferry due to interisland stops) from Swartz Bay (32 km/20 mi north of Victoria); 13 nautical mi (50-min ferry ride) from Tsawwassen (39 km/24 mi south of Vancouver).*

The activities on Galiano Island are almost exclusively of the outdoor type. The long, unbroken eastern shoreline is perfect for leisurely beach walks, while the numerous coves and inlets along the western coast make it a prime area for kayaking. Miles of trails through forests of Douglas fir beg for exploration by foot or bike. Hikers can climb to the top of **Mount Galiano** for a view of the Olympic Mountains in Washington or trek the length of **Bodega Ridge.** The best spots to view **Active Pass** and the surrounding islands are Bluffs Park, Bellhouse Park, and Centennial Park; these are also good areas for picnicking and bird-watching.

Biological studies show that the straits between Vancouver Island and the mainland of British Columbia are home to the largest variety of marine life in North America. The frigid waters offer superb visibility, especially in winter. Acala Point, Porlier Pass, and Active Pass are top locations for scuba diving. Fishermen head to the point at Bellhouse Park to cast for salmon from shore, or head by boat to Porlier Pass and Trincomali Channel.

Lodging

$$$ ☎ **Woodstone Country Inn.** This serene inn sits on the edge of a forest overlooking a meadow that's fantastic for bird-watching. Stenciled walls and tall windows bring the pastoral setting into spacious bedrooms furnished in a mixture of wicker, antiques, and English country prints. Most rooms have fireplaces and patios, and a few have oversize soaker tubs. The room rates include a hearty gourmet breakfast. Guests and nonguests can have four-course dinners here (reservations essential). Smoking is not permitted at the inn. ⊠ *Georgeson Bay Rd., R.R. 1, V0N 1P0,* ☎ *250/539–2022 or 250/539–5198. 12 rooms. Restaurant. AE, MC, V.*

$ ☎ **Sutil Lodge.** The simple guest rooms at this 1927 British colonial bungalow have throw rugs on dark hardwood floors and beds tucked into window nooks; the shared bathrooms have antique ball-foot tubs and small corner sinks. The kayak center on the property attracts folks from around the world who want to paddle the still coves of the Gulf Islands (rentals and guided trips are available). The room rates include breakfast. ✉ *637 Southwind Rd., Montague Harbour V0N 1P0,* ☎ *250/539–2930,* FAX *250/539–5390. 7 rooms share 3 baths. Dining room, hiking. MC, V.*

Outdoor Activities and Sports

BICYCLES

Bike rentals are available from **Galiano Bicycle** (☎ 250/539–9906).

BOATING, DIVING, AND FISHING

For dive charters on Galiano, contact **Martin Karakas** (☎ 250/539–5186) or **George Parson** (☎ 250/539–3109). Call **Mel-n-i Fishing Charters** (☎ 250/539–3171) or **Bert's Charters** (☎ 250/539–3109) to charter a fishing boat.

GOLF

The nine-hole, par-32 course at **Galiano Golf and Country Club** (☎ 250/539–5533) is moderate in difficulty. The greens fee is $17; power carts are not available.

KAYAKING

For equipment rentals and guided kayak tours, contact **Gulf Islands Kayaking** (☎ 250/539–2442). **Canadian Gulf Islands Seakayaking** (☎ 250/539–2930) has rentals and tours.

Mayne Island

㉝ *28 nautical mi from Swartz Bay (32 km/20 mi north of Victoria); 22 nautical mi from Tsawwassen (39 km/24 mi south of Vancouver).*

Middens of clam and oyster shells give evidence that tiny Mayne Island—only 21 square km (13 square mi)—was inhabited as early as 5,000 years ago. It later became the stopover point for miners headed from Victoria to the goldfields of Fraser River and Barkersville, and by the mid-1800s it had developed into the communal center of the inhabited Gulf Islands, with the first school, post office, police lockup, church, and hotel. Farm tracts and orchards established in the 1930s and 1940s and worked by Japanese farmers until their internment during World War II continue to thrive today, and a farmers' market is open each Saturday during harvest season. There are few stores, restaurants, or historic sites here, but Mayne's manageable size (even if you're on a bicycle) and slow pace make it very popular.

Starting at the ferry dock at Village Bay, head toward Miners Bay on Village Bay Road. About ½ mi from the ferry landing on the left is the unmarked path to **Helen Point** (pull off on the shoulder near the grouping of power lines that cross the road), previously a native reservation but currently without inhabitants. You'll pass middens by the bay and remains of log cabins in the woods on the hour-long hike out to Helen Point, where you can look out across Active Pass (named for the turbulent waters).

A quarter mile farther on the right side of Village Bay Road is the entrance to **Mount Parke,** declared a wilderness park in 1989. Drive as far as the gate and the sign that reads NO VEHICLES PAST THIS POINT. From here it's a 15- to 20-minute hike to the highest point on the island and a stunning, almost 360-degree view of Vancouver, Active Pass, and Vancouver Island.

Continue on Village Bay Road toward **Miners Bay,** a little town 2 km (1 mi) away. Here, you'll find Plumbers Pass Lockup (closed from September to June), built in 1896 as a jail and now a minuscule museum chronicling the island's history.

From Miners Bay head east on Georgia Point Road to **St. Mary Magdalene Church,** a pretty stone chapel built in 1898 that now doubles as an Anglican and United church. The graveyard beyond is also interesting; generations of islanders—the Bennets, Georgesons, Maudes, and Deacons (whose names are all over the Mayne Island map)—are buried here. A stairway across the road leads down to the beach.

At the end of Georgia Point Road is the **Active Pass Lighthouse,** built in 1855, which still signals ships into the busy waterway. The grassy grounds, open daily from 1 to 3, are great for picnicking.

Head back down Georgia Point Road and turn left on Waugh Road, which turns into Campbell Bay Road. There's a great pebble beach for beachcombing at shallow (and therefore warmer) **Campbell Bay.** Look for a pull-out on the left just past the bottom of the hairpin turn. A fence post marks the entrance to the path leading to the beach. Campbell Bay Road ends at Fernhill Road; turn right here and you'll end up back in Miners Bay.

Dining and Lodging

$$$-$$$$ ✕⊞ **Oceanwood Country Inn.** This Tudor-style house on 10 forested
★ acres overlooking Navy Channel has English country decor throughout. Fireplaces, ocean-view balconies, and whirlpool or soaking tubs make several rooms deluxe; all are inviting, with cozy down comforters on comfortable beds, cheerful wall stenciling, and cushioned chairs in brightly lighted reading areas. The waterfront dining room (no lunch) serves outstanding regional cuisine. Afternoon tea and breakfast are included in the room rates. ⊠ *630 Dinner Bay Rd., V0N 2J0,* ☎ *250/ 539–5074,* ⅢX *250/539–3002. 12 rooms. Restaurant, no-smoking rooms, hot tub, sauna, hiking, jogging, beach, bicycles, library, meeting room. MC, V.*

$$-$$$ ✕⊞ **Fernhill Lodge.** Constructed of wood from the property, this 1983 West Coast cedar structure has fantastic theme rooms—Moroccan, East Indian, Edwardian, Japanese, Colonial, Jacobean, and French. Two of them have outdoor hot tubs. Hosts Mary and Brian Crumblehulme prepare historical dinners (Rome, Chaucer, and Cleopatra, to name a few themes) several nights a week; reservations are essential for nonguests. Breakfasts, included in the room rate, are less exotic. This is a no-smoking inn, and pets are not allowed. ⊠ *Fernhill Rd., R.R. 1 C-4, V0N 2J0,* ☎ *250/539–2544. 7 rooms. Dining room, no-smoking rooms, sauna, bicycles, library. MC, V.*

Outdoor Activities and Sports

You can rent bicycles at the **Miner's Bay gas station.**

Saltspring Island

❸❹ *28 nautical mi from Swartz Bay (32 km/20 mi north of Victoria); 22 nautical mi from Tsawwassen (39 km/24 mi south of Vancouver).*

Named for the saltwater springs at its north end, Saltspring is the largest and most developed of the Gulf Islands. Among its first nonnative settlers were black Americans who came here to escape slavery in the 1850s. The agrarian tradition they and other immigrants established remains strong, but tourism and art support the local economy. A government wharf, two marinas, and a waterfront shopping complex at Ganges serve a community of more than 8,500 residents.

In **Ganges,** a pedestrian-oriented seaside village and the island's cultural and commercial center, you'll find dozens of smart boutiques, galleries, and restaurants. **Mouat's Trading Company** (⊠ Fulford-Ganges Rd.), built in 1912 and still functioning as a community store, is worth

Saltspring Island

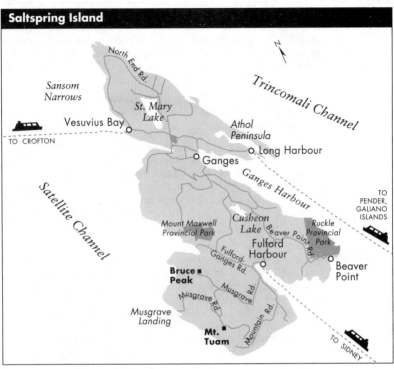

a peek. Ganges is the site of **ArtCraft,** a summerlong festival of arts, crafts, theater, music, and dance. Dozens of artists' studios are open to the public; pick up a studio tour map at the chamber of commerce on Lower Ganges Road.

From Ganges, you can circle the northern tip of the island by bike or car (on Vesuvius Bay Road, Sunset Road, North End and North Beach roads, Walker Hook Road, and Robson Road) past fields and peekaboo marine views. You can take a shortcut on North End Road past **St. Mary Lake,** your best bet for warm-water swimming.

Near the center of Saltspring, the summit of **Mount Maxwell Provincial Park** (⊠ Mt. Maxwell Rd., off Fulford-Ganges Rd.) affords spectacular views of south Saltspring, Vancouver Island, and other of the Gulf Islands. It's also a great picnic spot. The last portion of the drive is steep, winding, and unpaved.

From Mount Maxwell, follow Fulford-Ganges Road south, and then turn east on Beaver Point Road to reach **Ruckle Provincial Park,** site of an 1872 heritage homestead and extensive fields still being farmed by the Ruckle family. The park also has camping and picnic spots and trails leading to rocky headlands.

Dining and Lodging

$$ ✕ **House Piccolo.** Broiled sea scallop brochette, roasted British Columbia venison with juniper berries, and the salmon du jour are good choices for dinner at this casual restaurant. But save room for homemade ice cream or the signature chocolate terrine. ⊠ *108 Hereford Ave., Ganges,* ☎ *250/537–1844. Reservations essential. AE, DC, MC, V. Closed Jan. No lunch.*

$–$$ ✕ **Pomodori.** Earthenware pots with dried flowers, antique farm im-
★ plements, battered wooden tables, bent-willow chairs, and international
folk music set an eclectic tone for an eatery with a menu that changes
daily. Roasted tomato, red pepper, and Italian feta in balsamic-vine-
gar and olive-oil dressing with home-baked focaccia for dipping;
chicken, prawn, and mussel jambalaya; and fresh vegetable and herb
stew appear often. ✉ *Booth Bay Resort, 375 Baker Rd., Ganges,* ☎
250/537–2247. Reservations essential. MC, V. No lunch Mon.–Sat.

$$$$ ✕⊞ **Hastings House.** The centerpiece of this luxurious 30-acre seaside
★ farm estate is a Tudor-style manor built in 1940. Guest quarters are
in the manor or the farmhouse, in cliff-side or garden cottages and in
suites in the reconstructed barn. All are furnished with fine antiques
in an English country theme, with extras such as eiderdowns, fireplaces,
and covered porches or decks. Formal, prix-fixe dinners (reservations
essential) are served in the manor house. ✉ *160 Upper Ganges Rd.,
Box 1110, Ganges, V0S 1E0,* ☎ *250/537–2362 or 800/661–9255,* ⛶
*250/537–5333. 3 rooms, 7 suites, 2 2-bedroom suites. Restaurant, mini-
bars, no-smoking rooms, croquet, beach, mountain bikes. AE, MC, V.
Closed Jan.–mid-Mar.*

$$$ ⊞ **Beach House on Sunset.** Two upstairs rooms in this B&B have pri-
vate entrances and balconies; a romantic cedar-lined cottage with a
wraparound porch sits over the boathouse at water's edge. There's also
a suite with a cathedral ceiling, broad windows framing lovely sea views,
and a private deck with an outdoor shower. Extras include eiderdown
comforters, thick terry robes, slippers, fruit platters, decanters of
sherry, fresh flowers, and a bountiful breakfast. ✉ *930 Sunset Dr., V8K
1E6,* ☎ *250/537–2879,* ⛶ *250/537–4747. 4 rooms. Library. MC, V.
Closed Dec.–Feb.*

$$$ ⊞ **Old Farmhouse Bed and Breakfast.** The style of the main house, a
registered historic property built in 1895, is echoed in a four-room wing
added in 1989 that has rooms furnished with pine bedsteads, down
comforters, lace curtains, and wicker chairs. Breakfast in the dining
room begins with fresh-baked goods followed by a hot entrée such as
a smoked salmon soufflé. ✉ *1077 Northend Rd., V8K 1L9,* ☎ *250/
537–4113,* ⛶ *250/537–4969. 4 rooms. Breakfast room, no-smoking
rooms, boating. MC, V.*

$$$ ⊞ **Salty Springs Resort.** Perched on a 50-ft bluff on the northern shore
of Saltspring, this is the only property to take advantage of the island's
natural mineral springs. The one-, two-, and three-bedroom pon-
derosa-pine cabins have arched Gothic ceilings, fireplaces, kitchenettes,
and whirlpool massage bathtubs that tap into the mineral springs. ✉
1460 N. Beach Rd., V8K 1J4, ☎ *250/537–4111,* ⛶ *250/537–2939.
12 units. Picnic areas, kitchenettes, refrigerators, boating, bicycles, recre-
ation room, coin laundry. MC, V.*

Outdoor Activities and Sports

For bicycle rentals on Saltspring, try **Island Spoke Folk** (☎ 250/537–
4664) at the Trading Company Building in Ganges.

Shopping

There are bargains galore at Saltspring Island's **Saturday markets,** held
from April to October. Fresh produce, seafood, crafts, clothing, herbs
and aromatherapy mixtures, candles, toys, home-canned items, and more
are available at two markets; one is at the top of the hill (next to the
Harbour House) overlooking Ganges Harbour, the other in the center
of town between Fulford-Ganges Road and Centennial Park.

Gulf Islands Essentials

Arriving and Departing

BY BOAT

B.C. Ferries (☎ 250/386–3431; 888/223–3779 in British Columbia only) provides service from outside Vancouver and Victoria to Galiano Island, Mayne Island, and Saltspring Island (reserve ahead). When you travel with a vehicle in summer, arrive at the terminal well in advance of the scheduled sailing time.

BY PLANE

Harbour Air Ltd. (☎ 250/537–5525 or 800/665–0212) and **Hanna Air Saltspring** (☎ 250/537–9359; 800/665–2359 in British Columbia) operate 20- to 30-minute daily floatplane flights from Ganges on Saltspring Island to Coal Harbour in downtown Vancouver and to the Vancouver airport.

Getting Around

BY BUS

Salt Spring Transit (☎ 250/537–4737) routes include one between the ferry terminal and Ganges.

BY CAR

The roads on the islands are narrow and winding. Exercise extreme caution around the many cyclists, who are especially thick on the roads in summer.

Contacts and Resources

CAR RENTAL

Car rentals are available on Saltspring Island through **Heritage Rentals** (☎ 250/537–4225).

EMERGENCIES

Ambulance (☎ 911). **Police** (☎ 911).

Lady Minto Hospital (✉ Ganges, Saltspring Island, ☎ 250/537–5545).

VISITOR INFORMATION

Galiano Island Visitor Information Centre (✉ Sturdies Bay, Box 73, Galiano V0N 1P0, ☎ 250/539–2233). **Mayne Island Chamber of Commerce** (✉ General Delivery, Mayne Island V0N 2J0, no phone). **Saltspring Island Visitor Information Centre** (✉ 121 Lower Ganges Rd., Ganges V8K 2T1, ☎ 250/537–5252).

NORTH OF VANCOUVER ISLAND

The gateway to Alaska and the Yukon, the vast, rugged region north of Vancouver Island, is marked by soaring, snowcapped mountain ranges, scenic fjords, primordial islands, and towering rain forests. Once the center of a vast trading network, the "North by Northwest Region" is home to First Nations (native) people who have lived here for 10,000 years and more recent immigrants drawn by the natural resources of fur, fish, and forest. You can explore the ancient native villages of the Queen Charlotte Islands and Hazelton, fish for rainbow trout or giant halibut, and tour cities such as Prince Rupert and Prince George, which grew out of important fur trading posts.

Inside Passage

★ ㉟ *507 km (314 mi), or 274 nautical mi, between Port Hardy on northern Vancouver Island and Prince Rupert.*

The Inside Passage, a sheltered marine highway, follows a series of natural channels behind protective islands along the green-and-blue shaded

British Columbia coast. The undisturbed landscape of rising mountains and humpbacked islands has a striking, prehistoric look. You can take a ferry cruise along the Inside Passage or see it on one of the more expensive luxury liners that sail along the British Columbia coast from Vancouver to Alaska.

The ferry **Queen of the North,** which holds 800 passengers and 157 vehicles, takes 15 hours (almost all in daylight during summer sailings) to make the Port Hardy to Prince Rupert trip. Reservations are required for the cruise and advised for hotel accommodations at ports of call. ⊠ *B.C. Ferries, 1112 Fort St., Victoria V8V 4V2,* ☎ *250/386–3431 or 604/669–1211.* 📠 *Cost varies according to cabin, vehicle, and season.* ☉ *Sailings Oct.–Apr., once weekly; May, twice weekly; June–Sept., daily, departing on alternate days from Port Hardy and Prince Rupert; departure time 7:30 AM, arrival time 10:30 PM; call to verify schedule.*

Prince Rupert

36 *1,502 km (931 mi) by highway and 750 km (465 mi) by air northwest of Vancouver; 15 hrs by ferry northwest of Port Hardy on Vancouver Island.*

Prince Rupert, the final stop on the B.C. Ferries route through the Inside Passage, has a mild but wet climate, so take rain gear. The town lives off fishing, fish processing, logging, saw- and pulp-mill operations, deep-sea shipping, and tourism.

The **Museum of Northern British Columbia** has one of the province's finest collections of coastal native art; some of the artifacts date back 10,000 years. Native artisans work on totem poles in the carving shed, and in summer the museum runs a 2½-hour boat tour of the harbor and Metlakatla native village. ⊠ *1st Ave. and McBride St.,* ☎ *250/624–3207.* 📠 *Donations accepted.* ☉ *Sept.–May, Mon.–Sat. 10–5; June–Aug., Mon–Sat. 9–9, Sun. 9–5.*

The **North Pacific Cannery Village Museum** in Port Edward, 20 km (12 mi) south of Prince Rupert, is the oldest salmon cannery on the west coast. You can step back in time here, touring the cannery buildings, mess hall, company store, and managers' houses, where interpretive displays about the canning process and cannery village life are set up. ⊠ *1889 Skeena Dr., Port Edward V0E 1G0,* ☎ *250/628–3538.* 📠 *$5.* ☉ *May–Sept., daily 10–7; Oct.–Apr., Wed.–Sun. 10–4.*

Dining and Lodging

$$$ ✕🏨 **Crest Motor Hotel.** Warm and modern, the Crest stands on a bluff
★ overlooking the harbor. Some rooms have minibars and whirlpool tubs. The restaurant, pleasantly decorated with brass rails and beam ceilings, has a waterfront view and specializes in salmon and seafood dishes. ⊠ *222 1st Ave. W, V8J 3P6,* ☎ *250/624–6771 or 800/663–8150,* 📠 *250/627–7666. 102 rooms. Restaurant, coffee shop, lounge, in-room modem lines, no-smoking floor, room service, outdoor hot tub, steam room, exercise room, fishing, baby-sitting, dry cleaning, business services, meeting rooms. AE, D, DC, MC, V.*

$$ 🏨 **Best Western Highliner Inn.** This modern high-rise near the waterfront is in the heart of the downtown shopping district only one block from the airline terminal building. Ask for a room with a private balcony and view of the harbor. ⊠ *815 1st Ave. W, V8J 1B3,* ☎ *250/624–9060 or 800/668–3115,* 📠 *250/627–7759. 93 rooms. Restaurant, lounge, beauty salon, coin laundry. AE, DC, MC, V.*

Shopping

Native art and other local crafts are for sale at **Studio 9** (⊠ 516 3rd Ave. W, ☎ 250/624–2366).

Queen Charlotte Islands

★ ➂⑦ *93 nautical mi southwest of Prince Rupert; 367 nautical mi northwest of Port Hardy.*

The beautiful Queen Charlotte Islands, or Misty Islands, were once the remote preserve of the Haida natives; now they are easily accessible by ferry. Today the Haida make up only one-sixth of the population, but they continue to infuse the island with a sense of the Haida past and contribute to the logging and fishing industries, as well as to tourism. Haida elders lead tours—an essential service if you want to reach the isolated, abandoned villages.

In the Queen Charlottes, 150 km (93 mi) of paved road, most of it on Graham Island (the northernmost and largest of the group of 150), connect the city of Queen Charlotte in the south to Masset in the north. Some of the other islands are laced with gravel roads. The rugged, rocky west coast of the archipelago faces the ocean; the east coast has many broad, sandy beaches. The incredible scenery makes the islands an artisans' delight, and kayaking enthusiasts from around the world are drawn to waterways here. Throughout, the mountains and shores are often shrouded in fog and rain-laden clouds, adding to the islands' mystery.

Naikoon Provincial Park (☎ 250/557–4390), in the northeast corner of Graham, preserves a large section of wilderness where low-lying swamps, pine and cedar forests, lakes, beaches, trails, and wildlife combine to create an intriguing environment. Take the 5-km (3-mi) walk from the Tlell Picnic Site to the beach, and on to the bow section of the old wooden shipwreck of the *Pezuta*, a 1928 log-hauling vessel.

On the southern end of Graham Island, the **Queen Charlotte Islands Museum** has an impressive display of Haida totem poles, masks, and carvings of both silver and argillite (hard black slate). A natural-history exhibit gives interesting background on the wildlife of the islands. ⊠ *Box 1373, Skidegate V0T 1S1,* ☎ *250/559–4643.* ⚏ *$2.50.* ⊙ *Apr.–Oct., weekdays 9–5, weekends 1–5; Nov.–Mar., Wed.–Sun. 1–5.*

The **Ed Jones Haida Museum,** in Old Masset on the northern coast of Graham Island, exhibits totems and artifacts. Nearby, artists sell their work from their homes. South of Graham, in and around **South Moresby National Park Reserve,** lie most of the better-known abandoned Haida villages, which are accessible by water. Several days' travel time and careful planning for wilderness conditions are required to see some of the villages. Visitors must arrange their trips through Parks Canada (☎ 250/559–8818).

Dining and Lodging

There are many small B&Bs on the islands; contact the **Queen Charlotte Islands Travel Infocentre** (⊠ 3922 Hwy. 33, Box 819, Queen Charlotte V0T 1S0, ☎ 250/559–4742, ℻ 250/559–8188) for a list.

$$ ⌂ **Alaska View Lodge.** On a clear day, you can see the mountains of Alaska from the porch of this B&B. A long stretch of sandy beach borders the lodge on one side and woods on the other. With advance notice and at an additional cost, the owner makes a three-course dinner, using classical recipes based on Queen Charlotte fare, such as home-smoked salmon, scallops, and Dungeness crab. ⊠ *Tow Hill Rd., Box 227, Masset V0T 1M0,* ☎ *250/626–3333; 800/661–0019 in Canada;* FAX *250/626–3858. 4 rooms. Dining room, no-smoking rooms. MC, V.*

$$ 🏠 **Spruce Point Lodge.** This cedar-sided building, encircled by a balcony, attracts families and couples because of its low rates and downhome feel. Like most other Queen Charlotte accommodations, the Spruce Point tends to the rustic and has locally made pine furnishings. The rates include a Continental breakfast and an occasional seafood barbecue, with a menu that depends on the daily catch. Bunk rooms are usually available at a low rate. ⊠ *609 6th Ave., Queen Charlotte V0T 1S0,* ☎ FAX *250/559–8234. 7 rooms. Breakfast room, boating, fishing. MC, V.*

Outdoor Activities and Sports
Ecosummer Expeditions (⊠ 1516 Duranleau St., Vancouver V6H 3S4, ☎ 604/669–7741 or 800/465–8884) has multiday guided kayak tours. **Queen Charlotte Adventures** (⊠ Box 196, Queen Charlotte V0T 1S0, ☎ 250/559–8990 or 800/668–4288) also operates multiday guided kayak tours. For kayak equipment rentals, contact **Moresby Explorers** (⊠ Box 109, Sandspit V0T 1T0, ☎ 800/806–7633).

Shopping
Haida figurines are sold at the **Adams Family House of Silver** (☎ 250/ 626–3215), in Old Masset, behind the Ed Jones Haida Museum. **Joy's Island Jewellers** (☎ 250/559–4742) in Queen Charlotte carries a good selection of Haida art.

En Route To see interior British Columbia, take Highway 16 east from Prince Rupert. On the way you'll pass through or near communities such as **Terrace,** with a hot-springs complex at the Mount Layton Resort, skiing at Shames Mountain, and excellent fishing in the Skeena River. At **Kitimat** (Highway 37, off Highway 16 south of Terrace), at the head of the Douglas Channel, the fishing is superb.

Hazelton

❸❽ *293 km (182 mi) northeast of Prince Rupert on Hwy. 16; 439 km (272 mi) northwest of Prince George on Hwy. 16; 1,217 km (755 mi) northwest of Vancouver, Hwy. 99 to Hwy. 97 to Hwy. 16.*

★ Hazelton is rich in the culture of the Gitksan and Wet'suwet'en peoples. **'Ksan,** just outside town, is a re-created Gitksan village. The elaborately painted community of seven longhouses is a replica of the one that stood on the same site when the first European explorers arrived in the 19th century. The carving shed, often used by 'Ksan artists, is open to the public, and three other longhouses can be visited: One displays contemporary masks and robes, another has song-and-dance dramas in the summer, and the third exhibits pre-European tools of bone, sinew, stone, and wood. ⊠ *Box 326, V0J 1Y0,* ☎ *250/842–5544.* 🎫 *$8.* ⊙ *Apr.–Sept., daily 9–6; Oct.–Mar., Thurs.–Mon. 9–5; tour May– mid-Oct., on the hr.*

The **'Ksan Museum** displays works and artifacts from the Upper Skeena River region as well as modern-day regalia kept at the museum by local natives. ⊠ *Box 333, V0J 1Y0,* ☎ *250/842–5723.* 🎫 *Donation.* ⊙ *Mid-Apr.–May, daily 9–5; June–Sept., daily 9–6; Oct., Mon.–Sat. 9–5:30; Nov.–mid-Apr., weekdays 9:30–4:30.*

Prince George

 721 km (447 mi) east of Prince Rupert on Hwy. 16, 786 km (487 mi) north of Vancouver, Hwy. 99 to Hwy. 97.

At the crossroads of two railways and two highways, Prince George has grown to become the capital of northern British Columbia and the third-largest city in the province. Nestled on the edge of a vast forested plateau, it has an economy fueled by forest industries, from tree farms to logging to lumber and paper processing. **Canadian Forest Products Ltd.** (☎ 250/561–3947) provides free tours of the area's pulp and sawmills.

The **Fraser–Fort George Regional Museum** in Fort George Park holds a fine collection of artifacts illustrating local history. ⊠ *333 20th Ave.,* ☎ *250/562–1612.* ☑ *$3.* ☉ *May–Sept., daily 9–5; Sept.–Apr., Tues.–Sun. noon–5.*

A collection of photos, railcars, and logging and sawing equipment at the **Central BC Railway and Forest Industry Museum** traces the town's origin to the building of the railway and the development of logging. ⊠ *150 River Rd.,* ☎ *250/563–7351.* ☑ *$4.* ☉ *May–Sept., Thurs.–Mon. 9–5.*

The **Prince George Native Art Gallery** has traditional and contemporary works (carvings, sculpture, jewelry, literature) by the region's native peoples. ⊠ *144 George St.,* ☎ *250/562–7385.* ☑ *Free.* ☉ *June–Sept., daily 9–5; Oct.–May, Tues.–Sat. 9–5.*

Gold Rush Trail

Begins at Prince George and ends at Lilloet, 170 km (105 mi) west of Kamloops.

From Prince George you can turn south on Highway 97 toward Kamloops and the Okanagan Valley, following the 640-km (397-mi) Gold Rush Trail, along which frontiersmen traveled in search of gold in the 19th and early 20th centuries. It takes you through Quesnel, Williams Lake, Wells, and Barkerville and along the Fraser Canyon and Cache Creek. Most towns and communities through which the trail passes have re-created villages, history museums, or historic sites that help to tell the story of the gold-rush era. For more information contact the **Cariboo Chilcotin Coast Tourist Association** (⊠ Box 4900, Williams Lake V2G 2V8, ☎ 250/392–2226; 800/663–5885 in the U.S.; 𝔽𝔸𝕏 250/392–2838). Another source of information is **Heritage Attractions of British Columbia** (⊠ Ministry of Small Business, Tourism, and Culture, 800 Johnson St., Victoria V8V 1X4, ☎ 250/387–5129).

North of Vancouver Island Essentials

Arriving and Departing

BY BUS

Greyhound Lines of Canada (☎ 604/662–3222 in Canada; 800/231–2222 in the U.S.) stops in Prince Rupert and other towns in northern British Columbia.

BY CAR

The Trans-Canada Highway (Highway 1) heads east from Vancouver, connecting with **Highway 97,** which heads east toward Kamloops and north toward Prince George. **Highway 16** heads west from Prince George to Prince Rupert.

B.C. Rail (☎ 604/984–5246, 604/631–3500, or 800/663–8238) travels from Vancouver to Prince George. **VIA Rail** (☎ 800/835–3037) provides service between Prince Rupert and Prince George.

Getting Around
BY BOAT

The *Queen of Prince Rupert* (☎ 250/386–3431), a B.C. Ferries ship, sails six times a week between late May and September (three times a week during the rest of the year) and can easily accommodate recreational vehicles. The crossing from Prince Rupert to Skidegate, near Queen Charlotte on Graham Island, takes about six hours. Schedules vary and reservations are required. The **M.V. *Kwuna,*** another B.C. Ferries ship, connects Skidegate Landing to Alliford Bay on Moresby Island. Access to smaller islands is by boat or air; plans should be made in advance through a travel agent.

BY PLANE

Harbour Air Ltd. (☎ 250/627–1341 or 800/665–0212) runs scheduled floatplanes between Sandspit, Masset, Queen Charlotte City, and Prince Rupert daily except December 25 and 26 and January 1.

BY TRAIN

Esquimalt & Nanaimo Rail Liner (✉ 450 Pandora Ave., Victoria V8W 1N6, ☎ 250/383–4324; 800/561–8630 in British Columbia), operated by Via Rail, makes the round-trip from Victoria's Pandora Avenue Station to Courtenay; schedules vary seasonally.

Contacts and Resources
EMERGENCIES

Prince George Regional Hospital (✉ 2000 15th Ave., ☎ 250/565–2000; 250/565–2444 emergencies).

LATE-NIGHT PHARMACIES

Hart Drugs (✉ 3789 W. Austin Rd., Prince George, ☎ 250/962–9666).

VISITOR INFORMATION

Prince Rupert Convention and Visitors Bureau (✉ 100 McBride St., Box 669, Prince Rupert V8J 3S1, ☎ 250/624–5637 or 800/667–1994). **Queen Charlotte Islands Travel Infocentre** (✉ 3922 Hwy. 33, Box 819, Queen Charlotte V0T 1S0, ☎ 250/559–4742). **Tourism Prince George** (✉ 1198 Victoria St., V2L 2L2, ☎ 250/562–3700).

HIGH COUNTRY AND ENVIRONS

Diversity of setting differentiates High Country from the other regions of British Columbia. This roughly triangular territory, stretching from Valemount in the north just past Revelstoke in the southeast to Merritt, farther south and west, contains deep canyons carved by the Thompson and Fraser rivers and the towering ranges of the Rockies, Monashees, and Selkirks. If you're driving here from Prince George, continue on Highway 16 to Highway 5 for a spectacular drive through High Country to Kamloops.

The Okanagan Valley region, four hours east of Vancouver by car, or one hour by air, is part of a highland plateau between the Cascade Range on the west and the lower Monashees on the east. Though small in size (only 3% of the province's total landmass), the area contains the interior's largest concentration of people. Okanagan Lake is a vacation magnet for visitors from both the west coast and Alberta. In summer, rooms can be scarce here. The largest towns along the lake—Vernon at the north end, Kelowna in the middle, and Penticton to the south—

are actually one large unit. Okanagan Lake, bordered by Highway 97, is their glue, offering recreation, lodging, and restaurants. Between these towns, and along the lake, are the recreational and resort communities of Summerland, Peachland, Westbank, and Oyama, which are popular destinations and have camping facilities, motels, and cabins. The valley is the fruit-growing capital of Canada, producing apricots, pears, cherries, plums, apples, grapes, and peaches, plus clouds of fragrant blossoms from mid-April through early June.

Kamloops

40 *355 km (220 mi) northeast of Vancouver, Hwy. 1 to Hwy. 5*

Kamloops is a convenient passageway into the Okanagan Valley from Fraser Canyon and Thompson Valley, and a stop on the Canadian Pacific Railroad. Five hundred lakes with trout, Dolly Varden, and kokanee surround the town. In late September and October, however, attention turns to the sockeye salmon, when thousands of these fish, intent on breeding, return home to the waters where they were spawned, in the Adams River (65 km, or 40 mi, east of Kamloops off the Trans-Canada Highway).

Once every four years—the next times will be 1998 and 2002—the sockeye run reaches a massive scale, as more than a million salmon pack the waters and up to 500,000 visitors come to observe. The **Roderick Haig-Brown Conservation Area,** which protects the 11-km (7-mi) stretch of Adams River, is the best vantage point; call the B.C. Parks district office (☎ 604/851–3000) for information.

The **Kamloops Wildlife Park** houses 65 species in fairly natural habitats on 55 acres. Canyon hiking trails, a miniature railway, and adjacent water slides are other attractions. ⊠ *East of Hwy. 1, Box 698, V2C 5L7,* ☎ *250/573–3262.* ☞ *$6.50.* ☉ *Call for seasonal hrs.*

Dining and Lodging

$$ ✕🏨 **Lac le Jeune Resort.** With miles of hiking trails, a lake stocked with trout, and a restaurant that serves robust helpings, this resort lets you enjoy the outdoors. The rustic cabins have ample space and amenities for families, and pets are permitted. In the large, comfortable rooms in the main lodge, no phones or televisions distract from the beauty of the setting. ⊠ *Off Coquihala Hwy., 29 km (18 mi) southwest of Kamloops, Box 3215, Kamloops V2C 6B8,* ☎ *250/372–2722 or 800/561–5253,* FAX *250/372–8755. 28 rooms, chalet, 6 cabins. Restaurant, lounge, no-smoking rooms, sauna, boating, fishing, cross-country skiing, theater, meeting room. AE, D, DC, MC, V. Closed Oct.–Apr.*

$–$$ ✕🏨 **Corbett Lake Country Inn.** The inn's single and duplex cabins are
★ comfortable and basic, as are rooms in the main lodge. Every night the restaurant presents a different fixed menu; favorites include rack of lamb and chateaubriand. Fly-fishing for rainbow trout on the private lake is a big attraction here, and no fishing license is required. Small pets are allowed. The inn is in Merritt, 20 km (12 mi) south of Kamloops. ⊠ *Off Hwy. 5A, Box 327, Merritt V0K 2B0,* ☎ *250/378–4334. 3 rooms, 10 cabins. Restaurant, boating, fishing. V. Closed mid-Jan.– Apr. and Nov.–Dec. 23.*

Outdoor Activities and Sports

CANOEING AND KAYAKING

Mount Robson Adventure Holidays (⊠ Box 687, Valemount V0E 2Z0, ☎ 250/566–4386) operates canoe trips near Mount Robson Provincial Park. **Okanagan Canoe Holidays** (⊠ R.R. 1, 2910 N. Glenmore

Rd., Kelowna V1V 2B6, ☎ FAX 250/762–8156) runs day trips on more than a dozen rivers in the region.

Rivershore Golf Links (⊠ Off Old Shuswap Rd., ☎ 250/573–4211), a Robert Trent Jones–designed 18-hole, par-72 course, is one of British Columbia's longest. The greens fee is between $30 and $45; an optional cart costs $28.50.

Fraser River Raft Expeditions Ltd. (⊠ Box 10, Yale V0K 2S0, ☎ 250/863–2336; 800/363–7238 in Canada). **Mount Robson Adventure Holidays** (⊠ Box 687, Valemount V0E 2Z0, ☎ 250/566–4386).

With 2,844 ft of vertical drop, **Sun Peaks Resort** (⊠ Box 869, Kamloops V2C 5M8, ☎ 250/578–7222 or 800/807–3257) has 58 runs.

For High Country heli-skiing, contact **Mike Wiegle Helicopter Skiing** (⊠ Box 159, Blue River V0E 1J0, ☎ 250/762–5846 or 800/661–9170), **Cat Powder Skiing** (⊠ Box 1479, Revelstoke V0E 5S0, ☎ 250/837–5151).

Vernon

41 *117 km (73 mi) southeast of Kamloops on Hwy 97.*

The main businesses in Vernon are forestry and agriculture. The town borders two other lakes besides Okanagan, the more enticing of which is Kalamalka Lake. Vernon is also the town closest to the ski area and gaslight-era-theme village resort atop Silver Star Mountain.

Kalamalka Lake Provincial Park has warm-water beaches and some of the most scenic viewing points and hiking trails in the region. ⊠ *Off Hwy. 97, follow signs 16 km (10 mi) south of Vernon,* ☎ *250/494–6500.* ⌷ *Free.* ☉ *Daily 9 AM–dusk.*

★ The **O'Keefe Historic Ranch** provides a glimpse of cattle-ranch life at the turn of the century. The Victorian mansion is opulently furnished with original antiques. On the 50 acres are a Chinese cooks' house, St. Anne's Church, a blacksmith shop, a reconstructed general store, a display of the old Shuswap and Okanagan Railroad, and a modern restaurant and gift shop. Stagecoach rides are available. ⊠ *9830 Hwy. 97, 12 km (7 mi) north of Vernon,* ☎ *250/542–7868.* ⌷ *$5.* ☉ *Mid-May–mid-Oct., daily 9–5.*

Dining and Lodging

$$ ✕ **Craigellachie Dining Room.** The home-cooked meals in the dining room of the Putnam Station Hotel are filling rather than fancy. Soups and sandwiches are on the lunch menu, and old favorites like barbecue ribs, lasagna, pork chops, steaks, and pastas are offered in the evenings. The daily three-course special is generally a good deal. ⊠ *Silver Star Mountain Resort,* ☎ *250/542–2459. Reservations essential. AE, MC, V.*

$$–$$$ ✕⊡ **Swiss Hotel Silver Lode Inn.** Owner Isidore Borgeaud serves hearty helpings of real raclette or fondue in her cheerful Silver Lode Restaurant. The inn's no-frills rooms are the most reasonably priced in the village; some have kitchenettes. ⊠ *Silver Star Mountain Resort, Box 5, Silver Star Mountain, BC V0E 1G0,* ☎ *250/549–5105,* FAX *250/549–2163. 20 rooms. Restaurant, bar, lobby lounge, indoor pool, hot tub, bicycles, ski storage, meeting room. AE, MC, V.*

$$$ ⊞ **Vance Creek Hotel.** Looking more like the set of a spaghetti west-
★   ern than a modern hotel, the Vance Creek has a prime location in the
      heart of the resort. Rooms are simple, with coordinated decor and boxy
      bathrooms. Those on the first floor are equipped with kitchenettes, bunk
      beds, and private outside entrances. Willow furniture and fireplaces
      add a touch more comfort to suites in the 1993 annex. ⊠ *Silver Star
      Mountain Resort, Box 3002, Silver Star Mountain V0E 1G0,* ☎ *250/
      549–5191,* FAX *250/549–5177. 84 rooms. Bar, dining room, lobby
      lounge, kitchenettes, no-smoking rooms, refrigerators, bicycles, cross-
      country and downhill skiing, ski storage, coin laundry, meeting rooms.
      AE, D, MC, V. Closed mid-Apr.–mid-May.*

Outdoor Activities and Sports

GOLF

Predator Ridge Golf Resort (⊠ 360 Commonage Rd., ☎ 250/542–3436)
has an 18-hole, par-73 course. The greens fee is $60; an optional cart
costs $30.

SKIING

Silver Star Mountain Resort (⊠ Box 2, Silver Star Mountain V1B 3M1,
☎ 250/542–0224; 800/663-4431 in the U.S.), with more than 80 runs,
offers the extra bonus of well-lighted night downhill skiing.

Kelowna

㊷ *46 km (29 mi) south of Vernon on Hwy. 97; 68 km (42 mi) north of
Penticton on Hwy. 97.*

Kelowna is the largest town in the Okanagan Valley and the geo-
graphic center of the valley's wine industry. For information about tours,
call the individual wineries. **Calona Wines Ltd.** (⊠ 1125 Richter St.,
☎ 250/762–9144) is British Columbia's oldest and largest wine maker.
One of the area's more intimate wineries is **Gray Monk Estate Winery**
(⊠ 1055 Camp Rd., ☎ 250/766–3168), which is 8 km (5 mi) west of
Winfield, off Highway 97. **CedarCreek Estate Winery** (⊠ 5445 Lakeshore
Rd., off Hwy. 97, ☎ 250/764–8866) is 12 km (7 mi) south of Kelowna;
it's a smaller area winery.

Father Pandosy's Mission, the first nonnative settlement in the region,
was founded here in 1859. ⊠ *3685 Benvoulin Rd.,* ☎ *250/860–8369.*
🎫 *Donations accepted.* ⊙ *Daily 8–dusk.*

Dining and Lodging

$$–$$$ ✕ **Agapi's Greek Taverna.** This contemporary-looking restaurant has
        a Greek menu that lists seafood, lamb, and standards such as spanako-
        pita, dolma, hummus, and kabobs. ⊠ *375 Leon Ave.,* ☎ *250/763–
        0997. AE, DC, MC, V.*

$$$$ ⊞ **The Grand Okanagan.** On the shore of Okanagan Lake, this new
       resort is a five-minute stroll from the shops, theaters, and restaurants
       of downtown Kelowna. The guest rooms in the high-rise tower have
       peach decor and views of the lake and surrounding mountains. Wa-
       terfront condo units have fully equipped kitchens. ⊠ *1310 Water St.,
       V1Y 9P3,* ☎ *250/763–4500 or 800/465–4651,* FAX *250/763–4565.
       205 rooms. Restaurant, lounge, pool, exercise room, laundry service
       and dry cleaning, business services, convention center, meeting rooms.
       AE, DC, MC, V.*

$$$ ⊞ **Hotel Eldorado.** Rebuilt in the style of the 1926-vintage Eldorado
      Arms, which burned down in the early 1990s, the new Eldorado re-
      tains much of the original's charm. Rooms are cozy, with light carpets,
      floral patterns, and Canadian heritage furnishings; many have balconies

with views of Okanagan Lake. The dining room serves fresh rack of lamb and seafood dishes. ⊠ *500 Cook Rd., V1W 3G9,* ☎ *250/763–7500,* FAX *250/861–4779. 20 rooms. Restaurant, lounge, no-smoking rooms, boating. AE, DC, MC, V.*

$$$ ⊞ **Lake Okanagan Resort.** The rooms of this self-contained resort on
★ the west side of Okanagan Lake have either kitchens or kitchenettes and range in size from one-room suites in the main hotel to three-room chalets spread around the 300 acres. Large rooms, functional furnishings, wood-burning fireplaces, perfect views of the lake, and all the resort activities make this a good choice. ⊠ *2751 Westside Rd., V1Y 8B2,* ☎ *250/769–3511 or 800/663–3273,* FAX *250/769–6665. 150 rooms. Restaurant, café, no-smoking rooms, refrigerators, 3 pools, hot tub, sauna, 9-hole golf course, 7 tennis courts, exercise room, beach, dock, bicycles, video games, children's programs (ages 6–12), playground, coin laundry, laundry service and dry cleaning, meeting rooms, helipad. AE, DC, MC, V.*

Outdoor Activities and Sports

CANOEING AND KAYAKING

For guided trips along the region's waterways, try **Okanagan Canoe Holidays** (⊠ R.R. 1, 2910 N. Glenmore Rd., V1V 2B6, ☎ 250/762–8156).

GOLF

Gallagher's Canyon Golf and Country Club (⊠ 4320 Gallagher's Dr. W, Kelowna, ☎ 250/861–4240) has an 18-hole, par-72 course. The greens fee is $65; an optional cart costs $30. **Harvest Golf Club** (⊠ 2725 KLO Rd., East Kelowna, ☎ 250/862–3103) has an 18-hole, par-72 course. The greens fee is between $45 and $65; an optional cart costs $30.

HIKING

You can hike the rail bed of the **Kettle Valley Railway** network along Lake Okanagan between Penticton and Kelowna. The Visitors Bureau for Kelowna (☎ 250/861–1515) provides maps and information. **Kelowna Hike-Bike-Paddle Adventures** (⊠ R.R. 1, 2910 N. Glenmore Rd., V1V 2B6, ☎ 250/762–8156) arranges guided hikes.

SKIING

Big White Ski Resort (⊠ Big White Rd., 24 km [15 mi] east of Kelowna south of Hwy. 33, ☎ 250/765–3101 or 800/663–2772) has almost 70 downhill runs on about 12,000 acres of skiable terrain and is expanding rapidly. Night skiing is available five nights a week.

Shopping

At **Geert Maas Sculpture Gardens, Gallery, and Studio** (⊠ Reynolds Rd., ☎ 250/860–7012), in the hills above Kelowna, sculptor Geert Maas exhibits his distinctive bronze, stoneware, and mixed-media abstract figures in an indoor gallery and a garden. He also sells medallions, original paintings, and etchings. The **Okanagan Pottery Studio** (☎ 250/767–2010), on Highway 97 south of Kelowna in Peachland, sells handcrafted ceramics.

Penticton

43 *68 km (42 mi) south of Kelowna on Hwy. 97; 395 km (245 mi) from Vancouver, east on Hwy. 3 to Hwy. 3A (at Keremeos) and north (at Kaleden) on Hwy. 97.*

Penticton's winter population is about 25,000, but it numbers in summer near 130,000. Sixteen kilometers (10 miles) north of town, you can take a ride on the historic **Kettle Valley Steam Railway** (⊠ 10112

S. Victoria Rd., Summerland, ☎ 250/494–8422), which passes through 10 km (6 mi) of orchards, vineyards, and wooded mountain terrain along the 1915 line that opened up the interior of British Columbia by connecting Vancouver with the Kootenays.

The **Okanagan Game Farm** (☎ 250/497–5405), an 11-km (7-mi) drive south from Penticton on Highway 97, has more than 100 species of wild animals from around the world.

Dining and Lodging

$$–$$$ ✕ **Granny Bogner's.** The theme is determinedly homey: flowing lace
★   curtains, Oriental rugs, wood chairs, cloth-covered tables, and waitresses in long skirts. But the food at this mostly Continental restaurant is excellent. The poached halibut and roasted duck have contributed to the widely held belief that this is the best restaurant in the Okanagan. ⌂ 302 Eckhardt Ave. W, ☎ 250/493–2711. Reservations essential. AE, MC, V. Closed Sun.–Mon. and Jan. No lunch.

$$$ 🏨 **Clarion Lakeside Resort and Conference Center.** On the shore of Okanagan Lake, this is a peaceful retreat that's right in the center of the action. Vancouver businesspeople love the resort for its comfort and conference facilities. The rooms are bright and airy; half have lake views and some have whirlpool tubs. ⌂ 21 Lakeshore Dr. W, V2A 7M5, ☎ 250/493–8221 or 800/663–9400, ℻ 250/493–0607. 204 rooms. Café, coffee shop, dining room, in-room modem lines, no-smoking floor, room service, indoor pool, beauty salon, hot tub, massage, sauna, 2 tennis courts, aerobics, health club, jogging, shuffleboard, volleyball, beach, dock, bicycles, billiards, nightclub, recreation room, video games, baby-sitting, children's programs (ages 5–12), dry cleaning, concierge, business services, convention center, meeting rooms. AE, DC, MC, V.

$ 🏨 **Riordan House.** One bedroom at this B&B in a house built in 1921 by a Prohibition rum-runner has a fireplace, and one has a sitting area; all look out on the surrounding hills. The rates include a Continental breakfast of home-baked croissants, scones, muffins, and a selection of seasonal fruit; box lunches are packed on request. ⌂ 689 Winnipeg St., V2A 5N1, ☎ ℻ 250/493–5997. 3 rooms share 3 baths. Breakfast room, no-smoking rooms, in-room VCRs, bicycles, airport and beach shuttle. MC, V.

Outdoor Activities and Sports

Apex Resort (⌂ Apex Mountain Rd., 33 km [21 mi] west of Penticton, ☎ 250/492–2880 or 800/387–2739) has 56 trails, a vertical rise of 2,000 ft, and a peak elevation of 7,187 ft.

Cathedral Provincial Park

75 km (47 mi) from Penticton, Hwy. 97 south to Hwy. 3A west to Hwy. 3 west.

Off Highway 3 along the U.S. border, Cathedral Provincial Park (☎ 250/494–6500) preserves 82,000 acres of lakes and rolling meadows, teeming with mule deer, mountain goats, and California bighorn sheep. To reach the main part of the park, either take the steep, eight-hour hike, or arrange (and pay in advance) for the **Cathedral Lakes Lodge** (☎ 250/499–5848) to transport you by four-wheel-drive vehicle. There are 16 campsites in the park, which is open from mid-June to early October.

Outdoor Activities and Sports

Manning Park Resort (⌂ Hwy. 3, Hope, ☎ 250/840–8822), northwest of Cathedral Provincial Park, has excellent cross-country trails and downhill facilities.

En Route Heading west from Cathedral Provincial Park, Highway 3 connects with the Trans-Canada Highway (Highway 1), which parallels the Fraser River. To the north, a glimpse through the mists above roiling **Hell's Gate,** in scenic Fraser Canyon, hints at how the region got its name. An air tram (cable car) carries you across the foaming canyon above the fishway, where millions of sockeye salmon fight their way upriver to spawning grounds four times a year—April, July, August, and October. In addition to displays on the lifecycle of the salmon, you'll find a fudge factory, a gift shop, and a restaurant at the lower air-tram terminal. This site is about 2½ hours east of Vancouver. ⌂ *Hell's Gate Airtram, Exit 170 off Hwy. 1, Hope,* ☎ *604/867–9277.* ⌦ *$9.50.* ☺ *Mid-Apr.–mid-Oct., daily 9 AM; closing time between 5 and 7, depending on season.*

Harrison Hot Springs

㊹ *128 km (79 mi) northeast of Vancouver on Hwy. 1.*

The small resort community of Harrison Hot Springs lies at the southern tip of picturesque Harrison Lake. Vacationers flock here to relax in this almost pristine natural setting. Mountains surround the 64-km-long (40-mi-long) lake, which, ringed by pretty beaches, provides a broad range of outdoor activities in addition to the hot springs.

There's a spring-fed public pool at the **Harrison Hot Springs Hotel.** ⌂ *100 Esplanade,* ☎ *604/796–2244.* ⌦ *$7.50.* ☺ *Sun.–Thurs. 8 AM–9 PM, Fri.–Sat. 8 AM–10 PM.*

★ ☜ A tour of **Kilby Historic Store and Farm,** a heritage attraction in nearby Harrison Mills, takes you back to the British Columbia of the 1920s. Tour the general store and farm buildings of T. Kilby and other pioneers of the area, chat with the shopkeeper, sniff whatever is simmering on the wood-burning stove, and tramp through the orchards, stockroom, fueling station, barn, and dairy house on the grounds. The kids can enjoy feeding the farm animals. You can sample 1920s-style home cooking in the **Harrison River Tearoom.** This is a fine slice of living history. ⌂ *215 Kilby Rd. (1½ km/1 mi off Hwy. 7 on north shore of Fraser River; follow signs), Harrison Mills,* ☎ *604/796–9576.* ⌦ *$4.50.* ☺ *Mid-Apr.–June and Sept.–Nov., Thurs.–Mon. 11–5; July–Aug., daily 11–5.*

Dining and Lodging

$$ ✕ **Black Forest.** Ask the locals where to dine and they'll send you here, to a charming Bavarian dining room on Harrison Village Esplanade, overlooking the lake. It comes as no surprise that the specialties are German standards, from schnitzels to Black Forest cake, with a few Continental dishes (mainly steaks and seafood) for good measure. Hearty German beer and an array of wines round out the selection. ⌂ *180 Esplanade,* ☎ *604/796–9343. AE, MC, V. No lunch.*

$$$ ✕⊞ **Harrison Hot Springs Hotel.** Ever since fur traders and gold miners discovered the soothing hot springs in the late 1800s, Harrison has been a favored stopover spot. Built beside the lake in the 1920s, the hotel has grown over the decades. The most reasonably priced rooms, in the original building and the west tower, have an old English look, with Edwardian furnishings and ceiling moldings; the more modern and plush rooms in the east tower carry a heftier price tag. Amenities include a PGA-rated nine-hole golf course. ⊠ *100 Esplanade, V0M 1K0,* ☎ *604/796–2244 or 800/663–2266,* ᴬˣ *604/796–3682. 290 rooms, 16 cottages. 2 restaurants, lounge, no-smoking floors, room service, 2 indoor pools, 1 outdoor pool, beauty salon, hot springs, massage, 1 indoor tennis court, 2 outdoor tennis courts, exercise room, hiking, bicycles, playground, laundry service and dry cleaning, business services, meeting rooms. AE, DC, MC, V.*

Rosedale

45 *8 km (5 mi) southwest of Harrison Hot Springs; 120 km (74 mi) east of Vancouver on Hwy. 1.*

The attractions in Rosedale are a beautiful garden and a water park. The well-signed **Minter Gardens** is a 27-acre compound containing 11 beautifully presented theme gardens—Chinese, rose, English, fern, fragrance, and more—along with aviaries and ponds. There are playgrounds and a giant evergreen maze. ⊠ *Exit 135 off Hwy. 1, 52892 Bunker Rd.,* ☎ *604/794–7191; 800/661–3919 in Canada.* ⊠ *$10.* ☾ *Apr.–Oct., daily 9–dusk.*

☾ It's hard to miss the **Trans-Canada Waterslides,** a tremendously popular water park that has slides with such names as Kamikaze, Cannonball, Super Heroes, Black Hole, and Flash Flood, along with wave and soaking pools, snack bars, and sunbathing areas. ⊠ *Bridal Falls Rd.,* ☎ *604/794–7455.* ⊠ *$12.50.* ☾ *Mid-May–mid-June, weekends 10–8; mid-June–early Sept., daily 10–9.*

High Country and Environs Essentials

Arriving and Departing

BY CAR

From Vancouver, take the **Trans-Canada Highway** (Highway 1) and **Highway 5** to get to Kamloops. Highway 5 continues north to the Mount Robson Park area, where it joins **Highway 16** heading north to Prince George.

Contacts and Resources

EMERGENCIES

Kelowna General Hospital (⊠ 2268 Pandosy St., ☎ 250/862–4000). **Royal Inland Hospital** (⊠ 311 Columbia St., Kamloops, ☎ 250/374–5111).

LATE-NIGHT PHARMACIES

Kipp-Mallery I.D.A. Pharmacy (⊠ 273 Victoria St., Kamloops, ☎ 250/372–2531). **Pharmasave Drugs** (⊠ 235 Wallace St., Hope, ☎ 604/869–2486).

VISITOR INFORMATION

High Country Tourist Association (⊠ 2–1490 Pearson Pl., Kamloops V1S 1J9, ☎ 250/372–7770 or 800/567–2275). **North by Northwest Tourism** (⊠ 3840 Alfred Ave., Smithers V0J 2N0, ☎ 250/847–5227). **Okanagan–Similkameen Tourist Association** (⊠ 1332 Water St., Kelowna V1Y 9P4, ☎ 250/860–5999).

WHISTLER

Whistler and Blackcomb mountains, part of the Whistler Resort (☎ 800/944–7853), are the two largest ski mountains in North America and are consistently ranked the first- or second-best ski destinations on the continent. There's winter and summer glacier skiing, the longest vertical drop in North America, and one of the most advanced lift systems in the world. Whistler has also grown in popularity as a summer destination, with a range of outdoor activities and events.

Whistler Village

120 km (74 mi) north of Vancouver, Hwy. 1 to Hwy. 99.

At the base of the mountains are Whistler Village, Town Plaza, Market Place, and Upper Village—a rapidly expanding, interconnected community of lodgings, restaurants, pubs, gift shops, and boutiques. Locals generally refer to the entire area as Whistler Village. With dozens of hotels and condos within a five-minute walk of the mountains, the site is frenzied with activity, though all on foot: Whistler Village is a pedestrian-only community. Anywhere you want to go within the resort is at most five minutes away, and parking lots are just outside the village.

Dining
Dining at Whistler is informal; casual dress is appropriate everywhere. Japanese and Mediterranean offerings are especially strong in the village.

CATEGORY	COST*
$$$$	over C$40
$$$	C$30–C$40
$$	C$20–C$30
$	under C$20

per person for a three-course meal, excluding drinks, service, and sales tax

$$$ ✕ **Il Caminetto di Umberto and Trattoria di Umberto.** Umberto offers home-style Italian cooking in a relaxed atmosphere; he specializes in pasta dishes such as crab-stuffed cannelloni and four-cheese lasagna. Il Caminetto is known for its veal, osso buco, and zabaglione. The Trattoria has a Tuscan-style rotisserie. A pasta dish is served with a tray of chopped tomatoes, hot pepper, basil, olive oil, anchovies, and Parmesan so that you can mix it to be as spicy and flavorful as you like. ⊠ *Il Caminetto: 4242 Village Stroll,* ☎ *604/932–4442;* ⊠ *Trattoria: Mountainside Lodge, 4417 Sundial Pl.,* ☎ *604/932–5858. Reservations essential. AE, DC, MC, V.*

$$$ ✕ **Les Deux Gros.** The name means "the two fat guys," which may ex-
★ plain the restaurant's motto, "Never trust a skinny chef." Portions of the country French cuisine are generous indeed. Alsatian onion pie, steak tartare, juicy rack of lamb, and salmon Wellington are all superbly crafted and presented, and service is friendly but unobtrusive. Just southwest of the village, this is the spot for a special romantic dinner; request one of the tables by the stone fireplace. ⊠ *1200 Alta Lake Rd.,* ☎ *604/ 932–4611. Reservations essential. AE, MC, V. No lunch.*

$$ ✕ **La Rúa.** One of the brightest lights on the Whistler dining scene is
★ on the ground floor of Le Chamois (☞ Lodging, *below*). Reddish flagstone floors and sponge-painted walls, a wine cellar behind a wrought-iron door, modern oil paintings, and sconce lighting give the restaurant an intimate, Mediterranean ambience. Favorites from the Continental menu include charred rare tuna, loin of deer, rack of lamb, and baked sea bass fillet in a red-wine and herb sauce. ⊠ *4557 Blackcomb Way,* ☎ *604/932–5011. Reservations essential. AE, DC, MC, V. No lunch.*

$ ✕ **Zeuski's.** Wall murals of the Greek islands surround candlelit ta-
★ bles, helping to create a Mediterranean atmosphere at this friendly taverna. There's a patio for alfresco dining. It's hard to pass on the spanakopita, souvlaki, and other standards, but the house special, *katapoulo* (chicken breast rolled in pistachios and roasted), is not to

be missed, nor are the tender, delicately herb-battered calamari. ⊠ *Whistler Town Plaza, 4314 Main St.,* ☎ *604/932–6009. Reservations essential. AE, MC, V.*

Lodging

Accommodations in Whistler, including hundreds of time-share condos, can be booked through the **Whistler Resort Association** (☎ 604/932–3928 or 800/944–7853); summer rates are greatly discounted. The new **Pan Pacific Lodge** in Whistler Village, managed by Pan Pacific Hotels (☎ 800/937–1515), should be up and running by the time you read this.

CATEGORY	COST*
$$$$	over C$300
$$$	C$200–C$300
$$	C$125–C$200
$	under C$125

All prices are for a standard double room for two, excluding 10% provincial accommodation tax, 15% service charge, and 7% GST.

$$$$ ☒ **Chateau Whistler.** Canadian Pacific built and runs this large and friendly-looking fortress in the Upper Village at the foot of Blackcomb Mountain. The standard rooms are average, but the suites are fit for royalty, with specially commissioned quilts and works of art, complemented by antique furnishings. Expansion to be completed sometime in 1998 will add 220 more rooms and new meeting space. ⊠ *4599 Chateau Blvd., Box 100, V0N 1B0,* ☎ *604/938–8000; 800/441–1414 in the U.S. and Canada;* FAX *604/938–2055. 307 rooms, 36 suites. Restaurant, lobby lounge, tapas bar, indoor-outdoor pool, saunas, steam rooms, 18-hole golf course, 3 tennis courts, mountain bikes, ski shop, shops, piano, travel services. AE, D, DC, MC, V.*

$$$$ ☒ **Delta Whistler Resort.** The resort at the base of Whistler Mountain, catercorner to the Whistler Village Gondola and adjacent to the Whistler Golf Club, is a large complex, complete with shopping, dining, and fitness facilities. Rooms are very generous in size (almost all will easily sleep four). There are a few standard rooms, but most have fireplaces, whirlpool bathtubs, balconies, and/or kitchens. ⊠ *4050 Whistler Way, Box 550, V0N 1B0,* ☎ *604/932–1982; 800/877–1133 in the U.S.; 800/268–1133 in Canada;* FAX *604/932–7318. 276 rooms, 24 suites. Restaurant, sports bar, kitchenettes, pool, indoor and outdoor hot tubs, steam room, 2 indoor-outdoor tennis courts, shops, video games, coin laundry. AE, DC, MC, V.*

$$$$ ☒ **Edgewater.** Next to pretty little Green Lake nestles this intimate cedar lodge. In traditional Canadian shades of olive, crimson, pale yellow, and cloudy blue, the interior is simple and relaxing, a true country retreat. An extended Continental breakfast (juice, granola, fruit, and breakfast breads) is included in the tariff at this no-smoking establishment. ⊠ *Off Hwy. 99, 2½ km (1½ mi) north of village, Box 369, V0N 1B0,* ☎ *604/932–0688,* FAX *604/932–0686. 6 rooms, 6 suites. Dining room, bar, outdoor hot tub, hiking, boating, cross-country skiing, ski storage. MC, V.*

$$$–$$$$ ☒ **Le Chamois.** This luxury hotel enjoys a prime ski-in, ski-out loca-
★   tion at the base of the Blackcomb runs. Of the spacious guest rooms with convenience kitchens, the most popular are the studios with Jacuzzi tubs set in front of the living room's bay windows, overlooking the slopes and lifts. Guests can also keep an eye on the action from the glass elevators and the heated outdoor pool. ⊠ *4557 Blackcomb Way, V0N 1B0,* ☎ *604/932–8700; 800/777–0185 in the U.S. and Canada;* FAX *604/905–2576. 47 suites, 6 studios. 2 restaurants, kitchenettes, refrigerators, room service, pool, coin laundry. AE, DC, MC, V.*

$$$ 🕮 **Durlacher Hof.** Custom fir woodwork and doors, exposed ceiling beams, a *kachelofen* (tiled oven), and antler chandeliers hung over fir benches and tables carry out the rustic European theme of this fancy Tyrolean inn. The green and maroon bedrooms, all named for European mountains, contain more fine examples of custom-crafted wooden furniture. Two upgraded rooms on the third floor have added amenities such as double whirlpool tubs. A hearty European breakfast is included in the tariff. ⊠ *7055 Nesters Rd., V0N 1B0,* ☎ *604/932–1924,* FAX *604/938–1980. 7 double rooms, 1 suite. No-smoking rooms, hot tub, sauna, ski storage, airport shuttle. MC, V. Closed Nov.*

$$$ 🕮 **Pension Edelweiss.** Rooms here have a crisp, spic-and-span feel in keeping with the Bavarian-chalet style of the house; some have balconies and telephones. Breakfast is included in the room rate. A bus stop just outside provides easy access to Whistler Village. ⊠ *7162 Nancy Greene Way, Box 850, V0N 1B0,* ☎ *604/932–3641 or 800/665–2003,* FAX *604/938–1746. 8 rooms, 1 suite. No-smoking rooms, hot tub, sauna, bicycles, ski storage. AE, MC, V.*

$ 🕮 **Hostelling International Whistler Youth Hostel.** Although it's nothing to write home about, the hostel is the cheapest sleep in town, and there's a kitchen. ⊠ *Alta Lake Rd., V0N 1B0,* ☎ *604/932–5492,* FAX *604/932–4687. 30 beds in 5 dorms, 1 private room (no bath). Ski storage. No credit cards.*

Outdoor Activities and Sports

CANOEING, KAYAKING, RAFTING, AND WINDSURFING

Canoe, kayak, and sailboard rentals are available at **Alta Lake** at both Lakeside Park and Wayside Park. A spot that's perfect for canoeing is the **River of Golden Dreams,** either from Meadow Park to Green Lake or upstream to Twin Bridges. Kayakers looking for a thrill may want to try **Green River** from Green Lake to Pemberton. **Whistler River Adventures** (☎ 604/932–3532) operates half- and full-day rafting trips priced from $50 to $150.

The breezes are reliable for windsurfing on Alpha, Alta, and Green lakes. Call **Whistler Outdoor Experience** (☎ 604/932–3389), **Whistler Sailing and Water Sports** (☎ 604/932–7245), **Whistler Windsurfing** (☎ 604/932–3589), or **Sea to Sky Kayaking** (☎ 604/898–5498) for equipment or guided trips.

FISHING

Whistler Backcountry Adventures (⊠ 4314 Main St., No. 36, ☎ 604/938–1410) or **Whistler Fishing Guides** (⊠ Carlton Lodge, 4218 Mountain Sq. [base of both gondolas], ☎ 604/932–4267) will take care of anything you need—equipment, guides, and transportation. All five lakes around Whistler are stocked with trout, but the area around Dream River Park is one of the most popular.

GOLF

Robert Trent Jones II designed the championship 18-hole, par-72 course at the **Chateau Whistler Golf Club** (⊠ 4612 Blackcomb Way, ☎ 604/938–2092). The greens fee runs from $70 to $105, which includes a mandatory cart. The scenery at the 18-hole, par-72 course at the **Whistler Golf Club** (⊠ 4010 Whistler Way, ☎ 604/932–4544) is as beautiful as the back nine is difficult. The greens fee at this Arnold Palmer–designed course runs from $50 to $85; an optional cart costs $25.

RAFTING

Canadian River Expeditions (⊠ 301–9571 Emerald Dr., Whistler V0N 1B9, ☎ 604/938–6651; 800/898–7238 in Canada only) conducts rafting trips.

Skiing

CROSS-COUNTRY

The meandering trail around the Whistler Golf Club in the village is an ideal beginners' route. For more advanced skiing, try the 28 km (17 mi) of track-set trails that wind around scenic Lost Lake, Chateau Whistler Golf Club, and the Nicklaus North Golf Club and Green Lake. Cross-country trail maps and equipment rental information are available at the **Whistler Activity and Information Center** (☎ 604/932–2394) in the village.

DOWNHILL

The vertical drops and elevations at **Blackcomb** (☎ 604/938–7743, FAX 604/938–7527) and **Whistler** (☎ 604/932–3434, FAX 604/938–9174) mountains are perhaps the most impressive features here. The resort covers 6,998 acres of skiable terrain in 12 alpine bowls on three glaciers and on more than 200 marked trails, served by the most advanced high-speed lift system on the continent. Blackcomb has a 5,280-ft vertical drop, North America's longest, while Whistler comes in second, with a 5,020-ft drop. The top elevation is 7,494 ft on Blackcomb and 7,160 on Whistler. Blackcomb and Whistler have more than 100 marked trails each and receive an average of 360 inches of snow per year; Blackcomb is open from June to August for summer glacier skiing. Whistler Ski School and Blackcomb Ski School provide lessons to skiers of all levels.

HELI-SKIING

Mountain Heli-Sports (☎ 604/932–2070), **Tyax Heli-Skiing** (☎ 604/932–7007 or 800/663–8126), and **Whistler Heli-Skiing** (☎ 604/932–4105) have guided day trips with up to four glacier runs, or 12,000 vertical ft of skiing, for experienced skiers; the cost is about $350.

Whistler Essentials

Arriving and Departing

BY BUS

Maverick Coach Lines (☎ 604/255–1171) has buses leaving every couple of hours for Whistler Village from the depot in downtown Vancouver. The fare is about $34 round-trip. During ski season, the last bus leaves Whistler at 9:45 PM. **Perimeter Bus Transportation** (☎ 604/266–5386) has daily service, from November to April and June to September, from Vancouver International Airport to Whistler. Prepaid reservations are necessary 24 hours in advance; the ticket booth is on Level One of the airport. The fare is around $40 one-way. **Westcoast City and Nature Sightseeing** (☎ 604/451–1600 in Vancouver) operates a sightseeing tour to Whistler that allows passengers to stay over and return on their date of choice to Vancouver; call for seasonal rates.

BY CAR

Whistler is 120 km (74 mi), or 2½ hours, north of Vancouver on winding Highway 99, the Sea-to-Sky Highway.

BY TRAIN

B.C. Rail (☎ 604/984–5246) travels north from Vancouver to Whistler along a beautiful route. The Vancouver Bus Terminal and the North Vancouver Station are connected by bus shuttle. Rates are under $60 round-trip for the train only.

Getting Around

Streets in Whistler Village, Village North, and Upper Village are clearly marked and easy to negotiate by car, and pay parking is readily available. However, there's really no reason to use a car because the resort association operates a free public transit system that loops throughout the resort; call 604/932–4020 for information and schedules.

Contacts and Resources

B&B RESERVATION AGENCIES

Whistler Bed and Breakfast Inns (☎ 604/932–3282 or 800/665–1892) represents the leading inns of Whistler.

CAR RENTAL

Budget Rent-a-Car (☎ 604/932–1236) and **Thrifty Car Rental** (☎ 604/938–0302 or 800/367–2277) have rental outlets in the village.

EMERGENCIES

Dial 0 for **police, ambulance,** or **poison control.**

GUIDED TOURS

Alpine Adventure Tours (☎ 604/683–0209) conducts a Whistler history tour of the valley and a Squamish day trip. **Whistler Nature Guides** (☎ 604/932–4595) operates guided alpine hiking tours. Budget-priced, guided camping trips out of Vancouver are available through **Bigfoots Backpacker Adventure Express** (☎ 604/739–1025).

VISITOR INFORMATION

Whistler Resort Association (✉ 4010 Whistler Way, Whistler V0N 1B4, ☎ 604/932–4222; 604/664–5625 in Vancouver; 800/944–7853 in the U.S. and Canada).

BRITISH COLUMBIA A TO Z

Arriving and Departing

By Boat

See Victoria Essentials, *above.*

By Bus

Greyhound (☎ 604/662–3222; 800/661–8747 in Canada; 800/231–2222 in the U.S.) connects destinations throughout British Columbia with cities and towns all along the Pacific north coast.

By Car

Three main routes lead from other Canadian regions into British Columbia. Through Sparwood, in the south, take **Highway 3.** From Jasper and Banff, in the central region, travel on **Highway 1** or **Highway 5.** Through Dawson Creek, in the north, follow **Highways 2** and **97.** The driving time from Seattle to Vancouver on **I-5** to **Highway 99** is about three hours.

By Plane

British Columbia's main airport is **Vancouver International Airport** (✉ Grant McConachie Way, off Highway 99 south of downtown, ☎ 604/303–3602). *See* Vancouver A to Z *in* Chapter 6 for more information. *See* Victoria Essentials, *above,* for information about Victoria International Airport.

Getting Around

By Boat

B.C. Ferries (☎ 250/386–3431; 888/223–3779 in British Columbia only) provides frequent year-round passenger and vehicle service between Vancouver and Vancouver Island, from Tsawwassen (south of Vancouver) to Swartz Bay (30 minutes by car north of Victoria); Tsawwassen to Nanaimo; and Horseshoe Bay (north of Vancouver) to Nanaimo. B.C. Ferries also provides service from outside Vancouver and Victoria to the northern and southern Gulf Islands (reserve ahead), the Sunshine

Coast, Nanaimo, through the Inside Passage between Port Hardy and Prince Rupert, and from Prince Rupert to the Queen Charlotte Islands. When you travel with a vehicle in summer, plan to arrive at the terminal well in advance of the scheduled sailing time.

By Bus

Greyhound Lines of Canada (☞ Arriving and Departing, *above,* for phone numbers) serves the area north of Vancouver.

By Car

Major roads in British Columbia, and most secondary roads, are paved and well engineered. Mountain driving is slower but more scenic. There are no roads on the mainland coast once you leave the populated areas of the southwest corner near Vancouver.

By Train

B.C. Rail (☎ 604/984–5246, 604/631–3500, or 800/663–8238) travels from Vancouver to Prince George.

Contacts and Resources

B&B Reservation Agencies

Garden City Reservation Service (✉ 660 Jones Terr., Victoria V8Z 2L7, ☎ 250/479–1986, FAX 250/479–9999) specializes in Victoria reservations but can book bed-and-breakfast accommodations throughout British Columbia.

Car Rental

Most major agencies, including **Avis, Budget,** and **Hertz,** serve cities throughout the province (☞ Car Rental *in* the Gold Guide).

Emergencies

Except in Vancouver and Victoria (☞ Vancouver A to Z *in* Chapter 6 *and* Victoria Essentials, *above*), dial 0 for **police, ambulance,** or **poison control.** On the Gulf Islands, dial 911 for **police, fire,** or **ambulance service.**

Guided Tours

ECOLOGICAL TOURS

Ecosummer Expeditions (✉ 1516 Duranleau St., Vancouver V6H 3S4, ☎ 604/669–7741 or 800/465–8884), **Queen Charlotte Adventures** (✉ Box 196, Queen Charlotte V0T 1S0, ☎ 250/559–8990 or 800/668–4288), and the **Canadian Outback Adventure Company** (✉ 1110 Hamilton St., Vancouver V6C 3L6, ☎ 604/688–7206) run ecological tours of the Queen Charlotte and Gulf Islands.

ORIENTATION

Classic Holidays Tour & Travel (✉ 102-75 W. Broadway, Vancouver V5Y 1P1, ☎ 604/875–6377) and **Sea to Sky** (✉ 1928 Nelson Ave., West Vancouver V7V 2P4, ☎ 604/922–7339) operate tours throughout the province.

SPECIAL-INTEREST

The history and culture of the First Nations (native) people of the region are the focus of new summer tours, including **Lheit-Lit'en Nation Elders Salmon Camp Tours** (✉ Lheit-Lit'en Native Heritage Society, R.R. 1, Site 27, Compartment 60, Prince George V2N 2H8, ☎ 250/963–8451) on the mainland and **Yuquot History Tours** (✉ Ahaminaquis Tourist Centre, Box 459, Gold River V0P 1G0, ☎ 250/283–7464) on Vancouver Island. The **Canadian Outback Adventure Company** (✉ 1110 Hamilton St., Vancouver V6C 3L6, ☎ 604/688–7206) and **Queen Charlotte Adventures** (✉ Box 196, Queen Charlotte V0T 1S0, ☎ 250/559–8990 or 800/668–4288) offer unique summer tours of the abandoned Queen Charlotte Islands villages of the Haida Gwai, including the United Nations–designated World Heritage Site at Ninstints.

A few Vancouver Island–based companies that conduct whale-watching tours are **Jamie's Whaling Station** (⊠ Box 590, Tofino V0R 2Z0, ☎ 250/725–3919; 800/667–9913 in Canada); **Tofino Sea-Kayaking Company** (⊠ Box 620, Tofino VOR 2Z0, ☎ 250/725–4222) on the west coast; **Robson Bight Charters** (⊠ Box 99, Sayward V0P 1R0, ☎ 250/282–3833) near Campbell River; and, near Port Hardy, **Stubbs Island Charters** (⊠ Box 7, Telegraph Cove V0N 3J0, ☎ 250/928–3185).

Outdoor Activities and Sports

FISHING

A saltwater-fishing license for one day costs $3.75 for both Canadian residents and non-Canadians and is available at virtually every fishing lodge and sporting-goods outlet along the coast. Annual licenses are about $11 for Canadians who live outside British Columbia and $38 for non-Canadians.

For updated fishing information and regulations, contact the **B.C. Fish Branch** (⊠ Ministry of Environment, Parliament Bldgs., Victoria V8V 1X4, ☎ 250/387–9688). For a guide to saltwater fishing, contact the **Department of Fisheries and Oceans** (⊠ Recreational Fisheries Division, 555 W. Hastings St., Vancouver V6B 5G3, ☎ 604/666–3545).

GOLF

Tee-Time Central Booking Service (⊠ 412–4004 Bluebird Rd., Kelowna V1W 1X3, ☎ 250/764–4118 or 800/930–4622), for out-of-town golfers, lists courses throughout Vancouver Island and mainland British Columbia. It's open on weekdays between mid-May and mid-October from 9 to 5.

HIKING

B.C. Parks (⊠ 800 Johnson St., 2nd floor, Victoria V8V 1X4, ☎ 250/387–5002) offers detailed information. For heli-hiking information, contact **Highland Helicopter** (⊠ 1685 Tranmer, Agassiz V0M 1K0, ☎ 604/796–9610), **Crescent Spur Helicopter Holidays** (⊠ Crescent Spur V0J 3E0, ☎ 250/569–2730), **Peak Experiences** (⊠ 29 Oersted St., Kitimat V8C 1J6, ☎ 250/632–7512), and **Mount Robson Adventure Holidays** (⊠ Box 687, Valemount V0E 2Z0, ☎ 250/566–4386).

RAFTING

Hyak Wilderness Adventures (⊠ 204B–1975 Maple St., Vancouver V6J 3S9, ☎ 604/734–8622 or 800/663–7238), **Canadian River Expeditions** (⊠ 301–9571 Emerald Dr., Whistler V0N 1B9, ☎ 604/938–6651; 800/898–7238 in Canada only), **Alpine Rafting Company** (⊠ Box 1409, Golden V0A 1H0, ☎ 250/344–5016 or 800/663–7080), and **Suskwa Adventure Outfitters** (⊠ Box 3262, Smithers V0J 2N0, ☎ 250/847–2885) provide options ranging from lazy half-day floats to exhilarating white-water journeys of up to a week.

SKIING

The **Canada West Ski Areas Association** (⊠ 3313 32nd Ave., Suite 103, Vernon V1T 2M8, ☎ 250/542–9020) has information about the top heli- and Sno-cat ski operators in British Columbia.

Visitor Information

B.C. Parks Headquarters (☎ 250/387–5002). **Tourism B.C.** (⊠ 802–865 Hornby St., Vancouver V6Z 2G3, ☎ 604/660–2861 or 800/663–6000).

8 Southeast Alaska

Including Ketchikan, Juneau, Sitka, and Skagway

The Southeast encompasses the Inside Passage—a century ago the traditional route to the Klondike goldfields and today the centerpiece of Alaska cruises. Here are glacier-filled fjords and the justly famous Glacier Bay National Park. Juneau, the state's capital, is also in the Southeast, as are fishing villages such as Petersburg and Ketchikan, which is known for its totem-pole carving. An onion-dome cathedral accents Sitka, the onetime capital of Russian America. Each fall, up to 4,000 eagles gather outside Haines.

THE SOUTHEAST STRETCHES BELOW ALASKA like the tail of a kite. The largest concentration of coastal glaciers on earth can be viewed at Glacier Bay National Park and Preserve, one of the region's most prized attractions. Lush stands of spruce, hemlock, and cedar blanket the Southeast's thousands of islands. Bays, coves, lakes of all sizes, and swift, icy rivers provide some of North America's best fishing grounds. Many of Southeast Alaska's wildest and most pristine landscapes belong to the Tongass National Forest, which encompasses nearly 17 million acres—or 73% of the Panhandle's land.

By Mike Miller

Updated by
Bill Sherwonit

If you spend a week or more in the Southeast, you can count on showers during at least a few of those days. Die-hard southeasterners simply throw on a light slicker and shrug off the rain. Their attitude is philosophical: Without the rain, there would be no forests, no lakes, no streams running with world-class salmon and trout, and no healthy populations of brown and black bears, moose, deer, mountain goats, and wolves.

The Southeast's natural beauty and abundance of wildlife have made it one of the world's fastest-growing cruise destinations. About 20 big cruise ships ply the Inside Passage during the height of the summer. Regular air service to the Southeast is available from the lower 48 states and from mainland Alaska.

The native peoples you'll meet in the Southeast coastal region are Tlingit, Haida, and Tsimshian. These peoples, like their coastal neighbors in British Columbia, preserve a culture rich in totemic art forms, including deeply carved poles, masks, baskets, and ceremonial objects. Many live among nonnatives in modern towns while continuing their own traditions.

A pioneer spirit dominates the towns of Southeast Alaska. Residents—some from other states, some with roots in the "old country," some who can trace their ancestors back to the gold-rush days, and some whose ancestors came over the Bering Land Bridge from Asia tens of thousands of years ago—are an adventurous lot. The rough-and-tumble spirit of the Southeast often combines with a worldly sophistication: Those who fish are also artists, loggers are often business entrepreneurs, and homemakers may be native dance performers.

Pleasures and Pastimes

Dining
Given the region's coastal setting, it's not surprising that many of its restaurants and cafés specialize in seafood dishes—halibut, salmon, crab, shrimp, and clam chowder. Reservations are generally not necessary, but you should call ahead, particularly in the summer.

CATEGORY	COST
$$$$	over $40
$$$	$25–$40
$$	$10–$25
$	under $10

per person for a three-course meal, excluding drinks, and service

Lodging
Accommodations in Southeast Alaska include traditional urban hostelries, charming small-town inns, and rustic cabins in the boondocks. Ketchikan and Juneau offer the most options.

Southeast Alaska

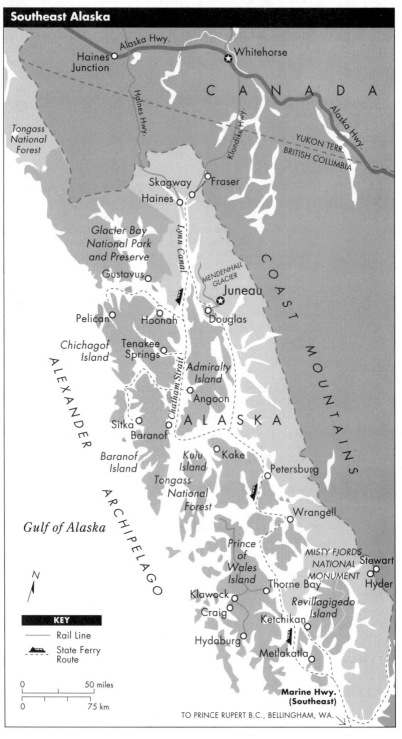

CANADA

Alaska Hwy.

Haines Junction

Whitehorse

Tongass National Forest

Haines Hwy.

Klondike Hwy.

Alaska Hwy.

YUKON TERR.
BRITISH COLUMBIA

Skagway   Fraser

Haines

Lynn Canal

Glacier Bay National Park and Preserve

MENDENHALL GLACIER

Juneau

Gustavus

Douglas

COAST

Pelican

Hoonah

Chichagof Island

Tenakee Springs

Chatham Strait

Admiralty Island

MOUNTAINS

Angoon

ALASKA

Sitka

Baranof

Baranof Island

Kuiu Island   Kake

Tongass National Forest

Petersburg

Gulf of Alaska

Wrangell

Prince of Wales Island

MISTY FJORDS NATIONAL MONUMENT

Stewart

Hyder

ARCHIPELAGO

Thorne Bay

Revillagigedo Island

Klawock

N

Craig

Ketchikan

KEY

——— Rail Line

⛴ State Ferry Route

Hydaburg

Metlakatla

0   50 miles

0   75 km

Marine Hwy. (Southeast)

TO PRINCE RUPERT B.C., BELLINGHAM, WA.

CATEGORY	COST*
$$$$	over $120
$$$	$90–$120
$$	$50–$90
$	under $50

All prices are for a standard double room, excluding 8%–10% tax.

Outdoor Activities and Sports

FISHING

The Southeast is a fisherman's paradise. There are saltwater salmon charter boats, salmon fishing lodges, fly-in mountain-lake lodges, and more than 150 remote but weather-tight cabins within the Tongass National Forest (☞ *below*).

HIKING AND BACKPACKING

Many of the trails in the Southeast are abandoned mining and logging roads. Others are natural routes that meander over ridges, through forests, and alongside streams and glaciers. A few, like the Chilkoot Trail out of Skagway, rate five stars for historical significance, scenery, and hiker aids en route. The Alaska Division of Parks Southeast regional office, in Juneau (☞ Contacts and Resources *in* Southeast Alaska A to Z, *below*), will send you a list of state-maintained trails and parks in the Panhandle; local visitor bureaus and recreation departments can also help.

Scenic Drives

The descent from the high, craggy Canadian mountain country to the Southeast Alaska coast makes both the Klondike Highway into Skagway and the Haines Highway to Haines especially memorable traveling. At the top of the passes, vegetation is sparse, and pockets of snow are often present, even in summertime. As you near the saltwater coast of the Panhandle, the forest cover becomes tall, thick, and evergreen. Both drives are worth an excursion, even if you don't intend to drive any farther than the Canadian border and return. Very few visitors bring their own cars to Southeast Alaska, but you can rent one (☞ Contacts and Resources *in* Southeast Alaska A to Z, *below*).

Shopping

Totem poles are among the most popular handicrafts made by the Tlingit and Haida in the Southeast Panhandle. Other items include wall masks, paddles, dance rattles, baskets, and tapestries with native designs. If you want to be sure of authenticity, buy items tagged with the state-approved AUTHENTIC NATIVE HANDICRAFT FROM ALASKA label. Other popular take-home items include salmon—smoked, canned, or otherwise packaged.

Exploring Southeast Alaska

The Southeast Panhandle stretches 500 mi from Yakutat at its northernmost to Ketchikan and Metlakatla at its southern end. At its widest the region measures only 140 mi, and in the upper Panhandle just south of Yakutat, it's a skinny 30 mi across. Most of the Panhandle consists of a sliver of mainland buffered by islands.

There are more than a thousand islands up and down the Panhandle coast—most of them mountainous, with lush covers of timber. Collectively they constitute the Alexander Archipelago. On the mainland to the east of the United States–Canada border lies British Columbia.

You can get to and around the area by ship or by plane, but forget traveling here by car or RV unless your destinations are Haines and Skagway; both those northern Panhandle communities are connected by road to the Alaska Highway. Elsewhere in the Southeast, the roadways that exist in these parts run at most a few dozen miles out from towns and villages and then dead-end. (If you're driving up the Alaska Highway and want to visit road-isolated communities, it is possible to reserve vehicle space on Alaska's state ferries.)

Most communities are on islands rather than on the mainland. The principal exceptions are Juneau, Haines, Skagway, and the native village of Klukwan. Island outposts include Ketchikan, Wrangell, Petersburg, Sitka, Metlakatla, native villages, and logging camps. Each town has its own ethnic lore, wildlife, and natural wonders.

Numbers in the text correspond to numbers in the margin and on the Ketchikan, Wrangell, Petersburg, Sitka, Juneau, Haines, and Skagway maps.

Great Itineraries

IF YOU HAVE 3 OR 4 DAYS

Begin your trip in ☷ **Juneau** ㊹–㊼. On your second day, go south via the state ferry to ☷ **Sitka** ㉞–㊸. Spend the next two or three days visiting White Sulphur Springs or paddling along Baranof Island's rugged coast. Or instead of going south from Juneau, travel north to ☷ **Gustavus** and nearby **Glacier Bay National Park and Preserve.**

IF YOU HAVE 7 DAYS

Starting at ☷ **Ketchikan** ①–⑳, known for its totem poles, the Alaska Marine Highway ferries regularly make stops at all of the region's larger communities: **Wrangell** ㉑–㉘, with its ancient petroglyphs; ☷ **Petersburg** ㉙–㉝, which has a strong Norwegian influence; ☷ **Sitka** ㉞–㊸, where many cultures meet; ☷ **Juneau** ㊹–㊼, the state capital; **Haines** ㊽–㊾, known for its bald eagles and native dance troupe; and ☷ **Skagway** ㊿–㊻, a gold-rush-era throwback; and several smaller communities, like **Kake, Angoon, Tenakee,** and **Hoonah.** Give yourself time to visit some out-of-town destinations, like **Admiralty Island** or the **Alaska Chilkat Bald Eagle Preserve.**

When to Tour the Southeast

The best time to visit is between May and September, when the weather is mildest, the daylight hours are longest, the wildlife most abundant, the fishing is best, and the festivals and tourist-oriented activities are in full swing.

Ketchikan

730 mi northwest of Seattle, 850 mi southeast of Anchorage.

Ketchikan, which has more totems than anywhere else in the world, perches on a large island at the foot of 3,000-ft-high Deer Mountain. The site at the mouth of Ketchikan Creek was a summer fish camp of the Tlingit until white miners and fishermen came to settle the town in 1885. Gold discoveries as the 19th century was coming to a close brought more immigrants, and valuable timber and commercial fishing resources spurred new industries. By the 1930s the town had dubbed itself the salmon-canning capital of the world. Some of the Southeast's best salmon fishing can still be had here.

Fishing and timber have traditionally been the mainstays of Ketchikan's economy, but in recent years tourism has played an important role, especially as local timber-mill operations have slowed down. If you visit in summer, historic Creek Street may be so packed with cruise passengers that just buying a T-shirt will be an ordeal. Ketchikan is one of the wettest Southeast cities—the average annual precipitation is more than 150 inches.

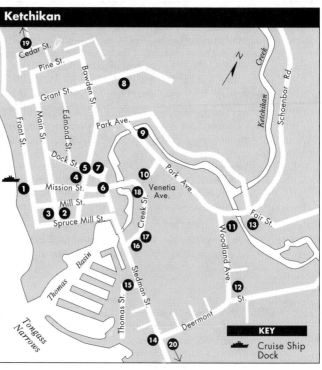

Ketchikan

❶ At the **Ketchikan Visitors Bureau,** you can pick up a free historic-walking-tour map. The bureau is next to the cruise-ship docks. ⊠ *131 Front St.,* ☎ *907/225–6166 or 800/770–3300.* ☾ *May–Sept., daily 8–5; additional hrs when ships are in port.*

❷ The U.S. Forest Service and other federal agencies provide information on Alaska's public lands at the **Southeast Alaska Visitor Center.** The center's exhibits focus on the resources, native cultures, and ecosystems of Southeast Alaska; a highlight is the rain forest exhibit. Another visitor-friendly feature is the "trip-planning room," especially helpful for independent travelers. While here you can also reserve public-use cabins in the Tongass National Forest or view a multimedia show, "Mystical Southeast Alaska," in the center's theater. The show runs every 30 minutes in the summer. ⊠ *Main and Mill Sts.,* ☎ *907/228–6220.* 🎟 *$3 (to enter center).* ☾ *May–Sept., daily 8:30–4:30; Oct.–Apr., Tues.–Sat. 8:30–4:30.*

❸ The **Spruce Mill Development** on Mill Street is modeled after 1920s-style cannery architecture. Spread over 6½ acres along the waterfront, its five buildings contain retail stores, souvenir shops, and restaurants.

❹ **St. John's Church** (⊠ Bawden St. between Mission and Dock Sts.), built in 1903, is the oldest house of worship in Ketchikan, its interior formed from red cedar cut in the native-operated sawmill in nearby Saxman.

❺ The **Seaman's Park,** next door to St. John's Church, was built in 1904 as a hospital. It later housed *Alaska Sportsman* magazine (now *Alaska*),

❻ which began publication in Ketchikan in 1936. **Whale Park,** catercorner from St. John's Church, is the site of the **Knox Brother Clock,** and the **Chief Johnson Totem Pole,** raised in 1989 and a replica of the 1901 totem in the same site.

7 At the **Tongass Historical Museum** you can browse among native arti-facts and pioneer relics of the early mining and fishing era. Among the exhibits are a big and brilliantly polished lens from Tree Point Light-house, the bullet-riddled skull of a notorious brown bear called Old Groaner, native ceremonial objects, and a model of a typical Alaskan salmon-fishing seine vessel. ⊠ *629 Dock St.,* ☎ *907/225–5600.* ⌨ *$2.* ☉ *May–Sept., daily 8–5; Oct.–Apr., Wed.–Fri. 1–5, weekends 1–4.*

At one time virtually all of Ketchikan's walkways and streets were made
8 from wooden trestles. But now only one remains, the **Grant Street Tres-tle** (⊠ Grant St. east of Bawden St.), constructed in 1908. Get out your
★ **9** camera and set it for fast speed at the **Salmon Falls, Fish Ladder,** and **Salmon Carving,** just off Park Avenue east of Bawden Street on Mar-ried Man's Trail. When the salmon start running in midsummer, thou-sands leap the falls (or take the easier ladder route) to spawn in Ketchikan Creek's waters farther upstream. Many can also be seen in the creek feeding the falls.

For fine dining and a stunning view of the harbor, hike up steep Vene-
10 tia Avenue to **Westmark Cape Fox Lodge** (☞ Dining and Lodging, *below*). The lodge operates funicular rides to and from Creek Street for $1.

Tens of thousands of salmon are annually dispersed into local waters
11 at **Deer Mountain Hatchery.** The hatchery, owned by the Ketchikan In-dian Corporation (☞ Guided Tours, *below*), has exhibits on traditional Native American fishing. ⊠ *Park Ave. at Woodland Ave.,* ☎ *907/225–6760.* ⌨ *$3.* ☉ *May–Sept., daily 8:30–4:30; Sept.–May gates some-times open for self-guided tours (call ahead).*

12 **Totem Heritage Center and Nature Park** is just south of the hatchery. Here you'll find totems dating back almost two centuries. ⊠ *Deermont St. at Woodland Ave.* ⌨ *$3.* ☉ *May–Sept., daily 8–5; Oct.–Apr., Tues.–Fri. 1–5.*

13 East of the hatchery is **City Park** (⊠ Park Ave. and Fair St.). If you fol-low Deermont Street west to Stedman Street you'll see the colorful wall
14 mural called **Return of the Eagle.** It was created by 21 native artists on the walls of the Robertson Building on the Ketchikan campus of the University of Alaska–Southeast.

15 At **Thomas Street,** enjoy the view of Thomas Basin, a picture-worthy harbor. One of four harbors in Ketchikan, it is home port to pleasure craft and workboats.

16 **Creek Street,** north off Stedman Street across from Thomas Basin, was Ketchikan's red-light district. Its small houses, built on stilts over the creek waters, have been restored as trendy shops. The street's most fa-
17 mous brothel, **Dolly's House,** has been preserved as a museum (open when cruise ships are in port), complete with furnishings, beds, and a short history of the life and times of Ketchikan's best-known madam.
18 Admission is $3. The view from the **Creek Street Footbridge** is great when the salmon are running.

The poles at Ketchikan's two most famous totem parks are, for the most part, 50-year-old replicas of older totems brought in from outlying vil-
☾ **19** lages as part of a federal-works project during the 1930s. **Totem Bight State Historical Park** (⊠ N. Tongass Hwy., ☎ 907/247–8574) is 10 mi north of town. On a scenic spit of land facing the waters of Tongass Narrows, it has many totems and a hand-hewn native tribal house.

★ ☾ **20** **Saxman Native Village** is 2 mi south of town, but don't try walking—there are no sidewalks. The village, named for a missionary who helped native Alaskans settle here before 1900, has a tribal house believed to be the largest in the world. There's also a carver's shed nearby where totems and totemic art objects are created and a stand-up theater where a multimedia presentation tells the story of Southeast Alaska's native peoples. You can see the **Totem Park** if you drive out on your own, but to visit the tribal house you must take a tour (☞ Guided Tours, *below*). ⊠ *S. Tongass Hwy.,* ☎ *907/225–4166 (Saxman City Hall).*

On the highway in either direction, you won't go far before you run out of road. The North Tongass Highway ends about 18 mi from downtown, at Settler's Cove Campground. The South Tongass Highway terminates at a power plant about 8 mi from town. Side roads soon end at campgrounds and at trailheads, viewing points, lakes, boat-launching ramps, and private property.

Misty Fjords National Monument (⊠ 3031 Tongass Ave., Ketchikan 99901, ☎ 907/225–2148) is a wilderness of mountains, steep-walled fjords, and islands with wildlife, recreational opportunities, and spectacular scenery. Misty Fjords affords breathtaking vistas when viewed up close in small boats. Travel on these waters can be an almost mystical experience, with the greens of the forest reflected in waters as still as black mirrors. You may find yourself in the company of a whale, see a bear fishing for salmon along the shore, or even pull in your own salmon for an evening meal. Drifting past the ice-blue face of a tidewater glacier, you may hear the great primeval sound of an avalanche of ice. White waterfalls make lace over sheer gray-black cliffs. The raucous conversation of ravens may ring out while a bald eagle feeds its young in the top of an ancient spruce tree. *See* Guided Tours, *below,* for tour information.

OFF THE
BEATEN PATH

BAILEY BAY – There's a hot-springs pool of sorts, big enough for two or three to lounge in, at this Tongass National Forest site on the mainland, north of Ketchikan's Revillagigedo Island. A 10-minute hike from a landing in a nearby lake or a 2-mi trek on an unmaintained but negotiable trail will bring you to the springs. Have your pilot fly over before you land to show you what your route on foot will be. Shelter here is a three-sided Adirondack lean-to. Request details and reservation information from the Southeast Alaska Visitor Center (☎ 907/228–6290) or call or write the U.S. Forest Service (⊠ 101 Egan Dr., Juneau 99801, ☎ 907/586–8751).

Dining and Lodging

$$–$$$$ ✕ **Clover Pass Resort.** For excellent seafood and a view of sportfishermen bringing home their catches, head out to this resort. ⊠ *Mile 15, N. Tongass Hwy.,* ☎ *907/247–2234. AE, MC, V.*

$$–$$$ ✕ **Salmon Falls Resort.** It's a half-hour drive from town, but the
★ seafood and steaks served up in this huge, octagonal restaurant make the trip worthwhile. At the center of the dining room, supporting the roof, rises a 40-ft section of 48-inch pipe manufactured to be part of the Alaska pipeline. The dining area overlooks the waters of Clover Passage, where sunsets can be vivid red and remarkable. Seafood caught fresh from adjacent waters is especially good; try the halibut and the prawns stuffed with crabmeat. ⊠ *Mile 17, N. Tongass Hwy.,* ☎ *907/225–2752; 800/247–9059 outside AK. AE, MC, V.*

$–$$ ✕ **Kay's Kitchen.** This simple restaurant, 1½ mi from downtown Ketchikan, is known for its soups and generous sandwiches. Other specialties include barbecued ribs and homemade desserts, including ice cream. ⊠ *2813 Tongass Ave.,* ☎ *907/225–5860. MC, V.*

$$–$$$ ✕🏨 **Gilmore Hotel.** The Gilmore has a European feel, and because of features such as its 1930s-style lobby, it's on the National Register of Historic Places. The rooms have some welcome modern touches, but there is no elevator in this three-story building. Annabelle's Keg and Chowder House is really two restaurants. The Keg and Chowder House serves seafood, pasta, steak, and prime rib. Specialties include oysters on the half shell and steamer clams. The more formal Annabelle's Parlor serves fine seafood in classic preparations. There's also an espresso bar and a semiformal lounge with a jukebox. ⊠ *326 Front St., 99901,* ☎ *907/225–9423 or 800/275–9423,* 𝔽𝔸𝕏 *907/225–7442. 40 rooms. 2 restaurants, bar. AE, D, DC, MC, V.*

$$$$ 🏨 **The Landing.** This Best Western property is named for the ferry landing site in the waters of Tongass Narrows across the street. The decor is modern and basic. Some rooms have microwaves and kitchenettes; the suites have all the comforts of home. ⊠ *3434 Tongass Ave.,* ☎ *907/ 225–5166 or 800/428–8304,* 𝔽𝔸𝕏 *907/225–6900. 76 rooms. Café, lobby lounge, exercise room. AE, D, DC, MC, V.*

$$$$ 🏨 **Waterfall Resort.** Remote, but with the ultimate in creature comforts, this lodge is on Prince of Wales Island near Ketchikan. At the former commercial salmon cannery, you sleep in the lodge or in Cape Cod–style cottages (formerly cannery workers' cabins, but they never had it so good); eat bountiful meals of salmon, halibut steak, and all the trimmings; and fish from your own private cabin cruiser under the care of your own private fishing guide. ⊠ *Box 6440, 99901,* ☎ *907/ 225–9461; 800/544–5125 outside AK;* 𝔽𝔸𝕏 *907/225–8530. 26 cabins, 4 suites, 10 lodge rooms. Restaurant. AE, D, MC, V.*

$$$$ 🏨 **Westmark Cape Fox Lodge.** One of Ketchikan's poshest properties has fantastic views of the town and harbor. Fine dining and a cozy but luxurious setting are other pluses. Rooms are spacious, with Shaker-style furnishings, the traditional Tlingit tribal colors (red, black, and white), and watercolors of native Alaskan birds. The town's main attractions are within walking distance, but guests can take the hotel's sky tram directly to Creek Street. ⊠ *800 Venetia Way, 99901,* ☎ *907/ 225–8001 or 800/544–0970 for reservations,* 𝔽𝔸𝕏 *907/225–8286. 72 rooms. Restaurant, lobby lounge, no-smoking rooms, room service, meeting rooms. AE, D, DC, MC, V.*

$$–$$$$ 🏨 **Cedars Lodge.** Nothing in the plain, square exterior of this hotel or in its spartan lobby hints at the deluxe accommodations within. Some rooms are split-level with circular stairways; all are carpeted and have a green color scheme with natural wood trim. Many have a full kitchen and a whirlpool bath. Large windows yield views of the busy water and air traffic in Tongass Narrows. Simple American fare is served at a buffet dinner and breakfast (summer only); meals can also be brought to your room from the Galley, which serves pizza and Asian food. ⊠ *1471 Tongass Ave. (Box 8331), 99901,* ☎ *907/225–1900,* 𝔽𝔸𝕏 *907/225– 8604. 12 rooms. Restaurant, room service, hot tub, sauna. AE, D, DC, MC, V.*

$$$ 🏨 **Ingersoll Hotel.** Patterned wallpaper, wood wainscoting, and etched-
★ glass windows on the oak registration desk set an old-fashioned mood at this three-story downtown hotel, built in the 1920s. Room furnishings are standard, with bright Alaskan art on the walls. Some rooms have a view of the cruise-ship dock and the waters of Tongass Narrows. ⊠ *303 Mission St. (Box 6440), 99901,* ☎ *907/225–2124 or 800/478– 2124,* 𝔽𝔸𝕏 *907/247–8530. 58 rooms. Meeting room. AE, D, DC, MC, V.*

Guided Tours

Alaska Cruises (☎ 907/225–6044 or 800/228–1905) runs harbor cruises of the Ketchikan waterfront and leads excursions from Ketchikan to Misty Fjords National Monument. Boat transport for kayakers is also offered to and from Misty Fjords. **Alaska Discovery** (☎ 800/586–1911 or 907/780–6226) organizes canoeing, sea kayaking, and wildlife-viewing trips within Tongass National Forest and explores Admiralty Island and Misty Fjords. The company offers boat transport for kayakers to and from Misty Fjords. **Alaska Sightseeing/Cruise West** (☎ 206/441–8687 or 800/426–7702) operates boat tours of Misty Fjords. **Cape Fox Tours** (☎ 907/225–4846) conducts tours (about $35; fee varies) of Saxman Native Village. **Ketchikan Indian Corporation** (☎ 907/225–5158 or 800/252–5158) conducts Native American heritage town tours focusing on traditional land and fishery use and native crafts.

Outdoor Activities and Sports

CANOEING AND KAYAKING

The **Ketchikan Parks and Recreation Department** (☎ 907/225–9579) rents canoes. **Southeast Exposure** (☎ 907/225–8829 in summer) rents canoes and kayaks, gives kayaking classes, and guides trips.

FISHING

Sportfishing for salmon and trout is excellent in the Ketchikan area, in either saltwater or freshwater lakes and streams. Contact the **Ketchikan Visitors Bureau** (☞ *above*) for information on guide services and locations.

HIKING

If you're a tough hiker, the 3-mi trail from downtown to the top of **Deer Mountain** will repay your efforts with a panorama of the city below and the wilderness behind. The trail begins at the corner of Fair and Deermont streets. **Ward Cove Recreation Area,** about 6 mi north of town, has easier hiking beside lakes and streams and beneath towering spruce and hemlock trees.

SCUBA DIVING

Alaska Diving Service (⌂ 4845 N. Tongass Ave., ☎ 907/225–4667) rents tanks and equipment.

Shopping

ART GALLERIES

Among the best of Southeast Alaska's galleries is the **Scanlon Gallery** (⌂ 318 Mission St., ☎ 907/247–4730 or 800/690–4730). It exhibits the work of major Alaskan artists (Byron Birdsall, Rie Muñoz, John Fahringer, Nancy Stonington) and local talent.

Soho Coho Art Gallery (⌂ 5 Creek St., ☎ 907/225–5954) carries an eclectic collection of art and clothing in modern Alaskan chic. The gallery features the work of Ray Troll, best known for his fish art, as well as that of other Alaskan artists.

BOOKS

Parnassus (⌂ 5 Creek St., ☎ 907/225–7690) specializes in northwestern art, Native American subjects, and women's studies; it also sells cards and CDs, with an emphasis on classical, new age, and jazz.

FOOD

For some of the Southeast's best canned or smoked salmon, try **Ketchikan's Salmon Etc.** (⌂ 322 Mission St., ☎ 907/225–6008), which is also the distributor for **Silver Lining Seafoods,** a Ketchikan-based company whose high-quality products are sold in food stores and gift shops throughout the Southeast.

Wrangell

80 mi northwest of Ketchikan.

Wrangell is on an island near the mouth of the fast-flowing Stikine River. The unassuming fishing community has existed under three flags. Known as Redoubt St. Dionysius when it was part of Russian America, the town was renamed Fort Stikine under the British.

You can see a lot in Wrangell on foot. A good place to start your tour
㉑ is at the tall totem pole at the **Wrangell Visitor Center** (⊠ 107 Stikine Ave., ☎ 907/874–3901 or 800/367–9745), which is close to the docks, in the **Stikine Inn Building.** It's open when cruise ships and ferries are in port and at other times throughout the summer. If you need information when the center is closed, call 907/874–2795.

㉒ **KikSadi Indian Park** (Front St. east of Stikine Ave.), a pocket park of Alaska greenery and impressive totem poles, is a pleasant spot for a stroll.

㉓ The collection at the **Wrangell Museum** includes a bootlegger's still, historic aviation and communication memorabilia, a totem pole, petroglyphs, woven native baskets, and other local artifacts. It's on the lower floor of the community center, between the Presbyterian church and the high school. ⊠ *318 Church St.,* ☎ *907/874–3770.* ▨ *$2.* ☉ *May–mid-Sept., weekdays 10–5, Sat. 1–4, Sun. when ferry or cruise ships arrive; mid-Sept.–Apr., Tues.–Fri. 10–4, or by appointment.*

㉔ **Chief Shakes's grave** (⊠ Case Ave. south of Bennett St.) is marked by two killer-whale totems. Buried here is Shakes V, who led the local Tlingits during the first half of the 19th century.

★ ㉕ **Chief Shakes Island** is Wrangell's number one attraction. Reached by a footbridge off the harbor dock, it has some of the finest totem poles in Alaska, as well as a tribal house constructed in the 1930s as a replica of one that was home to many of the various Shakes and their peoples. The interior contains six house totems, two of them more than 100 years old. ☎ *907/874–3747.* ▨ *$2 donation requested.* ☉ *When cruise ships are in port or by appointment.*

㉖ The **Irene Ingle Public Library** (⊠ 2nd St., ☎ 907/874–3535), behind the post office, has a small collection of ancient petroglyphs.

㉗ **Our Collections,** a private museum run by Elva Bigelow, is in a large metal building near the water. Thousands of Bigelow family items—clocks, animal traps, waffle irons, tools, etc.—are on display. ⊠ *Evergreen Ave. north of intersection of Stikine Ave. and 2nd St.,* ☎ *907/ 874–3646.* ▨ *Donations accepted.* ☉ *Call for hrs.*

㉘ **Petroglyph Beach** is one of the more curious sights in Southeast Alaska. Scattered among the rocks here are three dozen or more large stones bearing designs and pictures chiseled by unknown ancient artists. No one knows why the rocks were etched the way they were. Perhaps they were boundary markers or messages; possibly they were just primitive doodling. Because the petroglyphs can be damaged by physical contact, the state discourages visitors from creating a rubbing off the rocks. Instead, you can purchase a rubber stamp duplicate of selected petroglyphs from the city museum or from a Forest Service interpreter at the cruise dock for $4.50–$6.

There are other stones from the Wrangell area that you can take with you. These are natural garnets, gathered at Garnet Ledge, facing the Stikine River. The semiprecious gems are sold on the streets for 50 cents to $50, depending on their quality.

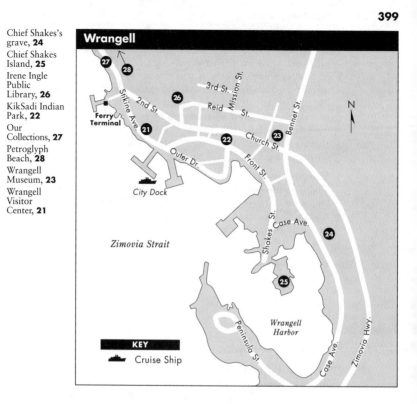

OFF THE BEATEN PATH

ANAN CREEK WILDLIFE OBSERVATORY – About 30 mi southeast of Wrangell in the Tongass National Forest, Anan is unique among Alaska's premier bear-viewing areas because black bears, not browns or grizzlies, are the principal attraction. Each summer, from early July to mid-August, as many as three dozen black bears gather at this stream to feed on pink salmon. For information on Anan, contact the Forest Service's Wrangell Ranger District (⊠ Box 51, 99929, ☎ 907/874–2323). *See also* Guided Tours, *below.*

Dining and Lodging

$$ ✕⭑ **Roadhouse Lodge.** This waterfront lodge 4 mi from downtown has a homestead atmosphere, with relics collected from all over the state; the walls here are practically a museum of early Alaska. The lodge's restaurant serves wholesome, tasty, and ample meals. Specialties include fresh halibut, local prawns (sautéed, deep-fried, or boiled in the shell) and Indian fry bread. ⊠ *Mile 4.5, Zimovia Hwy., Box 1199, 99929,* ☎ *907/874–2335,* FAX *907/874–3104. 10 rooms. Restaurant, bar, airport shuttle. MC, V.*

$$ ✕⭑ **Stikine Inn.** On the dock in the main part of town, this inn has great views of Wrangell's harbor. Rooms are simply decorated with plain, modern furnishings. Maggie's & Son restaurant has good views of the harbor. Seafood and steak are staples. ⊠ *Stikine Ave., 2 blocks from ferry terminal, Box 990, 99929,* ☎ *907/874–3388,* FAX *907/874–3923. 34 rooms. Restaurant. AE, DC, MC, V.*

$$ ⭑ **Harding's Old Sourdough Lodge.** This lodge sits on the docks in a beautifully converted construction camp. The Harding family welcomes guests with home-baked sourdough breads and local seafood in the open dining-living room. Rooms have rustic paneling and modest country-style furnishings; the exterior is hand-milled cedar. ⊠ *1104*

Peninsula St., Box 1062, 99929, ☎ *907/874–3613 or 800/874–3613,* FAX *907/874–3455. 19 rooms, 14 with bath. Sauna, steam room, boating, meeting room, airport shuttle. AE, D, DC, MC, V.*

$ ⌱ **Shakes Slough Cabins.** If you're a hot-springs or hot-tub enthusiast, these Forest Service cabins, accessible from Wrangell and Petersburg, are worth checking out. Request details and reservation information from the Forest Service office in Wrangell (☎ 907/874–2323) or the regional U.S. Forest Service Information Center (⌗ 101 Egan Dr., Juneau 99801, ☎ 907/586–8751). Reservations are required and no credit cards are accepted.

Guided Tours

Stikine Wilderness Adventures (☎ 907/874–2085) operates mild-to-wild jet-boat tours into the Stikine River wilderness country to Shakes Glacier, Shakes Hot Springs, and other historic and natural attractions, including Anan Bear Observatory. It does drop-offs and pickups within a 50-mi radius of Wrangell.

Sunrise Aviation (☎ 907/874–2319) is a charter-only air carrier that operates trips to the Anan Bear Observatory, Tracy Arm, and the LeConte Glacier and can drop you off at any number of places for a day of secluded fishing and hiking.

Petersburg

35 mi northwest of Wrangell.

Getting to Petersburg is an experience, whether you take the "high road" by air or the "low road" by sea. At sea level only ferries and smaller cruisers can squeeze through Wrangell Narrows with the aid of more than 50 buoys and range markers along the 22-mi crossing. The inaccessibility of Petersburg is part of its off-the-beaten-path charm. Unlike at several other Southeast communities, you'll never be overwhelmed by hordes of cruise passengers.

At first sight Petersburg may make you think you're in the old country, with neat, white, Scandinavian-style homes and storefronts with steep roofs and bright-colored swirls of leaf and flower designs (called rosemaling). Row upon row of sturdy fishing vessels in the harbor invoke the spirit of Norway. No wonder: This prosperous fishing community was founded by Norwegian Peter Buschmann in 1897.

You may occasionally even hear some Norwegian spoken, especially during the Little Norway Festival held here each year on the weekend closest to May 17. If you're in town during the festival, be sure to partake in one of the fish feeds that highlight the Norwegian Independence Day celebration. You won't find better beer-batter halibut and folk dancing outside Norway.

One of the most pleasant things to do in Petersburg is to roam among the fishing vessels tied up at dockside in the town's expanding harbor. This is one of Alaska's busiest, most prosperous fishing communities, and the variety of seacraft is enormous. You'll see small trollers, big halibut vessels, and sleek pleasure craft as well. Wander, too, around the fish-processing structures (you can't miss the pungent aroma). Watching shrimp, salmon, or halibut catches being brought ashore, you can get a real appreciation for this industry and the people who engage in it.

 From the **visitor center** (⌗ 1st and Fram Sts., ☎ 907/772–4636), wander to the **Hammer Slough reflecting pool** for a vision of houses and buildings on high stilts reflected perfectly in still, sloughy waters; it's

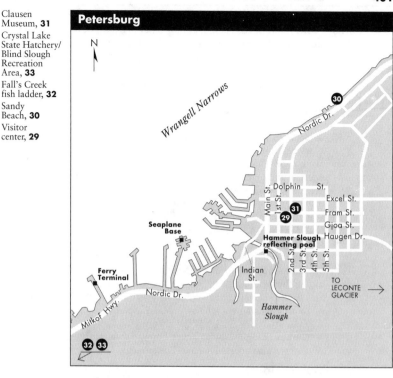

Petersburg

best seen at high tide. The large, white, barnlike structure on stilts that stands just south of the pool is the **Sons of Norway Hall**, headquarters of an organization devoted to keeping alive the traditions and culture of the old country.

30 For a longer scenic hike from the center of town, visit **Sandy Beach,** where there are picnic facilities and, frequently, eagles to view.

31 The **Clausen Museum** interprets commercial fishing and the cannery industry, the era of fish traps, the social life of Petersburg, and Tlingit culture. Don't miss the 126½-pound king salmon, the largest ever caught; as well as the Tlingit dugout canoe; two fish-trap anchors; the Cape Decision lighthouse station lens; and the *Earth, Sea and Sky* wall piece outside. ⌧ *203 Fram St., 99833,* ☎ *907/772–3598.* ⌐ *$2.* ☉ *May–mid-Sept., daily 9:30–4:30; winter schedule varies.*

32 The **Fall's Creek fish ladder,** at Mile 10.8 of the Mitkof Highway, is where coho and pink salmon migrate upstream in late summer and fall.

33 At the **Crystal Lake State Hatchery/Blind Slough Recreation Area,** at Mile 17.5 of the Mitkof Highway, more than 60,000 pounds of salmon and trout are produced each year.

OFF THE
BEATEN PATH

LECONTE GLACIER – Petersburg's biggest draw lies about 25 mi east of town and is accessible only by water or air. LeConte Glacier is the continent's southernmost tidewater glacier and one of its most active, often calving off so many icebergs that the lake at its face is carpeted bank to bank with floating bergs. Ferries and cruise ships pass it at a distance. For tour information, *see* Guided Tours, *below.*

Dining and Lodging

$–$$ ✕ **The Homestead.** There's nothing fancy here, just basic American fare: steaks, local prawns and halibut, a salad bar, and generous breakfasts. The fine homemade pies include peach, blackberry, and rhubarb. ✉ *217 Main St., ☎ 907/772–3900. AE, DC, MC, V.*

$ ✕ **Pellerito's Pizza.** This take-out place specializes in pizza, calzones, sub-style sandwiches, and ice cream. ✉ *Across from ferry terminal, ☎ 907/772–3727. No credit cards.*

$$ ▦ **Scandia House.** Rosemaling designs ornament the exterior of this Norwegian-flavored hotel on Petersburg's main street. All the squeaky-clean rooms have traditional Old West furnishings; some have kitchenettes, king-size beds, or both. Boat rentals are available on the premises. ✉ *110 Nordic Dr. (Box 689), 99833, ☎ 907/772–4281 or 800/722–5006, ℻ 907/772–4301. 33 rooms, 3 suites. Kitchenettes, minibars, boating, car rental. AE, D, DC, MC, V.*

$$ ▦ **Tides Inn.** This is the largest hotel in town, a block uphill from Pe-
★ tersburg's main thoroughfare. All the rooms are modern, with standard furnishings; some have kitchens. Rooms in the newer wing have views of the boat harbor. Coffee is always available in the small lobby, and in the morning you're welcome to complimentary juices, muffins, and pastries. ✉ *1st and Dolphin Sts. (Box 1048), 99833, ☎ 907/772–4288 or 800/665–8433, ℻ 907/772–4286. 48 rooms. Car rental. AE, D, DC, MC, V.*

$ ▦ **Shakes Slough Cabins.** These Forest Service cabins (☞ Wrangell, *above*) are also accessible from Petersburg.

Guided Tours

Pacific Wing, Inc. (☎ 907/772–9258) is an air-taxi operator that gets high marks from locals for its flightseeing tours over the Stikine River and LeConte Glacier. It also does drop-offs and pick-ups in the backcountry. **Viking Travel** (☎ 907/772–3818) is a travel agency that books whale-watching, glacier, and kayaking trips with local operators.

Nightlife

The name of the **Harbor Bar** (✉ Nordic Dr., ☎ 907/772–4526) suggests its decor—ship's wheels, ship pictures, and a mounted red snapper. Sample the brew at **Kito's Kave** (✉ Sing Lee Alley, ☎ 907/772–3207)—in the afternoon if you don't like your music in the high-decibel range—and examine the outrageous wall decor, which includes a Mexican painting on black velvet, a mounted Alaska king salmon, and two stuffed sailfish from a tropical fishing expedition.

Outdoor Activities and Sports

Because of its small size, most of Petersburg can be covered by bicycle. A good route is along the coast on Nordic Drive, past some lovely homes to the boardwalk. Coming back to town, take the interior route and you'll pass the airport and pretty churches before returning to the waterfront. **Northern Bikes** (☎ 907/772–3978) rents bicycles.

Shopping

Stores along Main Street carry imported Norwegian wool sweaters, metal Viking helmets complete with horns, and other Nordic items.

FOOD

Petersburg shrimp are a regional gourmet delicacy. Small (seldom larger than half your pinky finger), tender, and succulent, they're much treasured by Alaskans, who often send them "outside" as gifts. You'll find the shrimp fresh in meat departments and canned in gift sections at food stores throughout the Panhandle. You can buy fresh vacuum-packed Petersburg shrimp in Petersburg at **Coastal Cold Storage** (⊠ Main St., ☎ 907/772–4177 or 907/772–4171).

Sitka

110 mi west of Petersburg.

For centuries before the 18th-century arrival of the Russians, Sitka was the ancestral home of the Tlingit people, who fished the Alaskan Panhandle in canoes up to 60 ft long. The Russian territorial governor Alexander Baranof coveted the Sitka site for its beauty, mild climate, and economic potential. In the island's massive timbered forests he saw raw materials for shipbuilding; its location offered trading routes as far east as Hawaii and Asia and as far south as California.

In 1799 Baranof negotiated with the local chief to build a wooden fort and trading post 6 mi north of the current town. He called the outpost St. Michael Archangel and moved a large number of his Russian and Aleut fur hunters there from their former base on Kodiak Island.

The Tlingits took exception to the ambitions of their new neighbors. Reluctant to pledge allegiance to the czar and provide free labor, in 1802 they burned his buildings. Baranof was away at Kodiak at the time but returned in 1804 with a formidable force, including shipboard cannons. He attacked the Tlingits at their fort near Indian River (the site of the present-day 105-acre Sitka National Historical Park) and drove them to the other side of the island.

In 1821 the Tlingits came back to Sitka to trade with the Russians, who were happy to benefit from the tribe's hunting skills. Under Baranof and succeeding managers, the Russian-American Company and the town prospered, becoming known as the Paris of the Pacific. Besides the fur trade, the community had a major shipbuilding and repair facility, sawmills, forges, and a salmon salter, and it even initiated an ice industry. The Russians shipped blocks of ice from nearby Swan Lake to San Francisco. Baranof eventually shifted the capital of Russian America to Sitka from Kodiak.

The town declined after its 1867 transfer from Russia to the United States but became prosperous again during World War II, when it served as a base for the U.S. effort to drive the Japanese from the Aleutian Islands. Today its most important industries are fishing and tourism.

㉞ A good place to begin a tour of Sitka is the **visitors bureau** (⊠ Lincoln St., ☎ 907/747–5940) behind St. Michael's Cathedral, or at its information booth in the **Centennial Building**, which rests near a Tlingit war canoe on Harbor Drive. In the Centennial Building, you'll also find a museum, an auditorium, and an art gallery.

㉟ To get a feel for the town, head for **Castle Hill,** where Alaska was formally handed over to the United States on October 18, 1867, and where the first 49-star U.S. flag was flown on January 3, 1959, signifying Alaska's statehood. To reach the hill, which has one of Sitka's best views, head west on Harbor Drive and turn north (to the right) just before the John O'Connell Bridge. Walk past the **Baranof Castle Hill State Historic Site** entrance to the left of the Sitka Hotel. A gravel path takes you to the top of the hill, which once held several Russian residences, including Baranof's castle. **Totem Square,** below Castle Hill, has three anchors discovered in local waters and believed to be of 19th-century British origin. Look for the double-headed eagle of czarist Russia carved into the cedar of the totem pole in the park.

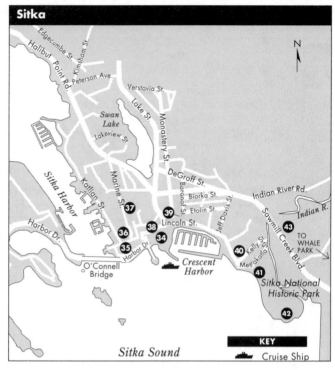

The large four-level, red-roof structure on the northeast side of Castle
Hill with the imposing 14-ft-high statue in front is the **Sitka State Pioneers' Home,** a state-run retirement home and medical-care facility.
The statue, symbolizing Alaska's frontier spirit, was modeled by an authentic pioneer, William "Skagway Bill" Fonda. It portrays a determined
prospector with pack, pick, rifle, and supplies on his back heading for
the gold country.

Most of Sitka's Russian dignitaries are buried in the **Russian and
Lutheran cemeteries,** off Marine Street. The most distinctive grave belongs to Princess Maksutoff, wife of the last Russian governor and one
of the most illustrious members of the Russian royal family to be
buried on Alaskan soil.

One of Southeast Alaska's best-known landmarks is **St. Michael's
Cathedral,** which had its origins in a log structure erected between 1844
and 1848. In 1966 the church was destroyed in a fire that swept
through the downtown business district. As the fire engulfed the building, townspeople risked their lives and rushed inside to rescue the
cathedral's precious icons, religious objects, vestments, and other treasures brought to the church from Russia.

Using original measurements and blueprints, an almost exact replica
of onion-domed St. Michael's was built and dedicated in 1976. Among
the icons on display are the much-prized *Our Lady of Sitka* (also
known as the *Sitka Madonna*) and the *Christ Pantocrator* (*Christ the
Judge*), on either side of the doors of the interior altar screen. Other
objects include ornate Gospel books, chalices, crucifixes, silver-gilt
wedding crowns dating to 1866, and an altar cloth made by Princess
Maksutoff. Visitors are welcome to attend services at the cathedral.
✉ *Lincoln St. west of Lake St.,* ☎ *907/747–8120.* ✎ *$1 donation requested.* ☺ *May–Sept., daily 7:30–5:30; Oct.–Apr., daily 1:30–5:30.*

39 Facing the harbor is the **Russian Bishop's House,** constructed by the Russian-American Company for Bishop Innocent Veniaminov in 1842. Inside the house, one of the few remaining Russian log structures in Alaska, are exhibits on the history of Russian America and the Room Revealed, where a portion of the house's structure is peeled away to expose Russian building techniques. ⊠ *Lincoln and Monastery Sts.,* ☎ *907/747–6281.* ▤ *Donation requested.* ☉ *Summer, daily 9–noon and 1–5; winter, by appointment.*

40 The octagonal **Sheldon Jackson Museum,** built in 1895, contains priceless native, Aleut, and Eskimo items collected by Dr. Sheldon Jackson in the remote regions of Alaska he traveled as an educator and missionary. Carved masks, Chilkat blankets, dogsleds, kayaks—even the helmet worn by Chief Katlean during the 1804 battle against the Russians—are on display here. The museum is just east of **Sheldon Jackson College,** founded in 1878. ⊠ *Lincoln St. north of Kelly St.,* ☎ *907/ 747–8981.* ▤ *$3.* ☉ *May 15–Sept. 15, daily 8–5; winter, Tues.–Sat. 10–4.*

Sitka National Historical Park celebrates the transfer of Alaska from Russia to the United States in 1867 and is on the site where the ex-
41 change took place. The **Sitka National Historical Park visitor center** has audiovisual programs and exhibits plus native and Russian artifacts. Often, Native American artists and craftspeople are on hand to demonstrate silversmithing, weaving, and basketry. ⊠ *Metlakatla St. at southern end of Lincoln St.,* ☎ *907/747–6281.* ▤ *Free.* ☉ *June–Sept., daily 8–5; Oct.–May, weekdays 8–5.*

A self-guided trail through Sitka National Historical Park to the site
42 of the **Tlingit Fort** passes by 15 skillfully carved totems. Some of the poles date back more than eight decades. Others are replicas of ones lost to time and a damp climate. ☎ *907/747–6281.* ▤ *Free.* ☉ *June– Sept., daily 8 AM–10 PM; Oct.–May, weekdays 8–5.*

43 At the **Alaska Raptor Rehabilitation Center** you can view American bald eagles and other wild Alaskan birds close-up. ⊠ *Sawmill Creek Blvd. (from Crescent Harbor take Jeff Davis St. north to Sawmill Creek Blvd. and turn right),* ☎ *907/747–8662.* ▤ *$10 in summer.* ☉ *Mid-May– Sept., whenever cruise ships are in town; Oct.–mid-May, Sun. open house 2–4, free of charge.*

About 6 mi from town on Sawmill Creek Boulevard is **Whale Park,** where you can get an excellent view of Sitka's largest annual visitors. Humpback whales frequent the waters off Sitka during the fall on their way toward their home in Hawaii.

Dining and Lodging

$$–$$$ ✕ **Channel Club.** The steak and the seafood here are equally good; halibut cheeks are a consistent favorite. The decor is nautical, with fishnet floats and whalebone carvings on the walls. ⊠ *Mile 3.5, Halibut Point Rd.,* ☎ *907/747–9916. AE, DC, MC, V.*

$$$$ ✕▥ **Westmark Shee Atika.** Native artworks at this hotel illustrate the
★ history, legends, and exploits of the Tlingit people. Many rooms overlook Crescent Harbor and the islands in the waters beyond; others have mountain and forest views. The Raven Room, a pastel-color restaurant with vaulted ceilings, serves seafood, pasta, and steak. Fried halibut nuggets are a top draw. ⊠ *330 Seward St., 99835,* ☎ *907/747– 6241 or 800/544–0970 for reservations,* ⅰ⅔⅘ *907/747–5486. 100 rooms. Restaurant, bar. AE, D, DC, MC, V.*

$$$$ 🏠 **Rockwell Lighthouse.** On an island ¾ mi from town, Burgess Bauder rents out his five-story lighthouse, hand-built in the 1980s with coastal woods and brass lights. The light at the top is built to Coast Guard specifications. There are accommodations for eight, and the price includes transportation to and from the lighthouse (in summer, visitors use a motorboat). ✉ *Box 277, 99835,* ☎ FAX *907/747–3056. 4 rooms. Dining room, boating. No credit cards.*

$ 🏠 **White Sulphur Springs Cabin.** This Tongass National Forest public-use cabin 65 mi outside Sitka is near a hot spring. For information on this or other Forest Service cabins in the Sitka region, call 907/747–6671 or contact the U.S. Forest Service's main Tongass office (✉ 101 Egan Dr., Juneau 99801, ☎ 907/586–8751).

Guided Tours

Prewitt Enterprises (☎ 907/747–8443) meets state ferries and operates city tours while vessels are in port, with stops at Sitka National Historical Park and the downtown shopping area. It also conducts a three-hour historical tour and a combined historical and raptor-center tour.

Nightlife and the Arts

BARS AND NIGHTCLUBS

Pilot House (✉ 713 Katlean St., ☎ 907/747–4707) is a dance club with a waterfront view. **Pioneer Bar** (✉ 212 Katlean St., ☎ 907/747–3456), across from the harbor, is a hangout for local fishermen. Tourists get a kick out of its authentic Alaskan ambience; the walls are lined with pictures of ships. **Rookies** (✉ 1617 Sawmill Creek Blvd., ☎ 907/747–3285) is a sports bar with pool, air hockey, darts, and a full dinner menu. A DJ plays dance music, and musicians occasionally perform.

DANCE

The **New Archangel Dancers of Sitka** perform authentic Russian Cossack–type dances whenever cruise ships are in port. Tickets are sold a half hour before performances; the Sitka Convention and Visitors Bureau (☎ 907/747–5940) will know the schedule.

MUSIC FESTIVALS

Southeast Alaska's major classical chamber-music festival is the annual **Sitka Summer Music Festival** (☎ 907/747–6774 in June only or 907/277–4852), a three-week June celebration of concerts and special events held in the Centennial Building.

Outdoor Activities and Sports

BIRD-WATCHING AND HIKING

Sitka has unveiled two bird-watching and hiking trails just outside town. The **Starrigavan Estuary Life Interpretive Trail** provides views of spawning salmon and of waterfowl. It has a platform for bird-watchers. The **Starrigavan Forest & Muskeg Interpretive Trail** has great views of the valley. Both trails are accessible to wheelchair users.

CANOEING AND KAYAKING

Alaska Travel Adventures (☎ 907/789–0052 in Juneau) conducts a three-hour kayaking tour in protected waters south of Sitka; instruction is provided and no experience is necessary. **Baidarka Boats** (☎ 907/747–8996) rents sea kayaks and operates guided trips in the Sitka area.

SCUBA DIVING

Southeast Diving & Sports (✉ 203 Lincoln Ave., ☎ 907/747–8279) gives diving instruction, rents tanks and equipment, and provides charter services.

Shopping

Great views of the harbor, high-quality fashions, and collectibles along with a quaint café can be found at the classy **Bayview Trading Company** (⌂ 407 Lincoln St.), Sitka's version of a mall, not far from St. Michael's Cathedral. **Old Harbor Books** (⌂ 201 Lincoln St., ☎ 907/747–8808) stocks books on the Southeast. The **Sheldon Jackson Museum** (☞ *above*) sells handcrafted Tlingit merchandise.

OFF THE
BEATEN PATH

NATIVE VILLAGES – To get a feel for how Southeast Alaska native people live today, fly or take the state ferry *LeConte* to **Kake, Angoon,** or **Hoonah.** You won't find much organized touring in any of these communities, but small, clean hotel accommodations are available (reservations are strongly recommended), and guided fishing, natural-history, and wildlife-watching trips can be arranged by asking around. In Kake, contact the Waterfront Lodge (⌂ Box 222, Kake 99830, ☎ 907/785–3472); in Angoon, contact Whalers Cove Lodge (⌂ Box 101, Angoon 99820, ☎ 907/788–3123); in Hoonah, contact Snug Harbor Lodge (⌂ Box 320, Hoonah 99829, ☎ 907/945–3636 in summer, 360/598–6463 in winter).

Juneau

100 mi north of Sitka.

Juneau, Alaska's capital and third-largest city, is on the North American mainland but cannot be reached by conventional road. The city owes its origins to two colorful sourdoughs, Joe Juneau and Dick Harris, and to a Tlingit chief named Kowee. In 1880 the chief led the two men to rich reserves of gold in the outwash of the stream that now runs through the middle of town and in quartz rock formations back in the gulches and valleys. Shortly after the discovery, a modest stampede resulted in the formation of first a camp, then a town, and finally, in 1906, the Alaska district government capital.

For 60 years or so after Juneau's founding, gold was the mainstay of its economy. In its heyday the AJ (for Alaska Juneau) gold mine was the biggest low-grade ore mine in the world. It was not until World War II, when the government decided it needed Juneau's manpower for the war effort, that the AJ and other mines in the area ceased operations. After the war mining failed to start up again, and government became the city's principal employer.

㊹ **Marine Park,** on the dock where the cruise ships tie up, is a little gem of benches, shade trees, and shelter, a great place to enjoy an outdoor meal purchased from Juneau's many street vendors. It also has a visitor kiosk staffed from 9 to 6 daily in summer. The **Mount Roberts Aerial Tramway** takes visitors from the cruise terminal 2,000 ft up the side of Mount Roberts. After the six-minute ride, you can take in a multimedia show on the history of the Tlingits, go for a walk on hiking trails, shop, or experience mountain-view dining. ⌂ *490 S. Franklin St.,* ☎ *907/463–3412 for tramway.* ⌸ *Park free, tramway $17.75.* ⊙ *Park open year-round; tramway May–Sept., daily 8 AM–10 PM, sporadically at other times of yr.*

㊺ The **Log Cabin Visitor Center** is a replica of a 19th-century structure that served first as a Presbyterian church and later as a brewery. ⌂ *Seward and 3rd Sts.,* ☎ *907/586–2201.* ⊙ *May–Sept., weekdays 8:30–5, weekends 9–5; Oct.–Apr., weekdays 9–5.*

★ **㊻** The decades-old **Red Dog Saloon** (⌂ 278 S. Franklin St.) is housed in quarters that echo its frontier past. It's one of several old and inter-

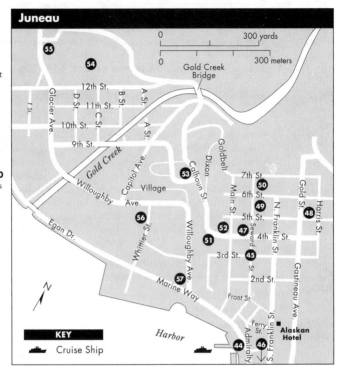

Juneau

KEY
🚢 Cruise Ship

esting buildings on South Franklin and Front streets. Many structures here reflect the architecture of the 1920s and '30s, and some are even older. The small **Alaskan Hotel** (⊠ 167 S. Franklin St.), which opened in 1913, is worth a visit; its barroom's mirrored, oak-wood back bar is accented by Tiffany lights and panels.

Also on South Franklin Street are the **Alaska Steam Laundry Building,** a 1901 structure with a windowed turret that now houses a coffee-house, a film processor, and other stores; the **Senate Building mall,** across the street; and numerous other curio and crafts shops, snack shops, and salmon shops.

47 The **Alaska State Capitol** has pillars of southeastern Alaska marble. The building, erected in 1930, houses the governor's offices and other state agencies. The state legislature meets here four months a year. ⊠ *Seward and 4th Sts.,* ☎ *907/465–2479.* ☉ *Tours mid-May–mid-Sept., daily 8:30–5; tours can also be arranged while the legislature is in session.*

48 Onion-domed **St. Nicholas Russian Orthodox Church,** the oldest original Russian church in Alaska, was erected in 1894. ⊠ *326 5th St.,* ☎ *907/586–1023.* 🎫 *Donation requested.* ☉ *Ask at visitor center about hrs.*

49 One of Juneau's finer totem poles, the **five-story totem,** stands uphill of the Capitol north of 5th Street.

50 The **House of Wickersham,** the former residence of James Wickersham, pioneer judge and delegate to Congress, contains memorabilia from the judge's travels throughout Alaska—from rare native basketry and ivory carvings to historic photos and a Chickering grand piano that came " 'round the Horn" to Alaska while the Russians still ruled here. The home, atop a steep hill, was built in 1899. ⊠ *7th St.,* ☎ *907/586–*

9001. ⊠ $2. ⊙ May–Sept., Mon.–Sat. noon–5; Oct.–Apr., by appointment.

⑤ At the **State Office Building,** you can have a picnic lunch like the state workers do and listen to organ music played in the four-story atrium on a grand old theater pipe organ, a veteran of the silent-movie era. ⊠ *4th St. west of Main St.*

☺ **⑫** The **Juneau-Douglas City Museum** interprets local mining and Tlingit history. On display are old mining equipment, historic photos, and pioneer artifacts, including a century-old store and kitchen. Also here are exhibits on commercial fishing and steamships, historic paintings, a Juneau time line, a hands-on area for children, and a half-hour video of Juneau's history. ⊠ *4th and Main Sts.,* ☎ *907/586–3572.* ⊠ *$2.* ⊙ *May–Sept., weekdays 9–6, weekends 10–6; Oct.–Apr., Fri.–Sat. noon–4, or by appointment.*

⑬ The **Governor's House,** a three-level Colonial-style home, was completed in 1912. No tours are given. The totem pole on the entrance side of the building is surely the only one of its kind to adorn the walls of a U.S. governor's mansion. ⊠ *Calhoun St. north of Dixon St.*

Many Juneau pioneers, including Joe Juneau and Dick Harris, are **⑭** buried in the **Evergreen Cemetery** (⊠ *12th St. west of Calhoun St.*). A meandering gravel road leads through the graveyard. At the end of the **⑮** lane you'll come to a monument commemorating the **cremation spot of Chief Kowee.**

★ **⑯** The **Alaska State Museum,** one of Alaska's top museums, contains natural-history exhibits (stuffed brown bears, a replica of a two-story-high eagle nesting tree), a walrus-hide whaling boat, a re-created interior of a Tlingit tribal house, mining exhibits, and contemporary art. ⊠ *395 Whittier St.,* ☎ *907/465–2901.* ⊠ *$3.* ⊙ *May 15–Sept. 15, weekdays 9–6, weekends 10–6; Sept. 16–May 14, Tues.–Sat. 10–4.*

⑰ **Centennial Hall** is the site of an excellent **information center** operated by the U.S. Forest Service. Movies, slide shows, and information about recreation in the surrounding Tongass National Forest and in the nearby Glacier Bay National Park and Preserve are available here. ⊠ *101 Egan Dr.,* ☎ *907/586–8751.* ⊙ *Mid-May–mid-Sept., daily 8–5; mid-Sept.–mid-May, weekdays 8–5.*

☺ **Gold panning** is fun, and sometimes you'll actually uncover a few flecks of the precious metal. You can buy a pan at almost any Alaska hardware or sporting-goods store. Juneau is one of the Southeast's best-known gold-panning towns; look for schedules of gold-panning excursions at visitor information centers.

★ Alaskan Amber, Pale, Frontier, and Smoked Porter beers are brewed and bottled in Juneau. Visitors are welcome at the **Alaskan Brewing and Bottling Company's microbrewery plant** and can sample the product after watching the bottling operation. ⊠ *5429 Shaune Dr.,* ☎ *907/ 780–5866.* ⊠ *Free.* ⊙ *May–Sept., Tues.–Sat. 11–5; Oct.–Apr., Thurs.– Sat. 11–5.*

Dining and Lodging

$$ ✕ **Gold Creek Salmon Bake.** Trees, mountains, and the rushing water
★ of Salmon Creek surround the sheltered, comfortable benches and tables at this salmon bake. Fresh-caught salmon (sometimes supplemented with ribs) is cooked over an alder-wood fire and served with a simple but succulent sauce of brown sugar, margarine, and lemon juice. For $22 you can enjoy the salmon, along with hot baked beans, salad, Jell-O, corn bread, and your choice of beer, wine, lemonade, tea,

or coffee. After dinner you can pan for gold in the stream or wander up the hill to explore the remains of the Wagner Gold Mine buildings. A free bus ride from downtown hotels is provided. ⊠ *1061 Salmon Lane Rd.,* ☎ *907/789–0052. MC, V. Closed Oct.–Apr.*

$–$$ ✕ **The Fiddlehead.** Light woods, stained glass, and historic photos
★ adorn Juneau's favorite restaurant. The healthful fare, served in generous portions, ranges from a light dinner of black beans and rice to pasta Greta Garbo (locally smoked salmon tossed with fettuccine in cream sauce). Homemade bread from the restaurant's bakery is laudable. Smoking is not permitted. ⊠ *429 Willoughby Ave.,* ☎ *907/586–3150. AE, D, DC, MC, V.*

$–$$ ✕ **Mike's Place.** This restaurant in the former mining community of Douglas has been serving up seafood, steak, and pasta for decades. Its treatment of the tiny Petersburg shrimp is particularly noteworthy. Rivaling the food is the view from the picture windows at the rear of the restaurant. Mike's looks over the waters of Gastineau Channel to Juneau and the ruins of the AJ mine. ⊠ *1102 2nd St., Douglas,* ☎ *907/364–3271. AE, D, DC, MC, V. Closed Mon. No lunch weekends.*

$$$ ✕🍽 **Silverbow Inn.** The main building of this small inn, for years one
★ of the town's major bakeries, was built in 1890. Century-old chairs, tables, and settings decorate the eponymous restaurant (reservations essential). Special dishes include the halibut in berries and port sauce, the mixed seafood grilled in lemon-garlic sauce, and several blackened meats; save room for the homemade ice cream and other rich deserts. The wine list is outstanding. ⊠ *120 2nd St., 99801,* ☎ *907/586–4146,* ⨝ *907/586–4242. 6 rooms. Restaurant. AE, D, DC, MC, V.*

$$–$$$ ✕🍽 **Inn at the Waterfront.** Antiques and modern amenities blend
★ seamlessly at this inn built in 1899. The inn is home to the Summit, the city's most prestigious dining spot (reservations essential). The intimate, candlelit restaurant prepares 25 entrées, mostly seafood but including a New York strip steak with blue cheese. The Summit has a luxurious brothel decor and, in fact, the inn was a brothel until 1958. Special accents include Italian sconce lamps and lace tablecloths. ⊠ *455 S. Franklin St., 99801,* ☎ *907/586–2050,* ⨝ *907/586–2999. 21 rooms. Restaurant. AE, D, DC, MC, V.*

$$$$ 🏨 **Baranof Hotel.** For half a century the Baranof has been the city's prestige address for business travelers, legislators, lobbyists, and tourists. That designation has been challenged in recent years by the Westmark (like the Baranof, a part of the Westmark chain). The art deco lobby and most rooms in this nine-story hostelry have tasteful woods and a lighting style reminiscent of 1931, when the hotel opened for business. The contemporary rooms have aqua blue, pink, or maroon color schemes. ⊠ *127 N. Franklin St., 99801,* ☎ *907/586–2660 or 800/544–0970,* ⨝ *907/586–8315. 193 rooms. Restaurant, coffee shop, lobby lounge, meeting rooms, travel services. AE, D, DC, MC, V.*

$$$$ 🏨 **Westmark Juneau.** A high-rise by Juneau standards, the seven-story Westmark is across Main Street from Centennial Hall and across Egan Drive from the docks. Rooms are modern in decor; deluxe ones have views of the Gastineau Channel. The lobby is distinguished by a massive carved eagle and wood paneling. Extensive wood-mural carvings adorn the Woodcarver Dining Room. ⊠ *51 W. Egan Dr., 99801,* ☎ *907/586–6900 or 800/544–0970,* ⨝ *907/463–3567. 105 rooms. Restaurant, lounge, meeting rooms. AE, DC, MC, V.*

$$$–$$$$ 🏨 **Country Lane Inn.** Only 4 mi from Mendenhall Glacier, this Best Western property has a charming sitting room–lobby with a couch and reading materials. Baskets of multicolor flowers hang along the entrance walk to the rooms and make for a pleasant welcome. Rooms are decorated with mauve and dusty blue fabrics in country style. Furnishings are kept to a minimum. Some rooms have a whirlpool bath and kitchenette. Complimentary Continental breakfasts are served. ⊠ *9300 Glacier Hwy., 99801,* ☏ *907/789–5005 or 800/528–1234,* FAX *907/789–2818. 50 rooms. Kitchenettes. AE, D, DC, MC, V.*

$$$–$$$$ 🏨 **Juneau Airport TraveLodge.** The rooms and furnishings here are pretty standard. The structure, like Micasa's Restaurant inside, is Mexican in design and decor. The motel is the only one in the community with an indoor swimming pool and whirlpool tub. Some rooms have mountain views. ⊠ *9200 Glacier Hwy., 99801,* ☏ *907/789–9700,* FAX *907/789–1969. 86 rooms. Restaurant, lobby lounge, indoor pool, hot tub, airport shuttle. AE, D, MC, V.*

$$$–$$$$ 🏨 **The Prospector.** A short walk west of downtown and next door to
★ the Alaska State Museum, this small but modern hotel is popular with business travelers and legislators. Very large rooms have contemporary furnishings, bright watercolors of Alaskan nature, and views of the channel, mountains, or city. McGuire's dining room serves steak, seafood, and outstanding prime rib. ⊠ *375 Whittier St., 99801,* ☏ *907/586–3737 or 800/331–2711,* FAX *907/586–1204. 60 rooms. Restaurant, lobby lounge. AE, D, MC, V.*

$$ 🏨 **Alaskan Hotel.** This historic 1913 hotel is 15 mi from the ferry ter-
★ minal and 9 mi from the airport (city bus service is available). Rooms are on three floors and have century-old antiques and iron beds. Four hot tubs can be rented by the hour. ⊠ *167 S. Franklin St.,* ☏ *907/586–1000 or 800/327–9347,* FAX *907/463–3775. 42 rooms, 22 with bath. Bar, 4 hot tubs. D, DC, MC, V.*

Guided Tours

BOATING

Alaska Travel Adventure (☏ 907/789–0052) conducts guided float trips below the Mendenhall Glacier, sea kayaking trips in the Juneau and Sitka areas, and sportfishing trips.

FISHING

Beartrack Charters (☏ 907/586–6945 or 800/586–6945) operates excursions for salmon and halibut. **Juneau Sportfishing** (☏ 907/586–1887) runs excursions for salmon and halibut, as well as whale-watching trips on its luxury yachts.

FLIGHTSEEING

Era Helicopters (☏ 907/586–2030) operates one-hour flightseeing trips that include alpine country, downtown Juneau, and the Juneau Icefield, with a touchdown on a glacier. **Temsco Helicopters** (☏ 907/789–9501) pioneered helicopter sightseeing over Mendenhall Glacier with an actual touchdown and a chance to romp on the glacier. On Temsco's pilot's-choice tour, visitors are taken to favorite destinations in the Juneau Icefield area.

NATIVE CULTURE

Alaska Native Tours (☏ 907/463–3231) employs Tlingit and Haida guides, who point out historic village sites in the Juneau and Douglas area, explaining native traditions along the way. Juneau is the embarkation point for two catamaran excursions from **Auk Nu Tours** (☏ 800/820–2628). One boat leaves downtown for sightseeing at Tracy Arm; the other operates as a ferry between Auke Bay and Gustavus before continuing to Icy Strait for wildlife watching. Both tours relate the lore of the areas visited from a Tlingit point of view.

PHOTOGRAPHY

Alaska Up Close (☏ 907/789–9544) arranges half-day nature photography tours in Juneau. At least a week's notice is recommended.

Nightlife and the Arts

BARS AND NIGHTCLUBS

The **Alaskan Hotel Bar** (⊠ 167 S. Franklin St., ☎ 907/586–1000) has live music.

The **Bubble Room** (⊠ 127 N. Franklin St., ☎ 907/586–2660), a comfortable lounge off the lobby in the Baranof Hotel, is quiet—and the site of more legislative lobbying than in the nearby state capitol.

The **Red Dog Saloon** (⊠ 278 S. Franklin St., ☎ 907/463–9954) carries on the sawdust-on-the-floor tradition, with mounted bear and other game-animal trophies on the walls and lots of historic photos. There's live music, and the crowd is lively, particularly when the cruise ships are in port.

MUSIC FESTIVALS

The annual **Alaska Folk Festival** (☎ 907/789–0292) is staged each April in Juneau, drawing singers, banjo masters, fiddlers, and cloggers from all over the state, the Yukon Territory, and beyond. During the last week of May, **Juneau Jazz 'n Classics** (☎ 907/463–3378) celebrates music from Bach to Brubeck.

THEATER

The **Naa Kahidi Theater** (☎ 907/463–4844) presents native dance and theater performers from throughout the state. **Perseverance Theater of Juneau** (⊠ 914 3rd St., ☎ 907/364–2421), a professional theater company, performs everything from Broadway plays to Shakespeare to locally written material.

Outdoor Activities and Sports

CROSS-COUNTRY SKIING

The **Parks and Recreation Department** (☎ 907/586–5226) sponsors a group ski and snowshoe outing each Wednesday morning and Saturday when there's sufficient snow. **Foggy Mountain Shop** (⊠ 134 N. Franklin St., ☎ 907/586–6780) rents skis, dispenses advice about local trails and ridges, and has climbing and camping gear.

DOWNHILL SKIING

The only downhill area in the Southeast, **Eaglecrest** (⊠ 155 S. Seward St., Juneau 99801, ☎ 907/586–5284 or 907/586–5330 for recorded ski information) on Douglas Island, 30 minutes from downtown Juneau, offers late-November to mid-April skiing and snowboarding on a well-groomed mountain with two double chairlifts, a beginner's platter pull, cross-country trails, a ski school (including downhill, Nordic, and telemark), a ski-rental shop, a cafeteria, and a tri-level day lodge. There's a vertical drop of 1,400 ft, runs up to 2 mi long, and 31 alpine trails. Knowledgeable skiers pack rain slickers along with other gear. On weekends and holidays there are bus pickups at hotels and motels.

HIKING

The **Parks and Recreation Department** (☎ 907/586–5226) sponsors a hike each Wednesday morning and on Saturdays in summer.

TENNIS

The **Juneau Racquet Club** (⊠ 2841 Riverside Dr., ☎ 907/789–2181), about 10 mi north of downtown, adjacent to Mendenhall Mall, will accommodate out-of-towners at its indoor tennis and racquetball courts. Facilities include a sauna, hot tub, exercise equipment, a snack bar, massage tables, and a sports shop. **JRC Downtown** (⊠ W. Willoughby, ☎ 907/789–2181 or 907/586–5773) is a smaller club. Both charge $12.50 per day for nonmembers.

Shopping

ART GALLERIES

The **Rie Muñoz Gallery** (✉ 2101 N. Jordan Ave., ☎ 907/789–7411) carries the creations of Rie Muñoz, one of Alaska's favorite artists, along with other artists' works.

CRAFTS AND GIFTS

The **Russian Shop** (✉ 175 S. Franklin St., ☎ 907/586–2778), on the first floor of the old Senate Building, on South Franklin between Ferry and Front streets, is a depository of icons, samovars, lacquered boxes, nesting dolls, and other items that reflect Alaska's 18th- and 19th-century Russian heritage.

Tongass National Forest

The country's largest national forest, the **Tongass** (✉ Centennial Hall, 101 Egan Dr., Juneau 99801, ☎ 907/586–8751) stretches the length of Alaska's Panhandle and encompasses nearly 17 million acres, or three-fourths of the Southeast region. Much of the forest is covered by old-growth, temperate rain forest, but it also includes rugged mountains, steep fjords, glaciers, and ice fields within its boundaries. Its lands and waters shelter black and brown bears, bald eagles, Sitka black-tailed deer, mountain goats, wolves, marine mammals, and dozens of sea- and shorebird species. Two national monuments, Admiralty Island (☞ *below*) and Misty Fjords (☞ Ketchikan, *above*), both within its borders, are especially popular with visitors.

Admiralty Island National Monument (✉ 8461 Old Dairy Rd., Juneau 99801, ☎ 907/586–8790) offers breathtaking vistas when viewed up close in small boats. Admiralty Island is best known as one of North America's richest brown-bear habitats. The island's earliest inhabitants called it Kootznoowoo, meaning "fortress of the bears." Ninety-six miles long, with 678 mi of coastline, Admiralty (the second-largest island in the Southeast) is home to an estimated 1,500 bears, or almost one per square mile. Since 1980 almost all of Admiralty's 1 million acres have been preserved as Kootznoowoo Wilderness. Among its chief attractions is **Pack Creek,** where visitors can watch brown bears feed on salmon. One of Alaska's premier brown-bear viewing sites, Pack Creek is co-managed by the Forest Service and the Alaska Department of Fish and Game. Permits are required during the main viewing season, from June 1 to September 10, and only 24 people per day are allowed to visit Pack Creek from July 10 to August 25. Reservations are available through the monument office beginning March 1. The monument also has a system of public-use cabins, a popular canoe route, the world's highest density of nesting bald eagles, and some of the region's best sea kayaking and sportfishing.

OFF THE
BEATEN PATH

TENAKEE SPRINGS – This tiny community clings to (in fact, hangs out over) the shores of Chichagof Island. It's accessible from Juneau by air or by the small Alaska ferry *LeConte* on an eight-hour run. The Tenakee Springs bathhouse is the centerpiece of the community's lifestyle. Between baths you can go crabbing, hiking, berry picking, or fishing for salmon and halibut. Tenakee Hot Springs Lodge (✉ Box 3, Tenakee Springs 99841, ☎ 907/736–2400), near the water, is a two-story, rustic spruce building with excellent views of the inlet. Sportfishing packages, which include airfare from Juneau and guided fishing off a 42-ft boat, are available. Five-day packages with all meals included start at $2,390 per person. For cabin rentals, write to Snyder Mercantile (✉ Box 505, Tenakee Springs 99841, ☎ 907/736–2205).

Guided Tours

Alaska Discovery (☎ 800/586–1911 or 907/780–6226) organizes canoeing, sea kayaking, and wildlife-viewing trips within Tongass National Forest and explores Admiralty Island.

Lodging

$$$$ ⚕ **Thayer Lake Lodge.** One of Southeast Alaska's pioneer lodges, Thayer Lake is on private land within Admiralty Island National Monument, near Juneau. Bob and Edith Nelson built this small, rustic lodge-and-cabins operation, which houses up to 10 people. They did it mostly with their own labor, using local timber for their buildings. Lake fishing is unsurpassed for cutthroat and Dolly Varden trout (though they're not overly large). Canoes and motorboats are available for guests who want to explore the 9-mi-long lake, which laps the sandy beach fronting the lodge. Simple family-style meals are available at the lodge. Rates vary, depending on whether people cook their own meals or eat at the lodge. ⊠ *Box 8897 or Box 5416, Ketchikan 99901,* ☎ *907/225–3343 or 907/247–8897,* 𝔽𝔸𝕏 *907/247–7053. 2 cabins. Dining room, kitchens, hiking, boating, fishing. No credit cards. Closed mid-Sept.–May.*

$ ⚕ **U.S. Forest Service Cabins.** Scattered throughout Tongass National Forest, these rustic cabins offer a charming and cheap escape. Most cabins have oil- or wood-burning stoves and bunk beds, but no electricity or running water. You provide your own sleeping bag, food, and cooking utensils. Reservations may be made up to 180 days in advance in person or by mail. Don't be surprised if the Forest Service recommends you carry along a 30.06- or larger-caliber rifle in the unlikely event of a bear problem.⊠ *U.S. Forest Service Information Center, Centennial Hall, 101 Egan Dr., Juneau 99801,* ☎ *907/586–8751. 150 cabins. No credit cards.*

Camping

$ ⚠ **U.S. Forest Service Campgrounds.** Eight Forest Service–maintained campgrounds are scattered through the Tongass Forest; all are accessible from Southeast communities (Juneau, Sitka, Ketchikan, and Petersburg). All have toilets and sites for RVs and tents, but not all provide drinking water. Sites may be reserved in advance at four of the campgrounds (Mendenhall, Starrigavan, Last Chance, and Signal Creek). ⊠ *U.S. Forest Service Information Center, 101 Egan Dr., Juneau 99801,* ☎ *907/586–8751 or 800/280–2267 for reservations. No credit cards.*

Glacier Bay National Park and Preserve

★ *50 mi by air from Juneau to town of Gustavus.*

Glacier Bay National Park and Preserve is one of the few places in the world where you can come within inches of 16 tidewater glaciers. Getting this close is not recommended, though, because of the dangers involved when chunks of the glaciers break off. The glaciers line the 60 mi of narrow fjords at the northern end of the Inside Passage and rise up to 7,000 ft above the bay. With a noise that sounds like cannons firing, icebergs the size of 10-story office buildings sometimes come crashing from the "snout" of a glacier. The crash sends tons of water and spray skyward, and it propels mini-tidal waves outward from the point of impact. **Johns Hopkins Glacier** calves so often and with such volume that the large cruise ships can seldom come within 2 mi of its face.

Glacier Bay is a recently formed (and still forming) body of water fed by the runoff of the ice fields, glaciers, and mountains that surround it. Captain James Cook and Captain George Vancouver sailed by Glacier Bay and didn't even know it. At the time of Vancouver's sailing in 1794, the bay was hidden behind and beneath a vast glacial wall of ice. The glacier face was more than 20 mi across and, in places, more than 4,000 ft in depth. It extended more than 100 mi to its origins in the St. Elias Mountain Range. Since then, because of warming weather and other factors not fully understood, the face of the glacial ice has melted and retreated with amazing speed, exposing nearly 60 mi of fjords, islands, and inlets.

It was Vancouver who named the magnificent snow-clad **Mount Fairweather** that towers over the head of the bay; popular legend says Vancouver named Fairweather on one of the Southeast's most beautiful blue days—and the mountain was not seen again during the following century! That's an exaggeration, to be sure, but overcast, rainy weather is certainly the norm here.

In 1879, about a century after Vancouver's sail-by, one of the earliest white visitors to what is now Glacier Bay National Park and Preserve came calling. He was naturalist John Muir, drawn by the flora and fauna that had followed in the wake of glacial withdrawals and fascinated by the vast ice rivers that descended from the mountains to the tidewater. The naturalist's namesake glacier, like others in the park, continues to retreat dramatically. Its terminus is now scores of miles farther up the bay from the small cabin he built at its face.

Glacier Bay is a marvelous laboratory for naturalists of all persuasions. Glaciologists, of course, can have a field day; animal lovers can hope to see the rare glacial "blue" bears of the area (a variation of the black bear, which is here along with the brown bear), whales feasting on krill, mountain goats (in late spring and early summer), and seals on floating icebergs. Birders can look for the more than 200 species that have been spotted in the park (if you're lucky, you may witness two bald eagles engaging in aerial acrobatics).

A remarkable panorama of plants unfolds from the head of the bay, which is just emerging from the ice, to the mouth, which has been ice-free for more than 200 years. In between, the primitive plants—algae, lichens, and mosses—that are the first to take hold of the bare, wet ground give way to more complex species: flowering plants such as the magenta dwarf fireweed and the creamy dryas, which in turn merge with willows, alders, and cottonwood. As the living plants mature and die, they enrich the soil and prepare it for new species to follow. The climax of the plant community is the lush spruce-and-hemlock rain forest, rich in life and blanketing the land around **Bartlett Cove.**

As you sail farther into the great bay, the conifers become noticeably smaller, and they are finally replaced by alders and other leafy species that took root and began growing only a few decades ago. Finally, deep into the bay where the glaciers have withdrawn in very recent years, the shoreline contains only plants and primitive lichens. Given enough time, however, these lands, too, will be covered with the same towering forests that you see at the bay's entrance. ⊠ *Park Headquarters: Upstairs in Glacier Bay Lodge; National Park Dr., 8 mi north of Gustavus,* ☎ *907/697–2230.* 📧 *Free.* ☉ *Visitor center mid-Apr.–mid-Dec., daily 8:30–7; park year-round.*

For airborne visitors, **Gustavus,** 50 mi west of Juneau and 75 mi south of Skagway, is the gateway to Glacier Bay National Park. The long, paved jet airport, built as a refueling strip during World War II, is one of the best and longest in Southeast Alaska, all the more impressive because facilities at the field are so limited. Alaska Airlines, which serves

Gustavus daily in the summer, has a large, rustic terminal at the site, and from a free telephone on the front porch of the terminal, you can call any of the local hostelries for a courtesy pickup. Smaller light-aircraft companies that serve the community out of Juneau also have on-site shelters.

Gustavus has no downtown. In fact Gustavus is not a town at all. The 150 or so year-round residents are most emphatic on this point; they regularly vote down incorporation. Instead, Gustavus is a scattering of homes, farmsteads, arts-and-crafts studios, fishing and guiding charters, and other tiny enterprises peopled by hospitable individualists. It is, in many ways, a contemporary exemplar of the frontier spirit in Alaska.

Dining and Lodging

$–$$ ✕ **Strawberry Point Cafe.** There's nothing fancy here, just wholesome fresh-baked breads, pastries, and deli sandwiches. Alaskan antiques and knickknacks, such as an eclectic bottle collection, enhance this small, homey establishment. Monday is pizza night; come for seafood on Saturday. ⊠ *On the dock road,* ☏ *907/697–2227. DC, MC, V. Closed in winter.*

$$$$ ✕⬚ **Glacier Bay Country Inn.** This picturesque, rambling log structure
★ with marvelous cupolas, dormers, gables, and porches was built from local hand-logged timbers yet has modern amenities. Some rooms have antiques and open log-beam ceilings; all have views of the Chilkat Mountains' rain forest and a mountain-modern ambience. Innkeepers Ponch and Sandi Marchbanks arrange sightseeing and flightseeing tours and charter their three boats, each of which sleeps four to six, into Glacier Bay and nearby waters. Ponch and Sandi run a gourmet kitchen ($$$), in which they prepare foods fresh from the sea and the inn's own garden; reservations are essential. Among guests' favorites are steamed Dungeness crab, homemade fettuccine, and rhubarb custard pie. Bears and moose might peek in at you from the hay fields. Meals are included in the room rate. ⊠ *Halfway between the airport and Bartlett Cove, Box 5, Gustavus 99826,* ☏ *907/ 697–2288 or 800/628–0912,* ⑆ *907/697–2289. 9 rooms. Restaurant, travel services. AE, MC, V.*

$$$$ ✕⬚ **Glacier Bay Lodge.** The lodge, the only one within the national
★ park, is constructed of massive timbers and blends well into the thick rain forest surrounding it on three sides. The modern yet rustic rooms (no televisions) are accessible by boardwalks; some have views of Bartlett Cove. If it swims or crawls in the sea hereabouts, you'll find it on the menu in the rustic dining room ($$–$$$), which has a water view. A guest favorite is the halibut baked *aleyeska,* a fillet baked in a rich sauce of sour cream, cheese, and onions. Activities include whale-watching, sportfishing, kayaking, and naturalist-led hiking; excursions up the bay leave from the dock out front. ⊠ *Bartlett Cove, Box 108, Gustavus 99826, or 520 Pike Tower, Suite 1400, Seattle, WA 98101,* ☏ *907/697–2226 or 800/451–5952,* ⑆ *206/623–7809. 5 rooms. Restaurant, travel services. DC, MC, V. Closed in winter.*

$$$$ ⬚ **Gustavus Inn.** Built in 1928 and established as an inn in 1965, Gus-
★ tavus Inn continues a tradition of gracious Alaskan rural living. In the original homestead building and in an attached newer structure, rooms are decorated in New England farmhouse style. Glacier trips, fishing expeditions, bicycle rides around the community, and berry picking in season are offered here. Many guests, though, prefer to do nothing but

enjoy the inn's tranquillity and its notable family-style meals. Hosts David and Jo Ann Lesh heap bountiful servings of seafood and fresh vegetables on the plates of overnight guests and others who reserve in advance. The farmhouse-style dining room is down-home cozy. ⊠ *Box 60, Gustavus 99826,* ☎ *907/697–2254 or 800/649–5220;* ☎ *913/649–5220 in winter;* ℻ *907/697–2255; 913/649–5220 in winter. 11 rooms with bath, 2 rooms share bath. Restaurant, travel services, airport shuttle. AE, MC, V. Closed winter.*

$$–$$$$ 🏠 **Puffin Bed & Breakfast.** These attractive cabins are in a wooded homestead and are decorated with Alaskan crafts. There's also a main lodge with an arts-and-crafts shop. A full breakfast is included. The owners also operate Puffin Travel for fishing, kayaking, sightseeing charters, and Glacier Bay cruises. A cabin for rent is not part of the B&B. ⊠ *Box 3, Gustavus 99826,* ☎ *907/697–2260,* ℻ *907/697–2258. 4 cabins, 3 with bath. Bicycles, travel services, airport shuttle. No credit cards. Closed in winter.*

Guided Tours

Glacier Bay is best experienced from the water, whether from the deck of a cruise ship, on a tour boat, or from the level of a kayak. During the several hours the ships are in the bay, National Park Service naturalists come aboard to explain the great glaciers; to point out features of the forests, islands, and mountains; and to help spot black bears, brown bears, mountain goats, whales, porpoises, and the countless species of birds that call the area home.

Uniformed Park Service naturalists travel aboard the *Spirit of Adventure* (☎ 800/622–2042), which operates daily from the dock at Bartlett Cove, near Glacier Bay Lodge.

Gray Line of Alaska (☎ 907/983–2241 or 800/544–2206) conducts Glacier Bay flightseeing tours.

Outdoor Activities and Sports

The most adventurous way to explore Glacier Bay is by paddling your own kayak through the bay's icy waters and inlets. But unless you really know what you're doing, you're better off signing on with the guided tours. You can book one of **Alaska Discovery**'s (⊠ 5449 Shaune Dr., Suite 4, Juneau 99801, ☎ 907/586–1911 or 800/586–1911) eight-day guided expeditions. Alaska Discovery provides safe, seaworthy kayaks and tents, gear, and food. Its guides are tough, knowledgeable Alaskans. Kayak rentals for unescorted Glacier Bay exploring and camping can be arranged through **Glacier Bay Sea Kayaks** (⊠ Box 26, Gustavus 99826, ☎ 907/697–2257). Twice a day, at 9 AM and 5 PM, its experienced kayakers give orientations on handling the craft, plus camping and routing suggestions. The company will also make reservations aboard the regular day boat so that kayakers can be dropped off and picked up in the most scenic country. **Sea Otter Kayak Glacier Bay** (⊠ Dock Rd., Box 228, Gustavus 99826, ☎ 907/697–3007) rents kayaks, instructs on their use, and supplies essentials like rubber boots, life jackets, maps, and tide tables.

Haines

80 mi northwest of Juneau.

Missionary S. Hall Young and naturalist John Muir picked the site for this town in 1879 as a place to bring Christianity and education to the native peoples. They could hardly have picked a more beautiful spot— a heavily wooded peninsula with magnificent views of Portage Cove and the Coastal Mountain Range.

Unlike most other cities in Southeast Alaska, Haines can be reached by road (the 152-mi Haines Highway connects at Haines Junction with the Alaska Highway). It's also accessible by the state ferry and by scheduled plane service from Juneau. The Haines ferry terminal is 4½ mi northwest of downtown, and the airport is 3½ mi west.

The town has two distinct personalities. On the northern side of the Haines Highway is the portion of Haines founded by Young and Muir. After its missionary beginnings the town served as the trailhead for the Jack Dalton Trail to the Yukon during the 1897 gold rush to the Klondike. The following year, when gold was discovered in nearby Porcupine (now deserted), the booming community was a supply center and jumping-off place for those goldfields as well.

South of the highway the town looks like a military post, which is what it was for nearly half a century. In 1903 the U.S. Army established a post—Fort William Henry Seward—at Portage Cove just south of town. For 17 years (from 1922 to 1939) the post (renamed Chilkoot Barracks to avoid confusion with the South Central Alaska city of Seward) was the only military base in the territory. That changed with World War II, but after the war the post closed down.

A group of World War II veterans purchased the property from the government. They changed its name to Port Chilkoot and created residences, businesses, and a Native American arts center out of the officers' houses and military buildings that surrounded the old fort's parade ground. Eventually Port Chilkoot merged with the city of Haines. The two areas are officially one municipality, but the old military post is referred to as Fort Seward.

The Haines–Fort Seward community is recognized for the enormously successful native dance and culture center at Fort Seward, as well as for the superb fishing, camping, and outdoor recreation to be found at Chilkoot Lake, Portage Cove, Mosquito Lake, and Chilkat State Park on the shores of Chilkat Inlet. The Alaska Chilkat Bald Eagle Preserve is a treasure; thousands of eagles come here annually in winter to feed on a late run of chum salmon, making it one of Alaska's premier wildlife-watching sites.

You can pick up walking-tour maps of Haines and Fort Seward at the
⑤⑧ visitor center (⊠ 2nd Ave. near Willard St., ☎ 907/766–2234).

⑤⑨ The core of the collection of the **Sheldon Museum and Cultural Center** came from one Alaskan family. Steve Sheldon began assembling native artifacts, Russian items, and gold-rush memorabilia, such as Jack Dalton's sawed-off shotgun, in the 1880s and started an exhibit of his finds in 1924. ⊠ *11 Main St.,* ☎ *907/766–2366.* ▨ *$3.* ☉ *Mid-May–mid-Sept., daily 1–5 and some mornings and evenings; mid-Sept.–mid-May, Sun.–Mon. and Wed. 1–4, Tues. and Thurs–Fri. 3–5.*

Dalton City, an 1890s gold-rush town re-created as a set for the 1991
⑥⓪ movie *White Fang,* is less than 1 mi from downtown on the **Southeast Alaska State Fairgrounds** (☎ 907/766–2476). Attractions include carriage rides, gold panning, native carvers, and keepsakes from the Dalton City shops. Admission is free except during the state fair. The fair, held each August, is one of several official regional fall blowouts, and in its homegrown, homespun way it's a real winner. Along with the usual barnyard animals, you'll find stellar examples of local cuisine,

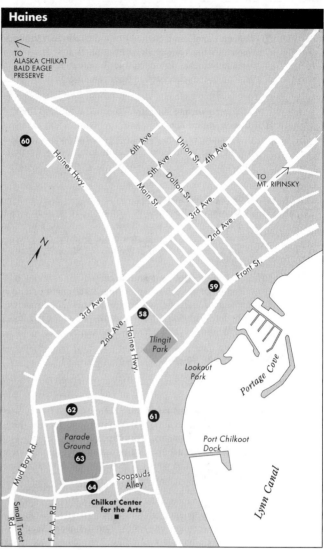

native dancers and displays of totemic crafts, and some fine art and photography.

The Haines Highway is completely paved on the American side of the border, and except for a few remaining stretches, it's almost entirely paved in Canada. At the base of the Haines Highway is **Mile 0,** the starting point of the 152-mi road to the Alaska Highway and the Canadian Yukon. Whether you plan to travel all the way or not, you should spend at least a bit of time on the scenic highway. At about Mile 6 there's a delightful picnic spot near the Chilkat River and an inflowing clear creek; at Mile 9.5 the view of the Takhinsha Mountains across the river is magnificent; and around Mile 19 there is good viewing of the **Alaska Chilkat Bald Eagle Preserve.** The United States–Canada border lies at Mile 40. If you're traveling on to Canada, stop at Canadian customs and be sure to set your clock ahead one hour.

The stately former home of Fort Seward's commanding officer is now
62 a part of the **Halsingland Hotel** (☞ Dining and Lodging, *below*). On
63 the flat but sloping parade ground of the **Fort William H. Seward National Historic Landmark,** the site of the first army post built in Alaska,
is a native tribal house, trapper's log cabin, and cultural center; walking tours are scheduled in summer. ⊠ *Box 530, 99827,* ☎ *800/458–3579.* ⊑ *Free.* ⊙ *Mid-May–mid-Sept., weekdays 2 PM.*

The fort's former hospital is now a workshop for the craftspeople of
64 **Alaska Indian Arts,** a nonprofit organization dedicated to the revival
of Tlingit art forms. Here, between the parade ground and the Center
for the Arts, you'll see carvers making totems and metalsmiths working in silver. ☎ *907/766–2160.* ⊑ *Free.* ⊙ *Weekdays 9–noon and 1–5.*

Dining and Lodging

$$–$$$ ✕ **Lighthouse Restaurant.** Come here for great views of Lynn Canal
and fine barbecued ribs, steak, and seafood. The restaurant's colorful
Harbor Bar is a popular watering hole for commercial fishermen. ⊠
Front St. on the harbor at the foot of Main St., ☎ *907/766–2442. AE, MC, V.*

$$ ✕ **Chilkat Restaurant and Bakery.** Family-style cooking is served in
a homelike, no-smoking setting. Lace curtains and plush green carpet add a touch of class. Seafood, steaks, and sandwiches are cooked
to order; on Friday the fare is all-you-can-eat Mexican. ⊠ *5th Ave.
near Main St.,* ☎ *907/766–2920. AE, MC, V. Closed Sun. in winter.*

$–$$ ✕ **Bamboo Room.** This unassuming coffee shop is popular for sandwiches, burgers, fried chicken, seafood, and breakfast. ⊠ *2nd Ave. near
Main St.,* ☎ *907/766–2800. AE, D, DC, MC, V.*

$$ ✕⌂ **Halsingland Hotel.** The officers of old Fort Seward lived in the
big, white structures that today constitute the Halsingland Hotel.
Many rooms have nonworking cast-iron fireplaces and original clawfoot bathtubs; all are carpeted and have photos of wildlife and historic sites on the walls. The restaurant serves seafood, burgers, and
fish-and-chips. There's a salad and potato bar, an extensive wine list,
and a choice of local beers. In summer, at the Tlingit tribal house nearby,
the Halsingland prepares a nightly salmon bake called the Port
Chilkoot Potlatch—$22 for all you can eat. ⊠ *Fort Seward, Box
1589, 99827,* ☎ *907/766–2000; 800/542–6363 in the U.S.; 800/
478–2525 in Yukon Territory and British Columbia;* ⅢX *907/766–2445.
58 rooms, 52 with bath. Restaurant, bar, travel services. AE, D, DC,
MC, V.*

$$$ ⌂ **Captain's Choice Motel.** Rooms in this conventional motel in downtown Haines have cable TV and telephones. The motel's decor manages to be contemporary and rustic at the same time. Ask for a room
with a view of Portage Cove. ⊠ *2nd and Dalton Sts., Box 392, 99827,*
☎ *907/766–3111 or 800/247–7153; 800/478–2345 in AK. 39 rooms
with bath, 5 suites. Room service, car rental, travel services. AE, D,
DC, MC, V.*

Nightlife and the Arts

Harbor Bar (⊠ Front St. at the Harbor, ☎ 907/766–2444). Commercial fisherfolk gather here nightly at this old (1907) bar and restaurant. Sometimes in summer there is live music.

The **Chilkat Indian Dancers** perform at the **Chilkat Center for the Arts,** which was the army post's recreation hall. Some performances may be at the tribal house next door; check posted notices for performance times. Masked performers wearing bearskins and brightly patterned dance blankets act out traditional stories. There are several performances weekly, more when cruises are in port. ⊠ *1 Theater Dr.,* ☎ *907/766–2160.* 🖃 *$10.* ☉ *May–Sept. 15.*

Outdoor Activities and Sports

HIKING

One of the most rewarding hikes in the area is to the north summit of **Mount Ripinsky,** the prominent peak that rises 3,610 ft behind the town. This is a strenuous trek that requires a full day. The trailhead lies at the top of Young Street, along a pipeline right-of-way. For other hikes, pick up a copy of "Haines Is for Hikers" at the visitor center.

RAFTING

Alaska Cross-Country Guiding and Rafting (☎ 907/767–5522) conducts fly-in, raft-out trips down the Tsirku River, plus photo trips into the Chilkat preserve.

SKIING

Alaska Nature Tours and Backcountry Outfitters (⊠ Box 491, 99827, ☎ 907/766–2876) operates a winter shuttle bus to flat-track skiing in the Chilkat Bald Eagle Preserve and telemarking at Chilkat Pass. Ski and snowboarding equipment may be rented here. The company also conducts bird-watching and natural-history tours in the Chilkat preserve and leads hiking treks in summer.

Skagway

13 mi north of Haines.

Skagway is a short hop north of Haines if you take the Alaska Marine Highway ferry. If you go by road, the distance is 359 mi, because you have to take the Haines Highway up to Haines Junction, Yukon, then take the Alaska Highway 100 mi south to Whitehorse, and then drive a final 100 mi south on the Klondike Highway to Skagway. North country folk call this popular sightseeing route the Golden Horseshoe or Golden Circle tour, because it takes in a lot of gold-rush country in addition to lake, forest, and mountain scenery.

However you get to Skagway, you'll find the town an amazingly preserved artifact from one of North America's biggest, most storied gold rushes. Most of the downtown district forms part of the Klondike Gold Rush National Historical Park, a unit of the national park system dedicated to commemorating and interpreting the frenzied stampede that extended to Dawson City in Canada's Yukon. Old false-front stores, saloons, and brothels—built to separate gold-rush prospectors from their grubstakes going north or their gold pokes heading south—have been restored by the federal government and Skagway's citizens. When you walk down Broadway, the scene is not appreciably different from what the prospectors saw in the days of 1898, except that the street is now paved.

When the Yukon gold rush began, the argonauts, as they liked to be called, swarmed to Dyea and the Chilkoot Trail, 9 mi west of Skag-

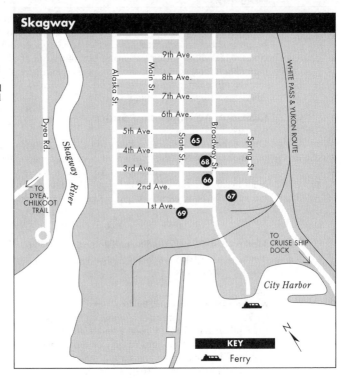

way. Skagway and its White Pass Trail didn't seem as attractive until a dock was built in town. Then it mushroomed overnight into the major gateway to the Klondike, supporting a wild mixture of legitimate businesspeople, con artists (among the most cunning was Jefferson "Soapy" Smith), stampeders, and curiosity seekers.

Three months after the first boat landed in July 1897, Skagway numbered perhaps 20,000 persons and had well-laid-out streets, hotels, stores, saloons, gambling houses, and dance halls. By the spring of 1898, the superintendent of the Northwest Royal Mounted Police in neighboring Canada would label the town "little better than a hell on earth."

A lot of the "hell" ended with a shoot-out one July evening in 1898. Good guy Frank Reid (the surveyor who laid out Skagway's streets so wide and well) faced down bad guy Soapy Smith on Juneau dock, downtown near the present ferry terminal. After a classic exchange of gunfire, Smith lay dead and Reid lay dying. The town built a huge monument at Reid's grave. You can see it in Gold Rush Cemetery and read the current inscription on it: "He gave his life for the honor of Skagway." For Smith, whose tombstone was continually chiseled and stolen by vandals and souvenir seekers, today's grave marker is a simple wooden plank.

When the gold rush played out after a few years, the town of 20,000 dwindled to 700. The White Pass & Yukon Railroad kept Skagway alive until 1982, when it began to run in summers only. By this time, however, the revenue from tourism was sufficient to compensate for the economic loss suffered as a result of the railroad's more limited schedule.

65 The **Skagway Convention and Visitors Bureau** (⌂ 5th Ave., ☎ 907/ 983–2854), on the first floor of the large, granite **city hall,** provides maps and information.

66 The **Arctic Brotherhood Hall/Trail of '98 Museum** is unlike anything else you'll see in Alaska. The Arctic Brotherhood was a fraternal organization of Alaskan and Yukon pioneers. To decorate the exterior false front of their Skagway lodge building, local members created a mosaic out of 20,000 pieces of driftwood and flotsam gathered from local beaches. At the Trail of '98 Museum inside the hall, Frank Reid's will is preserved under glass, as are papers disposing of Soapy Smith's estate. Gambling paraphernalia from the old Board of Trade Saloon is on display along with native artifacts, gold scales, a red-and-black sleigh, and a small organ. ⌂ *Broadway at 2nd Ave.,* ☎ *907/983–2420.* ▨ *$2.* ☉ *Mid-May–Sept., daily 9–5.*

★ **67** The **Klondike Gold Rush National Historical Park** is in what was the White Pass & Yukon Route rail depot. It contains exhibits, photos, and artifacts from the White Pass and Chilkoot trails and is of special interest if you plan to take a White Pass train ride, drive the nearby Klondike Highway, or hike the Chilkoot "Trail of '98." ⌂ *Broadway and 2nd St.,* ☎ *907/983–2921.* ▨ *Free.* ☉ *May–Sept., daily 8–7; Sept.–May, hrs vary (call ahead or visit administrative office on site to gain entrance).*

68 The **Golden North Hotel** (⌂ 3rd Ave. and Broadway), Alaska's oldest hotel, built in 1898, has been restored to its gold-rush-era appearance. Take a stroll through the lobby even if you're not staying here.

69 The **Klondike Highway,** which starts at the foot of State Street, often parallels the older White Pass railway route as it travels northwest to Carcross and Whitehorse in the Canadian Yukon. It merges south of Whitehorse for a short distance with the Alaska Highway, then heads on its own again to terminate at Dawson City, on the shores of the Klondike River. From start to finish, it covers 435 mi. Along the way the road climbs through steep, forested coastal mountains with jagged snow-covered peaks. It passes by deep, fish-filled lakes and streams in the Canadian high country, where mountain goats, moose, black bears, and grizzlies can often be spotted.

If you're driving the Klondike Highway north from Skagway, you must stop at Canadian Customs, Mile 22. If you're traveling south to Skagway, check in at U.S. Customs, Mile 6. And remember that when it's 1 PM in Canada at the border, it's noon in Skagway.

Each year, a journey along the historic **Chilkoot Trail** is the highlight of thousands of serious hikers' travels.

You can travel partway into gold-rush country on the **White Pass & Yukon Route** (WP & YR) narrow-gauge railroad over the "Trail of '98." The historic railroad's diesel locomotives chug and tow vintage viewing cars up steep inclines, hugging the walls of precipitous cliff sides, yielding views of lakes, forests, craggy peaks, and waterfalls. Two options are available. Twice daily the WP & YR leaves Skagway for a three-hour round-trip excursion to the White Pass summit. Sights along the way include Bridal Veil Falls, Inspiration Point, and Dead Horse Gulch. The fare is $75. Through service to Whitehorse, Yukon, is offered daily as well—in the form of a train trip to Fraser, where motorcoach connections are available on to Whitehorse. The one-way fare to Whitehorse is $95. For information call 907/983–2217 or 800/343–7373.

Dining and Lodging

$–$$ ✕ **Prospector's Sourdough Restaurant.** You'll meet as many Skagway folk here as you will visitors, particularly at breakfast time, when the sourdough hotcakes or snow-crab omelets are on the griddle. The sourdough recipes at this family-run restaurant are as old as the town. Salmon steak and halibut are favored in the evening. ✉ *4th Ave. and Broadway,* ☎ *907/983–2865. AE, DC, MC, V. Closed winter.*

$$$ ✕⌂ **Westmark Inn.** The inn's decor is gold-rush style but grander and more plush than anything the stampeders ever experienced, with rich red carpeting, brass trim, and historical pictures. The period furnishings are first class, in soothing ivories and soft greens. Rooms in the main structure are larger and more convenient to the restaurant and lounge than those in the annex. The Chilkoot Dining Room (☎ 907/983–6000), a rare find, prepares a diverse menu—everything from Thai sweet noodles to veal pastrami. Try to avoid the dining room's early-evening (5:30 PM) rush. ✉ *3rd and Spring Sts.,* ☎ *907/983–6000 or 800/544–0970,* ⨳ *907/983–6100. 220 rooms. Restaurant, 2 bars, meeting room, travel services, car rental. AE, D, DC, MC, V. Closed in winter.*

$$ ✕⌂ **Golden North Hotel.** This golden-dome hotel is Alaska's most his-
★   toric. Built in 1898 during the heyday of the gold rush, it has been re-stored to reflect that period. Pioneer Skagway families contributed furnishings to each of the hotel's rooms, and the stories of those families are posted on the walls of each unit. The third-floor lobby has a view of Lynn Canal. Popular choices in the Golden North Restaurant (closed in winter) include sourdough pancakes for breakfast; soups, salads, and sandwiches for lunch; and salmon or other seafood for dinner. ✉ *3rd Ave. and Broadway (Box 343), 99840,* ☎ *907/983–2451 or 907/983–2294,* ⨳ *907/983–2755. 31 rooms. Restaurant, pub. AE, D, DC, MC, V.*

$$ ✕⌂ **Skagway Inn Bed & Breakfast.** Each room in this downtown Vic-
★   torian inn is named after a different gold-rush gal. Color schemes vary, but rooms share a Victorian motif, with antiques and cast-iron beds; some have mountain views. The building, one of Skagway's oldest, was erected in 1897. The inn also has a fine summer-only restaurant, Lorna's. Owner and chef Lorna McDermott is a graduate of Le Cordon Bleu. ✉ *7th Ave. at Broadway (Box 500), 99840,* ☎ *907/983–2289,* ⨳ *907/983–2713. 12 rooms. Restaurant. D, MC, V.*

$$ ⌂ **Wind Valley Lodge.** A long walk or a short drive from downtown, the Wind Valley Lodge is one of Skagway's newer motels. Rooms are modern with typical motel furniture, and there's a free shuttle to downtown. A restaurant that prepares basic American fare is next door. ✉ *22nd Ave. and State St. (Box 354), 99840,* ☎ *907/983–2236,* ⨳ *907/983–2957. 29 rooms. AE, D, MC, V.*

Guided Tours

Skagway Street Car Co. (☎ 907/983–2908) lets you revisit the gold-rush days in 1937 White Motor Company streetcars, complete with costumed conductors who tell the story of the town's tumultuous history while showing you the sights.

Nightlife and the Arts

NIGHTLIFE

Moe's Frontier Bar (✉ Broadway between 4th and 5th Sts., ☎ 907/983–2238) is a longtime hangout of the locals. At the **Red Onion Sa-**

loon (⌂ Broadway at 2nd St., ☎ 907/983–2222) you'll meet at least as many Skagway people as you will visitors. The live music on Thursday night ranges from rock to folk. The Red Onion is closed in winter.

THE ARTS

At **Eagles Hall,** locals perform a show called *Skagway in the Days of '98.* You'll see cancan dancers, learn a little local history, and watch desperado Soapy Smith get the punishment he deserves. ⌂ *Broadway and 6th St., ☎ 907/983–2545 in summer, 801/489–7070 in winter.* 🎟 *$14. ⊙ Daily 2 PM and 7:30 PM and Tues.–Thurs. 10:30 AM, depending on cruise ship arrivals.*

Shopping

David Present's Gallery (⌂ Broadway and 3rd St., ☎ 907/983–2873) has outstanding works by Alaskan artists. For vintage items such as historical photos and old-fashioned newspapers, visit **Dedman's Photo Shop** (⌂ Broadway and 3rd St., ☎ 907/983–2353), a Skagway institution.

SOUTHEAST ALASKA A TO Z

Arriving and Departing

By Bus

Year-round service between Anchorage and Skagway is available from **Alaska Direct Bus Lines** (☎ 907/277–6652 or 800/770–6652). Though it's a long ride, you can travel **Greyhound Lines of Canada** (☎ 604/662–3222) from Vancouver or Edmonton to Whitehorse and make connections there with Gray Line buses (☞ Getting Around, *below*) to Southeast Alaska.

By Car

Only Skagway and Haines, in the northern Panhandle, and tiny Hyder, just across the border from Stewart, British Columbia, are accessible by conventional highway. To reach Skagway or Haines, take the Alaska Highway to the Canadian Yukon's Whitehorse or Haines Junction, respectively, then drive the Klondike Highway or Haines Highway southwest to the Alaska Panhandle. You can reach Hyder on British Columbia's Cassiar Highway, which can be reached from Highway 16 just north of Prince Rupert.

By Ferry

From the south, the **Alaska Marine Highway System** (☎ 800/642–0066 or 907/465–3941) operates stateroom-equipped vehicle and passenger ferries from Bellingham, Washington, and Prince Rupert, British Columbia. The vessels call at Ketchikan, Wrangell, Petersburg, Sitka, Juneau, Haines, and Skagway, and they connect with smaller vessels serving bush communities; in all, 14 Southeast towns are served by state ferries. One of the smaller ferries also operates between Hyder and Ketchikan. In the summer, staterooms on the ferries are always sold out before sailing time; reserve months in advance. For those planning to take cars on the ferry, early reservations for vehicle space are also highly recommended.

B.C. Ferries (☎ 250/386–3431) operates similar passenger and vehicle ferries from Vancouver Island, British Columbia, to Prince Rupert. From there, travelers can connect with the Alaska Marine Highway System.

By Plane

Alaska Airlines operates several flights daily from Seattle and other Pacific Coast and southwestern cities to Ketchikan, Wrangell, Petersburg, Sitka, Glacier Bay, and Juneau. The carrier connects Juneau to the northern Alaskan cities of Yakutat, Cordova, Anchorage, Fairbanks, Nome, Kotzebue, and Prudhoe Bay. In summer, **Delta Airlines** has at least one flight daily from Seattle to Juneau. *See* Airline Travel *in* the Gold Guide for airline numbers.

By Train

Southeast Alaska's only railroad, the **White Pass & Yukon Railroad** (☎ 800/343–7373), operates between Skagway and Fraser, British Columbia. The tracks follow the historic path over the White Pass summit—a mountain-climbing, cliff-hanging route of 28 mi each way. Bus connections are available at Fraser to Whitehorse, Yukon.

Getting Around

By Bus

Gray Line of Alaska (☎ 907/277–5581 or 800/544–2206) provides summertime connections between Whitehorse, Anchorage, Fairbanks, Haines, and Skagway with other stops en route.

By Ferry

The **Alaska Marine Highway System** (☞ Arriving and Departing, *above*) runs ferries to several Southeast Alaskan towns.

By Plane

Many communities in Southeast Alaska have air-taxi services that fly people from town to town and into remote wilderness areas. Local chambers of commerce (☞ Visitor Information, *below*) can provide lists of bush-plane services.

Contacts and Resources

B&B Reservation Service

The **Alaska Bed & Breakfast Association** (✉ 369 S. Franklin St., Suite 200, Juneau 99801, ☎ 907/586–2959 or 800/493–4453) books B&B accommodations in most Southeast communities.

Car Rental

Practical Rent-a-Car (☎ 800/424–7722) has locations in Juneau, Ketchikan, Petersburg, Sitka, and Wrangell. *See* Car Rental *in* the Gold Guide for the phone numbers of the national agencies.

Doctors and Dentists

Haines Medical Clinic (next to Visitor Information Center, ☎ 907/766–2521). **Skagway Medical Service** (✉ 11th Ave. between State St. and Broadway, ☎ 907/983–2255). **Wrangell General Hospital** (✉ Airport Rd., next to the elementary school, ☎ 907/874–3356).

Emergencies

Ambulance (☎ 911). **Police** (☎ 911).

Late-Night Pharmacies

JUNEAU

Juneau Drug Co. (✉ 202 Front St., ☎ 907/586–1233). **Ron's Apothecary** (✉ 9101 Mendenhall Mall Rd., about 10 mi north of downtown in Mendenhall Valley, next to Super Bear market, ☎ 907/789–0458). Ron's Apothecary's after-hours number for prescription emergencies is 907/789–9522.

Downtown Drugstore (⊠ 300 Front St., ☎ 907/225–3144). **Race Avenue Drugs** (⊠ 2300 Tongass Ave., across from Plaza Portwest shopping mall, ☎ 907/225–4151). After hours, call **Ketchikan General Hospital** (☎ 907/225–5171).

Rexall Drugs (⊠ 215 N. Nordic Dr., ☎ 907/772–3265). After hours, call **Petersburg Medical Center** (☎ 907/772–4291).

White's Pharmacy (⊠ 705 Halibut Point Rd., ☎ 907/747–5755). **Harry Race Pharmacy** (⊠ 106 Lincoln St., ☎ 907/747–8006).

Stikine Drugs (⊠ 202 Front St., ☎ 907/874–3422).

Outdoor Activities and Sports

For information about fishing, hiking, camping, or other recreational activities in Southeast parks, Tongass National Forest, and other areas, contact the following: **Alaska Department of Fish and Game** (⊠ Box 25526, Juneau 99802, ☎ 907/465–4112; 907/465–4180 for seasons and regulations; 907/465–2376 for license information). **Alaska Division of Parks** Southeast regional office (⊠ 400 Willoughby Ave., Juneau 99801, ☎ 907/465–4563). **National Park Service** (☎ 907/271–2737). **U.S. Forest Service** (⊠ 101 Egan Dr., Juneau 99801, ☎ 907/586–8751).

Visitor Information

Most of the information centers listed below are open between mid-May and August, daily from 8 to 5 and when cruise ships are in port, and between September and mid-May, on weekdays from 8 to 5.

Davis Log Cabin Visitor Center (⊠ 134 3rd St., Juneau, ☎ 907/586–2201). **Juneau Convention and Visitors Bureau** (⊠ 369 S. Franklin St., Suite 201, 99801, ☎ 907/586–1737). **Southeast Alaska Tourism Council** (⊠ Box 20710, Juneau 99802, ☎ 907/586–4777 or 800/423–0568).

Haines/Fort Seward Visitor Information Center (⊠ 2nd Ave. near Willard St., Box 530, Haines 99827, ☎ 907/766–2234 or 800/458–3579). **Ketchikan Visitors Bureau** (⊠ 131 Front St., 99901, ☎ 907/225–6166 or 800/770–3300). **Petersburg Visitor Information Center** (⊠ 1st and Fram Sts., 99833, ☎ 907/772–4636). **Sitka Convention and Visitors Bureau** (⊠ Lincoln St. behind St. Michael's Cathedral, Box 1226, Sitka 99835, ☎ 907/747–5940). The bureau also has a visitor information booth in the Centennial Building on Harbor Street. **Skagway Convention and Visitors Bureau** (⊠ 333 5th Ave., Box 415, Skagway 99840, ☎ 907/983–2854). **Wrangell Chamber of Commerce Visitors Center** (⊠ Stikine Ave., Box 49, Wrangell 99929, ☎ 907/874–3901 or 800/367–9745).

9 Portraits of the Pacific Northwest

Pacific Northwest Microbrews:
Good for What Ales You
In the Footsteps of the First Settlers
Books and Videos

PACIFIC NORTHWEST MICROBREWS: GOOD FOR WHAT ALES YOU

FRESHLY POURED ALE sparkles a rich amber in the light of a sun-dappled May afternoon on the loading-dock beer garden of the Bridgeport Brewpub in Portland, Oregon. To the south rise the office towers of downtown Portland, which supply not a few of Bridgeport's customers. To the north is the graceful span of the Fremont Bridge, the bridge from which the tiny brewery takes its name.

The customer tips back his glass and takes a long, thirsty swallow. The ale cascades along his tongue, tweaking taste buds that for years have known only pale, flavorless industrial lagers. A blast of sweet malt explodes at the back of his mouth, counterpointing the citrusy sting of the hops. *This* is flavor, something missing from American beer for far too long.

There's something inherently noble about a well-crafted pint, something ancient and universal. Anthropologists theorize that agriculture and brewing may have provided the stimulus for the very foundation of human civilization. Certainly there is nothing new in the idea of a city or region being served by a number of small, distinctive breweries. More than 5,000 years ago, in Egypt, the many breweries of ancient Pelusium were as famous as the city's university. (Even then, books, beer, and scholarly contemplation went hand in hand.) The ancient Greeks and Romans, though more partial to wine than grain beverages, drank beer; evidence shows that there were more than 900 public houses in Herculaneum before Mount Vesuvius sounded its fateful "last call" in AD 79.

Brewing wasn't perfected, however, until it was introduced to northern climes. Teutonic ancestors could imagine no greater paradise than Valhalla, a banquet hall with 540 doors and an inexhaustible supply of ale. For the Tudor English, ale was far more than an amusement—it was a staple of life, "liquid bread," a source of national strength. Brewers who cut corners and overcharged for an inferior product were fined heavily, imprisoned, or both. It may be a coincidence that during the 1970s

Britain's Campaign for Real Ale movement—credited with single-handedly restoring fine ale to United Kingdom pubs—paralleled the resurgence in the British economy and national pride. It may also be a coincidence that the return of the microbrewery ale to the Northwest signaled the end of a bitter recession here, and the beginning of a rapid climb into prosperity. The best place to sample the Northwest's hand-crafted ale is a well-run brew pub, which stimulates the human spirit with conviviality, pleasant warmth, intelligent conversation, the scent of malt, and hearty food. Combatting the region's chilly, damp climate, brew pubs become places of refuge where you can shake the tears of a hostile world from your umbrella, order a pint of cask-conditioned bitter, and savor a complex substance that caresses the senses.

Microbreweries (companies producing fewer than 20,000 kegs per year) can be found from Minneapolis to Maui, but it all started in the Pacific Northwest. On any given evening, several dozen locally brewed beers and ales are available for tasting in pubs in Portland and Seattle. Most East Coast entries in the microbrewing sweepstakes produce German-style lagers—the most familiar brewing style to American palates—but the microbrewers of the Pacific Northwest go for wildly adventuresome bitters, stouts, and porters.

These are beers, it should be noted, that would make a megabrewery marketing consultant blanch. Take Grant's Imperial Stout. So dark that even a blazing summer sun, viewed through a pint glass of the pitch-black stuff, yields not a glimmer, Imperial Stout is heavy with choice whole barley malt, citrusy Cascade hops, and honey; it contains twice the alcohol, four times the calories, and a hundred times the flavor of a Bud Light. At a time when everyone supposedly wants to stay skinny and sober, who in his right mind would brew such a beer?

BACK IN 1982, when Paul Shipman of the Redhook Brewery in Seattle and Bert Grant of Grant's Ales in Yakima trundled out the first kegs of microbrewery ale tapped in America since Prohibition, they little dreamed that they were ushering in an era of modest revolutionary ferment. Not that these tiny breweries have the Clydesdales quaking in their traces: Anheuser-Busch annually *spills* a thousand times more beer than Bridgeport—one of the most successful microbreweries in America—produces in a year. Still, as America's megabrewers respond to a growing demand for variety by dressing up their beers with labels like "extra gold" and "dry," then actually make their lack of flavor a selling point ("No aftertaste!"), the Northwest's thriving microbrewery industry provides a real alternative for those of us who like beer to taste like *beer*.

Whether it's business or brewing, no Portland micro is more respected than Bridgeport, the oldest. Founded in 1984 by Dick and Nancy Ponzi, Bridgeport combines expertly brewed English-style ales with one of the city's most popular pub operations. As originally conceived by the Ponzis and brewmaster Karl Ockert, the pub was little more than a tasting room, located in the same 1880s-vintage former rope factory as the brewery, with only a single tap, a few tables, and a dart board.

As anyone who has attempted to fight through the crush at the pub's bar on a Friday night can tell you, a slightly different attitude prevails at Bridgeport today. Though the atmosphere is still casual, the pub's highly regarded selection of light and dark ales, handmade pizza with a sourdough beer wort crust, and the opportunity to watch the brewers at work through steamy windows behind the bar pack the place every night of the week.

One of the things that sets Bridgeport apart from other Portland-area breweries is the pub's skill with true cask-conditioned ales. Made in the traditional English style, these ales are pumped unfiltered directly into a firkin keg at the end of fermentation, to lie undisturbed in a cool cellar for several weeks. There is no added carbon dioxide; cask-conditioned ales contain only the natural carbonation produced during the fermentation process. The result, drawn from one of the antique "beer-engine" hand pumps at the end of the bar, is a smoother, noticeably less fizzy pint, with all the rich flavors of malt and hops allowed to shine through.

In Seattle, gems such as the Trolleyman pub keep the Emerald City in the running with other Northwest brew pubs. Tucked away in a corner of Redhook's state-of-the-art facility in Fremont—just north of downtown Seattle—the Trolleyman poured its inaugural pint in 1988. The popular, low-key pub's taps dispense brewery-fresh Redhook ESB, coffee-hued Blackhook porter, unfiltered Hefe-Weizen, and seasonal brews such as Winterhook strong ale. There is one cask-conditioned tap, pouring a rotating selection of real ales.

So with all these beers to choose from, where do you begin? What should you look for in a microbrewery ale? First and foremost, variety. At any given time in Portland and Seattle, there are several dozen fresh, locally made brews on tap. They range in strength from a standard 3½% alcohol to an ominous 8½%.

And the flavor? Well, you'll just have to taste for yourself. There is the rich sweetness of malt, counterbalanced by good bitter hops. There are the mocha java overtones of roasted barley, used in stouts and porters, and the spiciness of malted wheat. There are sweet ales and tart ales, mild inconsequential ales, and ales so charged with flavor they linger on the palate like a fine Bordeaux.

Above all else, you should look for an ale you can savor, an ale you can taste without wanting to swallow too quickly. The dearest emotion to a brewer's heart is the beer drinker's feeling of regret that the last swig is gone.

— By Jeff Kuechle

IN THE FOOTSTEPS OF THE FIRST SETTLERS

THERE'S A SORT OF PRIMEVAL mystery about the majestic landscapes of the Pacific Northwest, something elemental and ancient that can give you a strange sense of being dislocated in time. Drive along the coastal roads of Washington's Olympic Peninsula, for example, and you'll pass magnificent rain forest, pounding surf, and partially submerged chunks of headland stranded at sea. Every bridge you cross takes you over an ancient fishing stream where prehistoric Indians harvested salmon. The oldest trees along the road bear scars where these Indians pulled off bark strips dozens of feet long, which they used for clothing, construction work, and rope making. Stop to look out over the water, and you feel the presence of ancient whale hunters scanning the horizon for spouts among the waves.

It isn't just a question of landscape, either. Elders in the Eskimo (Inuit is the preferred term in Canada) and Indian communities along the coast still pass on stories told to them by their ancestors, stories that can sometimes be traced as far back as 1,000 years, and their tribal art is a living expression of cultures whose origins are lost in the mists of prehistory.

Despite a lack of hard evidence, many archaeologists believe the first people to inhabit the New World arrived by way of the Pacific Northwest. Unlike Columbus and the seafaring Vikings, Polynesians, Chinese, and Japanese, all of whom crossed oceans to arrive at different points in North and South America, it is believed that the first Americans came on foot. If these pioneers had boats at all, they were small ones, not designed for long-distance travel across oceans. They came via Alaska and traveled through Canada into the western United States.

Although these assertions sound feasible, there aren't any known archaeological sites to support them. The oldest documented sites in the New World are believed to be about 20,000 years old; the oldest known sites in the Pacific Northwest are Indian settlements about 13,000 years

old. Why, then, is the Pacific Northwest believed to be the point of entry for the earliest settlers? Because it's the only place where people could have walked into the New World or used their small boats to travel along the coast without excessive danger.

The last ice age tied up so much water that ocean levels probably dropped by hundreds of feet around the world. On certain winter days today, a person can walk between Alaska and the Soviet Union on ice when the oceans freeze over. But during the Ice Age the oceans were so reduced that the seabed was temporarily exposed as dry land, supporting vegetation and game, with fish in the rivers and sea mammals on the coast. So much ground was exposed, in fact, that the Old World and the New were connected by dry land. And though their languages and blood types differ, evidence strongly suggests that the Eskimos and Indians have their roots somewhere in Asia.

Why, then, aren't there any sites to prove this migration theory? All human activity may have been confined to lower ground levels now hidden under the ocean, reason the archaeologists. Or people may have traveled in small numbers, so their remains aren't easily detected. Or we may have already found these sites without recognizing them as such. Even though the two American continents were not inhabited with people at the outset, they did have abundant herds of large game, animals that had no fear of humans. With such easy prey, hunters wouldn't stay in one place for long; as they killed off their local supply of meat, or as the animals learned how to avoid people, the hunters moved on. So it is possible that the settlers arrived in the Pacific Northwest, lived a nomadic life there for a while, and then roamed on to other parts of North America and into South America.

The first Americans came to a land we wouldn't recognize today. Most of Canada, Alaska, and the northern United States was still under ice. Arctic weather and the forests, animals, and plants that are found in today's far north were prevalent halfway down the lower 48 states. Then the weather changed: The ice sheets melted and the ice receded north. The animal and plant distributions we see today started to become established about 10,000 years ago. Rivers and streams that were previously frozen started to run fast and clear at low temperatures. Conditions for pioneering salmon became so ideal that by 5,000 or so years ago, there were huge runs extending hundreds of miles inland.

FOR HUNTERS it was a revolutionary time. Herds of large animals started to diminish or disappear, and the big-game hunters were increasingly confronted with more work and less to show for their efforts. Many hunters in the Pacific Northwest, particularly those in Washington, British Columbia, and southeastern Alaska, turned to fishing instead. Their nomadic life following the herds became a more settled one as they switched to fishing. And as they started to settle down, they were able to accumulate more material things.

The first Americans moved from Alaska to Canada, and then to the lower 48 states, and finally into Central America and South America. The more recent inhabitants who made their living from salmon fishing, however, headed in the opposite direction, from the lower Pacific Northwest up into Canada and Alaska. The art and culture of these people spread and flourished in the Pacific Northwest and continued to do so in the centuries preceding their contact with European explorers. Archaeological sites of these fishing peoples date back 2,500 years and more.

One of the best-known archaeological sites of these fishing peoples is Ozette, on the Makah Reservation in Washington's Olympic Peninsula. The finds of the site can be viewed by the public, and you can request permission to visit the site itself. The village of Ozette was partially covered by a mud slide several hundred years ago. This apparent catastrophe ironically turned out to preserve the village, however, for the wet mud provided an anaerobic environment hostile to most decay-causing organisms.

Archaeologists usually excavate with masons' trowels because they generally dig up stone and ceramics, objects that a skill-fully handled trowel won't harm. But at Ozette in the 1970s, there was a tricky obstacle to overcome. Basketry, cordage, clothing, and all kinds of soft materials had been preserved, but since they were preserved wet, they were soft, and the trowels cut through them like mud. Even experienced excavators couldn't feel the damage they were doing to the objects.

A whole new excavation approach was undertaken, called "wet site" archaeology. Using water hoses to excavate the village, the archaeologists discovered that mud and debris could be washed away, leaving artifacts intact. During the handlers' first clumsy attempts at hosing down the mud, artifacts could be seen tumbling downhill with the water, but after some trial and error, the workers were able to keep even small finds in place.

One of the most exciting aspects of the Ozette excavation was the support archaeologists received from Indians living in the region. The Makah tribe encouraged archaeologists to excavate Ozette and assisted in the fieldwork; tribal members provided logistical support and helped interpret finds. And the tribe even built a museum based on the artifacts on its grounds at Neah Bay.

The Indians also helped prepare artifacts for public display, which turned out to be quite a challenge. Generally, archaeological finds of stone and ceramic pieces are preserved simply by being cleaned first in water and then glued together. But Ozette produced all kinds of perishable artifacts, objects that quickly started to deteriorate once they were removed from their muddy entombment. So the Makah Tribe provided laboratory space and helped the archaeologists preserve and stabilize the finds.

These descendants of the ancient Indians went one step further and created a living experiment on the site. The Makah people worked outside to build a plank house, like those in Ozette, and then attempted to use the interior in the same ways their ancestors did. Life in the house was set up based upon the directions of tribal elders, historic accounts, and archaeological interpretations. In the end, the house looked as if one good mud slide would turn it into another ruined Ozette home. After this experimental period, the tribe dismantled the house and rebuilt it inside the Makah museum.

A LARGE DUGOUT CANOE was also built for the museum. The art of making canoes had almost died out, but it was revived to capture an important part of life in Ozette. Young and old worked together to build the boat and to pass on these ancient skills.

Other archaeological sites in the area can require a bit more effort to explore. From southern Alaska to Oregon, you can find hundreds of petroglyphs (rock carvings) and pictographs (rock paintings). Only a handful of them can be dated, however, so they can't be attributed to any particular group of people. Some are easily accessible, and seen by the public every day. Others are so hidden you can only find them if you happen to stumble upon them. Still other carvings are positioned at the tidal zone and consequently are under water at high tide.

Prehistoric Indians also carved petroglyphs on land, although most face the ocean or overlook a river or waterway. Pictographs, on the other hand, can be seen throughout the Northwest. Some of these detailed rocks have been jackhammered from their embedded frames and carted away; others have eroded, and still others lie beneath reservoirs. But the vast majority are right where they were created, and with permission from native or nonnative landowners, or government agencies, visitors can examine them. More than 500 sites are known. One protected site open to the public is Petroglyph Park in the town of Nanaimo, on Vancouver Island. Petroglyphs at Wrangell, Alaska, are also open to the public.

The ancient arts of North America's native peoples can provide another avenue of insight into their lives and cultures. The craft of carving giant totem poles out of trees has survived as a living art form, with plenty of demand for new poles—gift shops all over the region offer miniature reproductions. Many carvers work in public throughout the Pacific Northwest, at museums or on the grounds of institutions that have commissioned their artworks.

The totem pole is the best-known example of current Northwest tribal art, but masks, tools, and a variety of paintings and prints also continue the artistic tradition of the area. Artworks can be purchased at local galleries, many of which are located on Indian lands and are run by Indians. The choices are broader and the prices lower here than they are in the native art galleries of New York and California.

Museums offer another glimpse of Inuit and Native American life. The Royal British Columbia Museum in Victoria is an outstanding research center, with representation of all five species of salmon and almost every other fish that might have been harvested by prehistoric natives. Each fish skeleton has been mounted on wires, with all the bones together in proper anatomical order. Although this is a scientific collection, it verges on being a work of art in itself, with skeletal fish elongating and compressing into fantastic shapes.

In Vancouver, at the University of British Columbia's Museum of Anthropology, there are excellent collections that are very accessible to the public. Other artifacts can be seen at the Burke Museum of Natural History and Culture at the University of Washington in Seattle, and at the Alaska State Museum in Juneau, where they also have a first-rate collection of historic baleen (fibrous plates that hang from the roof of the whale's mouth) baskets. Only native hunters and artisans are legally permitted to own unprocessed baleen.

Any overview of Northwest archaeology inevitably leaves out more than it includes. Paleo-Indian sites; Russian fur-hunting activities; cave sites in Washington's channeled scablands; mastodons and mammoths; and cairns dug up 100 years ago can all be found along the Pacific Northwest coast. And if you visit searching for a glimpse of the past, researchers may invite you to observe their work, artisans will explain their ancient crafts, the museums will let you view even the most fragile artifacts, and native people will share their stories. For throughout the region, one thing remains constant: the people's eagerness to document and understand the past.

— By Glenn W. Sheehan

BOOKS AND VIDEOS

Books

The magical, mystical Pacific Northwest has inspired countless writers, whose works have pondered the region's landscape and history. Twenty writers closely connected with the Pacific Northwest discuss it in Nicholas O'Connell's *At the Field's End*. Richard Nelson won an award for natural-history writing for *The Island Within*, an account of a year he spent on an unnamed island in the Pacific Northwest. Nelson uses this specific locale to reflect on humans' relationship to the ecology and spirit of the places they live.

The imaginative novels of Tom Robbins offer a sometimes surreal take on the Northwest. Annie Dillard's first novel, *The Living*, is an evocative account of life in the Pacific Northwest at the end of the 19th century. A few of the bittersweet short stories of Raymond Carver are set in the region as well. Other writers for whom the Pacific Northwest has been a muse include the novelist and historical writer Norman MacLean and the science-fiction author Ursula Le Guin. The *Journals of Lewis and Clark* make for interesting reading as you follow in the 19th-century explorers' path. Ken Kesey's novel *Sometimes a Great Notion* is about a troubled Oregon logging dynasty.

In her memoir *Nisei Daughter*, Monica Itoi Sone recalls her time in Seattle before World War II, the social and other struggles of her family and other Japanese-Americans during the war, and life in the postwar era. The treatment of Japanese-Americans during World War II is one of the subjects of David Guterson's *Snow Falling on Cedars*. The novel, which takes place in the 1950s on an island north of Puget Sound, won the PEN/Faulkner award for fiction. For a historical take on the coastal region read *The Interwoven Lives of George Vancouver, Archibald Menzies, Joseph Whidbey, and Peter Puget: Exploring the Pacific Northwest* by John Michael Naish.

Above Seattle, with photos by Robert Cameron and text by Emmett Watson, provides, literally, an overview of the city, via historical and contemporary aerial photographs.

The late Bill Spiedel, one of Seattle's most colorful characters, wrote about the early history of the city in books replete with lively anecdotes and legends: *Sons of the Profits* and *Doc Maynard* are two of his best. David Buerge's *Seattle in the Eighteen Eighties* is difficult to find but worth the effort; it documents a period of great growth and turmoil. Buerge also compiled the history and photographs in *Chief Seattle*, part of a series about the Northwest. Quintard Taylor's scholarly *The Forging of a Black Community: Seattle's Central District, From 1870 Through the Civil Rights Era* studies race relations in the city through anecdotal and other research.

John T. Gaertner's *North Bank Road: The Spokane, Portland and Seattle Railway* outlines the impact that railroads had on the Northwest. The book is one of several titles on the subject published by Washington State University Press, whose other titles include *The Way We Ate: Pacific Northwest Cooking 1843–1900* and *Raise Hell and Sell Newspapers: Alden J. Blethen and The Seattle Times*.

Screaming Music: A Chronicle of the Seattle Music Scene, by Charles Peterson and Michael Azerrad, delivers the dish on the grunge and other musical eras. Rock music reporter Clark Humphrey covers the city's music scene from the 1960s into the 1990s in *Loser: The Real Seattle Music*.

Seattle has the largest municipal gardening program in the United States. You'll get a minitour of the city and some great recipe ideas from *The City Gardener's Cookbook: Totally Fresh, Mostly Vegetarian, Decidedly Delicious Recipes from Seattle's P-Patches*.

For a pulpy good time, read John Saul's best-selling *Black Lightning*, in which a Seattle journalist who has spent years tracking a serial killer finds herself facing new horrors when similar murders begin occurring after his execution.

Photographer Morton Beebe's beautiful *Cascadia: A Tale of Two Cities, Seattle and*

Vancouver, B.C. explores the cultural and natural wonders of Seattle, Vancouver, and the regions surrounding each city.

Pauline Johnson's *Legends of Vancouver* is a colorful compilation of regional native myths. Longtime Vancouver resident George Bowering wrote the lively *British Columbia: A Swashbuckling History of the Province.* Lois Simmie's children's book *Mister Got to Go* takes place in the Sylvia Hotel. Annette, the protagonist of Margaret A. Robinson's *A Woman of Her Tribe,* leaves her village to study in Victoria but feels alienated upon her return.

Wayson Joy's 1997 novel *The Jade Peony,* which takes place in 1940, tells the tale of three children of a Chinese immigrant family in Vancouver's Chinatown.

Rhodri Windsor Liscombe explores the city's architecture in *The New Spirit: Modern Architecture in Vancouver 1938–1963.* Gerald B. Straley's *Trees of Vancouver* is a good survey of the major and less-common varieties. Straley's book is one of many titles published by the press of the University of British Columbia about the Canadian Northwest.

Jack London's *The Call of the Wild* tells the tale of a man attempting to survive in the Alaskan wilderness during the Klondike Gold Rush of 1897–98, and the dog who befriends him. His *White Fang* is also set around the time of the gold rush. Other novels with rich descriptions of Alaska and its inhabitants include Ivan Doig's *The Sea Runners,* an adventure set in 1853, when the state belonged to Russia; *Athabasca,* an Alistair MacLean thriller set around the Alaska pipeline; and *Sitka,* by Louis L'Amour, the popular chronicler of the American frontier. James Michener's *Alaska* is a weighty history of the state from prehistoric to modern times.

Videos

The Pacific Northwest has become a major center of film and television production in the past two decades, but its roots go back nearly to the beginning of the cinema. The Oregon desert has supplied the backdrop for numerous westerns—as early as 1915, when the silent film *Where Cowboy Is King* was shot in and around Pendleton. The rugged mountains of Washington and British Columbia appear in many wilderness adventures, and the waterways of the Southeast Alaskan coast can be seen in seafaring tales.

A portion of the 1920 silent film *The Golden Trail* was shot in Portland. The 1923 western *The Covered Wagon,* about two wagon trains headed from the Midwest to Oregon, includes scenes shot in the eastern portion of the state. Though it takes place elsewhere, Buster Keaton shot parts of his 1927 masterpiece *The General* in Oregon. Much of the best version to date of *Call of the Wild,* the 1935 Loretta Young–Clark Gable vehicle, was filmed in northern California, but some scenes were shot in Oregon.

Young and Robert Mitchum star as the title characters in *Rachel and the Stranger,* a fine western, some footage for which was shot in the Eugene, Oregon, area. Baker City appears in the western–musical comedy *Paint Your Wagon* (1969), starring Lee Marvin, Clint Eastwood, and Jean Seberg. The film version of *Sometimes a Great Notion* (1970) was shot all along the central coast of Oregon. The Deschutes National Forest and the Rogue River were among the Oregon backdrops for the John Wayne western *Rooster Cogburn* (1975). Many of the frat-house antics in *National Lampoon's Animal House* (1978) were shot in the Eugene area. Much of Robert Towne's directorial debut, *Personal Best* (1982), about the relationship between two women training for the Olympic Games, was also filmed in and around Eugene.

Gus Van Sant has set all or part of several films in Portland, including his gritty debut, *Mala Noche* (1986), about a gay man who falls for an illegal alien from Mexico; *Drugstore Cowboy* (1988), about junkies who rob drugstores to pay for their drugs; and *My Own Private Idaho* (1991), in which River Phoenix and Keanu Reeves play a pair of hustlers (Reeves is the son of the Portland mayor in the film).

Recent films with scenes shot in Oregon include the two *Free Willy* films and Jim Jarmusch's *Dead Man.* Madonna lives on a Portland houseboat in the campy *Body of Evidence,* parts of which were filmed in Olympia, Washington. Richard Dreyfuss plays a Portland high school music teacher in *Mr. Holland's Opus.*

One of the first talking pictures with scenes shot in Seattle was the 1930s comedy *Tug-*

boat Annie, starring Marie Dressler (as the title character) and Wallace Beery. (Dressler's famous line: "And I didn't get the name pushin' toy boats around the bathtub either.") Lizabeth Scott, a star of the late 1940s and early 1950s, debuted in the sentimental *You Came Along* (gal on war-bond tour falls in love with a GI), parts of which were filmed in Seattle. Elvis Presley flew into town—literally; he played a crop-dusting pilot—for *It Happened at the World's Fair,* shot in 1962. The film is no great shakes, but it has some fine views of the fair and the city.

Stars continued to pass through Seattle in the 1970s as film production in and around the city increased. All or part of the James Caan sailor-on-leave vehicle *Cinderella Liberty,* John Wayne's *McQ* (he plays a Seattle police detective), and Warren Beatty's paranoid political thriller *The Parallax View* take place in the city.

Car thief Stockard Channing drove through Seattle in *Dandy the All-American Girl* (a.k.a. *Sweet Revenge*). Michael Sarrazin, James Coburn, and Walter Pidgeon picked pockets in Seattle and Salt Lake City in the peculiar *Harry in Your Pocket,* now more memorable for Pidgeon's performance and the location shots of the two cities (and also Vancouver) than the plot. The San Juan Islands were among the places through which Jack Nicholson drifted in director Bob Rafelson's *Five Easy Pieces,* which also includes scenes in Oregon and British Columbia. The town of Redmond, south of Seattle, appeared in Peter Fonda's futuristic *Idaho Transfer,* which was shot and released to little fanfare in the 1970s but revived in the 1990s as a "lost American independent classic."

Scenes from *Eleanor and Franklin* and other made-for-TV movies were shot in Seattle in the 1970s, but the pace of television production picked up in the 1980s with the feature-length *The Divorce Wars* (in which Tom Selleck and Jane Curtin spar) and *Jacqueline Bouvier Kennedy.* Parts of the pilot for David Lynch's idiosyncratic *Twin Peaks* series were shot in North Bend, Snoqualmie, and Everett. Major theatrical films shot during the 1980s in the area include *An Officer and a Gentleman, War Games, Trouble in Mind, Starman,* and *The Fabulous Baker Boys.*

The hits continued in the 1990s with *Singles,* director Cameron Crowe's tale of Seattle twentysomethings; *The Hand That Rocks the Cradle,* in which nanny from hell Rebecca de Mornay terrorizes a yuppie couple; *Disclosure,* in which corporate boss Demi Moore terrorizes employee Michael Douglas; and *Sleepless in Seattle,* in which the town provides a backdrop for love to conquer all for Tom Hanks and Meg Ryan. Most of the American footage in *Little Buddha,* Bernardo Bertolucci's tale of an American lama, was shot in the Seattle area. Contemporary Seattle is the setting for the television show *Frasier,* whose title character has a call-in show on a top-rated radio station.

Seattle became a haven for independent producers in the 1990s. Jeff Bridges starred in the major studio release *The Vanishing,* parts of which were shot here, but received better notices for his performance in the independently financed *American Heart,* also shot in the area, in which he plays a convict whose 12-year-old son rejoins him upon his release from prison. A grim view of the city can be seen in *Black Circle Boys,* in which a southern California swimmer moves to Seattle and gets caught up in Satanic rituals, drugs, and the underground music scene. For a cheerier portrait, see *Steaming Milk,* a hit at the 1997 Seattle International Film Festival. Its lead character, a struggling screenwriter, encounters a cross section of Seattleites at his day job at a Queen Anne espresso café. The 1997 documentary *Hype* is an alternately enlightening and creepy glimpse at the rise and fall of the grunge music scene.

Film and television production is a big business in British Columbia—in 1996, $537 million was spent making 34 feature films, 52 made-for-TV movies or feature-length pilots, and 16 series. Much of this activity takes place in Vancouver, including animation produced at a recently opened Disney facility.

Vancouver often stands in for other urban areas—including New York City in *Rumble in the Bronx* (1994) and *Friday the 13th: Jason Takes Manhattan* (1989)—but occasionally plays itself. The 1995 Canadian feature *The War Between Us* re-creates 1940s Vancouver as it explores the fate of a well-to-do family of Japanese descent whose members are interned in a camp in interior British Columbia following the outbreak of World War II. *Once in a Blue*

Moon (1995), another period piece shot in British Columbia, concerns a 10-year-old boy who comes of age in the suburbs of Vancouver in the late 1960s. For a peek at Vancouver's 1990s slacker culture, check out *Live Bait,* a 1995 homage to Woody Allen. The sometimes goofy sci-fi flick *Cyberjack* (1995) conjures up the Vancouver of the 21st century, complete with flying SeaBuses.

The 1990s are the heyday of British Columbia film production, but the area's cinematic roots go back several decades. Estelle Taylor, Thomas Meighan, and Anna May Wong starred in *The Alaskan,* a 1924 Paramount drama about a man who rescues Alaska from the clutches of corrupt robber barons. The 1945 *Son of Lassie* is not one of the lovable collie's best pictures, but it does contain scenes shot in British Columbia. Rugged Sterling Hayden starred in *Timberjack,* a 1954 offering from Republic Pictures. Oliver Reed starred in the 1966 film *The Trap,* about a 19th-century trapper and his wife in British Columbia.

Robert Altman shot scenes for two of his early films in British Columbia, *That Cold Day in the Park* and *McCabe and Mrs. Miller.* The well-crafted 1976 remake of the Orson Welles thriller *Journey into Fear,* starring Vincent Price, Shelley Winters, and Sam Waterston, was shot in and around Vancouver, as was the 1980 *The Grey Fox,* based on the life of an early 1900s stagecoach bandit. *Klondike Fever,* a 1979 picture starring Rod Steiger, concerns the 1897–98 gold rush.

Among the productions filmed in whole or in part in British Columbia in the past decade or so are *Roxanne, Stakeout, The Accused,* the *Look Who's Talking* movies, the Jean Claude Van Damme action picture *Time Cop, The Crush, Cousins, This Boy's Life, Stay Tuned, Jennifer Eight,* the Robin Williams fantasy *Jumanji,* the Adam Sandler comedy *Happy Gilmore,* the remake of *Little Women, Cyberteens in Love* (check your local video store for this curious Canadian production), *Bounty Hunters II, Mr. Magoo,* and *Deep Rising.*

The TV series *21 Jump Street,* which made Johnny Depp a star, was one of several 1980s television series filmed in Vancouver. Since then, production has increased greatly. Other small-screen shows shot here include *Poltergeist, Highlanders, Millennium,* and *The X-Files. Neon Rider, Northwood, The Odyssey,* and *Mom P.I.* are among the Canadian series produced in Vancouver or elsewhere in British Columbia in the 1990s.

The film of Edna Ferber's novel *Ice Palace* (1960), about Alaska's attainment of statehood, shows off the state's wilderness to glorious effect. The Disney adaptation of Farley Mowat's *Never Cry Wolf* (1983) was shot in the Skagway area. Disney also came north to shoot the third film version of Jack London's *White Fang* (1991), which is set during the gold-rush era. Dalton City, a gold-rush town re-created as a set for the movie, is now a tourist attraction. In the ultrasentimental *Leaving Normal* (1992), two women leave Wyoming for Alaska; much of the film was shot in Skagway and British Columbia.

INDEX

NOTES

Fodor's Travel Publications

Available at bookstores everywhere, or call 1–800–533–6478, 24 hours a day.

Gold Guides
U.S.

Alaska

Arizona

Boston

California

Cape Cod, Martha's Vineyard, Nantucket

The Carolinas & Georgia

Chicago

Colorado

Florida

Hawai'i

Las Vegas, Reno, Tahoe

Los Angeles

Maine, Vermont, New Hampshire

Maui & Lāna'i

Miami & the Keys

New England

New Orleans

New York City

Pacific North Coast

Philadelphia & the Pennsylvania Dutch Country

The Rockies

San Diego

San Francisco

Santa Fe, Taos, Albuquerque

Seattle & Vancouver

The South

U.S. & British Virgin Islands

USA

Virginia & Maryland

Walt Disney World, Universal Studios and Orlando

Washington, D.C.

Foreign

Australia

Austria

The Bahamas

Belize & Guatemala

Bermuda

Canada

Cancún, Cozumel, Yucatán Peninsula

Caribbean

China

Costa Rica

Cuba

The Czech Republic & Slovakia

Eastern & Central Europe

Europe

Florence, Tuscany & Umbria

France

Germany

Great Britain

Greece

Hong Kong

India

Ireland

Israel

Italy

Japan

London

Madrid & Barcelona

Mexico

Montréal & Québec City

Moscow, St. Petersburg, Kiev

The Netherlands, Belgium & Luxembourg

New Zealand

Norway

Nova Scotia, New Brunswick, Prince Edward Island

Paris

Portugal

Provence & the Riviera

Scandinavia

Scotland

Singapore

South Africa

South America

Southeast Asia

Spain

Sweden

Switzerland

Thailand

Toronto

Turkey

Vienna & the Danube Valley

Special-Interest Guides

Adventures to Imagine

Alaska Ports of Call

Ballpark Vacations

Caribbean Ports of Call

The Complete Guide to America's National Parks

Disney Like a Pro

Europe Ports of Call

Family Adventures

Fodor's Gay Guide to the USA

Fodor's How to Pack

Great American Learning Vacations

Great American Sports & Adventure Vacations

Great American Vacations

Great American Vacations for Travelers with Disabilities

Halliday's New Orleans Food Explorer

Healthy Escapes

Kodak Guide to Shooting Great Travel Pictures

National Parks and Seashores of the East

National Parks of the West

Nights to Imagine

Rock & Roll Traveler Great Britain and Ireland

Rock & Roll Traveler USA

Sunday in San Francisco

Walt Disney World for Adults

Weekends in New York

Wendy Perrin's Secrets Every Smart Traveler Should Know

Worldwide Cruises and Ports of Call

Fodor's Special Series

Fodor's Best Bed & Breakfasts

America

California

The Mid-Atlantic

New England

The Pacific Northwest

The South

The Southwest

The Upper Great Lakes

Compass American Guides

Alaska

Arizona

Boston

Chicago

Colorado

Hawaii

Idaho

Hollywood

Las Vegas

Maine

Manhattan

Minnesota

Montana

New Mexico

New Orleans

Oregon

Pacific Northwest

San Francisco

Santa Fe

South Carolina

South Dakota

Southwest

Texas

Utah

Virginia

Washington

Wine Country

Wisconsin

Wyoming

Citypacks

Amsterdam

Atlanta

Berlin

Chicago

Florence

Hong Kong

London

Los Angeles

Montréal

New York City

Paris

Prague

Rome

San Francisco

Tokyo

Venice

Washington, D.C.

Exploring Guides

Australia

Boston & New England

Britain

California

Canada

Caribbean

China

Costa Rica

Egypt

Florence & Tuscany

Florida

France

Germany

Greek Islands

Hawaii

Ireland

Israel

Italy

Japan

London

Mexico

Moscow & St. Petersburg

New York City

Paris

Prague

Provence

Rome

San Francisco

Scotland

Singapore & Malaysia

South Africa

Spain

Thailand

Turkey

Venice

Flashmaps

Boston

New York

San Francisco

Washington, D.C.

Fodor's Gay Guides

Los Angeles & Southern California

New York City

Pacific Northwest

San Francisco and the Bay Area

South Florida

USA

Pocket Guides

Acapulco

Aruba

Atlanta

Barbados

Budapest

Jamaica

London

New York City

Paris

Prague

Puerto Rico

Rome

San Francisco

Washington, D.C.

Languages for Travelers (Cassette & Phrasebook)

French

German

Italian

Spanish

Mobil Travel Guides

America's Best Hotels & Restaurants

California and the West

Major Cities

Great Lakes

Mid-Atlantic

Northeast

Northwest and Great Plains

Southeast

Southwest and South Central

Rivages Guides

Bed and Breakfasts of Character and Charm in France

Hotels and Country Inns of Character and Charm in France

Hotels and Country Inns of Character and Charm in Italy

Hotels and Country Inns of Character and Charm in Paris

Hotels and Country Inns of Character and Charm in Portugal

Hotels and Country Inns of Character and Charm in Spain

Short Escapes

Britain

France

New England

Near New York City

Fodor's Sports

Golf Digest's Places to Play

Skiing USA

USA Today The Complete Four Sport Stadium Guide

WHEREVER YOU TRAVEL, HELP IS NEVER FAR AWAY.

From planning your trip to

providing travel assistance along

the way, American Express®

Travel Service Offices are

always there to help

you do more.

American Express Travel Service
Offices are found in central locations
throughout the United States.
For the office nearest you, please
call 1-800-AXP-3429.

do more · AMERICAN EXPRESS · Travel

http://www.americanexpress.com/travel